Lecture Notes in Computer Science   10850

Commenced Publication in 1973
Founding and Former Series Editors:
Gerhard Goos, Juris Hartmanis, and Jan van Leeuwen

More information about this series at http://www.springer.com/series/7412

Lucio Tommaso De Paolis · Patrick Bourdot (Eds.)

Augmented Reality, Virtual Reality, and Computer Graphics

5th International Conference, AVR 2018
Otranto, Italy, June 24–27, 2018
Proceedings, Part I

 Springer

Editors
Lucio Tommaso De Paolis ⓘ
University of Salento
Lecce
Italy

Patrick Bourdot
University of Paris-Sud
Orsay
France

ISSN 0302-9743   ISSN 1611-3349   (electronic)
Lecture Notes in Computer Science
ISBN 978-3-319-95269-7   ISBN 978-3-319-95270-3   (eBook)
https://doi.org/10.1007/978-3-319-95270-3

Library of Congress Control Number: 2018947461

LNCS Sublibrary: SL6 – Image Processing, Computer Vision, Pattern Recognition, and Graphics

This Springer imprint is published by the registered company Springer Nature Switzerland AG
The registered company address is: Gewerbestrasse 11, 6330 Cham, Switzerland

Preface

Virtual Reality (VR) aims to develop computer systems that give humans the ability to perceive and interact in realistic multisensory motor ways, with 3D digital data or virtual worlds that are more or less realistic depending on the applications. Computer graphics is used to create a realistic visual scene, while physical-based rendering makes, for instance, 3D audio perception and haptic interactions possible. All this is meant to provide a feeling of immersion to the users (i.e., the sensation of being in a 3D world in a perceptive way), and even a feeling of presence (i.e., the sensation of being somewhere: apart from the immersive perception, this sensation targets cognitive factors, such as affordance of virtual objects and implication/involvement of users in their virtual activity).

Augmented Reality (AR) technology allows the real-time fusion of computer-generated digital content with the real world. Adding virtual content to reality makes it possible to understand information or knowledge of the real world that is not directly accessible, and/or may provide assistance to users during the execution of their tasks. Regarding the perception of immersion and feeling of presence, designing such 3D user interfaces remains challenging, but the result may greatly improve the accuracy of users' interaction in the real world, and the efficiency or even security of their activity.

Human–Computer Interaction (HCI) technology is a research area concerned with the design, implementation, and evaluation of interactive systems that make more simple and intuitive the interaction between user and computer.

This book contains the contributions to the 5th International Conference on Augmented Reality, Virtual Reality, and Computer Graphics (SALENTO AVR 2018) that has held in Otranto (Italy) during June 24–27, 2018. We cordially invite you to visit the SALENTO AVR website (http://www.salentoavr.it) where you can find all relevant information about this event.

SALENTO AVR 2018 intended to bring together researchers, scientists, and practitioners to discuss key issues, approaches, ideas, open problems, innovative applications, and trends in virtual and augmented reality, 3D visualization, and computer graphics in the areas of medicine, cultural heritage, arts, education, entertainment, as well as industrial and military sectors.

We are very grateful to the Program Committee and local Organizing Committee members for their support and for the time spent to review and discuss the submitted papers and for doing so in a timely and professional manner. We would like to sincerely thank the keynote and tutorial speakers who willingly accepted our invitation and shared their expertise through illuminating talks, helping us to fully meet the conference objectives.

In this edition of SALENTO AVR, we were honored to have the following invited speakers:

- Marco Sacco – ITIA-CNR, Italy
- Arcadio Reyes-Lecuona – Universidad de Malaga, Spain
- Roberto Pierdicca – Università Politecnica della Marche, Italy
- Marcello Carrozzino – Scuola Superiore Sant'Anna, Italy
- Donato Maniello – Studio Glowarp, Italy

We extend our thanks to the University of Salento for the enthusiastic acceptance to sponsor the conference and to provide support in the organization of the event.

We would also like to thank the EuroVR Association, which has supported the conference since its first issue, by contributing each year to the creation of the international Program Committee, proposing invited keynote speakers, and spreading internationally the announcements of the event.

SALENTO AVR attracted high-quality paper submissions from many countries. We would like to thank the authors of all accepted papers for submitting and presenting their work at the conference and all the conference attendees for making SALENTO AVR an excellent forum on virtual and augmented reality, facilitating the exchange of ideas, fostering new collaborations, and shaping the future of this exciting research field.

For greater readability, the papers are organized in two volumes and are classified into seven main parts:

- Virtual Reality
- Augmented and Mixed Reality
- Computer Graphics
- Human–Computer Interaction
- Applications of VR/AR in Medicine
- Applications of VR/AR in Cultural Heritage
- Applications of VR/AR in Industry

We hope the readers will find in these pages interesting material and fruitful ideas for their future work.

June 2018   Lucio Tommaso De Paolis
                                                                                    Patrick Bourdot

Organization

Conference Chair

Lucio Tommaso De Paolis   University of Salento, Italy

Conference Co-chairs

Patrick Bourdot   CNRS/LIMSI, University of Paris-Sud, France
Marco Sacco   ITIA-CNR, Italy
Paolo Proietti   MIMOS, Italy

Honorary Chair

Giovanni Aloisio   University of Salento, Italy

Scientific Program Committee

Andrea Abate   University of Salerno, Italy
Giuseppe Anastasi   University of Pisa, Italy
Selim Balcisoy   Sabancı University, Turkey
Vitoantonio Bevilacqua   Polytechnic of Bari, Italy
Monica Bordegoni   Politecnico di Milano, Italy
Davide Borra   NoReal.it, Turin, Italy
Andrea Bottino   Politecnico di Torino, Italy
Pierre Boulanger   University of Alberta, Canada
Andres Bustillo   University of Burgos, Spain
Massimo Cafaro   University of Salento, Italy
Sergio Casciaro   IFC-CNR, Italy
Marcello Carrozzino   Scuola Superiore Sant'Anna, Italy
Mario Ciampi   ICAR/CNR, Italy
Pietro Cipresso   IRCCS Istituto Auxologico Italiano, Italy
Arnis Cirulis   Vidzeme University of Applied Sciences, Latvia
Lucio Colizzi   CETMA, Italy
Mario Covarrubias   Politecnico di Milano, Italy
Rita Cucchiara   University of Modena, Italy
Yuri Dekhtyar   Riga Technical University, Latvia
Matteo Dellepiane   National Research Council (CNR), Italy
Giorgio De Nunzio   University of Salento, Italy
Francisco José Domínguez Mayo   University of Seville, Spain
Aldo Franco Dragoni   Università Politecnica delle Marche, Italy
Italo Epicoco   University of Salento, Italy

Robert Stone	University of Birmingham, UK
João Manuel R. S. Tavares	Universidade do Porto, Portugal
Daniel Thalmann	Nanyang Technological University, Singapore
Nadia Magnenat-Thalmann	University of Geneva, Switzerland
Franco Tecchia	Scuola Superiore Sant'Anna, Italy
Carlos M. Travieso-González	Universidad de Las Palmas de Gran Canaria, Spain
Manolis Tsiknaki	Technological Educational Institute of Crete (TEI), Greece
Antonio Emmanuele Uva	Polytechnic of Bari, Italy
Volker Paelke	Bremen University of Applied Sciences, Germany
Aleksei Tepljakov	Tallinn University of Technology, Estonia
Kristina Vassiljeva	Tallinn University of Technology, Estonia
Krzysztof Walczak	Poznań University of Economics and Business, Poland
Anthony Whitehead	Carleton University, Canada

Local Organizing Committee

Ilenia Paladini	University of Salento, Italy
Silke Miss	Virtech, Italy
Valerio De Luca	University of Salento, Italy
Cristina Barba	University of Salento, Italy
Giovanni D'Errico	University of Salento, Italy

Spatial Augmented Reality: A Way to Increase Content in Cultural Heritage Context (Tutorial)

Donato Maniello

Studio Glowarp, Italy

The technique called Spatial Augmented Reality – better known as video mapping – is constantly growing. Several fields of application have tested the potential and particularity of use. This contribution aims to discuss the well-known potential of this medium in the urban redevelopment through forms of "augmented architecture" and enhancement in the museum in the case of "augmented archaeology" and to expose some of the techniques used to map generic surfaces in relation to their complexity and size. This allows the construction of a workflow that transforms this raw data into useful contents to enhance the asset itself through multimedia installation and digital storytelling, taking care not to replace the asset itself.

In this way the user is not placed in front of the object in a detached manner, but is catapulted and projected into it, as if he were in a parallel reality. In this case video mapping becomes a medium through which the museum experience is integrated and completed, without going beyond the real world but simply making discernment easier and emphatic.

Keynote Speakers

Augmented and Virtual Reality Enabler for the "Factory 4.0"

Marco Sacco

ITIA-CNR, Italy

Manufacturing sector transformation (the so call Factory 4.0) requires the introduction of advanced tools for both the knowledge representation and simulation. For over 10 years, Virtual Reality and Augmented Reality have generated benefits in several sectors thanks to the potentialities offered by these visualisation technologies able to provide an added value to the contents and data enrichment.

Manufacturing companies, thanks to the reduction of cost and a widespread of devices, could now take advantage integrating AR/VR to simulation and emerging AI.

The result is a Virtual Factory, a full digital twin of the real plant, that could be used for several purposes, from design to monitoring and logistics, from reconfiguration to training. Some industrial applications will be presented.

3D Audio for VR Applications: Fundamentals and Practicalities

Arcadio Reyes-Lecuona

Universidad de Malaga, Spain

Immersive Virtual Reality has been experimenting a constant development and has become more and more popular in the last times. This development has been mainly focused in the visual modality. However, auditory stimuli can also be very powerful in creating immersive perceptions. In this context, three-dimensional localization of sound sources plays an important role in these systems.

3D audio techniques allow to produce the perception in the listener that a sound source is virtually located anywhere in the 3D space, including behind or above the listener. They are not new, but, with the advancements in computational power, it is now possible to perform the required processing in real time using affordable equipment. Therefore, the interest for 3D sound has been increasing.

Additionally, the environment modifies sound and this is especially relevant when simulating spatial sound. The perception of sound includes a combination of the original sound emitted by the source, modifications due to the environment and modifications produced by the listener's head. All those modifications can be characterized and applied in a simulation in order to virtually locate a source in a specific place within a given environment.

In this talk, the fundamentals of several techniques of 3D audio will be presented, with special attention to those more suitable for affordable Virtual Reality systems. More specifically, the potential of binaural audio and virtual Ambisonics will be presented. In addition to this, the role of the environment and how it can be considered will also be discussed. Finally, using 3D audio in a Virtual Reality system requires to know some basic concepts of real time audio, which will be addressed as well. Moreover, the main decisions and trade-off to be taken when implementing a 3D sound renderer will be discussed, presenting the practical implications of each of them.

Sensing Cultural Heritage: User-Centered Approaches Towards Senseable Spaces

Roberto Pierdicca

Università Politecnica della Marche, Italy

Cultural Heritage domain (both tangible and intangible) has witnessed, in the last decade, to a tremendous improvement on the way in which the users can be in contact with cultural goods. The reasons are many, but one can summarize all of them: ICT are everywhere, pervasive like never in the past, and at the same time more and more cheaper and available in the market. Following this wave, 3D reconstructions, new advanced interfaces, wireless connections and interactions are becoming the backbone for AR/VR experiences, which can be definitively defined as the mainstream for communicating and valorizing the priceless values of cultural goods in a more efficient way. State of art solutions for the development of such experiences are mature enough to allow an effective storytelling and are designed to be exploited by heterogeneous users.

However, several limitations still prevent the adoption of a real and efficient digital agenda for the management of Cultural Heritage. One of them, and probably the most urgent, is that digital experiences are developed by experts or insiders, without taking into account the real needs of the users. There is thus the necessity of adopting strategies to understand the users' behaviours by analysing and studying their habits, preferences and knowledge. Nowadays this process is made possible by the increasing miniaturization of new technologies, which allows providing contextual information to the users and, at the same time, to infer information from the digital footprints they leave (the so-called Users' Generated Data).

The talk, besides providing a complete overview of the latest achievements in the field of DCH, will provide prospective visions about a new paradigm of spaces (both indoor and outdoor) where a bidirectional exchange of information from the space to the user and vice versa is possible. These Spaces can be defined Senseable Spaces, which can be both indoor and outdoor scenario where the service to the users are designed following their behaviours and need, in a seamless way. To show the feasibility of such approach, some research projects (developed by a multi-disciplinary group) will be broadly discussed.

Opportunities of the Use of Embodied Agents in Virtual Reality for Cultural Heritage

Marcello Carrozzino

Scuola Superiore Sant'Anna, Italy

Virtual Reality is becoming an increasingly important tool for the research, the communication and the popularization of cultural heritage. However most of the available 3D interactive reconstructions of artefacts, monuments and sites often miss an important factor: human presence. Thanks to the advancements in the technology, in latest years Virtual Humans have started being used in a variety of cultural-related VR applications. From simple 2D characters to complex 3D avatars, technology continues to evolve and so is the adoption of virtual assistants in digital heritage. The acceptance of such tools deserves a greater attention from the scientific community.

This talk will explore the state-of-the-art on this subject, underlining the technological challenges and also analysing the effects of avatar interaction on user engagement, sense of immersion and learning effectiveness.

Contents – Part I

Virtual Reality

Augmented and Mixed Reality

Computer Graphics

Contents – Part II

Applications of VR/AR in Cultural Heritage

Applications of VR/AR in Industry

Human-Computer Interaction

Virtual Reality

Sense of Presence and Cybersickness While Cycling in Virtual Environments: Their Contribution to Subjective Experience

Marta Mondellini[1]([⊠]), Sara Arlati[1,2], Luca Greci[1],
Giancarlo Ferrigno[2], and Marco Sacco[1]

[1] Institute of Industrial Technologies and Automation,
National Research Council, Milan, Italy
{marta.mondellini, sara.arlati, luca.greci,
marco.sacco}@itia.cnr.it
[2] Dipartimento di Elettronica, Informazione e Bioingegneria,
Politecnico di Milano, Milan, Italy
sara.arlati@polimi.it

Abstract. Head mounted displays (HMDs) are visualization devices that provide high levels of immersion in virtual environments (VEs), which have been recently used to enhance the experience of subjects performing a physical exercise. However, the use of these devices in rehabilitation is discussed as it could cause cybersickness and other physical drawbacks. In this context, we conducted a preliminary study investigating the experiences of navigating in the same VEs using a cycle-ergometer and either a projected screen (PS) or a HMD, considering whether the "the Sense of Presence" influenced the device's preference. Thirty-three healthy young adults were enrolled and randomized in four groups to counterbalance the two conditions and to investigate the effects of 5-days washout. Most of the subjects (n = 26) preferred the HMD with respect to PS; sense of presence was higher using HMD than using projector (t = −11.47, p < 0.001), but the difference between conditions was higher for those who preferred the HMD (t = −14.64, p < 0.001), compared to those who chose projector (t = −2.70, p < 0.05). The correlation of presence with cybersickness revealed that, despite higher levels of sickness, sense of presence probably counts more in choosing the HMD as the preferred device.

Keywords: Presence · Virtual reality · Immersive environments

1 Introduction

Virtual reality (VR) has recently been proposed as a means for the physical and cognitive rehabilitation of users with severe cognitive impairments, such as Alzheimer's Disease patients [1], and people affected by age-related decline [2]. Indeed, physical and cognitive exercise increases individual skills and well-being [3], limiting symptoms of decline and thus enhancing users' quality of life [4]. In this context, the use of VR has been proved to increase the motivation of the patients through the provision of physical and/or cognitive tasks in a controlled, safe and ecological

© Springer International Publishing AG, part of Springer Nature 2018
L. T. De Paolis and P. Bourdot (Eds.): AVR 2018, LNCS 10850, pp. 3–20, 2018.
https://doi.org/10.1007/978-3-319-95270-3_1

environment, thus allowing the avoidance of real-life limitations and risks, and promoting the development of healthy habits [5].

However, to be engaging and to promote better performances, VR-based treatments must be able to induce in the users the sense of "being present" in the virtual world [6]. As a consequence, *presence* has become a more and more relevant concept. It should be always considered to evaluate, develop and improve Virtual Environments (VEs) and media systems [7], especially in a field – as physical and cognitive rehabilitation – in which users are requested to respond to virtual events and situations similarly to how they would act in a corresponding real environment [8].

In 2015, a research group developed Goji [9, 10], a preventive program based on the use of Virtual Reality and a cycle-ergometer aimed at preventing the occurrence of symptoms of dementia in elderlies with Minor Cognitive Impairment. The goal pursued with the project was trying of counteract the psycho-cognitive decline affecting these subjects [11, 12] by providing them with both a physical and a cognitive training. The intervention program was based on three different training scenarios dealing with activities of daily life: (1) riding a bike in a park, (2) crossing roads – avoiding cars – to reach a supermarket and, when arrived, (3) buy certain grocery items that are indicated on the shopping list.

For completing the former two scenarios, the users had to ride the cycle-ergometer and interact with the VEs – projected on a flat screen in front of them – using a PlayStation controller. Within these two scenarios, it has been hypothesized that the use of a Head Mounted Display (HMD) could enhance the navigational experience in the VEs, thanks to the increased sense of presence that the HMD can elicit [13]. In this way, in fact, it would be possible to increase the engagement of the patients leading them towards the achievement of better results during therapy [14].

However, it is also necessary to consider that VR and HMD in particular sometimes lead to the occurrence of physical malaise. The onset of cybersickness and other adverse events due to the disagreement between visual and vestibular feedback are not infrequent, though it may be somehow limited by taking into account some recommendations when designing the VE [15]. Thus, in order to promote a safe and engaging application of virtual reality in rehabilitation, sense of presence and cybersickness should be always taken in consideration: the positive effects of sense of presence and motivation must be not obscured by physical drawbacks [13, 16].

For these reasons, before taking advantage of this kind of immersive technologies in studies involving frail people, as elderlies with cognitive impairment, preliminary tests must be conducted on healthy subjects.

In this work, we report the results of a pilot study conducted on young adults with the aim of investigating how much sense of presence, considering the induced physical problems, counts in choosing the preferred device. Sense of presence and cybersickness were evaluated while cycling on a stationary bike in two different conditions, visualizing the VE using (1) a HMD or (2) a flat projected screen (PS).

2   Related Works

In recent years, technological developments eased the creation of VR indoor stationary exercise bike equipment [17] and many researches have designed and built VEs for stationary bicycles elderly rehabilitation and exercise in general [18].

Several studies showed in fact that physical exercises [19] and cognitive simulation [20] within VR could improve physical and cognitive control in the elderlies. Furthermore, older people seem to be open to use new technologies, provided there are not too many unnecessary learning processes [21]. For example, Brunn-Pedersen et al. [22] have proposed to the residents of a retirement home a cycling exercise enriched by an audio-visual virtual environment: the residents embraced the VE augmentation well, although they did not like the use of headphones for auditory inputs.

Another research [20] compared the cognitive and physical improvements of some elderly people who performed the training pedalling on a virtual reality-enhanced cyber-cycle, with age-matched controls training with the same effort on a traditional stationary bike. The first group showed greater improvements, especially in the cognitive domain, probably due also to the nature of the VE that was competitive. Authors reported that navigating in a 3D environment and competing with other people fortifies executive functions such as divided attention, focused attention and decision making.

The use of virtual reality to support physical exercise is particularly useful not only to tempt subjects to train in the short term, but also to modify the intrinsic motivation to perform the activity, thus promoting healthy behaviours that can prevent many diseases [23]. Data [22, 23] show, in fact, that virtual reality used during cycling on stationary bikes contributes to the desire to exercise longer, decreasing the fear of exercising and minimizing the focus on the exercise duration.

Bruun-Pedersen and colleagues observed the experience of some seniors while pedalling in an immersive environment using an HMD, in detail using an Oculus Rift [24]. In their experiment, the authors evaluated the system's usability and the intrinsic motivation during the exercise. Both qualitative comments and elderly behaviours during the exercise showed the positive effect of HMD on people's sense of presence; however, the authors did not quantitatively evaluate the sense of presence experienced and did not compare the use of the Oculus Rift with a non-immersive condition such as the use of a flat screen. The relationship between the subjective sense of presence and the system characteristics of immersion (in particular, the type of display) has been studied extensively over the last decades. As discussed by Slater et al. [25], there is a strong effect of immersion on presence.

All these results suggest that Virtual Reality and immersive VR in particular are able to provide very positive experiences for elderlies, though it is necessary to control the side effects that the immersive technologies may induce [13].

Finally, some theories assume that the time passing between two subsequent experiences in VR may affect subjective judgment about experience [26, 27], thus the differentiation in four groups – made to evaluate whether performing the task in two different days influences the results – have been performed.

3 Methods

3.1 Participants

Participants were enrolled among the employees of the Italian National Research Council; all the subjects gave informed written consent. Their characteristics are reported in Table 1.

Table 1. Sample characteristics. *= missing values.

Participants	N = 33
Age	31 ± 4.94
Sex (M/F)	23/10
Impaired vision:	
• Myopia, astigmatism	21
• No visual problems	9
Familiarity with VR (Y/N)*	6/26
Bike users*:	
• Yes	28
• No	4

No subjects had severe vision impairments. Participants with myopia and astigmatism were left free to wear their prescript glasses or to change the focal distance in the case of HMD. In both experimental conditions the pursued objective was making the subjects see the virtual environments as well as possible.

3.2 Study Design

A within-subjects repeated-measurements study in which participants performed the cycling tasks in two different experimental conditions was conducted. Both conditions used the same VEs and the same cycle-ergometer, but they differed in the devices allowing the visualization and interaction with the VEs (see in Sect. 3.3).

To control the order effects, subjects' exposure to each condition was counterbalanced; moreover, a balanced randomization scheme was used to study the effect of 5-days-washout period with respect to performing both conditions on the same day. This was made with the aim of investigating whether performing the same task after a certain time influenced the perception of sense of presence and the subjective judgement of experience in general. The final distribution of subjects in the study is shown in Table 2.

Table 2. Study randomization scheme.

	5-days-washout	Same day
HMD then PS	Group 1 (n = 10)	Group 3 (n = 6)
PS then HMD	Group 2 (n = 10)	Group 4 (n = 7)

3.3   Equipment

The two VEs – the park and the road-crossing – were developed using Unity 3D. The former (Fig. 1) represented a trail in the park that flows according to the pedals' velocity; an empirical estimation to identify the conversion factor between the cycle-ergometer velocity data – acquired in Round Per Minute (RPM) – and the flowing velocity of the visual representation had been made before this study. If the rider stops pedalling the environment continues to slide, as it would happen in reality, as the cycle-ergometer wheel continues rotating because of its inertia.

Fig. 1. A screenshot of the park scenario.

The aim of this VE was increasing engagement of the users and providing them with the information needed to control the exercise, such as RPM and remaining time, which are displayed as on-screen text.

The user travelled the path in first person following a predefined route, which included only slight bends to try to avoid the occurrence of cybersickness due to the expectation of lateral accelerations [13]; no interaction to deviate from the itinerary were allowed. In details, the path was created through the placement of subsequent nodes on the route, whose interpolation occurs in real-time using quaternion spherical linear interpolation (slerp). To increase the realism of the scene, trees' leaves and grass moved as the wind was blowing and, sometimes, wild animals appeared in the sky or on the trail sides. Moreover, realistic 3D sounds were implemented in the scene.

The latter VE (Fig. 2) represented an urban route in which the subjects had to face the crossing of five traffic-congested and non-regulated crosswalks. The aim of this VE was to train cognitive impaired patients' visuospatial abilities while performing a frequent and thus familiar activity. The subjects, in fact, were requested to reach the supermarket (at the end of street) crossing the road without being hit by any moving vehicles. They had to cycle to reach the sidewalk edge, brake, look around to check if the way is free and proceed only if it safe.

Fig. 2. A screenshot of the urban scenario.

Cars were randomly generated and had different velocities. Collisions with moving cars were signaled to the user via 3D sounds of car horns, braking and glass breaking. If an accident occurs, the user is brought in a safe-position and could restart to pedal as the cars disappeared from that cross in a few seconds.

The hardware equipment is composed by the cycle-ergometer, an upright stationary bike (Cosmed Eurobike 320), a Samsung GearVR HMD equipped with a Samsung S6 smartphone, a projector (EB-1430WI, Epson) and a computer handling the data exchange, as shown in Fig. 3.

Fig. 3. A schematic representation of the setup used in the PS condition (on the left) and in the HMD condition (on the right). Continuous lines represent cabled connection; the dotted line represent the client-server connection used to synchronize the visual flow with the user's velocity in the HMD condition.

The dimensions of the projected screen (1.30 × 2.35 m) were kept constant for all the trials, as well as the distance of the cycle-ergometer from the projected screen. The cycle-ergometer was connected to the PC using a serial port; thanks to its Software Development Kit (SDK) and a communication protocol developed ad-hoc, it was possible to get the users' cycling velocity as input, so that the visual flow in the VEs could be synchronized. For the HMD condition only, a client-server connection was set up to allow the PC to send the velocity data to the application running on the smartphone (Fig. 3).

More in detail, a standalone program – the server, running on the PC established a connection on demand and exchanged data over the network, thus allowing the client component in the VE to remotely access the devices via a wireless network. The two applications (the client on Android smartphone and the server on a Windows PC) communicate via a proper protocol, based on a TCP client-server connection. No issues due to end-to-end latency of the system were perceivable by human users.

The interactions with the VEs were implemented in two different ways. In PS condition, the PlayStation controller, connected to the PC via USB, regulated the interaction between the users and the VE: the joystick was used to look around, while X button simulated the brake. In HMD condition, the gyroscope integrated in the Samsung GearVR handled the rotation of the point of view; participants were able to freely look around with their head in the virtual environment, not to define their steering direction. The braking function was implemented as a result of the touching of the device touchpad.

The brake could be implemented only in the virtual world because, due to physical structure of the ergometer, it was impossible to access the wheel compartment and create a physical brake, able to stop the inertial wheel rotation. The complete stop of the visual flow was thus obtained in both cases decreasing linearly the velocity (i.e. the last value measured when the button/the touchpad was pressed). In both cases, the braking interactions were not handled in the most realistic way as possible, thus introducing in both of them a potentially distractive element for sense of presence.

In both conditions, to proceed forward after a stop, the user had to restart pedaling: the voluntary restarting of the cycling reset the system to the normal acquisition of data.

3.4   Study Protocol

All the enrolled subjects were instructed at the beginning of the test session about the scenario they would be presented and how to handle the interactions (rotating the point of view and braking). All of them were asked to perform the test navigating in the two VEs using both visualization devices, whose order was defined according to Table 2 (Sect. 3.2). For all groups, the presentation order of the VEs was kept unvaried. The first part of the test consisted of 5 min of cycling in a virtual park. Subjects were instructed to pay attention at maintaining the pedals' cadence between 50 and 70 RPM, since that was the pedal cadence used in our previous study [9], with the aim of inducing a training effect in the elderly patients. Within that setup, the workload was in fact adjusted according to the subject's heart rate; in this study, the workload was set to 0 to avoid inducing fatigue in the users, especially in the case in which the two conditions were performed in the same day.

After this task, the environment turned automatically into the urban route and the subject was asked to cross the road, avoiding accidents with moving cars. In this second scenario, participants thus performed different visuospatial and attentional tasks:

(1) pedalling to reach the border of the sidewalk, (2) brake when being near it, (3) check on both sides if there are cars moving closer and, if not, (4) restart pedalling to reach the following cross.

3.5 Measures

The subjective experience was assessed as a whole; therefore both scenarios together were assessed through questionnaires.

The sense of presence (SoP) was evaluated using the Igroup Presence Questionnaire (IPQ) [28] immediately after the administration of each condition.

Data on cyber sickness were also collected using the Simulator Sickness questionnaire (SSQ) [29].

Furthermore, after the completion of both conditions, participants were asked which device they preferred.

Participants' comments during and after the test were collected and analyzed, as they could be useful in providing qualitative information usually not detected through questionnaires [27]. Comments that were judged relevant to Sense of Presence were examined through thematic analysis [30].

3.6 Statistical Analysis

IBM SPSS was used to perform all the statistical analyses. Paired t-tests were run to compare the Sense of Presence in the two conditions. Unpaired t-tests were also used to compare SoP in sub-groups defined according to: (a) device's preference, (b) belonging to a specific Group (Table 2), (c) personal characteristics (Table 1).

A 2×4 mixed ANOVA was performed to evaluate the effects of the interaction [condition * group] and the two main effects of Condition and Group.

Cybersickness was compared between the two conditions in each group using Wilcoxon signed rank tests.

The effect size was measured too. Cohen's d was calculated when the two groups had similar standard deviations and were of similar size; Hedges' g was used where there were different sample sizes. Effect size for Wilcoxon signed rank tests was calculated following Pallant's indication [31].

Correlations of SoP with the cybersickness were evaluated using both Pearson's index correlation and partial correlations. Partial correlation was applied with the aim of examining the relationship between the two variables without the effect of the others. Since SSQ total scores have non-normal distributions [29], a square root transformation was performed before running this statistic.

Chi-squared test was run to establish whether the difference in device preference was generalizable. For this test, VR frequent users were excluded to avoid any bias of the sample.

4   Results

The results of three subjects were excluded: one did not perform the second condition for reasons independent from the study (Group 2), one did not express a preference between devices (Group 2) and the last was considered an outlier since she reported too high scores in SSQ in both conditions (Group 1).

4.1   Sense of Presence

Scores in IPQ ranges from 13 (minimum SoP) to 91 (maximum SoP). In both conditions, scores of SoP were verified to be distributed according to a normal distribution.

In condition PS, subjects got variable scores from 19 to 50(36.5 ± 8.32); with HMD, instead, scores were significantly higher with a minimum of 35 out of 91 (56.8 ± 10.39) (Table 3).

Table 3. Groups' differences in sense of presence measured using IPQ.

		SoP	p-value	Effect size
Group 1	PS	37.00 ± 9.17	$p < 0.05$	Cohen's $d = 1.9$
	HMD	55.89 ± 10.68		
Group 2	PS	33.00 ± 6.16	$p < 0.05$	Cohen's $d = 1.98$
	HMD	52.00 ± 12.10		
Group 3	PS	42.29 ± 7.63	$p < 0.001$	Cohen's $d = 2.16$
	HMD	60.86 ± 9.48		
Group 4	PS	24.43 ± 8.10	$p < 0.05$	Cohen's $d = 3.97$
	HMD	57.86 ± 8.71		

Considering separately those who preferred the projector or the HMD, the difference in sense of presence in the two conditions was statistically significant for both groups: t = −2.70, p < 0.05 and Cohen's d = 1.337 for the former and t = −14.64, p < 0.001, Cohen's d = 0.239 for the latter. The sense of presence of those who chose the projector as preferred device was 42.33 ± 6.563 using this device and 53.33 ± 9.61 using HMD; those who preferred the Samsung GearVR obtained 35.04 ± 8.17 in PS condition and 57.67 ± 10.59 in HMD condition.

Observing the four groups, no difference in IPQ's scores was found: all subjects experienced greater sense of presence in the HMD condition, regardless of the group they belonged to (Table 3).

The 2 × 4 mixed-ANOVA was performed (Condition: [PS, HMD; within] x Group [group 1, group 2, group 3, group 4; between]). The main effect of condition was statistically significant (F (1, 26) = 134.19, p < 0.001 and η2 = 0.59), whereas nor the main effect Group (F (3, 26) = 1.97, p > 0.05 and η2 = 0.14), neither the interaction between the two variables (F (3, 26) = 0.297, p > 0.05 and η2 = 0.009 were.

No effect of personal characteristics was found in SoP scores between the two conditions (Fig. 4). All subjects experienced more presence with HMD regardless of sex (t = 0.93, p > 0.05 and Edges' g = 0.41 for PS condition; t = 1.29, p > 0.05 and Edges' g = 0,05 for HMD condition); visual problems (t = −0.88, p > 0.05 and Edges' g = 0,034 with projector screen, t = −1.934, p > 0.05 and Edges' g = 0,46 with HMD); bicycle's use (t = −0.34, p > 0.05, Edges' g = 0.02 using PS, t = 1.06, p > 0.05 and Edges' g = 0.48 using HMD) and past experience with virtual reality (t = −0.59, p > 0.05 and Edges' g = 0.38 with PS; t = −1.49, p > 0.05 and Edges' g = 0.001 with HMD).

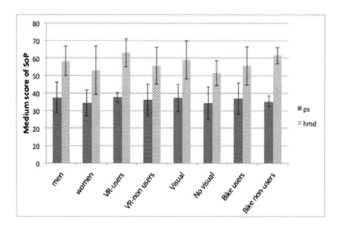

Fig. 4. Sense of Presence, measured with IPQ, according to personal characteristics. No significant difference was found between subgroups.

4.2 Cybersickness

SSQ-TS total scores as measured in the four Groups are reported in Table 4. All groups experienced greater discomfort using HMD.

Table 4. SSQ raw scores and Z-tests. Values are reported as median (minimum – maximum) values.

		SSQ-TS	Z-test	Effect size
Group 1	PS	1 (0–8)	−2,53 p > 0.05	r = 0.59
	HMD	8 (1–20)		
Group 2	PS	0.5 (0–6)	−2,53 p > 0.05	r = 0.63
	HMD	9 (1–26)		
Group 3	PS	4.5 (0–9)	−2,21 p > 0.05	r = 0.64
	HMD	9.5 (4–16)		
Group 4	PS	0 (0–7)	−2,37 p > 0.05	r = 0.63
	HMD	10 (4–50)		

4.3   Correlation Between SoP and Cybersickness

Using the HMD, cybersickness and sense of presence were correlated, but only when the simple correlation is run (r = −0.39, p < 0.05). The correlation disappears when the partial correlation test is performed, indicating that probably sense of presence is more strictly related with other feelings that may arise during the experience of the navigation in the VE. In the PS condition, there is no correlation between the two variables in any case (Fig. 5).

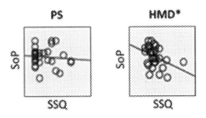

Fig. 5. Correlation between Sense of Presence, measured using IPQ, and cybersickness, measured with SSQ. Cyber-sickness and sense of presence were significantly correlated only in the HMD condition.

4.4   Device Preference

Data showed a significant difference in the device's preference between those who chose HMD (N = 24) and PS (N = 6): chi-square = 10.8, p < 0.001, even when considering only subjects who did not regularly use virtual reality systems (N = 25) to avoid any potential bias (chi-square = 6.76, p < 0.01).

4.5   Participants Comments and Free Notes

The participants' comments about the sense of presence experienced during the exercise were identified and separated from the others. To perform the thematic analysis, four different main areas related to SoP were identified: *realness, interaction, engagement* and *physical drawbacks*.

Comments labelled as *realness* dealt about the naturalness of the virtual environment and of the exercise, namely how similar the reality was perceived to the virtual experience. According to many of these comments, the lack of realism led to distraction from the experience in both conditions (e.g. "The change in bike's direction is not so natural", "I believe there are missing elements which can make the environment more realistic: walking people, animals"), thus reducing the SoP. Some criticisms were made on the poor fluidity of VE, pale images, too slow cars ("The environment is not very detailed", "The movement of cars is unrealistic", "The city is aseptic and fake") and, especially, on the static nature of cycle-ergometer in the bends ("The change in bike's direction is not so natural", "During the test, I felt detached from the ground"). Most of the participants complained that the braking was too unrealistic and immediate in both conditions and that the change of the point-of-view with PS was too sharp because of the joystick sensitivity.

Besides these comments relating to *realism*, which were the most numerous, others were related to self-efficacy and active control of the VE. Within these comments, classified under the label *interaction*, many subjects suggested an increase in the interaction with the virtual environment, even by adding mini-games in the first scenario ("I would have liked to be able to choose the path to follow", "I could not interact with the environment", "It would be nice if something happens at your passage: for example something that rolls and should be avoided"). In the PS condition, subjects reported issues in the interactions with the second VE, as "The change of the visual perspective with the joystick is too quick and unnatural", "The commands to change the point of view are unrealistic and increase the difficulty of the task". In the HMD condition, one subject complained that braking was unrealistic ("Braking is not so natural and distracts from the experience"); two subjects made clear comments on the increase engagement induced by the use of HMD ("The possibility to look around freely increases the level of realism of the experience and makes it more enjoyable and less static", "Exercising with HMD is more realistic and immersive: the environment surrounds the person and thus its visual exploration is more immediate").

Some subjects said that the experiment was, especially with the projected virtual environment, quite monotonous ("I found the exercise boring and therefore not very engaging"). Nevertheless, the same subjects reported also a contrast of emotions, reporting involvement with the Head Mounted Display ("It is to be improved, but I found the experience very fun", "The experience with HMD was engaging") and amusement at some points in the pathway. All these comments were grouped under the category *involvement*.

Finally, some subjects' comments related to the physical discomfort experienced during exercise. This category was named *physical drawbacks*. Mostly, people reported general discomfort and vision problems during the HMD condition "I had nausea and dizziness", "I had a slight sense of nausea", "The background was somewhat blurry and it caused a slight annoyance", "I did not feel comfortable, maybe because I did not see well"). While the latter were felt throughout the exercise, the former appeared mainly during bends ("During the curves, the trajectory was fragmented and this caused malaise" "I felt good on the straight path, but not in the curves"), in the first scenario, and after braking, in the second ("I felt pushed out of my body"). In two cases, malaises were reported also in the PS condition ("I had headache", "I felt a little dizzy").

5 Discussion

Results of this study, which compared Sense of Presence and other different aspects related to the visualization of virtual environments, showed that the preferred visualization device in a sample of healthy young adults was largely the HMD. It has to be highlighted that both those who preferred the projector and those who preferred the HMD experienced a greater sense of presence with Samsung GearVR; however, the difference between the two conditions was greater for those who preferred HMD. Thus, although there could be physical side-effects [13, 32], positive feelings induced by higher SoP seemed to have weighted more in the subjects' choice of the preferred device. In addition, the results of this experiment indicate that exposure mode to both devices does not affect the sense of presence experienced, but they are in contrast with previous studies [33].

Our study did not show any differences in the sense of presence depending on some user's characteristics. These data confirm some studies' conclusions about the differences for males and females for sense of presence [34], but are in contrast to the experiments that reported that virtual reality frequent users experience a higher sense of presence [35]. This may be due to the different way in which questions related to past experience with VR have been posed.

The obtained results also indicate that the physical discomfort (cybersickness) affects sense of presence, but only while wearing the HMD; since no difference in SSQ was found in the two conditions, however it may be possible that cybersickness participates indirectly in SoP determination, by weighing on other variables. This findings are in agreement with what Witmer and Singer's [36] reported in their study, i.e. the physical drawbacks turns the focus away from the virtual environment, decreasing involvement and, consequently, reducing the sense of presence.

Examining the participants' verbal productions, we found four categories of comments about sense of presence: realness, interaction, involvement and physical effects.

These categories correspond to the latent factors already identified in specific questionnaires created to investigate the sense of presence. First, the comments labelled "Realness" are completely comparable to those found in other studies; for example, in the IGroup Presence Questionnaire [28] authors talk of "Experienced Realism", while Witmer and Singer [36] named it "Interface quality". Our second category, namely "Interaction", is perceived as a part of the widest "Space Presence" category for Schubert, and Witmer and Singer insert it in the PQ's first cluster: "Involve/Control". Unlike in Witmer's PQ, that include involvement comments in the first subspace in addition to the VE's sense of control, we have separated these phrases in a single category ("Involvement"); in the Igroup Presence Questionnaire [28] this aspect is present in the first sub-scale, called by the authors "Spatial Presence".

What is interesting is that only one person explicitly reported the feeling of being present in the virtual environment ("I had the feeling of being in the park") but all comments in the "interaction" category contained the implicit reference to the interruption of the sense of presence ("I could not turn the handlebars and this distanced me from the virtual environment"). These outcomes have a twofold importance. On the one hand, they support Schubert and colleagues' proposal [28], which combine interaction and general sense of feeling present in the wider category "Spatial presence"; on the other hand, they suggest the possibility of assessing the sense of presence by alternative methods. In this context, Slater and Steed [37] conducted an experiment in which they asked the subjects to report how many times they were aware of the environment in which they were physically present in. Authors reported a significant correlation between the number of times that subjects reported a conscious transition between the virtual world and the real world, and the sense of presence evaluated through a questionnaire. The comments of subjects enrolled in this study confirmed that often the sense of presence is detected through an interruption.

At last, our "Physical Drawbacks" category is presented only in [7] (with the label "Negative Effects"); in this case, it has to be underlined that most of the physical reactions due to immersion into a virtual environment are evaluated with other specific questionnaires, such as the Simulator Sickness Questionnaire [29].

Many phrases of the subjects referred to the need for motivation in order to have fun and to feel more involved in the virtual environment. Although motivation was a variable we investigated separately, it is interesting how people have spontaneously linked it to the sense of presence. This can be explained by the influence that motivation has on involvement and, consequently, on the sense of presence. Other studies confirmed the strong correlation between motivation and sense of presence [38].

Dealing with the presented system, specific comments have been very helpful for future improvements of the tool. It appeared that cycling in both environments had been enjoyable, but bends and hard braking were judged too sharp and were identified as the main cause of malaise. This could be expected since during brakes and bends, the human body – and its vestibular system in particular – expects to perceive respectively frontal and lateral accelerations. These situations induce a strong conflict between visual and vestibular signals that increased physical discomfort [13, 39]. A correct design of the virtual environment, that has to be developed excluding all the elements that provoke symptoms in susceptible individuals, is indeed a recommendation that has to be pursued [32, 39]. Moreover, it seems plausible that adding some interactions with the environment, as suggested by this study participants, can be useful to increase future users' engagement, but also to reduce motion sickness as suggested in [32, 39, 40].

User comments have highlighted how the sense of presence is important. Though the sample may be biased with respect to the target population (i.e. young adults have more familiarity with VR) who did not complain about graphical features [9], their suggestions to improve the graphic and the technical features of the instrument, and adding sounds, highlighted how the realism of the scenarios is strongly linked to provision of a better experience.

6 Conclusion

In this study, the results of a preliminary test comparing the visualization of two VEs using a projector and a HMD while riding a cycle-ergometer are reported. In particular, the role of sense of presence has been investigated and discussed. The influence of cybersickness was also investigated and reported. It has been noticed that, despite HMD often caused higher discomfort, it was the preferred device for the majority of the subjects and obtained results indicate that this is due to the increased sense of presence that HMD elicited; this underlines the importance of designing engaging systems and exercises with clear and motivating goals. Moreover, the IP Questionnaire's scores obtained in this pilot study were not related to those of cybersickness, contrary to what studies on the antecedents of the sense of presence have reported [7], but this is probably due to the small sample.

Although in this experiment we have evaluated only two variables, it is evident that many others have to be studied when considering the sense of users' presence. It would be interesting to integrate future analyses with other variables: various researches revealed relationships between usability and sense of presence [41], between sense of presence and attention [36] or between usability and memory [27], without considering the role of perceived motivation. Other studies reported that user characteristics, such as cognitive abilities and the willingness to suspend disbelief can be important in influencing presence [36].

Further tests should also be conducted to consider the effect of time and of the habituation on the tolerability of the instrument [42] and the possibility of including objective measures, such as heart rate, skin conductance and/or postural instability. Other experiments, in fact, reported an association between sense of presence and these physiological parameters [43, 44].

Finally, since the study highlighted that the system can be improved to better respond to users' needs, some modifications will be implemented in order to engage more future users. First, since sharp bends and brakes were the main causes of malaise for most of the subjects, they will be improved with the aim of reducing motion sickness. The trajectory of the bike in the park, which resulted sometimes fragmentary, will be modified to create a smoother path, which should not induce in the user the expectations of centripetal accelerations. Moreover, the sensitivity of the braking device, especially in the case of the HMD, will be decreased, recreating the situation in which the velocity slowly decreases until the complete stop. The use of different HMDs, like Oculus Rift or HTC Vive, whose have higher performance than Samsung GearVR, and thus may induce less discomfort [45], will also be considered in future developments. The employment of these devices, in fact, will allow increasing the details of the VEs and the vertices of the objects displayed in the scene, thus leading to a plausible increased realism.

When the navigation and the interaction will be comfortably tolerated by a population of young adults, first tests on frail people and elderly – the target population of the designed physical and cognitive intervention – will be conducted taking into account the proper safety equipment (e.g. harness) and recommendations [32].

References

1. Serino, S., Pedroli, E., Tuena, C., De Leo, G., Stramba-Badiale, M., Goulene, K., Mariotti, N.G., Riva, G.: A novel virtual reality-based training protocol for the enhancement of the "Mental Frame Syncing" in individuals with Alzheimer's disease: a development-of-concept trial. Front. Aging Neurosci. **9**, 240 (2017)
2. Migo, E., O'Daly, O., Mitterschiffthaler, M., Antonova, E., Dawson, G., Dourish, C., Craig, K., Simmons, A., Wilcock, G., McCulloch, E., et al.: Investigating virtual reality navigation in amnestic mild cognitive impairment using fMRI. Aging Neuropsychol. Cogn. **23**(2), 196–217 (2016)
3. Ekelund, U., Steene-Johannessen, J., Brown, W.J., Fagerland, M.W., Owen, N., Powell, K.E., Bauman, A., Lee, I.-M., Lancet Physical Activity Series 2 Executive Committe, Lancet Sedentary Behaviour Working Group, et al.: Does physical activity attenuate, or even eliminate, the detrimental association of sitting time with mortality? A harmonised meta-analysis of data from more than 1 million men and women. Lancet **388**(10051), 1302–1310 (2016)
4. Lok, N., Lok, S., Canbaz, M.: The effect of physical activity on depressive symptoms and quality of life among elderly nursing home residents: randomized controlled trial. Arch. Gerontol. Geriatr. **70**, 92–98 (2017)

5. Holden, M.K., Todorov, E.: Use of virtual environments in motor learning and rehabilitation. In: Handbook of Virtual Environments: Design, Implementation, and Applications, Department of Brain and Cognitive Sciences, pp. 999–1026 (2002)

6. Bystrom, K.-E., Barfield, W., Hendrix, C.: A conceptual model of the sense of presence in virtual environments. Presence Teleop. Virtual Environ. **8**(2), 241–244 (1999)

7. Lessiter, J., Freeman, J., Keogh, E., Davidoff, J.: A cross-media presence questionnaire: the ITC-Sense of Presence Inventory. Presence Teleop. Virtual Environ. **10**(3), 282–297 (2001)

8. Jordan, J., Slater, M.: An analysis of eye scanpath entropy in a progressively forming virtual environment. Presence Teleop. Virtual Environ. **18**(3), 185–199 (2009)

9. Arlati, S., et al.: Virtual environments for cognitive and physical training in elderly with mild cognitive impairment: a pilot study. In: De Paolis, L.T., Bourdot, P., Mongelli, A. (eds.) AVR 2017. LNCS, vol. 10325, pp. 86–106. Springer, Cham (2017). https://doi.org/10.1007/978-3-319-60928-7_8

10. Greci, L.: GOJI an advanced virtual environment for supporting training of physical and cognitive activities for preventing the occurrence of dementia in normally living elderly with minor cognitive disorders. In: 12th EuroVR Conference (2015)

11. Bamidis, P.D., Fissler, P., Papageorgiou, S.G., Zilidou, V., Konstantinidis, E.I., Billis, A.S., Romanopoulou, E., Karagianni, M., Beratis, I., Tsapanou, A., et al.: Gains in cognition through combined cognitive and physical training: the role of training dosage and severity of neurocognitive disorder. Front. Aging Neurosci. **7**, 152 (2015)

12. Cheng, S.-T., Chow, P.K., Song, Y.-Q., Edwin, C., Chan, A.C., Lee, T.M., Lam, J.H.: Mental and physical activities delay cognitive decline in older persons with dementia. Am. J. Geriatr. Psychiatr. **22**(1), 63–74 (2014)

13. Nichols, S., Patel, H.: Health and safety implications of virtual reality: a review of empirical evidence. Appl. Ergon. **33**(3), 251–271 (2002)

14. Zimmerli, L., Jacky, M., Lünenburger, L., Riener, R., Bolliger, M.: Increasing patient engagement during virtual reality-based motor rehabilitation. Arch. Phys. Med. Rehabil. **94**(9), 1737–1746 (2013)

15. Hakkinen, J., Vuori, T., Paakka, M.: Postural stability and sickness symptoms after HMD use. In: IEEE International Conference on Systems, Man and Cybernetics, pp. 147–152 (2002)

16. Kiryu, T., So, R.H.: Sensation of presence and cybersickness in applications of virtual reality for advanced rehabilitation. J. Neuroeng. Rehabil. **4**(1), 34 (2007)

17. Nigg, C.R.: Technology's influence on physical activity and exercise science: the present and the future. Psychol. Sport Exerc. **4**(1), 57–65 (2003)

18. Maculewicz, J., Serafin, S., Kofoed, L.B.: A stationary bike in virtual reality. In: Biostec Doctoral Consortium, Lisbon (2015)

19. Donath, L., Rössler, R., Faude, O.: Effects of virtual reality training (exergaming) compared to alternative exercise training and passive control on standing balance and functional mobility in healthy community-dwelling seniors: a meta-analytical review. Sports Med. **46**(9), 1293–1309 (2016)

20. Anderson-Hanley, C., Arciero, P.J., Brickman, A.M., Nimon, J.P., Okuma, N., Westen, S.C., Merz, M.E., Pence, B.D., Woods, J.A., Kramer, A.F., et al.: Exergaming and older adult cognition: a cluster randomized clinical trial. Am. J. Prev. Med. **42**(2), 109–119 (2012)

21. Ijsselsteijn, W., Nap, H.H., de Kort, Y., Poels, K.: Digital game design for elderly users. In: Proceedings of the 2007 Conference on Future Play, pp. 17–22. ACM (2007)

22. Bruun-Pedersen, J.R., Serafin, S., Kofoed, L.B.: Augmented exercise biking with virtual environments for elderly users: considerations on the use of auditory feedback. In: ICMC-SMC Conference 2014, pp. 1665–1668. National and Kapodistrian University of Athens (2014)

23. Bruun-Pedersen, J.R., Serafin, S., Kofoed, L.B.: Motivating elderly to exercise-recreational virtual environment for indoor biking. In: 2016 IEEE International Conference on Serious Games and Applications for Health (SeGAH), pp. 1–9. IEEE (2016)

24. Bruun-Pedersen, J.R., Serafin, S., Kofoed, L.B.: Going outside while staying inside— exercise motivation with immersive vs. non–immersive recreational virtual environment augmentation for older adult nursing home residents. In: 2016 IEEE International Conference on Healthcare Informatics (ICHI), pp. 216–226. IEEE (2016)

25. Slater, M.: Place illusion and plausibility can lead to realistic behaviour in immersive virtual environments. Philos. Trans. Roy. Soc. Lond. B Biol. Sci. **364**(1535), 3549–3557 (2009)

26. McAuley, E., Duncan, T., Tammen, V.V.: Psychometric properties of the Intrinsic Motivation Inventory in a competitive sport setting: a confirmatory factor analysis. Res. Q. Exerc. Sport **60**(1), 48–58 (1989)

27. Sutcliffe, A., Gault, B., Shin, J.-E.: Presence, memory and interaction in virtual environments. Int. J. Hum. Comput Stud. **62**(3), 307–327 (2005)

28. Schubert, T., Friedmann, F., Regenbrecht, H.: The experience of presence: factor analytic insights. Presence Teleop. Virtual Environ. **10**(3), 266–281 (2001)

29. Kennedy, R.S., Lane, N.E., Berbaum, K.S., Lilienthal, M.G.: Simulator sickness questionnaire: an enhanced method for quantifying simulator sickness. Int. J. Aviat. Psychol. **3**(3), 203–220 (1993)

30. Braun, V., Clarke, V.: Using thematic analysis in psychology. Qual. Res. Psychol. **3**(2), 77–101 (2006)

31. Pallant, J.: SPSS Survival Manual. McGraw-Hill Education, Maidenhead (2013)

32. Sharples, S., Cobb, S., Moody, A., Wilson, J.R.: Virtual reality induced symptoms and effects (VRISE): comparison of head mounted display (HMD), desktop and projection display systems. Displays **29**(2), 58–69 (2008)

33. Ling, Y., Nefs, H.T., Brinkman, W.-P., Qu, C., Heynderickx, I.: The relationship between individual characteristics and experienced presence. Comput. Hum. Behav. **29**(4), 1519–1530 (2013)

34. De Leo, G., Diggs, L.A., Radici, E., Mastaglio, T.W.: Measuring sense of presence and user characteristics to predict effective training in an online simulated virtual environment. Simul. Healthc. **9**(1), 1–6 (2014)

35. Gamito, P., Oliveira, J., Morais, D., Baptista, A., Santos, N., Soares, F., Saraiva, T., Rosa, P.: Training presence: the importance of virtual reality experience on the 'sense of being there. Annu. Rev. Cyberther. Telemed. **2010**, 128–133 (2010)

36. Witmer, B.G., Singer, M.J.: Measuring presence in virtual environments: a presence questionnaire. Presence Teleop. Virtual Environ. **7**(3), 225–240 (1998)

37. Slater, M., Steed, A.: A virtual presence counter. Presence Teleop. Virtual Environ. **9**(5), 413–434 (2000)

38. Lourenco, C.B., Azeff, L., Sveistrup, H., Levin, M.F.: Effect of environment on motivation and sense of presence in healthy subjects performing reaching tasks. In: Virtual Rehabilitation, pp. 93–98. IEEE (2008)

39. Porcino, T.M., Clua, E., Trevisan, D., Vasconcelos, C.N., Valente, L.: Minimizing cyber sickness in head mounted display systems: design guidelines and applications. In: 2017 IEEE 5th International Conference on Serious Games and Applications for Health (SeGAH), pp. 1–6. IEEE (2017)

40. LaViola Jr., J.J.: A discussion of cybersickness in virtual environments. ACM SIGCHI Bull. **32**(1), 47–56 (2000)

41. Brade, J., Lorenz, M., Busch, M., Hammer, N., Tscheligi, M., Klimant, P.: Being there again–presence in real and virtual environments and its relation to usability and user experience using a mobile navigation task. Int. J. Hum. Comput Stud. **101**, 76–87 (2017)

42. Kennedy, R.S., Stanney, K.M., Dunlap, W.P.: Duration and exposure to virtual environments: sickness curves during and across sessions. Presence Teleop. Virtual Environ. 9(5), 463–472 (2000)

43. Insko, B.E.: Measuring presence: subjective, behavioral and physiological methods. In: Riva, G., IJsselsteijn, W.A., Davide, F. (eds.) Being There: Concepts, Effects and Measurement of User Presence in Synthetic Environments, pp. 109–119. IOS Press, Amsterdam (2003)

44. Meehan, M., Insko, B., Whitton, M., Brooks Jr., F.P.: Physiological measures of presence in stressful virtual environments. ACM Trans. Graph. (TOG) 21(3), 645–652 (2002)

45. Biocca, F.: Will simulation sickness slow down the diffusion of virtual environment technology? Presence Teleop. Virtual Environ. 1(3), 334–343 (1992)

Omero 2.0

Matteo Palieri[1,2](✉), Cataldo Guaragnella[1,2], and Giovanni Attolico[1,2]

[1] Institute of Intelligent Systems for Automation,
National Research Council of Italy, Via Amendola 122/D, 70126 Bari, Italy
matteo.palieri@sstlab.it
[2] Department of Electrical and Information Engineering,
Polytechnic University of Bari, Via Orabona 4, 70126 Bari, Italy

Abstract. The OMERO 2.0 system (Organized Multimodal Exploration of Relevant Virtual Objects) is an innovative system that enables visually impaired users to explore *and edit* 3D virtual models. It involves three interaction modalities: visual, haptic and auditory. Virtual models are properly designed to convey the information of interest in a polymorphous and redundant way: the user can therefore choose the sensorial modalities best suited to his/her characteristics, accounting for specific limitations and/or impairments. Virtual models are specially organized to help visually impaired people in building an integrated mental scheme of complex realities (cultural heritage objects and sites, large buildings, abstract concepts in fields such as geometry or chemistry etc.): a challenging task when using a serial sense such as touch. Different semantic layers of the scene (scenarios) convey logically different views of the scene at hand and can be selected separately or in combination depending on the user's needs: that prevents users from being overwhelmed by too many simultaneous details. The software tools used in this new version of OMERO increase the generality of the system and support a larger number of haptic devices. Moreover, the completely new Interactive Haptic Editor of OMERO offers an innovative haptic interface: the haptic properties of the virtual models can be edited even without using the GUI. This redundant combination of vision and touch improves the efficiency for sighted people and enables visually impaired users (that cannot use a GUI) to modify autonomously the rendering of virtual scenes. This results in their active involvement even in the design phase, improving their ability to match the rendering with their specific and individual needs.

Keywords: Virtual reality · Haptic user interface
Human computer interaction · Visual impairment
Scene cognition and understanding

1 Introduction

Virtual reality can be a powerful tool to help visually impaired people to deal with the difficult process of filling the gap between perception and knowledge acquisition and understanding.

Sight is a parallel sense that allows a top-down approach to perception and cognition: it provides at a glance a global and meaningful idea of the scene leaving to further explorations the detection of more details and their interpretation and

L. T. De Paolis and P. Bourdot (Eds.): AVR 2018, LNCS 10850, pp. 21–34, 2018.
https://doi.org/10.1007/978-3-319-95270-3_2

integration in the mental schema of the scene. Visually impaired people use mainly touch and hear to perceive the surrounding world. Touch is a serial sense: it generates long spatio-temporal sequences of data that need to be integrated to build a globally meaningful mental model through a bottom-up process. This difficult integration becomes even more challenging because physical objects exhibit always all the details: this huge amount of information makes very difficult a coarse to fine approach to acquisition and comprehension of the scene. Moreover, this sense is totally useless when dealing with objects that cannot be touched (due to their dimension, position, sensitivity to damages, etc.). Proper lenses can enable a multi-resolution visual perception of scenes while the single resolution available to touch depends on the relative dimension of the fingertips with respect to details and prevent the appreciation of details below a certain threshold. The use of several physical models (offering versions of objects at different scales) is expensive and require the difficult match of perceptions related to different versions of the same scene.

Moving touch inside properly designed Virtual Environments (VEs) can flexibly and effectively cope with these problems. Digital models can dynamically change their scale and resolution to support the haptic perception of details that can also be dynamically highlighted or hidden to focus the attention on the most relevant information. Haptic properties can change according to users' needs and characteristics. Virtual model can represent information that cannot be naturally perceived on real objects (such as measures provided by scientific instruments) and express information that is complementary with respect to the real experience. They can emphasize the perception and the comprehension of the desired informative content and tailor the representation of data to the interests and capabilities of the user.

When the combined haptic and acoustic rendering is used to make up the lack of visual information, the limited bandwidth of haptic must be compensated by well-defined interaction metaphors. The perception of VEs must support a fast comprehension of the overall meaning of the scene. Haptic rendering of VEs for visual impaired is a relatively recent research topic and it is possible for blind people to explore and interact with virtual objects in a virtual environment thanks to the use of haptic interfaces. Guidelines to make hapto-acoustic interaction more effective are available but not yet completely satisfactory.

Movements of the user in the real world generate corresponding movements of its avatar in the virtual world: when the virtual counterpart of the fingertip interacts with a virtual object, the haptic rendering detects a collision and supply through the haptic interface a force feedback that reproduces the same impression of touching a real object using the tip of a pencil. For example, a user can feel the solidity, shape and size of different objects (a wall, a car seat, an artistic piece, ...) (Fig. 1).

The first version of OMERO enabled the user to explore a properly designed Virtual Environment by touching and interacting with Virtual Objects, receiving acoustical and verbal information about the nature and meaning of environments and objects. It introduced the concept of "scenario" as a way to group semantically related objects/details and hide or show them on demand. It assessed several advantages of the virtual experiences as a way to collect knowledge and even to prepare real interaction with physical environments. Due to architectural choices, the first version of OMERO could be executed only on Windows platforms (Windows 2000) and only with

Fig. 1. Example of a haptic interface

Sensable's PHANTOM force-feedback haptic devices that provide high quality features but at prices that can be unaffordable for most people.

A first requirement of OMERO 2.0 has been to make the system available on more software platforms, on different OS and with a larger choice of haptic devices. This required a complete redesign and rewriting of the system using a new file format to encode VR and a new haptic software development tool to achieve the cross-platform capability and a greater independency on the haptic device.

Moreover OMERO 2.0 includes a new functional module called OMERO Interactive Haptic Editor that enables the interactive (and fully haptic) edit in real time of the haptic properties of objects in the scene.

In fact, this task does not use only a standard Graphical User Interface (that would be useless for a visually impaired person) but includes a redundant haptic interface to manage the whole editing process.

We claim that this totally tactile approach strongly simplifies the editing process and make it more natural and effective also for sighted persons. The resulting editing task is also completely available for visually impaired people.

Therefore, it promotes the blind person from final user of the virtual world created by the programmer to co-protagonist of the creative process: he/she is allowed to interactively edit the haptic properties of the VE according to his/her preferences/needs in order to improve the effectiveness of the process of moving from experience to knowledge.

2   Software Architecture

The first version of OMERO used:

- the VRML format to describe the virtual scene
- the OpenHaptics SDK for haptic rendering
- the Coin3D for visual rendering
- the C++ language for programming the interaction with the scene

VRML is an old file format for representing 3-dimensional interactive vector graphics: it is basically a scene graph that contains the visual information of the virtual scene. As mentioned before, the problem of the SDK used for haptic rendering was that OpenHaptics is designed to work specifically with Sensable's PHANTOM force-feedback haptic devices that can be unaffordable for most people: due to this choice the first version of OMERO could be executed only on Windows platforms (Windows 2000) and only with Sensable's haptic interfaces.

OMERO 2.0 uses:

- the X3D format to describe the virtual scene
- the H3D for haptic and visual rendering
- the Python language for programming the interaction with the scene

X3D is a royalty-free open standard including a file format and a run-time architecture to represent and communicate 3D scenes and objects using XML. It is basically a scene graph containing both the visual and the haptic descriptions of the virtual scene.

H3D is an open source haptic software development platform that uses one unified X3D scene graph to handle both graphic and haptic rendering at the same time. The main advantage of H3D is that it is cross platform and independent on the haptic device. It enables audio integration as well as stereography on supported displays.

Python scripts are easy to write and allow rapid development of efficient interaction paradigms with the scene.

OMERO 2.0 is now cross-platform and independent on the haptic device. A more in-depth view of the software architecture is presented in the following sections.

2.1   The X3D File Format

X3D is a scene graph containing both visual and haptic descriptions of the virtual scene: scene graphs are general data structures used to hierarchically organize and manage the contents of a collection of nodes in a tree structure. Each node is an object that is composed of a set of data elements, known as fields that describe the parameters of the node. A node may have many children but often only a single parent. The effects of a parent are applied to all its child nodes. An operation performed on a group automatically propagates its effect to all of its members. A common feature, for instance, is the ability to group related shapes/objects into a compound object that can then be moved, transformed, selected, etc. as a single object. Scene graph programming models support a variety of operations through traversals of the graph data structure that typically begin with the root node. Graph traversals are required for a number of operations (including rendering activities) related to transformations, clipping and culling, lighting and interaction operations such as collision detection and picking. Starting from the root node, operations are recursively applied (often the updating and rendering operations are applied one after the other) moving down the scene graph until a leaf node is reached. We report below a simple X3D code that describes a water molecule made up of a big blue hard sphere representing the oxygen and two smaller and softer red spheres representing the hydrogen (Fig. 2).

```
<X3D>
<Scene>

<Group DEF="WATER_MOLECULE">

<Shape>
<Appearance>
<Material emissiveColor="0 191 255"/>
<FrictionalSurface stiffness="0.9"/>
</Appearance>
<Sphere DEF="O" radius="0.07"/>
</Shape>

<Transform translation='-0.15 -0.1 0'>
<Shape>
<Appearance>
<Material emissiveColor="255 0 0"/>
<SmoothSurface stiffness="0.8"/>
</Appearance>
<Sphere DEF="H1" radius="0.05"/>
</Shape>
</Transform>

<Transform translation='0.15 -0.1 0'>
<Shape>
<Appearance>
<Material emissiveColor="255 0 0"/>
<SmoothSurface stiffness="0.8"/>
</Appearance>
<Sphere DEF="H2" radius="0.05"/>
</Shape>
</Transform>

</Group>

</Scene>
</X3D>
```

Fig. 2. Example of a simple X3D file representing a water molecule

For each object in the scene we can specify position, color, haptic characteristic and geometry (as illustrated above) by setting the desired values in the correct field of the proper node.

2.1.1   X3D Nodes

The *<Transform>* node enables the programmer to specify the position of a certain object in the virtual world coordinates by setting the desired values in the *translation*, *rotation*, *center* and *scale* fields: this is indeed a grouping node that defines a coordinate system for its children that is relative to the coordinate systems of its ancestors.

The *<Shape>* node has two child nodes, *<Appearance>* and *<Geometry>*.

The *<Appearance>* node specifies the visual attributes (e.g. material and texture) to be applied to the geometry and shall contain the following child nodes: *<Material>*, *<Surface>*, and *<ImageTexture>*.

The *<Material>* node specifies surface material properties for the associated geometry nodes and is used by the X3D lighting equations during rendering.

The *<Surface>* node is H3D-specific and encapsulates information about the haptic properties of the item. There are 3 surface types currently implemented in H3D:

- *SmoothSurface*
- *FrictionalSurface*
- *MagneticSurface*

The *<SmoothSurface>* node specifies a surface with no friction at all, and has the following fields: *stiffness* (whose value should be in the range [0, 1] where 1 is the maximum stiffness the haptics device can handle) and *damping* (the velocity based damping of the surface). An object with a high stiffness value will be perceived as hard on touch while an object with a low stiffness value will be perceived as soft on touch.

The *<FrictionalSurface>* node specifies a surface with friction and, besides *stiffness* and *damping*, it has the fields: *staticFriction* (the friction that is experienced upon initial movement when resting on the surface and whose value should be in the range [0, 1]) and *dynamicFriction* (the friction that is experienced when moving along the surface and should be a value in the range [0, 1] as well).

The *<MagneticSurface>* node specifies a surface where the proxy of the haptic device is attracted and forces are generated to keep the proxy on the surface; beside *stiffness*, *damping*, *staticFriction* and *dynamicFriction* it has the following field: *snapDistance* (the distance from the surface within which forces are generated to pull the proxy towards the surface). If the device is pulled outside the distance from the surface it will be freed from the magnetic attraction.

The *<ImageTexture>* node defines a texture map by specifying an image file and general parameters for mapping to geometry. The texture is read from the URL specified by the *url* field and the image file should be placed in the same directory of the X3D scene file.

The *<X3DGeometryNode>* is the base node type for all geometry in X3D and stores the geometry that will be used for haptics as well as graphics. This node has the following fields: *isTouched* (tells if a HapticDevice has been in contact with the geometry in the last scenegraph loop), *force* (the last force delivered by this geometry to the haptics device), *contactPoint* (the last contact point of the HapticDevices on the geometry), *contactNormal* (the normal at the last contact point of the HapticDevice on the geometry). We inherit all the different geometries from this base class: commonly used geometries in VEs are 'Sphere', 'Cone', 'Box', 'IndexedFaceSet', 'ElevationGrid', etc.

2.2   H3D

H3D is a dual license, open-source and commercial, cross-platform, scene-graph API: it uses one unified X3D model to handle both graphic and haptic rendering at the same time. H3D is written entirely in C++ and uses OpenGL for graphics rendering and

HAPI for haptics rendering. Using X3D syntax, applications containing animated virtual worlds can be created: for more advanced animations and behaviors in the world Python can be used. H3DAPI is device independent and supports multiple currently available commercial haptics devices such as devices from Sensable, devices from Force Dimension, Falcon device from Novint, HapticMaster device from Moog FCS Robotics.

H3DAPI is distributed with two small programs written in C++ called H3DLoad and H3DViewer that can be used to load the X3D file. Loading with H3D Viewer the above mentioned X3D file will enable us to see it in 3 dimensions and touch it with the haptic stylus (Fig. 3).

Fig. 3. Example of an X3D water molecule loaded in H3D Viewer

3   Interactive Virtual Environments

Different interactive virtual environments have been created in order to test the efficiency of the system in helping the visually impaired user to acquire a mental model of complex sites that should then come in handy during a real inspection.

3.1   Labyrinth Example

A first VE called 'Labyrinth' is presented in Fig. 4.

The scene is made up of four rooms: the entrance (ROOM_1), a room with a television (ROOM_2), an empty room (ROOM_3) and a room with an exit (ROOM_4). Walls, floors and ceilings are modeled as simple 'Box'-es and are properly positioned in the VE through the <*Transform*> node.

Being ROOM_1 the starting point of the simulation, this Interactive VE has been created in order to measure the time needed and the difficulties encountered by the visually impaired user to understand the surrounding environment and successfully complete the labyrinth: as it can be seen in Fig. 4 ROOM_1 and ROOM_2 are

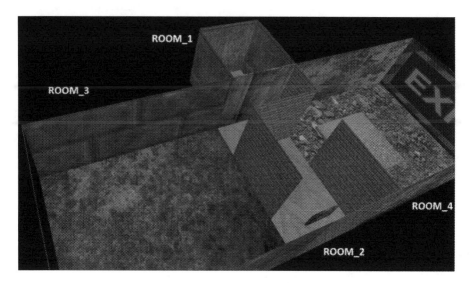

Fig. 4. First example of interactive virtual environment: Labyrinth

separated by a door that must be opened to proceed with the exploration and reach the exit located in ROOM_4.

Custom interaction paradigms can be added to the scene by incorporating Python scripts in the X3D model using the *<PythonScript>* node. In order to open the door, for example, the user needs to touch it and keep pressed the *mainButton* of the haptic interface for more than 2 s: this event will trigger the execution of a Python script that will take care of raising and lower the door within a prefixed interval of time.

In particular, in order to implement the above mentioned functionality we need to insert in the X3D model: a *<TimeSensor>* node (used to generate events as time passes), a *<PositionInterpolator>* node (used to linearly interpolate among a list of 3D vectors to produce an *SFVec3f value_changed_event*) and a *<DynamicTransform>* node as shown in Fig. 5.

```
<DynamicTransform DEF="MOVEMENT_DOOR">
<Shape DEF="SHAPE_DOOR">
<Appearance>
<Material DEF="MATERIAL_DOOR" diffuseColor="0 0 1" />
<FrictionalSurface stiffness="0.5" />
<ImageTexture DEF="TEXTURE_DOOR" url="texture3.jpg" />
</Appearance>
<Box DEF="DOOR" size="0.08 0.2 0.005" />
</Shape>
</DynamicTransform>
```

Fig. 5. X3D moving door code snippet

By properly routing the events generated by the haptic device and the X3D scene graph data flow to a dedicated Python script it is possible to accomplish the desired task, causing the door to rise and lower within an interval of 15 s, giving to the user the chance to go from one room to the other and proceed with the inspection.

Another important feature implemented in this VE is the possibility that is given to the user to ask the system about what he/she is touching at any time: pressing the *mainButton* of the haptic device while touching a certain object in the scene will trigger the execution of a Python script that will take care of reproducing a.wav file containing an audio description of the selected object. This will help the user with visual impairments in localizing his/her position, time after time, in the virtual environment.

3.2 Apulia Region Example

A second VE called 'Apulia Region' has been carefully designed to help visually impaired people to acquire the available information in a progressive and ordered way: a virtual scene reproducing a complex environment can contain a big amount of information and providing all the contents at the same time can overburden the blind user, making hard an effective navigation and comprehension of the VE.

To simplify the user interaction with the virtual scene and organize information on the basis of their semantic meaning, VEs can be designed exploiting the scenarios metaphor: the user can, by simply pressing the function keys on the keyboard, introduce a progressive level of detail to the scene navigating therefore in different scenarios each reproducing data related to a particular semantic view of the region. This approach enables the user in building a progressively growing mental schema of the territory and its peculiarities.

A first scenario of the region model concerns the shape of the territory and the disposition of provinces, their borders and the borders between Apulia, the neighborhood regions and the sea. In the second scenario, the hydrographic network of the region is added: rivers and lakes have been respectively realized as canyon and ditches in which the user avatar can fall and move to provide perceptions about their course and shape.

A third scenario includes the location of the major towns while the fourth and last view adds the connections between different towns: roads are haptically represented as canyons connecting two towns.

All elements have been defined as acoustic active objects enabling the user to get vocal explanations of the current touched item on demand.

A visualization of the scenario N.4 (Region shape + Provinces + Cities + Roads) is presented in Fig. 6.

The dynamic display of the different semantic scenarios is made possible by inserting in the X3D model, beside a *<PythonScript>* node, a *<KeySensor>* node and various *<ToggleGroup>* nodes: a *<ToggleGroup>* node gives the chance to the user to enable/disable haptics and graphics rendering of its children nodes.

It is important to note that the acquisition and comprehension of the elements in the scene is critically related to the representation of each elements. The design must therefore be accomplished paying attention to prevent confusion and sense of disorientation that can easily arise when touch and hearing are the only available sensorial modalities.

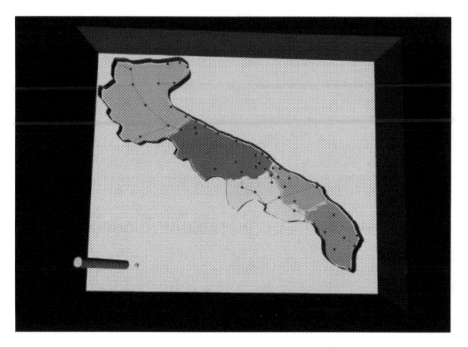

Fig. 6. Apulia region – Scenario N.4

4 Interactive Haptic Editor

OMERO 2.0 includes a completely new Interactive (fully) Haptic Editor. This tool enables the user to edit in real time the haptic properties of the virtual scene using a completely haptic interaction that does not requires the use of a GUI and is therefore available also to blind users. Visually impaired people can be promoted from being just the final users of an experience designed by sighted persons to be active part of the creative process by interactively editing the haptic properties of the virtual environment to best fit their needs and characteristics.

The editing starts by opening the X3D-model of the VE through the H3DViewer: the virtual WORLD module appears and a vocal message explains how the system works and how to use it.

To modify the haptic properties of an object the user needs to touch it and keep pressed the *mainButton* of the haptic interface for more than 3 s (Fig. 7).

That disables the haptic and graphic rendering of the ToggleGroup "WORLD", while a gentle force leads the haptic stylus towards a specific position that when reached activates the haptic and graphic rendering of the ToggleGroup "EDITOR": a vocal message notifies the user that he/she is now in the EDITOR module and that he/she can move across the double box editor (Fig. 8) to set the desired haptic properties for the selected object.

Fig. 7. Interactive haptic editor: WORLD module

Fig. 8. Interactive haptic editor: EDITOR module

The double box editor, centered in a void environment, has the following characteristics:

– Moving along the x-axis of the left box modifies the stiffness
– Moving along the y-axis of the left box modifies the damping

– Moving along the x-axis of the right box modifies the staticFriction
– Moving along the y-axis of the right box modifies the dynamicFriction

The user continuously experiences the setting changes and can therefore properly and efficiently look for the desired combination of properties. This procedure is much simpler than the use of GUI also for sighted people.

To save the setting the user has to keep pressed the button of the haptic interface for more than 3 s. The haptic and graphic rendering of the ToggleGroup "EDITOR" is disabled and a gentle force takes the user back to the target point in the WORLD where the EDITOR had been invoked: once this position is reached the haptic and graphic rendering of the ToggleGroup "WORLD" is enabled again. Now the user can press again the *mainButton* of the haptic interface to be detached from the target point and continue the exploration. A special care has been used in the system design in order to prevent the user from experiencing a loss of his/her sense of position/orientation in the VE.

The haptic rendering of the edited object will immediately reflect any change made.

5 Experimental Results

Different applications of OMERO have been designed and proposed to visually impaired users in order to test the efficiency of the system in helping the blind to quickly acquire an exhaustive mental model of complex environments. VEs have been carefully designed in order to allow the blind user to overcome some of the difficulties he encounters in acquiring spatial information in the everyday life. Very different navigation contexts have been proposed to visually impaired users in several occasions: we report below the experimental results obtained with the VE of the Apulia Region. This VE has been constructed from GIS data in order to allow the user to acquire a proper knowledge of the territory from different perspective: as previously mentioned it is multi-layered and, by pressing the function keys on the keyboard, it is possible to navigate among four different scenarios each reproducing data related to a particular semantic view of the region. The described model has been proposed to twenty visually impaired users. Some of them did not have any previous knowledge of the region features. Users started their test exploring the first scenario of the model in order to construct a cognitive map of the shape of the region and its provinces, their borders, names and relative positions. Then they went through the next scenarios to progressively increase their knowledge of the VE. The scene querying interaction modality helped the users during the exploration allowing them to organize all the vocal information provided by the system on button demand in an effective learning. Most of the users were able to correctly locate rivers, lakes and towns with respect to the regional and/or provincial territories and with respect to each other. Furthermore, after a complete and accurate exploration of all the semantic levels offered by the model, they were easily able to find any given object again. The more curious and interested subjects were able to reach towns following a suitable pathway, even when they were very distant from each other. All of the users were able to learn new information about the region and found the haptic/acoustic interaction very stimulating and almost all of the users judged the proposed system a valid and more flexible alternative to tactile maps.

6 Conclusion and Future Works

The new characteristics of the system OMERO 2.0 and the advantages of its Interactive (fully) Haptic Editor have been described.

OMERO 2.0 is now platform independent and supports a larger variety of haptic devices. Its new Interactive Haptic Editor can significantly simplify the editing of haptic properties for sighted people and opens new possibilities to visually impaired users: they are not only final users but can actively design the rendering of virtual models even without using the GUI. Moving from sensations to knowledge when using a serial sense such as touch is difficult and a relevant cooperation of final users in the design and customization of rendering can be critical to succeed. While developed in cooperation with blind people, the system now needs an extensive validation of its efficiency through a larger number of individuals with a wide variety of visual impairments and of personal history and experiences.

The extended tests on the previous release of OMERO have assessed the efficacy of virtual exploration of models of real objects and sites in making the construction of a mental model quicker and easier. The use of virtual reality improves the flexibility and versatility of the interaction and its adaptation to the specific needs of final users. Virtual models can be used to acquire a rough but effective concept of the real world that can therefore be refined and completed by the direct experience. The virtual exploration of virtual maps of sites and territory can increase the autonomy of visually impaired users. The new version of the system can make wider the use of the system (by decreasing its cost depending on the accuracy required by the application) and can involve each single person in the design phase. This increased customization is expected to further improve the efficacy of OMERO and the amount and kinds of knowledge that can be made available to visually impaired people using this new paradigm.

References

1. De Boeck, J., Cuppens, E., De Weyer, T., Raymaejers, C., Coninx, K.: Multisensory interaction metaphors with haptics and propioception in virtual environments. In: Proceedings of NordiCHI 2004, Tampere, FI, October 2004
2. De Boeck, J., Raymaekers, C., Coninx, K.: Are existing metaphors in virtual environments suitable for haptic interaction. In: Proceedings of the 7th International Conference on Virtual Reality, pp. 261–268 (2005)
3. De Felice, F., Gramegna, T., Renna, F., Attolico, G., Distante, A.: A portable system to build 3D models of culturale heritage and to allow their explorations by blind people. In: IEEE Proceedings of HAVE 2005, Ottawa, Ontario, Canada, October 2005

4. De Felice, F., Renna, F., Attolico, G., Distante, A.: A haptic/acoustic application to allow blind the access to spatial information. In: Proceeding of WorldHaptics 2007, Tzukuba, Japan, March 2007
5. De Felice, F., Attolico, G., Distante, A.: Configurable design of multimodal non-visual interfaces for 3D VEs. In: Proceedings of HAID 2009 4th International Conference on Haptic and Audio Interaction Design, Dresden, Germany, September 2009, p. 71 (2009)
6. Lahav, O., Mioduser, D.: Haptic-feedback support for cognitive mapping of unknown spaces by people who are blind. Int. J. Hum Comput Stud. **66**, 23–25 (2008)
7. Lecuyer, A., Mobuchon, P., Megard, C., Perret, J., Andriot, C., Colinot, J.: Homere: a multimodel system for visually impaired people to explore virtual environments. In: Proceedings of IEEE Virtual Reality, pp. 251–258 (2003)
8. Okamura, A., Cutkosky, M.: Haptic exploration of fine surface features. In: Proceedings of IEEE International Conference on Robotics and Automation, pp. 2930–2936 (1999)
9. Ott, R., Vexo, F., Thalmann, D.: Two-handed haptic manipulation for CAD and VR applications. Comput. Aided Des. Appl. **7**(1), 125–138 (2010)
10. Badcock, D.R., Palmisano, S., May, J.G.: Vision and virtual environments. In: Hale, K.S., Stanney, K.M. (eds.) Handbook of Virtual Environments: Design, Implementation, and Applications, 2nd edn, pp. 39–86. Taylor & Francis Group Inc., Boca Raton (2014)
11. Wuillemin, D., van Doom, G., Richardson, B., Symmons, M.: Haptic and visual size judgements in virtual and real environments. In: Proceedings of IEEE World Hapics Conference, pp. 86–89 (2005)
12. Yoon, W.J., Hwang, W.-Y., Perry, J.C.: Study on effects of surface properties in haptic perception of virtual curvature. Int. J. Comput. Appl. Technol. **53**, 236–243 (2016)
13. Maidenbaum, S., Levy-Tzedek, S., Chebat, D.R., Amedi, A.: Increasing accessibility to the blind of virtual environments, using a virtual mobility aid based on the "EyeCane": feasibility study. PLoS One **8**(8), e72555 (2013). https://doi.org/10.1371/journal.pone.0072555
14. Picinali, L., Afonso, A., Denis, M., Katz, B.F.G.: Exploration of architectural spaces by blind people using auditory virtual reality for the construction of spatial knowledge. Int. J. Hum Comput Stud. **72**(4), 393–407 (2014). https://doi.org/10.1016/j.ijhcs.2013.12.008
15. Jaimes, A., Sebe, N.: Multimodal human-computer interaction: A survey. Comput. Vis. Image Underst. **108**(1–2), 116–134 (2007)

Geometry Extraction for Ad Hoc Redirected Walking Using a SLAM Device

Christian Hirt[(⊠)], Markus Zank, and Andreas Kunz

ETH Zurich, Innovation Center Virtual Reality, 8092 Zurich, Switzerland
{hirtc,mzank}@ethz.ch, kunz@iwf.mavt.ethz.ch

Abstract. Redirected walking applications allow a user to explore large virtual environments in a smaller physical space by employing so-called redirection techniques. To further improve the immersion of a virtual experience, path planning algorithms were developed which choose redirection techniques based on the current position and orientation of the user. Furthermore, additional algorithms were developed to guarantee the user's safety at all times. In order to ensure a reliable performance, both safety and planning algorithms depend on accurate position tracking which is commonly provided by an external tracking system. The disadvantage of this kind of tracking is the time-consuming preparation of the physical environment, which renders the system immobile. A possible solution to eliminate this dependency is to replace the external tracking system with a state-of-the-art inside-out tracker based on the concept of Simultaneous Localization and Mapping (SLAM). SLAM algorithms track the position and orientation of a sensor by fusing various measurements and using a continuously generated and expanding map of its surroundings. However, the information contained in this map is not suitable for existing safety and planning algorithms due to its feature-based localization properties.

In this paper, we present an approach in which we attach a commercially available SLAM device to a head-mounted display to track the head motion of a user. From sensor recordings of the device, we extract environmental information specifically suitable for existing path planner and safety algorithms of a redirected walking application using a sequence of algorithms. Accordingly, the resulting spatial data consists of 2D coordinates describing closed polygons which are used to approximate the geometry of the walkable area. This geometrical data can then be streamed to the redirected walking application.

Keywords: Human-centered computing – Virtual reality
Computing methodologies – Tracking

1 Introduction

Redirected walking (RDW) is used in immersive virtual reality applications and allows a user to explore an extensive virtual environment in a smaller physical

© Springer International Publishing AG, part of Springer Nature 2018
L. T. De Paolis and P. Bourdot (Eds.): AVR 2018, LNCS 10850, pp. 35–53, 2018.
https://doi.org/10.1007/978-3-319-95270-3_3

space while walking freely. In order to achieve RDW, the user's real walking path is manipulated by applying so-called redirection techniques (e.g. scaling translational mapping of the user's movement between the real and the virtual world). Early approaches mainly focused on simple behaviour like guiding a user away from physical boundaries such as walls (e.g. Steer-to-Center, S2C [13]), whereas newer, more sophisticated algorithms (e.g. MPCRed [10], FORCE [19]) actively plan for future situations. However, it is still inevitable that a user will at some point approach a physical boundary which may lead to a collision. To prevent such a collision, different safety measures were developed over the years (e.g. resets [17], wall warners [18]). For both, the path planners and safety measures, it is crucial to have access to accurate information about the user's position and orientation with respect to the real physical space. Therefore, state-of-the-art RDW applications rely on external tracking systems, which render the whole system immobile and inflexible due to time-consuming calibration and set-up processes. In order to address this issue, we replace the external tracking system with a commercially available inside-out tracker which is based on a simultaneous localization and mapping (SLAM) algorithm. In SLAM tracking, the environment is continuously recorded, points of interests, so-called features, are extracted using feature detection algorithms (e.g. SIFT [9]) and a map is generated, in which these feature locations are stored. The algorithm then continuously refers to this map to determine the orientation and position of the tracker by recognizing previously recorded features. However, these features have no geometrical meaning in a spatial sense, because they are basically simple pixel clusters with specific properties (e.g. strong change of contrast along a specific axis). Since safety and planning algorithms for RDW specifically require spatial polygonal information describing the geometry of the surroundings, a way of providing a map in a suitable form is required.

In this paper, we show a sequence of algorithms which extract spatial information about the geometry of the surroundings by evaluating raw data captured by a Google Tango Yellowstone tablet[1]. To this end, this spatial information was provided manually to the system by identifying the 2D coordinates of the corners of the rectangular tracking space. Consequently, the goal is to automatically represent physical boundaries or obstacles similarly in the form of closed polygons, each described by a set of control points (i.e. 2D coordinates). After discussing the related work, the paper introduces the system architecture for extracting spatial data from the point cloud that is suitable to be used for a later RDW algorithm (i.e. a S2C). Since such an extraction is computationally expensive, it cannot be run on the tablet only, but instead a suitable workload distribution between the tablet and an external notebook is proposed. The remainder of the paper shows the individual components of this algorithm more in detail and concludes with the presentation of achieved results and an outlook on future work. For completeness, all relevant design variables used in the algorithms are listed in the appendix.

---

[1] https://developers.google.com/tango/.

2   Related Work

RDW was first introduced by Razzaque et al. [14], showing that a virtual room can be larger than the available physical space by employing a simple redirection technique which manipulated the user's rotation around his own axis (i.e. rotational gain). Further redirection techniques, such as scaling translational movement [16] and altering the walking path by adding a curvature distortion [12], were introduced in the following years. Furthermore, Field et al. [4] described target-oriented approaches such as steer-to-orbit which are used to select the most suitable redirection techniques based on the current position and orientation (i.e. state) of the user. Later, Zmuda et al. [19] introduced the first approach evaluating potential future user states for the selection of redirection techniques. Nescher et al. [10] further presented a model predictive controller MPCRed, which is used as a path planner solving a receding horizon optimal control problem in order to choose the most appropriate redirection technique.

Since the user cannot see the real environment, it is crucial to have reliable safety measures which stop him if a collision with any physical object or boundary would occur otherwise. A commonly used technique to stop a user from colliding is a reset mechanism (or also called reorientation) which was shown by Williams et al. [17]. During a reset, a user is instructed to turn on the spot, while a rotational gain is applied which scales the mapping between the real and the virtual viewing direction. Besides reset techniques, a more recent approach is a multi-phase wall warner by Zank et al. [18], which gradually overlays real world boundaries to the virtual environment if a collision is imminent based on walking speed and distance to the wall.

Due to technical limitations, SLAM-based RDW implementations have not been realised so far. However, Bachmann et al. [1] mentioned a potential application for SLAM integration into a low-cost portable immersive virtual environment system. But this approach was focused on a 1:1 mapping of a user's motion between the real and the virtual worlds. Further, a more specific proposition was shown by Nescher et al. [11] introducing a concept for ad hoc free walking in virtual environments and RDW. This concept mainly showed a potential hardware setup and additionally pointed out that existing planning algorithms cannot be applied directly because of missing information (e.g. for S2C, a clear center point cannot be defined without known system boundaries). A different approach by Sra et al. [15] focused on the extraction of a walkable area from a prerecorded scan of the environment, which may potentially be used as an input for planning and safety algorithms, however, the algorithmic part was performed offline. More recent approaches to an algorithmic online extraction of planning data from SLAM point clouds were introduced by Hirt et al. in [6,7].

3   Methodology

As proposed in Nescher et al.'s ad hoc free walking, we use a Google Tango Yellowstone tablet in our paper. The tablet provides a six degrees of freedom

SLAM tracking by fusing various sensor measurements. It is attached to the front of a head-mounted display to align the user's and the tablet's field of view. Consequently, the head position and orientation of the user can be calculated at any given time using the tablet's tracking data and a previously measured static offset between the tablet and the user's head. As explained before, the SLAM algorithm continuously populates a map with features found in the recorded environment, but this particular map is unsuitable for the existing planning and safety algorithms due to its fundamentally different structure. Both algorithms were originally designed to receive a set of 2D coordinates (i.e. control points) forming a closed polygon which describes the physical boundary of the tracking space. The previously employed external tracking system covered a rectangular tracking area which was defined by four control points in the respective corners. Since the dedicated tracking area was stationary, the coordinates were manually measured and entered into the system. For SLAM, the tracking space is not known beforehand and is continuously expanding. Consequently, the map needs to be updated regularly. Since it cannot be assumed that the tracking area is completely free of obstacles, it is important to detect the outer boundary as well as obstacles lying within this tracking area.

In our approach, we access the measurements of the IR depth sensor on the rear side of the tablet, which scans its surroundings with 5 Hz up to a distance of 3 m. The reflected infrared rays are analysed using time-of-flight which results in a 3D point cloud containing coordinate triplets. Each of these coordinate triplets represents a reflection of a single IR ray in the environment and thus the cloud describes the surface of recorded objects. These triplets are recorded with respect to the origin of the coordinate system which is initialised at the tablet's position when the application is launched. Due to the large amount of data in such a point cloud, it cannot be transferred directly over the network for further processing, but needs some preprocessing to reduce the amount of data. However, the tablet's CPU power is very limited and the SLAM algorithm already requires most of its capacity. Thus, a careful distribution of the workload on the tablet and on a remote notebook is important, also taking into account the available network bandwidth.

Using this data recorded by the tablet's depth sensor, we apply a sequence of algorithms in order to extract a spatial description of the environment, which can later be used for RDW algorithms. Accordingly, the final representation will consist of a set of 2D control points describing the outer physical boundary as well as of objects lying in the vicinity. The system architecture of the data extraction process is shown in Fig. 1. The recorded 3D point cloud is fed into a preprocessing step on the tablet which continuously generates two different maps (a wall map and an occupancy map) of the surroundings. This preprocessing needs to be done on the tablet due to the limited network bandwidth. Additionally, splitting the preprocessing into two separate maps is necessary to achieve both, a fast and accurate representation. Since the Tango tablet also runs the SLAM algorithm as well as the two preprocessing stages, further computations are severely limited. Therefore, the wall map and the occupancy map are transmitted via wireless network to a more powerful notebook. The notebook is used to run the computationally more demanding tasks of fusing the sub-maps into a world map and extracting geometrical shapes in the form of control points from it. Finally, the tracking information determined by the SLAM algorithm and the extracted set of control points are transferred to a RDW application (i.e. RDW Minimal) running on the notebook, which consists of a basic virtual environment with a simple S2C algorithm and safety measures (i.e. a wall warner and resets). The following subsections will describe this architecture more in detail.

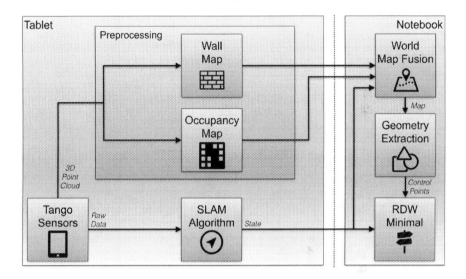

Fig. 1. System architecture showing the individual subroutines.

3.1 Wall Map

The wall map has the purpose of representing an outline of large vertical structures such as walls of the tracking space. The update rate is slower compared to the second sub-map, however, the accuracy is higher. This is essential to maximise the walkable area while ensuring the safety of a user at the same time. The wall map extraction consists of several subroutines that are described more in detail next.

2D Projection. So far, path planners in RDW were only realised for walking in 2D. Hence, the 3D point cloud is projected along the gravitational axis onto a grid with 10×10 mm resolution which is parallel to the floor. At the same time, all measurements belonging to the actual floor are eliminated, since these are not required for identifying vertical structures. The resulting projected and discretised 2D point cloud is shown in Fig. 2 next to a sketch of an evaluation space (2.5×5.5 m).

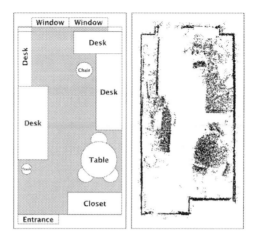

Fig. 2. 2.5 × 5.5 m evaluation space (left) and a 2D projection of several 3D point clouds recorded in the area (right).

Confidence Filter. The projected 2D point cloud contains walls as well as noisy measurements and obstacles which hinders a clean extraction of the walls. Consequently, a filter is designed to address this issue. It is expected that high vertical structures like walls projected onto a horizontal plane will result in areas of higher point density compared to horizontal objects or noise. Thus, an integer value is calculated for each cell of the grid on which the point cloud is projected. This integer value is increased with each projected point into the respective grid cell. Next, a confidence threshold c_T is used to distinguish between low and high confidence grid cells. Even applying low thresholds removes low confidence cells which already reduces noise considerably. Increasing c_T results in a cleaner outline of the physical space by suppressing obstacles as well, which simplifies further calculations significantly. Figure 3 shows a comparison of different values for the confidence threshold.

Line Extraction. The purpose of line extraction is to find line segments within a given set of points. Applying such a line extraction allows reducing the description of a single wall segment from a set of points to a pair of coordinates. Due to its low complexity while still maintaining accuracy, a Random Sample Consensus (RANSAC [5]) is implemented here. Figure 4 shows the line extraction applied to a scan of the evaluation space. The line extraction runs in real-time and terminates with 40 line segments on average for our evaluation space. The RANSAC algorithm detects the lines reliably, but tends to extract segments which are short in length (ca. 1.5–3 m).

Alignment. In a final step, short line segments are merged to longer lines such that slight orientation differences are smoothed and close segments are

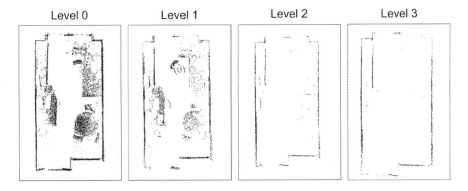

Fig. 3. Comparison of different threshold values $c_T = \{0, 1, 2, 3\}$ for the confidence filter, c_T increasing from left to right.

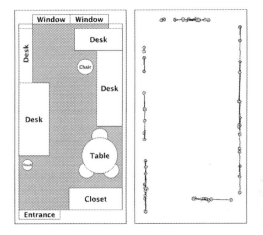

Fig. 4. Applying the line extraction to the projected point cloud results in 40 line segments on average which are roughly 1.5–2 m in length.

connected. The alignment algorithm needs to be fast and must not remove crucial spatial information such as open doorways. Consequently, a simplified version of the approach shown by Liu and Huang [8] is implemented, which merges two segments based on the smallest Euclidean distance d_A and their difference in orientation α_A. Applying the alignment algorithm to the extracted line segments reduces the number of lines to 8 line segments on average (see Fig. 5).

3.2   Occupancy Map

The wall map which is specifically used for walls and similar objects, works precise, but slow. Additionally, objects within the tracking space are discarded for a cleaner extraction. Therefore, a second representation is needed to compensate for the slow update rate and the discarded measurements. For this reason,

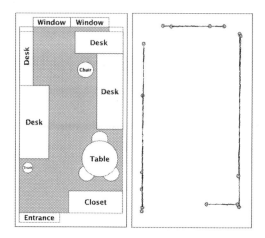

Fig. 5. Applying the alignment to the extracted line segments reduces the average number of segments from 40 to 8 which vary in length but are able to cover the full length (6 m) of the evaluation space.

an occupancy grid [3] is designed using a 2D array. The grid covers an area of 6×6 m, which is limited by the depth sensor's range, with the device located in the center. The occupancy grid is oriented parallel to the floor and consists of cells that contain the real objects' outlines. In this case, each cell of the grid can have one out of three states: *PENDING*, *FREE* or *OCCUPIED*. In order to limit the amount of data that needs to be transmitted, the grid cell resolution is gradually reduced with the distance to the device (see Fig. 6). The smallest cell size is defined as $A_0 = 100 \times 100$ mm and the maximum size is set to $A_{max} = 1200 \times 1200$ mm. Furthermore, the occupancy map needs to include moving objects in the scene. Thus, the grid is generated anew with each recorded point cloud and is immediately transferred to the notebook.

For every update of the occupancy map, each cell is initialised to the *PENDING* state and the recorded 3D point cloud is separated into a floor cloud and an obstacle cloud (see Fig. 7). Note that in contrast to the wall map, points belonging to the floor are not discarded. In order to populate the map, the floor cloud is projected onto the occupancy map first. Each cell holds an integer value n denoting the number of projected points. If a previously determined threshold n_{free} is exceeded, the state of the cell is changed to the *FREE* state. When all floor points are mapped to the grid, n is reset to 0 for all grid cells. Then, the same mapping procedure is repeated for the obstacle cloud, but changing the state to *OCCUPIED* if n exceeds a second threshold n_{occ}. The order of projection is crucial from a safety perspective, since it may occur that measurements are taken in the floor space and the obstacle space simultaneously for the same cell (see Fig. 7). Using this order allows cells to switch from *PENDING* to *FREE* first and finally to *OCCUPIED*, but not the other way around.

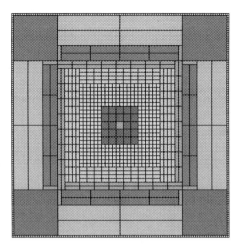

Fig. 6. The occupancy grid, each color indicates a different cell size between $100 \times 100\,mm$ (yellow) up to $1200 \times 1200\,mm$ (purple), with the device located in the center cell (green). Note that the depth sensor has a lower range limitation at $400\,mm$ (red) given by hardware. (Color figure online)

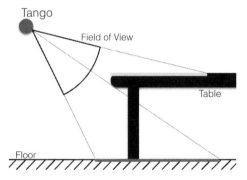

Fig. 7. Projection of the point cloud - the point cloud is split into a floor cloud (blue) and an obstacle cloud (yellow). Projecting both clouds may result in overlapping areas. (Color figure online)

3.3   World Map

Both maps are transferred with a different frequency to the external notebook and differ considerably in structure. It is therefore necessary to have a method that reliably fuses the information contained in both maps. Due to its simplicity and compatibility with the two sub-maps, a high resolution ($10 \times 10\,mm$) occupancy grid is chosen which allows the states *PENDING*, *FREE* and *OCCUPIED*. In order to take the varying accuracy of the two recorded sub-maps into account, a value Γ_c is introduced which describes the occupancy of each grid cell c. In general, definition (1) for Γ_c holds for the world map at all times.

$$\text{cell state} = \begin{cases} PENDING & \text{if } \Gamma_c = 0 \\ FREE & \text{if } \Gamma_c < 0 \\ OCCUPIED & \text{if } \Gamma_c > 0 \end{cases} \tag{1}$$

The initial value of Γ_c is 0 for all cells, which indicates that no information has been recorded yet for this cell. During recording, this value is calculated iteratively for each cell c as shown in Eq. (2).

$$\Gamma_c = \Gamma_{c,old} + s_c \cdot w_c \tag{2}$$

with s_c being the state value and w_c denoting a weighting coefficient. The state values s_c are defined as shown in definition (3) and are directly extracted from the transmitted occupancy map.

$$s_c = \begin{cases} 0 & \text{if the cell is } PENDING \\ 1 & \text{if the cell is } OCCUPIED \\ -1 & \text{if the cell is } FREE \end{cases} \tag{3}$$

The weighting coefficient w_c is used to compensate for the decreasing depth sensor accuracy in the map fusion. Since the grid cells of the occupancy grid are already adjusted accordingly, the size of the smallest cell A_0 is used to calculate w_c for each cell c size as shown in Eq. (4).

$$w_c = \frac{A_0}{A_c} \tag{4}$$

with A_c being the size of cell c. This allows high resolution areas of the occupancy map to have a higher influence on the world map than lower resolution areas.

Because addressing the single cells in the world map is done repeatedly, the values for Γ_c need to be limited to ensure that the world map can dynamically adjust to moving objects or a changing environment. To prevent an unbounded growth, an upper and a lower saturation value Γ_{max} and Γ_{min} are defined. These values are defined symmetrically with respect to 0 (i.e. $\Gamma_{min} = -\Gamma_{max}$).

The wall sub-map is transmitted in the form of coordinate pairs denoting the corners of line segments. In order to fill in the line segment between the respective corners, a modified Bresenham algorithm [2] is used to approximate the line. In general, the Bresenham algorithm is an approximation algorithm that determines the shortest connection between two points in a tessellated environment using an error minimization model. The algorithm therefore approximates a straight line addressing the single cells in between. Moreover, because the wall map is considered to be more accurate than the occupancy map, the respective value Γ_c for each affected cell c is set to the upper saturation value as shown in Eq. (5).

$$\Gamma_c = \Gamma_{max} \tag{5}$$

The algorithms are tested in a larger room ($6 \times 6\,\text{m}$), adding a single obstacle in the area to simplify the evaluation. The results are shown in Fig. 8. Whereas the geometry of the surroundings is clearly recognizable in the world map, there are lots of artefacts close to walls and objects.

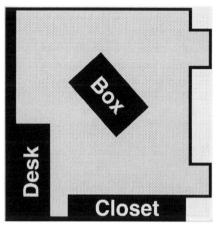

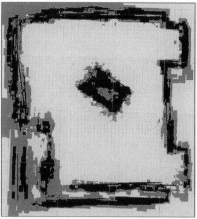

(a) Model of the evaluation space for the world map with labeled objects - black: occupied, grey: free.

(b) Recorded world map for the evaluation space - black: occupied (saturated), dark grey: occupied, light grey: free.

Fig. 8. Testing the map generation in an evaluation space (6×6 m).

3.4 Geometry Extraction

As shown previously, the desired input for the path planner and safety algorithms is a set of 2D coordinates describing closed polygons. One of the polygons describes the outline of the walkable area, while each object within the area is represented separately by an additional closed polygon.

Outline Detection. The first step of the geometry extraction is to isolate all grid cells in the world map which are considered to lie on the outline of an object or a boundary. Consequently, all relevant cells belonging to an outline are adjacent to the walkable area. Therefore, a modified flood fill algorithm is implemented that searches the world map for grid cells satisfying these properties. In general, flood fills are simple tools used to find the area connected to a given node. In our case, the algorithm searches for the connected area starting from an initial cell, but only stores the information about the boundary instead. The algorithm described in (1) spreads in all cardinal and ordinal directions from the initial cell until an occupied cell (i.e. a wall or an obstacle) is hit. In order to do so, a first-in-first-out stack is created containing the initial cell. Removing the cell from the stack, all cardinal and ordinal directions are checked for their state: *OCCUPIED* cells are added to the outline list and *FREE* or

PENDING cells are added to the end of the stack. Each cell that has been checked is marked accordingly to prevent the algorithm from evaluating it multiple times. This process is continued until the stack is empty, meaning that all connected *FREE* or *PENDING* cells are checked and thus the complete outline is identified.

Algorithm 1. Flood Fill

1: UserPosition ← SLAM Tracking
2: Add $c_{UserPosition}$ to Stack
3: **while** Count(Stack) > 0 **do**
4:     c ← Remove First Element
5:     **for all** Directions **do**
6:         **if** state(c_{temp}) == *OCCUPIED* **then**
7:             Add c_{temp} to Outline list
8:         **else**
9:             Add c_{temp} to the End of Stack

Using such a flood fill means that two major issues need to be addressed which are the choice of the initial position and prevention of infinite searches. The initial position always has to be within the same walkable area the user is in to only detect the relevant outlines. Therefore, the algorithm is initialised from the cell $c_{UserPosition}$, on which the user is currently standing. Furthermore, the recorded map may not enclose the user completely, which would result in an unbound flood spread due to not hitting any boundary conditions (i.e. occupied cells). In order to avoid this, a temporary, rectangular bounding box sized 15×15 m is placed around the initial user position (see Fig. 9(a)). Each edge of this bounding box is dynamically expanded and moved further away from the user when he approaches as shown in Fig. 9(b).

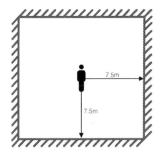

(a) An artificial bounding box (purple) is placed around the user to avoid an infinite spread using the flood fill algorithm.

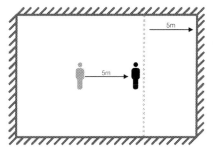

(b) The bounding box is dynamically adjustable and is pushed further back when a user approaches.

Fig. 9. Confining the flood fill algorithm using a bounding box.

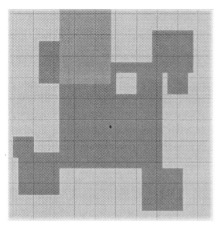 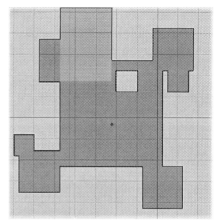

(a) Model of a simplified, artificial eval-
    uation space. It features an obstacle
    in the walkable area and a pending
    space.

(b) Outline detection - the flood fill is
    initialised from the red user position
    and detects all cells connected to the
    walkable area.

Fig. 10. Simulating the outline detection in a simplified artificial environment - red:
user position, green: free space, cyan: pending space, grey: occupied space, black: identified outline. (Color figure online)

Note that for using this flood fill, it is necessary to treat *PENDING* cells
equal to *FREE* cells in order to allow exploration. Otherwise, the user would be
immediately engulfed by safety measures early on, since all cells are initialised
to a *PENDING* state. This would prevent further exploration and thus stopping
the expansion of the world map. Applying the outline detection to a simplified evaluation space (see Fig. 10(a)) results in the outline drawn in black in
Fig. 10(b).

Polygon Conversion. The result of the outline detection contains all cells
belonging to an outline of an object or the outer boundary of the physical space.

Algorithm 2. Polygon Extraction

1: **while** Count(Outline) > 0 **do**
2:　　$c_{init} \leftarrow$ withdraw a cell c from Outline list
3:　　Initialize Polygon P
4:　　$c_{tmp} \leftarrow c_{init}$
5:　　**do**
6:　　　　$c_{tmp} \leftarrow$ Move one step along the Outline
7:　　　　**if** Change of Direction **then**
8:　　　　　　Add c_{tmp} to P
9:　　　　Remove c_{tmp} from Outline list
10:　　**while** $c_{tmp} \neq c_{init}$

However, the cells are arranged in the order in which they were found and are not categorised by objects. The polygon conversion is used to reduce these isolated outline cells to polygons each described by a set of control points (see Algorithm 2).

The conversion starts by withdrawing the first cell c_{init} in the outline list and initializes the first polygon P using this particular cell. This initial cell belongs to an outline which means that two of the neighbouring cardinal cells are part of the same outline. Identifying such a neighbouring cell yields a direction of movement which is used to follow the outline. While moving along the outline, the algorithm removes each cell from the outline list. If the next cell along the direction of movement is not element of the outline list, a change of direction is required (see Fig. 11). In this case, the respective corner cell is added to P and a new cardinal direction of movement is determined. Repeating this procedure until the outline of the specific object or boundary is closed (i.e. the next temporary cell is the initial cell), the polygon is stored and the next polygon is initialised. When the list of the outline cells is empty, all polygons have been identified and the conversion algorithm terminates as shown in Fig. 12(b).

Applying the complete sequence of algorithms to a recording of the 6×6 m evaluation space (see Fig. 8(a)) results in roughly 100 polygons. Clearly, the ideal number of polygons for this particular room would be two (one for the outer boundary and one for the obstacle in the center). However, the creation of artefacts during the fusion of the different sub-maps adds a polygon per artefact regardless of its size. The number of artefacts significantly increases the run-time

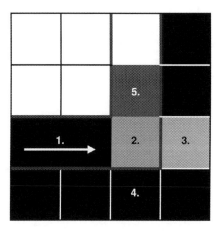

Fig. 11. Change of direction during polygon conversion. 1. algorithm moves along the outline (red); 2. Cell (light grey) on the outline is evaluated, not yet identified as a corner cell; 3. Cell (yellow) is not element of the outline list, since it is not part of the outline. Therefore, the light grey cell is identified as a corner cell and is added to the polygon; 4. Cell south of the corner is checked, but not found in the outline list; 5. Cell in the north is checked, detected in the outline list and the direction of movement is changed towards north. (Color figure online)

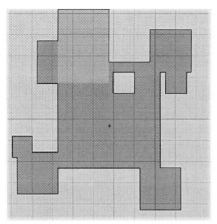
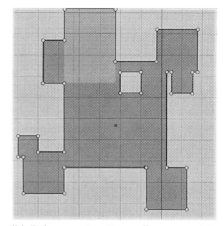

(a) *Outline determination - the flood fill is initialised from the red user position and detects all cells connected to the walkable area.*

(b) *Polygon extraction - all corner points of the obstacle and the boundary are identified and marked.*

Fig. 12. Simulating the polygon extraction - red: user position, green: free space, cyan: pending space, grey: occupied space, black: identified outline, yellow: identified corners forming the polygons. (Color figure online)

and may exceed 100 ms per geometry extraction, which renders the algorithm sequence inapplicable for a real-time implementation.

4 S2C Initialization

The run-time poses a significant issue for an S2C implementation relying on the information provided by the geometry extraction alone. Additional calculations and rendering put even more strain on the notebook which further reduces the framerate of the geometry extraction. In order to avoid this issue, a simple tracking space is initialised with a squared base area which needs to be free of obstacles. In that way, even though the information from the geometry extraction is not available during the first few frames, the S2C can refer to a safe environment. This square starts with 2×2 m edge length and forms a dynamically allocated artificial boundary. The size of this boundary is then continuously expanded as soon as an area close-by is explored. Since the initial square starts with the user located in the center, the boundary of the initial tracking space is at least 1 m away in each direction which coincides with the high resolution area of the occupancy map allowing for a fast expansion. In this manner, the tracking space continuously grows until the physical boundaries are eventually met. After each iteration in which the size or form of the tracking space is altered, the center point of this current tracking space is updated such that the S2C can adjust accordingly (see Fig. 13). Note that only the initial square needs to

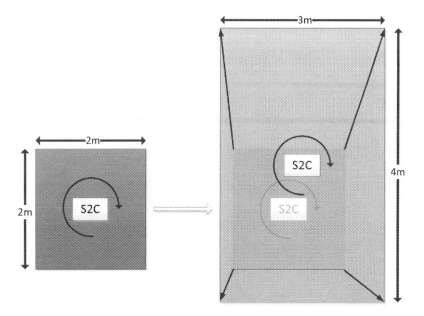

Fig. 13. S2C algorithm - the center of the tracking area is adjusted based on the current tracking space. Green: free space before the expansion; grey: free space after the expansion. (Color figure online)

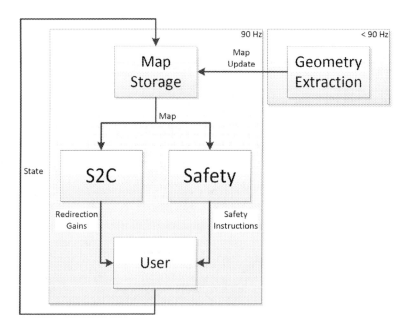

Fig. 14. System Distribution - Splitting the systems running with different frequencies into subsystems to be calculated separately.

be free of obstacles whereas any sort of obstructions are continuously added to the tracking space. However, these objects cannot be considered in the standard S2C algorithm. Nevertheless, every object is displayed using the wallwarner and is considered as an obstacle and thus triggers a reset.

With this implementation, the S2C and safety algorithms form a separate system which runs independently from the geometry extraction (see Fig. 14). Whenever spatial information is generated by the extraction, a map update is pushed to this main system. That way, the S2C and safety algorithms always rely on the newest information and do not need updates with a constant framerate.

5   Discussion

Potential software improvements include applying smoothing filters to the world map or discarding undersized objects to remove artefacts. Other than that, upgrading the CPU of the SLAM device in order to have more computational resources available would also allow to increase the resolution of the occupancy grid which will also decrease the amount of artefacts. Additionally, the wireless connection between the tablet and the external notebook poses a major issue. Under the best conditions, a lag of roughly 60 ms is measured, which may already be detected by a user in VR. Therefore, the best solution for this case would be a wired connection to the sensor. In that case, the complete point cloud would be available on the notebook allowing a higher resolution for the occupancy map. However, even though a real-time implementation using only spatial data from the sequence of algorithms presented here is not feasible at the moment, the separation of the single systems shown in the implementation works reliably and the S2C algorithm performs well for each individual iteration of the tracking space. Accordingly, the longer the system runs, the larger and more detailed the tracking space becomes. This results in the S2C algorithm triggering fewer resets and less intrusive gains can be used.

6   Conclusion

In this paper, we showed an approach that bridges the gap between a mobile SLAM tracking device and an existing RDW application on a conceptual level with a simple initialization strategy. Both sub-maps created using depth measurements of the tablet run well in real-time, however, there are major run-time issues during data transmission and processing in later stages which is addressed with the shown initialization. Whereas an alternative connection for data transfer seems unavoidable for real-time spatial updates, both the world map fusion and the geometry extraction can be improved on an algorithmic level by applying filters (e.g. a Gaussian or a Laplacian filter for artefact removal) or other optimizations. Concluding, the algorithms described in this paper operate reliably and can be adapted to any other system which provides a 3D depth point cloud (e.g. an ARCore device). Tests with these algorithms using upgraded hardware, for example with a system, where the SLAM device is separated from a depth sensor to improve the run-time, should be conducted in the future.

7   Future Work

Besides run-time performance issues that were previously described, there are a lot of unanswered questions regarding the handling of the environmental representation in the RDW application itself. So far, a RDW algorithm that relies only on the current state of the user was used. However, if an active planning algorithm would be tested which evaluates potential future states (e.g. MPCRed), the concept of the initialization would need to be redesigned, since the unknown space needs to be considered for the planning horizon as well. Further, the planner needs to decide how the unknown space will be handled in general. Potential approaches would involve a discount-based or a risk-based system, which emphasizes or penalizes exploration in unknown space respectively.

A   Design Variables

The design variables that have been used during the evaluations are listed in Table 1. Note that these variables have been tuned for the sensors of the Google Tango Yellowstone tablet and may not be used for other devices.

Table 1. Design variables used during the evaluation processes.

Design variable	Value
Confidence Threshold c_T	3
RANSAC Iterations k	5
Alignment Distance d_A	20 mm
Alignment Orientation α_A	5°
Occupancy Map n_{free}	5
Occupancy Map n_{occ}	5
Occupancy Map n_{cells}	756
Saturation Value $\Gamma_{max,min}$	±5
Smallest Bounding Box	±7.5 m

References

1. Bachmann, E.R., Zmuda, M., Calusdian, J., Yun, X., Hodgson, E., Waller, D.: Going anywhere anywhere: creating a low cost portable immersive VE system. In: 2012 17th International Conference on Computer Games (CGAMES), pp. 108–115. IEEE (2012)
2. Bresenham, J.E.: Algorithm for computer control of a digital plotter. IBM Syst. J. 4(1), 25–30 (1965)
3. Elfes, A.: Occupancy grids: a stochastic spatial representation for active robot perception. In: Proceedings of the Sixth Conference on Uncertainty in AI, vol. 2929 (1990)

4. Field, T., Vamplew, P.: Generalised algorithms for redirected walking in virtual environments (2004)
5. Fischler, M.A., Bolles, R.C.: Random sample consensus: a paradigm for model fitting with applications to image analysis and automated cartography. Commun. ACM **24**(6), 381–395 (1981)
6. Hirt, C., Zank, M., Kunz, A.: Real-time wall outline extraction for redirected walking. In: VRST 2017 Proceedings of the 23rd ACM Symposium on Virtual Reality Software and Technology, p. 72. ACM (2017)
7. Hirt, C., Zank, M., Kunz, A.: Preliminary environment mapping for redirected walking. In: 25th IEEE Conference on Virtual Reality and 3D User Interfaces (IEEE VR 2018). IEEE (2018)
8. Liu, Y., Huang, T.S.: Determining straight line correspondences from intensity images. Pattern Recogn. **24**(6), 489–504 (1991)
9. Lowe, D.G.: Object recognition from local scale-invariant features. In: The Proceedings of the Seventh IEEE International Conference on Computer vision, 1999, vol. 2, pp. 1150–1157. IEEE (1999)
10. Nescher, T., Huang, Y.-Y., Kunz, A.: Planning redirection techniques for optimal free walking experience using model predictive control. In: 2014 IEEE Symposium on 3D User Interfaces (3DUI), pp. 111–118. IEEE (2014)
11. Nescher, T., Zank, M., Kunz, A.: Simultaneous mapping and redirected walking for ad hoc free walking in virtual environments. In: IEEE Virtual Reality Conference, pp. 239–240. IEEE (2016)
12. Nitzsche, N., Hanebeck, U.D., Schmidt, G.: Motion compression for telepresent walking in large target environments. Presence Teleoperators Virtual Environ. **13**(1), 44–60 (2004)
13. Razzaque, S.: Redirected Walking. University of North Carolina at Chapel Hill (2005)
14. Razzaque, S., Kohn, Z., Whitton, M.C.: Redirected walking. In: Proceedings of EUROGRAPHICS, Manchester, UK, vol. 9, pp. 105–106 (2001)
15. Sra, M., Garrido-Jurado, S., Schmandt, C., Maes, P.: Procedurally generated virtual reality from 3D reconstructed physical space. In: Proceedings of the 22nd ACM Conference on Virtual Reality Software and Technology, pp. 191–200. ACM (2016)
16. Williams, B., Narasimham, G., McNamara, T.P., Carr, T.H., Rieser, J.J., Bodenheimer, B.: Updating orientation in large virtual environments using scaled translational gain. In: Proceedings of the 3rd Symposium on Applied Perception in Graphics and Visualization, pp. 21–28. ACM (2006)
17. Williams, B., Narasimham, G., Rump, B., McNamara, T.P., Carr, T.H., Rieser, J., Bodenheimer, B.: Exploring large virtual environments with an HMD when physical space is limited. In: Proceedings of the 4th Symposium on Applied Perception in Graphics and Visualization, APGV 2007, pp. 41–48. ACM, New York (2007)
18. Zank, M., Yao, C., Kunz, A.: Multi-phase wall warner system for real walking in virtual environments. In: 2017 IEEE Symposium on 3D User Interfaces (3DUI), pp. 223–224. IEEE (2017)
19. Zmuda, M.A., Wonser, J.L., Bachmann, E.R., Hodgson, E.: Optimizing constrained-environment redirected walking instructions using search techniques. IEEE Trans. Visual Comput. Graphics **19**(11), 1872–1884 (2013)

Wrist-Worn Sensor-Based Tangible Interface for Virtual Percussion Instruments

Abassin Sourou Fangbemi[1] and Yanxiang Zhang[2(✉)]

[1] School of Software Engineering, University of Science and Technology
of China, Hefei, Anhui, China
abassino@mail.ustc.edu.cn
[2] Department of Communication of Science and Technology,
University of Science and Technology of China, Hefei, Anhui, China
petrel@ustc.edu.cn

Abstract. Virtual musical instruments (VMIs) are Augmented Reality (AR) or Virtual Reality (VR) based applications that focus on the interaction with real or virtual musical objects through AR or VR mediums. For such purpose, different interaction tools and techniques such as fiducial markers, RGB and depth cameras, VR and AR headsets are used. Though modern AR and VR devices provide better interaction interfaces, they are more expensive than traditional ones that are unfortunately not robust as the modern devices. To provide a robust and affordable AR and VR interaction interface for real-time applications, we investigate the use of affordable body-worn inertial measurement unit (IMU), a web camera, an RGB light as a simple, cheaper and reliable solution for the interaction with virtual percussion instruments. The performance of the proposed system was evaluated through a series of feedback from fifteen users. In general, the framework was considered as intuitive and tangible.

Keywords: Virtual musical instruments · Percussion · Augmented Reality
Virtual Reality · Inertial measurement unit

1 Introduction

In recent years, advances in AR and VR technologies have extended their application to almost every area of our life, including musical arts. Hence, to allow users to experience with musical instruments without necessarily buying the real instruments that are expensive in some cases, various kind of AR and VR virtual musical instruments applications have been created. Some of the early works in building virtual musical instruments include the Augmented Groove [1, 2] and the reacTable [3] projects. In Augmented Groove, users can play music together, with or without traditional music instruments, simply by picking and manipulating physical cards on a table, resulting in changes in musical elements such as timbre, pitch, rhythm, distortion, and reverb. A similar result was achieved with the reacTable project which used Computer Vision (CV) solution to capture users' hand and other objects shape and position on a table and generate visual and audio feedback based on their change in position on the table. Though such applications offer a cost-effective way for the user to learn or play with

© Springer International Publishing AG, part of Springer Nature 2018
L. T. De Paolis and P. Bourdot (Eds.): AVR 2018, LNCS 10850, pp. 54–66, 2018.
https://doi.org/10.1007/978-3-319-95270-3_4

musical instruments, they still require additional devices to make the interaction between the users and the virtual instruments possible. Among those additional devices, some provide better interaction interface and immersive experience than other but are usually more expensive to acquire. That is the case for the Oculus Rift and the High Tech Computer (HTC) Vive virtual reality headsets. On the other hand, other peripheral devices which are cheaper and easier to configure (for example, fiducial markers with a traditional web camera) do not always provide the best immersive and interactive experience.

Meanwhile, we are currently assisting in the increased production of smart body-worn devices with precise sensors (accelerometer, gyroscope, barometer, etc.) integrated into those devices at an affordable price. With data captured by the sensors embedded in those devices, it is possible to model different activities or body related behavior of the users. Though many researchers, especially in the medial area, are currently trying to explore those data at their full potential, there is still a very limited application or use such data in the field of AR and VR. To close this gap, in this paper we proposed a new AR framework that uses acceleration data captured by a wrist-worn sensor to model a hit gesture as performed by percussion instrument musicians and use it as an event trigger for the AR application. For our case study, we implemented both a virtual drum and a virtual xylophone as examples. In addition to the wrist-worn sensor, a simple and cheap web camera is also used to detect the position of the hit relatively to the virtual drums or xylophone. Fifteen participants tried and evaluated the performance of the system through a questionnaire and a satisfactory feedback was observed in general with few suggestions made by the participants to improve the system.

After performing a literature review of existing AR and VR based virtual musical instruments, in the next section, we provide a more detailed explanation of the design and the implementation of the proposed framework. In Sect. 4 we present the evaluation criteria used to evaluate the performance of the system together with the corresponding feedback collected from the participants. We then conclude this paper in Sect. 5, by presenting some ideas for improving the performance and functionalities of the system in our future work.

2 Related Work

Learning new musical instruments can easily be subject to some challenges or limitations such as budgets cuts, fear of playing on stage, etc. In order to overcome such challenges, different studies have been conducted to create virtual musical instruments applications that mimic the interaction with real instruments. With VMI applications, the user can interact with virtual musical instruments or characters which are either overlay on real objects (AR-based) or fully integrated into a virtual environment (VR-based) through different interactive interfaces. In their work, Karjalainen and Teemu [4] used wired data gloves to capture users' gestures as input to interact with four different virtual instruments including a virtual xylophone, membrane, Theremin and Air Guitar. However, their system was limited by low spatial and temporal resolution and latency decrease efficiency. Within their virtual studio environment [5], the authors used an infrared-laser-based multi-touch device to interact with a virtual screen, which is augmented in front of the user. Using a CV solution similar to [3] and that tracks hand and finger movements with a color-based Sequential Monte Carlo algorithm, Olivie et al. [6] also created sound from virtual musical instruments. In their work, Rastogi and Joshi [7] introduced an interface that allows users to simulate a musical instrument by printing a template on a sheet of paper and placing it in view of the webcam of their laptop. The appropriate sound is generated by calibrating the template, detecting the marker position, identifying the hit position and playing notes corresponding to that position. The V-Drum [8] is an AR-based drum kit that provides a low-cost, portable drum kit whose implementation allows any person to learn and play percussion instruments. Using CV techniques, the input image is filtered to include only the chosen colors of the drumstick beads. By tracking the beads colors, drum sound can be generated when the tracked bead is within an active range of a drum.

Instead of creating virtual musical instruments, other works have combined real musical instruments with AR and VR techniques to enhance the efficiency of the learning process. The authors of [9] implemented a visual feedback for their AR drum Kit in order to keep intrinsic motivation by offering playful features, such as a game-like user interface and a variety of tasks with different difficulty levels. Using the same approach but with a head-mounted display, [10] combined superposed fiducial AR makers on top of real dreams to provide visual feedback in addition to the auditory feedback in order to improve drum learning experience. Fernandez et al. [11] also created an AR-based piano playing experience, which allows the user to interact with a virtual character through the sounds generated by a real piano. The interaction between the virtual character through the generated piano's sound is designed mainly to evaluate the psychological benefits of music learning in order to make the learning experience interesting and keep the users' motivation during the learning process as in [9].

Most of the works mentioned above are mainly based on CV techniques and fiducial markers as opposed to some recent works that make use of more modern AR and VR technologies. In order to create a flexible and easy to use interface that would allow the user to choose the scale and distance between notes, Cabral et al. [12] introduced a virtual music instrument where the notes of a given music key are arranged and replicated on a grid that minimizes jumps across the musical scale. The visualization and interaction with their system were implemented with the Oculus Rift and a Razer Hydra as gesture input whereas [13–15] used the leap motion as user input device for their virtual musical instrument. The skeleton data generated by Microsoft Kinect was used in [16] to create, in addition to a virtual drum and a virtual guitar, a new virtual musical instrument, namely the Spider King, which is represented as spider web centered on the user. The outmost circular layer of the web positioned around the user is divided into several intervals that correspond to different keys with which the user can interact to compose a music. The volume of the generated sound is also controlled by the distance of the hand from the circumference of the web. [17] used a 3D blob tracking technology with the Microsoft Kinect to create a virtual xylophone. However, though the system allows a tangible experience, it also requires additional physical material representing the xylophone.

Though VMIs are mainly designed as an education or entertainment tool, they have also been used as a medical solution to assist people with disability to improve their conditions. In their application, [18] used fiducial markers as an interactive tool for their AR-based computer-assisted music therapy for children with cerebral palsy rehabilitation. Within their system, each card is represented by a virtual colored virtual cube (for visual feedback) and correspond to a different musical note in the timbre of a given musical instrument. The system generates sound when the user covers the center of a card with one of their hands. In order to allow people with hearing disability or muscular weakness to play music, Chouvatut and Jindaluang [19] created an AR real-time virtual piano experience with interaction based on automatic card detection. In order to generate sounds, users only have to place their finger on the virtual key to cover some part of it and get both visual and auditory feedback.

Though a lot of progress has been made in developing more immersive VMIs systems, the interaction interface offered by such application are either based on ready-to-use modern technologies (such as HTC Vive controller), fiducial markers combined with CV techniques, or data gloves, with less research on the integration of body-worn sensors for AR and VR application. With their lower cost, such devices can represent an ideal substitute for expensive AR and VR devices or for cheap and less robust ones. Hence, in this work, we explore the capabilities of a wrist-worn IMU to implement an interactive interface for AR and VR based virtual musical instruments. The small size of all the components used to build the system in addition to their relatively low price (Table 1) does not only make it affordable but also easy to transport and install anywhere.

Table 1. Price comparison of real musical instruments, some AR and VR devices and the devices used in our virtual percussion system

Real instruments		Modern AR and VR devices		Virtual percussion devices	
Name	Price	Name	Price	Name	Price
Drum kit [23]	$ 299.99	Kinect2 [26]	$ 359.95	MetaMotion R [27]	$ 78.00
Xylophone [22]	$ 159.99	Oculus Rift [25]	$ 421 00	LED [28]	$ 0.16 (CYN 1)
		HTC Vive [24]	$ 527 12	Drum stick [29]	$ 0.80 (CYN 5)

3 System Design and Implementation

3.1 Design

Playing percussion instruments requires a constant motion of hands. The hand has to be moved from a still position A to a high position B before brought down on another still position C (Fig. 1) which corresponds to the hit or contact position between the stick and the instrument. The design of our virtual musical instrument (Fig. 2) takes advantage of the possibilities wireless wrist-worn sensors offer us in capturing acceleration data without obstructing the user when using such motion as a hit gesture for the interaction between the stick and the instrument. Hence, the wrist-worn sensor is used to compute in real-time the acceleration and deceleration of the user's hand motion; we then use such changes in motion to detect when the impact between the stick and the instrument happens. In addition to the wrist worn-sensor, we also use a web camera to track the position of the stick's bead in order to detect which part of the virtual instrument has been hit. By using a CV blob tracking technique, we can detect and track in real time a LED light placed on the bead of the stick. Hence, by simply moving the stick in front of the camera, the detected blob moves accordingly on top of the virtual instrument. During the process, if the tracked blob is positioned over any part of the virtual instrument (for example a key of the xylophone or a drum of the drum kit), then that particular part is immediately highlighted with a blue glow color to inform the user that he/she can interact with that specific part at that precise moment. This provides the user an accurate and real-time visual feedback. Additionally, using a real percussion stick than a virtual one (empty hand), not only allow for an accurate tracking system of the interaction tool but also provides a tangible interface that creates a real sense of connection between the user and the virtual instrument for better immersive experience. Finally, a sound of the key hit is generated whenever the user hit the corresponding part of the virtual instrument as the auditory feedback.

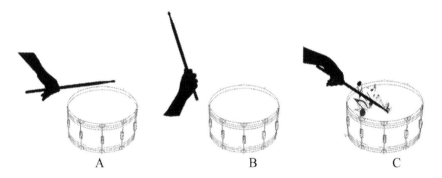

Fig. 1. Changes in hand motion used to perform a percussion gesture detection

To evaluate the performance of the proposed framework, we designed and implemented two virtual musical instruments (a virtual drum kit and a virtual xylophone). The drums composing the drum kit are arranged at a spatial distance one from each other, requiring the user to perform a notable change in the hand motion to hit drums positioned at different coordinates on the screen. Whereas with the xylophone, though a notable motion of the hand is also required when hitting two different keys distant one from each other, the lateral arrangement of the keys make it easy to master.

3.2   Implementation Details

The system was implemented in Python on an Ubuntu 16.04 virtual machine on an i7-6700HQ (2.60 GHz) processor laptop with a random access memory of 4 GB. The hardware includes the MbientLab MetaMotion R wrist-worn sensor, an HD webcam which can capture video images at a maximum of 60 fps, a drumstick, and an RGB LED to ease the detection of the drumstick bead (Fig. 3). The interaction with the

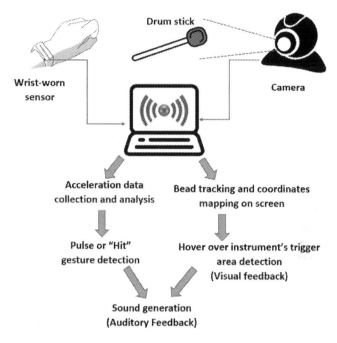

Fig. 2. System overall diagram

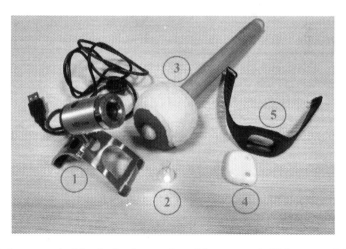

Fig. 3. Hardware required for the implementation of the system: 1. Web camera, 2. LED light, 3. Drumstick, 4. MetaMotion R, 5. Wristband

virtual system shown in the diagram Fig. 2 is achieved by combining the hit gesture recognition implemented with the wrist-worn sensor and the tracking of the stick's LED light by the camera.

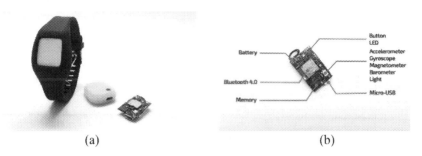

Fig. 4. MetaMotion R: (a) With the wristband and the case, (b) Detailed view

"Hit" Action recognition and volume control subsystem with MetaMotion R. The MetaMotion R (Fig. 4) is a motion sensing platform that includes multiples sensors with an additional 10 axis of motion sensing (3-axis accelerometer, 3-axis gyroscope, 3-axis magnetometer, altimeter, barometer, pressure) that provide a robust absolute orientation vector in the form of quaternion or Euler angles. The algorithm fuses the raw sensor data from 3-axis accelerometer, 3-axis geomagnetic sensor, and 3-axis gyroscope intelligently to improve each sensor's output. Including algorithms for offset calibration of each sensor, monitoring of the calibration status and Kalman filter fusion provide distortion-free and refined orientation vectors [20]. Powered by a 100 mAH lithium-ion 3.7 V rechargeable battery, the board is based on the nRF52 SOC from Nordic built around an ARM® Cortex™ M4F CPU and Bluetooth Low Energy. For our project, the sensor has been used to implement two main functionalities that consist of the detection of a hit gesture and the control of the volume based on the acceleration data collected from the sensor.

Upon start, we first create and initialize the MetaMotion R; we establish communication with the board through a Bluetooth Low Energy connection. Then, after starting the accelerometer, we can start streaming the acceleration data from the sensor to our computer which can then be processed and analyzed by the data processing unit included in the board API, specifically, the pulse processor. The hit gesture recognition is implemented by analyzing a consecutive number of acceleration data within a sample interval. As shown in Fig. 1., a hit gesture can be characterized by an upward motion of the hand followed by a downward motion. Hence, such motion can be represented by the curve on Fig. 5 which shows the changes in the acceleration in the y-axis overtime when performing one hit gesture. With a pulse defined as a minimum number of data points that rise above then fall below a predefined threshold, it is possible to use the pulse processor [21] to detect and quantify a pulse variation which is similar to a hit gesture (upward followed by downward motion). Hence, by raising or lowering the threshold value, we can control how soon or late a pulse or hit gesture can be detected.

Volume Control. By using the acceleration data sent from the sensor, we are able to control the volume level at which each sound is generated to mimic the realist effect fast or slow percussion action has on the level of the sound produced on real instruments. With the percussion impact happening during the downward motion of the hand, we calculate the absolute acceleration norm at the time the hit action (pulse) is

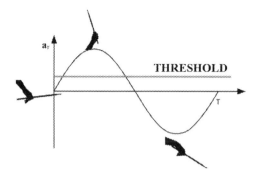

Fig. 5. Hit gesture represented by a pulse moving above then under a predefined threshold

detected and use it as a multiplication factor to amplify or reduce the original audio sound's amplitude (volume) whenever the user performs a hit gesture. Hence creates an additional control of the user over the generated sound for a better immersive experience. Figure 6 Show the detailed flowchart of the data sent on one side by the MetaMotion R, and on the second side captured by the Web camera (LED data).

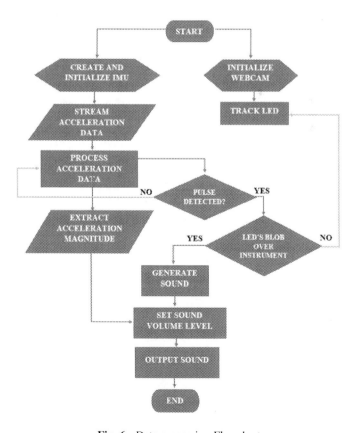

Fig. 6. Data processing Flowchart

4   Experimental Results and Analysis

The interaction space was set up as shown in Fig. 7(b) and (c) with the camera facing the ceiling while the user performs a hit action on top of it with the MetaMotion R worn on his/her wrist. Hence, with the drumstick in the user's hand placed above the camera's field of view, the camera can detect and track the LED light attached to the bead of the drumstick. The highlighted key or drum in a blue glow color represents the element that can be currently hit (active elements). Fifteen students were asked to evaluate the performance of the system by interacting with both virtual drum and xylophone. The majority of the participants are Chinese (12 participants) with age between 20 and 27 years old and composed by ten (10) males and two (2) females. The remaining three (3) participants are all males with two from Yemen and one from Ghana of age between 24 and 31 years old. Though all participants are interested in music in general, only few of them had previous experience with some musical instruments, especially the drum kit. In addition to performing simple interaction tasks (just playing randomly with the virtual instruments), the participants were also asked to learn and play a simple "Happy birthday to you" melody in order to test their aptitude at mastering how to play the virtual xylophone. We chose to test this more complex interaction scenario only with the virtual xylophone because it is simpler to play than the drum kit especially for users who are not professional musicians. The feedback in the form of questions-answers collected from each participant after testing the system was used to evaluate its performance. Below are the questions and the overall feedback.

Question one: Have you ever played a real drum kit or a real xylophone?

Surprisingly, none of the participants had previous experience with a real drum kit, though seven of them have occasionally played a single drum. Only three of them had the opportunity to play with a real xylophone.

Question two: What did you like the most about the system?

Most of the participants were thrilled by the idea of hitting a virtual (non-material) instrument while still being able to get auditory feedback as if hitting a real instrument.

Question three: How would you evaluate the interaction with the virtual instruments?

All participants find the interaction with virtual instruments intuitive and easy to grasp since it consists in one simple motion. However, they also deplored the absence of feedback that occasionally happens when a hit gesture is not correctly detected. Additionally, because the current system is designed with only one drum-stick, some of the participants suggested the use of two sticks instead of one especially with the virtual drum kit as that would be the case with real drums.

Question four: How would you appreciate the auditory and visual feedback of the system?

Except for the few occasional absence of feedback due undetected hit gesture, all participants were in general satisfied with the auditory and visual feedback.

Question five: How difficult was it to learn and play the "Happy birthday to you" melody with the virtual xylophone?

All users agreed that it was challenging at first mostly because it was their first time to interact with such system and additionally because most of them did not have prior

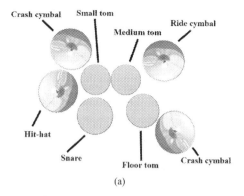

(a)

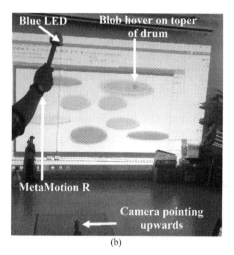

(b)

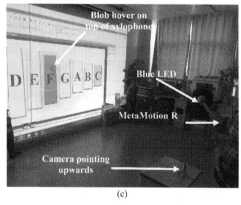

(c)

Fig. 7. System setup: (a) Five piece drum set design without brass drum used for designing the virtual drum kit, (b) Interaction with the virtual drum kit, (c) Interaction with the virtual xylophone

experience with a real xylophone. But four of the participants among which two who previously have experience with a real xylophone quickly mastered how to play the song while it took a little more time for other participants to feel comfortable in playing the melody. This was expected since learning any new instrument or subject always require some time.

5   Conclusion

The rapidly evolving market of body-worn smart devices with IMU sensors integrated into them can provide new possibilities for creating robust and cost-effective AR and VR interaction interfaces. In this paper, we proposed a new virtual musical instrument framework that can be used to learn and play percussion instruments, mainly drum kit and xylophone. Using a simple wireless wrist-worn IMU device, we were able to model in real-time a hand gesture that is used to trigger sound generation whenever a virtual key or drum is hit. The drumstick, together with a LED for easy tracking of the bead of the stick by camera provide a tangible interface for the user without being cumbersome. Thanks to the cheap cost involved in implementing the system, our framework represents a good alternative to real instruments that require expensive means to purchase with a very good tradeoff between cost and performance. Though the framework provides accurate feedback most of the time, it fails on very few occasions to detect the hit gesture. To overcome such shortage, we plan in our future work to design and implement a more robust hit recognition algorithm based on deep learning techniques one multiple types of data captured by the sensor and on top of which additional gestures can be built for diverse applications.

Acknowledgments. The research was sponsored by CAS-TWAS President's Fellowship.

References

1. Poupyrev, I., Berry, R., Kurumisawa, J., Nakao, K., Billinghurst, M., Airola, C., Kato, H., Yonezawa, T., Baldwin, L.: Augmented groove: collaborative jamming in augmented reality. In: ACM SIGGRAPH 2000 Conference Abstracts and Applications, p. 77 (2000)
2. Poupyrev, I., Berry, R., Billinghurst, M., Kato, H., Nakao, K., Baldwin, L., Kurumisawa, J.: Augmented reality interface for electronic music performance. In: Proceedings of HCI, pp. 805–808 (2001)
3. Jordà, S.: Interactive music systems for everyone: exploring visual feedback as a way for creating more intuitive, efficient and learnable instruments. In: Proceedings of the Stockholm Music Acoustics Conference, pp. 6–9, August 2003
4. Karjalainen, M., Maki-Patola, T.: Physics-based modeling of musical instruments for interactive virtual reality. In: 2004 IEEE 6th Workshop on Multimedia Signal Processing, pp. 223–226. IEEE (2004)
5. Wöldecke, B., Marinos, D., Pogscheba, P., Geiger, C., Herder, J., Schwirten, T.: RadarTHEREMIN-Creating musical expressions in a virtual studio environment. In: 2011 IEEE International Symposium on VR Innovation (ISVRI), pp. 345–346. IEEE (2011)

6. Olivieri, D., Conde, I.G., Vila-Sobrino, X.A.: AR-based virtual musical instruments using SMC tracking. In: 2011 6th Iberian Conference on Information Systems and Technologies (CISTI), pp. 1–7. IEEE (2011)
7. Rastogi, A., Joshi, A.: Virtual Musical Instruments (2015)
8. Lobo, N.: V-Drum: an augmented reality drum kit. Int. J. Adv. Res. Comput. Commun. Eng. **4**(10), October 2015
9. Yamabe, T., Asuma, H., Kiyono, S., Nakajima, T.: Feedback design in augmented musical instruments: a case study with an ar drum kit. In: 2011 IEEE 17th International Conference on Embedded and Real-Time Computing Systems and Applications (RTCSA), vol. 2, pp. 126–129. IEEE (2011)
10. Nilsson, S., Vechev, V., Yeh, A., Hedler, C.: Holo beats: design and development of an AR system to teach drums. In: Proceedings of SIDeR 2016, The 12th Student Interaction Design Research Conference, Malmö (2016)
11. Fernandez, C.A.T., Paliyawan, P., Yin, C.C., Thawonmas, R.: Piano learning application with feedback provided by an AR virtual character. In: 2016 IEEE 5th Global Conference on Consumer Electronics, pp. 1–2. IEEE (2016)
12. Cabral, M., Montes, A., Roque, G., Belloc, O., Nagamura, M., Faria, R.R.A., Teubl, F., Kurashima, C., Lopes, R., Zuffo, M.: Crosscale: a 3D virtual musical instrument interface. In: 2015 IEEE Symposium on 3D User Interfaces (3DUI), pp. 199–200. IEEE (2015)
13. Fillwalk, J.: Chromachord: a virtual musical instrument. In: 2015 IEEE Symposium on 3D User Interfaces (3DUI), pp. 201–202. IEEE (2015)
14. Moore, A.G., Howell, M.J., Stiles, A.W., Herrera, N.S., McMahan, R.P.: Wedge: a musical interface for building and playing composition-appropriate immersive environments. In: 2015 IEEE Symposium on 3D User Interfaces (3DUI), pp. 205–206. IEEE (2015)
15. Hariadi, R.R., Kuswardayan, I.: Design and implementation of Virtual Indonesian Musical Instrument (VIMi) application using Leap Motion Controller. In: 2016 International Conference on Information & Communication Technology and Systems (ICTS), pp. 43–48. IEEE (2016)
16. Hsu, M.-H., Kumara, W.G.C.W., Shih, T.K., Cheng, Z.: Spider King: virtual musical instruments based on microsoft kinect. In: 2013 International Joint Conference on Awareness Science and Technology and Ubi-Media Computing (iCAST-UMEDIA), pp. 707–713. IEEE (2013)
17. Burks, N., Smith, L., Saquer, J.: A virtual xylophone for music education. In: 2016 IEEE International Symposium on Multimedia (ISM), pp. 409–410. IEEE (2016)
18. Correa, A.G.D., Ficheman, I.K., do Nascimento, M., de Deus Lopes, R.: Computer assisted music therapy: a case study of an augmented reality musical system for children with cerebral palsy rehabilitation. In: Ninth IEEE International Conference on Advanced Learning Technologies, ICALT 2009, pp. 218–220. IEEE (2009)
19. Chouvatut, V., Jindaluang, W.: Virtual piano with real-time interaction using automatic marker detection. In: 2013 International Computer Science and Engineering Conference (ICSEC), pp. 222–226. IEEE (2013)
20. MbientLab. https://mbientlab.com/product/metamotionr/
21. MbientLab. https://mbientlab.com/cppdocs/latest/dataprocessor.html#pulse
22. Guitar Center. http://www.guitarcenter.com/Sound-Percussion-Labs/Bell-Kit-w-Rolling-Cart-2-1-2-OCTAVE-1385392679518.gc?pfm=item_page.rrt1|ClickCP

23. Guitar Center. http://www.guitarcenter.com/Sound-Percussion-Labs/Kicker-Pro-5-Piece-Drum-Set-with-Stands-Cymbals-and-Throne-Silver-Metallic-Glitter-1395067583347.gc? cntry = us&source = 4WWRWXGP&gclid = Cj0KCQiAh_DTBRCTARIsABIT9MYwb MgfMMDaQJZ91WMf6cj6G_4SnvzlOcfDEA2EGzIKW9p2afuIz1UaArMCEALw_ wcB&kwid = productads-adid^78244844802-device^c-plaid^146600819322-sku^1395067583347@ADL4GC-adType^PLA
24. Amazon.   https://www.amazon.com/HTC-VIVE-Virtual-Reality-System-pc/dp/B00VF5NT 4I/ref=sr_1_1?s=electronics&ie=UTF8&qid=1518159685&sr=1-1&keywords=htc% 2Bvive&th=1
25. Amazon.   https://www.amazon.com/Oculus-Rift-Virtual-Reality-Headset-pc/dp/B00VF0IX EY/ref=sr_1_4?s=electronics&ie=UTF8&qid=1518159763&sr=1-4&keywords=oculus+rift
26. Amazon.   https://www.amazon.com/Microsoft-Windows-Development-Requires-Dedicated/ dp/B00KZIVEXO/ref=sr_1_1?ie=UTF8&qid=1518420355&sr=8-1&keywords=kinect +windows+v2
27. Amazon.   https://www.amazon.com/MBIENTLAB-Meta-Motion-Sensor-Fusion/dp/B01N9 C3HVU/ref=sr_1_1?s=electronics&ie=UTF8&qid=1518420762&sr=1-1&keywords= metamotion+r
28. Taobao. https://item.taobao.com/item.htm?spm=a1z09.2.0.0.34792e8dG0R4A6&id=558971 532837&_u=c8icdh45a36
29. Tmall. https://detail.tmall.com/item.htm?id=12513799511&spm=a1z09.2.0.0.34792e8dG0R 4A6&_u=c8icdh47c30&skuId=3433523876996

Training for Bus Bodywork in Virtual Reality Environments

Danny F. Herrera$^{(\boxtimes)}$, S. Bolívar Acosta$^{(\boxtimes)}$,
Washington X. Quevedo$^{(\boxtimes)}$, Jhon A. Balseca$^{(\boxtimes)}$,
and Víctor H. Andaluz$^{(\boxtimes)}$

Universidad de las Fuerzas Armadas ESPE, Sangolquí, Ecuador
{dfherrera4, bvacosta, wjquevedo,
jabalsecal, vhandaluzl}@espe.edu.ec

Abstract. This document presents a virtual training system oriented for learning of electric welding applied to automotive body assembly industry. The training tasks are developed in a virtual immersion environment created with Unity 3D graphic software, in order to improve the user's skills and welding skills through a teaching-learning process that allows the virtual manipulation of industrial instruments. In this way, the experience in welding task is obtained, risks of industrial accidents are reduced and waste is eliminated. The experimental results show the behavior of the system and the evolution of the user's skills.

Keywords: Electric welding · Virtual reality · Bodyworks assembly

1 Introduction

Virtual reality is a world created in computer, where the user has the feeling of being internal in this one. The applications of this tool grow with great expectation due to the creation of immersion technologies, such as Oculus Rift, HTC, Leap Motion, etc. The same ones that allow to increase the sensation of realism and the interaction with the virtual environment [1]. In recent years, virtual reality applied to learning allows to develop significant and necessary skills to act in real processes, simplifying the training of professionals in diverse areas where learning activities have a certain level of risk in case of not performing correctly, in [2] it is shown that the fidelity of the immersion is a feature of great relevance which involves the realism of the input devices and their interaction, the fidelity of the screen or output devices and finally the loyalty of the stage that corresponds to the realism of the environment simulated [3]. Currently, virtual reality is involved in several areas and allows the development of several applications such as *(i) Medical,* for physical rehabilitation systems, surgical training for surgeries, [4]; *(ii) Psychologists,* in applications relating to social interaction training for people with autism, [5]; *(iii) Entertainment*, such as the development of motion platforms for video game immersion, [6]; *(iv) Education,* focused on technology with virtual reality for education, [7]; *(v) Industry,* training in a technical environment regarding risk prevention and various industrial maintenance techniques, [8].

© Springer International Publishing AG, part of Springer Nature 2018
L. T. De Paolis and P. Bourdot (Eds.): AVR 2018, LNCS 10850, pp. 67–85, 2018.
https://doi.org/10.1007/978-3-319-95270-3_5

Currently, virtual reality training in the industry allows technical operators to train safely as they can manipulate protection elements and industrial equipment, as well as the visualization of technical diagrams facilitating the understanding of the process and the connections related in it, as explains in the work presented in [9]. In the work described in [10], it affirms this idea when proposing a welding training system that allows feedback to identify patterns of wrong movements for correction, thus optimizing training by improving welding quality and reducing production times, very important data in the metallurgical industry [11], of infrastructures [12] and automotive [13].

For this reason the virtual reality within the automotive engineering has become a main tool that through cooperation with software of design of mechanical components of vehicles, simplifies many procedures such as the schematization and creation of basic parts in the construction of vehicles such as is exposed in [14], the development of virtual laboratories allows research associated with the need to observe safety measures within the manufacture of vehicles as well as the use of equipment used in the training of engineers as it is an economical alternative [7], In this way, construction work is provided that demonstrates a high level of reliability in each piece that makes up the automotive [15].

Considering the above, this work presents in a first instance the simulation in virtual reality of a bus assembly plant which allows the immersion of an individual with the aim of strengthening the recognition of automotive assembly processes, in addition in second instance, the user is virtually trained in electric welding tasks, specifically in the main joints of the metallic body, which is coupled and assembled on the common chassis existing in the ecuadorian market.

Therefore, the presentation of this document is structured as follows: the parameters of the electric welding is exposed in Sect. 2, the development of the structure of the virtual reality system described in Sect. 3, the virtualization of the electric welding process is explained in part IV and finally the Analysis of Results in the Sect. 6 with their respective conclusions defined in Sect. 7.

2 Parameters of Electric Welding

Electric welding is one of the most common tools in the construction of metal structures, because it represents an accessible instrument whose quality depends exclusively on the skills and experience of the welder, who through a series of factors can determine a good appearance. The drawback of this practice is that such skill is only obtained with experience, generating waste of resources, also the demand by industry requires trained employees to ensure quality work with the elements available in the plant. Likewise, good industrial safety and quality management practices promote a good work environment suited to the needs of each process [16]. Here is the correct use of protections, such as gloves, mask, glasses, as well as the correct selection of electrodes and current intensity to perform this work.

In this work we propose the development of a virtual application where the user is able to develop physical and psychological skills with the advantage of reducing waste in a virtual environment where their physical integrity is not exposed to risks in case of mistakes, optimizing time work and increasing production.

The welding training procedure starts with: *(i) Electrode,* the correct selection of the electrode dependent on the material to be welded, such as galvanized iron, carbon steel, A36 steel, etc. *(ii) Position,* where refers to the type of orientation of the weld either vertical or horizontal; *(iii) Machine,* in the practical case an AC welding machine is presented. For the selection of the electrode, its numbering must be recognized: this code allows knowing the parameters *i, ii,* and *iii* mentioned above, this depends on the quality of the weld that depends on the resistance exerted by the welding per square inch, therefore, for the selection of the electrode to be used, Table 1, standardized by the AWS, is used. (Society American Welding) for the selection of its penultimate number [17].

Table 1. Classification of the penultimate number according to AWS

Classification AWS	Coating	Welding position	Electric current
E 6010	High cellulose, sodium	F, V, OH, H	CC (+)
⋮	⋮	⋮	⋮
E 7018	Under hydrogen, potassium, iron powder	F, V, OH, H	CA ó CC (+)

Where, according to the AWS standards, the welding positions are: F: flat; H: horizontal; H_Filete: horizontal fillet; V_Descending: vertical descending; V: vertical; OH: ceiling or overhead. In the same way the currents for each electrode are: AC: Alternating current; CC (+): Positive polarized direct current; CC (−): Negative polarized DC current. From this selection it is obtained that the electrode to be used must have 1 as the penultimate number because it allows welding in any position and also the use of the alternating welding machine which is used in the virtual environment.

For the selection of the last number of the electrode, the Table 2 of the last number of electrodes exposed in the AWS standard is taken as a basis [17].

Table 2. Classification of the last number according to AWS standards

Last digit	Current	Cladding	Arc type	Penetration
E XX11	CA ó CCPI Reverse polarity	Organic	Strong	Deep
⋮	⋮	⋮	⋮	⋮
E XX18	CA ó CCPI Reverse polarity	Low hydrogen	Medium	Median

In this way it is determined that the electrode suitable for the practice of body welding would be the electrode: E_7018.

Once the electrode to be used is established, the current necessary to be applied by the machine is identified, the wrong current is selected, faults that damage the welded material are produced. Also, when applying too low an amperage, the weld bead will not be uniform and the electrode will stick in the weld. While if the amperage is very high there is a lot of splashing and the piece to be welded will be perforated. The amperage needed to perform the electrical welding is within a set range with values that can be identified in the electrode's datasheet or it can be found analytically using the formula 1

$$I = (\phi - 1) * 50 \tag{1}$$

where: I is the intensity; ϕ is the diameter of the electrode. As shown in Fig. 1 of amperage limits of an electrode in this case for a diameter of 3.25 its optimum amperage is calculated as follows:

$$I = (3.25 - 1) * 50$$
$$I = 112.5 \, [A] \cong 110 \, [A]$$

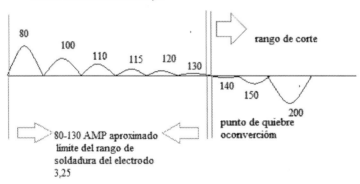

Fig. 1. Amperage limits for an electrode 3, 25

Once the electrode is established and the level of intensity to be used, the time in which the heat must be applied to the solder is established. For this purpose, the heat transfer equation presented below in formula 2 is determined:

$$Q = R * I^2 * t \tag{2}$$

where Q is energy in the form of heat expressed in Joules; R resistance in ohms; I intensity applied in amperes; t time in seconds. For the correct welding of a material it is necessary to follow steps and essential parameters that are commonly performed empirically producing waste of both economic resources and raw materials, for this reason the development of a virtual training environment gives us the possibility to develop the skill needed to perform this task correctly.

3   Structure in Virtual Reality

The proposed application is developed in the Unity 3D engine for graphics with the aim of associating the virtual assembly and welding operations with the input and output devices which allow to interact with the process as shown in Fig. 2. The application uses the Steam VR plugin able to use the controls and interact with simple instructions.

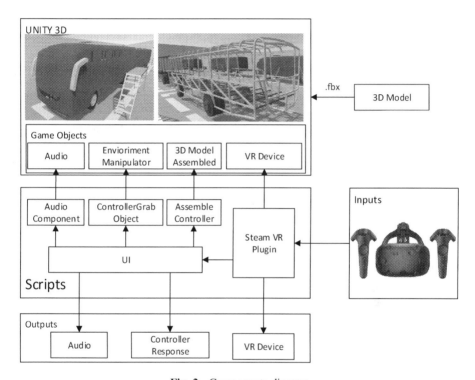

Fig. 2. Components diagram

Virtual reality programming is performed for the simulation stage of each work scenario, where the components of the bodywork and the assembly controller are linked, in this phase is the respective configuration of physical properties, coupling and welding of parts that simulates a realistic assembly process.

In the data input and output stage the HTC VIVE device is considered to interact with the environment, connected to a computer using a HDMI port, which adds all the visual quality of the environment and the IR cameras connected by USB reads the movements of the hand controls in the environment. The communication is established due to the Steam VR software and its respective libraries that allow programming the interaction with the control actions, in addition to the compatibility with Unity 3D software.

The Scripts phase contains the communication with the I/O devices, as well as the development of the virtual interface that interacts in the different assembly areas which obey industrial safety regulations since it is where each of the pieces of the environment to obtain the respective response of the output device, emphasizing audio responses with surround sound because it plays a very important role in the user's immersion.

The simulation is a stage of great importance, the presented application has pieces developed parametrically in CAD format software, in this case SolidWorks is used due to the friendly interface and the versatility to create 3D models, as well as 2D planimetries that facilitate the dimensional comprehension of the assembly.

These pieces are exported to the 3DSMax software to convert them an extension file .FBX which is compatible with Unity 3D, the main program of the application that gathers the characteristics for communication and interaction with stations of assembly, sheathing and painting of the bodywork. In this way the body assembly is recorded in the following order where the structure of the bodywork is composed of several main stages.

4   Bodywork Structure

The application presents the assembly of the metallic structure of a bus, which depends exclusively on the design provided by the manufacturer. Even so, every bodywork contains quite similar structures with elements and sets of basic parts which are described below.

Chassis. This element is defined by a Torpedo-type chassis as shown in Fig. 3, with an engine ahead of the front axle and mechanical crossbow type suspension, this type of chassis covers 90% of national bus production.

Fig. 3. Torpedo-type chassis

Anchors. These elements allow anchoring the floor of the bodywork to the main chassis, obeying the rules of the chassis manufacturer which strictly prohibit welding directly to the main beams, as indicated in Fig. 4. These elements are adjusted with screws in perforations specified by the manufacturer in order to distribute the weight in an equitable manner.

Fig. 4. Anchorage

Floor. Visible in Fig. 5, it is comprised of a structure of square steel tubes of 50 × 50 mm, uniform structure, mesh type, welded vertically, and coupled to the anchors with electric welding.

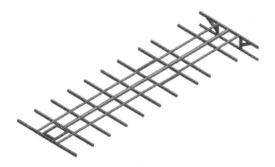

Fig. 5. Floor of the bodywork

Body. This structure is shown in Fig. 6, is comprised of galvanized iron tubes, arranged in specific sizes and shapes to support the roof and lined with the bus, this body is composed of serrated, frontal, rear and lateral supports, these elements are located individually and are welded together with vertical welding.

Fig. 6. Body of the bodywork

Ceiling. The roof structure is as light as possible so that the center of mass of the vehicle is as close as possible to the ground, as shown in Fig. 7, made up of square galvanized iron tubes and small tool plates to distribute the weight towards the searches.

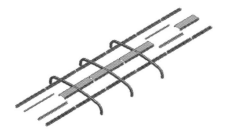

Fig. 7. Ceiling of the bodywork

Lined. The final stage of the assembly of bodyworks comprises a coating of tool plates, as indicated in Fig. 8, which provide firmness, stability and aerodynamics to the working conditions of the vehicle.

Fig. 8. Lined of the bodywork

The elements described above are part of the virtual application, and can be manipulated by the user through the controls of HTC VIVE device, in addition to the free movement of the user in the virtual plant including stairs that allow access to the assembly on the roof of the body, providing a realistic environment that facilitates the immersion of the human being in Virtual Reality.

5   Process Programming

For the immersion in the presented application the realism of the elements is indispensable, for that reason the design of the parametric model in a CAD software is made. In this case, the Solidworks software is used, a tool focused on mechanical design in 2D and 3D since it allows modeling individual pieces and in sets, besides

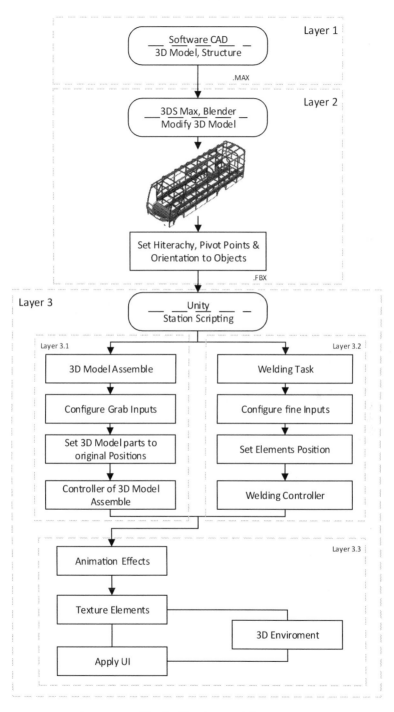

Fig. 9. Structure model

extracting from them planimetries or any other technical information of the element, its versatility is that once the piece has been made, all the extractions (planes and exchange files) are done in a automated way.

This document proposes a multi-layer scheme focused on immersion and the development of virtual applications for automotive assembly and electric welding tasks as shown in Fig. 9.

(i) Layer 1. In this section the design of each 3D CAD model corresponding to the parts that interact in the assembly of bodyworks such as anchors, bars, searches and linings, elements designed to work in Unity 3D is developed, for this the use of the 3ds Max software. So, in *(ii) Layer 2,* based on the assembly references, the hierarchy and orientation of each piece of the model is determined as well as standardizing them in the same coordinate system. Thus, it establishes the axes of rotation or pivots of each element for tasks of rotation. By completing this process you get a .FBX file compatible with the Unity 3D graphics engine where the next layer of the process is developed: *(iii) Layer 3,* characterized by a Unity software scene, which was initially responsible for defining the process station and the task to be performed, here the interaction between the input and output devices is performed with the environment where the application is executed. This section contains 3 subroutines established by *Layer 3.1. Assembly tasks,* the programming of the application made in C language, contains Scripts linked to each element that interacts in the process. In the assembly subroutine the entrances are configured for the movement interaction of the bodywork parts towards their respective position in relation to the original 3D model, task carried out with HTC VIVE & Gear VR devices, directed by the assembly controller with *Trigger functions* where it compares the current position of a piece in space with its respective position to the original model which retains the invisible feature. Thus, the drag of the piece is assigned to the TRIGGER button of the HTC control, visible in Fig. 10.

Fig. 10. Drag parts

The consequent subroutine is called as *Layer 3.2. welding tasks.* Where the inputs of the HTC VIVE device are configured in such a way that the application interacts with tiny movements of the electrode, associated with the HTC VIVE device to perform the corresponding animations around these movements. The welding effect is represented by several solid elements, visible in Fig. 11, which appear sequentially by keeping the electrode in correct position for a defined period of time. Finally, the *Layer 3.3, Animación.* consists of immersion effects defined by specific effects of each task such as *(i)* assembly animation where the assembly plans are visualized when the HTC VIVE control is located in a space delimited on the wall of the simulation, as shown in Fig. 12. *(ii)* For welding tasks, particle systems are used, which provide visual effects of sparks, smoke and welding flames, visible depending on the position of the virtual electrode with respect to the welded pieces.

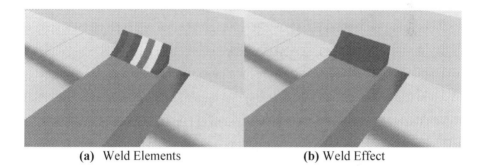

(a) Weld Elements   **(b)** Weld Effect

Fig. 11. Weld effect

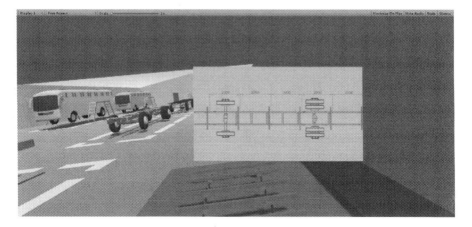

Fig. 12. Display of planes

6 Analysis of Results

The section presents a virtual environment of a bodyworks assembly plant, see Fig. 13, where user immersion is allowed when interacting with assembly and welding tasks in a realistic manner. The bus bodyworks factory has two main areas: *(i)* office area, where the administrative staff works, management and customer service. *(ii)* production area, where the manufacturing process is completely carried out to transform a chassis into a passenger bus with all available services.

Fig. 13. Bus bodywork factory

The assembly of bus bodyworks is composed of three main stages, grouped by the similarity of their tasks: *(i)* Assembly, *(ii)* Welding and *(iii)* Lining and painting. These tasks are developed with the HTC VIVE device, which provides the ideal feedback in order to develop a realistic environment. Next, each process is described individually.

Assembly. This process considers four sections of work with their respective pieces as shown in Figs. 14, 15, 16, 17 and 18, these pieces initially appear unarmed on a work table. The main objective is to use the HTC control to take and move each piece to the chassis in order to assemble the metal structure of the bus by placing each element in its corresponding position according to the layout of each planimetry. The first parts to be placed on the chassis are the anchors, the chassis manufacturer indicates the quantity and number of parts necessary considering the use of the vehicle, since they support the total weight of the structure. In the work carried out, a total of seven anchors are joined to the bodywork. See Fig. 14.

Fig. 14. Anchors area

For the assembly task it is required to interact with the planimetry of each section, see Fig. 15, and use the HTC VIVE control to move each piece to its corresponding position, in the case that the task is carried out successfully, the color of the piece changes and it is restricted to continue with the movement. See Fig. 16.

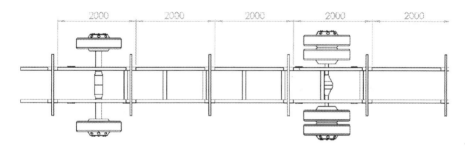

Fig. 15. Anchors station plans

(a) White Anchor while moving.   (b) Black Anchor, correct position

Fig. 16. Assembly animations

For tasks of displacement in the environment, it is possible to walk within the area established by HTC VIVE, while, if you want to travel greater distances or move a piece, you must press the touch panel of the remote control and choose the desired location with the pointer that moves on the floor. See Fig. 17. It is possible to use a control for scrolling while an object is dragged by another control.

Fig. 17. Teleportation

The floor structure is welded on the anchors, this mesh is constituted by two main support bars on which rest twelve bars located transversely, as shown in Fig. 18, in this way the weight of the structure is held uniformly.

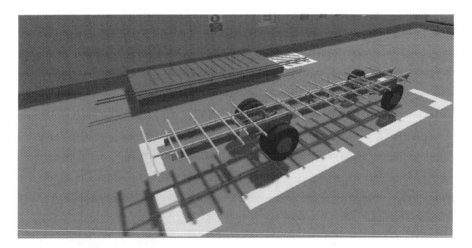

Fig. 18. Floor area

The next work station corresponds to the placement of eight searches, welded to the crossbars of the floor as shown in Fig. 19, form the main frame of the bus where it is possible to perceive its most basic dimensional characteristics.

Fig. 19. Main structure area

Finally, approximately 120 pieces of square pipe are located and welded between the searches and the floor to form the main skeleton of the bus, see Fig. 20. In this way they form a solid and resistant structure ideal for the harshest conditions of passenger transport.

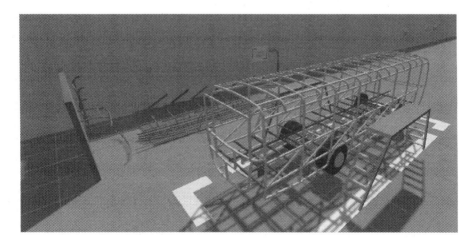

Fig. 20. General structure area

Welding. This process is involved in the whole assembly stage, since a strong and resistant joint between pieces is necessary to guarantee the quality of the structure. For the virtualization of this task several elements are considered such as welding machine, mask, electrodes of different characteristics and electrode holder. See Fig. 21.

Fig. 21. Welding area

The welding task provides a detailed sequence in which Unity 3D software initially considers the selection of the corresponding electrode for the material to be welded, the amperage selection and subsequent ignition of the soldering machine to finally manipulate the handle of the electrode holder, it is here where the displacement of the electrode is considered to produce visual effects, such as sparks, smoke and flames of colors and tactile sensory effects, which involves the vibration of the HTC VIVE control, in this way determining the state of the process and its correct development. See Fig. 22. The user can perform horizontal and vertical welding tasks as a sequential and realistic process.

Fig. 22. Welding task

Lining and Painting. The metallic structure of the bus is subjected to a coating process, covered and sealed with metal sheets, as well as the front and rear pieces made with fiberglass. See Fig. 23. They use the recurring dynamics of taking pieces with HTC VIVE controls and place them in their corresponding positions.

Fig. 23. Cover area

Figure 24 represents the area of facilities where the seats are placed and electrical and pneumatic connections are made. This stage of the bodywork is virtualized with the purpose of its theoretical knowledge.

Fig. 24. Seats and connections area

The painting area, visible in Fig. 25, consists of selecting and moving a predetermined color of several available, to paint the bus, according to the user's decision.

Fig. 25. Paint area

7   Conclusions

In this article, we propose a virtual training system for tasks of assembly and welding of bus bodyworks. A virtual reality environment developed with a graphics engine in Unity 3D is the fundamental basis of the system presented. In this way it allows the user to immerse during the teaching-learning process in order to reduce waste, optimize infrastructure, time and other variables. The experimental results obtained show the efficiency of the system which is generated due to the human-machine interaction oriented to develop psychosomatic abilities in the area of metallic bodywork industries.

Acknowledgements. The authors would like to thanks to the Corporación Ecuatoriana para el Desarrollo de la Investigación y Academia–CEDIA for the financing given to research, development, and innovation, through the CEPRA projects, especially the project CEPRA-XI-2017-06; *Control Coordinado Multi-operador aplicado a un robot Manipulador Aéreo;* also to Universidad de las Fuerzas Armadas ESPE, Universidad Técnica de Ambato, Escuela Superior Politécnica de Chimborazo, and Universidad Nacional de Chimborazo, and Grupo de Investigación en Automatización, Robótica y Sistemas Inteligentes, GIARSI, for the support to develop this work.

References

1. Turner, C.J., Hutabarat, W., Oyekan, J., Tiwari, A.: Discrete event simulation and virtual reality use in industry: new opportunities and future trends. IEEE Trans. Hum. Mach. Syst. **46**, 1–13 (2016)
2. Buttussi, F., Chittaro, L.: Effects of different types of virtual reality display on presence and learning in a safety training scenario. IEEE Trans. Vis. Comput. Graph. 1–14 (2016)
3. Pais, F., Patrao, B., Menezes, P.: Virtual reality as a training tool for human interactions. In: 4th Experiment@ International Conference, vol. 4, pp. 119–120, June 2017

4. Wang, R., Yao, J., Wang, L., Liu, X., Wang, H., Zheng, L.: A surgical training system for four medical punctures based on virtual reality and haptic feedback. In: IEEE Symposium on 3D User Interfaces (3DUI), L.A., pp. 215–216, March 2017

5. Mourning, R., Tang, Y.: Virtual reality social training for adolescents with high-functioning autism. In: IEEE International Conference on Systems, Man, and Cybernetics Budapest, Hungary, pp. 4848–4853 (2016)

6. Hament, B., Cater, A., Oh, P.Y.: Coupling virtual reality and motion platforms for snowboard training. In: 14th International Conference on Ubiquitous Robots and Ambient Intelligence (URAI), Korea, pp. 556–560, July 2017

7. Makarova, I., Khabibullin, R., Belyaev, E., Bogateeva, A.: The application of virtual reality technologies in engineering education for the automotive industry. In: IEEE International Conference on Interactive Collaborative Learning, Italy, pp. 536–544 (2015)

8. Cigert, J., Sbaouni, M., Segot, C.: Virtual reality training of manual procedures in the nuclear sector. In: IEEE Virtual Reality Conference, France, pp. 381–382, March 2015

9. Cordeiro, C., Paludo, J., Tanaka, E., Dominguez, L., Gadbem, E., Euflausino, A.: Desenvolvimento de Ambiente de Realidade Virtual Imersivo para Treinamento de Eletricistas Habilitados em Subestações. In: IEEE XVII Symposium on Virtual and Augmented Reality, pp. 142–146 (2015)

10. White, S., Prachyabrued, M., Baghi, D., Aglawe, A., Reiners, D., Borst, C., Chambers, T.: Virtual welder trainer. In: IEEE Virtual Reality, USA, March 2009

11. Benkai, X., Quiang, Z., Liang, Y.: A real-time welding training system based on Virtual Reality. In: 2015 IEEE Virtual Reality (VR), pp. 309–310 (2015)

12. Andaluz, V.H., et al.: Immersive industrial process environment from a P&ID diagram. In: Bebis, G., et al. (eds.) Advances in Visual Computing, ISVC 2016. LNCS, vol. 10072, pp. 701–712. Springer, Cham (2016). https://doi.org/10.1007/978-3-319-50835-1_63

13. Khastgir, S., Birrell, S., Dhadyalla, G., Jennings, P.: Development of a drive-in driver-in-the-loop fully immersive driving simulator for virtual validation of automotive systems. In: IEEE 81st Vehicular Technology Conference, pp. 1–4 (2015)

14. Quevedo, W.X., Sánchez, J.S., Arteaga, O., ÁV, M., Zambrano, V.D., Sánchez, C.R., Andaluz, V.H.: Virtual reality system for training in automotive mechanics. In: De Paolis, L. T., Bourdot, P., Mongelli, A. (eds.) AVR 2017, Part I. LNCS, vol. 10324, pp. 185–198. Springer, Cham (2017). https://doi.org/10.1007/978-3-319-60922-5_14

15. Wu, X., Fei, G.: Research of virtual reality technology in automotive engine assembly teaching. In: 6th IEEE Joint International Information Technology and Artificial Intelligence Conference, vol. 1, pp. 167–169 (2011)

16. Freschi, F., Giaccone, L., Mitolo, M.: Arc welding processes: an electrical safety analysis. IEEE Trans. Ind. Appl. **53**(2), 819–825 (2017)

17. Manual de Electrodos para Soldar, 2nd edn. INFRA, pp. 4–5 (2009)

Market Study of Durable Consumer Products in Multi-user Virtual Environments

Washington X. Quevedo[⊠], Olga J. Benavides[⊠],
Verónica A. Rocha[⊠], Cristian M. Gallardo[⊠], Aldrin G. Acosta[⊠],
Julio C. Tapia[⊠], and Víctor H. Andaluz[⊠]

Universidad de las Fuerzas Armadas ESPE, Sangolquí, Ecuador
{wjquevedo,ojbenavides,vlrocha,agacosta,jctapia3,
vhandaluzl}@espe.edu.ec, cmgallardop@gmail.com

Abstract. This article describes an analysis of the demand of a product or service through virtual environments to measure the acceptance of it in consumers. The developed system consists of a virtual reality environment, which involves both designers in the characterization of the prototype and users in measuring the acceptability of the product in the market, in order to optimize human and economic resources for the company. The developed application considers a multi-user system where a user should enter at the beginning of the application inviting a certain number of people to participate in the analysis of the prototype of the product and make the changes that are considered convenient. Modification options allow users to interact simultaneously with the product, creating different models. The interaction of users subject to testing, contributes to the measurement of the acceptability of the characteristics of the product through manipulation and observation in virtual environments.

Keywords: Virtual reality · Product designers · Consumers
Analysis of demand · Multi-user

1 Introduction

Entrepreneurship as an important part in the search for opportunities that a company has for the development of it, involves different factors such as the creation of ideas, ingenuity, risk taking and invention with a greater imaginative power [1–3]. The latest strategies cannot leave aside the professional and at the same time novel approach to generate profits in companies [4, 5]; strategic entrepreneurship can be taken as a starting point, which allows focusing on how the organization will compete in the market and at the same time in different areas such as the launch of a new product, organizational renewal and recreation of the existing commercial model [6]. When applying the area of entrepreneurship in the launching of new products it is necessary to know the feasibility which it possesses, so a financial analysis is inevitable.

At the time of launching a different product in the market, considerable amounts of resources are put into play, which can be represented in human and financial capital [7]. For it, employers select evaluation strategies which mainly involve measures of financial performance KPI (Key Performance Indicators) which is a technique managed

© Springer International Publishing AG, part of Springer Nature 2018
L. T. De Paolis and P. Bourdot (Eds.): AVR 2018, LNCS 10850, pp. 86–100, 2018.
https://doi.org/10.1007/978-3-319-95270-3_6

by financial researchers to assess the financial environment of an organization and the ease of decision making [8, 9]. This analysis allows us to understand if there are enough resources of the organization to achieve the objectives as well as be prepared to face possible risks depending on the scenario in which it is located [10]. Continuously to the financial analysis, it is necessary to adapt the production to the client needs and preferences so it is necessary to implement marketing strategies.

Marketing is identified as a set of systematic steps for decision making in order to reach the proposed goals based on the fact that consumer needs must be considered in all activities of the organization [11]. Traditional marketing uses various tools where advertisers pay to the markets of broadcast chains, radio, online news sites and magazines, through which audience and consumers are reached [12]. New trends for marketing make traditional strategies adapt to changes such as online development, acquisitions, services and assistance [13].

A tool to the acceptance of the product for consumers and designers is the virtual reality, described as a set of methods which allow individuals to appreciate a virtual world [14, 15]. Describing virtual reality as the result of the power of technology to create simulated realities, these can be an important tool for diverse fields of study and market. Through elements such as helmets, glasses and haptic devices, the user can be immersed in an alternate reality to consume intangible products. In this aspect, virtual reality represents an element which organizations can use to develop their processes, evaluate, and introduce new products more quickly in the market and in a more profitable way [16]. Previous research emphasizes the importance of virtual reality in organizations, which has generated competitive advantages by providing facilities for product design, form, simulations, tests, and verification. For instance, [17] proposes a framework for positioning the level of VR consumer engagement based on location and interactivity. The paper rounds off with a discussion of the future of VR and a number of problems that need to be solved. In the same way, [18] investigates the persuasive power of virtual reality (VR) imagery for destination marketing by assessing the roles of spatial presence in influencing attitude and behavior toward tourism destinations. In this way, diverse conflicts can be solved before being used in their production practices, avoiding the loss of resources providing an environment for observation in a three-dimensional space and manipulation with objects and optimize decision making in qualitative and quantitative perspectives [19–21]. A clear difference between the traditional sources of information (internet) and the VR is the immersion level, allowing to experiment in first person a close real world.

The present proposal shows the analysis of a market study that is done before and during the launch of products such as simulated tests using platforms in virtual environments, which allow not only the visualization of the design but the interaction and manipulation of the prototype for any change that is required according to the needs of consumers and designers. These changes can be given in color, texture, size, and so on, according to the options presented in the platform, making it easier for organizations to take a decision about the launch of a product or modifications in order to be more acceptable in the market, decreasing the costs and the time that is invested in a traditional market study.

This article is split into 6 Sections, including the introduction. Section 2 presents the formulation of the problem in the market study of products and the resources that are implemented for it. The structure of the multi-user virtual reality system is shown in Sect. 3. Section 4 presents the results of the experimentation applied to designers and consumers, while Sect. 6 presents the conclusions of the work.

2 Problem Formulation

In a production process it is necessary to satisfy the needs of the user, which is why the participation of personnel trained in the characteristics of the design is required, who give a constructive criterion for the improvement of the product [22]. This grouping brings with it several adverse factors, such as the concentration of tactics in any place, requiring the presence of several experts. However, there are problems such as the availability of people's time due to their different occupations, scheduling conflicts due to their location in different time zones, logistics costs that entail lodging, transportation, time spent for meals, and so on, affecting the economic health of the company [23].

Companies increasingly involve customers in the generation of ideas to maintain their competitive advantages. For this, it is necessary to use high economic resources in the inclusion of consumers as test subjects to measure the degree of acceptance before, during and after the launch of new products or services. This inclusion process involves the creation of an appropriate logistics which allows reaching the consumer with the prototype under test, generating costs in the production of physical versions of the product as mobilization, assembly and new marketing strategies to attract potential consumers [24] (Fig. 1).

In view of the rapid changes that are generated in the market, it is seen the need for companies to use information technology to improve the detection capacity of the market to simplify operational factors, knowing that the process of introducing a new product or service involves a set of complex research, development, and distribution activities [25].

The first blocks of the diagram show the process of conceptualizing an idea for the generation of a new product or service that comes from the needs and desires of customers, which is optimized in order to minimize errors in the selection of the best option based on a more elaborate version of the insight according to the consumer's mentality. The marketing strategy is continuously developed, which allows describing the size of the target market, the price of the distribution strategy, sales goals and long-term profits through an estimate of marketing. This process gives way to the development of product concept through a physical prototype of one or more versions that meets the needs of consumers. Market tests are carried out to obtain feedback from consumers about the strategic characteristics of the prototype. Through these results, it is decided to continue with the commercialization stage in which the companies face the decision making when the product must be introduced, at the same time identify the most attractive geographical with the best groups of consumers, in order to coordinate the launch schedule [26].

As described above, this article focuses on the stage of creating the prototype through virtual environments, where the personnel in charge of the design can modify the physical characteristics of the product. The interaction of the staff is simultaneous in real time, which allows modifying the prototype in its characteristics of size, material,

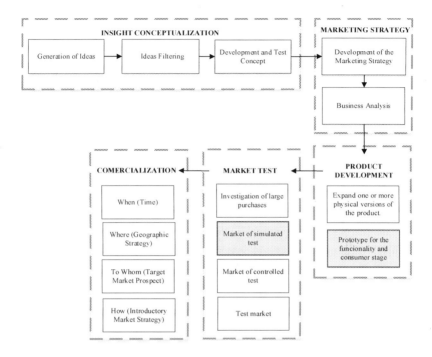

Fig. 1. Diagram of development, test and launch of new products and services.

texture and combination of colors, based on design regulations. Through voice chat, an attempt is made to reach consensus among experts to determine a final prototype, allowing the simulated test to be executed through virtual reality in the market stage. This allows consumers to participate in the measurement of acceptance of the prototype through the application of a satisfaction survey, after the virtual manipulation of the product or service.

3   System Structure

This section presents a diagram of a cyclic operation of the proposed application in virtual reality, see Fig. 2. The diagram consists of 4 main blocks, which includes: the design stage of the scenes in virtual reality with the use of 3D resources, the functions programming block for each scene in C#, and the blocks of Inputs/Outputs which are related to the hardware destined to execute the application.

In the *Unity block*, the main design modules of the design and validation environments are added. These will be accessible through the home and Configuration Window, allowing to select the initial parameters of each environment. For the graphics creation of each scene, the 3D models have been classified using generic Game Objects described as follow: The Product module is a Game Object that represents the 3D model of the prototype which is evaluated for acceptance; Avatar G.O. it is the representation of the user within the virtual environment which allows replicating the

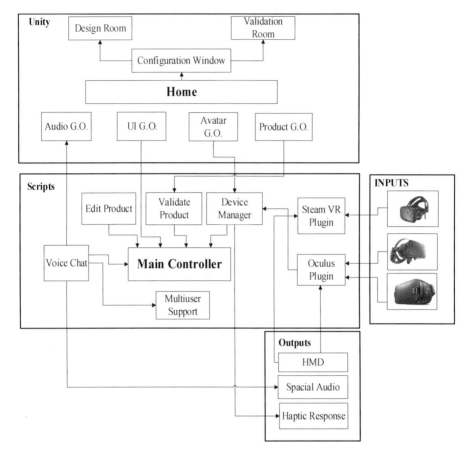

Fig. 2. Virtual reality app cyclic diagram

movements and actions carried out in the real world; U. I. G. O. (User Interface Game Object) shows the indications, editing controls, and methods of interaction with the environment available for each activity, and finally, the G.O. contains audible sources that generate audio effects within the virtual environment.

In the *Scripting block* are programmed scripts in C# language, grouped into specific function modules. The modules pass through the Main Controller, which centralizes and combines the functions of each of the modules in a single result. The predominant modules are those of Edit Product and Validate Product, because they contain the programming of the Validation and Design Room scenes behaviour. The Edit Product module integrates an algorithm which allows the user to edit the basic characteristics of the product: colour, texture, size, and information; while the algorithm of Validate Product allows informing of the characteristics and advantages of the product while the user manipulates it. Both modules can modify the Product G.O. according to the results of the algorithm. In order for the application to support the interaction with more users in real time, the implementation of the Multiuser Support module is necessary, which integrates the functions of Unity: Network Manager, Identity, Animation, and so on. In addition, for the exchange of voice messages in real time, the Voice Chat module is used, which manages an independent communication channel for all the concurrent users in the room. The device manager module selects prefabricated scripts to manage the inputs of different virtual reality devices from the SteamVR plugin (Eyewear Manager HTC VIVE) and Oculus Library (Oculus Rift and GearVR glasses manager).

The *Input block* shows the possible connection of three virtual reality devices: HTC VIVE, Oculus Rift, and GearVR. Each device has characteristics which make them suitable for the present application. HTC VIVE has a system of continuous tracking without blind spots, Oculus Rift has a massive system of distributions of apps and GearVR offers portability when running the application on a smartphone.

In the *Output block* there are the items audio, haptic and visual response to virtual reality interaction. Visual response is shown in the HMD of the virtual reality device, Audio response catch the special audio effects in the headset device, finally de haptic response creates some small vibrations in the controllers to feedback the action when the user interacts with an object or function.

4   Procedure

The present application is used as a tool to evaluate the acceptability of the product from the perspective of the personnel in charge of the modifications in a virtual environment, by editing the characteristics of the product as: color, texture, shape and size defined according to the contribution of each competitor. The interaction through voice chat between the designers allows reaching consensus and facilitates decision making about the product. While potential consumers manipulate and visualize the characteristics of the product to subsequently fill a survey which helps to determine the satisfaction generated by the product. The app uses multi-user native services of Unity software to support multiple persons using the app in real time to interact with each other. The native modules to multiuser support are enough to this app because the users at the same time is maximum 6 persons and the movements to stream to the other user are limited to the hands movement when the user manipulate the smartphone and position when the user is walking around the room until found a free space to work.

The development of the research is done with the GearVR headset and hand-controls to manipulate the prototype. In the part of designers, a group of 5 tech designers specialized in front end product design according to the target market to sell the smartphone. They are asked to know the latest technological advances which allow to create or modify innovative products. In the case of consumer participants, ten groups of 5 people are considered as potential consumers of the product, to which they are requested to carry out the following tasks.

The group of designers have access to the platform by deploying the modules for the modifications of size, color and texture characteristics in order to make changes based on the knowledge that each one possesses. When executing the application, a mode selection screen is displayed (Fig. 3) as a designer or as a consumer in each scenario are the functions programmed in Sect. 3.

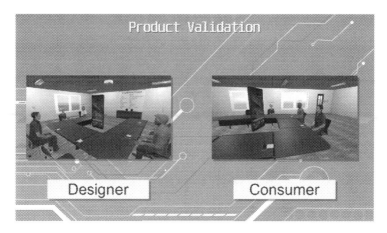

Fig. 3. Home screen app

In the next screen you have the registration information request specifically for the multiplayer function in which the identification of each user will be established, see Fig. 4.

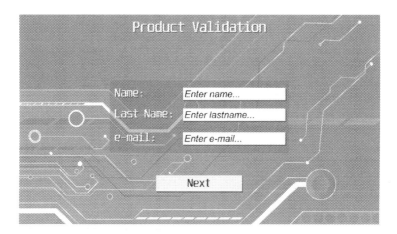

Fig. 4. User information form view

4.1 Designer Mode

At the initial design mode, the room is configured so that the editable elements of the product are accessible to the designer user. The designer appears inside the room and visualizes the other users already connected and those who are entering, see Fig. 5.

(a) TPV of Designer Room

(b) FPV and UI of Designer Mode

Fig. 5. First ingress to designer room

When taking a seat around the meeting table, the organizer of the room explains the context of the prototype and invites to collaborate in the external design of the prototype, see Fig. 6.

To change the characteristics of: color, texture and size of the prototype, it is necessary to use the tools available in the user interface, see Fig. 7.

Finally, through voice chat you can explain the design made by each guest and select the most suitable and it projected with a gigant model in the middle of the meeting room, see Fig. 8.

4.2   Consumer Mode

For the second phase of the experiment, the consumer option is chosen in the main application menu. Followed by filling the personal identification data until you reach

(a)Verifyng design

(b)View from meeting table

Fig. 6. Prototype viewing

the required position. The user in his HUD can see the indications and the status in which he is. In this mode, the manipulation of the smartphone and the reading of its main characteristics are only enabled for the user, see Fig. 9.

5 Analysis of Results

In order to denote the validation of this proposal, there are diverse methods which can be taken into account. In this way, the proposed virtual reality system will be validated through the SUS summary evaluation method which allows measuring attitudes towards the usability of the System [27]. The questions commonly applied in this questionnaire have negative and positive elements (see Table 1), where the weighting ranges from 1 to 5 denotes a complete disagreement or agreement, respectively.

a)   Color selector

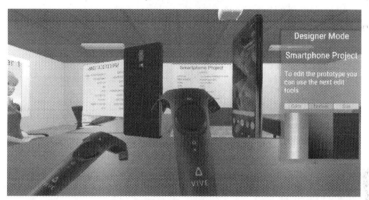

b)   Texture selector

c)   Screen Size selector

Fig. 7. Edit product features

Fig. 8. Discuss about the final design of product

(a) Consumer inside the room

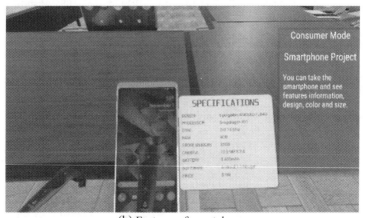

(b) Features of smartphone

Fig. 9. Virtual view in consumer mode

To obtain the final score of the SUS test, the assessment of each item is added, having a weight of 0 to 4 in questions 1, 3, 5, 7, and 9, and the final grade will be the score minus 1. For questions 2, 4, 6, 8, and 10, the weighting will be 5 minus the score given by the participant. For the generation of the final results of the SUS Test, the final score of the 10 items is added and multiplied by 2.5 [28]. The result will be within the range of 0 to 100. For the application of what is described, proceed to Table 1.

Table 1. Survey results

No	Questions	Score	Operation
1	I think I would like to use this system frequently	4	4 − 1 = 3
2	I find this system unnecessarily complex	1	5 − 1 = 4
3	I think the system is easy to use	4	4 − 1 = 3
4	I think you would need technical support to make use of the system	2	5 − 2 = 3
5	I find the various functions of the system quite well integrated	4	4 − 1 = 3
6	I have found too much inconsistency in this system	1	5 − 1 = 4
7	I think most people would learn to make use of the system quickly	4	4 − 1 = 3
8	I found the system quite uncomfortable to use	2	5 − 2 = 3
9	I have felt very safe using the system	4	4 − 1 = 3
10	I would need to learn a lot of things before I can manage the system	1	5 − 1 = 4
	TOTAL		**33**

The total sum of the SUS test results is 82.5, which indicates that the usability of the application is appropriate and the beneficiary accepts it for its management and can recommend its use, but the process of improvement is not ruled out in order to get a perfect score, being 100 points the highest score that can be reached.

Table 2. Survey results

Attributes	Purchase intention scale				
	I would buy it without doubt	I would probably buy it	I could buy it or not	I would probably not buy it	I would certainly not buy it
Utility/benefit	56%	22%	4%	10%	8%
Design	50%	24%	8%	8%	10%
Price	22%	20%	22%	10%	26%
Characteristics	36%	22%	24%	8%	10%
Quality	44%	24%	14%	10%	8%

Each group of consumer participants will be able to manipulate the product for 5 min, fully visualizing each physical detail through virtual reality. At the end of the simulation, consumer participants must conduct a survey in order to collect information which allows measuring the purchase intention through the characteristics of the product as well as evaluating the operation and acceptance of the platform. To achieve this end, the application of the purchase intention evaluation method [29] is used, which is based on developing detailed balanced questions with a neutral position that make it easier for the consumer to select the answer that most resembles his criteria.

There are 5 physical attributes of the product to know the degree of importance in the consumer at the time of purchase (see Table 2), whose evaluation scale has five levels that have a correlation between -I would buy it without doubt- and -I would certainly not buy it-, marking available only one of the scales in each of the attributes to choose.

Consumers who participated in the virtual reality platform selected the answers according to their perspectives, then preceded the sum of the answers to obtain the percentages shown in Table 2. The most relevant results indicate that 56% of consumers would buy the product for the profit and benefit it has, however 26% would not acquire the product for the suggested price, taking these results as an opportunity for improvement by reducing of costs.

6   Conclusions

In this article, the analysis for the market study of durable products in a multi-user virtual environment is proposed. The platform consists of a virtual reality environment which allows the participants to interact and visualize the product in the perspective of the designer and the consumer, improving the optimization of resources for the launch of products to the market as well as the use of new technologies for the development of companies and the processes used in them. The development of the proposal is structured in blocks to improve the interpretation of the application, where the operating schemes and the main components are described. Finally, the experimental results are shown to validate the operation of the application, denoting the robustness in the multi-user platform.

Acknowledgements. The authors would like to thanks to the Corporación Ecuatoriana para el Desarrollo de la Investigación y Academia –CEDIA for the financing given to research, development, and innovation, through the CEPRA projects, especially the project CEPRA-XI-2017-06; Control Coordinado Multi-operador aplicado a un robot Manipulador Aéreo; also to Universidad de las Fuerzas Armadas ESPE, Universidad Técnica de Ambato, Escuela Superior Politécnica de Chimborazo, and Universidad Nacional de Chimborazo, and Grupo de Investigación en Automatización, Robótica y Sistemas Inteligentes, GI-ARSI, for the support to develop this work.

References

1. Chen, J.K., Altantsetseg, P.: Entrepreneurship of professional managers in high-tech firms to enhance service innovation: case study of Hsinchu Science Park and Silicon Valley Park. In: 2017 Portland International Conference on Management of Engineering and Technology (PICMET), pp. 1–15. IEEE, July 2017
2. Audretsch, D.B., Kuratko, D.F., Link, A.N.: Making sense of the elusive paradigm of entrepreneurship. Small Bus. Econ. **45**(4), 703–712 (2015)
3. Ferreira, J.J., Fernandes, C.I., Kraus, S.: Entrepreneurship research: mapping intellectual structures and research trends. Rev. Manag. Sci. 1–25 (2017)
4. Bloodgood, J.M., Hornsby, J.S., Burkemper, A.C., Sarooghi, H.: A system dynamics perspective of corporate entrepreneurship. Small Bus. Econ. **45**(2), 383–402 (2015)
5. Acs, Z.J., Stam, E., Audretsch, D.B., O'Connor, A.: The lineages of the entrepreneurial ecosystem approach. Small Bus. Econ. **49**(1), 1–10 (2017)
6. Kuratko, D.F., Hornsby, J.S., Hayton, J.: Corporate entrepreneurship: the innovative challenge for a new global economic reality. Small Bus. Econ. **45**(2), 245–253 (2015)
7. Stummer, C., Kiesling, E., Günther, M., Vetschera, R.: Innovation diffusion of repeat purchase products in a competitive market: an agent-based simulation approach. Eur. J. Oper. Res. **245**(1), 157–167 (2015)
8. Bruton, G., Khavul, S., Siegel, D., Wright, M.: New financial alternatives in seeding entrepreneurship: microfinance, crowdfunding, and peer-to-peer innovations. Entrepr. Theory Pract. **39**(1), 9–26 (2015)
9. Block, J.H., Colombo, M.G., Cumming, D.J., Vismara, S.: New players in entrepreneurial finance and why they are there. Small Bus. Econ. 1–12 (2017)
10. Pushkar, D.I., Dragunova, E.V.: Financial analysis as a tool for company strategy developing, pp. 1–5 (2016)
11. Tomczak, T., Reinecke, S., Kuss, A.: Introduction. In: Strategic Marketing, pp. 1–18. Springer Gabler, Wiesbaden (2018). https://doi.org/10.1007/978-3-658-18417-9_1
12. Chen, W., Li, F., Lin, T., Rubinstein, A.: Combining traditional marketing and viral marketing with amphibious influence maximization. In: Proceedings of the Sixteenth ACM Conference on Economics and Computation, pp. 779–796. ACM, June 2015
13. Gerrikagoitia, J.K., Castander, I., Rebón, F., Alzua-Sorzabal, A.: New trends of intelligent e-marketing based on web mining for e-shops. Procedia-Soc. Behav. Sci. **175**, 75–83 (2015)
14. Castro, J.C., et al.: Virtual reality on e-Tourism. In: Kim, K., Kim, H., Baek, N. (eds.) IT Convergence and Security 2017. LNEE, vol. 450, pp. 86–97. Springer, Singapore (2018). https://doi.org/10.1007/978-981-10-6454-8_13
15. Acosta, A.F., Quevedo, W.X., Andaluz, V.H., Gallardo, C., Santana, J., Castro, J.C., Quisimalin, M., Córdova, V.H.: Tourism marketing through virtual environment experience. In: Proceedings of the 2017 9th International Conference on Education Technology and Computers, pp. 262–267. ACM, December 2017
16. Castellanos, E.X., García-Sánchez, C., Llanganate, W.B., Andaluz, V.H., Quevedo, W.X.: Robots coordinated control for service tasks in virtual reality environments. In: De Paolis, L. T., Bourdot, P., Mongelli, A. (eds.) AVR 2017. LNCS, vol. 10324, pp. 164–175. Springer, Cham (2017). https://doi.org/10.1007/978-3-319-60922-5_12
17. Barnes, S.: Understanding virtual reality in marketing: nature, implications and potential, pp. 1–50. King's College London, London (2016)
18. Tussyadiah, I., Wang, D., Jia, C.: Exploring the persuasive power of virtual reality imagery for destination marketing. In: Tourism Travel and Research Association, vol. 1, no. 1, pp. 1–8 (2016)

19. Mujber, T.S., Szecsi, T., Hashmi, M.S.: Virtual reality applications in manufacturing process simulation. J. Mater. Process. Technol. **155**, 1834–1838 (2004)
20. Martinez, F.J.P.: Present and future of virtual reality technology. In: Creativity and Society, p. 16 (2011)
21. Rai, A., Kannan, R.J., Ramanathan, S.: Multi-user networked framework for virtual reality platform. In: 2017 14th IEEE Annual Consumer Communications & Networking Conference (CCNC), pp. 584–585. IEEE, January 2017
22. Aurich, J.C., Fuchs, C., Wagenknecht, C.: Life cycle oriented design of technical product-service systems. J. Clean. Prod. **14**(17), 1480–1494 (2006)
23. Aguilar Santamaría, P.A.: An inventory classification model to increase the level of customer service and the profitability of the company. In: Thought & Management, no. 32, pp. 148–160 (2012)
24. Day, G.S.: The capabilities of market-driven organizations. J. Mark. **58**(4), 37–52 (1994)
25. Cappa, F., Del Sette, F., Hayes, D., Rosso, F.: How to deliver open sustainable innovation: an integrated approach for a sustainable marketable product. Sustainability **8**(12), 1341 (2016)
26. Kotler, P.: Marketing management: analysis, planning, implementation and control. Master in Administration-Part Time, pp. 40–43. ESAN (2001)
27. Sauro, J., Lewis, J.R.: When designing usability questionnaires, does it hurt to be positive? In: Proceedings of the SIGCHI Conference on Human Factors in Computing Systems, pp. 2215–2224. ACM, May 2011
28. Brooke, J.: SUS-A quick and dirty usability scale. In: Usability Evaluation in Industry, vol. 189(194), pp. 4–7 (1996)
29. Dillon, W.R., Madden, T.J., Firtle, N.H.: Market research in a marketing environment, pp. 328–329. Irwin, Madrid (1996)

Guiding the Viewer in Cinematic Virtual Reality by Diegetic Cues

Sylvia Rothe[(✉)] and Heinrich Hußmann

LMU Munich, Munich, Germany
{sylvia.rothe, hussmann}@ifi.lmu.de

Abstract. Cinematic Virtual Reality has been increasing in popularity the last years. Watching 360° movies with a Virtual Reality device, viewers can freely choose the viewing direction, and thus the visible section of the movie. In order to ensure that the viewer observes all important details, we investigated three methods of implicitly guiding the attention of the viewer: lights, movements, and sounds. We developed a measurement technique to obtain heat maps of viewing direction and applied statistical analysis methods for spatial data. The results of our work show that the attention of the viewer can be directed by sound and movements. New sound induces the viewer to search for the source of the sound, even if not all participants paid attention to the direction of the sound. In our experiments, lights without movements did not draw more attention than other objects. However, a moving light cone changed the viewing direction considerably.

Keywords: Cinematic Virtual Reality · 360° movie · Guiding attention
Spatial sound · Directing gaze

1 Introduction

360° movies are attracting widespread interest and have many possible applications, e.g. telling stories about exciting locations in the world or ancient places of interest in history. Especially, museums and other educational institutions can take advantage of this.

In Cinematic Virtual Reality (**CVR**) the viewer watches 360° movie using a Head Mounted Display (**HMD**) or other VR devices. Thus, the viewer is inside the scene, and can freely choose the direction of view. Accordingly, the viewer determines the visible section of the movie – the field of view (**FoV**). Therefore, it is not always possible to show the viewer what is important for the story. Several conventional filmmaking methods for guiding the viewer's line - such as close ups or zooms - are not practicable in CVR. For other methods, it needs a closer analysis of whether they are suitable to direct the attention of the viewer to important details in a CVR environment. In this paper, we focus on some traditional alertness methods of filmmaking which we think are transferable to CVR: sound, lighting, and movements.

Electronic supplementary material The online version of this chapter (https://doi.org/10.1007/978-3-319-95270-3_7) contains supplementary material, which is available to authorized users.

L. T. De Paolis and P. Bourdot (Eds.): AVR 2018, LNCS 10850, pp. 101–117, 2018.
https://doi.org/10.1007/978-3-319-95270-3_7

From film theory, we absorb the terms **diegetic** and **non-diegetic**. Diegetic cues are part of the scene – for example, a musician playing music. Non-diegetic cues come from outside – for example, film music or a voice over. The cues considered in this paper are diegetic cues.

We want to investigate if diegetic cues are suitable for drawing the attention of the viewer. For this the following questions should be studied:

- Which **type** of cues are more effective for guiding the attention: sound, light or movements?
- Which **combination** of cues sound/light, light/movement, movement/sound are efficacious for guiding the attention?
- Can a diegetic **audio** cue draw the attention of the viewer to it, even if it not in the field of view in the moment the cue appears? How important is the direction of the sound for guiding?
- Can a diegetic **moving** cue draw the attention of the viewer to it, even if it not in the field of view all the time?

For answering these questions, a short movie was produced, which was shown to 27 participants. The head tracking data were recorded for generating heatmaps and analysing the data. For finding significant hotspots spatial statistics methods were used.

2   Related Work

360° movies are not new and not only produced for HMD. Investigations for 360° videos on a desktop [1] and in full domes [2, 3] provide general background information.

Much research in recent years has focused on **presence** in VR environments [4–7] – these results can be adapted to CVR. Poeschl et al. [8] and Serafin and Serafin [9] have shown that spatial sound is important for a high level of presence in virtual environments. In our study, we concentrated on guiding the attention of the viewer. However, we considered the results of these investigations and endeavoured to ensure that our methods do not interfere with the presence.

Syrett et al. [10] have discovered that some viewers feel distracted by the freedom to choose the viewing direction. In their experiments, it happened that important parts of the storyline were missed. In the literature [11–13] several methods for guiding the viewer are explored for non-VR environments, such as salient objects, sounds, lights, or moving cues. Our work examines how this can be adapted to CVR, even if an object is not in the FoV of the viewer.

Van der Burg et al. [14] showed that audio cues (pop) synchronized to a salient visual cue (pip) reduces the search time, even if the audio cue does not have any location information. Hoeg et al. [15] enhanced this experiment to Virtual Reality with sound cues from the same direction as the visual cue. They demonstrated that binaural cues lead to shorter search times, even though the visual cue was not always visible at the moment the audio cue was presented. In the experiments, the participants were given a search task in an abstract VR environment. In our study in comparison to [14, 15], we move closer to a real cinematographic setting by using a realistic scene instead of abstract symbols and by not giving a concrete task to the participants but letting them choose freely what to do next.

Several investigations are focused on **non-diegetic** methods. Lin et al. [16] compared two focus-assistance tools. The first one, an autopilot, adjusts the field of view automatically, so the viewer can see the target. The second tool uses visual signs that show the direction which the viewer should follow. Both tools assist the viewer to find an intended target. Questionnaires were used for investigating ease of focusing, presence, and discomfort. The results illustrate that the preferred method depends on the viewer's preferences and the content of the movie.

Brown et al. [17] describe several gaze attraction techniques for VR which are also useable for CVR: two guided camera techniques and two voluntary distractor methods. The first technique is a scene transition by fading out the previous scene and fading in the subsequent scene with the important section in the FoV. The second method is a forced camera rotation, similar to the autopilot of Lin et al. [16]. The authors expect disruption and disorientation of the viewer through this method. Additionally, two distractor techniques are described. First, a firefly drifts in the FoV until the viewer changes the viewing direction to the target following the firefly. Secondly, spatial sound is used for guiding the attention. The investigations are not finished yet and the results not published.

Few researchers have addressed how to guide the viewer's attention in CVR by **diegetic** cues. In 1996 Pausch et al. [18] examined how the attention of the viewer can be drawn to a desired spot. For that, they used the characters as diegetic cues. Similarly, Sheikh et al. [19] connected several diegetic cues (motion, gestural, and audio cues) to the main character of a scene. In the experiment, the cues with an audio component were more helpful than just visual cues, even if the sound was not fully spatialized. However, the main character of a movie attracts more attention, in general, even without any special cues. In our approach, we investigate if it is possible to guide the view with cues connected to neutral objects that the viewer has not seen before.

Nielsen et al. [20] compared a diegetic cue (firefly) with a non-diegetic cue (forced rotation) and no guidance. Using a questionnaire, they figured out that the diegetic cue (firefly) was more helpful than the non-diegetic cue (forced rotation). Furthermore, the results demonstrate that the non-diegetic cue may decrease the presence.

For determining which cues attract the attention of the viewer and can change the viewing direction, we decided not to use questionnaires. Instead, the head direction was recorded and evaluated to obtain more precise results. For this, we developed a tool that generates heatmaps for every timecode in the movie.

3   Methods

Material
To investigate whether diegetic cues can guide the attention of the viewer, we produced a movie which contains various diegetic cues

- sound from a certain direction (**s**)
- lighted objects (**l**)

- **m**ovements of stationary objects – for example swinging (**m**)
- **lo**comotive objects - movements with change of position (**lo**)

In the scenes which are relevant for the test, the sound is spatial and connected to visual objects. In the scenes which are used for randomizing the viewing direction, the sound is not spatial.

The field of view of every viewer was recorded, so it was possible to evaluate if the view was influenced by the cues. For every timecode of the movie a heatmap was generated.

Participants

27 Participants (10 women and 17 men) watched the movie with a head-mounted display (Samsung Galaxy S6 with google cardboard) and headphones (Ultrasone HFI 780). The voluntary participants were in the age between 16 and 73 (mean = 40). One participant was a sound engineer and was removed from the data set. He explored how spatial sound worked in the test environment by unusual head movements. In the concluding interview, we noticed that his attention was not on the movie.

We chose a within-subject test design – all participants watched the same movie. Standing they turned head and body to watch the movie. There was no special task, they should look around and follow the objects they are interested in.

After watching the movie, a short interview was conducted. The participants enumerated the objects which they could remember spontaneously. Afterward, they were asked whether they have seen the other objects or not. Our research did not investigate the influence on cognitive assimilation, however this additional information helped to interpret the measured data.

Movie

The movie consists of 4 sections. The sections are separated by a neutral scene: a forest which looks similar in every direction (Fig. 1), the sound is not spatial. This scene makes sure that the viewing direction at the beginning of the next scene is random.

Fig. 1. The forest separates the tests scenes to make the viewing direction for the start of the next scene random.

All the other scenes are of the same place - a mystery kitchen of an old castle (Fig. 2). Objects with different cues appear and disappear from time to time. The sound in these scenes is spatial and connected to the appearing objects. We used Unity for attaching the sounds to the objects in the movie.

Fig. 2. The place of the test scenes

In the first part of the movie (scene 1 and 2) the objects do not change their positions. Objects with movements are swinging or flickering. Other objects are lighted or connected with sound. All the objects are there from the start to the end of the scene. It was investigated if these objects can attract the attention of the viewer.

The aim of the second part (scene 3 and 4) is to evaluate if we can modify the viewing direction of the participant by objects, which are not necessarily in the FoV at the beginning. In scene 3 objects are associated with sounds. In scene 4 we use locomotive objects.

In the **first scene**, the investigated objects are connected to only one cue. There is one moving object (m), one object with spatial sound (s), and one lighted (l) object in the room.

In the **second scene**, every object is provided with two cues:

- a lighted moving object (m, l),
- a moving object with spatial sound (s, m),
- a lighted object with spatial sound (l, s).

Thus, all combinations of the three methods are in the scene. Figure 7 shows the arrangement of the objects.

In the **third scene,** we explored if it is possible to change the direction of view using objects with sounds. For this, several objects with and without sound appear and disappear in the kitchen. At the beginning, there is a ticking alarm clock followed by a whistling tea kettle and a cuckoo clock at different positions. Subsequently, two phones – only one with sound - appear. After they have disappeared again, a gramophone (with sound) and an old record player (without sound) are visible in the kitchen – succeeded by an old radio. The objects are positioned at several positions (Fig. 3) and not always in the FoV of the participants. All the sounds are spatial.

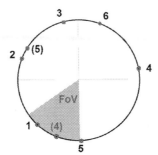

Fig. 3. The arrangement of the objects in the room, the shaded segment shows the size of FoV (60°), the numbers show the sequence of appearing: 1-alarm clock, 2-kettle, 3-cuckoo clock, 4-phone (4)-silent phone, 5-gramophone (5)-silent record player, 6-radio

The **fourth scene** explores locomotive objects changing their position (lo) with and without additional cues. We tested three different methods for guiding the view to another direction:

- locomotive object without sound – feather (lo)
- locomotive light without sound – light cone (lo, l)
- locomotive object with spatial sound – bee (lo, s)

Statistical Evaluation

In a first step, we inspected the heatmaps for relevant timecodes in the movie. We found several hot spots which had to be verified for significance. Therefore, we used spatial statistical methods.

The collected data are point incident data. Point incident data are points connected to an event – in our case the viewer looked to this point. We were interested in significant clusters. To find such clusters, we used the Getis-Ord Gi* statistic [21] – a spatial statistic method for examining spatial data. This statistical method requires values for the investigated points. In order to use this method, the incident data were aggregated and incident counts established. The incident counts – in our case the number of views - are the attribute values which are analyzed by the method.

The Getis-Ord Gi* statistic is given as:

$$G_i^* = \frac{\sum_{j=1}^{n} w_{i,j} x_j - \overline{X} \sum_{j=1}^{n} w_{i,j}}{S \sqrt{\frac{\left[n \sum_{j=1}^{n} w_{i,j}^2 - \left(\sum_{j=1}^{n} w_{i,j} \right)^2 \right]}{n-1}}}$$

where x_j is the attribute value for point j, $w_{i,j}$ is the spatial weight between point i and j, n is equal to the total number of points and:

$$\overline{X} = \frac{\sum_{j=1}^{n} x_j}{n}$$

$$S = \sqrt{\frac{\sum_{j=1}^{n} x_j^2}{n} - (\overline{X})^2}$$

To apply this statistical method, the GIS software ArcGIS Pro was used. For every point in the incident data set, the p value was calculated and can be displayed by double-clicking on the point. The p value is the probability that the observed pattern was created randomly. A small p value means that the pattern is most likely caused by a cluster. Segments with p values smaller than 0.01, which means 99% confidence, are displayed in red. Figure 4 shows the color for the different confidence levels. These legend is used for interpreting the results in the next chapter.

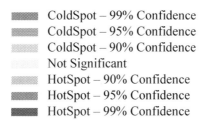

ColdSpot – 99% Confidence
ColdSpot – 95% Confidence
ColdSpot – 90% Confidence
Not Significant
HotSpot – 90% Confidence
HotSpot – 95% Confidence
HotSpot – 99% Confidence

Fig. 4. Legend for the significance test of the hotspots (Color figure online)

4   Results

Scene 1
In the first scene three objects with one cue were examined: socket (lighted), ladle (moving/swinging), dripping water (sound). Figure 5 demonstrates the locations of the objects in this scene.

We could not observe any greater attention to one of the cued objects. As can be seen in Fig. 6 the hot spots were distributed over the whole room, except the bottom and the ceiling.

The significance test (Fig. 6, right) showed limited hotspots. The sound object and the moving object each have a significant cluster. At the position of the light (not moving), there was no significant cluster. Instead there were clusters on other objects.

The scene takes 17 s (0:20–0:37). In the interview, socket and water were listed by only 3 persons. The ladle was swinging until the end of the movie and enumerated by 16 participants. In a detailed review of the data, we saw that most people inspected the ladle later for a longer time, not in the first scene.

Fig. 5. Objects with one feature: socket - light (l), ladle - movement (m), water - sound (s)

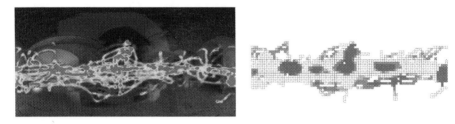

Fig. 6. In scene 1 many little hotspots were generated

Scene 2

The second scene has three cued objects: a flickering lamp (m, l), a pot on the fire (s, m), and a ticking clock (l, s). The arrangement of the objects is displayed in Fig. 7.

As can be seen in Fig. 8, two significant hotspots arose around the objects with sounds (fire, clock). The lighted flickering lamp (without sound) was not recognized by the participants. In addition to the absent sound this could be due to the position of the lamp. It is located higher than the other objects.

The scene takes 18 s (0:49–1:07). No participant mentioned the lamp, the fire was listed by 18 people and the clock by 12.

Investigating the beginning of the scene (0:50–0:52) we discovered that most participants first looked to the fire.

Scene 3

In the third scene, several objects with spatial sounds appear and disappear. It starts with a ticking alarm clock, 10 s later added by a whistling tea kettle and after another 10 s by a cuckoo clock, all at different positions (Fig. 9).

For each of these objects, most participants changed the viewing direction when the objects with sound appeared. As can be seen in Figs. 10 and 11 significant hotspots were generated in all three cases.

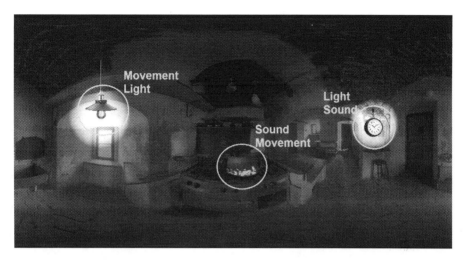

Fig. 7. Objects with two cues: lamp (m, l), pot (s, m), clock (l, s).

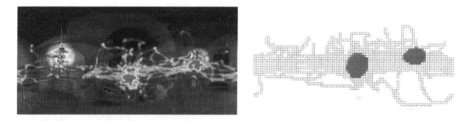

Fig. 8. There are hotspots on the fire and the clock, but no hotspot on the lamp.

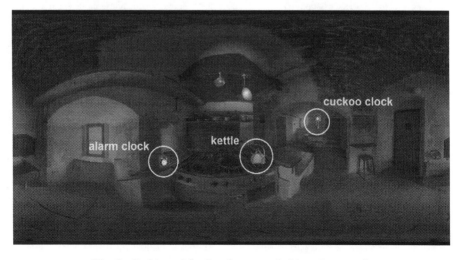

Fig. 9. Position of the first three sound objects in scene 3.

Fig. 10. Heatmap and hotspot for the alarm clock

Fig. 11. Left: hotspot for the whistling kettle, right: hotspot for the cuckoo clock

Afterwards, two phones – only one with sound – appear (Fig. 12). Around both objects a hotspot has formed even though only one phone was ringing (Fig. 13).

Fig. 12. Two objects: phone with sound (right), phone without sound (left)

Analysing the data, we found out that the phone with sound has a stronger effect. In the interview, more people listed the ringing phone near the door, (11 participants) than the phone without sound near the window (8 participants). Seven participants listed both phones.

In the next step, this experiment was repeated with other objects: a gramophone (playing an old melody) and an ancient record player (without sound). Even if both objects caused significant hotspots (Fig. 14), this time more people were looking to the

Fig. 13. Heatmap and hotspots for the phones with and without sound

sound object than in the test before. A reason for this could be that the gramophone was closer to the phone in the last test. Asking a participant, we got the answer that for him it was a learning process. He recognized the two phones in the test before. Therefore, this time he was looking for the object with sound.

Fig. 14. Gramophone with sound (left), record player without sound (right), 2 s after the objects appeared

In the final step of this test section, we increased the angle to the following object – to nearly 180° (Fig. 5). A radio appeared opposite the gramophone. This time it took longer until the hotspot was built (Figs. 15 and 16).

Fig. 15. Heatmap and hotspots for the radio - 2 s after the radio appeared

Scene 4

The **fourth scene** includes **lo**comotive objects (**lo**) with and without additional cues:

- a feather (lo)

Fig. 16. Heatmap and hotspots for the radio - 5 s after the radio appeared

- a moving cone of light (lo, l)
- a humming bee (lo, s).

When an object reaches a target position a music instrument appears and starts playing. The locomotive object disappears. The music instruments stay present and play until the end of the sequence. In this way, the scene is becoming more and more complex – visually and aurally.

The sequence starts with a moving feather (Fig. 17). Most participants followed this cue, even the time interval was relatively long (20 s). In Fig. 17 the distance from the start point (SP) to the end point (EP) is illustrated. The heatmap and the significance of the hotspots can be seen in Fig. 18.

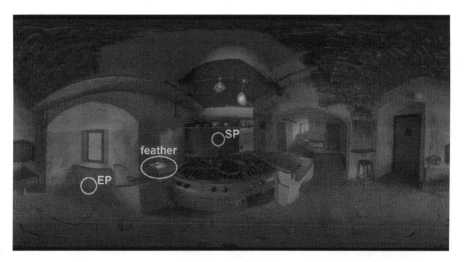

Fig. 17. Moving feather. The feather hovers from the starting point (SP) to the end point (EP) - it takes 20 s

For the next test, we chose a bigger distance and time interval (47 s). A light cone moves to the far side of the scene (Fig. 19).

At the beginning of the test interval there was only one hotspot (Fig. 19). Later (around 10 s) the participants were looking around, mostly to the playing instruments.

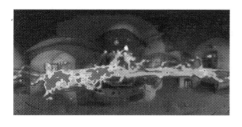

Fig. 18. Heatmap and hotspots for the moving feather

Fig. 19. The moving light cone – one hotspot at the beginning of the test interval

Fig. 20. The moving light cone – three split hotspots in the middle of the test interval

Three hotspots were formed (Fig. 20). Nevertheless, mostly they returned back to the light cone and at the end of the movement there was only one hotspot again (Fig. 21).

The last test – a moving bee with sound - was shorter (10 s). Thus, the covered distance was shorter, too. As a consequence, it was more difficult to identify if the participants really followed the bee or were looking at the instruments, because the bee

Fig. 21. The moving light cone – hotspot at the end of the test interval

Fig. 22. A hotspot around the moving humming bee

was flying from one instrument to the other one. Even if a hotspot was built, there is not only the bee in this area but also the instruments (Fig. 22).

Accordingly, for all three methods investigated in scene 4, significant hotspots were built around the cues.

5   Discussion

The presented results show that diegetic cues are useful for guiding the attention of viewers in Cinematic VR.

In our first experiment (scene 1) applying the single cues simultaneously, we could not find a type of cue more efficient as the other ones. The hotspots are distributed in the room (Fig. 6). A reason for that could be that the cues are subtle and not so flashy as in the next scenes. Furthermore, at the beginning of the movie all objects are new and cues have less effect.

Comparing combination of two cues in our second experiment (scene 2), the combinations including sounds (s, m) and (l, s) resulted in hotspots, but the lamp (m, l) was not noticed by the viewers. It needs further experiments if this result was influenced by the position of the object, which was higher than the others. In our study the combination of movement and sound had the most power for drawing the attention.

Analysing the data of scene 3, we could find, that objects connected with sound can attract the attention of the viewer, even if they are not in the FoV in the moment the sound starts. This method, is more effective if the sound is coming from the direction of the object. However, it works also in other cases. Thus, the sound itself seems to be more important than the direction of the sound.

In addition, moving objects can influence the viewing direction (scene 4). Even if the movements are for a longer period of time, viewers looking around in the meantime but mostly return to the movements. In our experiment the moving objects and lights guided the attention even without additional sound.

In **summary**, we found the following results:

- Objects connected with sounds attract more attention than without sound
- Objects connected with sounds can guide the viewing direction even if the sound is not spatial or is coming from another direction
- Moving objects or lights can guide the viewing direction even without any sounds

- It is difficult to guide the viewer at the beginning of a new scene
- Non-moving lights had no effects in our tests.

For finding these results we used heatmaps and spatial statistical methods for determining significant hotspots. In our interviews we experienced, that some people are afraid of missing something. Therefore, guiding can be helpful for making the enjoyment of Cinematic Virtual Reality more enjoyable.

6   Limitations

In our research, we tracked the head movements – not the eyes. Through that, we could follow the viewing direction in general, however not in detail. This was sufficient for a first approach and the most experiments led to evaluable data. Tracking the eyes instead the head would give more detailed information.

In the first scene of our tests the cues did not generate more attention than other objects in the room. We are not sure, if the reason is the weakness of the cues or the novelty of the room. In further tests we will replicate the first scene at the end of the movie.

In the last part of our experiments – we investigated if the viewer follows the bee for a short distance - we can see only a hotspot in the middle of its flight. The bee was flying between two music instruments which were visible at this time and so most people fixed the direction of the head between the instruments. The flight of the bee was short and the viewers could follow it by moving their eyes and not their heads – so the instruments stayed in the FoV. In this case eye tracking would be helpful for the analysis.

We tried to give the objects equivalent properties. However, sometimes there was an impact which we did not expect. It seems that objects in Cinematic Virtual Reality which are a little bit higher are not equivalent to objects straight ahead or a little bit lower. This might be due to the fact that we rarely look upwards in real life.

Even if we randomized the direction of view between the sections, within the sections the objects were correlated. In our experiment, we tested the sequence of cues. In the analysis of the data we found plausible additional assumptions which should be verified in further experiments where the cues are independent:

- Objects with spatial sound from the side of the viewer attract attention more and faster than objects which lie behind the viewer
- Higher objects attract attention less than objects ahead or below.

7   Conclusion

This research was our first step in investigating how a viewer can be guided in Cinematic Virtual Reality. We showed that sound draws the attention of the viewer. However, also objects without any sound can be used for guiding the viewer to other directions. The participants followed a locomotive cone of light and also locomotive objects.

These results can be used for integrating diegetic cues in a movie for guiding the viewer to things which are important for the story. The investigated methods require the integration of cues in the movie. This is not always possible. The viewer should have several possibilities to find an own way in the story. In our future research, we plan to examine non-diegetic methods for viewer guiding which should not decrease the presence.

In our research we looked for a method to analyze the collected data. Our data - the tracked FoV - are points on a sphere changing over time. Our approach using spatial statistical methods has proved of value and we will develop this method further in our research.

References

1. Boonsuk, W.: Evaluation of Desktop Interface Displays for 360-Degree Video. Iowa State University, ProQuest Dissertations Publishing, Ames, Iowa (2011)
2. Overschmidt, G., Schröder, U.B. (eds.): Fullspace-Projektion: Mit dem 360°lab zum Holodeck. Springer, Heidelberg (2013). https://doi.org/10.1007/978-3-642-24656-2
3. von Chamier-Waite, C.: The cine-poetics of fulldome cinema. Animat. Pract. Process Prod. 3, 219–233 (2013)
4. Slater, M., Usoh, M., Steed, A.: Depth of presence in virtual environments. Presence Teleoperators Virtual Environ. 3, 130–144 (1994)
5. Slater, M., Wilbur, S.: A Framework for Immersive Virtual Environments (FIVE): speculations on the role of presence in virtual environments. Presence Teleoperators Virtual Environ. 6, 603–616 (1997)
6. Hendrix, C., Barfield, W.: The sense of presence within auditory virtual environments. Presence Teleoperators Virtual Environ. 5, 290–301 (1996)
7. Cummings, J.J., Bailenson, J.N.: How immersive is enough? A meta-analysis of the effect of immersive technology on user presence. Media Psychol. 19, 272–309 (2016)
8. Poeschl, S., Wall, K., Doering, N.: Integration of spatial sound in immersive virtual environments- an experimental study on effects of spatial sound on presence. In: Proceedings of the IEEE Virtual Reality Conference 2013, Piscataway, NJ, pp. 129–130. IEEE Computer Society Press (2013)
9. Serafin, G., Serafin, S.: Sound design to enhance presence in photorealistic Virtual Reality. In: Proceedings of ICAD 04-Tenth Meeting of the International Conference on Auditory Display, Sydney, Australia. International Community for Auditory Display (2004)
10. Syrett, H., Calvi, L., van Gisbergen, M.: The Oculus Rift film experience: a case study on understanding films in a head mounted display. In: Poppe, R., Meyer, J.-J., Veltkamp, R., Dastani, M. (eds.) INTETAIN 2016 2016. LNICST, vol. 178, pp. 197–208. Springer, Cham (2017). https://doi.org/10.1007/978-3-319-49616-0_19
11. Goldstein, E.B.: Sensation and Perception. 8th International Edition. Hague, J., Perkins, J. (eds.) Wadsworth, Belmont (2010)
12. Coren, S., Ward, L.M., Enns, J.T.: Sensation and Perception, 5th edn. Harcourt Brace College Publishers, San Diego (1999)
13. Veas, E.E., Mendez, E., Feiner, S.K., Schmalstieg, D.: Directing attention and influencing memory with visual saliency modulation. In: Proceedings of the SIGCHI Conference on Human Factors in Computing Systems (CHI 2011), Vancouver, Canada, pp. 1471–1480. ACM Press (2011)

14. Van der Burg, E., Olivers, C.N.L., Bronkhorst, A.W., Theeuwes, J.: Pip and pop: nonspatial auditory signals improve spatial visual search. J. Exp. Psychol. Hum. Percept. Perform. **34**, 1053–1065 (2008)
15. Hoeg, E.R., Gerry, L.J., Thomsen, L., Nilsson, N.C., Serafin, S.: Binaural sound reduces reaction time in a virtual reality search task. In: IEEE 3rd VR Workshop on Sonic Interactions for Virtual Environments (SIVE), Los Angeles, CA, pp. 1–4. IEEE (2017)
16. Lin, Y.-C., Chang, Y.-J., Hu, H.-N., Cheng, H.-T., Huang, C.-W., Sun, M.: Tell me where to look: investigating ways for assisting focus in 360° video. In: Proceedings of the 2017 CHI Conference on Human Factors in Computing Systems, Denver, Colorado, pp. 2535–2545. ACM (2017)
17. Brown, C., Bhutra, G., Suhail, M., Xu, Qi., Ragan, E.D.: Coordinating attention and cooperation in multi-user Virtual Reality narratives. In: 2017 IEEE Virtual Reality, Los Angeles, CA, pp. 377–378. IEEE (2017)
18. Pausch, R., Snoddy, J., Taylor, R., Watson, S., Haseltine, E.: Disney's Aladdin: first steps toward storytelling in virtual reality. In: Proceedings of the 23rd Annual Conference on Computer Graphics and Interactive Techniques, New Orleans, LA, pp. 193–203. ACM (1996)
19. Sheikh, A., Brown, A., Watson, Z., Evans, M.: Directing attention in 360-degree video. In: IBC 2016 Conference, Amsterdam, pp. 29–38. IET (2016)
20. Nielsen, L.T., Møller, M.B., Hartmeyer, S.D., Ljung, T., Nilsson, N.C., Nordahl, R., Serafin, S.: Missing the point: an exploration of how to guide users' attention during cinematic Virtual Reality. In: Proceedings of the 22nd ACM Conference on Virtual Reality Software and Technology, Munich, Germany, pp. 229–232. ACM (2016)
21. Getis, A., Ord, J.K.: The analysis of spatial association by use of distance statistics. Geogr. Anal. **24**, 189–206 (1992)

Virtual System for Teaching-Learning of Initial Education Using a Haptic Device

Marco Pilatásig[1(✉)], Emily Tobar[1(✉)], Lissette Paredes[1(✉)],
Franklin M. Silva[1(✉)], Andrés Acurio[1(✉)], Edwin Pruna[1(✉)],
Ivón Escobar[1(✉)], and Zulia Sánchez[2(✉)]

[1] Universidad de las Fuerzas Armadas ESPE, Sangolquí, Ecuador
{mapilatagsig,ektobar,mlparedes2,fmsilva,adacurio,
eppruna,ipescobar}@espe.edu.ec
[2] Unidad Educativa Mario Cobo Barona, Ambato, Ecuador
zulia.sanchez@educacion.gob.ec

Abstract. This article proposes a teaching-learning system for children of initial education through haptic devices and 3D Unity software. The system has several virtual interfaces that will be chosen according to the age, skills and knowledge that the child needs to acquire or improve. The interface allows to view the environment where the user must do a task or activity by the teacher in charge. Which it can listen to the instructions issued by the system and then be executed, also it has an introduction that remembers the objective to be fulfilled according to the interface. Through the haptic device geomagic Touch, a trajectory tracking control is carried out, which allows the child to perceive by means of feedback of forces if the movement and the direction with which he makes the stroke is the correct one. In addition, it allows to acquire the input signals the same that are sent to an algorithm that validates the stroke of the uppercase, lowercase vowels and basic figures made by the child. Also, it indicates to the teacher the results in a qualitative way.

Keywords: Virtual reality · Haptics devices · Initial education
Learning strategies

1 Introduction

Currently the teaching-learning process uses new emerging technologies such as: virtual reality and haptic devices [1]. These components have participated in various studies, having a high degree of success and usefulness [2]. Haptic devices are used in different fields such as: rehabilitation through virtual games and education, which allow to attract the attention of the user in order to develop the tasks in a proper way [3, 4]. In this context, there are jobs related to this topic, in [5] presents a multi-touch panel that includes virtual reality in games for infants with a dynamic interface to make drawings and identify figures. In [6] shows the interaction between virtual reality and the visual haptic device that allows to increase the fluency in the production of handwriting by hand in kindergarten children. A virtual reality game to improve the performance of students in the area of mathematics is presented in [7].

© Springer International Publishing AG, part of Springer Nature 2018
L. T. De Paolis and P. Bourdot (Eds.): AVR 2018, LNCS 10850, pp. 118–132, 2018.
https://doi.org/10.1007/978-3-319-95270-3_8

The development of the virtual system has three main features: the simulation of an environment, a didactic and interactive element and an immersive component. The immersion is integrated through haptic technology, which has been used, for example as a guide in systems of navigation and feedback of forces in which the touch sense allows the interaction between the user and the system [8–10].

The basis for educational development must be fostered from the home to the school, all with new technologies that allow structuring levels such as: interaction, which is the capacity of the human being to interact with a virtual environment. The immersion must have as a primary goal to capture the full attention of the user, which with its imagination will seek that the experience in virtual reality resemble as much as possible to the reality. The virtual tools applied to children present results of great validity, because they have high motivational degree and interaction [11–13]. In the development of educational systems have highlighted virtual applications aimed at teaching and didactic guide in the management of processes as it appears in [14–16].

Virtual reality (VR) allows to create realistic and dynamic images, which acquire sensory information that allow the interaction with the 3d virtual model [15]. This is presented in applications oriented to different purposes, from entertainment to interactive teaching for engineering or medical training [17, 18]. It has also been found that the application of VR for teaching increases the interest of students, either by the novel of the technology or by the challenges that may arise during the use of the application which motivates the user to finish the task in a correct way [19].

The children have a great cognitive capacity since the first years of life which allows them to learn quickly from their surroundings. By applying the appropriate stimuli to them in a continuous teaching process is possible to develop their skills quickly and upgraded [20–22]. Initial education is intended to be based on the best techniques and methods of teaching basic knowledge in early ages [23]. The methods for taking a proper initial education are varied, but all of them require resources that are attractive to the students, from colorful images to interactive games and much more, therefore, the qualitative method is very important in validating the learning process in children of young age [24]. At present a considerable percentage of students present a lack of interest in the conventional methods of didactic teaching taught by the teacher, being necessary the integration of new tools to capture the attention of the students in the classrooms [25]. In this context, the integration of VR into systems for the initial teaching process can provide great educational benefits for both the student and the teacher. The use of haptic devices offers an improved experience when interacting with the environment, the new advances of these devices have made it possible to stimulate other senses in people, besides the visual and auditory [26], which would allow to cover some methods of motor learning in the teaching of children.

With the aim of updating the methods of teaching of initial education, this work proposes the creation of a virtual tool didactic, for the teaching-learning of basic knowledge on: primary colors, secondary, strokes to realize the writing of basic figures, uppercase and lowercase vowels of the alphabet. The system is implemented through the use of interactive virtual reality interfaces and controlled through the analysis of signals from a haptic device.

The present work is divided into five sections, including the introduction, Sect. 2 methodology used for the development of the system, Sect. 3 multilayer development plan, Sect. 4 developed environments, Sect. 5 use mode, Sect. 6 shows the tests and results and, finally, Sect. 7 conclusions.

2 Methodology Used for the Development of the System

This section describes the stages of the virtual system as shown in Fig. 1.

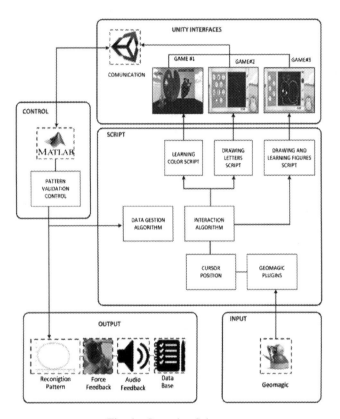

Fig. 1. Operative Scheme

A. *Input peripherals*

The virtual system uses the haptic device Geomagic Touch as an input peripheral. It has 6 degrees of freedom and digital encoders that allow the user to move into the three spatial dimensions and translate these positions into readable variables for the system, the communication used is Ethernet.

B. *Script development*

Scripts developed in c# language in visual studio are responsible for system administration and the control of outputs depending on input. The control algorithm of each game starts with the acquisition of signals, manages the required information according to the interaction interface, runs, and if the object has weight or collides with another object, the haptic device supplies a feedback of forces as shown in Fig. 2. The scripts are compatible with unity and communicate with the haptic device geomagic touch via plugins. This allows its manipulation by making the times of a pointer, also control the audio output, for which, starts with the selection of the desired game. An audio feedback is obtained with the instructions and the objective that the user must reach in the environment, indicating at the same time if the actions performed are correct, incorrect or if it should improve.

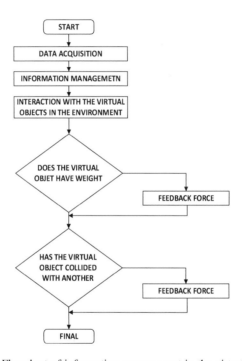

Fig. 2. Flowchart of information management in the virtual system

The validation and trajectory-generation controls have been developed in MATLAB software, which, through interaction with unity, receives the information necessary to send a response to the haptic device or to unity, as the case might be. To validate the input data, classifiers are used, which allow to calculate the Euclidean distance, to validate the stroke made by the child with a pattern stroke. The goal of the trajectory generation control is to get the haptic geomagic Touch device to move according to a variable signal in the time received from Unity, a sinusoidal signal for instance. For this procedure, a PID control is applied to each of the device's position inputs.

3   Multilayer Development Plan

This section describes the multi-layered scheme for the development of virtual applications of a teaching-learning system in children of initial education. This schema presents in an orderly manner the development of the application, has the following layers: (i) Layer 1 preselection of materials to be used in the objects that compose the interfaces; (ii) Layer 2 2D and 3D object editing; (iii) Layer 3 development and implementation of the virtual environment in Unity; (iv) Layer 4 Script development and interaction with virtual interfaces; and finally (v) Layer 5 data acquisition for the validation of the educational activities carried out by the child, as shown in Fig. 3.

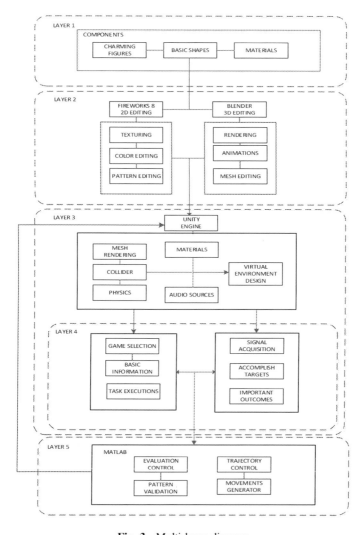

Fig. 3. Multi-layer diagram

Layer 1. This layer defines the resources and materials used in the design process, based on the theory of Vygotsky, which indicates that children acquire their knowledge through games related to their daily environment. To which you have: images that relate colors with objects (orange color-image carrot), vowels with images of animals (the vowel 'a' with a picture of a spider), sounds, audio of basic instructions, colors and textures.

Layer 2. Design of the objects used in the virtual environment, through the Fireworks 8 software and taking into consideration the resources of the previous layer, 2d drawings are designed; Textures, palettes and shapes highlight their details to make them attractive to the user. 3d objects are built with the blender software, giving realism to the object by implementing meshes, rendering and creation of bones in a hierarchical way that allows to give life to it through the animations provided by Unity.

Layer 3. All resources to be used are exported to a working environment in 3d Unity. Each virtual object is assigned the respective properties according to the function that must be fulfilled within the design of the game. Each element that could be touched has different features to provide the sense of reality to the environment. Materials used in the writing area imitate the shape and color of an academic blackboard. The other elements in the environment are presented with colors and shapes that are pleasant and appealing to children. All games have audio to explain the procedures and indicate if the task is done in the correct way to orientate the child during the development of the activity. There are animations in the Unity environment which help the user in the development of the task and dynamize the interfaces.

Layer 4. The reproduction of the programs is done through the scripts of each interface, they run the script to start each game with their respective elements, they also allow the functions to be handled in an organized way to link the different environments and access each one. Once started the game these scripts activate the corresponding audio source to make known the objective of the activity to be realized. The scripts contain the plugins for the use of the haptic device as input and output of the system. They accept the input data which are evaluated according to determined parameters and depending on these one has a feedback of forces of the haptic device.

The development of writing in the virtual environment is done editing the texture of the blackboard object. By using several scripts is calculated the position of the cursor on the 3d element and the force applied to it, with these calculations modify the color of the original texture at the exact point where the cursor is placed multiplying by a certain radius and establishing the definition of the stroke on the blackboard that will be proportional to the force applied. It means with a small force applied the stroke will be very subtle, and with a stronger the stroke will be very definite and with more color. The environment has a reset button to return the original texture to the blackboard object when you want to delete the strokes made, as well as you can choose between seven different colors to do the writing.

Layer 5. Finally, in this layer there are two controllers that meet different functions. The first one is a controller by classifiers which performs the evaluation of the strokes made, checking the trajectory followed and similarity of the stroke with a pattern. It is found both in writing of the vowels of the alphabet as in writing of initial strokes. The second controller is used for the generation of movement in the haptic device, while the child holds the manipulator of the geomagic, it moves on a surface (blackboard) indicating the movements that the child should perform with his hand to do the stroke. This process uses a PID control [27] that is applied on the output of the geomagic to carry out the feedback of forces.

4   Developed Environments

Three different games were designed with their results interface. In the application of secondary colors are used 2D and 3D objects. It presents a palette of colors that can be perceived by the haptic device as a real object, also there are figures of vegetables and fruits to be colored, these are only visible to user, but you can't touch it with the cursor. The writing games show an object similar to a blackboard on which the haptic device simulates writing, there are some buttons with different functions. There is an avatar with animations in all environments and each application has a second interface where the results of each game are indicated, as shown in Fig. 4

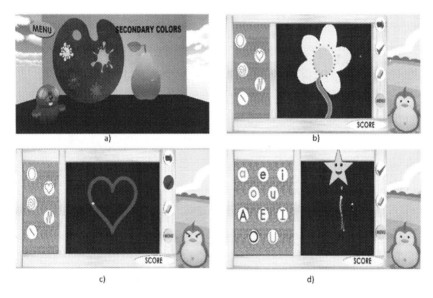

Fig. 4. Environment development (a) Secondary Colors Interface, (b) y (c) Figures drawing Interface and (d) Vowel Writing Interface

5   How to Use

The application displays a main menu, it has 3 games with the following parameters: secondary colors, stroke drawing and vowel writing respectively.

In Fig. 4 the virtual environment of the first game is shown where the theme of this game are the secondary colors. It starts with an introduction of the combination that has to be performed between the primary colors to form each one of the secondary colors (Fig. 5(a)); it presents an illustration with the silhouette of a vegetable or fruit

(Fig. 5(b)), the audio mentions that type of vegetable or fruit and its color, asking the child to select the respective primary colors to form the requested color. When the correct colors are chosen, the illustration is colored and continues with the next secondary color (Fig. 5(c)), the audible response indicates when the selected color is correct or incorrect, objects appear and disappear according to the color secondary to be colored. Once the game is complete, a button appears that when pressed, it leads to a different environment where the child's performance during the activity will be shown (Fig. 5(d)).

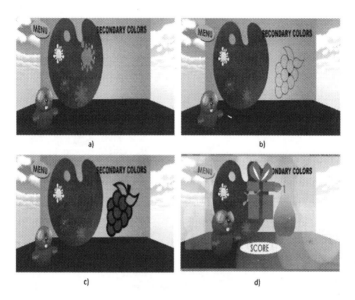

Fig. 5. First game virtual environment (Color figure online)

In the second game there is a surface as an academic blackboard in order to the child can learn to make the first strokes as an initial help for the learning of writing. There are five buttons to the left of the blackboard, which are chosen according to the stroke of the desired figure to practice (circle, heart, spiral, wave and straight line). When one of the buttons is selected an audio sounds, which in conjunction with the animations, explain how the stroke should be performed (trajectory and starting point). On the right side of the blackboard there are five more buttons, the first one is for trajectory generation. The following buttons are complete, delete, menu and results.

For the third game, the upper and lowercase vowels must be written. Like the previous game, the auditory feedback and animations are presented to indicate the trajectory to follow in each letter. Each vowel is chosen with the buttons on the left and on the right, there are buttons for ending, deleting, menu and results. Similarly, colorful animations are presented at the end of each letter correctly.

6 Tests and Results

A. *Test*

The system should always be used under the supervision of the teacher or tutor's child, who will evaluate the performance of it. The main menu of the game is presented where the teacher in charge selects the game that he believes is suitable according to the age, knowledge or skills of the child.

In the first level the child hears the way the secondary colors are formed and proceeds to perform the task (Fig. 6(a)). When the selection is incorrect, it is sent a denial hearing response (Fig. 6(b)) for that the child understands and chooses the right color. Once this is done, the silhouette is colored on the screen with the resulting color (Fig. 6(c)) and continues with the next color until the game ends (Fig. 6(d)).

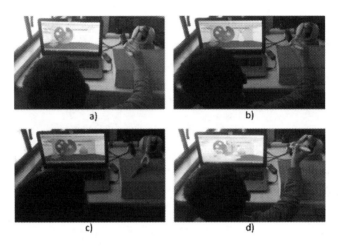

Fig. 6. First game used by the user

For the development of the second level a button is pressed to perform one stroke at a time. When the desired figure has been chosen, the indications are heard of how the stroke should be performed (Fig. 7(a)). By pressing the button to view the tutorial, the scene changes and is possible to perceive the displacement of the haptic device following the path of the stroke to be written (Fig. 7(b)). The child proceeds to complete the dotted lines forming the figure (Fig. 7(c); If the stroke is performed correctly, a positive auditory response is heard and the respective animations in the environment (Fig. 7(d)). Otherwise, the audio indicates to the child that try to do it again.

In the last game the vowels must be written (Fig. 8(a)). Just as in the previous game the sounds along with the animations show to child how the vowel should be written (Fig. 8(b)). The child performs the layout of each vowel and at the end presses the button with the tick (Fig. 8(c)); The system evaluates the trajectory and the order, if

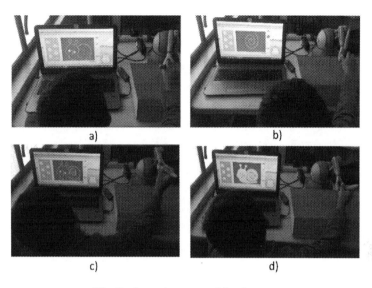

Fig. 7. Second game used by the user

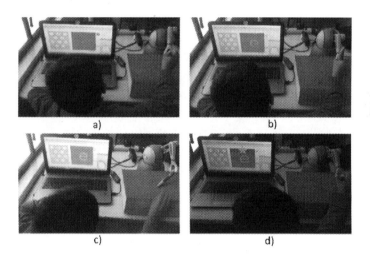

Fig. 8. Third game used by the user

they are correct it presents the animations and positive sounds (Fig. 8(d)), when one makes a mistake the child is told to continue practicing.

B. *Results*

The results tables for each of the games are presented in the next section. In Fig. 9 the evaluation of the game of the secondary colors showing the successes and failures are indicated, as well as the respective qualitative qualification.

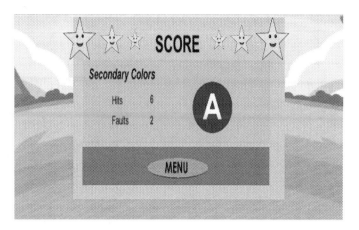

Fig. 9. Game results secondary colors

In the second game the user chooses between: (a) learn how to perform the stroke or (b) perform the stroke, to which if the user chooses option (a) a trajectory control is executed, in which two aspects are experimental: the trajectory described by haptic device geomagic touch (Fig. 10(a)), and the control errors (Fig. 10(b)), where you can see that the errors tend asymptotically to zero.

For the results corresponding to the second game is necessary to do a control by sorter which compares the similarity of the stroke made by the child with the data of a pattern, in Fig. 11(a) The pattern of the heart figure (blue Line) is indicated along with the child's stroke (red color line). In the same way for the third game the same control by sorter is applied, as shown in Fig. 11(b) the pattern and the stroke made by the child in the vowel 'e' lowercase are shown. Once the comparison is made the control reveals a numerical result, this value varies according to the type of stroke (if it is a capital, lowercase vowel or a figure) that is performed, this result is transformed to a qualitative qualification (form of qualification Managed by the initial education teachers) with the following evaluation parameters: A, EP and I (see Fig. 12(a)) and (Fig. 12(b)); where they correspond to acquired (very satisfactory performance), in process (satisfactory performance) and insufficient (incorrect performance), respectively.

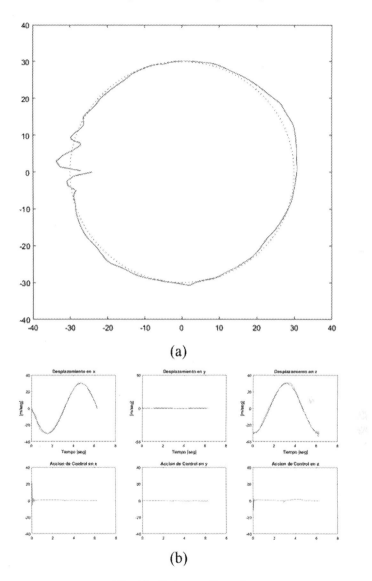

Fig. 10. Trajectory Control

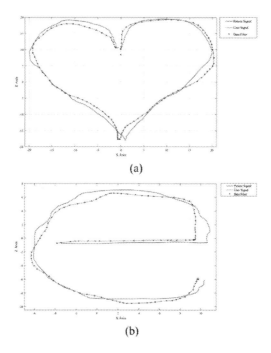

(a)

(b)

Fig. 11. Validation of letters and figures using a control by classifier (Color figure online)

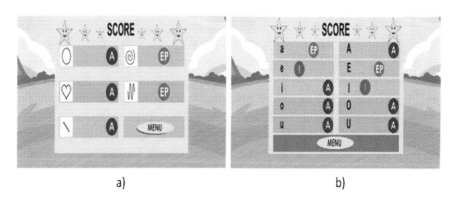

a)   b)

Fig. 12. Results (a) game strokes basic figures (b) game vocal stroke

7 Conclusion

The teaching-learning process for children of initial education can be complemented with the virtual system presented in this article, and it is very useful as a support for the teacher. In order children to focus their attention on the virtual environments designed. It must be eye-catching and most of their objects should be related to elements of daily life. As well as it is necessary to get the attention of the infant and encourage him to learn with the use of audio and animations within the virtual environment. The motion control developed in MATLAB allows to execute a trajectory tracking in the haptic device geomagic Touch and helps to develop skills for the writing of the children.

Acknowledgements. We thank the "Universidad de las Fuerzas Armadas ESPE" for financing the inves-tigation project number 2016-PIC-0017.

References

1. Greenwald, S., Kulik, A., Kunert, A., Beck, S., Fröhlich, B., Cobb, S., Parsons, S., Newbutt, N., Gouveia, C., Cook, C., Snyder, A., Payne, S., Holland, J., Buessing, S., Fields, G., Corning, W.: Technology and applications for collaborative learning. In: 12th International Conference on Computer Supported Collaborative Learning (CSCL), pp. 719–726 (2017)
2. Hite, R., Pereyra, M., Chesnutt, K., Corin, E., Childers, G., Jones, M.: Pedagogical perceptions of novel 3-D, haptic-enabled virtual reality technology. Int. J. Educ. Inf. Technol. **10**, 73–81 (2016)
3. Brown, A., Green, T.: Virtual reality: low-cost tools and resources for the classroom. TechTrends **60**(5), 517–519 (2016)
4. Pruna, E., Acurio, A., Escobar, I., Albiol, S., Zumbana, P., Meythaler, A., Álvarez, F. A.: 3D virtual system using a haptic device for fine motor rehabilitation. In: WorldCIST 2017: Recent Advances in Information Systems and Technologies, pp. 648–656 (2017)
5. Yu, X., Zhang, M., Xue, Y., Zhu, Z.: An exploration of developing multi-touch virtual learning tools for young children. In: 2010 2nd International Conference on Education Technology and Computer (ICETC), vol. 3, pp. V3–4. IEEE, June 2010
6. Palluel-Germain, R., Bara, F., De Boisferon, A. H., Hennion, B., Gouagout, P., Gentaz, E.: A visuo-haptic device-telemaque-increases kindergarten children's handwriting acquisition. In: EuroHaptics Conference, 2007 and Symposium on Haptic Interfaces for Virtual Environment and Teleoperator Systems, World Haptics 2007. Second Joint, pp. 72–77. IEEE, March 2007
7. Frade, B.V., Gondim, P.H.C.C., de Sousa, P.M.: The use of virtual reality as the object of mathematics learning. In: 2015 XVII Symposium on Virtual and Augmented Reality (SVR), pp. 137–141. IEEE, May 2015
8. Anthes, C., García-Hernández, R., Wiedemann, M., Kranzlmüller, D.: State of the Art of Virtual Reality Technology. In: IEEE Aerospace Conference (2016)
9. Wu, C.-M., Hsu, C.-W., Lee, T.-K., Smith, S.: A virtual reality keyboard with realistic haptic feedback in a fully immersive virtual environment. In: Virtual Reality, pp. 19–29 (2017)
10. Chen, J., Glover, M., Yang, C., Li, C., Li, Z., Cangelosi, A.: Development of an immersive interface for robot teleoperation. In: Conference Towards Autonomous Robotic Systems, pp. 1–15 (2017)
11. Sun Joo, A., Kyle, J., James, M., Scott, B., Melanie, B., Catherine, B.: Using virtual pets to increase fruit and vegetable consumption in children: a technology-assisted social cognitive theory approach. Cyberpsychology Behav. Soc. Networking **19**(2), 86–92 (2016)
12. Bailey, J., Bailenson, J.: Considering virtual reality in children's lives. J. Children Media **11**(1), 107–113 (2017)
13. Fowler, C.: Virtual reality and learning: Where is the pedagogy? Br. J. Educ. Technol. **46**(2), 412–422 (2015)

14. Chenga, M.T., Lin, Y.W., She, H.C.: Learning through playing Virtual Age: exploring the interactions among student concept learning, gaming performance, in-game behaviors, and the use of in-game characters. Comput. Educ. **86**, 18–29 (2015)
15. Minocha, S., Tudor, A.D., Tilling, S.: Affordances of mobile virtual reality and their role in learning and teaching. In: The 31st British Human Computer Interaction Conference (2017)
16. Hung, Y.H., Chen, C.H., Huang, S.: Applying augmented reality to enhance learning: a study of different teaching materials. J. Comput. Assist. Learn. **33**(3), 252–266 (2016)
17. Dinis, F.M., Guimarães, A.S., Carvalho, B.R., Martins, J.P.P.: Development of virtual reality game-based interfaces for civil engineering education. In: 2017 IEEE Global Engineering Education Conference (EDUCON), pp. 1195–1202. IEEE, April 2017
18. Elliman, J., Loizou, M., Loizides, F.: Virtual reality simulation training for student nurse education. In: 2016 8th International Conference on Games and Virtual Worlds for Serious Applications (VS-Games), pp. 1–2. IEEE, September 2016
19. Psotka, J.: Immersive training systems: virtual reality and education and training. Instr. Sci. **23**(5–6), 405–431 (1995)
20. Ary, D., Jacobs, L.C., Irvine, C.K.S., Walker, D.: Introduction to Research in Education. Cengage Learning, Boston (2018)
21. Chaney, C.: Language development, metalinguistic skills, and print awareness in 3-year-old children. Appl. Psycholinguist. **13**, 485–514 (1992)
22. Clements, D., Swaminathan, S., Zeitler, M., Sarama, J.: Young children's concepts of shape. Journal for Research in Mathematics Education **30**(2), 192–212 (1999)
23. Muijs, D., Reynolds, D.: Effective Teaching: Evidence and Practice. SAGE, London (2017)
24. Grajewski, D., Górski, F., Hamrol, A., Zawadzki, P.: Immersive and haptic educational simulations of assembly workplace conditions. In: International Conference on Virtual and Augmented Reality in Education, p. 359–368 (2015)
25. Cortés, H., García, M., Acosta, R., Santana, P.: Diseño y Desarrollo de un Dispositivo Háptico con Aplicaciones para Entornos Educativos. En Memorias de la Novena Conferencia Iberoamericana en Sistemas, Cibernética e Informática (CISCI 2010) (2010)
26. Kirkman, M.A., Ahmed, M., Albert, A.F., Wilson, M.H., Nandi, D., Sevdalis, N.: The use of simulation in neurosurgical education and training: a systematic review. J. Neurosurg. **121**(2), 228–246 (2014)
27. Mohammadi, A., Tavakoli, M., Jazayeri, A.: Phansim: a simulink toolkit for the sensable phantom haptic devices. In: Proceedings of the 23rd CANCAM, Canada, vol. 11, pp. 787–790 (2011)

VirtualCruiseTour: An AR/VR Application to Promote Shore Excursions on Cruise Ships

Sara Arlati[✉], Daniele Spoladore, Davide Baldassini,
Marco Sacco, and Luca Greci

Institute of Industrial Technologies and Automation,
National Research Council, Milan, Italy
{sara.arlati,daniele.spoladore,davide.baldassini,
marco.sacco,luca.greci}@itia.cnr.it

Abstract. This work presents VirtualCruiseTour, an AR/VR-based application dedicated to ship cruises' guests for the promotion of organized shore excursions. It can be exploited also in travel agencies to showcase future customers the sites of interest that can be visited during the cruise. The AR module allows augmenting a map showing the cruise route, the ship current position and the ports in which the liner will stop. Tapping one of the port (or the ship), the user is shown more details about the shore excursions organized for that stop (or the ship facilities) and has the chance to experience the site of interests watching 360° pictures or videos either in an immersive (VR) or non-immersive mode. A pilot study to validate the application as a marketing tool is foreseen. The experiment evaluates the customers' purchase intentions and their knowledge of the product in comparison to traditional marketing media (web sites and brochures). Preliminary results of the study conducted enrolling nine participants are presented and discussed.

Keywords: Augmented reality · Virtual Reality · Tourism · Marketing

1 Introduction

The use of Virtual and Augmented Reality (VR/AR) in the tourism field represents a topic of growing interest for both researchers and companies [1]. Due to their characteristics and their capability of entertaining the users, in fact, AR and VR have found different applications within this sector, such as enhancing the touristic visits [2], increasing the accessibility of fragile or remote areas [3], educating and guiding the tourists [4] and broadening the global interactions among travelers [5].

Indeed, the potential of VR and AR applications can be exploited also to promote trips to specific destinations, thus influencing travelers' decisions with the final aim of increasing the visits of certain sites [1]. Being aware of this, tourism companies are trying to enhance visual representations – that are currently the main means to promote tours – by introducing VR/AR technologies in their marketing campaigns. In this way, in fact, they can provide the potential customers with the possibility to experience a virtual world and to "feel present" in another place (i.e. with immersive environments), thus helping them in making more informed decisions and creating realistic expectations

© Springer International Publishing AG, part of Springer Nature 2018
L. T. De Paolis and P. Bourdot (Eds.): AVR 2018, LNCS 10850, pp. 133–147, 2018.
https://doi.org/10.1007/978-3-319-95270-3_9

on how the real experience would be [6]. Moreover, recent studies reported that the common audience has become more resistant towards traditional visual media as sources of information [7], and thus it is plausible to hypothesized that only information conveyed in an innovative way and within an enriched-data context are capable of captivating new potential customers. AR and VR may represent a solution to this issue, also taking into consideration that, nowadays, making use of VR/AR have become widely accessible, thanks to the new generation of mobile devices supporting these technologies and the diffusion of low-cost devices for the visualization of 3D and VR content as the CardBoard.

In this context, VR and AR-based marketing tools can be helpful for travel agencies, to incentivize the purchase of specific holiday packages, and they could represent a key marketing element and value proposition also during the travel, when the guests of a cruise liner are offered to buy one or few-day excursions to interesting sites nearby the ship port [1].

In this work, a mobile phone-based application dedicated to cruise ships' guests for the presentation of the excursions offered in each port is presented. *VirtualCruiseTour (VCT)* exploits both AR and VR to provide the end user with information about the cruise's route, the excursions proposed at each stop and immersive experiences in the sites of interests that can be visited – through organized excursions – during the vacation. Besides, it offers the opportunity for travel agencies to show in advance to potential customers the ship features, the different typologies of staterooms and of the places that can be visited during the whole cruise tour. In this way, future tourists can make their decision while being aware of how the real future experience will be.

One of the aim of this work is to evaluate whether AR and VR technologies provided by the VCT application can be effectively used as marketing tools to promote shore excursions to cruise passengers, investigating their purchase intentions and consumer learning compared to traditional marketing media (brochures and web pages).

2   Related Works

As already mentioned, VR and AR technologies have great potential as promotional instruments to encourage customers to visit a specific destination or purchase a service. In recent years, several examples of application have been presented both in the scientific literature and, especially, in the commercial scene.

In the former area, Fritz et al. [4] introduced the PRISMA project, which foresaw the development of an application dedicated to cultural tourism; their system, based on a video see-through device, exploits AR to enhance the real scenes by multimedia personalized interactive information, such as text, photographs, maps, video and 3D reconstructions. In 2015, Kourouthanassis et al. [8] developed and tested on the field a mobile augmented reality (MAR) travel guide, which supports personalized recommendations while visiting the Greek isle of Corfu. Martinez-Grana et al. [9] developed a virtual tour for a natural park, using geological layers and topographic and digital terrain models that can be overlaid in a 3D model. They used augmented reality to allow the users to access these georeferenced thematic layers and overlay data, in real time, on their mobile devices.

Dealing with the use of VR, some examples may be represented by the works of Potter et al., who developed a VR experience in a nature based environment [10], and Lee et al. who reconstructed five Korean heritage sites to allow visitors to see them as they originally were in ancient times [11].

In the field of marketing products, Hilton [12] and Marriot [13] – two of the major hotel brands – offer to visit their facilities and some of the cities in which they have accommodations, through immersive experiences that can be experienced using Cardboards. Moreover, many countries, cities and heritage sites have developed their own virtual or augmented tour to promote their visits. Among these, South Africa [14], London [15], the Duomo of Milan [16], the Quirinale palace in Rome [17].

Although there are not many works investigating the role that VR and AR-based technologies have in tourism marketing, several authors analyzed the effects of these technologies in marketing strategies. Bulerca et al. [18], despite highlighting the scarceness in benchmarks, examined the benefits for brands and companies deriving from the adoption of AR technologies and AR Experiential Marketing by testing them in a focus group. The results of the study underlined the perceived benefits of AR technologies, such as an impression of timesaving, sense of playfulness while using the technology and satisfaction. Furthermore, trustworthiness and reliability of the brand adopting AR technologies has emerged as one of the most relevant element of the brand attitude. Nah et al. [19] conducted a study to assess whether telepresence provided by 3D environments could enhance or deteriorate the brand equity and found these types of environment can indeed increase the brand equity by offering immersive and enjoyable VR-supported experiences. Several researches also showed that telepresence provided by VR technologies can positively influence consumers' knowledge of a product [6], as well as consumers' brand attitude and purchase intentions [20, 21]. With regards to the tourism marketing, in 1995 Williams and Hobson [22] stated that VR applied to tourism marketing has "the potential to revolutionize the promotion and selling of tourism". For instance, it has been proved by Wan et al. [23] how VR is a more powerful advertising tool than brochures for the promotion of theme and natural parks. Several researches suggested to incorporate AR and VR technologies into tourism website to provide a more effective advertising techniques [24, 25].

3   The VirtualCruiseTour Application

The main aim of VCT is supporting the promotion of one-day organized shore excursions in the ports where the cruise ship stops. It is dedicated to cruise liner's guests who can book these trips on-board being aware of what they will visit. As a secondary aim, VCT can act as a marketing tool to be used both on the cruise and in travel agencies to showcase the shore excursions available for each destination; it offers the possibility to potential customers to see in advance which will be the sites of interests along the cruise route.

VCT relies on both AR and VR; when used in the AR mode, it augments a map showing the cruise route and stops. If the user is on-board, he/she can also see the ship position and data dealing with the covered distances, traveling times, current velocity, etc. While in this mode, the cruise stops are highlighted and the user can select one of the augmented ports to discover which are the sites of interests and the shore excursions that can be made. When a site is selected, the user can consult written description and/or choose to explore cultural and natural sites of interest through 360° videos and pictures either while using the mobile in a classic mode, or wearing a CardBoard to experience the proposed sites in an immersive way.

The application has been developed to run on Android and iOS smartphones for several reasons. First, being the cruise customers the main target, it can be supposed that almost everybody owns his/her own device. Thus, neither the ship owners, nor the travel agencies are committed to buy special AR/VR equipment in order to provide all the passengers with the VCT application. Finally, the majority of smartphones supports the VR modality – the screen splitting in two halves – that, coupled with biconvex lenses (e.g. cardboards lenses), allows the user to feel immersed in a virtual world. These lenses, conversely to AR/VR equipment, can be provided to the cruise guests with a small economical effort: it is enough to think that Google Cardboards are sold for $7. In addition, they can be customized with the company logo for further marketing purposes.

VCT has been developed using Unity 3D to exploit its ability to target the developed application to multiple platforms (Android, iOS).

3.1 The Application Workflow

The VCT application is characterized by the two different modules: the AR module and the 360°/VR module (Fig. 1). The AR module allows the user to select a port to access more information about the nearby sites of interest. In addition, the interface shows – while on-board – the cruise liner's current position and some details about the itinerary and the ship itself. Once the user has tapped a port, he/she is provided with an interface where to select the site of interest to be explored with 360° videos or pictures. The user can then tap on one of the site of interest to access these multimedia contents either in an immersive or non-immersive way.

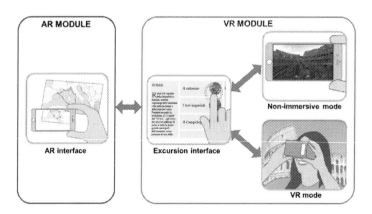

Fig. 1. The application workflow.

An important requirement that was taken in consideration in the design phase of the VCT application was the possibility for the ship owners or the travel agencies to easily modify or add new multimedia contents, especially when dealing with 360° pictures and videos. To do this, an external configuration file, easily modifiable by non-programmers, has been used.

The AR Module

The AR module has been developed in Unity 3D using Vuforia, a Software Development Kit (SDK) designed to integrate AR in mobile applications [26]. The AR module has been built using a marker-based approach; with this approach, when a marker (typically an ad-hoc 2D image) is framed with a camera, it is recognized by the application and used as reference system to place and orient the virtual content to be superimposed onto the real world.

The marker chosen for the VCT application is a map showing a cruise route in the Mediterranean Sea (Fig. 2). At the application launch, the user's smartphone camera is activated, so that when the user frames the map, the augmented multimedia contents appear superimposed on the map. The position of the ship along its route and each stop of the cruise, are displayed as icons, which can be interacted by tapping them. Moreover, the user can access augmented contents showing real time information about the cruise route and the ship, such as speed, covered distances and traveling times. All these pieces of information are retrieved in real time using a client-server architecture; the cruise ship position is interpolated along the route starting from covered distance data.

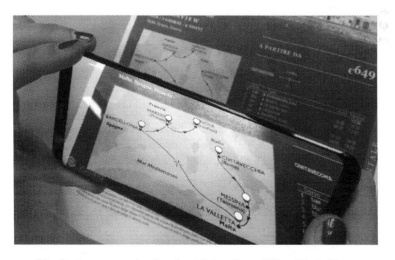

Fig. 2. A user experiencing the AR interface of VirtualCruiseTour.

The VR Module

When the user taps an AR interactive icon, a new interface (excursion interface, see Fig. 2) providing a brief description of the shore excursions (or the ship) and a list of buttons showing nearby sites of interest (or the cruise ship facilities) is shown. 360° pictures or videos associated to the site of interest (or to the ship) can be further accessed by tapping one of the buttons. At this point, the user can choose to visualize the multimedia content using two different visualization modes:

- Non-immersive: with this mode, the user can explore the 360° view of the multi-media content by orienting the smartphone in different directions or by dragging the content with a finger on the screen.
- VR: in this case, the user has to put the smartphone inside the cardboard provided by the ship owner. He/she can then explore the sites of the excursion or the ship facilities in an immersive way, by moving his/her head.

The user can switch from the non-immersive to the VR mode, and vice versa, respectively by tapping on the screen or pointing the gaze toward a designated button.

3.2   The Customization and the Accessibility of Media Contents

As mentioned before, particular attention has been dedicated to the flexibility of the VCT application after its deployment. The ship owners or the travel agencies must be able to easily modify the multimedia contents (360° photos or videos) without accessing the source code. To reach this goal, an external XML-based configuration file containing all the relevant information about the media contents has been used.

Media contents can be either stored locally and, thus, downloaded with the VCT application, or downloaded in real time. A control algorithm prevents the visualization of buttons – that are instantiated dynamically – associated to online contents when internet connection is not available. However, even without internet connection, users can still use VCT since it is provided with a set of pre-loaded contents (two lightweight multimedia contents for each site of interest or ship facility). Online contents that are changed after the download of the application (by modifying the configuration file) are made accessible through periodic application updates.

4   Proposed Validation

The validation proposed to test the effects of VCT relies on some basic assumptions. Firstly, the current state of the art of Virtual and Augmented Reality technologies allows the users to interact with representations of products mainly with two senses, vision and hearing. Secondly, VR is able to enhance telepresence [27].

Following the theoretical background provided in [20], the validation experiment relies on Vessey's Theory of Cognitive Fit [28]. According to this theory, there is a positive correlation between task performances and the modality with which the task is presented. Hence, a match between IT applications and users' tasks should be realized in order to promote better results. By applying this theory, Suh and Lee stated that products with attributes that can be experienced through Virtual Reality technologies benefit from an enhanced presentation to the consumers, since their salient attributes become completely obvious and apparent thanks to both visual and auditory cues [20].

Basing on this assumption, Suh and Lee classified products into virtually high experiential (VHE) and virtually low experiential (VLE). The former category indicates those products whose evaluation requires the consumer to exploit vision and hearing (i.e. paintings, clothes), while the latter describes products whose evaluation is best performed using other senses than vision or hearing (i.e. food, beverage).

4.1   Validation Goals

In this work, we reprise the classification of [20] with the aim of investigating whether the offer of cruises' shore excursions can fit the category of VHE – basing on the assumption that these products can be indirectly experienced by customers mainly through vision and hearing. As a consequence, it is plausible to hypothesize that consumers' purchase intentions are positively influenced by the use of AR/VR technologies.

On the other hand, it is also true that AR/VR still represent a novelty for the general public, thus inducing a "wow" effect (at least during the first experience) that can induce a sense of being engrossed, thus limiting the task performances and the learning of the proposed information [29]. Within this context, the aims of this work are therefore the testing of the following hypotheses:

(1a)   shore-excursions are VHE, thus AR/VR technologies are able to increase purchase intentions;

(1b)   sense of presence positively influences consumers' purchase intentions.

(2)   AR/VR technologies induce a "wow" effect, during the first experience that limits consumers' learning.

4.2   Selected Product and Advertising Materials

The enrolled participants are shown advertising materials regarding a five-day long Mediterranean cruise starting from the port of La Spezia and reaching, in order: Marseille, Palma de Mallorca, La Valletta, Trapani and Civitavecchia (Rome). The materials provide information and details on a shore excursion in Rome that includes visits, among others, of four main attraction sites that will be the object of guided tours: the Colosseum, the Circus Maximum, St. Peter's Basilica and Caracalla's thermal baths. These four areas of interest are described with short text while the whole excursion is described with essential details, such as cost, duration, difficulty of the excursion (whether the excursion is suggested only for persons in a good shape or for any passenger, even in wheelchair) and possible in-excursion activities (possibility of lunch, local products tasting, shopping, etc.).

The shore excursion is described in three different types of advertising materials (Fig. 3):

(a)   a tri-fold brochure describing the excursion and its interesting sites with two pictures for each site and a table summarizing the essential details (cost, duration, difficulty, possible in-excursion activities);

(b) a web-page containing the same text provided for the brochure and the same pictures, with a picture for each main attraction, a frame showing sliding pictures of the same sites and two frames illustrating 360° pictures for two monuments; the page is also provided with the same essential details of the brochure next to a "purchase" button;

(c) an AR/VR set composed of a Cardboard and smartphone running the VCT application; the content of VCT showcases the same sites of interest depicted in (a) and (b) using eight 360° pictures, but presents the same text used in the brochure and in the web-page.

Fig. 3. The three types of the provided advertising material: (a) the trifold brochure, (b) a screenshot of the web page and (c) the Cardboard, the marker and a smartphone running the VCT application.

4.3   Experimental Procedure

The experiment is aimed at investigating whether (1) the offer of shore excursions can be positively represented by AR and VR technologies, thus indicating that these products fit in the VHE category, and (2) the "wow" effect limits consumers' learning.

Participants enrolled in the study are randomly divided into three groups. The first group (A) is provided with a standard tri-fold brochure describing the product; the second group (B) is provided with a web page, while the third group (C) is provided with a Cardboard and a smartphone running the VCT application.

Before starting the experiment, each participant is presented the shore excursion to Rome as a facultative guided visit to the city that can be purchased while being a passenger on a cruise ship sailing in the Mediterranean Sea. Group C receives also a brief explanation of the functioning of the VCT application. This is made not to prevent the provision of specific information within the application; it is assumed, in fact, that all the subjects are familiar with both printed-paper and web pages, whereas they may not be so skilled in the experience of a mobile app presented them for the first time.

After a maximum of 10 min of exposure (subjects were told they could stop whenever they felt good with the information they had) to the specific media, the participants are administered a questionnaire asking about personal information (age, gender, year of schooling, employment) and regarding the offer they learned about. In details, the questionnaire investigates the following outcomes:

- *Sense of presence*; presence is the sense of "being there" in an environment by means of a communication medium. Presence is mainly investigated in scenarios involving VR, however it can be elicited also by different media (as a book or a movie). Sense of Presence is investigated using the questionnaire developed by Usoh et al. [30]. Questions have been adapted to the context of this trial, modifying the term "office space", which authors used in their version, with "Rome's sites of interest/local attractions".
- *Perceived product knowledge*; three Likert-scale items, adapted from the questionnaire developed by Smith and Park [31], aimed at investigating how well the customer feel informed about the content of the excursion.
- *Mode of product evaluation*; this section contains two Likert-scale items which intend to investigate how much the quality of the product (i.e. the excursion) is evaluable from the experience provided by media (i.e. the brochure, the web page, VCT app).
- *Product attitude*; in this section, participants are asked how they feel about the product, using five 7-point Likert items (*bad/good, not appealing/appealing, unpleasant/pleasant, unattractive/attractive, boring/interesting*).
- *Purchase intention*; a 7-point Likert Scale question asks the participant if he/she would take into consideration to purchase the proposed excursion.
- *Actual product knowledge*; four open questions investigate the product information's retention by the subject. In details, the questions are about: the price and the duration of the excursion, the possibility for people with mobility issues to join it, and the main touristic attractions that will be presented through guided tours. These answers are rated 0, if the answer is wrong or not given, 1 if the answer is correct; for the last question, each correct attraction is rated 0.25.

At the end of this first step of validation, the participants of C group are asked to complete a questionnaire for User Interaction Satisfaction [32], aimed at evaluating their experience with the AR/VR interface.

4.4 Preliminary Results

At the moment of this publication, nine subjects (age: 35.5 ± 7.3; 6 males, 3 females; years of schooling > 18) have been enrolled among the employees of Italian National Research Council. No inclusion criteria were specified; exclusion criteria were severe visual impairment and inability to read or speak Italian language. All subjects gave their informed consent.

Task times were measured during each trial; results, reported in Fig. 4, showed an increase in the duration of the experience as the means become more interactable.

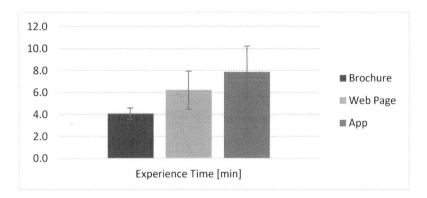

Fig. 4. Task duration for each group.

Sense of presence was unexpectedly found to be higher in the case of the brochure (3.5 ± 2.0) as shown in Fig. 5; VCT application elicited a sense of presence (3.2 ± 1.2) just a little higher with respect to the web page (3.1 ± 1.7).

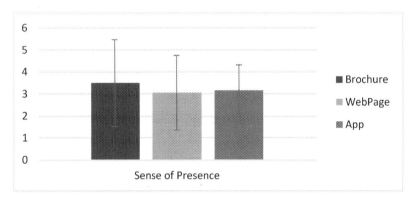

Fig. 5. Sense of Presence evaluated with Usoh et al. questionnaire [30]. Values are up to 7.

For *perceived knowledge*, the brochure (5.1 ± 1.3) was the means that made the consumers feeling more confident about the knowledge they acquired, both with respect to the web page (4.4 ± 1.9) and VCT application (4.3 ± 1.4). The evaluation of the product through visual means resulted more reliable in the case of the web page (5.2 ± 1.5); results obtained by the brochure (4.2 ± 2.3) and VCT application (4.3 ± 1.9) were comparable.

Dealing with the *product attitude*, VCR application received the best score (4.8 ± 0.7), the web page was rated 3.9 ± 1.7, whereas the brochure was the less appreciated with a score of 3.1 ± 1.8 (Fig. 6).

Fig. 6. Brand attitude: the subjects evaluated how much the product was good, appealing, pleasant, attractive and interesting on a scale 7 [31].

Purchase intentions were considerably higher in the case of VCT app: all subjects rated 5 their will to buy the shore excursion; the web page obtained a score of 4.0 ± 1.0, whereas the brochure caused the excursion to have a lower appeal (2.7 ± 2.0).

The *actual knowledge*, evaluated through four questions investigating information retrieval after the experience, resulted quiet high for the brochure (2.7 ± 1.2) and for the web page (2.7 ± 1.0), whereas in the case of VCT application, the score was lower (1.8 ± 1.0). Perceived and actual knowledge are compared in Fig. 7.

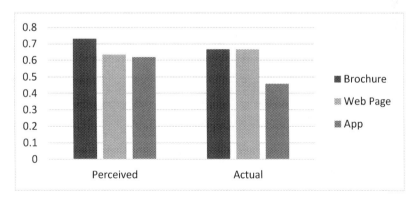

Fig. 7. Comparison between actual and perceived knowledge; values were normalized to ease the visual comparison.

Finally, the administration of the User Interaction Satisfaction questionnaire to the subjects enrolled in Group C resulted in a score of 6.4 ± 1.7. No statistical tests were run due to the small sample recruited up to the date of this manuscript preparation.

4.5   Discussion

VR and AR technologies are gaining more and more prominence during recent years and their application in the marketing field is growing proportionally; this tendency can be explained by the possibility, provided by these technologies, to experience a product before its purchase, alleviating consumers' lack of physical contact [20].

In this context, the preliminary results of the conducted study – though with several limitations – introduce some interesting findings. First, the time dedicated to the means' consultation was considerably higher in the case of the VCT application. This is undoubtedly due the time 'wasted' to insert the smartphone in the Cardboard and to the longer experience that the navigation in a 360° picture can elicit; however, it has to be noticed that the subjects were not required to look at all the media contents: it was therefore their choice to spend more time consulting several pictures. This outcome is in agreement with results obtained by Suh and Lee, who reported an increase in *flow* for all subjects experiencing either a VHE or a VLE product when the media was indeed VR [20]. Flow, firstly defined by Csikszentmihalyi, indicates a state of well-being in which people can be depicted as intrinsically motivated, unconscious of themselves while performing the tasks, and oftentimes losing the sense of physical time [33]; it is believed to be responsible of users' engagement and motivation: hence, the longer experience time may be the result of the generation of such positive mental status.

This fact is in agreement with the assessment made for product attitude (the VCT app was the most appreciated) and user satisfaction, but appears in contrast with the results obtained from the Usoh et al. questionnaire, aimed at evaluating subjects' sense of presence. The brochure resulted in fact as the media capable of eliciting the highest presence. However, this unexpected result can be explained because all the enrolled subjects, with the exception of one (in Group B) have already visited the city of Rome. This fact, which surely represent a bias in the sample, led the groups to perform an evaluation of the sense of presence basing on to two different principles: people in Group A and B answered the questions relying on the memories they had of the city which were recalled by the media contents, while Group C answered thinking more specifically of the application. This hypothesis is confirmed by some comments the subjects made during the questionnaire compiling; two subjects in Group A and B said that their memories were mixed with the real ones, while two subjects in Group C commented about features related with the application ('I would have liked to walk inside the sites', 'I did not feel so present because I could not focus images properly').

Another interesting observation that could be made by looking at the obtained results deals with the comparison of perceived and actual knowledge. The former resulted higher in the case of the brochure and comparable for the web page and the application. However, when evaluating the acquired knowledge, this resulted considerably lower only for the VCT app. This confirms – at least preliminarily – hypothesis (2), and goes in favor of the relationship between the onset of a "wow" effect that still emerges in the general public when it comes to VR/AR technologies, and the limitations in task performances, already noticed in previous studies [29, 34].

Nonetheless, purchase intentions were higher in Group C, meaning that the media could play an important role in the marketing field. Only one participants in Group C remembered how much the shore excursion would cost, but all voted 5 (up to 7) when asked if they would consider to buy the proposed excursion. This result would suggest that perceived knowledge, together with the product attitude, the users' satisfaction and the flow, account for more when consumers' are proposed with a product – a shore excursion – to buy, making it a VHE.

As already mentioned, these results are only preliminary, and the presented study has several limitations. First, the sample was too small to draw any conclusion on the generalizability of the obtained results. In addition, all subjects were researchers, had a higher education degree and almost all have already visited Rome: these aspects may have biased also other results, different from sense of presence.

Therefore, before proceeding with the experiment, it is needed to increase the catchment area adding subjects with different age, years of schooling and profession; changing the city in which the excursion take place with a less-known one may also be of help to eliminate biases in sense of presence due to memory recall. The possibility to change the instrument used to evaluate sense of presence will also be taken into consideration: Usoh et al.'s questionnaire is in fact a brief set of question that results very useful not to lengthen too much the evaluation times, but, on the other hand, it does not address all the domains related to presence, as, for instance, the ITC-SOPI developed by Lessiter et al. does [35]. Thus, replacing the questionnaire with a more detailed one could help to increase the sensitivity of the instrument in detecting differences and in better addressing the motivation for a reduced or an enhanced sense of presence.

5   Conclusion and Future Works

This work presents an Augmented and Virtual Reality-based application, VCT, for supporting the promotion of one-day organized shore excursions in the ports where the cruise ship stops. VCT is dedicated to cruise liner's guests, who can experience in advance the sites of interests, in order to make a more informed decision before purchasing the organized trips. Moreover, the application can act as a marketing tool to be exploited in travel agencies with the aim of show-casing the shore excursions available for each destination and the ship liner's facilities. The architecture and the features of VCT are described, together with the experiment and its preliminary results to validate the marketing opportunities it can provide.

Future works for VCT foresee the deployment of the application and the conclusion of the validation experiments, addressing the limitation presented in paragraph 4.5. Analyzing the results of the questionnaires, it will be possible to assess whether AR/VR technologies represents a potential vehicle for the promotion of cruises and shore excursions.

In addition, the results coming from the Questionnaire for User Interaction Satisfaction will be useful to evaluate the interactions between the users and the application in terms of usability. These data will also allow to identify shortcomings related to the interface, the application and/or the use and to address future improvements of the whole application.

Acknowledgments. This study is part of Project AGORÀ, a Research and Innovation project coordinated by Fincantieri S.p.A. with the participation of the National Research Council (CNR); the project receives grants from the Italian Ministry of Infrastructures and Transport (MIT).

References

1. Griffin, T., Giberson, J., Lee, S.H., Guttentag, D., Kandaurova, M., Sergueeva, K., Dimanche, F.: Virtual reality and implications for destination marketing. In: Travel and Tourism Research Association International Conference, Quebec City, QC, Canada, June 2017
2. Healy, N., van Riper, C.J., Boyd, S.W.: Low versus high intensity approaches to interpretive tourism planning: the case of the Cliffs of Moher, Ireland. Tour. Manag. **52**, 574–583 (2016)
3. Pierdicca, R., Frontoni, E., Malinverni, E.S., Colosi, F., Orazi, R.: Virtual reconstruction of archaeological heritage using a combination of photogrammetric techniques: Huaca Arco Iris, Chan Chan, Peru. Digit. Appl. Archaeol. Cult. Herit. **3**(3), 80–90 (2016)
4. Fritz, F., Susperregui, A., Linaza, M.T.: Enhancing cultural tourism experiences with augmented reality technologies. In: 6th International Symposium on Virtual Reality, Archaeology and Cultural Heritage (VAST) (2005)
5. Huang, Y.-C., Backman, S.J., Backman, K.F., Moore, D.: Exploring user acceptance of 3D virtual worlds in travel and tourism marketing. Tour. Manag. **36**, 490–501 (2013)
6. Klein, L.R.: Creating virtual product experiences: the role of telepresence. J. Interact. Mark. **17**(1), 41–55 (2003)
7. Fransen, M.L., Verlegh, P.W., Kirmani, A., Smit, E.G.: A typology of consumer strategies for resisting advertising, and a review of mechanisms for countering them. Int. J. Advert. **34**(1), 6–16 (2015)
8. Kourouthanassis, P., Boletsis, C., Bardaki, C., Chasanidou, D.: Tourists responses to mobile augmented reality travel guides: the role of emotions on adoption behavior. Pervasive Mob. Comput. **18**, 71–87 (2015)
9. Martnez-Graña, A.M., Goy, J., Cimarra, C.: A virtual tour of geological heritage: valourising geodiversity using Google Earth and QR code. Comput. Geosci. **61**, 83–93 (2013)
10. Potter, L.E., Carter, L., Coghlan, A.: Virtual reality and nature based tourism: an opportunity for operators and visitors. In: Proceedings of the 28th Australian Conference on Computer-Human Interaction, pp. 652–654. ACM (2016)
11. Lee, J., Lee, J., Kim, J.W., Kang, K., Lee, M.H.: Virtual reconstruction and interactive applications for Korean traditional architectures. SCIRES-IT-SCIentificRESearch Inf. Technol. **6**(1), 5–14 (2016)
12. Samuely, A.: Hilton checks in virtual reality push via 360-degree video experience. http://www.mobilemarketer.com/ex/mobilemarketer/cms/news/video/22759.html. Accessed 25 Sept 2017
13. Dua, T.: Marriott taps Oculus Rift for virtual reality tours of Hawaii, London. https://digiday.com/marketing/take-virtual-reality-tour-hawaii-london-thanks-marriott-hotels-oculus-rift/. Accessed 25 Sept 2017
14. South Africa Tourism Board, VR Travel Experience for South African Tourism. http://visualise.com/case-study/vr-travel-south-african-tourism. Accessed 25 Sept 2017
15. London Virtual Tours. https://360.visitlondon.com/. Accessed 25 Sept 2017
16. Veneranda Fabbrica del Duomo di Milano, Duomo di Milano. www.duomomilano.it/it/vr. Accessed 25 Sept 2017

17. Presidenza della Repubblica: Virtual Tours. http://www.digitallighthouse.it/index.php/it/works/projects/quirinale-3d-vr. Accessed 25 Sept 2017
18. Bulearca, M., Tamarjan, D.: Augmented reality: a sustainable marketing tool. Glob. Bus. Manag. Res. Int. J. 2(2), 237–252 (2010)
19. Nah, F.F.-H., Eschenbrenner, B., De Wester, D.: Enhancing brand equity through flow and telepresence: a comparison of 2D and 3D virtual worlds. MIS Q. 35, 731–747 (2011)
20. Suh, K.-S., Lee, Y.E.: The effects of virtual reality on consumer learning: an empirical investigation. MIS Q. 29, 673–697 (2005)
21. Li, H., Daugherty, T., Biocca, F.: Impact of 3-D advertising on product knowledge, brand attitude, and purchase intention: the mediating role of presence. J. Advert. 31(3), 43–57 (2002)
22. Williams, P., Hobson, J.P.: Virtual reality and tourism: fact or fantasy? Tour. Manag. 16(6), 423–427 (1995)
23. Wan, C.-S., Tsaur, S.-H., Chiu, Y.-L., Chiou, W.-B.: Is the advertising effect of virtual experience always better or contingent on different travel destinations? Inf. Technol. Tour. 9(1), 45–54 (2007)
24. Doolin, B., Burgess, L., Cooper, J.: Evaluating the use of the Web for tourism marketing: a case study from New Zealand. Tour. Manag. 23(5), 557–561 (2002)
25. Fotakis, T., Economides, A.A.: Art, science/technology and history museums on the web. Int. J. Digit. Cult. Electron. Tour. 1(1), 37–63 (2008)
26. Vuforia. https://www.vuforia.com. Accessed 25 Sept 2017
27. Witmer, B.G., Singer, M.J.: Measuring presence in virtual environments: a presence questionnaire. Presence 7(3), 225–240 (1998)
28. Vessey, I.: Cognitive fit: a theory-based analysis of the graphs versus tables literature. Decis. Sci. 22(2), 219–240 (1991)
29. McMahan, R.P., Bowman, D.A., Zielinski, D.J., Brady, R.B.: Evaluating display fidelity and interaction fidelity in a virtual reality game. IEEE Trans. Vis. Comput. Graph. 18(4), 626–633 (2012)
30. Usoh, M., Catena, E., Arman, S., Slater, M.: Using presence questionnaires in reality. Presence Teleop. Virtual Environ. 9(5), 497–503 (2000)
31. Smith, D.C., Park, C.W.: The effects of brand extensions on market share and advertising efficiency. J. Mark. Res. 29(3), 296 (1992)
32. Harper, B.D., Norman, K.L.: Improving user satisfaction: The questionnaire for user interaction satisfaction version 5.5. In: Proceedings of the 1st Annual Mid-Atlantic Human Factors Conference, pp. 224–228 (1993)
33. Csikszentmihalyi, M.: Flow and the Psychology of Discovery and Invention, p. 39. HarperPerennial, New York (1997)
34. Whitton, M.C.: Making virtual environments compelling. Commun. ACM 46(7), 40–47 (2003)
35. Lessiter, J., Freeman, J., Keogh, E., Davidoff, J.: A cross-media presence questionnaire: the ITC-Sense of Presence Inventory. Presence Teleoper. Virtual Environ. 10(3), 282–297 (2001)

Perception of Absolute Distances
Within Different Visualization Systems:
HMD and CAVE

Mihalache Ghinea[1(✉)], Dinu Frunză[2], Jean-Rémy Chardonnet[3],
Frédéric Merienne[3], and Andras Kemeny[3,4]

[1] Department of Machines and Manufacturing Systems,
University POLITEHNICA of Bucharest, sector 6, 060042 Bucharest, Romania
ghinea2003@yahoo.com
[2] Jaguar Land Rover, Warick CV35 0RR, UK
justkior@gmail.com
[3] LiSPEN EA7515, Arts et Métiers, UBFC, HeSam, Institut Image,
71100 Chalon-sur-Saône, France
{jean-remy.chardonnet, frederic.merienne}@ensam.eu
[4] VR and Immersive Simulation Center, Renault, Guyancourt, France
andras.kemeny@renault.com

Abstract. Many studies on distance perception in a virtual environment exist. Most of them were conducted using head-mounted displays (HMD) and less with large screen displays such as CAVE systems. In this paper, we propose to measure the accuracy of perceived distances in a virtual space ranging from 0 to 15 m in a CAVE system compared to an HMD. Eight subjects with different vision performances took part in an experiment. Results show that the HMD provides the best results for distances above 8 m while the CAVE provides the best results for close distances.

Keywords: Virtual immersion · Absolute distance · HMD · CAVE
Human vision

1 Introduction

Since a couple of years, Virtual Reality (VR) is more and more used in several domains some of which are: health industry (to treat phobias or in surgeon simulation), entertainment (video games, advertisement, tele-immersion), automotive and aerospace industries (driving simulations, numerical layouts visualization and virtual prototyping), preservation of culture heritage (historical places and old building reconstruction), scientific visualization (meteorology, architecture, urbanism), and in dangerous business sectors like chemical or nuclear industries.

The goal of VR technologies is to get a perceptual approximation of future environments that is as close as possible to reality, so that rapid comparison and iteration can be performed before concretization of the products or the services. However, when using VR systems, a problem arises. Past work showed that distances are misperceived in virtual environments; more precisely, they are underestimated [17].

© Springer International Publishing AG, part of Springer Nature 2018
L. T. De Paolis and P. Bourdot (Eds.): AVR 2018, LNCS 10850, pp. 148–161, 2018.
https://doi.org/10.1007/978-3-319-95270-3_10

In this paper, we propose to study the accuracy of two VR display systems in restituting distances. Though most of past work conducted studies with HMDs, we propose here to compare between a CAVE system and an HMD. We measure the standard deviation between the distance of a virtual object as supposed by observers and the real distance, called here a reference distance. We investigate how this deviation evolves with the distance for each of the VR systems.

The paper is organized as follows. In the next section, we present a literature review on previous work dealing with distance estimation, then in Sect. 3, we present the user study we made comparing a CAVE system and an HMD. We then expose the results and discuss them.

2   Previous Work

2.1   Distance Estimation

To find the spatial position of a virtual object, our visual system relies on the distance and on depth indicators available within a virtual scene. Ten depth indicators are usually available: binocular disparity, adjustment, convergence, motion parallax, aerial and linear perspective [9], occlusion, size of the field of view, shadows and textures [7]. For both the real and the virtual environments, distances always influence these depth indicators.

Numerous past studies showed that estimated distances in virtual environments are compressed (underestimated) [14, 17, 27], with the underestimation increasing with the distance [2]. Whereas in real environments, distance estimation is fairly accurate [26]. The reasons for this phenomenon are multiple and different.

Past studies reported the display system to have the most significant role in the compression phenomenon, and not the image quality, as previously thought [24]. Among the factors contributing to the limitation of the display system, we mention: the vergence - accommodation conflict, the image quality, the light and dimension of the field of view (FOV), motion parallax.

In a real environment, vergence and accommodation will target the same point. In a virtual environment, on the contrary, vergence and accommodation will dissociate in two different points. This well-known vergence - accommodation conflict results in headaches after a long period of use [8].

The importance of the FOV in distance estimation has been widely studied in previous studies. Especially these have shown that the size of the FOV in a real environment is decisive in distance estimation. For example, a vertically limited FOV (21° or less) leads to an underestimation in a real environment [29] and to the degradation of some distance indicators (linear perspective and relative dimension) [28]. However, in an HMD, it has been shown that for medium distances (from 2 to 15 m) a vertically limited FOV does not influence the observers' appreciation regarding absolute distances estimation [12].

Even though the FOV is not such an important factor in absolute distance estimation, together with others factors (inertia, weight of the HMD), it can contribute to compression appreciations in virtual environments [25], influencing the observers perception [19].

Presence is also a source of misperception of distances [23]. Indeed, perceiving both the real and virtual environments as being different may induce a lack of presence, which will affect distance perception [10]. Therefore, to reduce the source of compression, the effect of high fidelity of virtual immersive environments has been studied, showing very good results in absolute distances estimation (around 95%). Also, distance compression can be reduced if those distances are well known (that means distance underestimation is not necessarily defined by the used technology) [10].

Mohler et al. showed that using a precise avatar instead of an own observer image/body will lead to a smaller number of errors when absolute distances are estimated [18].

In HMD systems, observers are totally shielded from the real environment. Whereas these systems allow increased presence and interaction with the virtual world, past research on absolute distance perception using HMDs showed an important underestimation (than can be up to 50%) in certain situations (depending on the immersive systems used, the textures, the quality of the system parameters) [14]. However, recently launched HMDs showed much less severe distance underestimation [11], as they provide much higher image resolution.

With large screens displays, despite fewer literature, distance estimations are found to be more accurate compared to HMDs, though distances are still underestimated [6, 21]. Piryankova et al. found similar results but they identified an effect of stereoscopy on distance perception [20]. Marsh et al. showed that observers use physical cues, more specifically the physical boundaries of the CAVE, to estimate distances, however still underestimating them [15]. Bruder et al. studied the effect of parallax on distance perception in a CAVE system [1]. They showed that distance perception is more accurate when target objects are in front of the screen or at screen-depth.

Dorado et al. presented a study comparing a low cost HMD and a CAVE system to select the best opera seat [3]. In this study, observers had to select the best seat in an opera theater from their point of view based on the view to the scene and on auditory considerations. Results showed that observers' decisions were not substantially affected by the display system; however their performance judgment could be affected by the display factors.

Examples of comparison between a CAVE system and an HMD are still rare in the literature (most of past work concentrate on one system at a time but do not compare both of them together). We propose here to fill this gap.

2.2   Evaluation Methods

Several evaluation methods for distance estimation have been used in past work: verbal estimation, perceptive adjustment or measurement based on motor behaviors (blind walking, triangulation). However, the choice of the method may influence results [22].

The simplest method to evaluate distance perception is verbal estimation, where observers stand still within the virtual environment and just estimate the distances counting certain measurement units or using the size of a virtual object to measure a specific distance (for example [20]). Obviously, it is widely accepted that this method is less accurate than measurements based on motor behavior (action-based metrics) [14].

Another static method based on visual perception is the distance bisection method. Observers must, using a joystick, find the middle point on the distance between them and the target [16].

Blindfolded walking is an action-based method requiring observers to go to the target, blindfolded [10, 26]. This method was demonstrated to be useful for distances below 20 m, otherwise distances were strongly underestimated.

Another action-based method is triangulated walking, where observers have to go to the target seen before. This method was shown to be well suited for long distances [4]. Perception adjustment is another motor-based technique to evaluate distances. Observers estimate distances by moving the target object to the expected right position. Adjustment is done manually, however recent work proposed a correction algorithm for HMDs allowing users to maintain the distance perception equal in both the real and the virtual spaces [30].

Here we select evaluation methods that can comply with the VR systems we want to use, namely an HMD and a CAVE. Because the CAVE does not allow for large displacements, we choose the perception adjustment method.

3   User Study

3.1   Problem Definition

Consider in a virtual environment an object is located at a reference distance D_{ref} to the observer, the problem is to determine the minimal distances $d+$ and $d-$ leading to the detection of differences in the depth (Fig. 1). The distances $D_{ref} + d+$ and $D_{ref} - d-$ are the planar coordinates of the object found by the subjects while adjusting their view. The theoretical objective is to measure $d+$ and $d-$ for several values of D_{ref}.

Determining $d+$ and $d-$ will offer a global idea on the smoothness of the space representation within the virtual environment. Recall that the appreciations on observed distances are smaller in VR than in the real world and this compression increases with the distance. Therefore studying $d+$ and $d-$ will allow understanding this evolution as a function of the distance.

After several trials, this evolution will be plotted to visualize and compare the results for both VR systems (HMD and CAVE). This will represent an important indicator regarding the systems capabilities to offer an accurate measured depth.

3.2   Experimental Conditions

We used a four-sided CAVE system (vertical screens: 2.74 × 3.00 m; ground screen: 3 × 3 m). The images are produced at a 60 Hz frame rate by eight Projection Design F30 video-projectors, two for each screen (one for each eye) with a resolution of 1160 × 1050 pixels per side. Passive technology is used for stereoscopy and an ART tracking system is used to track the subjects.

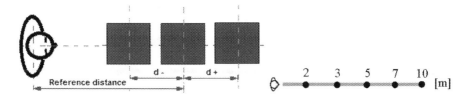

Fig. 1. Representation of the reference distance D_{ref}, $d+$ and $d-$ (left) and different values of the reference distance (right).

Regarding the HMD, we used a VFX 3D HMD that can have a resolution up to 1600×1200 pixels (64 frames/sec). Note that though this HMD does not offer today's available HMDs capabilities, it allows to compare more easily with the CAVE as the image quality is close. No tracking of the subjects were performed to simplify the setup. A small calibration was made, in order to establish the eye position of each subject, as past literature showed HMD calibration to have an effect on distance estimation [13].

To interact with the virtual environment, a Flystick is used in the CAVE while a keyboard is used with the HMD.

To avoid any biases during the experiment, head movements are not allowed either in the CAVE, either in the HMD, while vergence is accepted. Also, a head support was designed ensuring the subjects do not use motion parallax during the experiment in the CAVE. The subjects are therefore asked to put their head on it all along the experiment in the CAVE. Also, as no tracking is used in the HMD, this support allows reproducing the same eye position in the CAVE as in the HMD. Figure 2 shows the design of the head support, where θ is the deflection angle, H the eye position, and h the cube position on the vertical axis. These dimensions are used to calculate the absolute distance from the subject eyes to the virtual cube displayed in the virtual space. The deflection angle can be used to calculate the absolute distance when h is a known parameter. Modifying this variable can also alter the perceived distance for the objects in the virtual/real environment [5, 19].

The virtual environment is composed of a corridor, with many visual cues regarding distances (linear perspective, relative size, light, etc.). The environment is textured to provide more realistic conditions to subjects, however, studying the influence of the textures will be beyond the scope of this paper.

For the experimental study, eight subjects (two women and six men) participated on a voluntary basis. They were asked to perform with each visualization system distance estimation for the five different reference distances shown in Fig. 1 right and 20 times for each distance. The distances were displayed in a random order. After each series of tests, the subjects took a small break. The subjects performed the experiment seated.

Before and after the experiment, the subjects had to fill two questionnaires: the first one related to issues and performance of their vision system and to previous experiences in VR, while the second one was related to technical aspects such as immersive visualization and virtual interaction.

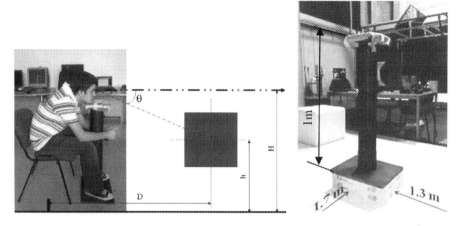

Fig. 2. Variables used to calculate the absolute distance to the cube (left) and position of the head support (right).

3.3 Experimental Protocol

For each test, the subjects performed the following steps:

1. **Preparation:** the subject visualizes the target (a blue cube) placed exactly in front of him (the initial position of the cube) (Fig. 3, left). In order to move the cube, the subject must press the trigger button of the Flystick (in the CAVE mode) or press the Space key of a keyboard when the HMD system is used.

Fig. 3. The initial position of the cube in the virtual space (left) and its final position (right). (Color figure online)

2. **Learning:** the blue cube is automatically moved instantly from its initial position to the final one (one of the reference distances, Fig. 3, right). The subject sees the cube position for only two seconds. Then, the cube disappears and reappears at its initial

position. At this point, to facilitate the understanding of the distance between the start and the end positions, the subject can see the first reference distance ($D_{ref.perc}$) that is an internal representation of D_{ref} ($D_{ref.perc} = f(D_{ref})$) (Fig. 4, left).

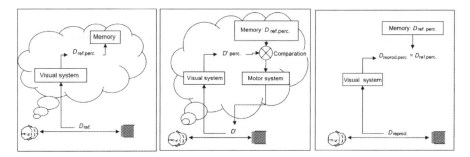

Fig. 4. Representation of the internal processes during the learning phase (left), during the adjustment phase (middle) and after the adjustment phase (right).

3. **Adjustment:** the subject is asked to reproduce the reference distance as learned in the previous phase. To set the cube position, the subject can use the grid displayed on the floor. In order to see much better the grid, the position of the object is set at a height of 0.5 m from the floor. Using the Flystick in the CAVE or the keyboard for the HMD, the subject moves the cube toward the final position. The supposed final position is validated by pushing the trigger button of the Flystick or twice on the <Space> key. The adjustment is done when the perceived distance D'_{perc} is equal to the memorized reference distance ($D_{ref.perc}$) (Fig. 4, middle). After adjusting the distance, the subject takes the reproduced distance D_{reprod} as being equal to D_{ref} ($D_{reprod} = D_{ref}$). More precisely, the perceived distance is equal to the perceived reference distance $D_{reprod.perc} = D_{ref.perc}$. As we propose to characterize the distance perception by the visual system, we get $D_{reprod.perc} = f(D_{reprod})$. Also, we have f ($D_{reprod}$) = f ($D_{ref}$), therefore, by simplifying, we have $D_{reprod} = D_{ref}$ (Fig. 4, right).

Fig. 5. Tests with the HMD (left) and the CAVE system (right).

4. **Data recording:** all the data from the subjects' performance are recorded. Figure 5 shows the two conditions as performed by the subjects.

3.4   Hypothesis

For each test, a standard deviation σ is calculated in order to establish the dispersion of the reproduced distances D_{reprod} depending on the reference distance D_{ref}. We make the following hypotheses:

1. the dispersion of the standard deviation is wider in the HMD than in the CAVE system (Fig. 6), meaning that the CAVE allows more accurate estimations than with the HMD.

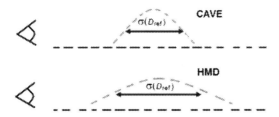

Fig. 6. Evolution of the dispersion for both the CAVE and the HMD systems.

2. the dispersion of the standard deviation as a function of the reference distance increases following a power law, for example Weber's law, with the following relation (Fig. 7):

$$\sigma\left(D_{ref}\right) = k \cdot D_{ref}^{\beta} \tag{1}$$

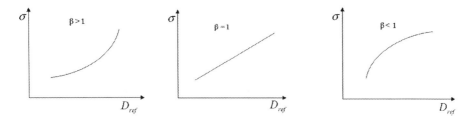

Fig. 7. Evolution of the data dispersion depending on D_{ref} for all three values of β.

4   Results

For each subject, the standard deviation σ was calculated as follows:

$$\sigma\left(D_{ref}\right) = \sqrt{\frac{1}{N}\sum_{i}\left(D_{reprod,i} - D_{ref}\right)^2} \tag{2}$$

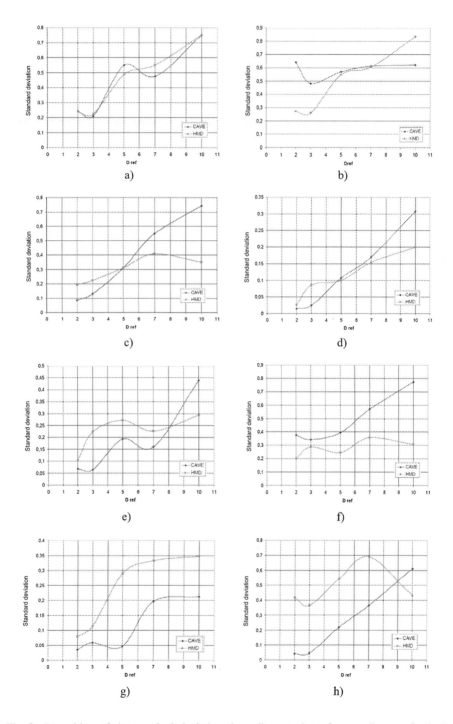

Fig. 8. Repartition of the standard deviation depending on the reference distance for both immersion systems for each subject.

where N denotes the number of tests. The reproduced distances were grouped depending on D_{ref}. On the same graph, for each subject, we plotted the results in each condition (CAVE and HMD). We can therefore find which distance indicator globally influences the accuracy of the perceived distances. Figure 8 shows the results for all eight subjects. Table 1 summarizes the analysis of the results from Fig. 8.

Table 1. Analysis from Fig. 8

Subject no.	Same precision $D_{ref,CAVE} = D_{ref,HMD}$ D_{ref} [m]	Better precision [m] CAVE $\sigma_{CAVE} < \sigma_{HMD}$	HMD $\sigma_{HMD} < \sigma_{CAVE}$	Weber law (see Fig. 7)
S1	2, [3...5], [5...7], 10	3, 7	5	NO
Obs. Fig. 8, a	The unequal repartition of distributed values shows that this subject used the visual cues in the virtual space, or a distance indicator degradation appeared (a vergence-accommodation conflict, a relative size, etc.). The curve's in the HMD mode shows that the subject did not use the virtual cues for the distances between 3...10 m			
S2	[7...10]	10	2, 3, 5, 7	NO
Obs. Fig. 8, b	For the farthest distances, the CAVE system seems the most performant; for distances up to 7 m, the HMD system is more precise. Regarding the curve's shapes, with the HMD, it can be observed an important evolution of data dispersion with the reference distance. For both systems, it can be observed a positive slope over 3 m that may be caused by some similar factors as for subject 1			
S3	5	2, 3	7, 10	CAVE $\beta > 1$ HMD $\beta < 1$
Obs. Fig. 8, c	Contrary to the previous subjects, a good perception appears when distances are small (2 to 5 m) in the CAVE. With the HMD, the situation is the opposite, all the good results appear over 5 m			
S4	[3...5]	2, 3	5, 7, 10	CAVE $\beta > 1$
Obs. Fig. 8, d	This subject faced a specific situation: for several distances the deviations are much smaller than with the other subjects. However, we observe a response bias at 3 m with the HMD. A possible explanation of this phenomenon is a degradation of the distance indicators in this zone (for example the vergence-accommodation conflict)			
S5	[7...10]	2, 3, 5, 7	10	NO
Obs. Fig. 8, e	When studying the values of dispersion with the CAVE, three zones where the subject perception was strongly affected can be drawn. An explanation can be the large number of cues in the virtual scene that the subject took involuntarily into account in the adjustment phase. Another reason can be the same degradation of the distance indicators			
S6	–	–	2, 3, 5, 7, 10	CAVE $\beta > 1$
Obs. Fig. 8, f	Unique situation: when using HMD system, the results are always better than when using the CAVE system			

(continued)

Table 1. (*continued*)

Subject no.	Same precision $D_{ref,CAVE} = D_{ref,HMD}$ D_{ref} [m]	Better precision [m]		Weber law (see Fig. 7)
		CAVE $\sigma_{CAVE} < \sigma_{HMD}$	HMD $\sigma_{HMD} < \sigma_{CAVE}$	
S7	–	2, 3, 5, 7, 10	–	HMD β > 1
Obs. Fig. 8, g	Supposing that the curve's shape for the CAVE was caused by the vergence-accommodation conflict or an increased number of cues within the virtual scene, it cannot be neglected that the curve's shape with the HMD respects the previously enounced theory, despite that the distance deviations are much higher than with the CAVE system			
S8	[7…10]	2, 3, 5, 7	10	CAVE β > 1
Obs. Fig. 8, h	The curve's shape for the CAVE corresponds to the hypothesis enounced above. This means that the dispersion changes in the same way as the distance (following Webber's law). For the farthest distances, the precision increased with the HMD			

Figure 9 presents the average standard deviations versus the reference distances. We conducted a statistical analysis to determine whether the display system had an influence on distance perception. A t-test did not return a significant difference for any of the reference distances.

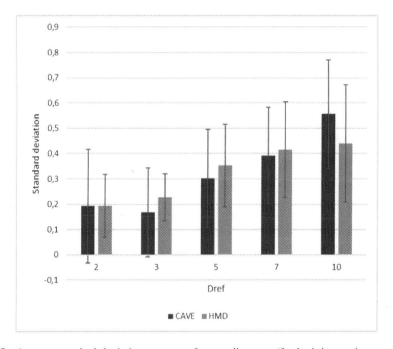

Fig. 9. Average standard deviations versus reference distances (for both immersive systems).

5   Discussion and Conclusions

Our goal was to measure the precision of the perceived distances in a 3D virtual environment displayed in different systems: a CAVE and an HMD. Past research has assumed that the deviation increases with distances. Excepting few situations, our study follows these findings.

For the distance range (5...10 m), dispersion curves respect Weber's law. The study of the standard deviation values for each distance range revealed that the dispersion increases with the increase of D_{ref} (especially for closer distances, 2...3 m).

Recalling the first hypothesis, it was estimated that the subjects were more precise in the CAVE system than with the HMD, for any reference distance. Contrary to our hypothesis, the measurement spectrum is strongly different for each system and for each subject. For the CAVE system, almost all the subjects were more precise for close distances (2...3 m and 5...7 m). On the other hand, all the good results for the HMD are found over 7 m, though it was not significantly different.

A possible explanation for incorrect appreciations in the CAVE system can be the shape, accuracy, dimensions and resolution of all the virtual cues designed in the virtual space. In the close distances case, the subjects could distinguish the graphical elements of the cues, and thus their task was more precise. These observations were mentioned by almost all subjects in their final questionnaire. As a second hypothesis, we supposed that the deviations would increase following a power law, for example Weber's law (the subjective discrimination threshold of a stimulus depends linearly on its intensity). Here, in some cases, Weber's law was not confirmed. An important reason can be a degradation in the distance indicators (vergence-accommodation conflict, relative size, etc.) or an excessive density of some indicators [2]. Finally, it must be mentioned that each subject has a personal strategy to pass the experiment. Thus, to improve the results, as a future work, a much higher number of subjects should be part of the experiment.

References

1. Bruder, G., Argelaguet, F., Olivier, A.H., Lcuyer, A.: CAVE size matters: effects of screen distance and parallax on distance estimation in large immersive display setups. Presence Teleoperators Virtual Environ. **25**(1), 1–16 (2016). https://doi.org/10.1162/PRES_a_00241

2. Cutting, J.E., Vishton, P.M.: Perceiving layout and knowing distances: the integration, relative potency, and contextual use of different information about depth. In: Perception of Space and Motion, pp. 69–117 (1995). https://doi.org/10.1016/B978-012240530-3/50005-5

3. Dorado, J.L., Figueroa, P., Chardonnet, J.R., Merienne, F., Hernandez, T.: Comparing VR environments for seat selection in an opera theater. In: IEEE Symposium on 3D User Interfaces (3DUI), pp. 221–222 (2017). https://doi.org/10.1109/3DUI.2017.7893351

4. Fukusima, S.S., Loomis, J.M., Da Silva, J.A.: Visual perception of egocentric distance as assessed by triangulation. J. Exp. Psychol. Hum. Percept. Perform. **23**(1), 86–100 (1997). https://doi.org/10.1037/0096-1523.23.1.86

5. Gardner, P., Mon-Williams, M.: Vertical gaze angle: absolute height-in-scene information for the programming of prehension. Exp. Brain Res. **136**(3), 379–385 (2001). https://doi.org/10.1007/s002210000590

6. Grechkin, T.Y., Nguyen, T.D., Plumert, J.M., Cremer, J.F., Kearney, J.K.: How does presentation method and measurement protocol affect distance estimation in real and virtual environments? ACM Trans. Appl. Percept. 7(4), 26:1–26:18 (2010). https://doi.org/10.1145/1823738.1823744

7. Howard, J.P., Rogers, B.J.: Stereoacuity. In: Seeing in Depth. University of Toronto Press (2002)

8. Huckauf, A.: Virtual and real visual depth. In: APGV 2005 Proceedings of the 2nd Symposium on Applied Perception in Graphics and Visualization, p. 172 (2005). https://doi.org/10.1145/1080402.1080456

9. Iachini, T., Logie, R.: The role of perspective in locating position in a real world, unfamiliar environment. Appl. Cogn. Psychol. 17, 715–732 (2003). https://doi.org/10.1002/acp.904

10. Interrante, V., Anderson, L., Ries, B.: Distance perception in immersive virtual environments, revisited. In: Proceedings of the IEEE Conference on Virtual Reality, pp. 3–10 (2006). https://doi.org/10.1109/VR.2006.52

11. Kelly, J.W., Cherep, L.A., Siegel, Z.D.: Perceived space in the HTC Vive. ACM Trans. Appl. Percept. 15(1), 1–16 (2017). https://doi.org/10.1145/3106155

12. Knapp, J.M., Loomis, J.M.: Limited field of view of head-mounted displays is not the cause of distance underestimation in virtual environments. Presence Teleoperators Virtual Environ. 13, 572–577 (2004). https://doi.org/10.1162/1054746042545238

13. Kuhl, S., Thompson, T., Creem-Regehr, S.: HMD calibration and its effects on distance judgments. ACM Trans. Appl. Percept. 6(3) (2009). https://doi.org/10.1145/1577755.1577762

14. Loomis, J.M., Knapp, J.M.: Visual perception of egocentric distance in real and virtual environments. In: Virtual and Adaptive Environments, pp. 21–46 (2003)

15. Marsh, W.E., Chardonnet, J.-R., Merienne, F.: Virtual distance estimation in a CAVE. In: Freksa, C., Nebel, B., Hegarty, M., Barkowsky, T. (eds.) Spatial Cognition 2014. LNCS (LNAI), vol. 8684, pp. 354–369. Springer, Cham (2014). https://doi.org/10.1007/978-3-319-11215-2_25

16. Meng, J., Rieser, J., Bodenheimer, B.: Distance estimation in virtual environments using bisection. In: APGV 2006 Proceedings of the 3rd Symposium on Applied Perception in Graphics and Visualization, p. 146 (2006). https://doi.org/10.1145/1140491.1140523

17. Messing, R., Durgin, F.: Distance perception and the visual horizon in head mounted displays. ACM Trans. Appl. Percept. 2(3), 234–250 (2005). https://doi.org/10.1145/1077399.1077403

18. Mohler, B., Bülthoff, H., Thompson, W., Creem-Regehr, S.: A full-body avatar improves egocentric distance judgments in an immersive virtual environment. In: APGV 2008 Proceedings of the 5th Symposium on Applied Perception in Graphics and Visualization, p. 194 (2008). https://doi.org/10.1145/1394281.1394323

19. Ooi, T.L., Wu, B., He, Z.J.: Distance determined by the angular declination below the horizon. Nature 414, 197–200 (2001). https://doi.org/10.1038/35102562

20. Piryankova, I.V., de la Rosa, S., Kloos, U., Bülthoff, H.H., Mohler, B.J.: Egocentric distance perception in large screen immersive displays. Displays 34(2), 153–164 (2013). https://doi.org/10.1016/j.displa.2013.01.001

21. Plumert, J., Kearney, J., Cremer, J.: Distance perception in real and virtual environments. In: APGV 2004 Proceedings of the 1st Symposium on Applied Perception in Graphics and Visualization, pp. 27–34 (2004). https://doi.org/10.1145/1012551.1012557

22. Renner, R.S., Velichkovsky, B.M., Helmert, J.R.: The perception of egocentric distances in virtual environments - a review. ACM Comput. Surv. 46(2), 23:1–23:40 (2013). https://doi.org/10.1145/2543581.2543590

23. Ries, B., Interrante, V., Anderson, L., Lindquist, J.: Presence, rather than prior exposure, is the more strongly indicated factor in the accurate perception of egocentric distances in real world co-located immersive virtual environments. In: APGV 2006 Proceedings of the 3rd Symposium on Applied Perception in Graphics and Visualization, p. 157 (2006). https://doi.org/10.1145/1140491.1140534
24. Thompson, W.B., Willemsen, P., Gooch, A.A., Creem-Regehr, S.H., Loomis, J.M., Beall, A.C.: Does the quality of the computer graphics matter when judging distances in visually immersive environments? Presence Teleoperators Virtual Environ. **13**(5), 560–571 (2004). https://doi.org/10.1162/1054746042545292
25. Willemsen, P., Colton, P., Creem-Regehr, S., Thompson, W.: The effects of head mounted display mechanics on distance judgments in virtual environments. In: APGV 2004 Proceedings of the 1st Symposium on Applied Perception in Graphics and Visualization, pp. 35–38 (2004). https://doi.org/10.1145/1012551.1012558
26. Willemsen, P., Gooch, A.: Perceived egocentric distances in real, image-based, and traditional virtual environments. In: Proceedings of the IEEE Virtual Reality Conference 2002, p. 275 (2002). https://doi.org/10.1109/VR.2002.996536
27. Witmer, B.G., Kline, P.B.: Judging perceived and traversed distance in virtual environments. Presence Teleoperators Virtual Environ. **7**(2), 144–167 (1998). https://doi.org/10.1162/105474698565640
28. Witmer, B.G., Sadowski, W.: Nonvisually guided locomotion to a previously viewed target in real and virtual environments. Hum. Factors **40**(3), 478–488 (1998). https://doi.org/10.1518/001872098779591340
29. Wu, B., Ooi, T., He, Z.: Perceiving distance accurately by a directional process of integrating ground information. Nature **428**, 73–77 (2004). https://doi.org/10.1038/nature02350
30. Yang, U., Kim, N.G., Kim, K.H.: Perception adjustment for egocentric moving distance between real space and virtual space with see-closed-type HMD. In: SIGGRAPH Asia 2017, pp. 23:1–23:2 (2017). https://doi.org/10.1145/3145690.3145721

e-Tourism: Governmental Planning and Management Mechanism

Aldrin G. Acosta$^{(\boxtimes)}$, Víctor H. Andaluz$^{(\boxtimes)}$, Jessica S. Ortiz$^{(\boxtimes)}$,
Franklin M. Silva$^{(\boxtimes)}$, Julio C. Tapia$^{(\boxtimes)}$, Christian P. Carvajal$^{(\boxtimes)}$,
and Washington X. Quevedo$^{(\boxtimes)}$

Universidad de las Fuerzas Armadas ESPE, Sangolquí, Ecuador
{agacosta,vhandaluz1,jsortiz4,fmsilva,jctapia3,
wjquevedo}@espe.edu.ec, chriss2592@hotmail.com

Abstract. This article proposes the development of a virtual application as a planning and government management tool, focused on the digitization of objects, monuments-buildings, and real environments using 2D and 3D virtualization techniques. The application considers two modes of use: PLANNER for use by managers and planners of offices and technical units linked to tourism; and TOURIST created for travelers, hikers or tourists in general. The first allows recreating new scenes incorporating objects that make it attractive to the tourist recourse, and thus achieve a projected image of the vision of development proposed by the planner; and the second designed to recreate touristic environments and program circuits, provoking a tourist avatar through HTC VIVE, Oculus Rift and GearVR Headsets to make the application available to the largest market segment of virtual reality viewers. In addition, the app allows the interaction of several users in the same scenario to exchange information and experiences of the place.

Keywords: Audiovisual stimulation · Wearable devices · Virtual reality
Unity3D

1 Introduction

The universality of the use of Information and Communication Technologies (ICT) has allowed countries to develop their interconnection capacity, increasingly effective in times and distances in order to achieve speed of communication, information transfer and technological evolution. Through the use of the internet and other computer networks, it has been possible to generate greater and better communication flows in society, spreading, virtual communities that are formed, organized and promoted through online services, which according to Howard Rheinhold, in his book "The virtual community", are a society without borders, which are structured by social and relational aggregations in cyberspace around common interests, forming computer networks of communication [1–5].

The incorporation of technology and internet services in the tourism business have meant the characterization of e-Tourism, defined as a virtual society of travel agents and tourism managers that, through the use of ICTs, supported by the use of Internet

© Springer International Publishing AG, part of Springer Nature 2018
L. T. De Paolis and P. Bourdot (Eds.): AVR 2018, LNCS 10850, pp. 162–170, 2018.
https://doi.org/10.1007/978-3-319-95270-3_11

and other networks, mainly social, allow interactions in multiple destinations and users, often in real time, to show the city's attractions or attractions as well as all the services that make up the tourist offer of the destination. Tourism destinations today must provide technological tools capable of offering interactive and dynamic information, especially when the evolution of mobile devices has caused a change in the way in which tourists interact and obtain information [6–9].

This reality leads to projecting new ways of planning and activating a tourist destination, since the intensive and widespread use of ICTs are increasingly necessary in the management of a company and destination. Virtual Reality (VR) and Augmented Reality (AR) begins to appear as an alternative technology for tourism because it allows the interaction of the subject with the physical and real world around super-virtual objects. With VR you can recreate natural environments and show cultural manifestations of a destination, expanding the real world scene, projecting its history, culture and showing complementary information through the RA; achieving the vir-tualization of spaces to promote tourism, according to the vision of the tourism man-ager and planner, as well as the characteristics of the tourist [10–12].

For this reason, the VR and AR is taking part in the actions and dynamics of the tourist destinations of a country, even more so when several cities are already incor-porating digital information in the attraction sites so that they serve as support for the tourist during their journey and visit. This current situation means that tourism planning requires technological systems and tools that help to project tourist destinations and promote the characteristics of attraction and recreation of a city, region or country, so that through these projected environments make decisions related to the management of the destination; In addition, nowadays, technological services and facilities must be provided to help carry out activities at the visit site and give support to tourists during their stay [13, 14].

Therefore, this research proposes the development of a VR/AR APP for the vir-tualization of spaces with attraction and projection towards tourism, to be used in the planning and management of destination cities and natural areas for tourist visits. These trends pose a challenge: the incorporation of ICT in the planning and management processes of a tourist destination as well as in the design of products related to the VR and AR: Tourist Destinations 3.0 that will be deployed through a generated system by a computer and a technological application of multiple users and destinations, with the purpose of facilitating the design and formulation of new projects as part of the planning and management processes of a tourism space. In addition to promoting tourism products by immersing the tourist in fully recreated spaces of a destination, creating a "tourist avatar" with sensations and surrounding experiences around virtual scenes and computer applications [15–17].

This article is divided into 4 Sections: 1. Introduction, where ICTs are contextu-alized and the e-tourism approach, presenting the research problem; 2. Description of the System, which describes the operation of the application; 3. Results, where the experimental performance of the VR application oriented to the virtualization of tourist environments is presented; and 4. Conclusions of the investigation.

2 System Description

In the tourism industry, the idea of visiting destinations through virtual worlds is being promoted, where tourists are brought closer to the reality of their visit, by combining virtual information with real data, provoking an innovative experience with your mobile device; with which, a competitive advantage is generated, by managing your time and your visit program according to your needs and desires, moving away from the concept handled until today by tourist packages, since the use of ICT in tourism is leading to the trips are more individualized with more personalized experiences.

For this reason, this article refers to the development of an application in VR oriented to management of the tourist space as well as an aid for the tourist in the programming of circuits and travel itineraries. This section describes the operation structure of the VR application, using blocks: graphic composition SCENE VR, behavior coding of the SCRIPTS app and INPUTS/OUTPUT hardware, according to the graphic reference indicated in Fig. 1.

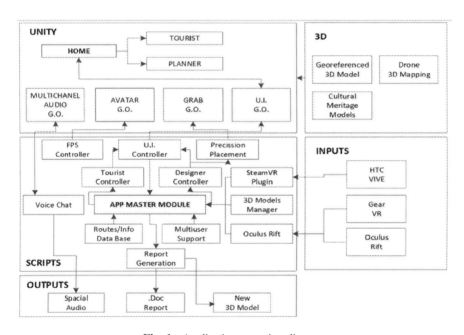

Fig. 1. Application operating diagram

The virtual development is carried out in the SCENE VR block, where the resources obtained in the 3D resources block are located and which are represented by generic blocks called Game Objects (G.O.). The main scenes are generated from a HOME module from which two components of execution and use of the application are deployed: PLANNER and TOURIST, which will allow to observe virtualized 3D scenes of the site and tourist resources. The resources used are grouped into generic G.O. modules: MULTICHANEL AUDIO, AVATAR, GRAB, UI, which allow the user different ways of interacting with the environment such as recreating sound effects from the real world, manipulating objects through a virtual avatar, navigating by the available options of each environment, etc.

The programming of the interaction of the VR application is implemented in the control modules and execution of activities in the SCRIPTS block. The main module of the blocks is the Master Module app, which manages the resources and functions of the application through auxiliary modules that perform specific tasks. The SteamVR Plugin and Oculus Library modules manage the data generated by the user using HTC VIVE, Oculus Rift and GearVR devices. The behavior of each scene is given by the modules of Tourist and Designer Controller, the first one allows recreating visitor environments and programming tourist circuits through the consumption of information from the Routes/InfoDataBase module; and the second module modifies the virtualized environment by incorporating 3D objects into the scene, the result of editing the scene is stored in the Report Generator module.

The user is represented in the virtual environment by means of a customized avatar to navigate through the FPS Controller module; interact/visualize graphic and audible information through the module U.I. Controller; Place objects from 3D Models Manager to the environment that can be modified using the Precision Placement module, as appropriate for the chosen scene. Multiuser and Voice Chat modules interact with each other to create social rooms as a meeting point for several users to interact with the environment, and with each other. The modules share data of transform, animation and voice of each client with the host of the system in real time.

In the INPUTS block you can find the devices to access the virtual reality environments, each device has its advantages in each scene presented in the following way: HTC VIVE and Oculus Rift are focused on the Planner scene due to their large workspace and the fine tracking of the controls, while GearVR is ideal for the Tourist scene due to the mobility and ease of acquisition of the device that matches the segment of users you want to reach. Finally, in the OUTPUTS block, the spatial audio module is shown as a response to the user's interaction with other users and the environment, a textual response module and its graphic representation of the changes made to the environment through the 3D New Model.

3   Experimental Results

This section presents the experimental performance of the application of VR oriented to the virtualization of environments and tourist attractions of a city in order to be used as a tool for planning digital cities and government management, specifically the offices and units responsible for the actions of tourism in a city, region and country. For the present test of application and visualization of results, some tourist attraction sites of the city of Baños de Agua Santa in the Province of Tungurahua, a Priority Destination for the development of tourism in Ecuador, have been digitized.

In the technical section, the virtual reality headset is used: HTC VIVE & Oculus Rift (tethered) and GearVR (mobile). The gathering of information for the construction, projection and recreation of virtual tourist environments is done with the inventories of tourist attractions in the country, because they constitute an official register with specific information that allow the selection of attractiveness based on their hierarchy (importance of visit), category, type and subtype. Information that feeds the database of the present application. When the app is run for the first time, a welcome screen is displayed and it lands on a home screen where you can see the usage modes: Tourist and Planner, Fig. 2.

Fig. 2. Screenshot of the app developed

Both to enter the Tourist and Planner mode the user is indicated that it is necessary to log in by filling out a basic information form to start the session in the multi-user server, see Fig. 3.

By choosing the Tourist mode the user can navigate within the reconstructed 3D environment of the tourist place by means of a preloaded touristic circuit. The circuit shows the user the stops of the so-called "The route of the waterfalls", in which each point of interest shows information (directions, signage of trails), animations and sounds (waterfalls, the wind blowing through the branches of the trees, local fauna, etc.). The lighting and effects of the environment are affected by the current time of the tourist place and its weather forecast in real time. The conjunction of these variables makes the visit become a unique and different experience in each execution (dynamic environment) see Fig. 4.

Immediately the user is at the starting point of the tourist circuit. An information balloon serves as a guide for the user throughout the tour (as a tutorial) to avoid disorientation and ignorance of the next step to follow, see Fig. 5. If the user wishes, he can deactivate the balloon of indications and perform an autonomous tour through the circuit.

While the user is doing the tour, he can relate to other tourists who are using the app in real time by using gestures with the headset controllers (HTC VIVE and GearVR).

Fig. 3. Login form data

a) Information and signaling   b) Waterfalls and fauna of the place

c) Environmental lighting   d) Weather effects

Fig. 4. Graphics functionalities of the tourist scene

The system also allows to listen and speak to all the users who are near the sender of the message and see the nickname and origin of each connected tourist. See Fig. 6.

The Planner mode allows the user to edit the surface-graphic features of the digitized environment. Inside the virtual reality environment, the user has tools to add:

Fig. 5. Information balloon in the tourist scene

Fig. 6. Multi-user view in the tourist mode

information, external 3D models, animations and new touristic circuits, see Fig. 7. These tools are available from the user interface and accessed through the device's Controllers.

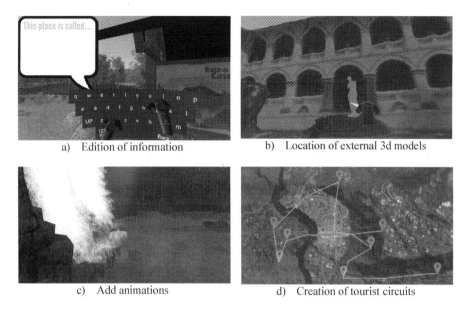

a)   Edition of information   b)   Location of external 3d models

c)   Add animations   d)   Creation of tourist circuits

Fig. 7. Planner mode editing tools

4   Conclusions

In this article, a virtual reality application was developed in order to manage and plan tourist destinations; the development of the application considers general virtual environments that allow the interaction and immersion of multiple users either to obtain tourist information and formulate new projects as part of the planning and management processes of a tourist area. The results presented show the correct performance of the developed application, in which multiple users can interact with each other, virtual environment and the tools to edit it.

Acknowledgements. The authors would like to thanks to the Corporación Ecuatoriana para el Desarrollo de la Investigación y Academia – CEDIA for the financing given to research, development, and innovation, through the Grupos de Trabajo, GT, especially to the GT-eTURISMO; also to Universidad de las Fuerzas Armadas ESPE, Universidad Técnica de Ambato, Escuela Superior Politécnica de Chimborazo, Universidad Nacional de Chimborazo, and Grupo de Investigación en Automatización, Robótica y Sistemas Inteligentes, GI-ARSI, for the support to develop this work.

References

1. Law, R., Buhalis, D., Cobanoglu, C.: Progress on information and communication technologies in hospitality and tourism. Int. J. Contemp. Hospitality Manag. **26**(5), 727–750 (2016)
2. Wang, X., Li, X.R., Zhen, F., Zhang, J.: How smart is your tourist attraction? Measuring tourist preferences of smart tourism attractions via a FCEM-AHP and IPA approach. Tour. Manag. **54**, 309–320 (2016)
3. Guerra, J.P., Pinto, M.M., Beato, C.: Virtual reality-shows a new vision for tourism and heritage. Eur. Sci. J. ESJ, **11**(9) (2015)
4. Leiva, J.L., Guevara, A., Rossi, C., Aguayo, A.: Augmented reality and group recommendation systems: a new perspective on tourism destination systems (2014)
5. Requena, J.V., Sellens, J.T., Masllorens, J.L., Tamajón, L.G.: Information and communication technologies, innovation and tourism: towards the networked company (2007)
6. Castro, J.C., et al.: Virtual reality on e-Tourism. In: Kim, K.J., Kim, H., Baek, N. (eds.) ICITS 2017. LNEE, vol. 450, pp. 86–97. Springer, Singapore (2018). https://doi.org/10.1007/978-981-10-6454-8_13
7. Acosta, A., et al.: Tourism marketing through virtual environment experience. In: International Conference on Education Technology and Computers, pp. 262–267 (2018)
8. Ukpabi, D.C., Karjaluoto, H.: Consumers' acceptance of information and communications technology in tourism: a review. Telematics Inform. **34**(5), 618–644 (2017)
9. Gretzel, U., Sigala, M., Xiang, Z., Koo, C.: Smart tourism: foundations and developments. Electron. Markets **25**(3), 179–188 (2015)
10. Huang, Y.C., Backman, K.F., Backman, S.J., Chang, L.L.: Exploring the implications of virtual reality technology in tourism marketing: an integrated research framework. Int. J. Tourism Res. **18**(2), 116–128 (2016)
11. Sorrentino, F., Spano, L.D., Scateni, R.: Superavatar children and mobile tourist guides become friends using superpowered avatars. In: Interactive Mobile Communication Technologies and Learning (IMCL), pp. 222–226 (2015)
12. Geszten, D., Hámornik, B.P., Hercegfi, K.: User experience in a collaborative 3D virtual environment: a framework for analyzing user interviews. In: IEEE International, pp. 207–210 (2015)
13. Jung, T., tom Dieck, M.C., Lee, H., Chung, N.: Effects of virtual reality and augmented reality on visitor experiences in museum. In: Information and Communication Technologies in Tourism 2016, pp. 621–635 (2016)
14. McGrath, J.L., Taekman, J.M., Dev, P., Danforth, D.R., Mohan, D., Kman, N., Bond, W.F.: Using virtual reality simulation environments to assess competence for emergency medicine learners. Acad. Emerg. Med. **25**(2), 186–195 (2018)
15. Stevens, J.A., Kincaid, J.P.: The relationship between presence and performance in virtual simulation training. Open J. Model. Simul. **3**(2), 41 (2015)
16. Quevedo, W.X., Sánchez, J.S., Arteaga, O., Álvarez, M., Zambrano, V.D., Sánchez, C.R., Andaluz, V.H.: Virtual reality system for training in automotive mechanics. In: International Conference on Augmented Reality, Virtual Reality and Computer Graphics, pp. 185–198 (2017)
17. Ortiz, J.S., et al.: Realism in audiovisual stimuli for phobias treatments through virtual environments. In: De Paolis, L.T., Bourdot, P., Mongelli, A. (eds.) AVR 2017. LNCS, vol. 10325, pp. 188–201. Springer, Cham (2017). https://doi.org/10.1007/978-3-319-60928-7_16

Geolocation and Counting of People with Aerial Thermal Imaging for Rescue Purposes

Córdova C. Andrea[1,5], Jiménez Q. Byron[1], Pardo I. Jorge[2,4],
Toalombo CH. Inti[1], and Wilbert G. Aguilar[3,6(✉)]

[1] DEM, Universidad de las Fuerzas Armadas ESPE, Latacunga, Ecuador
[2] UGT, Universidad de las Fuerzas Armadas ESPE, Latacunga, Ecuador
japardo@espe.edu.ec
[3] CICTE Research Center, Universidad de las Fuerzas Armadas ESPE,
Sangolquí, Ecuador
wgaguilar@espe.edu.ec
[4] Facultad de Ingeniería, Pontificia Universidad Católica del Ecuador,
Quito, Ecuador
[5] Aerospace Engineering Department, The Pennsylvania State University,
State College, PA, USA
[6] GREC Research Group, Universitat Politècnica de Catalunya,
Barcelona, Spain

Abstract. Thermography has become more frequently used in rescue operations when used together with flight technologies such as unmanned aerial vehicles (UAVs). This is due to its non-invasive and powerful supervision characteristics in the spectrum range not perceivable for the human eye or for a standard camera. This paper presents a developed system based on the synergy of a UAV and a counting and geolocation algorithm that detects people with aerial shots in areas of difficult access. The system integrates a thermal camera to a UAV, thus being useful in different scenarios such as floods, fires or wooded areas. For this purpose, the UAV navigation paths are configured from an earth station using a telemetry-specific software. Thermal images will be recorded during the mission at a height determined by the operator, which will later be processed to filter, discriminate, count and geolocalize people at risk. The processing of the images is done by means of artificial vision tools combined with Artificial Neural Networks (ANN).

Keywords: Geolocation · ANN · Telemetry · Thermography
UAVs

1 Introduction

The use of thermal imagery in military and industrial applications has awaken a growing interest in the research community, who have been experimenting with its uses in search and rescue applications. While image processing with artificial vision tools in the range of visible light has been studied for decades and recently combined with

© Springer International Publishing AG, part of Springer Nature 2018
L. T. De Paolis and P. Bourdot (Eds.): AVR 2018, LNCS 10850, pp. 171–182, 2018.
https://doi.org/10.1007/978-3-319-95270-3_12

machine learning techniques for the visual detection of objects with extremely fast image processing, research in the field of methodologies for developed applications in thermal imagery is becoming more popular [1, 6]. Likewise, the trend in recent years has been the development of flight technologies such as UAVs, and similarly to thermography, its initial applications were merely military. The benefits provided by aerial vehicles have enabled researchers to use these technological devices in various applications. Due to advances in the autonomous performance of the UAV, the intervention of an operator has been reduced and has resulted in these devices with some degree of intelligence being used in a wide range of assignments considered dangerous or difficult to perform by human beings [1]. This includes Search and Rescue (SAR) applications, which involve identifying and extracting information of people in emergencies caused by natural disasters.

The analysis of the thermal images is done on board the air vehicle, greatly reducing the need for a fast and stable communication with the earth station and avoiding delays in the decision-making process. The system is able to track several objects simultaneously, where the user has direct control over the types of objects that wants to follow [2]. The technique presented detects humans at a speed of 25 Hz, first analyzing the thermal image to find human temperature silhouettes and then using the regions corresponding to the color of the silhouette to classify human bodies. In addition, the system detects human positions, which are geolocalized to then build a map with points of interest [3].

SHERPA project has created collaborative robots to help in tasks of rescuing people in hostile environments or in emergencies in the Italian Alps. They work with small-scale airplanes, drones and autonomous small helicopters called "Hawks", they are used to transport technical materials like scanners and thermal cameras, but also food and water. The project has the advantage of not interrupting search activities during the night or when the visibility is limited. The operator establishes the mission, delimits the area of interest and with the push of a button gets the plans by scanning the area for postprocessing [4].

The Cotopaxi volcano is considered one of the most dangerous volcanoes in Ecuador. According to the Geophysical Institute (IG) of the National Polytechnic School, a research center in Ecuador for the diagnosis and monitoring of seismic and volcanic hazards, there have been five major eruptions since its activation in 1532 affecting more than 300,000 people [5]. The eventual reactivations of the Cotopaxi volcano have prompted efforts to develop a prototype of SAR; the first in Ecuador, of low cost that helps rescue agencies to optimize resources, in search missions and locating people in areas of difficult to access [5].

The paper is organized as follows. Firstly, the selection of components such as the UAV and the Thermal Camera is done. Next, the development of the SAR system is described, which integrates the configuration of the autonomous trajectories of the UAV, the algorithm designed that allows to process thermal images, sampling for ANN training, counting and geolocation. Finally, the conclusion of the paper analyzes and evaluates the system performance, based on collected data from several flight tests.

2   Devices Selection

2.1   Thermal Camera

For our project it is necessary to acquire aerial thermal images, obtained with the help of a thermal camera without radiometric functions because in this particular case these functions are not relevant. The technical characteristics of three thermal cameras have been analyzed: the Zenmuse XT, Workswell Wiris, and Flir Vue. The three cameras share similar functionalities varying slightly in their characteristics. The main difference is that the first two cameras have radiometric functions allowing to make thermal point measurements of the image in the range of −40 °C to 1500 °C and the third does not have such functions. Therefore, the Flir Vue Pro thermal camera was selected, which has the necessary functionalities to be used in a SAR. Its technical characteristics are described in Table 1.

Table 1.   Technical characteristics of thermal camera.

Parameter	Value
Sensor	Uncooled VOx Microbolometer
Sensor Resolution	640 × 512, 336 × 256
Spectral Band	7.5–13.5 um
Frame Rates	7.5 Hz
Size	63 mm × 44.4 mm × 44.4 mm
Weight	92.1–113.4 g
Image Optimization for sUAS	Yes
Color Palettes	Yes-Adjustable Via PWM
Input Voltage	4.8–6.0 VDC
Operating Temperature Range	−20 °C to +50 °C
Operative Altitude	+12000 m
Analog Video Output	Yes

2.2   UAV

The most suitable device for the development of the project is the drone Phantom 3 Professional of the DJI brand, this is considered as the best option as it has optimal characteristics such as: Safety, Useful Load, Stability, Maximum Distance, Flight Modes.

One of the most important features that the Phantom 3 Pro has is flight safety, which proves a RETURN TO HOME option automatically, in case of an anomaly during the flight. It is also proven that the payload that can lift with great stability can be up to 2.5 lbs according to evidence gathered in the investigation. Through its internal sensors, its GPS system and positioning by vision allows a stability at each flight point that is located. Other important features are the maximum distance which has a range of up to 5 km, as well as a maximum speed of 16 m/s. In addition, it has several intelligent flight modes which are defined in its DJI GO application, which are: Follow Me, Course Lock, Waypoints, Home Lock, Point Of Interest.

3 System

The system follows the next sequence, it consists in identifying, filtering, counting and geolocating people by processing images obtained with a thermal camera mounted on a UAV as is described in the following image (Fig. 1).

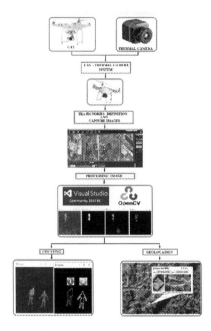

Fig. 1. SAR system diagram

3.1 Autonomous Trajectories

The DJI GS "Ground Station" Pro application is used for the definition of trajectories, which allows an autonomous flight of the UAV without the need of operating it by radio control, allowing us to load the Phantom 3 Pro trajectories defined by waypoints, delimiting in this way the area of search or interest. In addition, the application shows other flight characteristics such as takeoff parameters, actions to be taken at each point, speed, which according to tests performed for the acquisition of suitable images will be 2 m/s and finally return home or starting point.

The application allows to have programmed control of the UAV, it calculates and presents functions such as total distance traveled, flight time, and GPS coordinates during the mission. In addition, it divides the terrain with a sweep which allows to cover the entire search area, taking a parallel path or focus on a point of interest according to its configuration.

3.2   Image Acquisition

With the thermal camera mounted on the Phantom3 and with defined trajectories, several flyovers were carried out over areas of interest at a height of 20 m above the ground. The camera is set to recording mode and one of the nine palettes available in the camera is selected, for our project the GreenHot and IronBow palettes are used. Additionally the frames are configured to 10 fps and the scene where it is going to work in this particular case is outdoors.

During the flight the camera is able to capture images of the possible victims which are of our interest, but also captures any type of body that radiates heat, such as animals, automobiles, fire, etc. Once the UAV finishes its route returns to the ground station where information is extracted from the memory card to a computer.

3.3   Segmentation

Segmentation consists in distinguishing and separating each of the objects present in the scene and filtering only the objects of interest. In the particular case of this project, it is necessary to separate thermal silhouettes of people from the background of the image. Since an image sequence is to be processed, that is to say a video, the histogram will be different in each frame because the UAV records different scenes during its course. In Fig. 2(a) and (b) thermal captures of a person with their respective histogram are observed using the GreenHot palette where the variation of intensities of the pixels can be seen. It should be noted that the same thing happens when using the IronBow palette.

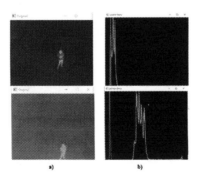

a)   b)

Fig. 2. (a) Thermal captures, (b) Histograms (Color figure online)

To facilitate segmentation, the image with color is converted to gray levels. This technique consists in calculating the average of each intensity for the matrices of the colors Red (R), Green (G) and Blue (B). The equation that rules this transformation is as follows.

$$I = Round\left\{\frac{1}{3}(R + G + B)\right\} \tag{1}$$

Later binarization is used as segmentation technique specifically the Otsu method, which is based on the variation of intensity between the pixels of the object of interest and the pixels of the background, assuming that the image contains two classes of pixels. The Otsu method calculates the optimal threshold that minimizes the intra-class variance and maximizes the inter-class variance automatically, so it does not need supervision. According to research by J. Kittler and J. Illingworth the ruling equations of the Otsu method are described below [6].

The process starts from a grayscale image with N pixels and L possible different levels.

$$p_i = f_i/N \tag{2}$$

Where f_i is the repetition frequency of the ith gray level with $i = 1, 2, \ldots, L$.

In the case of thresholding in two levels, or also called binarization, the pixels are divided into two classes, $c_1 [1, 2, \ldots, t]$ and $c_2 [t+1, \ldots, L]$. Where the probability distribution of gray levels for the two classes is as follows.

$$c_1 = \frac{p_1}{\omega_1(t)}, \ldots, \frac{p_t}{\omega_1(t)} \tag{3}$$

$$c_2 = \frac{p_{t+1}}{\omega_1(t)}, \frac{p_{t+2}}{\omega_2(t)}, \ldots, \frac{p_L}{\omega_2(t)} \tag{4}$$

Where

$$\omega_1(t) = \sum_{i=1}^{t} p_i \quad \& \quad \omega_2(t) = \sum_{i=t+1}^{L} p_i \tag{5}$$

The average for class c_1 and class c_2 is

$$u_1 = \sum_{i=1}^{t} \frac{iP_i}{\omega_1(t)} \quad \& \quad u_2 = \sum_{i=t+1}^{L} \frac{iP_i}{\omega_2(t)} \tag{6}$$

If is u_T the average intensity of the whole image, it is shown that

$$\omega_1.u_1 + \omega_2.u_2 = u_T \quad \omega_1 + \omega_2 = 1 \tag{7}$$

Using discriminant analysis Otsu defines the variance between two classes of a threshold image as follows.

$$\sigma_B^2 = \omega_1(u_1 - u_T)^2 + \omega_2(u_2 - u_T)^2 \tag{8}$$

For two level thresholding, the optimal threshold t* is chosen so that σ_B^2 will be maximum, this is

$$t^* = Max_t\{\sigma_B^2(t)\} \quad 1 \leq t \leq L \tag{9}$$

Considering that thermal images have a clear difference between the objects to be extracted or filtered from the background of the scene, the Otsu method described mathematically is very useful for our purpose because it has a good response in situations of the real world. After applying the segmentation to the infrared image, the following results are obtained, with the IronBow palettes (Fig. 2(a) and (b)) and GreenHot (Fig. 3(a) and (b)).

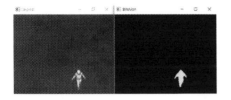 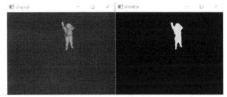

Fig. 3. (a) Thermal image, (b) Segmented image

Fig. 4. (a) Thermal image, (b) Segmented image

3.4 Sampling

After segmentation of the objects of interest, it is required to obtain binary samples of all types of bodies such as: human, animal, automotive, or any other object that radiates heat. Samples of people are stored as positive samples and anybody other than a person is saved as a negative sample. Negative and positive samples are required because ANN needs to learn which silhouette corresponds to a person and which does not (Fig. 4).

To obtain the samples an algorithm was developed that consists of detecting contours of the silhouettes of the bodies. From the silhouettes found by the program, areas of all contours are calculated and the largest area is selected. Lastly, a Region of Interest (ROI) is created from the biggest area and only that region is clipped to save the sample to the computer's hard disk.

3.5 ANN Structure

The ANN select for this project is a multilayer perceptron whit retro propagation because this network is ideal for real world situations and the recognition is faster. Thus, the model was conformed by an input layer where a binary image of 32 × 32 pixels is received, next the net has eight hidden layers where the input information is processed and finally has an output layer which will give the final result of whether or not it is a person. The activation function of the perceptron is the standard sigmoid symmetric function and the activation values range from −1 to 1. Based on experimental evidence in this particular case the probability of prediction returned by network has been set at 0.5, if the values exceed this value the silhouette is identified as person otherwise not. The resulting model of the ANN is showing in Fig. 5.

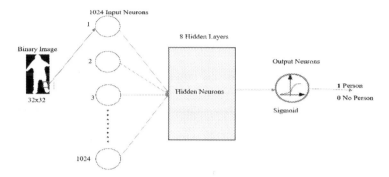

Fig. 5. Artificial Neuronal Network structure

3.6   ANN Learning or Training

The process of training or learning is completely analogous to teaching something to a child the algorithm has to be taught what to learn and what not, therefore there has to be a set of training pairs, enter them into the network and wait for the answer, if the answer is not correct you must perform the training again and so on until you achieve the desired result, the process of performing the training several times is called the period [1].

Previous to ANN training, samples must be prepared for which two algorithms are used. The first algorithm allows to give the mirror effect to all the images to obtain a total of 3288 positive samples from 1664 original samples, the same procedure is done with the negative samples, obtaining a total of 300.

The other algorithm allows to resize the sample images of any size to a size of 32×32 pixels, resulting in images with a total of 1024 pixels, this is done in order to have a fixed number of pixels in all images. The same algorithm allows to generate and save in the computer a file called "training.ocv" which is a file format distributed in rows and columns that stores the training data of both the positive samples as well as the negative samples in the form of text flat.

For training and recognize person silhouette it was necessary to use the multilayer perceptron using backpropagation algorithm, that model was created with the library "ml" of OpenCV that allows to develop common models of machine learning. Backpropagation algorithm works by determining the loss or error at the output and the propagating it back into the network. To minimize the error the weights are updated in each iteration until an acceptable error is obtained [11].

After performing the training it is necessary to save the characteristics of the ANN, for this purpose, a file called "parametros.xml" is generated. With this file format it is possible to arbitrarily store complex OpenCV data structures, as well as data types such as integers and floating-point numbers, as well as chain-text chains that are part of the designed ANN characteristics.

The results returned by the network are presented in Fig. 6 and after the training an accuracy of 95.4% was obtained in the recognition of the silhouettes of people.

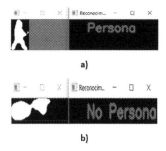

Fig. 6. (a) Person detection, (b) Other object detection

3.7 Counting and Geolocating

The detection of people through an ANN was used to perform the counting of human bodies. When a person was detected a counter set at zero at the beginning of the route was increased, so that by the end of the route it will have the total number of people detected.

Thanks to the GPS positioning system of the Phantom 3 Pro, precise parameters of latitude, longitude and height can be determined by means of coordinates that are shown on the screen in real time, thus indicating the exact position of the device in every second of Flight, as well as a histogram with all the information of the mission which after an analysis will facilitate the geolocation of each person.

For the tests performed it is possible to observe in Fig. 6 thanks to the DJI GS application, the defined trajectory that the drone must follow. Within the tour 10 people were positioned who are animated in the image as 8 green circles (people who were later identified as such) and 2 red circles (unidentified people), since the application image available is an offline map. Also, in the lower part of the image you can observe the people with their respective label (P) and geolocation (LAT and LON), as well as those that were not counted by the ANN that are in red color which are P5 and P8 (Fig. 7).

Fig. 7. Map of trajectories of geolocation (Color figure online)

Finally, the geolocation of each person or a group of people is delimited by the area of the vision range or focal length of the thermal camera [9]. The camera is positioned at an angle $\alpha = 45°$ with respect to the drone height. The triangulation of two images taken from different positions in the air, but focused towards the same point, allows us to find the distance between these two vectors for the geolocation of the point of interest [10]. Based on these investigations and considering that the height of the drone is $h = 15$ m, a right triangle is formed between the surface of the ground, the UAV and the identified person, as it is shown in the Fig. 8 below.

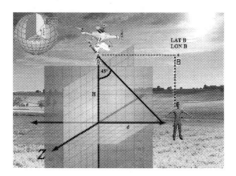

Fig. 8. Calculation of coordinates

This involves finding a distance d, which will serve as a reference to locate the real position of the person at the point $(B - h)$ for which the following formula was applied.

$$d = tg\, \alpha * h \tag{10}$$

Once $d = 15$ m is obtained, an estimation of how long it will take the drone to travel this distance and to overfly the point B was done. The same point gives the coordinates in latitude and longitude (LAT B and LON B) knowing that the device travels At a speed $v = 3$ m/s.

$$t = \frac{d}{v} \tag{11}$$

After having completed a $t = 5$ s trip, the GPS coordinates of the person or the people identified are accurately known. Moreover, as shown in the lower part of Fig. 6, the variation in latitude and longitude is minimal and does not change its value significantly according to where the body is. This will also depend on the magnitude of the area to be studied.

4   Test and Results

System tests were performed at different heights and a UAV displacement speed of 2 m per second, with 10 people located at different points of the defined trajectory. The error e in detection of the people is calculated as follows, where N_t is the theoretical number of people that the system must detect and N_r is the real number of people that the system detects.

$$e = \left| \frac{N_t - N_r}{N_t} \right| * 100\% \tag{12}$$

Table 2. People detection

Height	Detected people	Geolocation	% error
15 m	10	Yes	0
17 m	10	Yes	0
19 m	12	Yes	20
21 m	9	Yes	10

Therefore, the results obtained for the counting of people are shown in Table 2. The tests performed in terms of geolocation were verified by means of the GPS that the Phantom 3 has. Once the mission is finished, the drone is placed in the location of each person to take the data of Latitude and Longitude, obtaining an error less than 1% as is shown in the Table 3.

Table 3. Latitude and longitude test and error

Person	Calculate value	Real value	% error
P1	LAT: −0.9352	LAT: −0.9350	0.02
	LON: −78.6114	LON: −78.6115	0
P2	LAT: −0.9352	LAT: −0.9352	0
	LON: −78.6114	LON: −78.6115	0
P3	LAT: −0.9355	LAT: −0.9354	0.01
	LON: −78.6114	LON: −78.6114	0
P4	LAT: −0.9358	LAT: −0.9358	0
	LON: −78.6114	LON: −78.6114	0
P6	LAT: −0.9359	LAT: −0.9360	0.01
	LON: −78.6111	LON: −78.6111	0

5   Conclusions

The Search and Rescue System (SAR) was able to identify and geolocate people from a UAV, for which a total of 3588 samples were used, being one of the investigations with the largest number of images used in the training of an Artificial Neural Network for identification of people for rescue purposes. Furthermore, the algorithm designed segmented thermal images, independently of the scenario in which people were. The Otsu method applied in the segmentation of thermal images allowed to obtain suitable samples to train the ANN in order to identify and classify people correctly. Based on several experimental flight tests, it was determined that the range of heights at which the lowest error rate in the identification of persons is obtained is from 15 m to 17 m and the appropriate speed of the UAV is 2 m/s, using a 9 mm lens for the thermal camera. Considering the curvature of the earth and knowing that the system was tested near the equatorial line, a large displacement is required in order to have major changes in length and latitude parameters. The results obtained by the tests were compared with coordinates of Google Maps and drone GPS, which show a minimal variation in the order of the fourth decimal. This precision allows us to ensure that the method proposed can be applied efficiently in the geolocation of people.

References

1. Portman, J., Lynen, S., Chli, M., Siegwart, R.: People detection and tracking from aerial thermal views. In: IEEE International Conference on Robotics & Automation (ICRA), Hong Kong, China (2014)
2. Leira, F.S., Johansen, T.A., Fossen, T.I.: Automatic detection, classification and tracking of objects in the ocean surface from UAVS using a thermal camera. In: 2015 IEEE Aerospace Conference, Big Sky, MT, USA (2015)
3. Rudol, P., Doherty, P.: Human body detection and geolocalization from UAV search and rescue missions using color and thermal imagery. In: 2008 IEEE Aerospace Conference, Big Sky, MT, USA (2008)
4. Sherpa: sherpa-project.eu, 23 March 2017. http://www.sherpa-project.eu/sherpa/workshop-SR-2017. Último acceso: 20 Feb 2017
5. Instituto Geofísico: igepn.edu.ec (2016). http://www.igepn.edu.ec/cotopaxi. Último acceso: 16 Mar 2017
6. Viola, P., Jones, M.: Rapid object detection using a boosted cascade of simple features. In: Proceedings of the 2001 IEEE Computer Society Conference on Computer Vision and Pattern Recognition, CVPR 2001, Kauai, Hi, USA (2003)
7. Kittler, J., Illingworth, J.: On threshold selection using clustering criteria. IEEE Trans. Syst. Man Cybern. 15(5), 652–655 (1985)
8. Izurieta, F., Saavedra, C.: Redes Neuronales Artificiales. U. d. C. Departamento de Física, Ed., Concepción (2006)
9. Gibbins, D., Roberts, P., Swierkowski, L.: A video geo-location and image enhancement tool for small unmanned air vehicles (UAVs). In: Proceedings of the 2004 Intelligent Sensors, Sensor Networks and Information Processing Conference, Melbourne, Vic., Australia (2005)
10. Okello, N., Musicki, D.: Emitter geolocation with two UAVs. In: 2007 Information, Decision and Control, IDC 2007, Adelaide, Qld., Australia (2007)
11. Vladimir, V., Rauf, I.: Knowledge transfer in SVM and neural networks. Ann. Math. Artif. Intell. 81(1–2), 3–19 (2017)

Discrete Rotation During Eye-Blink

Anh Nguyen$^{(\boxtimes)}$, Marc Inhelder, and Andreas Kunz

Innovation Center Virtual Reality, ETH Zurich, Zürich, Switzerland
`nngoc@ethz.ch`

Abstract. Redirection techniques enable users to explore a virtual environment larger than the real physical space by manipulating the mapping between the virtual and real trajectories without breaking immersion. These techniques can be applied **continuously** over time (using translational, rotational and curvature gains) or **discretely** (utilizing change blindness, visual suppression etc.). While most attention has been devoted to continuous techniques, not much has been done on discrete techniques, particularly those utilizing visual suppression.

In this paper, we propose a study to investigate the effect of discrete rotation of the virtual environment during eye-blink. More specifically, we describe our methodology and experiment design for identifying rotation detection thresholds during blinking. We also discuss preliminary results from a pilot study.

Keywords: Redirected walking · Eye-blink
Rotation detection threshold · Visual suppression

1 Introduction

Compared to other methods of navigating in a virtual environment (VE) such as using controllers or walking-in-place, real walking has been shown to have better integrity and provide better immersion [1]. However, the challenge arises when the VE is much larger than the physical space. One of the solutions to this problem is the use of redirection techniques (RDTs). Depending on how these techniques are applied, Suma et al. categorized them into **continuous** and **discrete**. These techniques can be further divided into **overt** and **subtle** depending on whether they are noticeable or not [2]. Overt continuous RDTs involve the use of metaphors such as seven league boots [3], flying [1] or virtual elevators and escalators. Subtle continuous RDTs involve continuously manipulating different aspects of the users' trajectory such as translation - users walk faster/slower in the VE than in real life, rotation - users rotate faster/slower in the VE than in real life and curvature - users walk on a different curvature in the VE than in real life [4]. When applied within certain thresholds, these manipulations remain unnoticeable and immersion is maintained. Discrete RDTs refer to instantaneous relocation or reorientation of users in the VE. Some examples of overt discrete RDTs are teleportation [5] and portals [6]. Subtle discrete

© Springer International Publishing AG, part of Springer Nature 2018
L. T. De Paolis and P. Bourdot (Eds.): AVR 2018, LNCS 10850, pp. 183–189, 2018.
https://doi.org/10.1007/978-3-319-95270-3_13

RDT can be performed when users fail to notice the reorientation and relocation due to change blindness [7] or during visual suppression caused by saccadic eye movement or blinking [8,9]. Although overt RDTs offer higher range of motion and enable users to travel in a much larger VE, it has been shown that subtle RDTs produce fewer breaks in presence [2] and therefore are generally prefered for a more immersive VR experience. Among the subtle RDTs, most attention has been paid on continuous RDTs including research on detection thresholds and factors that influence them [10,11], or research on the implementation of these techniques in real walking applications such as steer-to-center, steer-to-orbit, steer-to-predefined-target [4], model predictive control [12]. Up to now, current research on discrete RDTs, especially using eyetracker information (e.g. eye movements, blinks, gazes) is quite limited, probably due to the lack of head mounted displays (HMDs) with an integrated eyetracker.

With the development of new HMDs with affordable integrated eyetrackers such as HTC Vive or FOVE, it is promising that research on subtle discrete RDTs using eyetracker information could be widely applicable in the future. In this paper, we propose the application of subtle discrete RDTs, more specifically **rotation**, in real walking during **blinking**. We first describe our methodology for blink detection and threshold identification. Furthermore, we discuss our experiment design and setup, and the results from a pilot study.

2   Related Work

We blink spontaneously 20–30 times per minute [13] to moisturize our eyes and each blink lasts about 100–150 ms [14]. During blinking, the eyelids cover the pupils and prevent light and visual inputs from entering the eyes, resulting in a disruption of the image on the rectina. Nevertheless, we rarely notice this disruption due to the fact that our brain suppresses visual information during blinking, so-called visual suppression. Interestingly, because of this suppression, people sometimes fail to notice changes happening to the scene during blinking such as color change, target appearance/disappearance or target displacement [15]. While visual suppression during blinking is undesirable in tasks that require constant monitoring of visual input such as driving, it offers a new posibility for discrete subtle redirection in the context of redirected walking. There is, however, a limit to how much redirection could be applied to the scene without the user noticing it. The only study that addresses this question is by Ivleva where a blink sensor was created and used with the HTC Vive to identify the detection thresholds for reorientation and repositioning during blinking [9]. While results from this study can not be used in a redirected walking application, they concluded that it could be a potential method. There are also a few limitations of this study such as users in the study were not performing locomotion, and the scene used may have contained reference points that give clues to the users where they have been redirected. In other contexts not related to redirected walking, many studies have been conducted to confirm the fact that people do not notice target displacement during blinking. However, to our knowledge, there exists no other study that quantifies this displacement.

3   Methodology

3.1   Blink Detection

Figure 1 shows typical pupil diameter recordings of a participant walking in a VE. It can be seen that during blinking the eyetracker loses track of the eyes and the pupil sizes become zero. However, it is worth to notice that the left and right eyes do not open or close at the same time and there is occasionally spurious noise like in Fig. 1(b). Since redirection should only be applied during blinking, it is important that blinks are detected reliably and there can not be any false positive. Therefore, in our blink detection algorithm, the following two conditions need to be satisfied for an event to be considered a blink: (i) both eyes' pupil diameters should change from nonzero to zero and remain zero for a certain amount of time; (ii) once the first condition is satisfied, the subsequent step from nonzero to zero will only be considered after a predefined amount of time to eliminate irregular blinks or noise like in Fig. 1(b).

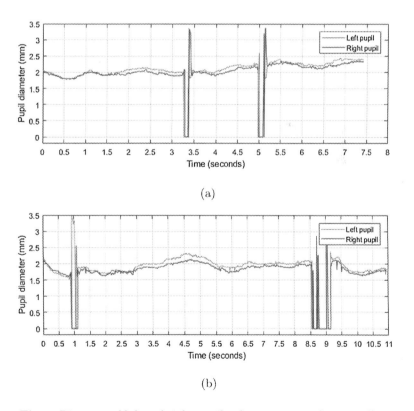

(a)

(b)

Fig. 1. Diameter of left and right pupils of a participant during walking

3.2   Threshold Identification

The detection of a stimulus could be modeled by a psychometric curve where the x-axis represents the stimulus value and the y-axis represents the percent of correct response. Threshold identification refers to the process of identifying this psychometric function. The classical method to identify the whole psychometric function is called the constant stimuli method (CSM), where the whole range of stimulus is presented in random order. However, this method requires a large number of repetitions and is not efficient since most of the time, only certain aspects of this psychometric function such as the 75% correct response point, or the slope are of interest. In contrast to CSM, adaptive methods such as staircase method, bayesian adaptive methods, etc. select the next stimulus level based on previous responses and do not present the whole range of stimulus. These methods require fewer trials but only identify one point on the psychometric curve and/or the slope.

While most existing studies on redirected walking adopt the CSM for threshold identification [8,10], to reduce experiment time, we select the Bayesian adaptive method called QUEST, whose details are provided by Watson and Pelli [16].

4   Experiment Design and Setup

The aim of this study is to identify the detection threshold for scene rotation during blinking. While in other redirected walking thresholds studies the participants were informed about the purpose of the study and asked if they notice the manipulation correctly, the same design can not be used in our experiment. If the participants are informed that during blinking the scene will be rotated, they will potentially try to fixate on a reference point and deliberately blink to identify the rotation direction. As a result, the real aim of the study can not be disclosed. Instead, a cover story is given to the participants that they are testing a new system which may contain some technical bugs and are encouraged to inform the experimenter whenever such bug occurs. When a subject reports a bug, the experimenter first makes sure that a scene rotation has just been applied and then verifies if the subject has really noticed the rotation rather than something else. When it is confirmed that the subject has noticed the rotation, it will be considered a correct detection response. Otherwise, when a stimulus has been presented after a blink, without the user making any comment, it will be considered a no detection response. Depending on the type of responses, the next stimulus level is selected accordingly. In addition, since there may be asymmetry in users' ability to detect scene rotation of different directions, we identify thresholds for left and right rotations separately.

In this study, users are required to walk around a maze-like environment (Fig. 2(a)) to search for a target. The maze is much larger than the existing available tracking space (Fig. 2(b)) and therefore whenever users approach the physical wall, a reset action will be performed which reorients the users towards the center of the physical space. Once the target has been found, a new scene will be randomly generated and loaded. The experiment is completed after the users have been exposed to 40 stimulus values per rotation direction.

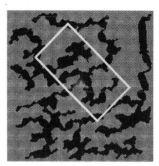

(a) User view of the VR scene   (b) Top view with real physical space overlay

Fig. 2. Scene used in the study

Our setup consists of an Oculus DK2 head mounted display (HMD) with an integrated SMI eyetracker providing eyetracking data such as gaze position, pupil diameters, etc. at 60 Hz. An Intersense IS-1200 optical tracking system is attached on top of the HMD and provides 6 DOF position tracking at a rate of 180 Hz. The system is powered by a backpack-mounted laptop and the game play was made with Unity. The environment was optimized to run constantly at the HMD's maximum frame rate of 75 Hz. The available tracking space is $13 \, m \times 6.6 \, m$.

5 Pilot Study and Preliminary Results

A pilot study was performed to verify the applicability of the proposed experiment protocol and the cover story. Five naive subjects (3 males and 2 females, age range: 20–29) who were all students from the university volunteered to participate in the study. The subjects were not informed about the real purpose of the study but instead were told the cover story. The first pilot subject remembered to mention to the expetimenter everytime he noticed a technical "bug" such as: "the color is weird", some things "seem a bit blur", or "the scene just glitched". However, the next two subjects were too immersed in the VE that they did not mention anything even though the scene rotation was increased up to its predefined maximum of 15°. When asked if they had noticed anything, they replied "I sometimes saw the scene jump" and "I have seen it for a while now but forgot to mention it". Since it is crucial that the user's responses are timely collected, we changed the experiment protocol for the last two pilot subjects and added a training session. In this training session, the subjects were exposed to the same environment but the scene rotation was always 15°.

This ensured that the subjects experienced the stimulus and understood what they should point out during the experiment. Moreover, keywords were assigned to each "bug" that the subjects discovered in the training session such as: "blur", "jump", "color", etc. This way, during the final study, the subjects only need to use these keywords when they detect a "bug" and do not have to stop and explain in full sentence what just happened. This adjusted protocol worked well for the last two pilot subjects and will be adopted for the final study. After the experiment, a series of questions was used to debrief the subjects, to determine the effectiveness of the cover story and whether the subjects had realized that the scene rotations were linked to blinking. When asked if they could guess why the technical bugs occured, all the subjects recited the cover story and none of them identified that they were associated with their blinks.

An average detection threshold could not be obtained from this pilot study due to the limited number of subjects and varied experiment protocol between subjects. However, it was observed that scene rotations below $5°$ were on average not detected by the subjects. This estimation is close to the detection threshold during saccadic eye movements found by Bolte and Lappe [8].

6   Conclusion

In this paper, we proposed an experiment design for identifying detection thresholds for scene rotation during blinking. Without being told the true purpose of the study, users were asked to walk around a VE looking for a target and encouraged to report when they detect some technical bugs, i.e. scene manipulation. The performed pilot study enabled us to refine the experiment design, showed that the cover story was effective and resulted in a rough estimation of the detection threshold. Further studies with large enough sample size are required to identify the detection threshold of not only scene rotation but displacement during blinking.

References

1. Usoh, M., Arthur, K., Whitton, M.C., Bastos, R., Steed, A., Slater, M., Brooks Jr., F.P.: Walking > walking-in-place > flying, in virtual environments. In: Proceedings of the 26th Annual Conference on Computer Graphics and Interactive Techniques, SIGGRAPH 1999, pp. 359–364. ACM Press/Addison-Wesley Publishing Co., New York (1999)
2. Suma, E.A., Bruder, G., Steinicke, F., Krum, D.M., Bolas, M.: A taxonomy for deploying redirection techniques in immersive virtual environments. In: 2012 IEEE Virtual Reality Workshops (VRW), pp. 43–46, March 2012
3. Interrante, V., Ries, B., Anderson, L.: Seven league boots: a new metaphor for augmented locomotion through moderately large scale immersive virtual environments. In: 2007 IEEE Symposium on 3D User Interfaces, March 2007
4. Razzaque, S., Kohn, Z., Whitton, M.C.: Redirected walking. In: Eurographics 2001 - Short Presentations, Geneva, Switzerland, pp. 1–6. Eurographics Association (2001)

5. Bowman, D.A., Koller, D., Hodges, L.F.: Travel in immersive virtual environments: an evaluation of viewpoint motion control techniques. In: Proceedings of IEEE 1997 Annual International Symposium on Virtual Reality, pp. 45–52, 215, March 1997

6. Freitag, S., Rausch, D., Kuhlen, T.: Reorientation in virtual environments using interactive portals. In: 2014 IEEE Symposium on 3D User Interfaces (3DUI), pp. 119–122, March 2014

7. Suma, E.A., Clark, S., Krum, D., Finkelstein, S., Bolas, M., Warte, Z.: Leveraging change blindness for redirection in virtual environments. In 2011 IEEE Virtual Reality Conference, pp. 159–166, March 2011

8. Bolte, B., Lappe, M.: Subliminal reorientation and repositioning in immersive virtual environments using saccadic suppression. IEEE Trans. Vis. Comput. Graph. **21**, 545–552 (2015)

9. Ivleva, V.: Redirected Walking in Virtual Reality during eye blinking. Bachelor's thesis, University of Bremen (2016)

10. Steinicke, F., Bruder, G., Jerald, J., Frenz, H., Lappe, M.: Estimation of detection thresholds for redirected walking techniques. IEEE Trans. Vis. Comput. Graph. **16**, 17–27 (2010)

11. Neth, C.T., Souman, J.L., Engel, D., Kloos, U., Bülthoff, H.H., Mohler, B.J.: Velocity-dependent dynamic curvature gain for redirected walking. In: 2011 IEEE Virtual Reality Conference, pp. 151–158. IEEE, New York, March 2011

12. Nescher, T., Huang, Y.-Y., Kunz, A.: Planning redirection techniques for optimal free walking experience using model predictive control. In: 2014 IEEE Symposium on 3D User Interfaces (3DUI), pp. 111–118, March 2014

13. Sun, W.S., Baker, R.S., Chuke, J.C., Rouholiman, B.R., Hasan, S.A., Gaza, W., Stava, M.W., Porter, J.D.: Age-related changes in human blinks. Passive and active changes in eyelid kinematics. Invest. Ophthalmol. Vis. Sci. **38**(1), 92–99 (1997)

14. VanderWerf, F., Brassinga, P., Reits, D., Aramideh, M., Ongerboer de Visser, B.: Eyelid movements: behavioral studies of blinking in humans under different stimulus conditions. J. Neurophysiol. **89**(5), 2784–2796 (2003)

15. Kevin O'Regan, J., Deubel, H., Clark, J.J., Rensink, R.A.: Picture changes during blinks: looking without seeing and seeing without looking. Vis. Cogn. **7**(1–3), 191–211 (2000)

16. Watson, A.B., Pelli, D.G.: Quest: a Bayesian adaptive psychometric method. Percept. Psychophys. **33**, 113–120 (1983)

Towards Visual Comfort: Disciplines on the Scene Structure Design for VR Contents

Yanxiang Zhang[✉] and ZhongBei Wang

Department of Communication of Science and Technology,
University of Science and Technology of China, Hefei, Anhui, China
petrel@ustc.edu.cn, Wanzhongbei110@163.com

Abstract. Inappropriate designed VR contents may cause visual discomfort (dizziness, vertigo) to users when they experience with VR head mounted displays (HMDs), This paper explored the human factors of binocular stereoscopic effects and provide some guidelines on how to achieve visual comfort in VR games.

Keywords: VR games · Human factors · Binocular stereoscopic effects
Discomfort

1 Introduction

With the popularization of VR head mounted displays (HMDs) such as HTC Vive, Oculus, etc. VR games are increasingly developed for entertainment purposes. These games allow the users to experience binocular stereoscopic effects through VR HMDs, but a widely existing issue is that many users experience VR sickness while they are playing VR games. Virtual reality sickness occurs when exposure to a virtual environment causes symptoms that are similar to motion sickness symptoms [5]. Users may feel discomfort, headache, stomach awareness, nausea, vomiting, pallor, sweating, fatigue, drowsiness, disorientation, and apathy when they experience VR sickness [4].

There are many reasons that may cause VR sickness. In some motion simulation virtual environments, the discrepancies between the visual aspects and body may cause simulator sickness. In binocular stereoscopic systems such as 3D stereo movies, visual discomfort is a widely existing issue, as VR HMDs are also based on binocular stereo effects, so in HMD based VR games, VR sickness could also be caused by the visual discomfort that existed in 3D stereo movies. Bad quality of 3D-stereo effects will also cause discomfort to the audiences who can experience dizziness vertigo, and this will greatly destroy the entertainment experience that VR games could bring to audiences. Visual discomfort in HMD based VR games is usually caused from inappropriate scene structure design of the games that exceed the threshold of human's visual system. For 3D-stereo vision based VR contents, users usually experience it in cinema or through VR HMDs. In such situations, the users have very few and weak controls over the 3D-stereo effects, hence the importance of designing the game scene towards visual comfort is obviously. Although there are many researches on the theory of cybersickness [9] and motion sickness [10], but there is still very few available guidelines for

© Springer International Publishing AG, part of Springer Nature 2018
L. T. De Paolis and P. Bourdot (Eds.): AVR 2018, LNCS 10850, pp. 190–196, 2018.
https://doi.org/10.1007/978-3-319-95270-3_14

the VR contents producers, this paper tried to provide some guidelines on VR scene structure design towards visual comfort.

2   Main Factors in Visual Comfort

Both experimental [1, 2] and experience studies [3] show that users with normal stereoscopic vision often have trouble fusing stereo image pairs into a single 3D image.

From the human's factor, the limits of near point of convergence in human's eye are usually no less than 25 cm, or it can't be fused into a single object. And the inter pupillary distance is usually at 6.5 cm; so at the nearest point of convergence, the angle between two pupil and the nearest point is $2 \times \tan^{-1}((25/6.5))$, which is about 12.24°. So in VR HMDs, at the nearest point of convergence, the angle between two pupil and the nearest point can't exceed the limit of 12.24°, it which represents the threshold below which VR content could be viewed as binocular stereoscopic effects in HMDs.

On the other side, usually there are more than one objects in a game scene. When human are looking at something in the near point in the game scenes, usually there are other objects just at the far point. In such situation, human's binocular vision system could not always produce a single stereoscopic vision in the brain. Panum's research found that in human's visual system, two retinal points near the retina could be combined into a single image only when they are within a small area, it is called the Panum's Fusional Area [6].

As shown in Fig. 1, when a point B is closer than the fixation point F, it is imaged on the two retina at the non-corresponding point bl and br on the left side of the line of sight of the left eye and the line of sight of the right eye. This is called cross parallax. The opposite point A is further than the fixation point F, in a single horizon left eye line of sight on the right side of the right eye line of sight on the left, called non-cross parallax. Although Point B and Point A are not in the retina, if they are in the Panum's Fusional Area, in the cerebral cortex under the combined analysis can still be integrated into a single image.

Panum's Fusion Area shows that not all images formed on both retinas with binocular parallax can form a single stereoscopic vision in the brain, and only a stereoscopic image pair that satisfies a certain binocular parallax can be fused into a single stereoscopic image.

In 1995, M. Wopking proposed that under the condition of natural viewing, binocular parallax angle difference of more than 1° will cause discomfort to the human's eye [7]. This value is know generally as the human eye comfortable viewing area of the rule of thumb. Longjian Di has discussed deep vertical space, the choice of shooting scenes when the clear prospects and background division and multi-level non-overlapping images help to create a better three-dimensional effect [8]. This is similar to the 1° angle of view, when we choose to shoot an object, the object with a small depth can helps to maintain a comfortable area with a 1° difference viewing angle. In 3D movies, in the same scene usually there are many different depths of field in

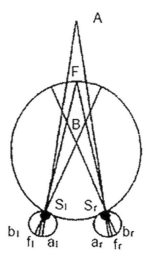

Fig. 1. Cross parallax and non-cross parallax

different part which will be beyond the human eye fusion capacity, 1° angle difference of view of the depth of the three-dimensional depth is clearly more comfortable.

The human's eyes' perception of the stereoscopic image is shown in Fig. 2. T is the object thickness, F1, F2 is the visual point of view and near point, the parallax of the stereoscopic image is controlled within 1°. The value of α and β should satisfy the parallax angle less than 1°, that is $|\alpha - \beta| \leq 1°$.

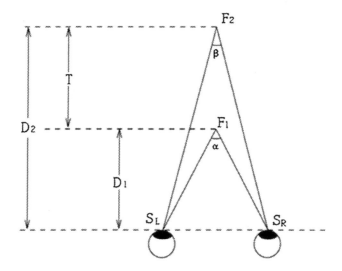

Fig. 2. 1° poor perspective

3   VR Scene Structure Design Principle for Visual Comfort

(1) Don't use motion simulation scenes if the users are sitting in a still chair

In many VR games, users are just sitting in the chair or standing in front of the computer screen on which the running games are displayed. With a HMD on the head, the movements that users could perform are very limited. If the users are playing a game that consists of driving a car or riding a sliding rail, the discrepancies between the visual environment and body will make users feel dizzy.

With the Oculus game names *Incell* (Fig. 3) in which users could explore the cell world by riding on a sliding rail, users' visual system will feel very fast movement while their body do not actually move at all; so they will start feeling heavily dizzy soon after they begin playing.

Fig. 3. Screen shot from VR game *incell,* in this game, user could see he/she is riding on the rail, but actually he/she is just seating in a normal chair

(2) The angle between the nearest point of virtual images and user's pupils should be less than 12°

This principle is to avoid seeing the image pair that is beyond the human's limits of binocular stereo system; if virtual images of an object in the scene is nearer than 25 cm to the user's eye, or the angle between the nearest point of virtual images and user's pupils should be less than 12°, it cannot be imaged as a single object in human's visual system.

(3) Design scene in a thin structure

According to Panum's Fusion Area, not the whole range within the angle of 12° could be fused as stereo vision, even if everything in the scene is within the threshold of 12°, but if the angle difference of two objects in the scene is large than 1°, it will also cause visual discomfort.

As shown in Fig. 4, the closer objects are from the eyes, the narrower the range of visual comfort will be; so it is not a good idea to design scene with very large span, in another word, the game scene should be designed in a thin structure.

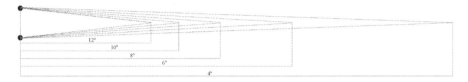

Fig. 4. Range change of visual comfort

For example, in the VR game *Arcade Saga* (Fig. 5), the scene was designed as virtual rooms which has limited spans, the closest objects to the eyes is the floor. But when users are playing, they are usually standing and looking up and don't look at the floor, and when the ball is flying, users' eye focus on the ball itself; so during the playing time, the angle difference of the eyes is almost always very small resulting in a feeling of comfort for the eyes.

Fig. 5. VR game *Arcade Saga*

(4) Using an independent visual background

Usually the game designers hope to provide users with wonderful and complicate scenes, but such scenes often breaks the threshold of 1° of angle difference. An alternative scheme is to use 3D geometries in closer scenes but use a 2D background as an independent visual background in the game scenes and which has no stereo parallax in the left and right eyes in the HMDs but could change angle and perspective with the movement of the payers.

The following scenes from stereo photography show the difference between a normal scene and another scene that replace the background using a 2D background. The left one was captured from a real scenery spot which has large span in depth, but as it contains both closer object and background that are far away. The angle difference of eyes between closer point and far point is obviously larger than 1°, so it is not comfortable for our eyes to view it; in the right one, the backgrounds that are far away in stereo pairs were removed and replaced with a same 2D background. This results in a much more comfortable stereo effects (Fig. 6).

Fig. 6. Using an independent visual background

In many game engines, the similar effects could also be realized by using lens blur rendering on far away objects in the scenes, but compare to using an independent visual background; such approach will consume many system resources and thus slows down the fluency of the game and playing experience.

4 Conclusion

The cause of visual discomfort is very complicate, this paper just provide some guidelines from the perspective of scene structure design in VR contents creation, but the display environments are also closely related with the visual discomfort, for example, the threshold of viewing angle and angle difference maybe vary in different display environments, so it should also be taken into account.

References

1. Surdick, R.T., Davis, E.T., King, R.A., Hodges, L.F.: The perception of distance in simulated displays. Presence **6**(5), 513–531 (1997)
2. Yeh, Y.-Y., Silverstein, L.D.: Limits of fusion and depth judgments in stereoscopic color displays. Hum. Fact. **32**(1), 45–60 (1990)
3. Lipton, L.: Foundations of the Stereoscopic Cinema: A Study in Depth. Van Nostrand Reinhold, New York (1982)
4. Kolasinski, E.M.: Simulator sickness in virtual environments (ARI 1027). U.S. Army Research Institute for the Behavioral and Social Sciences. www.dtic.mil. Accessed 22 July 2014
5. LaViola Jr., J.J.: A discussion of cybersickness in virtual environments. ACM SIGCHI Bull. **32**, 47–56 (2000). https://doi.org/10.1145/333329.333344
6. Grinberg, V.S., Podnar, G., Siegel, M.W.: Geometry of binocular imaging, pp. 56–65 (1994)
7. Wopking, M.: Viewing comfort with stereoscopic pictures: an experimental study on the subjective effects of disparity magnitude and depth of focus. J. Soc. Inf. Disp **3**, 101–103 (1995)
8. Di, L.: The influence of selecting and setting of 3D shooting scene to stereo effects, 012, p. 118 (2014). (in Chinese)
9. Rebenitsch, L., Owen, C.: Review on cybersickness in applications and visual displays. Virtual Real. **20**(2), 101–125 (2016)
10. Keshavarz, B., Riecke, B.E., Hettinger, L.J., Campos, J.L.: Vection and visually induced motion sickness: how are they related? Front. Psychol. **6**, 472 (2015)

"Changes": An Immersive Spatial Audio Project Based on Low-Cost Open Tools

Edoardo Bellanti, Alice Corsi, Andrea De Sotgiu,
and Gianni Vercelli[(⊠)]

Università degli Studi di Genova - DIBRIS, Genoa, Italy
{edoardo.bellanti,andrea.desotgiu}@edu.unige.it,
alice.corsi@dibris.unige.it, gianni.vercelli@unige.it

Abstract. An immersive multimedia project, namely "Changes", is presented to show the potential and effectiveness of an immersive experience based on spatial audio narration. The experience allows the listener to live an experience that begins by immersing him in a natural environment, then taking him to a war scenario and then back again to nature. The purpose of the paper is to explain the importance of the audio component in a multi-sensory storytelling.

Also, the will of the experience is to use free or low cost tools, in order that other people can easily take up the work and continue it or modify it.

Keywords: Spatial audio · Binaural audio · Virtual reality · Augmented reality Storytelling

1 Introduction

In recent years the terms "binaural audio" and "spatial audio" have assumed particular importance, mainly linked to the growing development and interest of virtual reality, which allows the immersive use of multimedia, video and audio contents. This technology is often automatically associated with the visual immersion, but, in reality, the sound component is crucial to increase the realism of the overall scene and, consequently, the involvement of the audience [1]. An example is the so-called Cinematic VR, which allows the use of 360° video through a head-mounted display equipped with headphones. In this particular field of virtual reality, in which the content is composed of an audio stream and a video stream, the sound component represents 50% of the experience [2]. Furthermore, virtual reality is only one of the application areas of spatial audio.

"Changes" is an immersive multimedia project entirely based on the spatial audio technology [3]. The main goal is to create an immersive audio-based storytelling, trying to underline the value that the sound component can bring to a multi-sensory experience (ex: Virtual Reality, Augmented Reality). To do so, a virtual scene has been created, in which the audience is witness to the unfolding of a great change. All this was created using only sound stimuli coming from different directions in the virtual space surrounding the spectator. Furthermore, free resources were used to implement the project, to underline how this type of technology is now available to everyone.

© Springer International Publishing AG, part of Springer Nature 2018
L. T. De Paolis and P. Bourdot (Eds.): AVR 2018, LNCS 10850, pp. 197–204, 2018.
https://doi.org/10.1007/978-3-319-95270-3_15

2 Related Works

In 2012, Dolby made a major breakthrough in cinema sound reproduction technologies, introducing Dolby Atmos [4]. This system, thanks to the Atmos CP850 processor, supports 64 speakers inside a theater, placed both on the walls and on the ceiling. Up to 128 tracks can flow to the speakers. This technology clearly distances itself from the previous one, the Dolby Digital Plus 7.1, generating an almost total immersion. With this system it is possible to fix the point of origin of a sound and give it an address from a speaker (or from an array of speakers) to others in the room. For example, during the passage of a helicopter over our head, the effect can be reproduced by the speakers on the ceiling with a sound shift from a point A to a point B of the room. As expressed in the Dolby White Paper, linked to Atmos technology, if a character looks at a source outside the screen, the sound will follow the effect expressed by the image. The position of the listener will also be decisive in this process. During the CES 2017, in Las Vegas, new Atmos systems for home theater were introduced via headphones and soundbar, making this technology also available for the consumer market (PCs and smartphones).

An example of experience that uses an audio-only narration to create an effective storytelling is Sleuth: An Audio Experience, an immersive audio game prototyped using VRML 2.0 and Java [5]. The concept of this game is the basis for the classic board game, Clue[1], but without any visual aspects of the game. The setting is a dinner party and the victim is the host of the estate, all of the guests are suspects. Somewhere in the many rooms of the house is the murder weapon. It is up to the player, the investigator, to determine the murderer, the weapon, and where it happened in the house. The events unfold as the detective navigates the rooms of the house and the investigator is surrounded by a world of sound.

A step forward is represented by A Blind Legend[2], an adventure game with hack-and-slash combat made for the visually impaired, that take advantage of the sensory experience of binaural 3D sound. The game features full 3D environments, outlined in details through directional audio and cues, and numerous styles of gameplay from stealth, horse-riding, combat, and even careful navigation of treacherous terrain.

Moreover, the panorama of contents produced in spatial audio today extends to an ever wider audience, with immersive productions recorded with binaural microphones and shared via social network. An example is Virtual Barber Shop, a binaural audio experience, recorded with microphones placed inside a dummy head that approximates a human head, in order to reach a 3D audio realism. Originally created in 1996, the complete version is also available on YouTube[3].

---

[1] Clue is registered trademark of Hasbro, Inc.

[2] http://www.ablindlegend.com/.

[3] https://www.youtube.com/watch?v=IUDTlvagjJA.

3 Motivations

Edison Research conducted a study in 2014 on the effects that new technologies and new media have on listening to music [6]. According to data collected on 2096 Americans over the age of 13, average listening in a day is four hours and five minutes. This tells us how much people listen to music, even passively, and certifies that music and sound play a fundamental role in our society, as much as the video component.

Based on Chap. 2, the importance of sound storytelling within a virtual experience [7], whether it is entirely based on audio, or part of a multi-sensorial experience, is evident. However, it also emerges that the audio is underestimated and, in the collective imagination, takes second place, for example, to the visual stimuli that are part of the content we are using (movies, VR, games, etc.). For this reason, the will to create an experience that was totally based on sound has grown, in order to exploit the spatial audio technology as a means to create an effective storytelling, allowing the exploration of the narrative power of this instrument. Moreover, the intention is to demonstrate how it is now possible to create this type of content even at low cost and with hardware and software tools available for everyone. This represents a fundamental component for the diffusion of any new technology and language.

4 The Experience

The creation of an immersive audio experience such as "Changes" can be dealt with in different ways, and includes a series of specific choices regarding hardware, software and storytelling techniques, which we illustrate below.

4.1 Content Design

The "Changes" project consists of an audio track that represents an immersive experience for the listener, to be heard through the headphones. The intent is to reproduce a sound environment that represents nature through some small changes, such as the addition or nuance of new sounds (animals, a river, etc.). In small steps the listener becomes accustomed to the environment, he imagines the distances and reconstructs in his own mind a fantastic image of an abstract environments. Then, suddenly, a big change takes place, the imminent war scenario that disorients the listener for a few seconds, but immediately catapults him into a new imaginary, only to return again to nature and stillness. The spatial perception, the concentration of the listener, change relatively the sense of space and time, allowing his memory [8] to leave a trace of the experience from the first listening, based on the emotions that transmit the sound immersion [9].

4.2 Content Creation

In the pre-production phase the story was chosen and, consequently, storytelling was designed. "Changes" had to allow free use, through something that everyone had available, like a pair of headphones. Furthermore, it had to be recreated or modified by any person who owned a computer. So, in order to work better, free resources and accessible to everyone were needed. Recording using binaural or ambisonic micro-phoning techniques [10] has been excluded since these microphones have costs that are difficult to sustain.

Through the search for free and shareware software and plug-ins, it was decided to create a virtual environment using monophonic sounds, taken from free libraries, leaving most of the work to the post-production phase. Monophonic samples were selected in order to be able to precisely choose the position of the sound in space. If we had chosen stereo files, some parameters, like the relationship between the left and right channels, would have been less modifiable. The desire to create an audio-only narra-tion, without the association of images or video, wants to emphasize the importance of hearing in a virtual immersion. The elimination of any visual input in the case of "Changes" stimulates the fantasy exponentially and enhances the immersion [11], for this reason it is expected to listen with eyes closed.

First of all, we have chosen the positions of the sounds, even before positioning them. In the first part of the experience, the storytelling imposes a natural scenario, all the elements have a precise position in space with respect to the listener (a river, a group of frogs, a group of birds, an eagle, etc.). The sound objects were positioned without transitions in the scene. The river was placed behind the listener, at sea level and at a distance of about fifteen meters from him. Subsequently, a group of frogs, after a few seconds, begins to make itself heard to the left of the listener at a distance of about five meters. While a bird's sound is perceived on the right (considering also a vertical height of a hypothetical tree), in the distance, it joins the sound of the river the sound of a flock of birds in a wood, all this in the same position behind the listener, but with a different height and distance.

Since the sounds have different amplitudes and volumes, once positioned in space, it was evaluated whether at a perceptive level the distance of each sound from the viewer was consistent with the unit of measurement (meters) inserted in the software. When the perception of the distance of a sound was not consistent with the distance established, a mix was made to make the volumes of the individual sounds reflect the distance in which they were placed. At this stage a qualitative evaluation component comes into play.

The only moving element of the naturalistic part of the experience was an eagle, which whizzes through the sky at a considerable distance from the listener, but it is always clear when it expresses its own sound in nature. Inside the virtual scene a circular motion of the eagle has been created, which flies around the listener starting from the $45°$ of a circumference to reach $-135°$ - Fig. 1. When manipulating sounds in motion, it is necessary to try to respect the Doppler effect [12] and the reverberations because this allows to increase the perception of reality [13].

The second part of the experience is short but intense. The outbreak of an imminent war is perceived by the arrival of a bomber, which is another element of transition from a point A to a point B and placed above the head of the listener. The bomber releases three bombs, one far away, one at mid distance and one relatively close to the listener, which in this way finds itself catapulted into a new scenario.

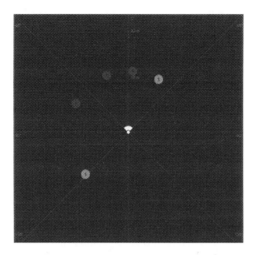

Fig. 1. The image is taken from the Facebook plugin Audio360 - Spatial Workstation and represents the movement on the X, Y axes of the eagle sound. To give a feeling of flying around the listener, the sound was placed far from the center and made a circular motion from 45° to about −135°.

Now instead of the river, there is the recurring sound of a moving tank. In the distance there is a guerrilla noise in the background, placed behind the listener. This sound is barely perceptible, but gives color to the scene.

The listener is above the tank and hears shots coming from right and left (as happened with frogs and birds in the part of experience dedicated to nature). It is the listener who takes up a machine gun and performs a barrage of shots (new transition element) from right to left. At the end of the flurry, the war also disappears and the old natural elements in a different order come back into fading.

In the mix phase it was not possible to use signal processors (equalizers, compressors, etc.) because the file, being nine channels (second-order ambisonic format), would have been manipulated incorrectly if processed with two-channel stereo instruments. The mix, therefore, was done using fades and automations that adjusted levels and transitions made possible by the plug-in and DAW (Digital Audio Workstation).

4.3   Tools

The DAW used for the experiment is Reaper[4], compatible with the plug-ins contained in the Facebook suite Audio360 - Spatial Workstation[5]. Specifically, as an audio card, we opted for an external solution: a Focusrite Scarlett 2i2[6] was used, but any other alternative is usable. After a few tests, we found that the headphones recommended for

---

[4] Reaper: https://www.reaper.fm/

[5] Facebook Audio360 – Spatial Workstation: https://facebook360.fb.com/spatial-workstation/

[6] Focusrite Scarlett 2i2: https://us.focusrite.com/usb-audio-interfaces/scarlett-2i2

listening must meet the following minimum requirements: frequency band from 100 Hz to 18 kHz. Possibly, the earphones are not recommended, if not in-ear. In the case of headphones with an even more restricted frequency band, the result is not fully guaranteed. It is not expected to listen through front speakers, since the 360° spatial perception would disappear because the sounds placed behind the listener would be perceived frontally. The sound library used for the project is FreeSfx [14].

4.4 Formats

The samples used are in mp3 format, 320 kbps of bitrate (44.100 Hz). It should be remembered that, despite the lossy compression conditions determining a variation in the quality of the files, the will to make accessible and replicable the creation of this type of content by anyone is a fundamental component of this experiment. Within the Reaper software, both in the input phase and in the output phase, it is possible to choose from how many channels the project reproduction is composed (2, 4, 8, 9, etc.). In the case of "Changes", the 9-channel format B-Format ambiX (2nd order ambisonics) was chosen. There are some playback issues, since classic players are not yet ready for decoding and playback of 4-8-9 or more channels, so the tests were done using the Reaper project for listening.

5 Preliminary Tests

A series of preliminary tests were carried out on a small group of 15 people in order to have a first qualitative feedback. The group consisted in different types of people (students, professors, workers of different categories), from an age of 20 to an age of 55. Various types of headphones were tested, these tests led to the selection of minimum requirements.

People kept their eyes closed for the whole time of the experiment (the duration of the track is 1 min and 53 s) because with open eyes the visual stimuli of the surrounding environment would have altered the sensations.

In fact, it has been found that closed-eye experience is much more powerful and stimulates precise images in the listener's mind. In addition to this, we found that after the listening experience, the audience's memory evokes visual images, like what happens after reading a book. The perception of the flow of time expands, many people thought they had listened for about 3–4 min and not 1 min and 53 s (the real duration of the track).

From the answers to some questions, it was understood that listening is experienced equally by everyone at the superficial level as regards the distinction of the main sounds, but with subjective differences instead on specific details.

Listeners perceived that they were totally immersed in nature. All this has a strong impact on the emotions of individuals, who lived an intense experience, amplified by the power of their imagination.

The position of the moving sound objects, such as the plane, the bombs and the eagle, were perceived correctly, according to the intent of the authors.

Instead, in the layering of different static sound objects within the mix, some of these have sometimes been interpreted differently.

For example, the flow of the river was perceived by some as a frontal cascade (despite being placed behind the listener). In the change from nature to the war scenario, it was clear that while listeners first felt immersed in nature, they rarely felt themselves to be protagonists of the conflict but rather external spectators. It is to underline the sense of amazement of the interviewees, a symptom of the fact that the experience is totally foreign to normality.

6   Conclusion

Sound is not only particularly present in new media, but continues to evolve from its birth. Presently, the sound encloses different worlds that are intertwined in different technologies, from cinema to music, from sound branding to social media. The audio component is often diminished and underestimated in a conception of the "image society", which almost always reminds only the visual component, forgetting the audio component that is currently very present in the coexistence between images and sound. As we have seen, spatial audio, combined with virtual reality and augmented reality techniques, allows a total immersion in an unreal space. The possibility of creating sound storytelling experiences, detached from the visual component, opens the way to new ways of using media content for different types of installations. The sound immersion stimulates the imagination, the emotions, the short and long-term memory, the spatio-temporal perception, catapulting the listener into a world recreated by his own mind, therefore extremely bound to subjective experiences.

With the project "Changes" we performed a few preliminary tests on users about the potential of an effective storytelling through spatial audio, and the results obtained encourage us to further deepen this field. To do this, future developments will be more focused on the collection and analysis of quantitative data related to the use of this type of immersive experience.

References

1. Mcmullen, K.A.: The potentials for spatial audio to convey information in virtual environments. In: 2014 IEEE VR Workshop: Sonic Interaction in Virtual Environments (SIVE) (2014)
2. Jaunt Inc.: The Cinematic VR Field Guide - A Guide to Best Practices for Shooting 360 (2017)
3. Herre, J., Hilpert, J., Kuntz, A., Plogsties, J.: MPEG-H 3D audio—the new standard for coding of immersive spatial audio. IEEE J. Sel. Topics Sig. Process. 9(5), 770–779 (2015)
4. Dolby Laboratories: Dolby® Atmos® Next-Generation Audio for Cinema. White Paper Dolby Laboratories (2017)
5. Drewes, T.M., Mynatt, E.D., Gandy, M., Mynatt Maribeth G, E.D.: Sleuth: an audio experience. In: Proceedings of ICAD (2000)

6. Edison Research: First ever share of ear measurement. http://www.edisonresearch.com/edison-research-conducts-first-ever-share-of-ear-measurement-for-all-forms-of-online-and-offline-audio/

7. Faria, R.R.A., Zuffo, M.K., Zuffo, J.A.: Improving spatial perception through sound field simulation in VR. In: IEEE Symposium on Virtual Environments, Human-Computer Interfaces and Measurement Systems (2005)

8. Baldis, J.J.: Effects of spatial audio on memory, comprehension, and preference during desktop conferences. In: Proceedings of the SIGCHI Conference on Human Factors in Computing Systems, CHI 2001. ACM, March 2001

9. Dinh, H.Q., Walker, N., Hodges, L.F., Song, C., Kobayashi, A.: Evaluating the importance of multi-sensory input on memory and the sense of presence in virtual environments. In: Proceedings of IEEE Virtual Reality. Cat. No. 99CB36316 (1999)

10. Hammershøi, D., Møller, H.: Methods for binaural recording and reproduction. Acta Acustica united with Acustica, vol. 88(3). S. Hirzel Verlag, May/June 2002

11. Murphy, D., Pitt, I.: Spatial sound enhancing virtual story telling. In: Balet, O., Subsol, G., Torguet, P. (eds.) ICVS 2001. LNCS, vol. 2197, pp. 20–29. Springer, Heidelberg (2001). https://doi.org/10.1007/3-540-45420-9_3

12. Iwaya, Y., Suzuki, Y.: Rendering moving sound with the doppler effect in sound space. Appl. Acoust. **68**(8), 916–922 (2007). Elsevier

13. Chowning, J.M.: The simulation of moving sound sources. J. Audio Eng. Soc. **19**(1), 2–6 (1971)

14. FreeSfx: http://freesfx.co.uk - Free sound libraries

Mnemosyne: Adapting the Method of Loci to Immersive Virtual Reality

Joakim Vindenes[1,2(✉)], Angelica Ortiz de Gortari[1], and Barbara Wasson[1,2]

[1] Centre for the Science of Learning and Technology (SLATE),
University of Bergen, Bergen, Norway
{joakim.vindenes, angelica.gortari,
barbara.wasson}@uib.no
[2] Department of Information Science and Media Studies,
University of Bergen, Bergen, Norway

Abstract. "Mnemosyne" is an Immersive Virtual Reality (VR) application designed to increase memory recall. The application simulates the processes of the ancient mnemonic "the Method of Loci" (MOL), also referred to as the "Memory Palace" technique. The application allows users to create personalised Memory Palaces by navigating and storing "memory cubes" in a Virtual Environment (VE) through a Head-Mounted Display (HMD). Results from a pilot study with 18 participants indicate that those with higher spatial reasoning abilities benefit more from use of the MOL. An evaluation of the pilot study raised a number of interesting issues to take into consideration in the redesign of a larger study.

Keywords: Memory application · Immersive Virtual Reality
Virtual environment · Method of Loci · Head-Mounted Display

1 Introduction

The MOL is an ancient mnemonic that works by combining visual and spatial cues to aid memorization. The method is highly effective [1, 12], and is used by champions in memory competitions worldwide. Watlin (2009) defines the MOL as "a memory strategy in which items to be learned are associated with a series of physical locations" [18, p. 489]. To apply the technique, one must choose a location (locus, pl. loci) to act as the Memory Palace. Within this palace one isolates a travel route: a fixed set of sub-locations in a certain order (e.g., your hallway, bathroom, and living room, etc.). Further, one visualizes the memory items one would like to recall at the different loci (e.g. a milk carton in the bathroom sink). To reinforce or recall the memory items, one mentally revisits the Memory Palace.

This combination of spatial and visual cues is in theory a great match for the medium of Immersive VR. By creating a Virtual Environment (VE) and enabling the user to place objects within this environment, the processes of the MOL can be simulated in VR. Potential benefits could include ease in performing the MOL and greater success in the memorization. As the medium of Immersive VR can provide an actual

© Springer International Publishing AG, part of Springer Nature 2018
L. T. De Paolis and P. Bourdot (Eds.): AVR 2018, LNCS 10850, pp. 205–213, 2018.
https://doi.org/10.1007/978-3-319-95270-3_16

visual and spatial environment, rather than an imaginary one as traditionally used with the MOL, the visuo-spatial impression might prove to be powerful in terms of memory.

The implementation of the MOL to VR can provide several benefits. Potential applications areas include students' learning, such as recalling content material they are learning, but can also exist within healthcare. The MOL itself has previously been used to aid several kinds of memory-impaired patients, with some success [13, 20]. The usefulness of the MOL, however, would be limited by the amount of time needed to train individual patients [13]. For this purpose an application that aids the user may be more adequate than the MOL alone. As the application simulates both the spatial environment and the visual cues, it may be easier to deploy a method which otherwise is complicated to perform on ones own, especially for elderly with reduced cognitive abilities.

In this paper, we review related work, describe the Mnemosyne application, the pilot study and results, and our improvements for a larger study.

2   Related Work

Several researchers have previously combined the MOL with VEs. Most related works provide the user with a VE through a screen, and the user performs the conventional MOL by mentally visualizing the memory items. Thus, the applications only provide the location for a Memory Palace, and the user has to perform the method without any aid from the system. Examples include the work by Legge et al. (2012) who compared two groups: one in which the participants used a virtual location presented on a screen, and another group which used a known physical location [8]. They found the performance of the two groups to be equivalent, a promising result for the use of VEs with the MOL. Another work is presented by Huttner and Robra-Bissantz (2017), who presented VEs to two groups: one using a laptop, and the other using an HMD. They found that the VR group outperformed the laptop group in terms of accuracy [5]. Although the applications in these studies did not let the user visualize and place memory objects within the VE, the results indicate that VEs fruitfully can be used as a basis on which to employ the MOL, and that an HMD is an effective way of displaying the Memory Palace.

Some work, however, has also been done where the MOL is performed through the application. Jund et al. (2016) simulated the MOL in a "semi-immersive" VE using a 3D monitor with 3D glasses [6]. The aim of their study was to compare the difference between an allocentric and an egocentric view, to evaluate which offered the best spatial cues to aid memorization. They found the results of the egocentric reference to be better than the allocentric. Similar to Jund et al.'s study, is the work presented by Fassbender and Heiden (2006) who created a Virtual Memory Palace for a desktop PC where the users could navigate through the palace and place images locally stored on the computer [2]. The results of their scoping study indicated a benefit for long term memory with the Virtual Memory Palace. Both the work by Jund et al. and Fassbender and Heiden, however, was done in a desktop VR scenario, and did not offer the natural orientation within the VE that head tracking with an HMD provides. This kind of orientation is important for spatial learning, as it is how we navigate and remember locations in real life. Utilizing natural orientation as a means to support spatial learning, is elementary to support the MOL. As the basic concept of the MOL is that if you remember the place (i.e. the Memory Palace), you remember the content, spatial learning may prove to be an essential part of the MOL which again could be supported by natural orientation.

Most similar to our work is the work by Mann et al. [9]. Their VE is delivered through a CAVE system, a series of wall projectors encompassing the user in the VE. They compared memory scores between the immersive group and three other groups: (1) using their usual method of memorizing, (2) the normal MOL, and (3) a desktop VR group. Although the Immersive VR group were most successful, the results were not statistically significant, and ceiling effect and uneven sample size made further analysis difficult [9]. Our work is differentiated from that of Mann et al. as we employ an HMD as the VR technology for executing the method. In short, our work is distinguished from the related works by performing the MOL through the application and visualizing the memory items within the VE in Immersive VR through an HMD.

By employing Immersive VR for our application, the user will experience the VE from a First-Person View, a feature that contributes to learning in VR [11]. Moreover, the application will allow the users to experience the spatial environment as we experience spatial environments in real life. As studies on spatial learning in VR and real life deliver similar results [4, 15], the application may allow for exploiting the way spatial information is seen and learned in the most basic sense. There is evidence suggesting that spatial knowledge from virtual environments are transferable to the real world [17, 19]. This is essential to the concept of the MOL, as the content to be recalled is embedded visually and spatially in the environment.

The hypothesis underlying this study is that the immersion, and the potential succeeding feeling of presence, will be of importance for the utilization of the visuo-spatial Memory Palace for memory recall purposes. The methodology of the pilot study which this paper presents, aims to isolate the effects of these different levels of immersion and presence and relate it to the memory scores in the experiment. For this purpose, the Mnemosyne application was created both for Immersive VR and Desktop VR, to be able to differentiate between these levels of immersion.

3   Application

Vindenes (2017) presents the "Mnemosyne" application [16]. The application was designed through a Research Through Design process, to be an "integration of many technical research contributions from a variety of disciplines into a single working system" [21, p. 498]. The design incorporates elements from research on Virtual Reality Learning Environments (VRLEs), and psychology research on cognitive load, spatial cognition, memory and learning. Effectively, this means that the design of the application is inspired by research on the important role of spatial navigation and visual impressions on memory. In addition to this, research on cognitive load and learning are taken into consideration. In this way, the Mnemosyne application functions as an "embodiment of theory and technical opportunities" [21, p. 498], and can be used to investigate the effects of the visuo-spatial dominant technology of VR on memory. The application will be used to investigate the hypothesis that Immersive Virtual Reality supports the visuo-spatial elements of the MOL. By comparing a group using the application in Immersive VR to other approaches, we will try and isolate to which degree immersiveness aids memorization.

3.1 Application Requirements

The system requirements for Mnemosyne were based on (1) a literature review, and (2) requirements set to simulate the mechanics of the MOL. From the literature review, three distinct requirements were identified. First, the users should be able to play 'themselves' from a FPV to get a first order experience [11], as opposed to controlling a character in a third-person view. Second, the design should allow the users to be autonomous, free to move where they want in the environment [3, 11], as opposed to navigation along a fixed route (carousel navigation). Third, the design of the rooms should be simplistic. This latter requirement draws on research on VR and cognitive load that suggests being careful and selective with content in the VEs so as to not overfill the environment [7]. Other requirements were set by the nature of the MOL itself. Requirements identified by the mechanics of the MOL state that a Memory Palace is needed, i.e. a three-dimensional VE. It has to be possible to navigate and orient oneself within this environment through an HMD. It must also be possible to instantiate and place objects, i.e. images, to any given association one might have. In this way, the MOL can be simulated, and the VE populated so it "becomes the physical representation of the knowledge to be taught" [14, p. 345]. According to Sanchez, Barreiro and Maojo (2000), this is the characteristic which distinguishes VR as an educational technology: "the possibility of creating symbolic spaces capable of embodying knowledge" [14, p. 360]. When a user has filled the Virtual Memory Palace with the memory objects, that instance of the VE will act as a virtual representation of the information he or she wants to recall.

3.2 Application Design

Mnemosyne was created with the A-Frame Web API for the Samsung GEAR VR HMD and displayed in the Carmel Developer browser. In the HMD, the Samsung S7 phone is used as the screen, while the GEAR VR provide lenses, a touchpad and a more precise internal measurement unit than what is present in the smartphone. The Memory Palace is presented as a building comprising five different rooms, and three memory items can be placed in each room (see Fig. 1). Thus, the application can be used to memorize a total of 15 items. The items to be memorized are entered into a smartphone application on the Samsung S7 as text keywords before the smartphone is inserted into the HMD. To support the ability to visualize almost any memory object, these keywords are further connected to a Web Image Search API that returns images the user can place within the VE. In this way, the user can enter any keyword he or she wants to memorize into the application. To be viewable from all sides within the 3D VE, these images are attached to the sides of a cube, creating a "memory cube" (see Fig. 2). The placement of memory cubes is performed by gaze interaction, by looking at blank memory cubes at pre-defined locations (see Fig. 1). Within the VE, the user has free navigation, and moves in the direction of the gaze by pressing the touchpad on the side of the HMD. The memory cubes are placed in the order that they were indexed in the word list. When the user has populated the Memory Palace, the environment is free to be navigated and inspected for memory reinforcement.

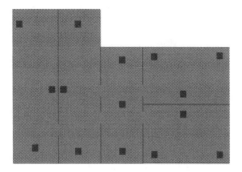

Fig. 1. Allocentric view

4   Pilot Study

To evaluate the application and research methodology before a full-scale study, we conducted a pilot study with 18 participants. These participants were divided into three groups of six participants each. The participants were university students, equally distributed in gender, aged between 20 and 32, with a mean age of 25 years. The students were recruited from a variety of fields, e.g. anthropology, media studies, pedagogy, information science, marine biology, etc. Information science had most representatives, with 6 out of 18 participants. Group 1 used the application in Immersive VR; group 2 used the application in Desktop VR, and group 3 used the MOL without any technological aids (i.e., the conventional MOL). The aim of the research design was to be able to compare results from the Immersive VR group to the desktop VR group, and from the desktop VR group to the conventional MOL-group. The reason for the three groups was to isolate which effects came from being immersed in the VE, which effects came just from a visualization, and which effects simply came from the MOL itself.

As spatial learning is important in the context of the MOL, each participant across all groups were required to take a test of their spatial reasoning abilities. The spatial test consisted of five "mental rotation" tasks. Each correct answer would give a score of 1, the max score in the spatial ability test being 5. When this test was completed, the participants were taught the concept of the MOL and were informed on how to execute the method. The VR groups (i.e., group 1 & 2) were also exposed to the VE before-hand, to ensure that as little time as possible was lost in the interaction with the application. In this training phase they were given instructions on how to navigate and perform the placement of the memory cubes. While Group 1 & 2 was training in employing the MOL in VR, Group 3 was trained in using the MOL without techno-logical aids. After the experiment, the participants answered a questionnaire, and

Fig. 2. Two memory cubes

participated in a short interview, which both addressed their experience of performing the MOL. The steps of the experiment for all three groups can be summarized as such: (1) Spatial task, (2) Training, (3) Memory task, (4) Interview & Survey.

5   Results

The group who used the conventional MOL outperformed both the VR groups in the memory experiment. More specifically, the Immersive VR group recalled on average 13.1 items, the Desktop VR group recalled 14.3 items, and the group using the conventional MOL recalled all 15 items. As for long term memory, similar results were found one week after the exposure to various experimental conditions (Immersive VR: 10.6, Desktop VR: 12, Conventional MOL: 13.8). On first glance, these results suggest that the MOL does not benefit in terms of effectiveness when combined or adapted to technological aids. We explored this further.

5.1   Spatial Ability

Further examination of the results, however, reveals other differences between the participants than just simply the mediums used. The spatial ability for instance, varied significantly between the groups. The conventional MOL group scored the highest with 3.8 points on average, the Desktop VR group scored 3.3, while the Immersive VR group had an average score of 1.8. There is thus a correlation between high spatial ability scores and high memory scores. To further examine this, we examined the relationship between spatial ability and memory scores between all participants regardless of groups. We found that those participants who had a spatial ability score of 1 remembered on average 12.25 items, while those who had a spatial ability score of 2, remembered on average 13.5 items. Those who had a spatial ability score of 3, remembered on average 14.8 items, while all of the participants who had a spatial ability score of 4 or 5, remembered 15 items.

These results support the ability-as-enhancer hypothesis as presented by Mayer and Sims, which states that high spatial ability learners should benefit more from 3D environments as they would use less cognitive effort [10]. This then allows more cognitive power for mental model construction. By this hypothesis, low spatial ability learners would not benefit from VR support in the performing of the MOL, as this would cause them to experience cognitive overload more often than the others. This theory may help to explain the low scores of the Immersive VR group.

5.2   Interaction Time

The Immersive VR group also had a higher interaction time, or method performing time, than the other groups. Having to navigate within the spatial environment "physically", had a disadvantage in terms of time versus only performing it mentally. This makes it harder to do time-based evaluations of the effectiveness of Virtual Memory Palaces. Two out of the six participants in the Immersive VR group reported stress due to time constraints in execution of the MOL, whereas none of the participants in the other groups reported such. The number of participants who were "finished" and thus had more time to walk around to memorize the items was also far higher in the Desktop VR group and the group using the conventional MOL than in the Immersive VR group.

6   Discussion

The medium of Immersive VR provides a promising venue for new visual information environments. By designing applications that exploit our brains visuo-spatial memory schema creation, the medium could allow us to create VEs filled with the content we want to recall or learn. The results from this pilot study, however, points out that this might not equally benefit everyone. The results indicate that low spatial learners benefit less from the MOL and using the MOL in a Virtual Memory Palace. These results should be controlled in future studies with larger sample size and using statistical analysis. For example, future studies on VRLEs should evaluate the impact of spatial ability on the outcomes of the learning content. If high spatial ability is a prerequisite for benefiting from VRLEs due to cognitive load, this may impact how VRLEs should be incorporated and for whom.

Although the study shows correlations between Immersive VR and low memory scores, it is questionable whether it is the features of Immersive VR causing these results, or if it is the factors following the Immersive VR group. Because of the disadvantages of the VR groups in terms of interaction time and lower spatial abilities of the participants, this pilot study cannot with certainty comment on the effectiveness of Virtual Memory Palaces. To be able to evaluate the effectiveness of the MOL with control groups, the interaction and navigation time could be eliminated so that valuable memorization time is not lost in the interaction with the system. This could be addressed with automatic rather manual placement of memory cubes. If a user is presented to an already-filled Memory Palace, the user could focus on just navigating through the different rooms. The interaction, however, may be important, and future studies would be needed to evaluate this. As spatial ability scores may affect the execution of the MOL, participants should also be placed in groups based on their spatial ability skills.

7   Conclusions

This study presented "Mnemosyne", an Immersive VR application simulating the MOL. A pilot study was conducted with the application, to evaluate the effects of the application on memory, and the research design of the study. Time lost in navigation with the VR interface and low spatial ability of the Immersive VR group makes it hard to conclude on the effects of the application on memory. The outcomes of this pilot study indicate that spatial ability was important for the effect of the MOL across all groups. For our future full-scale experiment, the implications of this study will be taken into consideration. In the next study, with an increased sample size, the application will be modified to reduce interaction time, and the groups will be sorted based on pre-tested spatial abilities. To avoid the ceiling effect, the number of items, and therefore also the size of the memory palace will be increased. The full-scale study will also gather more information about the participants, such as their subjective feeling of presence, as this is related to the varying degree of immersiveness. By employing statistical analysis on the results, we hope that the full-scale study will be able to isolate which effects different degrees of immersion and presence can have on their memory scores.

References

1. De Beni, R., Cornoldi, C.: Effects of the mnemotechnique of loci in the memorization of concrete words. Acta Psychologica **60**(1), 11–24 (1985). https://doi.org/10.1016/0001-6918 (85)90010-1
2. Fassbender, E., Heiden, W.: The virtual memory palace. J. Comput. Inf. Syst. **2**(1), 457–464 (2006). https://www.researchgate.net/publication/229059664_The_Virtual_Memory_Palace
3. Hanson, K., Shelton, B.E.: Design and development of virtual reality: analysis of challenges faced by educators. Educ. Technol. Soc. **11**(1), 118–131 (2008). http://www.ifets.info/journals/11_1/9.pdf
4. Hardiess, G., Mallot, H.A., Meilinger, T.: Virtual reality and spatial cognition. In: Wright, J.D. (ed.) International Encyclopedia of the Social & Behavioral Sciences (second edition), pp. 133–137. Elsevier, Oxford (2015). http://dx.doi.org/10.1016/B978-0-08-097086-8. 43098-9
5. Huttner, J., Bissantz-Robra, S.: An immersive memory palace: supporting the method of loci with virtual reality. In: 23rd Americans Conference on Information Systems (2017). http://aisel.aisnet.org/amcis2017/HumanCI/Presentations/20/
6. Jund, T., Capobianco, A., Larue, F.: Impact of frame of reference on memorization in virtual environments. In: 2016 IEEE 16th International Conference on Advanced Learning Technologies, pp. 533–537 (2016). https://doi.org/10.1109/ICALT.2016.77
7. Lee, E.A.L., Wong, K.W.: Learning with desktop virtual reality: low spatial ability learners are more positively affected. Comput. Educ. **79**, 49–58 (2014). https://doi.org/10.1016/j. compedu.2014.07.010
8. Legge, E.L.G., Madan, C.R., Ng, E.T., Caplan, J.B.: Building a Memory Palace in minutes: equivalent memory performance using virtual versus conventional environments with the method of loci. Acta Psychologica **141**(3), 380–390 (2012). https://doi.org/10.1016/j.actpsy. 2012.09.002

9. Mann, J., Polys, N., Diana, R., Ananth, M., Herald, B., Platel, S.: Virginia tech's study hall: a virtual method of loci mnemonic study using a neurologically-based, mechanism-driven, approach to immersive learning research. In: 2017 IEEE Virtual Reality (VR), Los Angeles, CA, pp. 383–384 (2017). http://dx.doi.org/10.1109/VR.2017.7892337

10. Mayer, R.E., Sims, V.K.: For whom is a picture worth a thousand words? Extensions of a dual-coding theory on multimedia learning. J. Educ. Psychol. **86**(3), 389–401 (1994). http://visuallearningresearch.wiki.educ.msu.edu/file/view/Mayer+%26+Sims+(1994).pdf/50533673/Mayer+%26+Sims+(1994).pdf

11. Mikropoulos, T.A., Natsis, A.: Educational virtual environments: a ten-year review of empirical research (1999–2009). Comput. Educ. **56**(3), 769–780 (2011). https://doi.org/10.1016/j.compedu.2010.10.020

12. Nelson, D., Vu, K.-P.L.: Effectiveness of image-based mnemonic techniques for enhancing the memorability and security of user-generated passwords. Comput. Hum. Behav. **26**(4), 705–715 (2010). https://doi.org/10.1016/j.chb.2010.01.007

13. Richardson, J.T.E.: The efficacy of imagery mnemonics in memory remediation. Neuropsychologia **33**, 1345–1357 (1995). https://doi.org/10.1016/0028-3932(95)00068-E

14. Sánchez, A., Barreiro, J.M., Maojo, V.: Design of virtual reality systems for education: a cognitive approach. Educ. Inf. Technol. **5**(4), 345–362 (2000). https://doi.org/10.1023/A:1012061809603

15. Tüzün, H., Özdinc, F.: The effects of 3D multi-user virtual environments on freshmen university students' conceptual and spatial learning and presence in departmental orientation. Comput. Educ. **94**, 228–240 (2016). https://doi.org/10.1016/j.compedu.2015.12.005

16. Vindenes, J.: A virtual mind palace: adapting the method of loci to virtual reality. Unpublished Master's thesis (2017)

17. Wallet, G., Sauzon, H., Pala, P.A., Larrue, F., Zheng, X., N'Kaoua, B.: Virtual/real transfer of spatial knowledge: benefit from visual fidelity provided in a virtual environment and impact of active navigation. Cyberpsychol. Behav. Soc. Netw. **14**(7–8), 417–423 (2011)

18. Watlin, M.: Cognition, 7th edn. Wiley, Hoboken (2009)

19. Witmer, B.G., Bailey, J.H., Knerr, B.W., Parsons, K.C.: Virtual spaces and real world places: transfer of route knowledge. Int. J. Hum.-Comput. Stud. **45**(4), 413–428 (1996)

20. Yesavage, J.A.: Imagery pretraining and memory training in the elderly. Gerontology **29**, 271–275 (1983). https://doi.org/10.1159/000213126

21. Zimmerman, J., Forlizzi, J., Evenson, S.: Research through design as a method for interaction design research in HCI. In: SIGCHI Conference on Human Factors in Computing Systems, pp. 493–502 (2007). https://doi.org/10.1145/1240624.1240704

Web-Based Real-Time LADAR Data Visualization with Multi-user Collaboration Support

Ciril Bohak[1][✉], Byeong Hak Kim[2], and Min Young Kim[2]

[1] Faculty of Computer and Information Science, University of Ljubljana,
Večna pot 113, 1000 Ljubljana, Slovenia
ciril.bohak@fri.uni-lj.si

[2] School of Electronics Engineering, Kyungpook National University,
1370 Sankyuk-dong, Buk-gu, Daegu, Korea
durumy98@hanmail.net, minykim@knu.ac.kr

Abstract. In this paper we present a web-based visualization system developed for visualizing real-time point cloud data obtained from LADAR (or other) sensors. The system allows direct visualization of captured data, visualization of data from database or visualization of preprocessed data (e.g. labeled or classified data). The system allows the concurrent visualization from same or different data-sources on multiple clients in the web browser. Due to the use of modern web technologies the client can also be used on mobile devices. The system is developed using modern client- and server-side web technologies. The system allows connection with an existing LADAR sensor grabber applications through use of UDP sockets. Both server- and client-side parts of the system are modular and allow the integration of newly developed modules and designing a specific work-flow scenarios for target end-user groups. The system allows the interactive visualization of datasets with millions of points as well as streaming visualization with high throughput speeds.

Keywords: LiDAR · LADAR · Point cloud data · WebGL
Data visualization

1 Introduction

There are many different ways of storing and presenting the data describing the world around us. One of more popular ways in the recent years is use of point cloud representation — a set of points in space which store different parameters and information regarding the specific spatial location. Such representation is mostly used for representing the shapes of the objects and surrounding world, but it can also be used for storing other information (e.g. meteorological data, physical measurements, simulation data etc.). In our case the point cloud data is representing the surrounding world and objects in it.

ⓒ Springer International Publishing AG, part of Springer Nature 2018
L. T. De Paolis and P. Bourdot (Eds.): AVR 2018, LNCS 10850, pp. 214–224, 2018.
https://doi.org/10.1007/978-3-319-95270-3_17

Point cloud data for shape representation can be acquired using several different sensors (e.g. depth camera [1], LiDAR [2] or LADAR [3]) or can be even extracted from image data [4]. In our case the LiDAR and/or LADAR sensors were used to acquire the point cloud data representing the shape of the world (terrain, vegetation, buildings, etc.). While the LiDAR data is acquired from the planes (see Fig. 1a) the LADAR data is acquired from stationary ground position using gimbal system (see Fig. 1b).

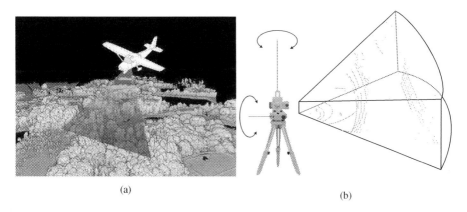

(a)   (b)

Fig. 1. Figure shows the acquisition process for LiDAR terrain data by plane (a) and an example of LADAR sensor structure (b)

Point cloud data obtained with LADAR or LiDAR system are mostly used for detection and tracking purposes [5,6], but to get better perception of the data it is crucial to visualize them. Real-time visualization of large point cloud data sets with up to tens or hundreds of millions of points poses a challenge even with today's GPU hardware. This is even more true if we want to display real-time streaming data with lots of newly added points per time frame (e.g. hundreds of thousands of points per second). To achieve such performance even on consumer accessible hardware (or even on mobile devices) several limitations have to be defined. A well accepted approach for processing as well as visualization of point cloud data is presented in [7] where authors present a programming library for platform specific applications. An immersive visualization using dedicated platform specific software for CAVE setup is presented in [8]. Some approaches convert the point cloud data into mesh geometry before visualization. Such approach which uses rapid Delaunay triangulation for generating the mesh model is presented in [9].

A very important aspect for fast real-time visualization of large point cloud data sets is also the ability to process and provide such large amount of data fast enough to the visualization system. LASTools [10] were developed for such purpose, which are fast command line tools for simple processing of point cloud data. For streamed data this speed is defined by speed of input sensors, but providing the already stored large amount of data at high speed is also important [11].

While the data visualization for as single user is the main goal, it is often appreciated if the same data visualization can bee seen by multiple users at the same time or even if those users have an option of mutual interaction with the data. Such collaborative approach is well known in online productivity tools (e.g. Google Docs) and even in some specialized scientific tools. Such example for collaborative annotation of medical data with use of modern web technologies [12] does not only allow the collaboration between user at a distance but also allows replacement of specialized software and hardware with a modern web browser. A similar concept is exploited in the presented system.

In the following section we present the developed system for real-time visualization of 3D point cloud data with support for real-time data streaming, collaborative viewing and labeling of the data. In Sect. 3 we present evaluation of the developed system and it's results. In the final Sect. 4 we present the conclusions and give the pointers for possible future work.

2   Developed System

The main goal was to determine whether it is possible to develop a real-time massive point cloud visualization system with support for visualization of real-time streamed data with support for multi-user viewing and labeling of the displayed data. Figure 2 shows the basic structure of the system: (1) Data Sender[1] is a standalone application for reading raw sensor data and sending it to desired application, (2) Data Preparation Module is a server based application for acquiring the data, packaging the data into desired form and sending the data to (3) Data

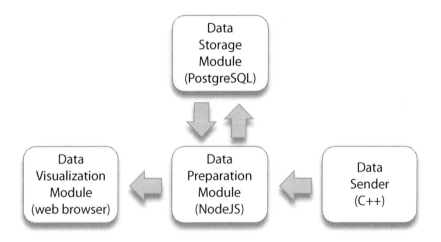

Fig. 2. The basic system structure.

---

[1] The application is developed in C++ and does was not developed as part of the presented work.

Storage module or (4) Data Visualization Module – a web application with support for WebGL for real-time visualization of point cloud data. The developed modules (2–4) are presented in more detail in the following subsections.

2.1   Data Preparation Module

The Data Preparation Module is a NodeJS[2] based server-side application developed for linking the Data Visualization Module with data resources. Data resources can be either real-time data provider such as Data Sender or off-line providers such as Data Storage Module. While data from Data Sender is acquired from sensors and directly sent to Data Visualization Module, it is up to the Data Preparation Module to request the data from Data Storage Module.

The application supports multiple connections and can simultaneously handle multiple data streams (live streams and data storage requests) and pipe them to multiple users individually. This allows multiple users to request data from diverse data sources. The module will prepare the data and send it to the users who requested it. The system does not support user management, but distinguishes between clients using uniquely generated tokens. The layer of security was not implemented at this stage of development due to specific use-cases where there is not such need (completely independent computer network or single computer deployment).

The Data Preparation Module also allows to simultaneously send the data obtained from Data Sender to data storage module, where the data is stored, and to multiple data visualization modules where the data is displayed in real-time. The communication between Data Preparation Module and Data Visualization Module is implemented using Socket.IO[3] – a library for fast and reliable continues communication. The communication with Data Sender is implemented using standard UTP sockets.

The data from Data Sender is received in form of binary blocks, where each block contains information from 200 points. Each point is represented with x, y and z position values with 32-bit float precision. Each package is directly submitted to all the clients (Data Visualization Modules) who are subscribed to live data streaming.

For preparation of stored data, module allows customization of query commands sent to the Data Storage Module. Some parameters of for query commands can also be defined by users through settings in Data Visualization Module. The data obtained from the Data Storage Module is packed and sent in JSON form to the client which requested it, but can also be packed into binary form for faster transmission.

While the basic functionality of module is to obtain, prepare and send the point cloud data, it can be easily extended for use with data from other domains as well. Such example might be the use of ortho-photo data or other GIS data for purposes of better/different final visualization.

---

[2] https://nodejs.org/.

[3] http://socket.io/.

2.2 Data Storage Module

Data Storage Module consists of a NodeJS based server-side application for interfacing with PostgreSQL[4] relational database with Pointcloud extension[5]. The extension deals with the variability of point dimensionality by using custom database schema which describes the content of individual point in the database. This takes care of number of point dimensions and their data types and possible scaling and/or offsets between the actual values and values stored in database.

The above presented storage is not the fastest possible option for storing large amounts of point cloud data, but offers a good trade-off between complexity of use, speed and price [11].

2.3 Data Visualization Module

The Data Visualization Module was developed as web application using Angular[6] and Bootstrap[7] for implementing interactive responsive GUI, and ThreeJS[8] and Potree [13] for implementing fast and reliable 3D visualization using WebGL technology.

The module's GUI consists of two parts as can be seen in Fig. 3: (1) preferences panel on the left, where users can select the data source and set the

Fig. 3. The data visualization module GUI.

---

[4] https://www.postgresql.org/.

[5] https://github.com/pgpointcloud/pointcloud.

[6] https://angular.io/.

[7] http://getbootstrap.com/.

[8] https://threejs.org.

parameters of the visualization and (2) visualization panel on the right, where users can see and interact with displayed data.

In preference panel users can select data source from one of the existing databases or they can turn on the live data receiving option. User can set next database point loading parameters:

Number of Concurrent Loading Patches: points in database are stored in patches containing several number of neighboring points according to their spatial position. This allows faster retrieval of neighboring points. We can choose how many patches of points we want to load in one call and thus speeding up the database response time.

Load Every n-th Point: in dense point clouds it is not necessary to load all the points to get the idea of the shape they are representing. For this reason users can choose the density of points they want to display selecting only every n-th point in the database according to the geolocation sorting. This also means that client will draw less points which will result in higher frame rate. An example of visualization of same data with different setting can be seen in Fig. 4. More complex methods of level-of-detail approach are planned for future work.

Progressive Loading: when the option of loading every n-th point has value higher than 1 this switch will define whether after every n-th point is loaded the loading will continue with incremented offset or not.

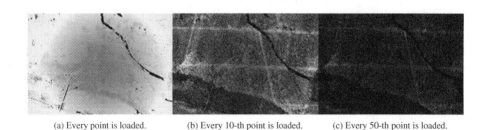

(a) Every point is loaded.   (b) Every 10-th point is loaded.   (c) Every 50-th point is loaded.

Fig. 4. The comparison of the same data visualization with different setting for loading every n-th point.

Users can navigate in the visualization scene with use of mouse and keyboard. Mouse is used for simple view rotation and zooming. The keyboard is used for moving the camera view through the scene, speed of navigation can be adjusted by changing the velocity multiplier.

When switch for Live data visualization is active the visualization module is waiting for the data to be piped from Data Sender through Data Preparation Module in real-time. If no Data Sender is connected to Data Preparation Module or no data is sent, the Data Visualization Module will wait and no data will be rendered.

Colors of visualization display the distance from camera to individual point. A jet color-map is used to represent distances from the viewpoint (red being closest and dark blue being the farthest away). Color-map is scaled for individual data set and can be adjusted easily. To make distance even more apparent the size of rendered points decreases with distance.

The visualization module also supports selection of desired points in the point cloud. Because the interaction with individual point would require too much overhead only selection of point groups is supported in the current version. The size of selection group can be defined as parameter. In our case the size of few thousands points per group in data set with millions of points proved to be best option for good performance. To allow faster selection of groups of points we allow two-level point selection: (1) single group under mouse cursor is selected and (2) all the groups with points under mouse cursor are selected. The focused points are rendered with pink color while selected points are rendered in white (both colors are not in jet color-map and are thus easily distinguishable from the rest). An example of focused and selected point groups can be seen in Fig. 5.

Fig. 5. The example of focused points (pink) and selected points (white). (Color figure online)

To get even better visualization experience, complete Potree visualization pipeline could be integrated, adding point shadowing and other more advanced visualization features. In our case we only followed few implementation solutions used in Potree library (point render size, server-client communication and few other features).

2.4   User Collaboration

Collaboration allows users to share their view on data with other users in real time similar to [14]. The user initiates sharing by activating share switch in preferences panel. Once activated other users can see such users in list of users (as shown in Fig. 6a) and connect to a selected user by clicking on button with his/her designation (see Fig. 6b). Users that want to join the shared session must do so before the host user initiates data loading. After the loading is initiated by host other users can not connect anymore. The initiation of the loading starts loading the data from same database for all the connected users. The data loading is independent for each user due to the different speeds of the network connections and request handling speed of individual client. Users can navigate the scene separately and change their view on the data as is presented in Fig. 6c (view of the main user) and 6d (view of the connected user).

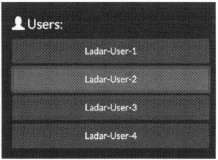

(a) List of users who are sharing their view.

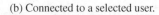

(b) Connected to a selected user.

(c) The view on the data for main user.

(d) The view for user connected to user (c)

Fig. 6. The sharing options.

The sharing is implemented as presented in the Fig. 7. Currently only the following types of sharing is supported by the system: (1) camera view parameters, (2) loading initiation cancellation and (3) data selection. While view and loading initialization are only shared in one direction (from host to connected users) the data selection is supported in both directions and the selection state is kept on the server. The framework supports simple implementation for sharing other data or parameters as well.

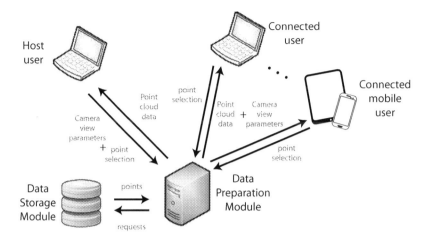

Fig. 7. The diagram is showing how the shared data is distributed.

3   Evaluation and Results

We only conducted preliminary evaluation of the system. The developed system allows interactive visualization of datasets with up to tens of millions of points on a consumer based hardware: i7 (2.3 GHz), 16 GB RAM, NVIDIA GeForce GT 650M 1024 MB. The visualization had on average more than 25 FPS. Streaming live data from the Data-Sender module on local network speed was approx. 200.000 points per second which presented the upper limit for the sending system. Streaming data from the server-side database system speed was approx. 30.000 points per second. The bottleneck in this case was the database system which ran on a low-end infrastructure, also the time for querying the database was a bit slow. The visualization test was performed with Autzen sample data supplied with liblas[9] library, which was imported into PostgreSQL database on virtual machine with single core (2.3 GHz) and 4 GB RAM. The loading of 10.6 million points in the dataset took on average 341 s while sending the data in JSON format over the wireless network connection.

The collaborative features worked fine on local network as well as over the Internet. This was expected since the data is sent to each client individually except the annotation information which is only sent between connected clients. As part of future work we are also planning more in-depth evaluation of the system.

4   Conclusion

The presented system is used for real-time visualization of real-time as well as stored point cloud data. The preliminary results show that the presented system

---

[9] https://www.liblas.org/samples/.

can be used in real-life scenarios. While there are some downsides to slow data streaming from the database it is still sufficient for the tested scenarios. However in the future we are planning to test different database solutions for faster data throughput. We are also planning on improving the client-side visualization implementation for easier user interaction and navigation as well as support for level-of-detail display of data with support for user defined detail parameters. Other possible future work contains reimplementation of user annotation and selection of the displayed data.

References

1. Du, H., Henry, P., Ren, X., Cheng, M., Goldman, D.B., Seitz, S.M., Fox, D.: Interactive 3D modeling of indoor environments with a consumer depth camera. In: Proceedings of the 13th International Conference on Ubiquitous Computing, pp. 75–84. ACM (2011)
2. Haala, N., Peter, M., Kremer, J., Hunter, G.: Mobile LiDAR mapping for 3D point cloud collection in urban areas - a performance test. Int. Arch. Photogrammetry Remote Sens. Spat. Inf. Sci. **37**, 1119–1127 (2008)
3. Molebny, V., McManamon, P.F., Steinvall, O., Kobayashi, T., Chen, W.: Laser radar: historical prospective-from the east to the west. Opt. Eng. **56**, 56 (2016). https://spie.org/publications/journal/10.1117/1.OE.56.3.031220?SSO=1
4. Rosnell, T., Honkavaara, E.: Point cloud generation from aerial image data acquired by a quadrocopter type micro unmanned aerial vehicle and a digital still camera. Sensors **12**(1), 453–480 (2012)
5. Wang, C.C., Thorpe, C., Suppe, A.: LADAR-based detection and tracking of moving objectsfrom a ground vehicle at high speeds. In: IEEE IV2003 Intelligent Vehicles Symposium. Proceedings (Cat. No.03TH8683), pp. 416–421, June 2003
6. Navarro-Serment, L.E., Mertz, C., Hebert, M.: Pedestrian detection and tracking using three-dimensional LADAR data. Int. J. Robot. Res. **29**(12), 1516–1528 (2010)
7. Rusu, R.B., Cousins, S.: 3D is here: Point cloud library (pcl). In: IEEE International Conference on Robotics and automation (ICRA) 2011, pp. 1–4. IEEE (2011)
8. Kreylos, O., Bawden, G.W., Kellogg, L.H.: Immersive visualization and analysis of LiDAR data. In: Bebis, G., Boyle, R., Parvin, B., Koracin, D., Remagnino, P., Porikli, F., Peters, J., Klosowski, J., Arns, L., Chun, Y.K., Rhyne, T.-M., Monroe, L. (eds.) ISVC 2008. LNCS, vol. 5358, pp. 846–855. Springer, Heidelberg (2008). https://doi.org/10.1007/978-3-540-89639-5_81
9. Su, T., Wang, W., Lv, Z., Wu, W., Li, X.: Rapid delaunay triangulation for randomly distributed point cloud data using adaptive hilbert curve. Comput. Graph. **54**, 65–74 (2016). Special Issue on CAD/Graphics 2015
10. Hug, C., Krzystek, P., Fuchs, W.: Advanced lidar data processing with lastools. In: ISPRS Congress, pp. 12–23 (2004)
11. van Oosterom, P., Martinez-Rubi, O., Ivanova, M., Horhammer, M., Geringer, D., Ravada, S., Tijssen, T., Kodde, M., Gonçalves, R.: Massive point cloud data management. Comput. Graph. **49**(C), 92–125 (2015)
12. Lavrič, P., Bohak, C., Marolt, M.: Collaborative view-aligned annotations in web-based 3D medical data visualization. In: MIPRO 2017, 40th Jubilee International Convention, 22–26 May 2017, Opatija, Croatia, proceedings, pp. 276–280 (2017)

13. Schütz, M.: Potree: Rendering Large Point Clouds in Web Browsers. Master's thesis, Institute of Computer Graphics and Algorithms, Vienna, University of Technology, Favoritenstrasse 9–11/186, A-1040 Vienna, Austria, September 2016
14. Marion, C., Jomier, J.: Real-time collaborative scientific WebGL visualization with WebSocket. In: Proceedings of the 17th International Conference on 3D Web Technology, pp. 47–50. ACM (2012)

Design of a Kind of Optimized Time-Lapse Macro VR Movie Recording System

YanXiang Zhang$^{(\boxtimes)}$ and Pengfei Ma

Department of Communication of Science and Technology,
University of Science and Technology of China, Hefei, Anhui, China
petrel@ustc.edu.cn, pfm@mail.ustc.edu.cn

Abstract. With the popularization of VR head mounted displays (HMD), the demands for VR movies are rising rapidly. Traditionally, time lapse movies are usually used for educational purpose, but they can be significantly more vivid if they can be viewed in VR ways. The authors designed a kind of automatic control system targeted to record VR movies showing the slow process of change such as plant growing, astronomical phenomena, etc. The system is mainly consist of hardware module and software part. The system hardware includes five parts consisting of the main-control chip using FPGA, dual H-bridge motor drive circuit using L298N drive chip, two channels relay circuit with isolation using optical coupler, the three channels DC output switched-mode power supply, a slide track with a two phase four wire step motor as mechanical parts, which are used to support the camera controlled by a cable release. For the software part, Quartus II and Verilog HDL were used to program and control. It has many advantages, including adjustable micro spur, simple design, unattended operation for a long time, safe and convenient operations.

Keywords: Time-lapse Macro VR movies · FPGA · Step motor
Liner slide rail

1 Introduction

The fast development of VR glass meet people's new demand of pursuing stereo content because of more realistic feelings. However, there are many stereo natural phenomenon in the domain of science, whose states change very slowly so that people can't notice the change. The authors usually use time-lapse videos to amplify the change, and need to shoot them in a relatively close distance as in Macro Photography.

There are three methods used by this kind of photography at present. However, traditional stereo camera has big spacing between two lens, and the spacing is not adjustable. Existing macro stereo lens usually lead to poor image quality [2], and imaging size will be reduced by a half [3]. Using two cameras synchronously to take photos results in a bigger spacing between the two lens on two cameras than when using the camera with a single stereo lens. Hence, using two cameras is not a good option to take macro effect photo. Currently, there is still no ideal solution for this kind of requirement.

© Springer International Publishing AG, part of Springer Nature 2018
L. T. De Paolis and P. Bourdot (Eds.): AVR 2018, LNCS 10850, pp. 225–234, 2018.
https://doi.org/10.1007/978-3-319-95270-3_18

Because object of time-lapse video changes very slowly, the authors then used a single camera by moving it on a liner slider rail. However, because the delay period may be for many days, the authors can't finish this kind of photography continuously by manual method. So the authors design an automatic control system based on FPGA [1], which can work automatically for a long time and has extra advantages of adjustable micro-interval, simple design, stable and convenient.

2 System Design

The hardware modules of automatic control system is designed based on FPGA as main-control chip, a power module, a liner slide rail, a step motor running on the liner slide rail, a L298N motor drive module, a two channels relay circuit module, the control principle of cable release, system machinery and power supply module. A camera was mounted on the liner slide rail, the shutter of the camera will be triggered by the cable release and the camera will move according to the step motor.

System logic was realized by software modules using Verilog HDL programming language in Quartus II software to drive and operate the whole system.

Figure 1 shows hardware modules diagram of the system.

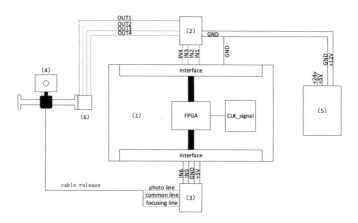

Fig. 1. System hardware modules block diagram (Color figure online)

2.1 Two Phase Four Wire Step Motor Timing Sequence

As the component (6) in Fig. 1, the system use a 42 series two phase four wire step motor, which contains four wires in red, yellow, green and blue corresponding to A+, B+, A−, B−. When FPGA pin sends a pulse to the motor, it will run 1.8°, and when FPGA sends pulses according to certain timing sequence, the motor will run incessantly. Here the authors use eight beats working mode because this mode can improve the system stability relative to four beats working mode [4]. The result is displayed in Table 1.

Table 1. Eight beats working mode timing sequence

	A	B	C	D	E	F	G	H
A+	1	1	0	0	0	0	0	1
B+	0	1	1	1	0	0	0	0
A−	0	0	0	1	1	1	0	0
B−	0	0	0	0	0	1	1	1

0 and 1 in table expresses given low and high level by FPGA relevant pins.

2.2 Main-Control Chip FPGA Module

Compared with the traditional design of step motor control, Altera ® FPGA has strong adaptive ability, adjustable DSP precision and effective electrical characteristics [5]. So the authors chose an Altera Cyclone EP1C3T144C8 FPGA mounted on a development board with 144 pins. In this part of work, as the component (1) in Fig. 1, the authors use totally 8 pins in FPGA, and their functions are given in Table 2.

Table 2. Pin numbers to name and corresponding function

Pin No. to name	Function
82 to IN1	Be used to link A+ wire of two phase four wire step motor
84 to IN2	Be used to link B+ wire of two phase four wire step motor
91 to IN3	Be used to link A− wire of two phase four wire step motor
96 to IN4	Be used to link B− wire of two phase four wire step motor
78 to IN5	Be used to link relay circuit module and finish auto-focusing function
98 to IN6	Be used to link relay circuit module and finish auto-photo function
100 to 5 V	Be used to act as power supply of relay circuit module
GND	Be used to form loop

The development board is equipped with a 48 MHz crystal oscillator in order to provide clock or pulse signal. In order to avoid resonance of step motor and slide rail [6], the system needs an appropriate step motor speed, so the authors used a 2400 Hz crossover module through instancing in the FPGA. This pulse frequency can avoid resonance effect after repeated experiments.

2.3 L298N Motor Drive Module

Step motor can be derived by relay or power transistor [7]. In the system, in order to adapt to the control requirement, for example, drive voltage, current, power, the authors design a dual H-bridge motor drive circuit based on L298N drive chip showed in the component (2) of Fig. 1, the module circuit is showed in Fig. 2.

L298N drive chip embeds dual H-bridge motor circuit, DriveOut(3) to DriveOut(0) respectively corresponds with 82, 84, 91, 96 pin of FPGA showed in Table 2, the four

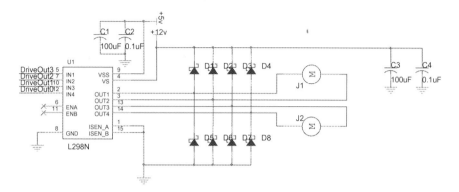

Fig. 2. L298N motor drive module circuit

wires can give same timing sequence as it in Table 1 to L298N so that the step motor will move without a break unless L298N receives a stop instruct (DriveOut(3) to DriveOut(0) is 4'b0) from FPGA.

C1, C2, C3, C4 are filter capacitors. In order to protect the step motor, the authors use eight freewheeling diode D1 to D8. J1, J2 are the load step motor symbols, and relevant motor control code will be stated in system software module part.

2.4   Two Channels Relay Circuit Module

In order to realize take photo and focusing automatically, the authors must accomplish communication automatically from FPGA to camera.

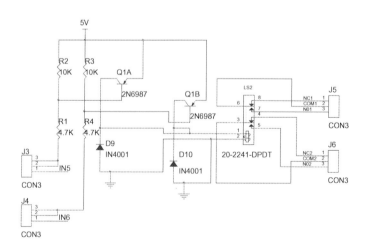

Fig. 3. Two channels relay module circuit

Two channels relay circuit and cable release are showed in the component (3) of Fig. 1. Figure 3 shows the detailed module circuit.

On the figure, IN5 and IN6 connect to FPGA number 78 and 98 pin and receive instruction from FPGA. The number 78 pin is for automatic focusing and the 98 pin for taking photo automatically. It can realize function switch on and off in fact when using the saturation conduction and cut-off character of transistor, but the load power of transistor is limited, so there should be a relay circuit amplification current from transistor [8]. The circuit uses low level to export from collector. R2 and R3 is pull-up resistor, the base will be high level when it is not offered pulse or voltage and now ungated because it is inverse transistor. It can be conductive when IN6 and IN5 offers low level to base, so when NO1 and NO2 is closed, NC1 and NC2 is opened with common port.

2.5   The Control Principle of Cable Release

In order to finish communication between relay module and camera, the authors use a strip of cable release to transmit signal. Its sketch map is showed in Fig. 4.

Fig. 4. Cable release sketch map (Color figure online)

The cable release consists totally of an interface and three lines [9]. The interface is used for inserting in camera. The purple line between is common. The orange line above used for taking photo, when the above and between line connect together, camera will open its shutter rapidly during a short time and take photo. Besides, camera will be focusing when the between lines and under dark green line connect together. But camera will open Blub gate when three lines connect together, this means that the camera will be exposed for a long time.

Figure 5 shows the interface of camera and relay module through cable release. The authors use FPGA number 98 pin to control J1 by first relay channel through IN5 pin of J3 and 78 pin to control J2 by second relay channel through IN6 pin of J4 in Fig. 3. When 98 pin gives low level to IN5 pin, the photo and common line will connect and camera will take photo.

Similarly, when 78 pin gives low level focusing and, the common line will be connected and the camera will be focusing.

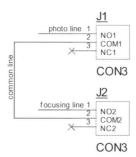

Fig. 5. The interface of camera and relay module

2.6   System Machinery and Power Supply Module

The camera can move and stop on the slide track that is about 220 mm long and has 8 mm screw pitch. System includes a three channels DC output Switch power supply represented by the component (5) of Fig. 1, it can offer +5 V, +12 V, +24 V power for our system, each channel maximal output current corresponding to 8 A, 2.5 A, 2 A respectively, so the power supply is enough for our L298N drive current. Figure 6 shows system setup.

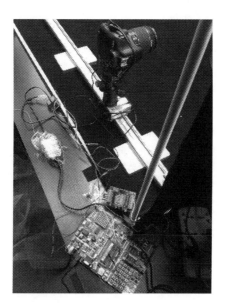

Fig. 6. System field entity

2.7   Software Modules and System Logic

System uses Verilog HDL programming language to implement function in Quartus II software. Figure 7 gives flow chart for achieving the requirement.

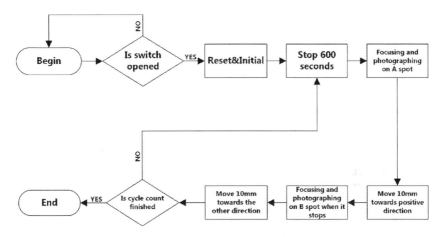

Fig. 7. Program flow chart.

3   Program Functionality Design and Application

In the basic logic of the time-lapse VR video recording, users could set spot A and spot B in the liner slide rail. The interval between A and B is adjustable freely so that system can reach micro spur target.

Usually the recorded objects change very slowly, in order to increase the production efficiency, the authors array a serials of objects in a line parallel to the liner slide rail, then record the objects one by one.

Another consideration is, in some situation, time-lapse VR videos might be displayed on naked eye stereoscopic displays, rather than a two-picture image pairs for traditional VR HMDs. Naked eye stereoscopic displays usually require four-picture image pairs, based on the above consideration, the recording method is designed as below (Fig. 8):

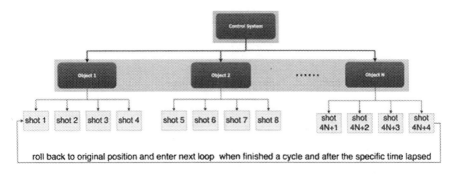

Fig. 8. Program functionality design

Four objects were arrayed parallel to the liner slide rail. For each object, four pictures were recorded in each loop. There is a gap of 5 mm between 2 adjacent shots for each object, and there is a 10-min interval between two loops, thus slightly changes could be recorded in detail.

4   Result Analysis

Three groups of pictures were selected to analyze the system, shown as Fig. 9.

Fig. 9. Selected recorded image groups

The first group were recorded from 2017/04/16/13:26 to 13:28, the second group were recorded from 2017/04/19/10:53 to 10:56, the third group were recorded from 2017/04/21/18:51 to 18:53, it lasted for 5 days and 5 and a half hours, 3872 pictures were recorded, there are 968 shots for each object, and 242 shots at each fixed position.

To check the stability of this system, we compare two pictures recorded at the same position at 2017/04/16/13:26 and 2017/04/21/18:51, as shown in Fig. 10. From the obtained results, it could be easily seen that the still objects in two pictures match perfectly in both horizontal and vertical directions, as shown in Fig. 11.

Fig. 10. Two pictures recorded at the same position at 2017/04/16/13:26 and 2017/04/21/18:51

Fig. 11. Two pictures match perfectly in both horizontal and vertical directions

Fig. 12. Four-picture stereo pairs for naked eye stereoscopic display

Also any two pictures from a four-picture stereo (Fig. 12) pairs could form very comfort stereo effects. When displaying the four-picture stereo pairs on a naked eye stereoscopic display, users could see very comfortable stereo effects from more than one angles.

The only one unexpected thing is that there is too large difference between the change speeds of the 4 objects. Actually, they are 4 kinds of plants, only one of them changes in the first 5 days and it changes too fast, while the other 3 plants almost didn't change a little, one of the 3 even have root rot.

5 Conclusion

By using a liner slide rail, FPGA board, step motor and its drive circuit using L298N IC, machinery system, and a program wrote by Verilog HDL, the authors developed a kind of system that could record stable time-lapse VR video contents automatically for long period. The users could define the numbers of pictures in an image pairs, gap between shots, the time gap between loops to realize a flexible time-lapse VR contents recording.

References

1. ALTERA Corporation: Optimized motor control design using integrated FPGA design flow. WP-01162-1.2 (2011)
2. Peng, B.: 3D Stereoscopic Photography. Zhejiang Photographic Publishing House, Hangzhou (2013)
3. Chen, J.: Research on the three - dimensional technique of flat image and the key technology in stereo photography. Doctoral thesis in Nankai University (2005)
4. Liu, B.: Research on precise control method of stepping motor. Doctoral thesis in Shan Dong University (2010)
5. Yang, Q.: Design of video image acquisition and processing system based on FPGA. Doctoral thesis in Huazhong University of Science and Technology (2013)
6. Shi, Y.: Research on high precision stepper motor control based on single chip microcomputer. Commun. World, 105–108 (2016)
7. Yang, M.: Research and Design of Relay Delay Time Measurement Circuit. Electronic design engineering (2014)
8. Liu, J.: Research and Application of Safe Driving Circuit for Electromagnetic relay. Measurement and Control Technology (2014)
9. Sha, L.: Research on the technique of delayed photography by digital camera. Lit. Life **6** (2012)

Catching Virtual Throws: An Immersive Virtual Reality Setup to Evaluate Human Predictive Skills

Antonella Maselli[1]([✉]), Benedetta Cesqui[1,2], Paolo Tommasino[1],
Aishwar Dhawan[3], Francesco Lacquaniti[1,2], and Andrea d'Avella[1,4]

[1] Laboratory of Neuromotor Physiology, Santa Lucia Foundation, Rome, Italy
a.maselli@hsantalucia.it

[2] Department of Systems Medicine and Center of Space Biomedicine,
University of Rome Tor Vergata, Rome, Italy

[3] Department of Biomechanics, Institute of Sukan Negara,
Kuala Lumpur, Malaysia

[4] Department of Biomedical and Dental Sciences and Morphofunctional
Imaging, University of Messina, Messina, Italy

Abstract. We present and validate a novel and portable IVR setup conceived for studying the predictive mechanisms associated to action observation. The setup implements an interactive throwing-catching task in which participants have to intercept balls thrown from a virtual character. To validate the setup, we performed a preliminary experiment in which participants had to intercept balls thrown by different throwers, under different ball/thrower visibility conditions. Non-expert adult participants were able to extract information from an observed throwing action to improve their interceptive performances. This ability was modulated by the throwing strategy (e.g. throwing from a fixed stance with respect to throwing with stepping corresponded to worse interceptive performances). These preliminary results validate our setup as a novel tool for exploring how humans access and make use of information from observed actions to optimize interpersonal interactions. Importantly, the proposed setup could be used as a tool for early diagnosis of pathologies in which predictive skills are progressively impaired.

1 Introduction

Catching a flying ball requires prediction to compensate for the intrinsic sensorimotor delays of the Central Nervous System (CNS) [1]. Indeed, a catcher needs to plan where and when to intercept the ball more than 100 ms ahead of the interception event, meaning that for fast balls (8–10 m/s) accurate predictions should be made when the ball is more than 1 m away. Experimental evidence suggests that this kind of predictions are typically made based on information from the initial part of the ball trajectory [2], with the support of an internal model used to extrapolate the observed motion according to the gravitational law of motion [3, 4]. Additional source of information, available for the early planning of more effective interceptive strategies, is embedded in the throwing kinematics. The throwing motion of the whole body leads

© Springer International Publishing AG, part of Springer Nature 2018
L. T. De Paolis and P. Bourdot (Eds.): AVR 2018, LNCS 10850, pp. 235–242, 2018.
https://doi.org/10.1007/978-3-319-95270-3_19

the ball to be released at a given combination of location, speed and time, and therefore determines the ball outgoing trajectory. Indeed, sports science literature has shown that the advance information available throughout the unfolding of an action (e.g. during the throwing action of a cricket bowler) is extensively used by elite players to improve their performances [5]. However, the possibility to exploit advance information kinematics for improving performances does not only depend on the ability of the observer (e.g. a catcher) to extract relevant information from the observed action, but also from the amount of information embedded in the action kinematics. The latter can be modulated on purpose, for example in deceptive throws, or can intrinsically vary according to individual throwing strategies.

In a previous study, we have quantitatively characterized the information available in the kinematics of the throwing action about the direction of the outgoing ball trajectories [6]. By analysing unconstraint overarm throwing kinematics from non-professional players, we showed that it is ideally possible to predict the side (right vs left) of a thrown ball already 400 ms before ball release with an accuracy above 80%. Furthermore, we showed that such early informative cues are associated to the kinematics of body segments, typically different from the throwing arm, that vary according to the individual throwing strategy.

Here we present a new Immersive Virtual Reality (IVR) setup designed to investigate whether and to what extent human adults are able to use information from an observed throwing action when performing an interceptive task. The setup is suited to address other potentially related effects, for example the dependence on the legibility of the throwing action (i.e., on the spatiotemporal structure of the information available in the throwing kinematics about the outgoing ball direction). The setup consists in a tracked Head Mounted Display (HMD) used to give participants a stereo and dynamical view of a virtual scenario representing a large room in which a humanoid avatar performs throwing actions leading to the consistent projection of a flying ball. Throwing animations may correspond to motion capture recordings of real throwing actions retargeted to the human avatar or reproduce synthetic kinematics (built or modified computationally). The system integrates a tracked wand that is given to participants as a racket for intercepting the approaching virtual balls.

To validate the setup, we performed a pilot experiment designed to test whether non-expert adult participants are able to use information from an observed throwing action during interceptive tasks, and whether there is a dependence of the kinematics strategy adopted by the thrower. Preliminary results confirm both hypotheses. This validates the IVR setup presented here as a robust tool for studying the predictive mechanisms associated to the observation of biological motion and the associated sensorimotor strategies underlying interpersonal interaction at distance.

2 Materials and Methods

2.1 VR Scenario and System

The virtual throwing and catching scenario was rendered using a virtual reality headset (HTC Vive) with a 90 Hz refreshing rate, a 110° field of view and with a display resolution of 1080×1200 pixels per eye. The HTC Vive system includes a "room scale" tracking technology used to track a headset and two handheld controllers, allowing the user to move in the 3D space and to interact with the virtual environment.

The virtual scene and the experiment were programmed in C# using the Unity cross-platform game engine and the SteamVR plugin. The virtual scene, shown in Fig. 1, consisted in a large empty room of 8×15 m^2 floor size and 5 m height, a 0.1 m diameter ball, a virtual "racket" used by subjects to intercept the virtual ball, and a throwing avatar. The virtual racket was designed by attaching a white disk (20 cm diameter, 3 cm thickness) to a virtual replica of the handheld controller. The spatial position and orientation of the racket were update with the position and orientation of the controller at each time sample.

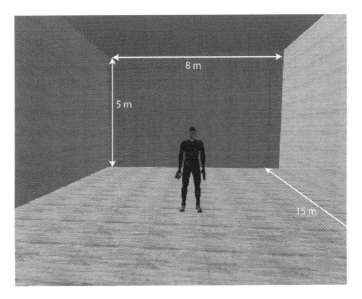

Fig. 1. Virtual scenario as seen from the participant's perspective.

The avatar was scaled so to match the size and relative proportions of four participants of a previous study [6]. The kinematics of the throwing actions and of the ball recorded by motion capture in that study were used to animate both the virtual thrower and the corresponding ball trajectories in the different experimental trails. Throwing motions were animated by retargeting kinematic data of real throwers with Motion Builder 2017. Up until the release time, the ball was attached to the avatar's right hand; from the release time onwards, the ball spatial position was updated at each time sample according to a 3rd order polynomial fit of the recorded trajectory.

2.2 Experimental Design

We adopted a 2×4 experimental design in which the two manipulated factors were: the throwing strategy of the thrower (4 individual throwers with different strategy) and

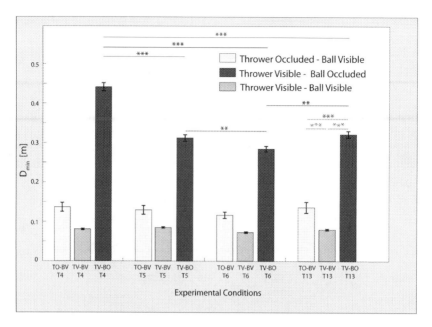

Fig. 2. Bar plots showing mean and standard error (averaged across participants) of the minimum hand-ball distance D_{min}. Horizontal lines and asterisks in black indicate significant comparisons (**p < 0.01, ***p < 0.001). Comparisons indicated in light gray refer to comparisons across visibility conditions (ExpCond) including data from all throwers.

the visibility of the ball flight (visible or occluded). Varying the throwing strategy allowed to test whether it affects the ability of an observer (the catcher-participant in this case) to predict the throw outcome. Changing the ball visibility forced participants to use advance information extracted from the observed throwing kinematics to perform the interceptive tasks. The ball visibility was either completely occluded from ball release to ball arrival, or visible throughout the whole flight. In the following, we refer to these two conditions as *TV-BO* and *TV-BV* (where *TV* stands for thrower visible, and *BV/BO* for ball visible/occluded). At the beginning of the experiment, participants additionally performed a training session in which the throwing phase was occluded and the ball appeared static at the release point for 1 s and then travelled along its prerecorded path (*TO-BV*).

To manipulate the throwing strategy, we selected four subjects from our previous experiment, each adopting different patterns of stepping during the throwing action and all having similar temporal profiles in the corresponding predictability of the outgoing ball direction. The selected subjects are P4, P5, P6 and P13 from [6], and will be referred to as T4, T5, T6 and T13 in the following. The average throwing kinematics of the four throwers is shown in Fig. 3 of [6] and corresponds to throwing while standing at place (T4), with a left step (T5), with a right step (T6) and with a double right-left stepping sequence (T13). We selected eight trials for each of the four throwers. The selection criteria were: (i) to include two successful throws for each of the four targets arranged on a rectangular layout (up-left, down-left, up-right, down-right) on a vertical plane placed at 6 m from the thrower, and (ii) to include trials which minimized the standard deviation of the flight time across all trials from all throwers. These selection criteria allowed to select 32 throws with similar flight time (mean ± std: 583 ± 10 ms) and, by groups of 8 throws, arriving at similar locations on the targets plane.

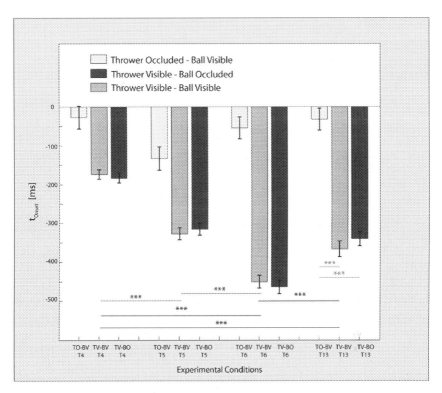

Fig. 3. Bar plots showing mean and standard error (averaged across participants) of the movement onset time, t_{onset}, measured with respect to ball release. Horizontal lines and asterisks in black indicate significant comparisons (**p < 0.01, ***p < 0.001). Comparisons indicated in light gray refer to comparisons across visibility conditions (ExpCond) including data from all throwers.

Participants could see the thrower at a distance of 5.5 m and were instructed to intercept the ball in all conditions, i.e. both with the ball visible or occluded. Each participant performed first a block of 64 trials in the *TO-BV* configuration (training session). Next, 512 trials with the thrower visible, including 8 blocks of the 32 trials in each of the two ball visibility conditions. Trials were presented in pseudo-randomized order (equal for all participants, to avoid potential presentation-order effects).

The spatial position and orientation of the racket were updated at each time sample with the position and orientation of the controller. For a successful catch, i.e. when the distance between the centre of the racket's disk and the ball was less than 20 cm, subjects received both an auditory feedback (a short tone) and haptic feedback (the vibration of the hand-held controller). Experimental data were logged at 100 Hz.

The experimental procedure was approved by the Ethical Committee of the Santa Lucia Foundation.

2.3 Participants

Eight participants (5 females) took part in the experiment (age: 35 ± 7 years, mean $\pm$ std), all with normal or corrected-to-normal vision and no history of neurological diseases. All participants signed an informed consent form before taking part to the study.

2.4 Assessment Variables and Statistical Analysis

Assessment variables were extracted from the kinematics of right hand tracked by the position of the hand-held controller. For each trial, we extracted the time of movement onset measured with respect to ball release (t_{onset}) and the minimum distance between the disk's centre trajectory and the ball trajectory (D_{min}). Trials for which $D_{min} < 20$ cm were considered successful. For each participant we then computed the individual score (S) as the percentage of successful trials.

A repeated measures two-way (3×4) ANOVA was performed to compare the assessment variables D_{min} and t_{onset} in different experimental conditions of ball and throwing kinematics visibility (*TO-BV* vs *TV-BV* vs *TV-BO*), and for different throwing strategies (T4, T5, T6, T7). We will refer to the two factors as *ExpCond* and *Thrower* when reporting the results. We used post-hoc Tukey tests with Bonferroni correction for pairwise comparisons between groups.

3 Results

Participants exhibited higher scores in the *TV-BV* condition ($99 \pm 1\%$, mean $\pm$ se across participants) with respect to both the *TV-BO* (25 ± 0.02 %) and the *TO-BV* (86 ± 0.04 %) conditions. ANOVA of the D_{min} variable revealed a significant effect for both factors, *ExpCond* ($F_{(2,4025)} = 60.2$, $p < 0.001$) and *Thrower* ($F_{(3,4025)} = 1809.6$, $p < 0.001$). Post-hoc comparisons revealed that all *ExpCond* groups were indeed statistically different from each other ($p < 0.001$ in all comparisons). When applied to the *Thrower* factor, post-hoc comparisons revealed significant differences between T4 and the other three throwers ($p < 0.001$ in all cases), as well as between T5 and T6 ($p = 0.006$) and between T6 and T13 ($p = 0.001$).

The means and standard errors across participants for D_{min} are shown in Fig. 2. The bar plot shows clearly how participants made significantly larger interception errors when the ball flight was occluded, which was an expected effect. Interestingly, when the ball was visible, interceptive accuracies were significantly modulated by the throwing kinematics visibility (*TV-BV* vs *TO-BV*). This suggests that also "non-expert" catchers are able to extract information from the observed throwing kinematics to improve interceptive performances. Nevertheless, the order effect (*TO-BV* was always performed before *TV-BV*) could play as a confound, as the improved performance could be also due to a learning effect. Future studies with completely randomized design across conditions should be implemented to remove such confound and confirm that improvements in performance are associated with the ability to extract information from the observed throwing kinematics.

The significant differences found across throwers are clearly visible for the *TV-BO* conditions, where the ball occlusion worked as intended in magnifying the effect of thrower kinematics on predictions. This result demonstrates that, as hypothesized, some throwing strategies are less informative than others.

Significant differences between groups where found also for the timing of the movement onset, t_{onset} (Fig. 3). ANOVA revealed a significant effect for both *ExpCond* ($F_{(2,4013)}$ = 122.7, p < 0.001), and *Thrower* ($F_{(3,4013)}$ = 95.5, p < 0.001). Post-hoc analysis revealed significant differences between the two thrower visibility conditions and the thrower occluded condition (p < 0.001 for both comparison). As expected, there was no difference between the *TV-BO* and *TV-BV* conditions (p = 0.932). Post-hoc comparisons applied to the factor *Thrower* revealed significant differences between T4 and the other three throwers (p < 0.001), as well as between T5 and T13 (p < 0.001) and between T6 and T13 (p < 0.001).

4   Conclusions

We designed a novel and portable IVR setup conceived for studying the mechanisms that allow humans to make predictions about the future outcome of an observed action (e.g. an overarm throw) and to exploit these predictions for planning anticipatory behaviour, which is crucial for optimizing interpersonal interactions.

The setup implements an interactive throwing-catching task in which participants were instructed to intercept balls thrown from a virtual character. In its current state, the setup allows to display (and occlude) a realistic human avatar throwing balls following pre-recorded whole-body throwing kinematics, and to display/occlude the corresponding ball trajectory.

We validated the setup and assessed its potential with an experiment in which participants had to intercept balls thrown by different throwers, under different ball/thrower visibility conditions. A preliminary analysis revealed that non-expert adult participants are able to extract information from an observed throwing action to improve their interceptive performances. Importantly, the impact of such predictive skills on both anticipatory behaviour and interceptive performance depends on the individual thrower. The latter result suggests that the legibility of a thrower is modulated by his/her individual throwing strategy. Future studies and more detailed analyses are required to explore more in details the sensorimotor mechanisms that underlying the observed differences.

Importantly, the proposed setup could be used as a tool for early diagnosis of pathologies in which predictive skills are progressively impaired.

Acknowledgments. This work was supported by Horizon 2020 Robotics Program CogIMon (ICT-23-2014 under grant Agreement 644727), by the Italian Education, University and Research Ministry (PRIN grant 2015HFWRYY), and by the Italian Space Agency (contract n. I/006/06/0).

References

1. Davidson, P.R., Wolpert, D.M.: Widespread access to predictive models in the motor system: a short review. J. Neural Eng. **2**, S313–S319 (2005). https://doi.org/10.1088/1741-2560/2/3/S11
2. Katsumata, H., Russell, D.M.: Prospective versus predictive control in timing of hitting a falling ball. Exp. Brain Res. **216**, 499–514 (2012). https://doi.org/10.1007/s00221-011-2954-y
3. Zago, M., McIntyre, J., Senot, P., Lacquaniti, F.: Internal models and prediction of visual gravitational motion. Vis. Res. **48**, 1532–1538 (2008). https://doi.org/10.1016/j.visres.2008.04.005
4. Russo, M., Cesqui, B., La Scaleia, B., Ceccarelli, F., Maselli, A., Moscatelli, A., Zago, M., Lacquaniti, F., d'Avella, A.: Intercepting virtual balls approaching under different gravity conditions: evidence for spatial prediction. J. Neurophysiol. jn.00025.2017 (2017). https://doi.org/10.1152/jn.00025.2017
5. Farrow, D., Abernethy, B., Jackson, R.C.: Probing expert anticipation with the temporal occlusion paradigm: experimental investigations of some methodological issues. Mot. Control **9**, 332–351 (2005)
6. Maselli, A., Dhawan, A., Cesqui, B., Russo, M., Lacquaniti, F., d'Avella, A.: Where are you throwing the ball? I better watch your body, not just your arm! Front. Hum. Neurosci. **11**, 1–19 (2017). https://doi.org/10.3389/fnhum.2017.00505

Virtual Reality as a Tool for the Cascade Control Learning

Edwin Pruna$^{(\boxtimes)}$, Mauricio Rosero, Rai Pogo, Ivón Escobar,
and Julio Acosta

Universidad de Las Fuerzas Armadas ESPE, Sangolquí, Ecuador
{eppruna, mgrosero4, rapogo, ipescobar,
jfacosta}@espe.edu.ec

Abstract. This work presents the development of an interactive didactic system for the learning of the cascade control technique of industrial processes, which uses an immersive virtual environment for the emulation of a plant behavior which can be monitored and controlled through an HMI (Human-Machine Interface). The virtual environment has been created through Computer Aided Design software and a graphic engine and, in addition, peripheral devices are used to achieve the immersion and interaction with the environment. Finally, the experimental results that validate the system when it is tested with a real or simulated process are presented.

Keywords: Virtual reality · Unity3D · Cascade control

1 Introduction

The automatic control has played a vital role in the advancement of engineering and science, this has become an important and integral part in the systems of space vehicles, in robotic systems, in modern manufacturing processes and in any industrial operation that requires the control of temperature, pressure, humidity, flow, among others [1, 8].

Among advanced control methods, there is a technique called cascade control, which is used when the manipulated variable suffers significant disturbances that excessively affect the controlled variable. The strategy consists in implanting a secondary control loop (nested) within the main loop, in order to control, independently, the manipulated variable itself [2].

In this context, education in technical areas, such as control engineering, has several factors that determine its quality. This needs to satisfy the students' needs in terms of theoretical and practical knowledge, which must be combined in a coherent and harmonious way [1, 3]. Since much of the engineering is based on the manipulation of materials, energy and information, it is obvious that the effectiveness of practical sessions is a determinant factor in the future performance of students, who should be able to investigate and solve problems efficiently and inside interdisciplinary teams, a characteristic that is not always well developed in engineering education [4]. All of this requires teaching methodologies that can have a positive impact on students, so that the knowledge imparted is enduring and makes their insertion process into the industry appropriate and successful [3–5].

© Springer International Publishing AG, part of Springer Nature 2018
L. T. De Paolis and P. Bourdot (Eds.): AVR 2018, LNCS 10850, pp. 243–251, 2018.
https://doi.org/10.1007/978-3-319-95270-3_20

To meet these objectives, nowadays, technology is being used much more frequently than before within modern teaching-learning techniques as a very influential method for an optimal knowledge transfer [5, 6]. The use of virtual reality, augmented reality, Internet of Things (IoT), artificial intelligence is increasingly common in the modern educational environment [7–9].

As it has been seen, virtual reality has taken a greater role as a computer simulation tool widely used for the advantages it provides in the educational process. The realism, versatility, immersive capacity and interaction that virtual reality provides are some of the elements that can significantly improve the learning experience. Its ability to provide information about real processes with different parameters of the system helps to evaluate the consequences of certain decisions. In addition, it allows to complement the process by showing the students the structures of the systems and the technological processes in the models [3, 10, 11]. Specifically, for education in control engineering, VR applications for training have been developed, where process plants with classic controllers applied to them are implemented [8].

Therefore, this article presents the development of an interactive virtual environment that contains an industrial plant and an HMI (Human-Machine Interface) that allows the monitoring and control of it, a cascade control technique is used for its regulation. The user is able to select the set-point for the control and can view the relevant process variables in measurement instruments and in the HMI itself. He also has the possibility of using his hands to complete the required tasks for which a gesture control device and a HMD (Head Mounted Display) have been used. The user's immersion in the environment increases thanks to the detail level of the objects and the sounds added to the plant. For the creation of the virtual environment, CAD (Computer Aided Design) tools have been used for the design of 3D objects, which are exported to a graphic engine for animation and characterization.

This article is organized into V sections including the Introduction. Section 2 describes the structure of the system. Section 3 details the creation of the virtual environment. In Sect. 4 the results are presented, and finally the conclusions and future work are exposed in Sect. 5.

2 System Structure

This work presents the development of an interactive didactic system for the process control learning, specifically cascade control. The system emulates the behavior of a real process according the change of its variables, this makes use of various software and hardware tools to achieve a high level of immersion and interaction between the user and the components of the environment.

The system is based on a virtual environment that contains an industrial level control plant of a tank and an HMI for its monitoring and control. The data corresponding to the process variables are obtained from a real control station or a simulation implemented externally, for which it is necessary to implement a method of data exchange between the programs that are part of the system.

The interaction between the peripheral devices and the used programs is shown in Fig. 1.

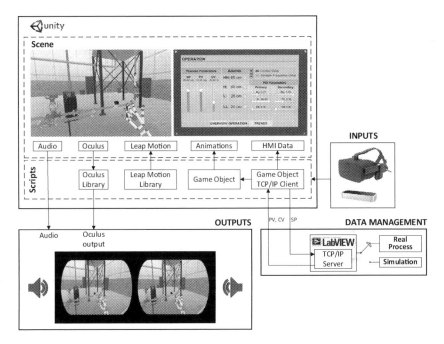

Fig. 1. System structure

The input stage consists of two dedicated devices for virtual reality, which for this case are: Oculus Rift and Leap Motion. The HMD Oculus Rift changes the vision angle according to the movements of the user's head and the Leap Motion handles the hands recognition to use them in the environment and thus interact with its components such as manual valves and the HMI screen, furthermore allowing the user to move along the environment by means of gestures in the direction in which displacement is desired. Thus the user can move freely around the environment and visualize each element that composes it. With the implementation of this feature the use of manual VR controllers is suppressed, making the experience more comfortable and realistic.

In the scripts stage, the communication between Unity3D, Labview and the input devices is implemented. The animations of the objects in the environment are designed so that they respond according to the process variables whose behaviors can be determined by data from a real control plant or by a simulation. In the first case, for a real control station, the control algorithm is performed in a Programmable Logic Controller (PLC) and the data is sent to Labview; in the second case, the matematical model of the real station is used to implement the simulation of the control in Labview. For both cases, Labview takes the set-point sent from Unity3D for the execution of the control algorithm and returns the data corresponding to the process and control variables themselves that are visualized in an HMI and in the indicators and process transmistters.

The data exchange between Unity3D and Labview is done using the TCP/IP protocolo, for which a Client-Server architecture is used, where Unity3D acts as client and

Labview as server. This method provides a real-time communication which allows a correct monitoring and control of the plant.

The output stage contains the components sounds of the virtual plant and its alarms, in addition to the visual immersion in the environment.

3   Virtual Environment Development

The virtual environment design is based on the P&ID diagram of a training station for cascade control of the level of a tank which is shown in Fig. 2.

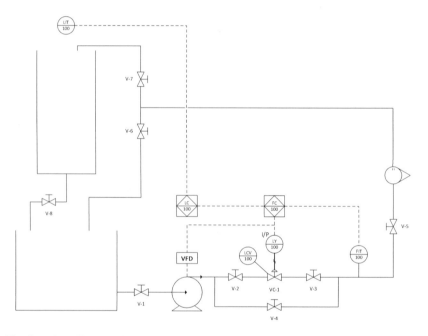

Fig. 2. P&ID diagram of a training station for the cascade control of the level of a tank

For the virtual environment creation, CAD tools and the Unity3D graphic engine are used. In addition, Labview is used as simulation and data management software. In Fig. 3 the diagram that describes the process used for the implementation of the VR application is shown.

3.1   CAD Design

One of the CAD tools used in this design stage is AutoCAD Plant 3D. This is a software oriented to the design of industrial plants and allows the interconnection of three-dimensional equipment in a realistic way. Figure 4 shows the base design of the virtual level control plant in AutoCAD Plant 3D.

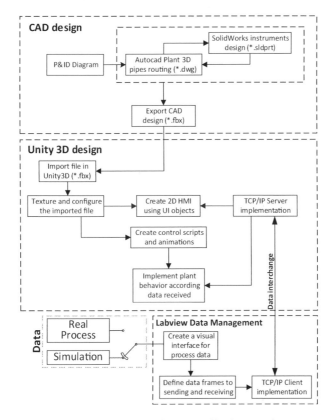

Fig. 3. Flow diagram for the application creation

Fig. 4. AutoCAD Plant 3D design

3.2 Unity3D Design

The implemented design in AutoCAD Plant 3D is imported in FBX format in Unity3D. In this stage the elements of the plant are animated and characterized, see Fig. 5.

Fig. 5. Virtual environment developed in Unity3D

The HMI for monitoring and control of the virtual plant has been designed using UI objects such as canvas, sliders and buttons. It consists of three screens: Overview, Operation and Trends. Figure 6 shows the screens of the implemented HMI that contains all the relevant information of the process. It is an important feature that the user has the possibility to manipulate the PID tuning constants of the two loops (primary and secondary) that make up the cascade control through the Operation screen of the HMI, which allows a more complete and optimal training by encompassing all the basic aspects related to cascade control of processes. The change of screens and the variation of the set-point and the tuning constants are made through Leap Motion.

(a) Overview screen

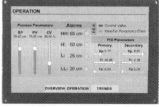

(b) Operation screen

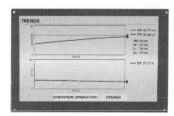

(c) Trends screen

Fig. 6. HMI screens

The elements of the plant have been animated so that their operation is identical to that of a real industrial plant. This feature allows students a greater acquisition of engineering knowledge with the advantage that there are no risks of equipment damage. In Fig. 7, it shows how the manual valves of the control valve bypass work according to the final control element used.

(a) Control valve like final control element

(b) Variable speed drive like final control element

Fig. 7. Manual valves work according the selected final control element

Another feature implemented to complement the process is the possibility of manipulating a load valve, which the user can operate through the Leap Motion to cause disturbances and visualize their effects in the control. This option is available only in simulation mode, see Fig. 8.

Fig. 8. Load valve

4   Results

To demonstrate the operation of the application, there are experiments that consist of
changing the set-point value and consequently the process and control variables values,
which can be visualized in the HMI and in the corresponding transmitters and indicators. Figures 9, 10 and 11 show the values of the process and control variable for
different set-point values when the system uses the actual control station.

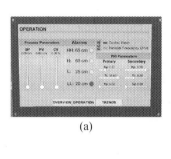 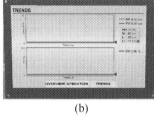 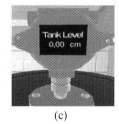

| (a) | (b) | (c) |

Fig. 9. SP = 0 cm

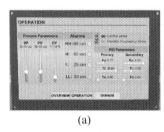 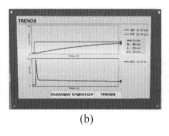 

| (a) | (b) | (c) |

Fig. 10. SP = 30 cm

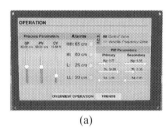 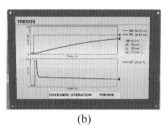 

| (a) | (b) | (c) |

Fig. 11. SP = 50 cm

5   Conclusion and Future Work

An interactive didactic system has been implemented for cascade control of processes.
The virtual environment provides a high degree of immersion by the level of detail of
the three-dimensional objects that make up the plant, a feature that generates a great
impact on users.

This system is capable of improving the teaching-learning process of engineering students since it contains all the basic aspects related to the cascade control of industrial processes. In addition, the user can experiment with the options provided by the environment to visualize and study the plant behavior in different conditions, which makes this application an effective educational alternative.

As future work, an evaluation of the proposed system with university students of control engineering is considered, who will have to carry out training sessions in the virtual environment to determine its effectiveness and usability.

References

1. Goodwin, G., Medioli, A., Sher, W., Vlacic, L., Welsh, J.: Emulation-based virtual laboratories: a low-cost alternative to physical experiments in control engineering education. IEEE Trans. Educ. **54**(1), 48–55 (2011)
2. Roca Cusidó, A.: Control de procesos. [Cambrils]: [L'autor] (2010)
3. Makarova, I., Khabibullin, R., Belyaev, E., Bogateeva, A.: The application of virtual reality technologies in engineering education for the automotive industry. In: 2015 International Conference on Interactive Collaborative Learning (ICL) (2015)
4. Häfner, P., Häfner, V., Ovtcharova, J.: Teaching methodology for virtual reality practical course in engineering education. Procedia Comput. Sci. **25**, 251–260 (2013)
5. Abulrub, A., Attridge, A., Williams, M.: Virtual reality in engineering education: the future of creative learning. Int. J. Emerg. Technol. Learn. (iJET), **6**(4) (2011)
6. Laseinde, O., Adejuyigbe, S., Mpofu, K., Campbell, H.: Educating tomorrows engineers: reinforcing engineering concepts through Virtual Reality (VR) teaching aid. In: 2015 IEEE International Conference on Industrial Engineering and Engineering Management (IEEM) (2015)
7. Li, M., Li, L., Jiao, R., Xiao, H.: Virtrul reality and artificial intelligence support future training development. In: 2017 Chinese Automation Congress (CAC) (2017)
8. Andaluz, V.H., et al.: Immersive industrial process environment from a P&ID diagram. In: Bebis, G., et al. (eds.) ISVC 2016. LNCS, vol. 10072. Springer, Cham (2016). https://doi.org/10.1007/978-3-319-50835-1_63
9. Turner, C., Hutabarat, W., Oyekan, J., Tiwari, A.: Discrete event simulation and virtual reality use in industry: new opportunities and future trends. IEEE Trans. Hum. Mach. Syst. **46**(6), 882–894 (2016)
10. Velosa, J., Cobo, L., Castillo, F., Castillo, C.: Methodological proposal for use of Virtual Reality VR and Augmented Reality AR in the formation of professional skills in industrial maintenance and industrial safety. In: Auer, M., Zutin, D. (eds.) Online Engineering & Internet of Things, vol. 22, pp. 987–1000. Springer, Cham (2017). https://doi.org/10.1007/978-3-319-64352-6_92
11. de Jong, T., Linn, M., Zacharia, Z.: Physical and virtual laboratories in science and engineering education. Science **340**(6130), 305–308 (2013)

Efficient Human Action Recognition Interface for Augmented and Virtual Reality Applications Based on Binary Descriptor

Abassin Sourou Fangbemi[1], Bin Liu[2(✉)], Neng Hai Yu[2], and Yanxiang Zhang[3]

[1] School of Software Engineering, University of Science and Technology of China, Hefei, Anhui, China
abassino@mail.ustc.edu.cn
[2] School of Information Science and Technology, University of Science and Technology of China, Hefei, Anhui, China
{flowice,ynh}@ustc.edu.cn
[3] School of Humanities and Social Science, University of Science and Technology of China, Hefei, Anhui, China
petrel@ustc.edu.cn

Abstract. In the fields of Augmented Reality (AR) and Virtual Reality (VR), Human-Computer Interaction (HCI) is an important component that allows the user to interact with its virtual environment. Though different approaches are adopted to meet the requirements of individual applications, the development of efficient, non-obtrusive and fast HCI interfaces is still a challenge. In this paper, we propose a new AR and VR interaction interface based on Human Action Recognition (HAR) with a new binary motion descriptor that can efficiently describe and recognize different actions in videos. The descriptor is computed by comparing the changes in the texture of a patch centered on a detected keypoint to each of a set of patches compactly surrounding the central patch. Experimental results on the Weizmann and KTH datasets show the advantage of our method over the current-state-of-the-art spatio-temporal descriptor in term of a good tradeoff among accuracy, speed, and memory consumption.

Keywords: Augmented Reality · Virtual Reality · Interaction
Human Action Recognition · Binary motion descriptor
Proximity patches · Real-time

1 Introduction

During the past recent years, many efforts have been devoted to developing more natural and better AR and VR interaction interfaces. Most popular interaction mediums include mobile devices, controllers, keyboard, mouse, fiducial AR makers, body worn-sensor, RGB and depth cameras... As part of the process of scene understanding, Human Action Recognition (HAR) can also be used as an interaction interface. However, though many researches have been conducted in recent years to develop efficient HAR frameworks, their integration in AR and VR is still a challenging task.

© Springer International Publishing AG, part of Springer Nature 2018
L. T. De Paolis and P. Bourdot (Eds.): AVR 2018, LNCS 10850, pp. 252–260, 2018.
https://doi.org/10.1007/978-3-319-95270-3_21

Indeed, the integration of HAR systems in real-time application requires them to be not only accurate but also fast and use a small amount of memory especially for memory limited devices such as mobile phones. In this paper, we address the challenging task of developing an HAR-based interaction interface for AR and VR applications, which is accurate, fast and does not require a lot of memory by exploring a novel method to represent dynamic features and that can efficiently describe motion in a video while achieving a good tradeoff among accuracy, speed, and memory. To do so, we introduce in this paper the following contributions: (1) we propose a new patch-based pattern for motion description in a video, namely the Proximity Patch pattern. In contrast to the previously used patterns, PP uses a compact structure to ensure that all pixel information surrounding a keypoint are used to compute the descriptor of the keypoint. (2) We introduce a new motion descriptor algorithm based on the PP pattern, namely the Binary Proximity Patches Ensemble Motion (BPPEM) descriptor that computes the change in texture at the same point from two consecutive frames using the PP pattern, in contrast to previous works who compute the descriptors using different positions. (3) We propose an extended version of BPPEM (eBPPEM) as a small size and fast motion descriptor using three consecutive frames and that achieves a competitive accuracy on the Weizmann and KTH datasets.

The remaining of the paper is organized as follow. In section two, we perform a literature review of existing HAR systems as an interaction interface for AR and VR applications and of existing binary motion descriptors. In section three, we describe the PP pattern and the BPPEM descriptor' algorithm followed by the analysis of the experiments conducted to evaluate the performance of the descriptor together with the performance analysis of its extension (eBPPEM) and its comparison with the state-of-the-art binary motion descriptors. We conclude in section five with different considerations for future works.

2 Literature Review

2.1 Human Action Recognition for AR and VR Applications

In the quest of developing less cumbersome interaction interface for AR and VR application, gestures and actions recognition systems have been used to capture and analyze user's motion with a camera for interaction purposes. With the introduction of depth cameras such as the Microsoft Kinect, it has become even easier to capture and use human body joints data in AR and VR systems [1, 2]. Though action representation using skeletal data generated by depth sensor is common in AR and VR applications, such approach requires a correct positioning of the depth camera at a certain distance from the user in order to be able to successfully generate the body skeletal data [3]. Additionally, the data generated by depth sensors are easily affected by noise, occlusion, and illumination that can make action representation and recognition more difficult.

Instead of using depth or their corresponding skeletal data to represent actions, RGB videos have proven to be a better alternative in addition to the extensive research already done on RGB images and video data for pose and action recognition. That is the case of the authors in [4] who proposed a real-time system that robustly tracks multiple persons in virtual environments and recognizes their actions through image sequences acquired from a single fixed camera. Unlike [4] which requires some pre-processing on the input data such as shadows and highlights removal in order to obtain a more accurate object silhouette and increase the computational cost, the action recognition method presented in this paper does not require any additional prepro-cessing step. Though, extensive researches have already been conducted to develop efficient HAR systems from RGB videos, very few as the ones mentioned above are dedicated to their application in AR and VR environment that require not only accurate performance but also fast and real-time performance.

2.2   Patch Based Binary Motion Descriptors

To develop HAR systems that can have possible applications in AR and VR envi-ronments, such systems should be simultaneously accurate, fast and use a limited amount of memory if they have to be integrated on low memory devices (mobile AR and VR). To developer faster HAR systems for real-time applications, many research have been focused on binary motion descriptors. In [5], Yeffet et al. proposed a patch-based self-similarity computational approach to characterize changes in motion from one frame to another. Their Local Trinary Patterns (LTP) combines the effective description of LBP with the flexibility and appearance invariance of patch matching methods. The Motion Interchange Patterns (MIP) [6] captures local changes in motion directions between three consecutive frames and includes a motion compensation component, which makes it more robust even in an unconstrained environment. In [7], Whiten and Bilodeau proposed a binary variation of MIP with a great improvement in speed. Recently, Baumann et al. [8] introduced a new and efficient spatio-temporal binary descriptor, namely the Motion Binary Patterns that combines the benefits of the volume local binary pattern (VLBP) and optical flow.

In the works introduced above, the neighborhood patches of the pattern used to compute the descriptors are positioned at a certain pixel distance from the patch cen-tered on the keypoint, leaving out some pixels. This can result in a loss of key information. Additionally, the squared root differences is often used as the similarity metric but it is not rotation invariant. Hence, aside of selecting a more compact pattern for the neighboring patches, our algorithm also uses the Frobenius Norm, which is invariant to rotation as a similarity metric.

3   Overview of the Proximity Patches Pattern and the BPPEM Motion Descriptor

3.1   The Proximity Patches Pattern

In previous literature, to compute binary motion descriptors using a patch-based approach [5–8], a 3 × 3 central patch centered at the coordinates of a detected moving keypoint is compared with a set of 3 × 3 surrounding patches, each positioned at a certain pixel distance from the central patch. Given a moving keypoint between a current and a next frame, the comparison of patches is carried out based on the assumption that the moving patch (central patch) from the current frame may be positioned at the location of one of the surrounding patches in the next frame. Through the computational process of a binary motion descriptor using such pattern, it is obvious that some pixel data surrounding the central frame are left out of the computation since there is a pixel distance gap between the central patch and each of the surrounding patches. In contrast to such exploded structure, we decided to investigate the impact a compact pattern structure can have on the performance of the descriptor. To do so, we propose the Proximity Patches (PP) pattern (Fig. 1(a)), a new patch-based pattern that has a set of surrounding patches compactly positioned around the central patch in order to ensure that all pixel information is included in the computation of the descriptor.

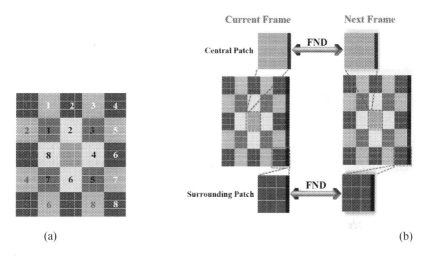

(a)   (b)

Fig. 1. The Proximity Patches (PP) pattern structure (a) and the computation of BPPEM (b).

3.2   The Binary Proximity Patches Ensemble Motion (BPPEM) Descriptor

BPPEM is a binary motion descriptor that focuses on the change in texture of a patch at the same location on two consecutive frames (Fig. 1(b)) in contrast to other methods that compute the descriptor at different locations on two consecutive frames. The computation of the descriptor is describe in Algorithm 1 and is as follows. After detecting a set of keypoints in a current frame with the SURF keypoint detector, BPPEM computes the Frobenius norms of the central patch in the current frame and the next frame; we then compute their difference as the variation in intensity (ΔcentPatch) of the central patch using Eq. 1. Similarly, we also compute the variation in intensity of each of the surrounding patches between the two consecutive (ΔsurrPatch). Knowing the variations of the central patch and of a surrounding patch, we can estimate the similarity in motion between both patches by computing the difference in their variation. If the difference in their variation is smaller than a predefined threshold θ, we return 1 to symbolize that both patches have a similar variation in intensity, otherwise, we return 0. By comparing the variation of each of the surrounding patches with the one of the central patch, we obtain a binary string of 24 bits grouped in three sets of 8 bits that are concatenated as a 3 bytes descriptor.

$$\Delta(A, B) = \left| \|A\|_F - \|B\|_F \right| = \left| \sqrt{\sum_{i=1}^{m} \sum_{j=1}^{n} |a_{ij}|^2} - \sqrt{\sum_{i=1}^{m} \sum_{j=1}^{n} |b_{ij}|^2} \right| \quad (1)$$

Algorithm 1 BPPEM One byte Computation

1: $INPUT$: $centPatchCurr, centPatchNext, surrPatchCurr[], surrPatchNext[], \theta$
2: $centPatchFN_1 = FrobeniusNorm(centPatchCurr)$
3: $centPatchFN_2 = FrobeniusNorm(centPatchNext)$
4: $\Delta centPatch = |centPatchFN_1 - centPatchFN_2|$
5: **for** $i = 0; i < 7; i + +$ **do**
6:       $surrPatchFN_1 = FrobeniusNorm(surrPatchCurr[i])$
7:       $surrPatchFN_2 = FrobeniusNorm(surrPatchNext[i])$
8:       $\Delta surrPatch = |surrPatchFN_1 - surrPatchFN_2|$
9:       **if** $|\Delta centPatch - \Delta surrPatch| < \theta$ **then**
10:            **return** $binary = 1$
11:      **else**
12:            **return** $binary = 0$
13:      **end if**
14:      $descriptor \Leftarrow binary$
15: **end for**
16: **return** $descriptor$

---

4 Experimental Results and Analysis

4.1 Experimentation Setup: Framework, Datasets, Evaluation Metrics

In order to evaluate the performance of our method, we adopted the bag-of-words representation together with an SVM classifier approach. After detecting keypoints of interest using the SURF detector and encoding them with the BPPEM descriptor, we generate a codebook by picking descriptors randomly and then compute the histogram distribution of each video to train an SVM model with the histogram intersection kernel. During the testing phase, we match each descriptor to the nearest codeword by Hamming distance and follow the same scheme to form k-dimension BoW histogram.

The performance of the descriptors was evaluate on two popular HAR datasets, namely the Weizmann [9] and KTH [10] datasets. The Weizmann dataset contains 10 human actions performed by nine persons and the KTH dataset contains six types of human actions performed by 25 subjects.

Three main metrics were used to evaluate the performance of the system and consist of the accuracy (average classification results with the leave-one-out SVM method), the speed in frame per-second computed during a recognition task from keypoint retrieval until classification, and the size of the descriptor.

4.2 Experimental Analysis

BPPEM

Table 1 shows experimental results of BPPEM and eBPPEM on the Weizmann and KTH. From the confusion matrix of the performance of BPPEM on both datasets, BPPEM (Fig. 2(a)) has more difficulty in differentiating between the Jump and Skip actions but also between the Jump and Run actions on the Weizmann dataset. In the former case, it is normal that BPPEM performs poorly because of the high similarly between the both actions with the main difference being that the Jump is performed on two legs while the Skip is performed on one leg. Similarly, on the KTH (Fig. 2(b)) dataset, BPPEM has more difficulty in recognizing the Jogging action, which is mostly confused with the Run and Walk actions, with the difference between both actions residing mainly in their speed of execution.

Table 1. Performance of BPPEM and eBPPEM on the Weizmann and KTH datasets

	Size (Bytes)	Weizmann		KTH	
		Accuracy (%)	Speed (fps)	Accuracy (%)	Speed (fps)
BPPEM	3	89.72	56.68	87.10	54.25
eBPPEM	6	92.22	50.64	91.14	46.28

	Bend	Jack	Jump	Pjump	Run	Side	Skip	Walk	Wav1	Wav2
Bend	100									
jack		100								
Jump			55				45			
Pjump				90		10				
Run					100					
Side						89		11		
Skip					20		80			
Walk							10	90		
Wav1									89	11
Wave2										100

(a) BPPEM on Weizmann

	Box	HC	HW	Jog	Run	Walk
Box	93	3				4
HC	6	93	1			
HW	6	3	91			
Jog	2			76	14	8
Run	2			17	80	1
Walk	3	1		2	2	92

(b) BPPEM on KTH

Fig. 2. Confusion matrix of BPPEM on the Weizmann (a) and KTH (b) datasets

eBPPEM

In the experiments performed above, we computed BPPEM by comparing patches from two consecutive frames whereas an alternative approach as done in [5, 6] consists of computing the descriptor using three consecutive frames. Hence, we also explore the impact the computation of BPPEM from three consecutive frames has on the performance of the descriptor by comparing patches from the current frame and the previous frames and patches from the current frame and the next frame. This result in an extended version of BPPEM (eBPPEM) with a twice increase in size (6 bytes).

Experimental results in Table 1 shows that the computation of the descriptor using three consecutive frames yields indeed to an improvement of the accuracy on both datasets. Figure 3 shows the confusion matrix of the performance of eBPPEM on the Weizmann (a) and KTH (b) datasets respectively, with eBPPEM being able to differentiate better between similar actions than BPPEM.

	Bend	Jack	Jump	Pjump	Run	Side	Skip	Walk	Wav1	Wav2
Bend	100									
jack		100								
Jump			89				11			
Pjump				100						
Run					80		20			
Side						89	11			
Skip					30		70			
Walk								100		
Wav1									100	
Wave2										100

	Box	HC	HW	Jog	Run	Walk
Box	95	4				1
HC	6	94				
HW	6	5	89			
Jog				89	9	2
Run				14	85	1
Walk	1	1		3	0	95

(a) eBPPEM on Weizmann   (b) eBPPEM on KTH

Fig. 3. Confusion matrix of eBPPEM on the Weizmann (a) and KTH (b) datasets

Comparison with the State-of-the-Art Spatio-Temporal Binary Descriptors

From the analysis performed above, it is clear that with eBPPEM, we are able to achieve a good tradeoff among accuracy, speed, and memory on both Weizmann and KTH dataset. Compared to the state-of-the-art accuracy, it can be seen that in contrast to previous works, our method does not require any preprocessing step as done in [8] for example. Moreover, our descriptor is totally a binary descriptor and focus on motion description whereas some of the state-of-the-art methods combined their motion descriptors to an appearance descriptor or other floating-pointing motion descriptors to achieve the highest accuracy. That is the case of [11] who combined the advantages of Hu invariant moments global descriptors with their local binary pattern descriptor to increase performance on the KTH dataset. Though the performance of our descriptor is still competitive to the current state-of-the-art spatio-temporal binary descriptor, it has the additional advantage of being faster and smaller than previous descriptors. Given a video data, the speed computed in frame per second (fps) corresponds to the number of frames that are processed per second during a recognition task, including the keypoint retrieval, feature extraction, vector quantization, bag-of-words and classification sub-steps. Experimental results show that eBPPEM can performs at 50.64 fps on the Weizmann dataset (Table 2) and 46.28 fps on the KTH dataset (Table 3), fast enough to be used for real-time HAR-based AR and VR applications. Though the use of an SVM classifier has yielded to satisfying results, it is not very suitable for a multi-class problem, and we can achieve better accuracy with our descriptor by using a better classifier such as Random Forest or a Decision Tree.

Table 2. Comparison of the performance of eBPPEM with the state-of-the-art binary motion descriptor on the Weizmann dataset

Methods	Classifiers	Accuracy (%)	Speed (fps)
[8] MBP	RF	**100**	N/A
[5] LTP	SVM	**100**	25
[11] DW_LBP +Moments	KNN and DT	91.4	N/A
eBPPEM	SVM	92.22	**50.64**

Table 3. Comparison of the performance of eBPPEM with the state-of-the-art binary motion descriptor on the KTH dataset

Methods	Classifiers	Accuracy (%)	Speed (fps)
[11] DW_LBP +Moments	KNN and DT	**96**	N/A
[6] MIP	SVM	93	N/A
[8] MBP	RF	92.13	N/A
[5] LTP	SVM	90.1	25
[7] MoFREAK	SVM	90	42.05
eBPPEM	SVM	91.14	**46.28**

RF: Random Forest, SVM: Support Vector Machine, KNN: K-nearest Neighbors, DT: Decision Tree

5 Conclusion

In augmented and virtual reality environments, the understanding of the scene and the correct interpretation of involved human gestures, actions or activities are key elements to develop natural and efficient interaction interfaces between the user and the virtual world. In this paper, we propose a new vision-based human-action recognition method to efficiently describe motion in a video. In contrast to previous methods that are also based on patches but used an exploded structure, we introduced a new compact patch pattern (PP pattern) that include all pixel information in the closest vicinity of a keypoint to describe its motion between three consecutive frames. The description is performed by computing a new binary motion descriptor based on the PP pattern (eBPPEM) that evaluates the changes in texture at the same pixel position of a patch and its surroundings from three consecutive frames. The proposed method has the advantage of being simultaneously fast, small and able to achieve a competitive accuracy on the Weizmann and KTH datasets, when compared to the current state-of-the-art spatio-temporal binary descriptor. In future works, we will explore the use of classifiers that are more suitable for multi-class problems such as random forest and together with the design and the implementation of an AR or VR application that used our method as interaction interface.

Acknowledgment. This work is supported by the CAS-TWAS Presidents Fellowship, the National Natural Science Foundation of China (Grant No. 61371192), the Key Laboratory Foundation of the Chinese Academy of Sciences (CXJJ-17S044), and the Fundamental Research Funds for the Central Universities (WK2100330002, WK3480000005).

References

1. Khotimah, W.N., Sholikah, R.W., Hariadi, R.R.: Sitting to standing and walking therapy for post-stroke patients using virtual reality system. In: International Conference on Information and Communication Technology and Systems (ICTS), pp. 145–150 (2015)
2. Sieluzycki, C., Kaczmarczyk, P., Sobecki, J., Witkowski, K., Maśliński, J., Cieśliński, W.: Microsoft Kinect as a tool to support training in professional sports: augmented reality application to Tachi-Waza techniques in judo. In: Third European Network Intelligence Conference (ENIC), pp. 153–158 (2016)
3. Tao, G., Archambault, P.S., Levin, M.F.: Evaluation of Kinect skeletal tracking in a virtual reality rehabilitation system for upper limb hemiparesis. In: International Conference on Virtual Rehabilitation (ICVR), pp. 164–165 (2013)
4. Choi, J., Cho, Y.I., Cho, K., Bae, S., Yang, H.S.: A view-based multiple objects tracking and human action recognition for interactive virtual environments. IJVR 7(3), 71–76 (2008)
5. Yeffet, L., Wolf, L.: Local trinary patterns for human action recognition. In: IEEE 12th International Conference on Computer Vision, pp. 492–497 (2009)
6. Kliper-Gross, O., Gurovich, Y., Hassner, T., Wolf, L.: Motion interchange patterns for action recognition in unconstrained videos. In: Fitzgibbon, A., Lazebnik, S., Perona, P., Sato, Y., Schmid, C. (eds.) ECCV 2012. LNCS, vol. 7577, pp. 256–269. Springer, Heidelberg (2012). https://doi.org/10.1007/978-3-642-33783-3_19
7. Whiten, C., Laganiere, R., Bilodeau, G.A.: Efficient action recognition with MoFREAK. In: International Conference on Computer and Robot Vision (CRV), pp. 319–325 (2013)
8. Baumann, F., Ehlers, A., Rosenhahn, B., Liao, J.: Recognizing human actions using novel space-time volume binary patterns. Neurocomputing 173, 54–63 (2016)
9. Blank, M., Gorelick, L., Shechtman, E., Irani, M., Basri, R.: Actions as space-time shapes. In: Tenth IEEE International Conference on Computer Vision (ICCV), vol. 2, pp. 1395–1402 (2005)
10. Schuldt, C., Laptev, I., Caputo, B.: Recognizing human actions: a local SVM approach. In: Proceedings of the 17th International Conference on Pattern Recognition, vol. 3, pp. 32–36 (2004)
11. Al-Berry, M.N., Salem, M.A.M., Ebeid, H.M., Hussein, A.S., Tolba, M.F.: Fusing directional wavelet local binary pattern and moments for human action recognition. IET Comput. Vis. 10(2), 153–162 (2016)

Virtual Training System for Crawling Skill in Infants Using Mapping 2D: Preliminary Test

Edwin Pruna[✉], Andrés Acurio, Ivón Escobar, Henry Cocha,
Silvia Alpúsig, and José Bucheli

Universidad de las Fuerzas Armadas ESPE, Sangolquí, Ecuador
{eppruna, adacuriol, ipescobar, hpcocha, sealpusig,
jgbucheli}@espe.edu.ec

Abstract. This paper describes the development of an interactive virtual tool, in order to encourage the ability to crawl in infants. The virtual environment in the system is implemented with the graphics engine Unity3D. The application is tested in the MagixBox platform with a high brightness projector. The environment has colorful and novel designs which are projected on a suitable floor space. User can interact with the projection due to the mapping that makes the infrared sensor and HD 2D camera in MagixBox. The sensor will continually scanning the objects that are close to the projection. The system helps in the process of activities record and saving important data for the assessment by the specialist.

Keywords: Virtual system · Therapeutic exercise · Unity 3D

1 Introduction

Crawling is moving capability baby through a quadruped position. This type of locomotion gives the child the opportunity to gain experience and basic movement patterns necessary for motor maturation. The crawling start plays a vital role in early development that involves changes to perceptual, cognitive, language, social and emotional level [1]. The transition to crawling supported on hands and knees can result in increasing the strength of the arms of infants. Diagonal or alternate crawling patterns are more efficient and stable. This sequence is useful for the walking preparation [2].

Cerebral Palsy is one of the major problems in decreasing skills and movements coordination; often the abilities that decline can be crawling skill [3]. For the treatment and therapy in infants have been used some virtual reality novel systems with other technological devices [4].

A study by the intervention of a mobile robot that helps children in crawling activities. The robot detects and analyzes the movements of the limbs. When the robot recognizes a valid movement moves in the same direction [5]. For tracking movement during crawling activity have been used different methods, such as markers placed on the body (IMUs placed in different parts of the body) and systems without markers in the body with infrared sensors and inertial tools [6]. The methods to capture crawling movements of infants are limited, but they have been effective to record the kinematics of the extremities of infants [7–9].

© Springer International Publishing AG, part of Springer Nature 2018
L. T. De Paolis and P. Bourdot (Eds.): AVR 2018, LNCS 10850, pp. 261–268, 2018.
https://doi.org/10.1007/978-3-319-95270-3_22

Other studies covered baby position in dorsal and ulnar movements. The crawling movements are captured with a system based in markers [10–12]. Recent studies cover the kinematics of baby movements without markers, through minimally invasive systems using sensors and cameras. These systems have shown to be more friendly and flexible [13, 14].

In this context, in recent years virtual reality has been involved in the development of new applications tested in motor rehabilitation. Virtual reality participates in studies with other technologies [15–18]. While devices with better technology are used, it will increase the efficiency of therapies and improve the immersion level experienced by the user. These kind of systems have become very popular, especially in the treatment of children with disabilities [17–21]. In many systems, a good response is obtained in the use of 2D and 3D mapping as scanning method high precision, creating a very reliable tracking method [22–24].

2   Structure of the System

A virtual and novel system is developed to enhance the crawling skill in infants, through the baby interaction with virtual objects, which move on a projection on the floor.

The system includes bright 3D environments, which the infants can interact in real time. To capture baby attention has been designed a friendly and attractive objects for the interface.

The interaction is due to mapping 2D, where infrared sensors made the infant movement scanning on the projection. In addition, the environment is harmonized with melodies and sounds feedback. Then the block diagram of the system is presented in Fig. 1.

3   System Development

This section describes the development of the system. The operation system diagram is shown in Fig. 2.

Next, the stages considered in the development of augmented reality system are presented:

Data Acquisition
The first stage corresponds to the system inputs. The infant movements performed while moving his body crawling on the projection is collected. This is done by using mapping 2D infrared sensor of Magixbox, which returns this information to the virtual interface.

Scripts Development
The flowchart in Fig. 3 explains the operation of the applications, according to the activities programmed in C#. At the time the application runs, the initialization of variables is made. When the infant is over the projection can interact with virtual

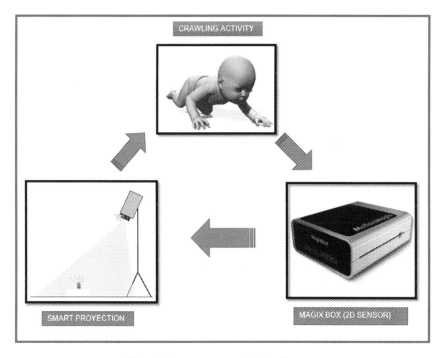

Fig. 1. System structure block diagram.

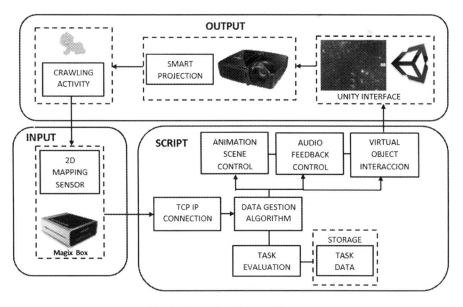

Fig. 2. Operating System Diagram.

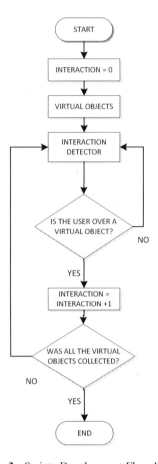

Fig. 3. Scripts Development Flowchart.

objects that are presented. A saving system where the user must go crawling over each object to increase the score is presented. In addition, it uses another virtual object that guides the baby towards the next target.

Environments Design

Animations of the environments are created in the Unity 3D graphic engine. The environments are designed with the topic "Sidereal Space", where stars and rockets are objects that the user will have to reach. These virtual environments will be projected on the floor in a designated work area. The user can interact with objects displayed in real time, in Fig. 4 environments created are presented.

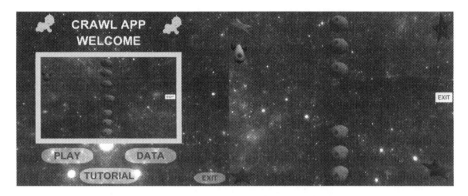

Fig. 4. Virtual Environment Design.

4 Test and Results

Test

The tests to be performed are aimed at determining the functionality of the system. A doll is used to perform the crawling activities on the virtual stage projected on the floor.

Several experiments are tested placing the projector in different angles. This proof determine the real time response of the interaction between the doll and the virtual objects. In addition, it verifies the functionality of the application. The tests follow the sequence in Fig. 5.

Fig. 5. Application Operation

Results

The results presented in Table 1 correspond to the tests performed by the doll in the crawling position in three different projection angles. According to the results projection around a 90° angle, it has a higher percentage of effectiveness (95%).

Table 1. Results of three projection angles

Angle projector/sensor	Number of tests	Number of right answers	Percentage of effectiveness
135°	20	16	80
112°	20	17	85
90°	20	19	95

Thus the effectiveness of a body (doll) to collect virtual objects in real time and sensitivity are in interaction with each object is also verified. An indicator is provided with a counter, which the number of items collected is recorded.

This test verified that the system has an optimum speed of response and acceptable sensitivity to run in real time. The speed with flowing virtual environment is 60 fps.

5 Conclusions and Future Works

The virtual system is reliable and has very attractive activity that motivates children as a crawling exercise alternative. Preliminary tests indicate that a projection in 90° has 95% of matching response and a speed of 60 fps.

As future work, the system will be implemented in dedicated therapies to improve infants in the crawling activity. A complete, attractive and intelligent system was developed, which is able to assess the level of progress that has a user in the capabilities development.

Acknowledgements. We thank the "Universidad de las Fuerzas Armadas ESPE" for financing the investigation project number 2016-PIC-0017.

References

1. Hernandez, G.M., Sanchez, Z.M.E., Villanueva, A.D., Pérez, M.J.C.: Dynamic model for assessment crawl. Am. J. Phys. Rehabil. Med. **28**(1–2), 28–32 (2016)
2. Patrick, S.K., Noah, J.A., Yang, J.F.: Interlimb coordination in human crawling reveals similarities in development and neural control with quadrupeds. J. Neurophysiol. **101**(2), 603–613 (2009)
3. Ghazi, M.A., Nash, M.D., Fagg, A.H., Ding, L., Kolobe, T.H.A., Miller, D.P.: Novel assistive device for teaching crawling skills to infants. In: Wettergreen, D.S., Barfoot, T.D. (eds.) Field and Service Robotics. STAR, vol. 113, pp. 593–605. Springer, Cham (2016). https://doi.org/10.1007/978-3-319-27702-8_39

4. Southerland, J.B.: Activity recognition and crawling assistance using multiple inexpensive inertial measurement units. Master's thesis, School of Computer Science, University of Oklahoma (2012)
5. Freedland, R.L., Bertenthal, B.I.: Developmental changes in interlimb coordination: transition to hands-and-knees crawling. Psychol. Sci. **5**(1), 26–32 (1994)
6. Xiong, Q.L., Wu, X.Y., Xiao, N., Zeng, S.Y., Wan, X.P., Zheng, X.L., Hou, W.S.: Antagonist muscle co-activation of limbs in human infant crawling: a pilot study. In: 2015 37th Annual International Conference of the IEEE Engineering in Medicine and Biology Society (EMBC), pp. 2115–2118 (2015)
7. Righetti, L., Nylen, A., Rosander, K., Ijspeert, A.J.: Kinematic and gait similarities between crawling human infants and other quadruped mammals. Front. Neurol. **6**(17) (2015)
8. Weiss, P., Tirosh, E., Fehlings, D.: Role of virtual reality for cerebral palsy management. J. Child Neurol. **29**, 1119–1124 (2014)
9. Cho, C., Hwang, W., Hwang, S., Chung, Y.: Treadmill training with virtual reality improves gait, balance, and muscle strength in children with cerebral palsy. Tohoku J. Exp. Med. **238**(3), 213–218 (2016)
10. Fetters, L., Sapir, I., Chen, Y.P., Kubo, M., Tronick, E.: Spontaneous kicking in full-term and preterm infants with and without white matter disorder. Dev. Psychobiol. **52**(6), 524–536 (2010)
11. Smith, B.A., Trujillo-Priego, I.A., Lane, C.J., Finley, J.M., Horak, F.B.: Daily quantity of infant leg movement: wearable sensor algorithm and relationship to walking onset. Sensors **15**(8), 19006–19020 (2015)
12. Wu, T., Artigas, J., Mattson, W., Ruvolo, P., Movellan, J., Messinger, D.: Collecting a developmental dataset of reaching behaviors: first steps. In: IROS 2011 Workshop on Cognitive Neuroscience Robotics (2011)
13. Olsen, M.D., Herskind, A., Nielsen, J.B., Paulsen, R.R.: Body part tracking of infants. In: 2014 22nd International Conference on Pattern Recognition, pp. 2167–2172 (2014)
14. Chen, X., Liang, S., Dolph, S., Ragonesi, C.B., Galloway, J.C., Agrawal, S.K.: Design of a novel mobility interface for infants on a mobile robot by kicking. ASME J. Med. Dev. **4**(3), 031006-1–031006-5 (2010)
15. Lorenzo, G., Lledo, A., Pomares, J., Roig, R.: Design and application of an immersive virtual reality system to enhance emotional skills for children with autism spectrum disorders. Comput. Educ. **98**, 192–205 (2016)
16. Ryu, J.-H., Park, S.-J., Park, J.-W., Kim, J.-W., Yoo, H.-J. Kim, T.-W., Hong, J.S., Han, S.-H.: Randomized clinical trial of immersive virtual reality tour of the operating theater before anesthesia in children. In: BJS, pp. 1628–1633 (2017)
17. Gamito, P., Oliveira, J., Coelho, C., Morais, D., Lopes, P., Pacheco, J., Brito, R., Soares, F., Santos, N., Barata, A.: Cognitive training on stroke via virtual reality Patients-based serious games. Disabil. Rehabil. **39**(4), pp. 385–388 (2015)
18. Wexelblat, A.: Virtual Reality: Explorations and Applications. Academic Press, Cambridge (2014)
19. Morina, N., Ijntema, H., Meyerbröker, K., Emmelkamp, P.: Can virtual reality exposure therapy gains to be generalized Real-life? A meta-analysis of studies applying behavioral assessments. Behav. Res. Ther. **74**, 18–24 (2015)
20. Howard, M.: A meta-analysis and systematic review of literature virtual reality rehabilitation programs. Comput. Hum. Behav. **70**, 317–327 (2017)
21. Labaf, S., Shamsoddini, A., Hollisaz, M., Sobhani, V., Shakibaee, A.: Effects of neuro developmental gross motor function on therapy in children with cerebral palsy. Iranian J. Neurol. Child. **9**(2), 36–41 (2015)

22. Valencia, R., Andrade-Cetto, J.: Mapping, Planning and Exploration with Pose SLAM. STAR, vol. 119. Springer, Cham (2018). https://doi.org/10.1007/978-3-319-60603-3
23. Hale, K.S., Stanney, K.M.: Handbook of Virtual Environments: Design, Implementation, and Applications. CRC Press, Boca Raton (2014)
24. Szewczyk, R., Zieliński, C., Kaliczyńska, M. (eds.): Progress in Automation, Robotics and Measuring Techniques. AISC, vol. 351. Springer, Cham (2015). https://doi.org/10.1007/978-3-319-15847-1

Virtual Reality-Based Memory Assistant for the Elderly

Fernando A. Chicaiza[1(✉)], Luis Lema-Cerda[1(✉)],
V. Marcelo Álvarez[1(✉)], Víctor H. Andaluz[1(✉)],
José Varela-Aldás[1,2(✉)], Guillermo Palacios-Navarro[2(✉)],
and Iván García-Magariño[2(✉)]

[1] Universidad de las Fuerzas Armadas ESPE, Sangolquí, Ecuador
{fachicaiza,lalema,rmalvarez,vhandaluz,
jlvarela}@espe.edu.ec
[2] University of Zaragoza, Zaragoza, Spain
{palanava,ivangmg}@unizar.es

Abstract. Older adults experience several diseases related to the habits of their daily lives, many times resulting in cognitive problems when they reach ages that overcome eighty years. This work presents the development of an application aimed at older adults, integrating scenarios in virtual reality to facilitate the immersion of people with signs of memory loss. Through the application, various tasks related to daily activities, professions, face recognition and weekend games are proposed, all evaluated to show scores at the end of the activities. As a result, the work presents real experiments executed to validate the proposal, showing first and third person views within several built virtual environments.

Keywords: Elderly · Virtual reality · Memory assistant
Third level immersion

1 Introduction

The human being goes through different stages during his development, initiating the process of aging at 65 years of age [1, 2]. An older adult integrates one of the most important groups within society, this consideration is determined given the tendency of the distribution of the population pyramid, mainly considering the new indexes identified towards life expectancy and the decrease in the fertility rate. According to the World Health Organization (WHO), the studies given in 2016 reflect that more than 22 countries exceeded on average 80 years of age, and in some cases exceeded 82 years. Furthermore, studies reveal that the growth of the adult population by 2050 will be 2000 million older adults, in contrast to the year 2000 where there were 605 million, estimating that soon the records of history will be surpassed with the greatest number of octogenarian individuals [3]. Likewise, by the year 2050, it is estimated that there will be a world population of approximately 395 million people in need of assistance, due to bad habits and exposure to toxic substances such as cigarettes,

© Springer International Publishing AG, part of Springer Nature 2018
L. T. De Paolis and P. Bourdot (Eds.): AVR 2018, LNCS 10850, pp. 269–284, 2018.
https://doi.org/10.1007/978-3-319-95270-3_23

alcohol and other narcotics which threaten the health of the population, having a direct impact on their mental performance [4].

Aging does not necessarily lead to health problems. According to medical studies, there are several ways to evaluate the consequences of the body's aging through the years, according to this, it can be identified some changes such as levels of consciousness, orientation in time and space; intellectual retardation, dementia; energy and motor function; attention horizon, sleep capacity; perceptions; emotions; high cognitive level, language management, and so on. In the same way, it is relevant to identify the changes given through sensory functions, in this sense, vision, hearing, balance and even pain management are evaluated. Besides, physiological changes produced by aging, i.e., cardiovascular functions, blood pressure, diabetes, hematology, immunology, tendency to suffer hypersensitivity, allergies, fatigue, and respiratory affection need to be taken into account [5].

The learning of new information, the ability to solve everyday problems, active listening, reading and writing ability, arithmetic, financial calculation, and so on, are developed given the conservation of memory and adequate cognitive conditions. Personal care is part of the aforementioned conservation, therefore, grooming, feeding, taking medication; that is, self-care can be affected when considering memory conditions. However, literature identifies ways to maintain mental lucidity in order to preserve personal interrelations and promote cognitive functions, often based on technology [6, 7].

Technological advances directly impact the development of human activities. Within the applications related to the conservation of health, the affections to memory have had a great research niche, generating some applications called Serious Games. Within this context, Table 1 identifies some of these applications [8].

Table 1. Support applications for the elderly

Nombre	Objeto
Gradior	Various exercises for cognitive functions
Rehacom	Training, maintenance and stimulation of cognitive functions
Smartbrain	Exercises of memory, language, calculation, orientation, attention, recognition
Tweri	Mobile application for distraction, ride in areas with security limit
NeuronUp	Neuropsychological rehabilitation
PSSCog Rehab	Rehabilitation system of cognitive therapy, memory improvement
C. Enhancement Therapy	Therapy based on individual exercises from the visual to spatial skills
Neuropsychonline	Cognitive multimodal rehabilitation, improvement of memory and abilities
Challenging Our Minds Cognitive	Rehabilitation parameterized in several stages according to the patient's requirement

(continued)

Table 1. (*continued*)

Nombre	Objeto
NeuroPersonal Trainer	Originally designed for patients with brain trauma and memory loss
CogniFit	Includes scientific questionnaires with cognitive abilities of patients
Lumosity	Training tools for patients with critical memory loss
MindMate	Fun and interactive games to improve the patient's cognitive skills
Elude	In a clinical context, it supports acute depression and dangerous conditions
RehaCom	Cognitive training solutions in different institutional, clinical and home environments

Under these conditions, this article focuses on identifying the support that information and communication technologies represent in the preventive process of patients with apparent memory loss. It is relevant to note that the applications identified have not yet included the benefits of virtual reality [9]. Within the virtual reality interfaces, there are applications which allow establishing activities around the management of the activities for the elderly, considering some criteria contributed by several authors [10, 11]. Additionally and under other perspectives, the following applications can be mentioned: Talking Tom 2, My Reef 3D, Let's créate! Pottery, Augment, FlowerGarden, MindMate, and so on [12].

As described in previous paragraphs, this work proposes the development of an application based on virtual reality (VR) oriented to preventive and corrective processes of memory loss. The proposed application mainly considers four interactive modules in which both the virtual user-environment interaction and three level immersion are considered: (*i*) *Home Tasks,* considers virtual environments related to home in order to perform different daily activities, e.g., laundry, shopping, grocery shopping, and so forth; (*ii*) *Professional Tasks*, poses tasks related to work activities in a factory; (*iii*) *Relatives recognition*, evaluates the answers given by the user and compares them with a pre-configured database for the recognition of people, and (*iv*) *weekend games*, provides environments for the execution of entertainment activities.

This work is split into 6 Sections, including the Introduction. The proposal is presented in Sect. 2; while the description of the application is presented in Sect. 3. Section 4 describes the workflow of the proposed assistant, showing the experimental results in Sect. 5. Finally, Conclusions are presented in Sect. 6.

2 Formulation Problem

According to several studies, three conditions required to consider cognitive problems in an older adult are recognized: (i) progressive deterioration in at least two domains of cognitive function, including memory, (ii) interference in a relevant way with natural behaviour in the person's social and family field and, (iii) absence of an alternative explanation for this disorder, for example, depression. The recognition of a problem related to the progressive memory deterioration continues with the identification of therapies to try to reduce the short or long term conditions of the diseases. Within these considerations, factors such as costs, the place of rehabilitation and the professionals involved must be taken into account prior to selecting an appropriate treatment.

In this context, the development of applications which work as support in the cognitive rehabilitation of patients can act as an innovative and economically profitable tool, where three fundamental categories can be considered to attract the user to this type of applications: (1) modification of environments, (2) compensatory strategies and (3) cognitive function restoration techniques. The present work focuses on the first two categories, in order to provide an assistant to avoid future difficulties which can arise as a result of memory problems. Figure 1 shows the simplified proposal of the application to be implemented, involving recognition activities, simple answer questions and various activities, where the execution results are evaluated to show the level of coincidence between the information stored and the user's response.

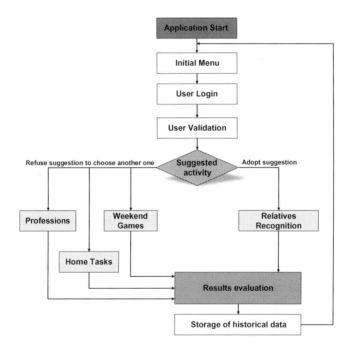

Fig. 1. Application proposal to strengthen memory of older adults

This work considers an application aimed at the use of virtual reality as a way to represent the daily environment of patients. Starting with the user's login, the application challenges the user to remember daily details through a validation question. Overcoming the short question implies that the user can choose an activity to develop, of which four different types of tasks are proposed. Through scenarios built in Unity 3D, everyday tasks such as making purchases, washing clothes, and so on are raised. In the same way, environments which recreate a factory for the execution of work tasks or the recognition of relatives are options which the application raises to maintain the user's concentration. Additionally, several games are designed to distract the user, where the set of input devices allow controlling the application. Considering that the application consumes geo-referenced time information, the activities are suggested depending on the day in which the older adult enters the system. Consequently, the application integrates an evaluation of results to display the level of coincidence between the expected responses and the generated responses and, finally, the data is stored in a database to analyse the evolution of the user.

3 System Structure

The system structure developed consists of four groups including: game objects (Unity Scenes), modules to control each game object (Scripts), information Input Devices, and Output Devices. Figure 2 shows the general structure of the system, where it is included all the components and how they are linked.

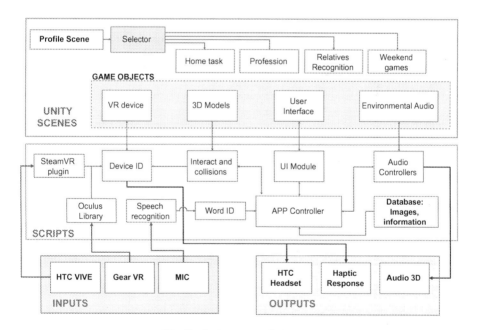

Fig. 2. System general structure

The *Unity scenes* contain the elements to build the virtual environments, depending on the selected scene. At this stage, characteristics such as gravity, haptic and audio responses, and other physical properties are set in order to recreate real interaction based scenarios. In addition, menus are created for accessing the different environments, in this case: home tasks, profession activities, relatives recognition and relaxation games, as well as auxiliary windows with guide information to execute each task. Each 3D model, virtual reality devices, interfaces and audio source are generically defined as a game object, by means of which scripting modules can modify their behaviour. All the elements of this stage are connected to modules and plugins to specify the game objects within the scenarios.

The Scripts group is the block which allows communicating the Unity Scenes with the input and output devices, perform mathematical calculations, control each of the game objects and generate execution sequences. Depending on the input device, the Oculus library or the SteamVR plugin can be activated to manage the resources provided by the hardware (Gear VR or HTC VIVE). Regardless of the connected device, the Interact and Collision module allows the dynamic interaction between the hardware and the game object modules, reusing the code of the n devices. In turn, the audio input can be provided by the microphone integrated to the selected hardware, which is connected to the speech recognition module to detect the user's interaction with the application through voice commands, where the speech fragment is analyzed by the word identification module to recognize keywords. The information provided by the - interact and collisions- modules and Word ID are administered by the APP controller, defined as the main scripting module. In addition, the UI module is called upon in order to control the navigation throughout all the scenes of the application; while the audio module manages the sound effects through a game object and in turn, it sends 3D audio hardware as a final response to the user. Finally, a database containing user-specific information is considered, which is used dynamically by the APP controller.

Remark 1: The scripting modules can be integrated by one or several scripts.

Remark 2: The application compatibility is developed for HTC VIVE and GearVR platforms in order to take advantage of each one. In the first case, the work area of 4×3 meters is used in which the user can move; while in the second case, the ease of execution without the help of third parties is exposed. In this way, the application can be used in a care centre for the first case, and an individual use for the second one.

The scripting block consumes the raw data of the inputs, processes them and sends results to the output module. In this way, the *Input Block* contains the HTC VIVE & GEAR VR devices, which are objective platforms for the application. Meanwhile, the *Output Block* contains three modules which receive dynamic visual, haptic, and audible feedback from the interaction.

4   Virtual Environment Interface Development

For the creation of the application and the functionalities of each of the scenarios, it is required to follow a set of steps, defined in this work as stages (Fig. 3). The stages are split into four parts, in which the creation of models in computer-aided design software is considered; the import of the models to Unity and the construction and programming of each one of the scenes. In *(i) the First Layer*, it is considered that the objects required to build each of the scenes are created by CAD software packages. These objects can be exported in a format compatible with Unity, but with the lack of necessary properties in the feature axis of scenes. To supply those properties, *(ii) the Second Layer* allows grouping objects by chains to form hierarchies, so that when executing movements of pieces of an object, all the pieces which have a mechanical relationship move in coordination with the displaced section. Additionally, this layer allows setting pivot points at the origin to each of the pieces that make up a model, individually or grouped. The result of this layer is an adaptable file format for 3D animation software (*.fbx), which is a file fully compatible with Unity 3D.

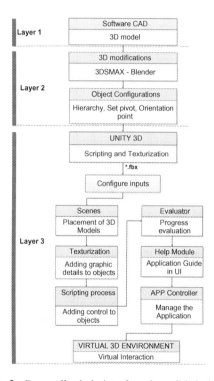

Fig. 3. Desarrollo de la interface de realidad virtual

Layer 3 runs completely in Unity 3D, allowing the textures assignment and evaluate the execution of the task to calculate results. In the configure inputs block, generic algorithms are made to manipulate interacting objects regardless of the input hardware. Next, the scenes are constructed using the 3D models resulting from the second layer and a layout of all 3D environments is obtained to later perform the texturing task (Fig. 4).

The texturization block includes the use of photorealistic colours, materials and textures to provide detail to each of the objects in the scene, where third-party complements can be used to achieve similarity in the colours recreation. In addition to this, lightning is configured in each environment to provide realism, depending on whether it is indoor or outdoor (Fig. 5). Although the so far elements have a close similarity to a

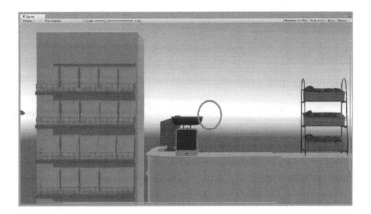

Fig. 4. Environment layout

Fig. 5. Application of texturing, colour and lightning to the stage

real environment and are distributed throughout the scene, they lack scripts which allow to include some type of control.

The scripting process allows to control the objects depending on the inputs generated by the user (audio, buttons of the input devices, etc.), to program the sequence in how the processes are executed, to perform mathematical calculations, to create animations, and so on (Fig. 6). The scripting process is directly related to the task evaluator, in charge of validating the subtasks executed, as well as calculating the total number of hits and the time spent by the activity to show results. Additionally, the Help module is activated when the inactivity time exceeds a predetermined value, using this factor to display help information if the user does not get hits or does not enter information into the system. Finally, all the modules are managed by the user through the APP controller,

Fig. 6. Use of scripting to control objects

allowing the sequence to converge in the interactive three-dimensional virtual environment and granting a level of third-degree immersion to the user.

5   Results

The results presented in this Section show the performance of the developed application. In order to reinforce self-identification, the first window identifies the user through his name and validates it with one of short questions pre-recorded at the beginning of the therapy. Short questions are parameters previously stored in a repository, while names are part of a dynamic memory that is fed back every time there is a new entry, so that the system can store profiles of users who previously used the program. The use of a short name and simple answer questions facilitates the work of the speech recognition module, where answers of less than 10 words are expected. Figure 7 (a) presents the welcome window to the memory trainer (in which new users can be included), continue with the session of the last user or search in the profile repository. The user selection continues with the user's validation (Fig. 7 (b)), where questions such as the name of a childhood pet, home address, telephone number, recognition of a family member, and so on, allow access to the exercises (Fig. 7 (c)).

Remark 3: The application includes a passive time counter which is activated when there is no response from the user or if the number of responses does not match the correct answers stored. In this case, a help method is displayed to guide the user to continue with the task (Fig. 6).

Depending on the day, the application suggests the execution of a specific task, where the activities that require greater concentration have preference during the week, while the tasks related to entertainment are suggested for the weekends (Fig. 8). Within

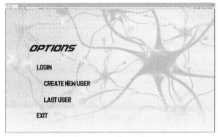

a) Options to select the user   **b)** Question to validate the user

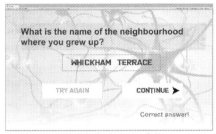

c) Validation succesfully

Fig. 7. Welcome windows

Fig. 8. Recommended task by the application dependent on the day

these exercises there are several options: daily tasks, tasks related to professions, relatives recognition, and entertainment tasks. Household chores, such as selecting a set of objects in a market with an assigned amount of money, cloths washing or repairing a piece of furniture, are referred to daily tasks, while tasks related to professions allow choosing a task that may be related to professional activities that the user played in previous years. On the other hand, face recognition is based on information stored in a database, where tagged photographs of people are enclosed to the patient's profile with the objective of the user citing his name and kinship.

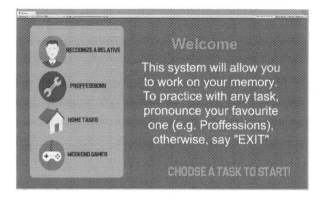

Fig. 9. Selectable task menu

Finally, the entertainment tasks are a complement to a set of exercises that may be difficult to execute. Unlike the rest of activities, the tasks of entertaining are based on exercises that the user can execute with the help of the arrangement of cameras and the HTC VIVE that the devices provide, such as tennis, target shooting, dancing, and so on. Figure 9 shows the menu of tasks to be selected, where messages are presented that are placed with the intention of guiding the user throughout the execution of the program.

The results shown are based on two experimental cases, which show the selection of two tasks: face recognition and related to a profession. Both show the execution of a specific task until obtaining results to determine the level of coincidences between the desired and the executed by the patient. In this way, the first experiment receives the activity suggestion, while the second one shows the selection of an additional task to that suggested by the application.

Fig. 10. Welcome message to the relative recognition application.

5.1 First Experiment

The First experiment is developed after the suggestion of the application, using the database which contains preloaded photographs of people related to the user's profile. The photographs are labeled to know the relationship between the user and the person shown in the photo, appearing in the application at random. Figure 10 shows the welcome message to the application, providing instructions for a successful execution.

At random, the application requests either the name of the person shown on the screen or the degree of kinship with the user (Fig. 11 (a–c)). The level of coincidences between the expected response and the responses generated by the user are counted by the application, showing the results once the questions are concluded (Fig. 11 (d)).

a)   Relative's name request

b)   Relative's name response

c)   Relative's kinship response

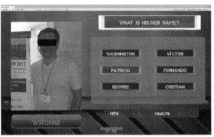

d)   Results of responses

Fig. 11.   Execution the relative recognition task.

Remark 4: Given the ease of response in the first acknowledgments, the application increases the level of difficulty if the number of hits is high, showing faces of more distant relatives or non-updated photographs of people when selecting the next level.

5.2 Second Experiment

Figure 12 shows the text displayed by the graphic engine when selecting work activities. The options are oriented to activities that the user can execute with the help of guides and examples included in the application. In this case, the tannery profession is shown, where the total work scenario is introduced and the places where the machinery, controls, elements, and material necessary to carry out the daily task are

Fig. 12. Selection of work activities

indicated (Fig. 13). It is important to emphasize that both this and the first experiment seek to demonstrate the functioning and applicability of the proposed system, but it does not demonstrate results on rehabilitated persons, therefore, the tests are developed by internal collaborators. Future works based on this research will propose to prove the effectiveness of the application.

Fig. 13. Tannery scenario

As an example, the objective of the task is to place a quantity of leather inside a drum and wash it. For this, the task is divided into seven stages, executed successively: (a) open the drum to place the material inside the drum, where a door which can be opened through the HTC VIVE controllers is presented; (b) pick the leather pieces up and place them inside the drum; (c) close and secure the drum door to start the washing process; (d) move to the control panel of the machinery and press the power button; (e) verify the operation of the process and wait a short time for the washing process; (f) turn the drum off and wait until it stops completely, and finally, (g) take out the processed leather pieces. The execution of all subtasks are shown in Fig. 14.

Fig. 14. Execution of the activity related to professions

Remark 5: Based on Literature [13, 14], it has been reported cases of aggressive behaviour in older adults with memory problems who cannot perform basic activities. In order to evaluate the reaction of these users, different avatar are placed in the work environment. Parallel to the main execution, avatars are programmed to develop specific and repetitive tasks, turning the work environment into a natural space that is easy to assimilate.

Fig. 15. Results of the task of the second experiment

Finally, a summary of results is shown, where recommendations to improve performance in future executions can be deployed. In this case, Fig. 15 shows a satisfactory execution of the user, at an appropriate time and without major recommendations.

6 Conclusions

An application to strengthen the memory of older adults through virtual reality is presented. In order to maintain the level of information retention of a person with memory problems, various environments are programmed, considering scenarios for recognition of relatives, domestic tasks, activities related to professions, and weekend games.

Each of the scenarios includes elements designed in CAD software, which are textured and coloured to recreate real environments, and can be controlled to generate the proposed tasks. Both sound and visual feedback try to achieve an immersion of third level in the user, where the older adult can interact with each of the elements distributed in the scenes. Additionally, speech recognition libraries are included to facilitate access to applications, as well as task evaluators to rate the development of the exercises. Finally, two experimental results are presented, showing the steps to execute the tasks satisfactorily.

Acknowledgements. The authors would like to thanks to the Corporación Ecuatoriana para el Desarrollo de la Investigación y Academia – CEDIA for the financing given to research, development, and innovation, through the CEPRA projects, especially the project CEPRA-XI-2017-06; *Control Coordinado Multi-operador aplicado a un robot Manipulador Aéreo*; also to Universidad de las Fuerzas Armadas ESPE, Universidad Técnica de Ambato, Escuela Superior Politécnica de Chimborazo, Universidad Nacional de Chimborazo, and Grupo de Investigación en Automatización, Robótica y Sistemas Inteligentes, GI-ARSI, for the support to develop this paper.

References

1. Inouye, S.K., Westendorp, R.G., Saczynski, J.S.: Delirium in elderly people. Lancet **383** (9920), 911–922 (2014)
2. Organization World Health, "World report on ageing and health 2016," Ageing and life-course, September 2016. http://www.who.int/mediacentre/factsheets/fs404/en/. Accessed 25 Mar 2015
3. World Health Organization, "Interesting facts about aging," Media centre, September 2015. http://www.who.int/ageing/about/facts/. Accessed 25 Mar 2018
4. World Health Organization, Mental health of older adults, Media centre, December 2017. http://www.who.int/mediacentre/factsheets/fs381/en/. Accessed 26 Mar 2018
5. Sotolongo, P.C., Carrillo, P.C., Carrillo, C.C.: Cognitive impairment in the third age. Rev. Cuba. Med. Gen. Integral **20**(5–6), 10–15 (2004)
6. World Health Organization, International Classification of Functioning, Disability and Health, ICF. World Health Organization, vol. 1, no. 1, pp. 1–15 (2001)
7. Gu, J., et al.: Multimorbidity and health-related quality of life among the community-dwelling elderly: a longitudinal study. Arch. Gerontol. Geriatr. **74**, 133–140 (2018)
8. Barbosa, H., Castro, A.V., Carrapatoso, E.: Serious games and rehabilitation for elderly adults. GSJ **6**(1), 275–280 (2018)
9. Andaluz, V.H., Pazmiño, A.M., Pérez, J.A., Carvajal, C.P., Lozada, F., Lascano, J., Carvajal, J.: Training of tannery processes through virtual reality. Augmented Reality Virtual Reality Comput. Graph. **10324**(1), 75–93 (2017)
10. Naranjo, C.A., Ortiz, J.S., Álvarez, V.M., Sánchez, J.S., Tamayo, V.M., Acosta, F.A., Proaño, L.E., Andaluz, V.H.: Teaching process for children with autism in virtual reality environments. Educ. Technol. Comput. **2017**(1), 41–45 (2017)
11. Andaluz, V.H., Guamán, S., Sánchez, J.S.: Autonomous March control for humanoid robot animation in a virtual reality environment. Comput. Kinematics **50**, 70–78 (2017)
12. Pang, H., Kwong, E.: Considerations and design on apps for elderly with mild-to-moderate dementia. Inf. Networking (ICOIN) **2015**(1), 348–353 (2015)
13. Brodaty, H., Low, L.: Aggression in the elderly. Eur. PMC **64**(4), 36–43 (2016)
14. Power, K.: Experiences of aggression and violence across dementia and adult acute psychiatric facilities. University of Warwick, England (2016)

Virtual Environments to Stimulate Skills in the Early Childhood Education Stage

Jorge S. Sánchez[1]($\boxtimes$), Jessica S. Ortiz[1]($\boxtimes$), Paola M. Velasco[1]($\boxtimes$),
Washington X. Quevedo[1]($\boxtimes$), Cesar A. Naranjo[1]($\boxtimes$),
Paulina X. Ayala[2]($\boxtimes$), Carlos X. Gordon[2]($\boxtimes$),
and Víctor H. Andaluz[1]($\boxtimes$)

[1] Universidad de las Fuerzas Armadas ESPE, Sangolquí, Ecuador
{jssanchez,jsortiz4,pmvelascol,wjquevedo,canaranjo,
vhandaluz1}@espe.edu.ec
[2] Universidad Técnica de Ambato, Ambato, Ecuador
{ep.ayala,cx.gordon}@uta.edu.ec

Abstract. This article describes the development of games within virtual reality environments oriented to early childhood education children between 3 and 5 years old. These games are developed according to the Cone of Learning and have been developed with a Unity 3D graphic engine. They are very attractive and allow children's learning through playing. They also stimulate the skills and abilities required to be developed and strengthened during this learning stage. The proposed games allow the teacher to select several difficulty levels on each game in order to stimulate the child to accomplish more complex tasks during this initial stage. At the end, the areas intended to be covered are presented according to the goals set.

Keywords: Virtual reality · Games · Unity3D · Pre-school education

1 Introduction

Traditional educational models are based on study programs where the teacher is the protagonist in the learning process. Through several methods such as lectures, magisterial conferences, among others, teaches students unilaterally. The permanent search for improving education quality creates nowadays a change on the educational paradigm. It tends to give the student an active role within the process, so they can discover and develop data through a bilateral process by sharing doubts, experiences, results, and more, with the teacher. This interaction teacher-student enables the student to auto manage his cognitive skills.

Cognitive development appears during the first childhood stages where development, physical, social, and emotional basis are established. A child's experiences shape the brain's architecture and design its future behavior. Therefore, it's essential to guarantee the basic nurturing, health, and early childhood education conditions among children [1].

Early childhood education considers various teaching-learning processes, which are focused on children's development for children from 0 to 5 years old. Several scientific researches have shown progressive advance that are significantly influenced by the theories from Froebel, Montessori, and Decroly. They supported the eventual participation of children to educational institutions [2]. The teaching-learning process in early childhood education mostly uses games as method, thus, enabling the teacher to stimulate cognitive, linguistic, physical, and social-affective development on each children. Therefore, technological tools must provide attractive ludic environment with didactic means that enable a child's learning by discovering knowledge.

The introduction of Communication and Information Technologies in education has made it possible to develop didactic resources, aiming at sharing knowledge between teacher and students by using tools such as: Virtual classrooms, email, forums, interactive chat rooms, videoconferences, Virtual Reality applications, among others [3, 4]. All these are currently being applied to face-to-face and distance education at high school and college levels. For early childhood and elementary education however, teachers need to supervise technology to manage children's cognitive development, skills, and abilities.

VR as a means allows the integration of sophisticated tools into the teaching-learning process though virtual working environments which enable children to interact within environments like the real ones. This way, it is possible to preserve creativity traits children have during this stage [5, 6]. Pedagogical innovation is directed to massive and effective global scopes. These scopes use VR environments on several topics and learning stages through efficient didactic strategies, thus, becoming a promising technology capable of changing the way to teach and learn [7, 8].

It is important to highlight that two scopes are considered to create VR environments; the constructivist scope, and the multiple intelligences scope. The constructivist scope is the pedagogical theory, which enables the creation of learning environments that stimulate students' expressions, attitudes, and emotions [3, 4], where emotions and intrinsic motivation promote learning [9]. Constructivism based on technologies, especially within VR environments, provides the conditions for autonomous learning and voluntary construction on knowledge structure [10]. Multiple intelligences focus on cognitive skills rather than emotional ones, personality, or culture. In addition, they allow knowledge development according to people's intelligence [7]. That is why VR environments are the right place to develop multiple intelligences on users such as: Logical-Mathematical, Physical-Kinesthetic, Musical intelligence, among others [10, 11].

This article talks about the creation of virtual environments applied to elementary education with the aim of encouraging creativity, concentration, mental stimulation, and logical, strategic, and visual thinking. It also aims at developing skills for problem solving [12] within an atypical environment, on children from 3 to 5 years old.

This work is organized into 5 sections, the Introduction describes in a general way the evolution of educational models and the use of technologies that are used as pedagogical tools. Section 2 presents the formulation of the problem based on the development of games in virtual environments. The general scheme of the applications developed and the description of the modules that intervene in the operation of the same in virtual reality are presented in Sect. 3. Section 4 presents the operation of the developed games, as well as analyzes of general form the expected learning achievements that are intended to be achieved; while the conclusions are shown in Sect. 5.

These areas use virtual reality environments in various topics and stages of learning through efficient teaching strategies, thus becoming a promising technology capable of changing the way we teach and learn [6].

This work is organized in 5 sections, the Introduction describes in a general way the evolution of the educational models and the use of the technologies used as pedagogical tools. Section 2 presents the formulation of the problem according to the development of games in virtual environments. The general scheme of the applications developed and the description of the modules involved in their operation in virtual reality are presented in Sect. 3. Section 4 presents the functioning of the games developed, as well as an overview of the expected learning achievements to be achieved, while the conclusions are shown in Sect. 5.

2   Problem Formulation

Stimulating children's interest to learn new things is carried out more effectively during the initial stage of the teaching-learning process. To do so, several methods must be implemented in the classroom to enable the teacher to propel learning through personal life experiences on this childhood stage. The methodology with greater implementation is detailed on Edgar Dale's "Cone of Learning" [13], see Fig. 1. It shows the various levels which the student goes through in the teaching-learning process. It also illustrates the achievements to be reached on each level according to the teacher's stimuli.

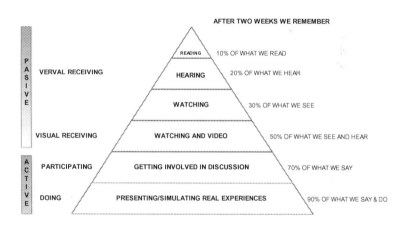

Fig. 1. Learning Pyramid

Levels shown on the cone integrate the teaching learning process. On top, verbal and visual activities are placed, where student's participation is passive since they only receive information, while at the bottom experiential activities are displayed. The student participates in the process and develops the activity from which he intends to learn. This contributes to the child's significant learning.

Didactic resources are part of the learning process when practice and life experiences take place. They contribute to developing the necessary skills and abilities for children's cognitive progress, for example body language and motricity, logical-mathematical relations, expression and communication, among others. Thereby, VR applications are considered as a didactic resource since they allow people to embrace all levels of methods shown in the Cone of Learning in an active manner toward the student.

VR breaks the paradigms of traditional education since it makes it easier for students to develop skills associated to tasks such as: exploring, communicating, analyzing, interpreting, and problem solving. The goal of VR applications is to offer an immersive experience to the student. They transform the classroom into a laboratory, into the bottom of a sea, or transport students to any time in history, thus, creating experiences, which are physically impossible in the real world. This intends to increase motivation and contribute with greater impact to the teaching-learning processes. Educationalist Alicia Canellas requests the participation of all teachers, educational centers, and institutions on the implementation of VR environments since "A 100% open mind to embrace a new framework in which the educational system adopts experiential practices and takes advantage of new technological opportunities to service teaching and learning, is necessary".

3   System Development

In this section, the modules, which participate in developing and executing the proposed virtual application, are described, taking as a reference the following diagram, see Fig. 2.

Several devices, which enable the observation of the virtual environment, are considered on the **Input block**, such as: virtual reality headsets (Oculus Rift, HTC VIVE and GearVR) and inout controls (Leap Motion and Manus VR) which make it possible to interact and manipulate objects within the developed environment. The code structure must be general in order to be compatible for various platforms without the need to reconstruct the project, and be able to detect automatically the previously mentioned devices.

The **Scripts Block** manages communication of each input and output device (Oculus Library, Environmental Audio) providing the required functionality to the virtual environment. It also implements the interface where the user is allowed to interact in different ways with the application (Manipulation Controllers, UI Controller, Leap Core Assets) displaying the different game options or activities (Games) that can be used through manipulating the environment objects with a sound response under the structure of a general controller (App Manager). Children's interaction with implemented games is preformed through the *leap motion* device which is neither invasive nor it requires complex instructions to be used.

Figure 3 shows the tracking from the child's hands moving in activities such as: reaching catching and manipulating an object according to the game dynamics.

Additionally, app controllers are implemented starting with the one for manipulating parts or pieces involved in the task, see Fig. 4. The local position of each part

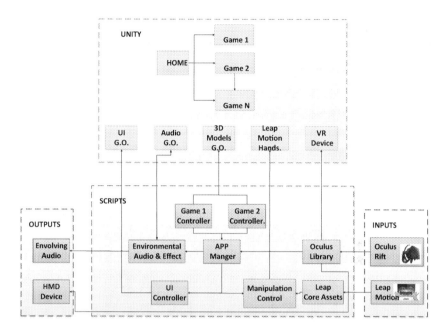

Fig. 2. Component interrelation diagram

involved is registered in order to compare the object and the position where the user must place it.

The **Scenes Block** refers to the Unity 3D environment. Here, the user manages scenes and the operation of applications (Games). On this block, generic objects that appear on each scene (Leap Motions Hands, 3D Model G.O, User Interface Game Object, Games Objects V.R Device y Audio G.O) are considered. These objects are modified according to their counterpart on the Scripts Block. They interact dynamically within the scene with the user and the application environment thus, making each execution different from the previous one. This way, it is possible to: get visual feedback, control applications, provide buttons, messages, and windows to the user to surf through the application. To create virtual game scenes, specialized programs, which enable the creation of 3D environments and objects, must be considered.

Figure 5 describes the virtualization process. The design of virtual environments begins by modeling real objects in 3D. This requires a CAD software. Once 3D objects are obtained, the elements must be texturized through Blender, in order to create an attractive environment for the user's interaction. It must be said that the Blender software can connect to Unity 3D. In addition, objects from Unity 3D are used; this combination enables the development of work virtual environments focused on interactive games.

Finally, the **Output Block** provides surround sound (En-voiving Audio) to the user. The sound response intensity is proportional to the distance between the user's virtual location and the source of the sound. It also provides visual feedback (HMD Device) which makes it possible to obtain a response according to head movements.

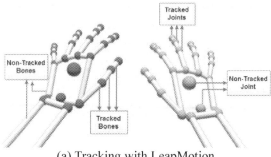

(a) Tracking with LeapMotion

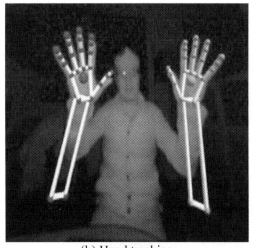

(b) Hand tracking

Fig. 3. Tracking from the child's hands

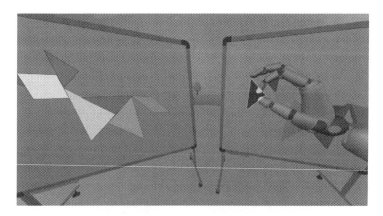

Fig. 4. Selecting an object

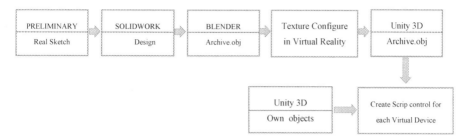

Fig. 5. Virtualization process

4   Applications Analysis and Description

In this section, the didactic specifications to develop skills and abilities in children through VR interactive games are established. To do so, it is important to include the environment characteristics such as mobile components (pieces objects), audio and visual indicators, attractive environments, among others, for children to be able to: identify basic color and size shapes, logically order activities, and generate spatial location notions. To do so, Vr devices are used, such as: VR headsets (Oculus Rift, HTC VIVE y GearVR) and leap motion, which enable interactions with the game

When the application is executed, the user is presented with a home page that consists of a playroom, Fig. 6, with audible indications that allows the child to intuitively access the activities; visual and auditory feedback at the child's input is important so that it can develop independently during the use of the application.

Fig. 6. Selection game

The user has the option to choose several games, based on the miniature animation of the mechanics of each of them, see Fig. 7. This paper shows the implementation of the Tangram games and a Recognition and Selection game.

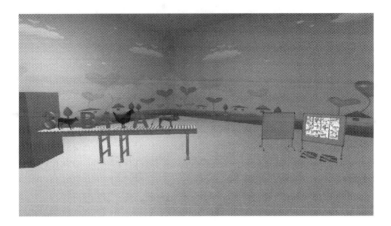

Fig. 7. Presentation of the games

A. *Tangram*

Tangram, an ancient Chinese game called "Chi Chiao Pan" which means wisdom chart or named the game of the 7 elements. It is composed of 7 pieces taken out from a square: 5 triangles of different sizes, 1 square and 1 parallelogram as illustrated on Fig. 8(a). Several figures can be represented using the same 7 pieces. There are more than 10000 shapes and figures which can be built out of the Tangram. Figure 8(b) shows the basic figures that are used for this interactive game. While the Fig. 9 shows a Tangram numbers.

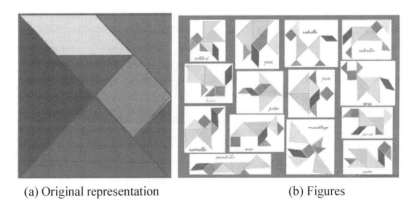

(a) Original representation   (b) Figures

Fig. 8. Tangram animals

This game is used as didactic material to stimulate logic, abstract, and mathematical thoughts. It is mainly used to: (i) recognize geometric figures and other shapes; (ii) develop spatial skills to build geometric figures and shapes; (iii) stimulate imagination through searching possible solutions to proposed figures to be built; (iv) introduce concepts of flat geometry, and promote the development of children's

Fig. 9. Tangram numbers

psychometric and intellectual capabilities, since it allows the user to link the concrete manipulation of materials with the creation of abstract ideas.

The virtual environment of the game has multiple playful activities, the pieces of the puzzle are in disorder, and the objective is that the child can assemble one of the possible figures in this game following a model already armed as seen in Fig. 10.

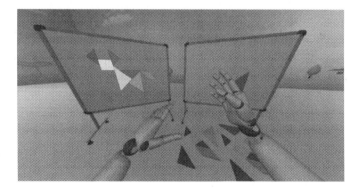

Fig. 10. Presentation of the Tangram game

The child takes the pieces with his hands and places them on a magnetic board, depending on the model presented, see Fig. 11.

When the child completes the figure, a visual animation is given off that motivates the child to continue playing, each figure demands a different level of dexterity in its assembly. There are three levels of difficulty, level 1, which guides the child to place the pieces in the correct position by marking the desired position with an outline;

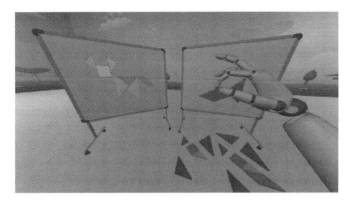

Fig. 11. Interaction with the game

Fig. 12. Completion of the task

level 2 does not provide visual aids for placing the pieces; and level 3 is a free construction mode where the child can create a creation according to his or her imagination, see Fig. 12.

B. Recognition and Selection

The goal of this game is for the child to develop sensorial attitudes, giving children the chance to record their impressions and classify them to combine and associate them with others. In addition, it allows the child to recognize object features, to choose what their senses perceive in order to build their judgement and act under the conclusions of this judgement.

In this game, a child is able to select images such as numbers, letters, or animals according to the instructions determined by the game, for instance, the type of figure to be recognized from the transporter band. Every time a task is completed, the child is rewarded in a visual and auditive manner to motivate him to continue with the game. The accomplished task is also recorded. Figure 13 shows the game interface.

Fig. 13. Initial game presentation

The game has a configuration section, in which the following items can be modified: (i) levels of difficulty, changing the speed of the movement of the objects on the conveyor belt, the randomness of the appearance of the objects and the selection characteristics such as type of element, colour and size, among others; (ii) the environment in which the activity is carried out and (iii) the time of execution of the task.

To evaluate the application, it is considered that the tasks to be executed work according to the following mechanisms: (i) perception is the integration of all data which gets into the brain and is related to a possible answer; (ii) decision consists of

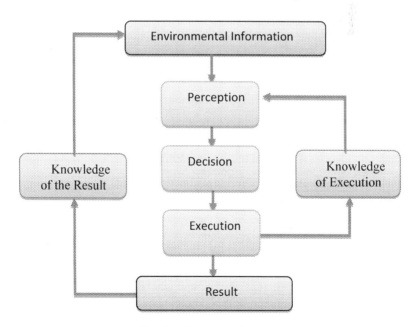

Fig. 14. Represents the cycle

data processing; (iii) execution implies the process to elaborate and issue the answer. Figure 14 shows a blocks diagram which represents the cycle performed when games are executed.

Therefore, it is possible to establish the level (initiated, processing, acquired) of the child's developed skilled when he uses the application. To do so, the teacher must observe the activity and determine whether the task has been accomplished or not. Table 1 shows a list of areas and indicators according to learning achievements.

Table 1. Learning achievements

Area	Indicator
Logical-mathematical relationships	A. *Attention:* Eye tracking, contact, visual, visual fixation, scanning
	B. *Limitation and monitoring of instructions:* execution of activities under instruction, execution of sequential actions
	C. *Discrimination:* grouping, placement of objects, marking, equalization
Body expression and motor skills	A. *Gross motor coordination:* displacement, static balance, coordinated movements
	B. *Fine motor coordination:* movements of hand, finger and wrist using digital clamp, precision axis-cution of movements

This application described above is a proposal that can be implemented as an alternative during regular classes in pre-school children, so that it will be possible to coordinate with the teacher the acceptability of the tool, as well as the extent to which the learning achievements of this age group are achieved.

5   Conclusions

Virtual reality offers facilities for the development of multiple playful games that can be applied in the initial stage of education, the games developed in this work are framed within the active levels of the Learning Pyramid. With the games implemented, the aim is to develop multiple intelligences, logical-mathematical relationships, and body expression and motor skills. In this work two games are presented (i) Tangram, with the objectives of: recognize geometric figures, develop spatial and geometric skills, and finally stimulate the imagination through the search for possible solutions to proposed construction figures; and (ii) Recognition and Selection, with the aim of developing sensory attitudes in children, image recognition, motor control, concentration, and arouse interest, attract and maintain their attention to the child (life experiences). Presenting specific tasks as a game arouses the child's interest, preventing the child from losing interest in the activity he or she is doing, and playing with difficulty levels becomes a challenge that the child wants to meet.

Acknowledgements. The authors would like to thanks to the Corporación Ecuatoriana para el Desarrollo de la Investigación y Academia – CEDIA for the financing given to research, development, and innovation, through the CEPRA projects, especially the project CEPRA-XI-2017-06; *Control Coordinado Multi-operador aplicado a un robot Manipulador Aéreo;* also to Universidad de las Fuerzas Armadas ESPE, Universidad Técnica de Ambato, Escuela Superior Politécnica de Chimborazo, and Universidad Nacional de Chimborazo, and Grupo de Investigación en Automatización, Robótica y Sistemas Inteligentes, GI-ARSI, for the support to develop this work.

References

1. J., Palacios, C.E.: Early childhood (0–6 years) and its future. Organization of Ibero-American States for Education, Science and Culture (2009)
2. Gálvez, I.: La educación inicial en el ámbito internacional: Situación y perspectivas en Iberoamérica y en Europa. Revista Iberoamericana de educación, n° 22 (2000)
3. Cózar Gutiérrez, R., De Moya Martínez, M.V., Hernández Bravo, J.A., Hernández Bravo, J. R.: Tecnologías emergentes para la enseñanza de las Ciencias Sociales. Una experiencia con el uso de Realidad Aumentada en la formación inicial de maestros. Digit. Educ. Rev. **27**, 138–153 (2015)
4. Dias, V., Gil, H., Gonçalves, T.: The Multimedia Interactive Whiteboard (MIW) in a supervised teaching practice in basic education. In: International Symposium on Computers in Education (SIIE 2015), Portugal, pp. 10–14. IEEE (2015)
5. Huang, H.M., Rauch, U., Liaw, S.S.S.: Investigar las actitudes de los alumnos hacia los entornos de aprendizaje de realidad virtual: Basado en un enfoque constructivista. Comput. Educ. **55**(3), 1171–1182 (2010). https://doi.org/10.1016/j.compedu.2010.05.014
6. Ortiz, J.S., Sánchez, J.S., Velasco, P.M., Sánchez, C.R., Quevedo, W.X., Zambrano, V.D., Arteaga, O., Andaluz, V.H.: Teaching-learning process through VR applied to automotive engineering. In: Proceedings of the 2017 9th International Conference on Education Technology and Computers, pp. 36–40. ACM, December 2017
7. Hamada, S.: Education and knowledge based Augmented Reality (AR). In: Shaalan, K., Hassanien, A.E., Tolba, F. (eds.) Intelligent Natural Language Processing: Trends and Applications. SCI, vol. 740, pp. 741–759. Springer, Cham (2018). https://doi.org/10.1007/978-3-319-67056-0_34
8. Quevedo, W.X., et al.: Virtual reality system for training in automotive mechanics. In: De Paolis, L.T., Bourdot, P., Mongelli, A. (eds.) AVR 2017. LNCS, vol. 10324, pp. 185–198. Springer, Cham (2017). https://doi.org/10.1007/978-3-319-60922-5_14
9. Pantelidis, V.S.: Razones para utilizar la realidad virtual en los cursos de educación y formación y un modelo para determinar cuándo utilizar la realidad virtual. Themes Sci. Technol. Educ. **2**(1–2), 59–70 (2010)
10. Hui-Min, Z.: Constructivism teaching mode of college English based on Multimedia. In: IEEE Taller sobre Investigación y Tecnología Avanzadas en Aplicaciones Industriales (WARTIA), pp. 147–149 (2014)
11. McLellan, H.: Realidad virtual e inteligencias múltiples: Potenciales para la educación superior. J. Comput. High. Educ. **5**(2), 33–66 (1994)
12. Suárez, J., Maiz, F., Meza, M.: Inteligências múltiplas: Uma inovação pedagógica para promo-ver o processo ensino-aprendizagem. Investigación y Postgrado, n° 25, pp. 81–94 (2010)
13. Sánchez, J.J.M., Ruiz, A.B.M., Olmos, A.: Augmented Reality (AR). Resources and proposals for educational innovation. Inter-Univ. Electron. J. Teach. Train. **20**(2), 183–204 (2017)

Augmented and Mixed Reality

Mixed Reality Stock Trading Visualization System

Dariusz Rumiński, Mikołaj Maik, and Krzysztof Walczak$^{(\boxtimes)}$

Poznań University of Economics and Business,
Niepodległości 10, 61-875 Poznań, Poland
{ruminski,maik,walczak}@kti.ue.poznan.pl
http://www.kti.ue.poznan.pl/

Abstract. In this paper, we present a novel mixed reality system for supporting stock market trading. The system is designed to enhance traders' working environment by displaying an array of virtual screens visualizing financial stock data and related news feeds within the user's surroundings. We combined the nVisor ST50 headset with InteriaCube4 and Leap Motion devices to enable tracking of head orientation and controlling the VR/AR environment with hands. Users can create and control the virtual screens directly using their hands in 3D space.

Keywords: Mixed reality · AR · VR · Visualization · Stock data
Natural interaction · Leap Motion

1 Introduction

Professional stock traders are responsible for buying and selling tradable financial assets such as shares, bonds, futures, options, and swaps – to name a few. They also conduct intensive and extensive research and observation of how financial markets perform, e.g., when new macroeconomic data or other important news are published. Stock market traders, in their daily work, use traditional trading workspaces that may be composed of multiple monitors, on which diverse financial information, charts, tables, and indicators are presented simultaneously, as shown in Fig. 1a. Moreover, to operate a stock trading system, a standard keyboard and mouse are typically used. Also, a landline is a common tool for traders to verbally communicate with managers, colleagues, or clients when there is a need to consult and make a buy/sell decision. Moreover, traders often simultaneously track live business TV channels or social media to 'catch' profitable news. In such an environment, a trader has to be focused all the time, while observing continuous changes in financial markets. It is easy to make a mistake when, e.g., some economic data are overlooked, and consequently, a trader might make a loss or miss a potential profit.

The use of mixed reality technology may aid traders' work by enabling creation of customized information spaces, in which relevant data are overlaid

© Springer International Publishing AG, part of Springer Nature 2018
L. T. De Paolis and P. Bourdot (Eds.): AVR 2018, LNCS 10850, pp. 301–310, 2018.
https://doi.org/10.1007/978-3-319-95270-3_25

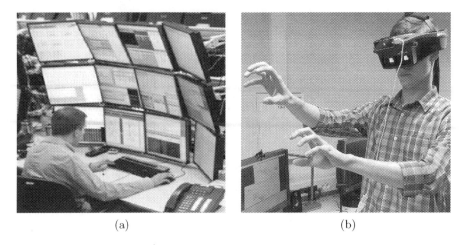

(a)   (b)

Fig. 1. Traditional trading workspace with multiple screens (a); AR trading workspace controlled with hand gestures (b).

onto users' real trading workspaces in the form of virtual screens supplementing physical screens or even completely replacing such complex computer setups with VR/AR interfaces. Visualization of abstract data in 3D VR/AR environments has been shown useful in many previous research works [2,19,20]. Within an AR system, traders could augment their surroundings with virtual screens displaying charts, tables, indicators, financial TV channels – as many as they need to observe, without running into hardware- or space limitations issues. Additionally, perception of changes in financial markets could be increased with the use of spatial sound in AR [12,15,23], and as a result, a trader could perform better by getting aural notifications triggered within his/her surroundings, e.g., when a particular financial value rapidly changes. In a different setup, a trader could be 'closed' within a VR trading system with the above-mentioned advantages of AR, but in this case, the trading environment, configuration of trading desktops, and the habits known to traders could be changed completely. Moreover, VR/AR technologies open new possibilities of remote collaboration within the financial domain, e.g., when there is a need to supervise the trading performance of employees. Previous studies have demonstrated that remote helpers have allowed local workers to perform real-world tasks better [1,5].

Such mixed reality stock trading system could be operated by hand gestures to manipulate information components in the user's environment. The introduction of motion gestures makes it possible to further enhance users performance while interacting with virtual objects. Nowadays, natural user interfaces play essential role in human-computer interaction by supporting – or even in some cases completely replacing – traditional computer input devices such as a mouse, keyboard, or touchpad to perform operations more precisely and faster [24]. With the introduction of the Microsoft Kinect in 2011 and the notable Leap Motion in 2015, technology for natural interaction is available at a price affordable to many consumers and researchers. Hand pose estimation is now achievable without the need for data gloves or specialized external sensing equipment [21]. This allows for designing more complex natural hand interaction within VR and AR applications than could be achieved in the past [3,6,7,9,17].

Despite the increasing prevalence of VR/AR interfaces, there is still a lack of interaction techniques that allow to fully benefit from these technologies – especially in the business domain. Therefore, it is essential to study mixed reality systems supported by natural hand interactions to learn their potential and limitations, especially in application areas not sufficiently explored by the scientific community, e.g., financial markets.

In this paper, we present a novel mixed reality stock trading visualization system allowing a user to create an array of virtual screens displaying stock data and related news feeds within the user's surroundings, and to manipulate the virtual screens directly in 3D space with user's hands.

In the remainder of this paper, first an overview of the related works is provided, then the technical setup is presented, followed by a description of the developed system. Finally, conclusions are provided, and directions for future research are discussed.

2   Related Work

Several studies that have had a great impact on VR as well as AR development have been conducted to analyze the possibilities of using hands for user interaction. For instance, Piumsomboon et al. provided a user-defined gesture set that can be used in AR systems and conducted an experimental study of guessability of hand gestures in AR. In this experiment, 800 gestures were elicited for 40 selected tasks from 20 participants [11]. Researchers found that most of the gestures obtained from the participants were physical gestures for tasks such as move, rotate, scale, and delete.

The knowledge from the previous study was used to improve the understanding of natural hand interaction and ultimately create novel natural hand interaction techniques that enhance user experience when interacting with 3D computer-generated content [10]. To better understand natural hand interaction, the authors developed an AR interaction framework, GSIAR, which provides two interaction techniques – so-called G-Shell and G-Speech. They have then demonstrated that direct free-hand interaction techniques can be natural, intuitive and precise. Additionally, the use of the G-Speech method, allowed to observe that ease of use and control is achievable for interactions without direct contact. Authors recommend combining both interaction techniques in a single AR interface to improve usability and enhance user experience.

The accuracy and precision of hand gestures have been tested with the use of the Leap Motion controller by Valentini and Pezzuti [18]. Authors conducted an experimental study for assessing the accuracy of the Leap Motion controller in tracking of fingertips. The assessment was performed in a real context using volunteers who were asked to point with fingers to a specific location in space.

Results show that Leap Motion is suitable for robust tracking of the user's hands. The results also unveil that there are preferable zones in which the tracking performance is better.

Wu et al. designed a novel 3D VR keyboard system with realistic haptic feedback [22]. The presented solution uses two five-fingered hand data to track finger positions and postures. Moreover, it uses micro-speakers to create vibrations, while an HMD is used to display virtual hands and keyboard. The results of this study show the advantages of the haptic VR keyboard – a keyboard that can appear at any location in a VR environment and can also be used to provide realistic key-click haptic feedback – over a physical keyboard used in VR. While the solution has been implemented for VR, it could be easily adapted to AR taking into account the lessons learned.

Khan et al. explored the effects of adding gesture interaction with 3D synthetic content in a 360 movie watching experience [8]. The presented system comprises a Leap Motion sensor to track users' hands in combination with a SoftKinetic RGB-D camera to capture the texture of the hands. It implements two different hand-visualization modes: point-cloud of the real hand and a rigged computer-generated hand. The results of the research demonstrate that participants preferred the conditions with realistic hand representation and they felt stronger embodiment and ownership. These results suggest that interaction with virtual objects should be performed using a real hand visualization instead of a virtual hand model.

Song et al. proposed a handle bar as an effective visual control metaphor between a user's hand gestures and the corresponding virtual object manipulation operations [16]. The authors performed three user studies to demonstrate the efficacy and intuitiveness of the proposed interaction techniques in different manipulation scenarios. The findings show that interaction based on the handle bar metaphor seems to provide an intuitive way for users to quickly learn how to map the action of their bi-manual hand gestures to corresponding visual manipulation tasks in a 3D virtual environment.

3   Technical Setup

In order to develop the presented mixed reality stock trading visualization system, we needed a high-resolution HMD device. We used nVisor ST50 (Fig. 2A), which is built with the use of high-contrast OLED micro-displays. The HMD provides 1280 by 1024 pixel resolution per eye in a low-power, 50° field of view compact design making the see-through compatible optics suitable for professional AR applications. The nVisor ST50 device supports the use of standard motion tracking devices from InterSense, Ascension, Polhemus, and others via a tracker platform mounted on the back of the HMD.

To detect the movement and position of the user's head, we used the InteriaCube4 device attached to the HMD (Fig. 2C). The InertiaCube4 sensor integrates the latest in MEMS inertial technology and utilizes advanced Kalman filtering algorithms to produce a full 360° orientation tracking. The sensor is

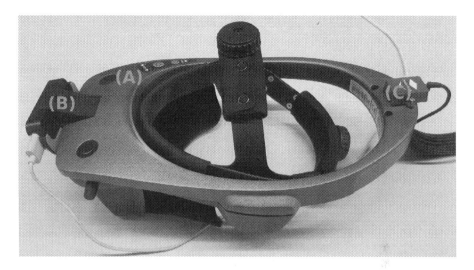

Fig. 2. The prototype of the mixed reality trading visualization system consisting of nVisor ST50 HMD (A), with attached Leap Motion (B) and InteriaCube4 (C) sensors.

compact and portable. The device is suitable for a wide range of applications including simulation, training, virtual and augmented reality, motion capture, and human movement analysis.

In order to control the mixed reality visual trading components with the use of hand gestures we used the Leap Motion controller and attached it to the front of the HMD (Fig. 2B). The Leap Motion controller is a small USB device designed for use either on a virtual reality headset or on a computer desk. It uses two monochromatic IR cameras and three infrared LEDs. The device observes roughly a hemispherical area, to a distance of about 1 m. The LEDs generate pattern-less IR light, while the cameras capture almost 200 frames per second of reflected light data. These data are then sent through a USB cable to the host computer, where they are analyzed by the Orion software.

4   System Software

The software part of the mixed reality trading visualization system consists of the MiddleVR and Orion libraries together with a custom application implemented in the Unity game engine. MiddleVR is a library responsible for handling input devices, stereoscopy, and clustering. Moreover, it offers an easy-to-use graphical user interface to configure VR/AR applications. The devices listed in Sect. 3 were integrated with the use of the MiddleVR GUI software which, as a result, generated a configuration file used by the above-mentioned MiddleVR module. In order to handle hand tracking in the 3D space, we used the Orion software. All components have been combined within the cross-platform Unity game engine (v.5.6.0f3 64-bit version). The trading visualization application has been implemented with the use of the C# language.

The financial component providing stock market data is based on Google Finance API.

The mixed reality trading visualization application consists of the following eight modules:

– *Chart* – responsible for drawing virtual charts;
– *VRkeyboard* – responsible for drawing virtual keyboard and interaction with this component;
– *FinancialAPI* – responsible for communication with the Google Finance service;
– *FXTools* – responsible for special graphical effects,
– *UI* – responsible for drawing the user interface elements,
– *LeapMotion* – based on the Orion library,
– *MiddleVR* – provided by MiddleVR for setting up hardware devices;
– *System* – integrating all components into a single VR/AR system.

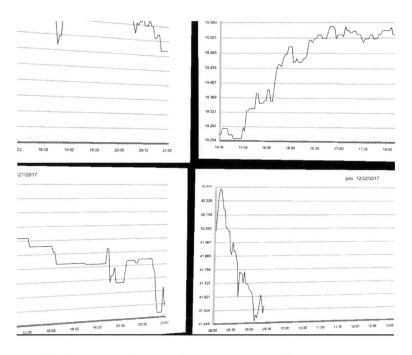

Fig. 3. An example view of a mixed reality trading workspace.

The system is designed to enhance stock traders' working environment by creating a panel of virtual screens visualizing stock data charts and presenting financial news video streams within user's surroundings. Figure 3 depicts a screen shot of an exemplary trading workspace configured with the use of the presented application.

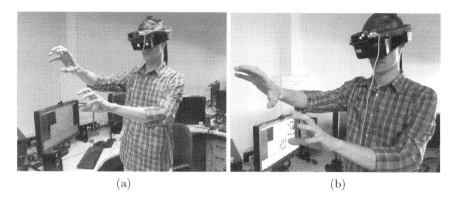

Fig. 4. A user performing in the AR mode (a) and the VR mode (b).

The application supports both VR and AR presentation modes. A user can quickly switch between the VR and AR modes throughout the entire scenario. By holding the right thumb down for three seconds, a user switches between the modes. In addition, the cover from the front of the goggles should be removed after switching to the AR mode (Fig. 4a) and inserted back when the user switches again to the VR mode (Fig. 4b).

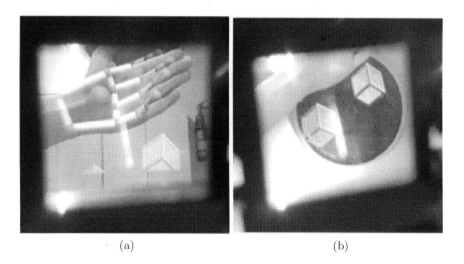

Fig. 5. A view through nVisor ST50 HMD with virtual hand visualization in the VR mode (HMD cover removed) (a) and virtual cubes used as interaction elements presented in AR mode – without virtual hand visualization (b). (Color figure online)

In the VR mode, a user sees a graphical representation of hands in the virtual space (Figs. 4b and 5a). In this mode, the view of the real hands and the real background is typically eliminated by the HMD cover (Fig. 4b). In the AR mode, a virtual sphere has been added at the palm of each hand, to indicate whether the Leap Motion controller is working correctly. When a user's hand is close to a virtual object, the color of the sphere changes to blue, signaling the user about the possibility of interacting with a virtual object.

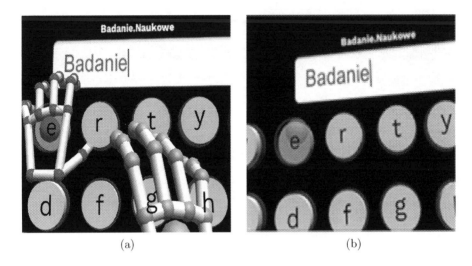

(a)   (b)

Fig. 6. Writing on a virtual keyboard in the VR (a) and AR (b) modes.

When the system starts, a menu appears informing users about possible modes of operation. The system supports three modes, which can be activated with the use of three virtual buttons in the menu. Each mode triggers a different procedure: (1) a demo of the system, (2) a tutorial for practicing basic operations, and (3) parametrization of the trading workspace.

While using the system in the third mode, a user can create any number of virtual screens showing financial data or news streams (e.g., YouTube streams). To create a screen with a chart or a video, a users needs to drag a virtual control element (a cube) from the left hand (Fig. 5b) to the desired location. For entering the names of assets and streams, the virtual keyboard is used (Fig. 6). The user can also grab and move any of the already configured virtual screens, or delete them when they are no longer needed.

5   Conclusions and Future Work

In this paper, we presented a novel mixed reality trading visualization system that can be used by stock market traders. The system can be operated both in VR and in AR modes. Our first tests show that the system is appealing to potential users, but users need training before they can effectively operate in such an environment.

There are many areas of potential future research. In particular, we plan to conduct experimental tests with non-experienced users. We would like to evaluate tasks completion times and users' experiences while learning principal functions of the system, i.e., creating and parameterizing virtual stock charts through the VR and AR interfaces. A long-term challenge is to enable building ubiquitous contextual AR environments, in which presentation of financial AR components is not dependent on a specific application, platform, or device. To "free" content and data from the above-mentioned constraints the CARE (Contextual Augmented Reality Environment) approach [13] supported with an architecture for distributed AR services could be used [14]. In such a mobile AR environment, a user could trade and analyze stocks anywhere and anytime. Last, but not least, the concept of customization of interactive three-dimensional content, supported with the use of semantic web techniques could be explored to enable generalized conceptual representation of visualization interfaces in the form of meta-scenes and on-demand customization of such interfaces with semantic queries [4].

Acknowledgements. This research work has been supported by the Polish National Science Centre (NCN) Grant No. DEC-2016/20/T/ST6/00590.

References

1. Billinghurst, M., Kato, H.: Collaborative augmented reality. Commun. ACM **45**(7), 64–70 (2002)
2. Cellary, W., Wiza, W., Walczak, K.: Visualizing web search results in 3D. Computer **37**(5), 87–89 (2004)
3. Fernandes, B., Fernández, J.: Bare hand interaction in tabletop augmented reality. In: SIGGRAPH 2009: Posters, p. 98. ACM (2009)
4. Flotyński, J., Walczak, K.: Customization of 3D content with semantic meta-scenes. Graph. Models **88**, 23–39 (2016). http://www.sciencedirect.com/science/article/pii/S1524070316300182
5. Gupta, K., Lee, G.A., Billinghurst, M.: Do you see what i see? the effect of gaze tracking on task space remote collaboration. IEEE Trans. Visual. Comput. Graph. **22**(11), 2413–2422 (2016)
6. Heidemann, G., Bax, I., Bekel, H.: Multimodal interaction in an augmented reality scenario. In: Proceedings of the 6th International Conference on Multimodal Interfaces, pp. 53–60. ACM (2004)
7. Kaiser, E., Olwal, A., McGee, D., Benko, H., Corradini, A., Li, X., Cohen, P., Feiner, S.: Mutual disambiguation of 3D multimodal interaction in augmented and virtual reality. In: Proceedings of the 5th International Conference on Multimodal Interfaces, pp. 12–19. ACM (2003)
8. Khan, H., Lee, G.A., Hoermann, S., Clifford, R., Billinghurst, M., Lindeman, R.W.: Evaluating the Effects of Hand-gesture-based Interaction With Virtual Content in a 360° Movie (2017)
9. Kolsch, M., Bane, R., Hollerer, T., Turk, M.: Multimodal interaction with a wearable augmented reality system. IEEE Comput. Graph. Appl. **26**(3), 62–71 (2006)

10. Piumsomboon, T., Altimira, D., Kim, H., Clark, A., Lee, G., Billinghurst, M.: Grasp-shell vs gesture-speech: a comparison of direct and indirect natural interaction techniques in augmented reality. In: IEEE International Symposium on Mixed and Augmented Reality (ISMAR) 2014, pp. 73–82. IEEE (2014)
11. Piumsomboon, T., Clark, A., Billinghurst, M., Cockburn, A.: User-defined gestures for augmented reality. In: Kotzé, P., Marsden, G., Lindgaard, G., Wesson, J., Winckler, M. (eds.) INTERACT 2013. LNCS, vol. 8118, pp. 282–299. Springer, Heidelberg (2013). https://doi.org/10.1007/978-3-642-40480-1_18
12. Rumiński, D.: An experimental study of spatial sound usefulness in searching and navigating through AR environments. Virtual Reality **19**(3–4), 223–233 (2015)
13. Rumiński, D., Walczak, K.: Semantic contextual augmented reality environments. In: The 13th IEEE International Symposium on Mixed and Augmented Reality (ISMAR 2014), pp. 401–404. IEEE (2014)
14. Rumiński, D., Walczak, K.: An architecture for semantic distributed augmented reality services. In: Proceedings of the 23rd International Conference on 3D Web Technology. Web3D 2018, ACM, New York, NY, USA (2018). http://doi.acm.org/10.1145/3208806.3208829
15. Sodnik, J., Tomazic, S., Grasset, R., Duenser, A., Billinghurst, M.: Spatial sound localization in an augmented reality environment. In: Proceedings of the 18th Australia Conference on Computer-human Interaction: Design: Activities, Artefacts and Environments, pp. 111–118. ACM (2006)
16. Song, P., Goh, W.B., Hutama, W., Fu, C.W., Liu, X.: A handle bar metaphor for virtual object manipulation with mid-air interaction. In: Proceedings of the SIGCHI Conference on Human Factors in Computing Systems, pp. 1297–1306. ACM (2012)
17. Taehee Lee, T., Handy, A.: Markerless inspection of augmented reality objects using fingertip tracking. In: IEEE International Symposium on Wearable Computers (2007)
18. Valentini, P.P., Pezzuti, E.: Accuracy in fingertip tracking using leap motion controller for interactive virtual applications. Int. J. Interact. Des. Manuf. (IJIDeM) **11**(3), 641–650 (2017)
19. Walczak, K., Cellary, W.: X-VRML-XML based modeling of virtual reality. In: Proceedings 2002 Symposium on Applications and the Internet (SAINT 2002), pp. 204–211. IEEE (2002)
20. Walczak, K., Rumiński, D., Flotyński, J.: Building contextual augmented reality environments with semantics. In: Proceedings of the 20th International Conference on Virtual Systems & Multimedia VSMM 2014, Hong Kong, 9–12 December 2014, pp. 353–361. IEEE (2014)
21. Wang, R., Paris, S., Popović, J.: 6D hands: markerless hand-tracking for computer aided design. In: Proceedings of the 24th annual ACM Symposium on User Interface Software and Technology, pp. 549–558. ACM (2011)
22. Wu, C.M., Hsu, C.W., Lee, T.K., Smith, S.: A virtual reality keyboard with realistic haptic feedback in a fully immersive virtual environment. Virtual Reality **21**(1), 19–29 (2017)
23. Zhou, Z., Cheok, A.D., Yang, X., Qiu, Y.: An experimental study on the role of software synthesized 3D sound in augmented reality environments. Interact. Comput. **16**(5), 989–1016 (2004)
24. Zocco, A., Zocco, M.D., Greco, A., Livatino, S., De Paolis, L.T.: Touchless interaction for command and control in military operations. In: De Paolis, L.T., Mongelli, A. (eds.) AVR 2015. LNCS, vol. 9254, pp. 432–445. Springer, Cham (2015). https://doi.org/10.1007/978-3-319-22888-4_32

A New Framework for Easy and Efficient Augmentation of Primary Level Books

Liaqat Ali[(✉)] and Sehat Ullah

Department of Computer Science and Information Technology,
University of Malakand, Chakdara, Pakistan
liaqat147@gmail.com, sehatullah@uom.edu.pk

Abstract. Augmented Reality (AR) helps students to understand abstract and invisible concepts in our daily life. There are several applications of AR in areas such as Medical, Cricket, Tourism, and in Education. AR delivers information (physical and abstract concepts) in a simple and meaningful ways which improve students learning along with increased motivation. In this paper, we propose a generalized framework for the automatic registration and augmentation of information (3D objects and audio information) of primary school books to achieve improved learning and motivation. A desktop based GUI is designed which uses an easy and step by step approach during the whole process. The experiments resulted in high accuracy with improved motivation and easiness.

Keywords: Augmented reality · Education · Technology
Preschool children's · Framework · 3D

1 Introduction

Augmented Reality is the superimposition of computer generated virtual information over a real scene to provide rich, relevant and meaningful information such as text, sound, graphics, and video to the user [1, 2]. To work successfully in the real-world AR offers clear and natural information for the users [3]. The goal of AR is to enhance information related to real world objects [4]. It is one of the newest technology that could be used as creativity promoting educational tool [5]. Users see the synthetic information mixed with the real scene, without losing the sense of reality [5]. AR is used and gaining popularity everywhere in our daily life [5, 6]. Different AR applications have been developed in different fields of life [7] such as Advertising and Marketing [8], Architecture and Construction [9], Entertainment [10], Medical [11], Military [12], Travel [13], and Education [14].

The use of AR in education is quite in initial stage [5]. In education, it was first used in 2000 when Sheldon et al. [5] developed an AR application for undergraduate education. They observe it useful for teaching, especially for abstract and invisible concepts that are hard to understand due to real world constraints [5]. In the next two-three years, AR will provide new opportunities for teaching and learning [15]. Overly of virtual information on the real-world scene is a source to increase learning experiences [15]. Using tablets and mobiles increase the value of AR applications in learning. AR has the power to help students to learn not only in the classrooms but also out of the

© Springer International Publishing AG, part of Springer Nature 2018
L. T. De Paolis and P. Bourdot (Eds.): AVR 2018, LNCS 10850, pp. 311–321, 2018.
https://doi.org/10.1007/978-3-319-95270-3_26

classrooms in students living spaces [4]. The use of AR technology in teaching and learning process will actively involve students in classrooms so they will be able to remember most of the information [7]. Researchers have shown that learning does occur in virtual environments and AR is the classroom of the future [4, 7]. Learners will learn and having fun if education and AR technologies are brought together [4].

The applications AR in education is very wide [16]. It is used in different fields of education [17] such as Chemistry [18], Physics [19], Biology [20], and Mathematics [21]. Researchers divided it into five groups such as Discovery-based learning, Object Modeling, Skills Training, AR Gaming, and AR Books [22]. Among these Augmented books have received the attention of the researchers and educators to enhance books with additional information [23]. AR books offer a new way of learning to actively engage and motivate learners [22]. The use of AR books in classrooms is a cost-effective approach and can be used in different levels of education [6]. AR book is a good example of the provision of virtual information to real worlds [6]. The capability to see and listen to additional computer generated information is the main advantage of AR to traditional teaching methodology [24, 25]. Different AR education systems have been developed such as Fun Learning with AR Alphabet book [26], Interactive Learning in Education [27], The Magic Book [28], and the Edutainment Story Book [29] etc.

There are different problems in the existing AR systems such as dependency on specific books, lack of a common framework for the augmentation, need of fiducial markers placed in the book, and manual drawing of borders around pictures for detection purposes. To deal with these problems we proposed an automatic generalized model for information augmentation.

In this paper, we proposed a new generalized framework for primary level books for the augmentation of virtual information in an easy, automatic, and efficient manner. The proposed system needs no manual work for augmentation (i.e. creating or placing markers in the book) or designing special books.

The rest of the paper is organized as follow. Section 2 discusses related work. The proposed system is presented in Sect. 3, while the evaluation and result are shown in Sect. 4. Finally, Sect. 5 gives the conclusion.

2   Literature Review

Augmented Reality is a very wide field. It is a difficult job to cover all area. However, several studies have been accomplished in the field of AR in education. This section explains the previous work on augmented books. The functionalities of existing systems have been discussed.

Fun learning with AR Alphabet Book [26] is an AR application developed for preschool children. The system used an external camera with a desktop computer for detection of fiducial markers placed on different pages of the book. For each alphabet, three different markers were used (i.e. for lower case, upper case, and 3D model). The system involves a considerable human effort due to manual generation, placement, and augmentation of markers in the book.

Abhishekh et al. [27] developed interactive Learning AR application. The system used fiducial markers, camera, and a computer with AR software. The system used AR glasses, a projector, or a monitor as output devices. The system display different animation based information upon detection of the fiducial markers placed on different pages in the middle of the book. The application needs physical work such as preparing, registering, printing and placement of the marker in a book.

The magic book [28] is developed by Billinghurst et al. for games and entertainment. The main components of the magic book application are a handheld augmented reality display (HHD), a computer with a camera and one or more physical books. The books consist of text and pictures. Pictures have thick black borders surrounding just like fiducial markers. The ARToolKit [29] is used for recognition of markers and visualization of 3D information. The system uses the 2D images of the book as fiducial markers by manually drawing the square shaped border around the images to cope with pasting external markers in the book. The manual work of drawing border around each image and costly nature of the system reduce its feasibility in school situations.

Rambli et al. [30] developed an AR based edutainment storybook for preschool children. The aim of this application system is learning numbers based on AR technology and an old folklore story. Multiple markers were placed in a sequence in the book to carry out the full story in the specified sequence. A magic wand is used to point to a specific marker to display the related 3D information. Use of special book (not related to course) and placement of markers leads to extra human efforts. Also, there is no strategy for the automatic generation, registration, and augmentation of 3D information. The system also depends on extra devices such as wand for pointing specific markers.

Augmented Story Book [23] is developed by Dunser et al. for children. ARToolKit, webcam, monitor, fiducial markers and two story books (big feet and little feet, looking for the sun) were used. Markers were placed in the physical books and special paddles (Using Markers) were designed for the main characters of the stories. Also, some additional files were printed and used as pages of the book. A user interface is used to start and interact with the story. The computer screen shows the stories and the navigation buttons to go next, back, skipping and listen to the story. The system needs a lot of manual work such as designing special story book, paddles, and placement of markers in the book.

The previous systems mostly have non-automatic nature for registration and augmentation of markers due to which they need extra time and efforts during registration and augmentation process.

In this paper, we propose a new generalize frame work for the automatic generation, registration, and augmentation of preschool books.

3   Proposed Solution

We proposed a new generalized framework for the registration and augmentation of primary level books. The frame work does not need any manual work such as designing markers or special books, printing markers, placement of markers on book pages and drawing borders around images. The main difference between the previous and the proposed system is shown in Table 1. This is desktop based AR system using Natural Feature Tracking (NFT) method for detection. C-sharp (C#), ARToolKit, Blender, Unity 3D, and Java software were used to develop this AR framework.

Table 1. Difference between previous and proposed system

Systems	Markers	Need special books	Special devices	Mixed reality	Common books	Frame work
Fun learning	Yes	Yes	No	No	No	No
Interactive learning	Yes	Yes	No	No	No	No
Magic book	Yes	Yes	Yes	Yes	No	No
Edutainment story book	Yes	Yes	No	No	No	No
Augmented story book	Yes	Yes	No	No	No	No
Proposed system	No	No	No	No	Yes	Yes

To achieve the goal, we developed the proposed system in four steps. The first step was to access the camera using the proposed system for this purpose we use C#. The second step was to provide a facility to the users to register an image instead of using the command line we use Java with ARToolKit. The third step was to design and develop 3D models and record audio information, we use Blender with Unity 3D for designing and audio recorder for audio information. The four step was to create a user interface (UI) for all these processes. We developed a UI in C# for easy access and operation as shown in Fig. 1. The UI consists of three main buttons Capture Image, Generate and augment 3D information.

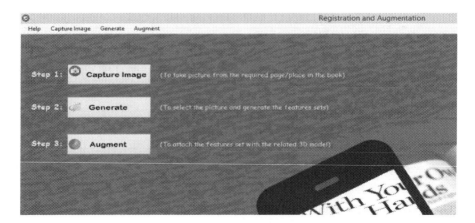

Fig. 1. User interface

The proposed framework works in three steps first to capture image from the required page or place to be used for augmentation. Second to generate features set of the image and third to augment the 3D information. A web cam is used for capturing the image from the book, to view the virtual models and to capture video of the real world as well as the book. In the marker generation, step feature set of the captured image is generated and stored in a database. The NFT feature of the ARToolKit is used for generation of the feature set. The augmentation step consists of retrieving the feature set and association (augmentation) of 3D model and audio information with it. The whole process is shown in the system model as shown in Fig. 2.

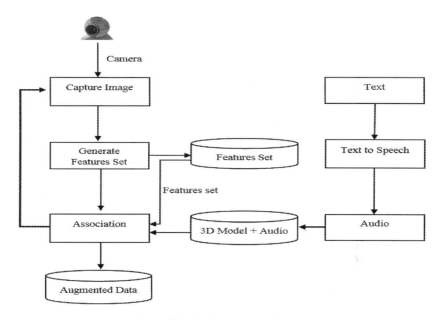

Fig. 2. System model

3.1 Working Mechanism

Figure 3 shows the working mechanism of the proposed system. After augmentation, the system uses a camera for capturing the desired image from the real-world scene. The camera uses ARToolKit software at the back ground for generating and comparing the specific feature of the image in the data base. When the camera finds a match then the associated 3D model and audio information are rendered on the screen as shown in Fig. 4. If the camera does not find a match, then the camera search for another image.

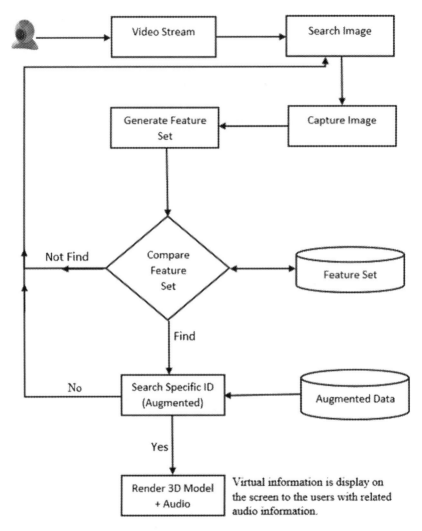

Fig. 3. Working mechanism

4 Evaluation and Results

For evaluation of the proposed system, an observational study was conducted at the primary school.

4.1 Protocol

Thirteen male primary school teachers participated in the experimental study. The evaluation was performed in six (6) different days. All the teachers were from six (6) different primary schools. They all have teaching experience. Two (2) teachers have nine (9) months, eight (8) teachers have two (2) to four (4) years, and three (3) teachers

Fig. 4. Augmented tree on book page (during experiments)

have five (5) to seven (7) years teaching experience. All the teachers are male having aged 25–30. All The teachers had used the computer but they have no experience with AR. Two books English from class nursery and Science from grade two were selected for evaluation.

4.2 Task

The teachers were first demonstrated about the use (registration and augmentation) of the system. The time taken on demonstration was twenty (20) to thirty (30) minutes. After that, they performed a pre-trial of registration and augmentation. Each teacher performs the pre-trail in ten (10) to fifteen (15) minutes. After the training, each of them performed the task. The task was to perform the whole process of registration and augmentation of an image from each of the two different primary level books. Task completion time and errors during registration and augmentation were recorded for each participant. Total fifty-two (52) pictures minimum two (2) and maximum five (5) pictures were augmented by each teacher. The time taken during the experiment by all thirteen teachers were 09, 24, 23, 25, 23, 24, 11, 28, 22, 26, 23, 18, and 22 min respectively. After the experiment, each participant filled a questionnaire for subjective analysis.

4.3 Results

Task Time. The mean task completion time and errors for each participant are 5.3 min and 0.7 as shown in Fig. 5. It means that the system is feasible as it takes a considerably less time in registration and augmentation process.

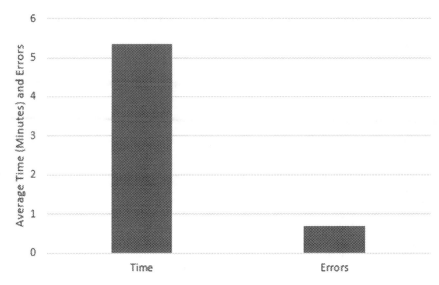

Fig. 5. Task time

Identification of Images. Two books each one having Twenty-six (26) pictures were used in the experimental study. Forty-three (43) pictures were correctly identified and only nine (9) pictures were not identified. The identification rate is 82.69%. Based on quality the identified pictures were divided into two groups i.e. strong identified and weak identified. Strong identified means that after augmentation using the books the proposed system identified the augmented pictures directly without any struggle while weak identified mean that the proposed system identified the pictures but after moving to left or right. The strongly identified rate of the proposed system is 76.74% and the weakly identified rate is 23.25%.

Easiness and Likeness. A questionnaire is filled by each teacher about easiness and likeness during registration, augmentation, and identification. The questionnaire included the following three simple questions:

Q1: Did you enjoy the work on the proposed system for augmentation?

  ☐ Yes ☐ No

Q2: Would you like to use the proposed system in education?

  ☐ Yes ☐ No

Q3: Do you think it was easy to use the proposed framework for augmentation?

  ☐ Easy ☐ Difficult

All thirteen teachers selected yes in response to question no 1 and 2. They all enjoyed and liked the proposed system and use of AR in education. The result of easiness and likeness is shown in Fig. 6. Ten (10) teachers selected that the system is easy. Three (3) teachers selected the option that it is difficult to use. The rate of easiness is 76.92% while the rate of difficulty is 23.07%. The result shows that the proposed system is easy and effective for augmentation of primary school books.

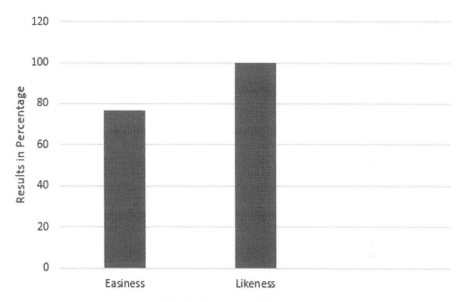

Fig. 6. Easiness and likeness

The results of our evaluation were satisfactory. Our study discloses that using common features instead of special materials is an attention grabber way to increase the use of AR. To increase user's enjoyment, engagement, usability and decrease cognitive load the use of a real book for the development of an AR book has shown positive effect [31]. In educational environments using AR books lead to active participation, authentic and collaborative learning [32].

5   Conclusion

In this research study, we have presented the development and evaluation of a new generalized framework for easy and effective augmentation of primary level books. The framework has a step by step and user-friendly interface for registration and augmentation of a book. One of the main advantages of the framework over other systems is that the framework does not need special skills (Designing Markers), materials (Fiduciary Markers), and books. The results of our experiments show that the framework is very useful for augmentation because of less time, accuracy, easiness and motivation. The use of AR in our daily life is difficult because of limited resources such as costly equipment's and required high skills. The proposed method is a positive step in this area.

References

1. Lee, K.: Augmented reality in education and training. TechTrends **56**(2), 13–21 (2012)
2. Adabala1, D., Kaushik, S.: Augmented reality: a review of applications. Int. Res. J. Eng. Technol. (IRJET), **3**(06), 1308–1312 (2016)
3. Rajasree, G., Varsha, K., Susmitha, E., Praveena, J., Harika, G.: Augmented reality on android platform. Int. J. Sci. Eng. Res. **4**(5), 1737–1744 (2013)
4. Rasalingam, R.R., Muniandy, B., Rasalingam, R.R.: Exploring the application of augmented reality technology in early childhood classroom in Malaysia. J. Res. Method Educ. (IOSR-JRME) **4**(5), 33–40 (2014)
5. Persefoni, K., Tsinakos, A.: Use of augmented reality in terms of creativity in school learning. In: Workshop of Making as a Pathway to Foster Joyful Engagement and Creativity in Learning (Make2Learn), p. 45 (2015)
6. Bower, M., Howe, C., McCredie, N., Robinson, A., Grover, D.: Augmented reality in education cases, places and potentials. Educ. Media Int. **51**(1), 115 (2014)
7. Mekni, M., Lemieux, A.: Augmented reality: applications challenges and future trends. In: Applied Computational Science Proceedings of the 13th International Conference on Applied Computer and Applied Computational Science (ACACOS 2014), pp. 23–25 (2014)
8. Carmigniani, J., Furht, B., Anisetti, M., Ceravolo, P., Damiani, E., Ivkovic, M.: Augmented reality technologies systems and applications. Multimedia Tools Appl. **51**(1), 341–377 (2011)
9. Webster, A., et al.: Augmented reality in architectural construction inspection and renovation. In: Proceedings of ASCE Third Congress on Computing in Civil Engineering (1996)
10. Bruns, E., Brombach, B., Zeidler, T., Bimber, O.: Enabling mobile phones to support large-scale museum guidance. IEEE Multimedia **14**(2), 16–25 (2007)
11. Bichlmeier, C., Wimmer, F., Heining, S.M., Navab, N.: Contextual anatomic mimesis hybrid In-Situ visualization method for improving Multi-Sensory depth perception in medical augmented reality. In: 6th IEEE and ACM International Symposium on Mixed and Augmented Reality 2007, ISMAR 2007, pp. 129–138 (2007)
12. Livingston, M., Rosenblum, L., Julier, S., Brown, D., Baillot, Y., Swan, J.E., Gabbard, J., Baillot, Y., Hix, D.: An augmented reality system for military operations in urban terrain. In: Interservice/Industry Training Simulation & Education Conference (I/ITSEC 2002), pp. 1–8 (2002)
13. Yang, J., Yang, W., Denecke, M., Waibel, A.: Smart Sight: a tourist assistant system. In: Proceedings of the 3rd IEEE International Symposium on Wearable Computers ISWC, pp. 73–78, October 1999
14. Chen, M.P., Liao, B.C.: Augmented reality laboratory for high school electrochemistry course. In: IEEE 15th International Conference on In Advanced Learning Technologies (ICALT), pp. 132–136 (2015)
15. Chen, P., Liu, X., Cheng, W., Huang, R.: A review of using Augmented Reality in Education from 2011 to 2016. Innovations in Smart Learning. LNET, pp. 13–18. Springer, Singapore (2017). https://doi.org/10.1007/978-981-10-2419-1_2
16. Billinghurst, M.: Augmented reality in education. In: New Horizons for Learning, vol. 12 (2002)
17. Yuen, S., Yaoyuneyong, G., Johnson, E.: Augmented reality: an overview and five directions for AR in education. J. Educ. Technol. Dev. Exch. **4**(1), 119–140 (2011)

18. Fjeld, M., Voegtli, B.M.: Augmented chemistry: an interactive educational workbench. In: Proceedings International Symposium on Mixed and Augmented Reality 2002, ISMAR 2002, pp. 259–321 (2002)
19. Enyedy, N., Danish, J.A., Delacruz, G., Kumar, M.: Learning physics through play in an augmented reality environment. Int. J. Comput. Supported Collaborative Learn. **7**(3), 347–378 (2012)
20. Marzouk, D., Attia, G., Abdelbaki, N.: Biology learning using augmented reality and gaming techniques. In: Proceedings of World Congress on Multimedia and Computer Science, ACEEE, Hammamet, Tunisia, pp. 79–86 (2013)
21. Kaufmann, H., Schmalstieg, D.: Mathematics and geometry education with collaborative augmented reality. Comput. Graph. **27**(3), 339–345 (2003)
22. Diegmann, P., Schmidt-Kraepelin, M., Van den Eynden, S., Basten, D.: Benefits of augmented reality in educational environments. a systematic literature review. In: Proceeding of the 12 International Conference Tagung Wirtschaftsinformatik, pp. 1542–1556 (2015)
23. Dnser, A., Hornecker, E.: An observational study of children interacting with an augmented story book. In: Proceedings of the 2nd International Conference on Technologies for e-Learning and Digital Entertainment, pp. 305–315, 11–13 June 2007
24. Liarokapis, F., Anderson, E.: Using augmented reality as a medium to assist teaching in higher education. In: Proceedings of the 31st Annual Conference of the European Association for Computer Graphics (Eurographics 2010), Education Program (2010)
25. Cai, S., Wang, X., Chiang, F.-K.: A case study of augmented reality simulation system application in a chemistry course. Comput. Hum. Behav. **37**, 31–40 (2014)
26. Rambli, D.R.A., Matcha, W., Sulaiman, S.: Fun learning with AR alphabet book for preschool children. Procedia Comput. Sci. **25**, 211–219 (2013)
27. Abhishekh, D., Reddy, B.R., Kumar, R.R., Rajeswarappa, G.: Interactive learning in education using augmented reality. Int. J. Sci. Eng. Res. **4**, 1 (2013)
28. Billinghurst, M., Kato, H., Pouprev, I.: The MagicBook: a transitional AR interface. Comput. Graph. **25**(5), 745–753 (2001)
29. ARToolKit.org
30. Rambli, D.R., Matcha, W., Sulaiman, S., Nayan, M.Y.: Design and development of an interactive augmented reality edutainment storybook for preschool. IERI Procedia **2**, 802–807 (2012)
31. Grasset, R., Duenser, A., Seichter, H., Billinghurst, M.: The mixed reality book: a new multimedia reading experience. In: CHI 2007 Extended Abstracts on Human Factors in Computing Systems, pp. 1953–1958. ACM, New York (2007)
32. Shelton, B.: How augmented reality helps students learn dynamic spatial relationships. PhD Thesis, University of Washington, Washington (2003)

Real-Time Multi-view Grid Map-Based Spatial Representation for Mixed Reality Applications

Pedro Girão$^{(\boxtimes)}$, João Paulo, Luís Garrote, and Paulo Peixoto

Institute of Systems and Robotics,
Department of Electrical and Computer Engineering, University of Coimbra,
Coimbra, Portugal
pedro.girao@uc.pt, {jpaulo,garrote,peixoto}@isr.uc.pt

Abstract. In this paper it is presented a markerless multi-view vision-based system to create a spatial representation of an indoor environment. Mixed reality integrates real-world elements into a virtual world. The modeling of such elements should be accurate to avoid interaction inconsistencies. The goal of this work is to achieve the virtualization of a room and its elements, providing seamless user navigation and interaction. This spatial representation based on grid maps provides a clear distinction between occupied and free cells. Scene objects are segmented using clustering techniques. The proposed approach has several potential applications, such as interactive virtual visits to heritage museums, real estate, and training scenarios. Preliminary qualitative results evidence a visually accurate modeling of the considered scenes, identifying elements and free space, encouraging future work towards the identification and tracking of static and dynamic elements on the scene.

Keywords: Mixed reality · Spatial representation · Grid maps
DB-SCAN · Kinect

1 Introduction

In recent years there has been a noticeable increase in the number of mixed reality technologies [1]. Mixed reality allows not only user interaction with a virtual environment, but also the interaction with physical objects on the immediate surroundings of the user that act as elements of interaction with the virtual environment. In this sense, mixed reality is a technology that seems to be the perfect solution to the immersion shortcomings of existing virtual reality systems.

However, systems based on mixed reality are heavily dependent on an adequate virtualization of real-world elements (objects and humans). These need to be correctly placed in the virtual world, requiring an accurate spatial representation of the real-world; this is a crucial step to achieve a coherent mixed reality experience.

© Springer International Publishing AG, part of Springer Nature 2018
L. T. De Paolis and P. Bourdot (Eds.): AVR 2018, LNCS 10850, pp. 322–339, 2018.
https://doi.org/10.1007/978-3-319-95270-3_27

With this work, we propose an innovative pipeline for the spatial representation of immersive rooms in a mixed reality context. The proposed system is based on a low-cost, multi-sensor, markerless, vision-based system that captures the environment from various angles in an easy-to-use deployment setup, requiring just a single initial calibration. The multi-sensor setup allows a more robust capturing of the environment by avoiding occlusions. The system works in real-time, detecting the elements of the scene, and can be scaled to adapt to the size of a given room depending on the number of used sensors. The sensor setup is composed of Microsoft's Kinect One cameras. The techniques used to achieve the real-world modeling employ background subtraction and clustering for scene segmentation. The spatial representation is based on occupancy grid maps, a methodology widely used in the robotics domain where it is applied typically in mapping for navigation purposes [2].

In this system, the user can navigate within a room using an headset, and the scene's elements can be detected and mapped into the virtual world where they can be interacted with while the system keeps tracking both user and scene elements in real-time.

This paper is organized as follows: Sect. 2 addresses the related work in this field, and provides some background on the occupancy grid maps techniques. Section 3 summarizes our proposal, while in Sect. 4 the full system is described in detail. Section 5 presents some preliminary qualitative results about the performance of the proposed system. Finally, Sect. 6 draws some conclusions and outlines future work.

2   Background

2.1   Work Context

The work presented in this paper was carried out as part of the HTPDIR project, "Human Tracking and Perception in Dynamic Immersive Rooms". The project aims to develop a low-cost, marker-less, and easy-to-setup system that (i) enables the reconstruction of a real-world environment in a grid-based virtual representation, and (ii) detect and track people and objects that are present in the environment.

2.2   Related Work

In the context of mixed reality interfaces, the authors were unable to find works that specifically attempt to model an entire room in real-time, as well as to simultaneously detect and track both user and objects. Most of the work in this field is based on user-worn headset's Point of View (POV) to detect objects immediately in front of the user, with which the user can interact, and are therefore not suitable for full scale room representations. On the other hand, some techniques have specifically evolved scene reconstruction to a high level of accuracy with low-cost sensors as is the case of the very well-know KinectFusion [3].

For spatial representation the works that deal with this task typically belong to other application domains outside the mixed reality context. Usually, approaches focusing on problems of environment representation, detection, and tracking of moving objects are related to perception for intelligent vehicles and robotics. Within the context of environment perception, environment representation deals with processing the data acquired by sensors to build an internal representation of the environment which can further be exploited for modeling static and dynamic parts of the scene. Nowadays, perception systems are able to sense and interpret surrounding environments in 3D, using sensors such as 3D LIDAR (light detection and ranging) [4,5], stereo vision [6,7] and RGB-D sensors. A combination of sensors is typically needed to provide data robust to all conditions.

In order to build an internal 3D representation of the environment, there are four main type of strategies typically used: (i) Point cloud-based [8,9]; (ii) Feature-based [10,11]; (iii) Grid-based [2]; (iv) Topological approaches [12].

Topological approaches represent the environment as a graph which is composed of nodes and links. Nodes represent distinctive places on the environment, and links represent information about movement between nodes. Topological approaches are usually built on top of grid-based or feature-based approaches by partitioning them into coherent regions. Therefore, due to its dependency on other approaches, we will only focus on those. Point cloud-based approaches directly use raw sensor data for environment representation. One can build a point cloud map by aggregating measured points of different scans using an iterative closest point (ICP) algorithm or its variants [2,13]. This approach generates an accurate representation, however, requires large memory and high computational power, and it does not provide a direct representation of free/unknown area. Feature-based methods use locally distinguishable features to model the environment (e.g. points [14], lines [15,16], rectangles or boxes [17,18], circles [19], superquadrics [20]). Using geometric primitives has a limitation of not being able to represent complex environments. Furthermore, since it is a sparse representation, the spaces between features remain undefined, which makes it inadequate for people to accurately navigate through the environment. Grid-based methods discretize the space into small grid elements in which each grid element contains information about the space it represents. Grid maps require a high amount of memory and computational power to represent a large outdoor environment. However, this issue can be mitigated if the map is limited to a smaller area [21,22]. The advantage of the grid map lies in the fact that it does not rely on any predefined features. It provides a detailed representation of the environment with information about free and unknown areas that makes it very useful for navigation tasks. A grid map is also useful to integrate different sensor measurements into a unified representation. These characteristics made the grid map a popular tool for representing environments in the intelligent vehicles and mobile robotics domains and was the reason why we considered the use of a 3D grid map-based representation of an indoor environment for this project.

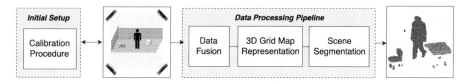

Fig. 1. High-level overview of the system architecture.

2.3   Theoretical Background

This section introduces the theoretical background and notation that will be employed throughout this paper.

A grid map M, in robotics, is usually defined as a two-dimensional environment representation whose indexes (i, j) are bounded between $([0, n_{rows}], [0, n_{cols}])$, row- and column-wise, and is composed by a set of cells $M_{2D} = \bigcup c_{ij}, i \in [0, n_{rows}], j \in [0, n_{cols}]$. Each cell c_{ij} is defined with constant dimensions and the number of points inside that cell that represent the existence of some object on the environment, provided by the integration of the sensors' measurements. In this work 3D grid maps are used. They add an extra dimension to the cell matrix representing height, $M_{3D} = \bigcup c_{ijk}, i \in [0, n_{rows}], j \in [0, n_{cols}], k \in [0, n_{height}]$.

3   Proposed System

This section describes the proposed system, starting with a top-level overview of the system's architecture and moving later to a detailed formulation of the developed modules.

3.1   System Overview

A high-level diagram representing the conceptual pipeline of the considered system is shown in Fig. 1. The key motivation of the presented work is, as aforementioned, the development of a low-cost system that could represent a real-world environment in a mixed reality application, creating the possibility of tasks such as object segmentation and efficient 3D user tracking.

The system processing pipeline is divided into two stages. The first one consists of an initial calibration module when the system is deployed on the environment. The second stage deals with the main processing pipeline, which is where synchronized data collected by the sensors is processed, first from local depth maps to a world reference, then to a unified point cloud (PCD), and finally into a 3D grid map where individual scene elements are then segmented.

3.2   Initial Considerations

In order to capture data from the environment, several technologies and sensors were studied. A particular constraint of the project was the overall cost of the sensor setup. In this sense, the Kinect family of products from Microsoft (Kinect V1 and Kinect One) proved to be affordable sensors that offered accurate RGB and spatial information. Even though these sensors were mainly designed for gaming, researchers have been using them for innovative applications in areas ranging from 3D environment reconstruction [3] to virtual and augmented reality [23].

Both versions of the Kinect sensors output a depth map of the environment from their given POV at a maximum rate of 30 Hz. Despite both models' depth sensors have good horizontal and vertical Field of View (FOV) and ranges, the process of reconstructing real-world environments with a static camera leads to the possibility of occlusions occurring, with a given object being obstructed by another from the sensors POV. By employing several of these sensors, a more robust and complete representation of the scenario can thus be obtained.

Besides some other differences between the two models, the Kinect V1's range sensor is based on structured-light (SL), producing depth images of resolution 320×240, while the latest Kinect One model is based on Time-of-Flight (ToF), and outputs images with a resolution of 512×424. The use of multiple Kinect v1 sensors brought up the problem of inter-sensor interferences, since each sensor sees the light patterns projected by other sensors. An intelligent solution was proposed by both Maimone *et al.* [24] and Butler *et al.* [25] by attaching a small DC motor to the Kinect, where each sensor would only see their own projected pattern correctly, with all other patterns being blurred. However, not only was the interference not completely mitigated, but the motion patterns induced by the motor were unpredictable and not easy to control. Sarbolandi *et al.* further specify in [26] that for depth-stereo systems the Kinect One can be a better suited sensor.

The proposed system utilizes four Kinect One sensors, creating an environment with an area ranging from about 9–$25\,\mathrm{m}^2$ depending on the expected accuracy of the data outputted by the sensors.

Finally, the data captured by all sensors is processed centrally on a single computer. Unlike solutions where a master-slave (or server-client) architecture was devised such as [27–29], the presented system has all the four sensors connected to the same computer. This was made possible by having each Kinect One connected to their own PCIe controller (one native to the motherboard and three addition external USB 3.0 controllers), eliminating the need of constantly sending data from several clients to a central server. The official Kinect SDK could not be used since it only supports a single sensor. As an alternative, the open source drivers for the Kinect One available in the `libfreenect2` project [30] were used, enabling our architecture to run on a single computer.

4   Methodology

This section provides a detailed description of each individual module of the system.

4.1   Calibration Procedure

All Kinect One sensors must operate in a common coordinate reference system, which can be achieved by having a co-registration of information between all of them. This procedure only requires a moderately sized checkerboard pattern (with an even-odd configuration of black and white squares) to be placed in the center of the room.

With the Kinect One depth sensor being based on ToF technology, each captured depth image pixel value at position (x, y) is the measured distance from the sensor lens' center to the real-world point where each beam is reflected. As such, by having 4 separate depth images of the same environment, a common reference system must be found to merge all of the depth data into an unified representation. To minimize the possible interference of the IR beams between the several sensors, the Kinect One sensors were placed at a height of $2.20m$ on top of aluminum profiles, facing downwards by an angle of $\sim 30°$.

The calibration module works as a one-pass procedure after the sensors are placed in the desired positions. Two types of calibration parameters need to be defined: intrinsic and extrinsic parameters. For the intrinsics estimation of each depth sensor, which include focal length (f_x, f_y), optical center (c_x, c_y) and skew coefficients of the lens, the well-known method proposed by Zhang in [31] was used. The result of this process is a camera intrinsic matrix K defined as:

$$K = \begin{bmatrix} f_x & 0 & 0 \\ 0 & f_y & 0 \\ c_x & c_y & 1 \end{bmatrix} \tag{1}$$

This data can then be used to transform a local 2D depth map to a local 3D PCD representation by applying the transformation in Eq. 2, where u and v represents a depth map pixel's column and row, respectively:

$$PCD_{(x,y,z)} = (d\frac{u - c_x}{f_x}, d\frac{v - c_y}{f_y}, d) \tag{2}$$

The extrinsic parameters are composed by a rotation and translation of each sensor reference frame to the world reference frame. The adopted extrinsic camera calibration procedures were based on works such as the one by Bouguet *et al.* [32] keeping in mind that, as mentioned by Rodehorst *et al.* [33], common relative pose estimation algorithms between reference systems offer "much more stable and accurate" rotational components in comparison to camera translations.

Calibration methods such as [32] use a 2D calibration object in the form of planar checkerboard patterns with known square sizes, where the detected internal corners are used as calibration points. In our case, we display a 9×6 checkerboard pattern with known square sizes in the center of the area defined by the placement of the cameras and find all extrinsic parameters in a single shot approach.

With the knowledge of each square's side size, the common (or *world*) reference system center is defined as starting on the first detected inner corner

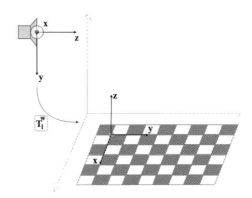

Fig. 2. Result of the extrinsics calibration for a given sensor.

of the real-world checkerboard pattern. A representation of the transformation between both reference systems can be seen in Fig. 2.

The problem of determining the extrinsics for each camera is then reduced to finding the rigid transformation that maps each sensor's local checkerboard corners in the PCD to the real-world corners, solving for R and t in Eq. 3, where PCD_{c_l} and PCD_{c_w} represent a PCD in both local and world reference frames, respectively:

$$PCD_{c_w} = R \times PCD_{c_l} + t \qquad (3)$$

The process of finding this optimal rigid transformation is composed of three steps: find the centroids $cent_l$ and $cent_w$ of PCD_{c_l} and PCD_{c_w}, move both point sets to the "origin" to find the optimal R, and finally find t. To find R, the N points are re-centered and the covariance matrix H is defined so that:

$$H = \sum_{i=1}^{N} \left((PCD_{c_l}^i - cent_l)(PCD_{c_w}^i - cent_w)^T \right) \qquad (4)$$

By applying the singular-value decomposition (SVD) to H one can find the optimal rotation R as:

$$[U, S, V] = SVD(H) \qquad (5)$$

$$R = VU^T \qquad (6)$$

Some special cases may happen when the SVD returns a *reflection matrix* that is mathematically correct but ends up calculating an incorrect R; if the determinant of R is negative, either the third column of V is multipled by -1 and R is recalculated, or the third column R is simply multiplied by -1, yielding the optimal rotation.

The last step, finding the translation between both point sets, is obtained by applying Eq. 7:

$$t = -R \times cent_l + cent_w \qquad (7)$$

The complete transformation matrix from each local to world PCD, T_l^w, can then be defined as:

$$T_l^w = \begin{bmatrix} R_{l_{3 \times 3}}^w & 0 \\ 0 & t_{l_{3 \times 1}}^w \end{bmatrix} \tag{8}$$

The single shot nature of the presented procedure was devised to overcome the hurdles of slow calibration procedures by favoring quickness in setup and calculation times.

4.2   Data Fusion

Having all 4 sensors connected to the main computer, data can be simultaneously acquired from each sensor. The data is captured at a given framerate of up to a maximum 30 FPS.

The data captured by the system is composed by 4 depth images per "frame". Each of these depth images is converted into a local PCD and afterward to a world PCD, with the latter process represented in Eq. 9. This data fusion process is applied at this low-level stage where all the PCD are merged into a unique representation, PCD_M, as given by Eq. 10.

$$PCD_{w_i} = T_i^w \times PCD_{l_i}^T, i \in \{1, \ldots, 4\} \tag{9}$$

$$PCD_M = \bigcup_{i=1}^{4} PCD_{w_i} \tag{10}$$

An example of one PCD local to a given sensor and the equivalent merged PCD can be observed in Fig. 3 with the axes on each image corresponding to their reference system.

4.3   3D Grid Map Representation

Having a fully condensed PCD, the next step is to obtain a 3D grid map representation of that data. Some preprocessing is applied beforehand in order to introduce only relevant scene elements into the 3D grid map.

Inter-Camera Planar Filter. The planar surfaces visible in the merged PCD in Fig. 3 correspond to walls and closets present in the room where the dataset was captured. Such cases can also happen on rooms where the system is meant to be deployed. With this in mind, an initial filtering of points outside the vertical volume defined by the cameras is used to solve this issue. Given a set of four points (base and height of the aluminum profiles for each pair of adjacent cameras) the plane that best fits those points is obtained by minimizing the sum of (perpendicular to the plane) quadratic distances between the plane and this set of points. Each plane will be characterized by a point and normal vector that points to the scene's center as illustrated in Fig. 4. We shall call PCD_{in} to the result of filtering PCD_M using this approach.

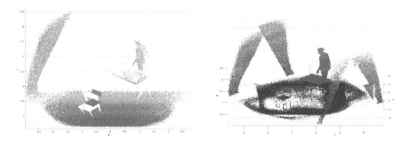

Fig. 3. A local PCD of one of the sensors (left) and the corresponding merged PCD (right).

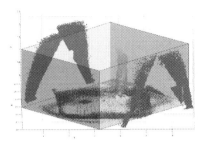

Fig. 4. Removal of points outside inter-camera planes.

Background Subtraction. Given the aforementioned physical setup, most of the captured information correspondent to points that belong to the ground. Referring back to Fig. 3, it can be seen that a very large percentage of the PCD information are in fact ground points and therefore not useful for the representation of users and objects present on the scene. In order to deal with this issue, a background model of the environment is created using an accumulating 2.5D grid map (or a height map) by capturing a sufficiently large number of images of the environment over a certain period of time.

The proposed 2.5D grid map $M_{2.5D}$ was based on the algorithm proposed by Garrote *et al.* [34]. The main idea of this approach is to create a meaningful representation of the environment so that new information entering the system is appropriately detected, acting as both a ground and noise removal process. $M_{2.5D}$ is composed by $m_x \times m_y$ cells with a given resolution $d_{r2.5D}$ (for the purposes of this project, a resolution $d_{r2.5D} = 0.05\ m$ was chosen). A given cell will contain information about the lowest and highest height values and the number of points from the PCD that fell within that cell. To map incoming PCD information into $M_{2.5D}$, each point's (x, y) value pair is projected onto the corresponding grid cell's (i, j) indexes $(i \leq m_x \wedge j \leq m_y D \wedge m_x > 0 \wedge m_y > 0)$ and c_{ij} parameters are updated based on the point's height, z. Examples of the 2.5D grid maps for the lowest and highest values in a given dataset can be observed in Fig. 5.

Fig. 5. Examples of 2.5D grid maps of the background model, representing the lowest (left) and highest (middle) value for each considered cell. On the right, a top down view of the 2.5D grid map, where the transparency of each height voxel is given by the percentage of points from the N frames that were mapped within the corresponding cell c_{ij}.

3D Grid Map Construction. The next step is to create the 3D grid map representation for the current frame. This 3D grid M_{3D} is composed of three-dimensional cells, c_{ijk}, with width, length and height equal to d_{r3D}, with $d_{r3D} = d_{r2.5D}$. To enter data from an incoming PCD_{in}, two main steps are needed: convert from a point's ($\phi_{(x,y,z)}$) 3D value to its corresponding (i,j,k) grid index and check whether it is mapped in a cell from $M_{2.5D}$ or not. If $M_{2.5D}$ cell c_{ij} is not empty, the current point's z-index value is compared to the minimum and maximum heights verified in c_{ij}. Hence, a point ϕ will not be added to M_{3D} if the following condition is met:

$$(|(\phi_z - min(c_{ij}))| \leq thresh_{3D}) \vee (|(\phi_z - max(c_{ij}))| \geq thresh_{3D});$$

If ϕ's z-index value falls between the minimum and maximum recorded heights for that cell, or if it is closer to either the minimum or maximum heights than a set threshold $thresh_{3D}$, ϕ is not added to the corresponding cell in M_{3D}. This threshold was implemented to deal with observable variance in the sensor readings (with an empirical value of $thresh_{3D} = 0.02m$ chosen after conducting tests for several studied scenes).

Information in M_{3D} will afterwards be used to segment the various elements in the scene. An information retrieval method from grid indexes to the 3D world reference system was also implemented where a simple statistical filter leaves out noise: given the total amount of occupied cells, it is expected that a much greater number of samples lie within some given cells (*e.g.* dense PCD representing an object in the middle of the room as opposed to noisy measurements from sensor crosstalk). In this sense, the standard deviation of the number of points across all occupied cells (σ_c) is calculated, and only cells that have at least ζ (*e.g.* $\zeta = \frac{\sigma_c}{2}$) points are retrieved. An illustration of this process can be observed in Fig. 6.

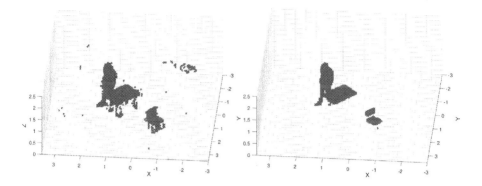

Fig. 6. Illustration of the process of conversion from PCD to 3D grid map. Depending on the value of ζ, an input filtered PCD gets converted to a 3D grid map representation such as in the left ($\zeta = 0$) or as in the right ($\zeta = \frac{\sigma_c}{2}$).

4.4   Scene Segmentation

With a solid 3D representation of the scene in a given frame, the last pipeline module is responsible for the segmentation of meaningful data present in the scene.

Data clustering had an enormous number of contributions along the years mainly due to the range of domains that can benefit from it. From a top-level view, the problem of segmentation by clustering can be considered to be fundamentally divided into two groups as suggested in [35]:

1. *Hierarchical techniques*: methods belonging to this group use a tree-based representation (dendrograms) that iteratively splits input data into subsets until a previously defined termination condition is met. These methods are however not recommend to discretize 3D information (in the shape of an unorganized PCD) due to the difficulty of choosing this termination condition. Another problem can arise in both space- and run-time requirements when larger input data and smaller cell sizes are considered;
2. *Partitioning techniques*: methods belonging to this group build sets (or *partitions*) of the input data into a set of k clusters where k is an input to the clustering algorithm. This implies that some knowledge about the scene exists, which is not a practical assumption for some applications. The output of such algorithms are clusters identified by their centroids or by parts of the cluster located near its center (*k-means* and *k-medoid* are examples, respectively).

The application of this type of algorithms to larger spatial data such as 3D PCD obtained by this system implies a minimal degree of knowledge about the scene in order to maintain computational efficiency for a larger amount of data. A partitioning technique seems to offer the most appropriate solution for the currently faced task.

The well-known query-based algorithm proposed by Ester *et al.* on [36], named Density-Based Algorithm for Discovering Clusters (*DBSCAN*) tries to solve this problem by requiring only two parameters other than the data to be clustered: a density threshold, specified by a minimum number of points (*minPts*) required to shape a dense region (or *cluster*); and an Eps-neighborhood (ε) search window.

As a starting condition, DBSCAN picks an arbitrary point p in space and obtains its ε-neighborhood. If that region (a 3D sphere) contains *minPts*, a cluster is created at point p, otherwise p is considered noise. From the problem formulation, if p is added to a cluster then so are p's ε-neighborhood points, as well as their own ε-neighborhood when they are also considered core points. Afterwards, a new arbitrary, non-visited point p is chosen and processed in the same fashion, finding new clusters or noise, until all point in the dataset have been visited. With DBSCAN, points initially labeled as noise can later on fall inside a cluster.

In this sense, a naïve implementation of the DBSCAN was implemented for scene segmentation from a 3D grid map. The estimation of the input parameters was done empirically by testing the implementation on several collected datasets, obeying however to some important assumptions. The first one is that, as a rule of thumb, the minimum number of points necessary to form a cluster can be automatically derived given the spatial data dimensionality of each point in the dataset, D, as $minPts \geq D + 1$. However, as stated by Schubert *et al.* [37], a bigger number of points should be considered for larger datasets with noise, as in the case of the proposed system, where this can be written as $minPts \geq 2 * D$. In turn, ε's value should be chosen so that a small fraction of points fall within this distance to each other.

Both values are heavily data-driven, so *minPts* and ε were attributed values based on empirical observations carried out on several trials for different datasets. In the particular case of ε, a neighborhood of the same size as M_{3D} cells means that, at most, the point returned by a cell that is completely surrounded by occupied cells will have 6 neighbors. Assuming that the implemented data retrieval only returns information from actual objects of interest in the scene, an ε-neighborhood that is too large or too little can, respectively, make DBSCAN produce dense regions that either encompass several different objects or various dense regions that, in reality, belong to the same object.

Finally, the output of the scene segmentation module is a set of the clusters identified in the current frame's 3D grid map. Due to the naïve implementation, some under or over-segmentation may occur in some cases, as will be discussed in the following section.

5 Results

To test the developed system, composed of four Kinect One sensors located in a rectangular area, several test datasets were collected to evaluate the proposed method. The first single shot dataset was captured for the purpose of extrinsic camera calibration. The considered real spatial disposition of the sensors was of $4.2m \times 5m$; due to the physical constraints of the room where the system was deployed, the smaller size could not be bigger than $4.2m$ and a decision was made to have the other side be of $5m$ so that, even though the room would not be in a square disposition, the available testing area would be greater. This information can be seen in Fig. 7, where the captured information of the checkerboard in the center of the room was used to calibrate all the sensors to the world reference frame.

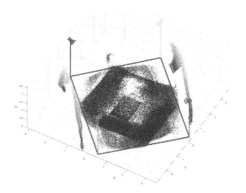

Fig. 7. Example of a captured IR image of the checkerboard (left) and the corresponding location of the sensors (right).

The extrinsic calibration procedure returns an area of $\sim 4.235m \times 4.944m$, close to the real measured distance between the cameras. Additional datasets were then captured with the same room setup, in order to evaluate the performance of the proposed processing pipeline. From the captured datasets, four will be highlighted in this section:

A. A user is alone in the center of the scene, with no other objects present in the room. The user's legs remain static while a user moves his arms in a given predefined gesture;
B. Two objects (a table and a chair) are placed near to the middle of the room, while keeping some distance between them (noting that the table has a fairly reflective surface);
C. While keeping the same objects from the previous dataset, a user enters and navigates the space in a slalom fashion, exiting the room afterwards;
D. A chair is placed in the middle of the room and a user enters the scene and sits on it.

Referring back to the works of [26], it is reported that the result produced by ToF cameras when mixing light beams reflected at object boundaries (with different depths) is a superimposed signal, or *flying pixels*. These pixels show a high variance in the measured depth along the captured frames. In the particular case of this system, flying pixels can be observed on most scenes starting at heights of $\sim 2m$, clearly introducing a problem when building the background model. A straightforward attempt to overcome this problem was the introduction of an additional constraint when building the background model so that only points whose height is lower than a given threshold, $z \leq thresh_{2.5D}$, contribute to the 2.5D grid map. This data processing is only applied when building the background model of the room. Results presented were obtained by using $thresh_{2.5D} = 1.80m$.

The processing pipeline was applied to each of these four datasets. The qualitative results obtained by the system on these datasets can be observed on Fig. 8, where each row represents datasets A. to D. and each column represents the output of a given module: initial merged PCD (after *Data Fusion*), the result of running the background subtraction module and the constructed 3D grid map (after *3D Grid Map Representation*) and the clusters outputted by the naïve DBSCAN method (after *Scene Segmentation*) displayed in different colors. All information from the 3D grid map that does not belong to any cluster is labeled as noise and present as a semi-transparent dark blob. The parameters used to obtain the displayed results, in agreement with the formulation on the previous section, are also presented in Table 1.

Table 1. List of considered system parameters

Parameter	Value
d_r	$0.05m$
ζ	$\frac{\sigma_c}{2}$
ε	$4 \times d_r$
$minPts$	σ_c

For dataset A., the system produces a single cluster that correctly identifies the stationary user. The statistical filter was not enough to remove the noise in the considered frame, seeing as some dense noise readings remain after applying the filter. The DBSCAN algorithm however is able to correctly distinguish between an actual object cluster and sporadic noise clusters due to the selected parameters.

The system's behavior is similar when processing dataset B., since both objects present on the scene are stationary; however, sporadic noise from sensor cross-talk as well as reflectiveness from the table surface sometimes deteriorate the clustering outcome, with really small clusters appearing briefly.

For dataset C., the system produces good results, showing distinct clusters while a user slaloms between the table and the chair left in the same spot from dataset B. While the user keeps a relative distance from both objects, as is shown in Fig. 8, the clustering module is successful at both removing noise and identifying the separate clusters.

When the distance between the user and an object decreases, this result tends to deteriorate and only one cluster is found characterizing both the user and the

PCD_M	Filtered PCD_M	M_{3D}	Identified Clusters

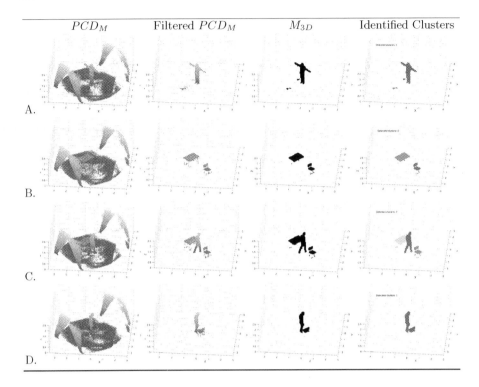

Fig. 8. Results produced by the system in various circumstances. Each row corresponds to a dataset, (A. to D.), and each column shows the outcome of a system module.

object. This effect is clearly shown in the last case, for dataset D., where the scene depicting a user preparing to sit in the chair gets segmented as a single cluster. This result can be mitigated with the implementation of tracking techniques as discussed in the next section.

6   Conclusion

In this work we presented a system capable of modeling an indoor scene, with the goal of creating a spatial representation for mixed reality applications. It is a low-cost scalable system, in the sense that it can be expanded to any room size, that allows the perception of both static obstacles and the perception and tracking of the users in the scene. The setup takes advantage of the commercially available Microsoft's Kinect One sensors, which are calibrated to create a holistic model of the room.

This system has the advantage of being markerless, taking the uncomfortable need for the user to wear constraining gear. The system can be used in parallel with any headset since the perception task is performed externally and not in the user's POV, not being dependent on the headset's perception sensors and capabilities.

The methodology developed in this work, takes advantage of a robust spatial representation used in the field of robotics, to generate a room model that is used to allow virtual user navigation. The detection of individual objects in the scene and users is achieved by using clustering techniques, which identify and each group of cells as belonging to a single entity (cluster).

Preliminary results show that for the evaluated scenes the objects were successfully modeled and the individual objects were identified.

Future work in the context of the undergoing project will focus in tracking methodologies to allow a clear distinction between all elements within the scene. The use of this tracking module will allow the mitigation of problems of crosstalk between clusters when elements come too close in the scene, and it will also allow the determination of the motion state of each cluster (either static or dynamic).

Acknowledgments. This work was supported by the project POCI-01-0247-FEDER-017644 HTPDIR - "Human Tracking and Perception in Dynamic Immersive Rooms" financed by the Portugal2020 program and European Union's structural funds.

References

1. Ricci, A., Piunti, M., Tummolini, L., Castelfranchi, C.: The mirror world: preparing for mixed-reality living. IEEE Pervasive Comput. **14**(2), 60–63 (2015)
2. Elfes, A.: Using occupancy grids for mobile robot perception and navigation. Computer **22**(6), 46–57 (1989)
3. Newcombe, R.A., Izadi, S., Hilliges, O., Molyneaux, D., Kim, D., Davison, A.J., Kohi, P., Shotton, J., Hodges, S., Fitzgibbon, A.: KinectFusion: real-time dense surface mapping and tracking. In: 2011 10th IEEE International Symposium on Mixed and Augmented Reality, pp. 127–136, October 2011
4. Urmson, C., Anhalt, J., Bagnell, D., Baker, C., Bittner, R., Clark, M., Dolan, J., Duggins, D., Galatali, T., Geyer, C., et al.: Autonomous driving in urban environments: boss and the urban challenge. J. Field Robot. **25**(8), 425–466 (2008)
5. Montemerlo, M., Becker, J., Bhat, S., Dahlkamp, H., Dolgov, D., Ettinger, S., Haehnel, D., Hilden, T., Hoffmann, G., Huhnke, B., et al.: Junior: the stanford entry in the urban challenge. J. Field Robot. **25**(9), 569–597 (2008)
6. Laugier, C., Paromtchik, I.E., Perrollaz, M., Yong, M., Yoder, J.D., Tay, C., Mekhnacha, K., Nègre, A.: Probabilistic analysis of dynamic scenes and collision risks assessment to improve driving safety. IEEE Intell. Transp. Syst. Mag. **3**(4), 4–19 (2011)
7. Pfeiffer, D., Franke, U.: Efficient representation of traffic scenes by means of dynamic stixels. In: Intelligent Vehicles Symposium (IV), 2010 IEEE, pp. 217–224. IEEE (2010)
8. Lu, F., Milios, E.E.: Robot pose estimation in unknown environments by matching 2D range scans. In: 1994 Proceedings of IEEE Conference on Computer Vision and Pattern Recognition, pp. 935–938, June 1994
9. Cole, D.M., Newman, P.M.: Using laser range data for 3D slam in outdoor environments. In: Proceedings 2006 IEEE International Conference on Robotics and Automation, 2006. ICRA 2006, pp. 1556–1563. IEEE (2006)

10. Leonard, J.J., Durrant-Whyte, H.F.: Simultaneous map building and localization for an autonomous mobile robot. In: IEEE/RSJ International Workshop on Intelligent Robots and Systems 1991. Intelligence for Mechanical Systems, Proceedings IROS 1991, pp. 1442–1447. IEEE (1991)
11. Dissanayake, M.G., Newman, P., Clark, S., Durrant-Whyte, H.F., Csorba, M.: A solution to the simultaneous localization and map building (slam) problem. IEEE Trans. Robot. Autom. **17**(3), 229–241 (2001)
12. Choset, H., Nagatani, K.: Topological simultaneous localization and mapping (slam): toward exact localization without explicit localization. IEEE Trans. Robot. Autom. **17**(2), 125–137 (2001)
13. Nuchter, A., Lingemann, K., Hertzberg, J., Surmann, H.: 6D slam with approximate data association. In: 12th International Conference on Advanced Robotics, 2005. ICAR 2005. Proceedings, pp. 242–249. IEEE (2005)
14. Montemerlo, M., Thrun, S., Koller, D., Wegbreit, B., et al.: FastSLAM: a factored solution to the simultaneous localization and mapping problem. In: AAAI/IAAI, pp. 593–598 (2002)
15. Siadat, A., Kaske, A., Klausmann, S., Dufaut, M., Husson, R.: An optimized segmentation method for a 2D laser-scanner applied to mobile robot navigation. IFAC Proc. Vol. **30**(7), 149–154 (1997)
16. Sack, D., Burgard, W.: A comparison of methods for line extraction from range data. IFAC Proc. Vol. **37**(8), 728–733 (2004)
17. Petrovskaya, A., Thrun, S.: Model based vehicle detection and tracking for autonomous urban driving. Auton. Robots **26**(2–3), 123–139 (2009)
18. Fayad, F., Cherfaoui, V.: Tracking objects using a laser scanner in driving situation based on modeling target shape. In: Intelligent Vehicles Symposium, 2007 IEEE, pp. 44–49. IEEE (2007)
19. Zhang, S., Adams, M., Tang, F., Xie, L.: Geometrical feature extraction using 2D range scanner. In: 4th International Conference on Control and Automation, 2003. ICCA 2003. Proceedings, pp. 901–905. IEEE (2003)
20. Pascoal, R., Santos, V., Premebida, C., Nunes, U.: Simultaneous segmentation and superquadrics fitting in laser-range data. IEEE Trans. Veh. Technol. **64**(2), 441–452 (2015)
21. Wang, C.C., Thorpe, C.: Simultaneous localization and mapping with detection and tracking of moving objects. In: IEEE International Conference on Robotics and Automation, 2002. Proceedings. ICRA 2002, vol. 3, pp. 2918–2924. IEEE (2002)
22. Vu, T.D.: Vehicle perception: localization, mapping with detection, classification and tracking of moving objects. Ph.D thesis, Institut National Polytechnique de Grenoble-INPG (2009)
23. Suma, E.A., Lange, B., Rizzo, A.S., Krum, D.M., Bolas, M.: FAAST: the flexible action and articulated skeleton toolkit. In: 2011 IEEE Virtual Reality Conference, pp. 247–248, March 2011
24. Maimone, A., Fuchs, H.: Reducing interference between multiple structured light depth sensors using motion. In: 2012 IEEE Virtual Reality Workshops (VRW), pp. 51–54, March 2012
25. Butler, D., Izadi, S., Hilliges, O., Molyneaux, D., Hodges, S., Kim, D., Butler, A., Molyneaux, D., Hilliges, O., Izadi, S., Hodges, S.: Shake'n'sense: reducing interference for overlapping structured light depth cameras. In: Proceedings of the 2012 ACM annual conference on Human Factors in Computing Systems, pp. 1933–1936, January 2012
26. Sarbolandi, H., Lefloch, D., Kolb, A.: Kinect range sensing: structured-light versus Time-of-Flight kinect. Comput. Vis. Image Underst. **139**, 1–20 (2015)

27. Martínez-Zarzuela, M., Pedraza-Hueso, M., Díaz-Pernas, F., González-Ortega, D., Antón-Rodríguez, M.: Indoor 3D Video Monitoring Using Multiple Kinect Depth-Cameras. arXiv preprint arXiv:1403.2895 (2014)

28. Leoncini, P., Sikorski, B., Baraniello, V., Martone, F., Luongo, C., Guida, M.: Multiple NUI device approach to full body tracking for collaborative virtual environments. In: De Paolis, L.T., Bourdot, P., Mongelli, A. (eds.) AVR 2017. LNCS, vol. 10324, pp. 131–147. Springer, Cham (2017). https://doi.org/10.1007/978-3-319-60922-5_10

29. Kowalski, M., Naruniec, J., Daniluk, M.: Livescan3D: a fast and inexpensive 3D data acquisition system for multiple kinect v2 sensors. In: 2015 International Conference on 3D Vision, pp. 318–325, October 2015

30. Blake, J., Echtler, F., Kerl, C.: libfreenect2 Project (2015). https://github.com/OpenKinect/libfreenect2

31. Zhang, Z.: A flexible new technique for camera calibration. IEEE Trans. Pattern Anal. Mach. Intell. **22**(11), 1330–1334 (2000)

32. Bouguet, J.Y.: Camera calibration tool-box for matlab (2002). http://www.vision.caltech.edu/bouguetj/calib_doc/

33. Rodehorst, V., Heinrichs, M., Hellwich, O.: Evaluation of relative pose estimation methods for multi-camera setups. In: International Archives of Photogrammetry and Remote Sensing (ISPRS 2008), pp. 135–140 (2008)

34. Garrote, L., Rosa, J., Paulo, J., Premebida, C., Peixoto, P., Nunes, U.J.: 3D point cloud Downsampling for 2D indoor scene modelling in mobile robotics. In: 2017 IEEE International Conference on Autonomous Robot Systems and Competitions (ICARSC), pp. 228–233, April 2017

35. Kaufman, L., Rousseeuw, P.J.: Finding Groups in Data: An Introduction to Cluster Analysis, vol. 344. John Wiley & Sons, Hoboken (2009)

36. Ester, M., Kriegel, H.P., Sander, J., Xu, X., et al.: A density-based algorithm for discovering clusters in large spatial databases with noise. In: KDD, vol. 96, pp. 226–231 (1996)

37. Schubert, E., Sander, J., Ester, M., Kriegel, H.P., Xu, X.: Dbscan revisited, revisited: Why and how you should (still) use dbscan. ACM Trans. Database Syst. (TODS) **42**(3), 19 (2017)

Framework for the Development of Augmented Reality Applications Applied to Education Games

Jorge Ierache[✉], Nahuel Adiel Mangiarua,
Martín Ezequiel Becerra, and Santiago Igarza

Applied Augmented Reality Team, Engineering Department,
National University of La Matanza (UNLaM),
Florencia Varela 1903, 1755 San Justo, Buenos Aires, Argentina
jierache@unlam.edu.ar

Abstract. Augmented Reality (AR) adds virtual elements to the real environment, providing relevant information to the user through the implementation of different IT infrastructures. Thus, the real environment is enriched with extra information that enhances the experience of the user. This technology can be applied in a wide range of areas, for instance: entertainment industry, healthcare, manufacturing industry and educational environment. This paper presents a framework designed for mobile platforms that allows the integration of augmented content like multiple choice questions and videos on a goose board game with the main purpose to reinforce concepts presented in class. We choose this gamification methodology because students can relearn concepts playing collaboratively with questions created by the teacher or students themselves.

Keywords: Augmented Reality · Mobile application · AR framework
AR in art · AR in education

1 Introduction

Augmented Reality is a technology that enhances our perception of reality, through which the real-world information is supplemented with digital information. The term refers to a group of methods that allows overlapping in real time, virtual content such as images, 3D models or drawings over images of the real world. It aims to create an environment in which information and virtual objects are fused with real objects, providing an immersive experience for the user. Recent technological advances have allowed AR experiences to be possible not only in personal computers, but also on high performance mobile devices such as tablets and smartphones, which have a great potential due to their mobility and widespread adoption.

To make AR applications possible, some specific hardware components are required. Firstly, an image capturing device, such as the camera of a smartphone or webcam. Secondly, a component to display the augmented contents like a screen or projector. Lastly, a powerful processing unit able to run the necessary algorithms of the AR application in real time. Additionally, an element or a set of elements are necessary

© Springer International Publishing AG, part of Springer Nature 2018
L. T. De Paolis and P. Bourdot (Eds.): AVR 2018, LNCS 10850, pp. 340–350, 2018.
https://doi.org/10.1007/978-3-319-95270-3_28

to act as triggers of the augmented contents. These elements can be physical markers or a GPS coordinate if the AR application supports geolocation.

In this paper the focus is on the development of a framework for the generation of AR games in the context of education. Applying the latest advances in ICT (Information and Communications Technology) we aim to create an engaging experience for both teachers and students through the interaction with virtual contents while playing a game. We propose to contribute to school learning environment by using the goose gamification strategy to relearn concepts presented in the classroom through the augmentation of multiple choice questions in video format over a physical game board. This strategy improves student-teacher interaction as well as the collaboration between students themselves to review concepts together. On one side, a group of students learn actively by making questions about the subject of study while on the other one, the rest of the student body can test their knowledge by answering questions. The proposal of this work is to provide a framework that allows the content creation (Questions with video uploads) using a web editor and a mobile application to play the goose game with the questions created. These augmented contents are organized in learning categories for proper distribution. By taking advantage of the popularity of mobile devices we expect an enrichment of the user experience in both inside and outside the classroom.

2   State of the Art

Concerning the state of the art of educational AR applications, we can find different projects that enrich teaching methods, such as AuthorAR [1]. Another example is Pictogram Room [2], which is a project that aims to improve the communication of people with autism spectrum disorder with the aid of an AR room. Additionally, Yuen et al. [3] describes the future of AR and how this will promote universal learning. AR will supply students with instant access to specific information collected and provided by different sources. Thornton et al. [4] expresses that Augmented Reality is an emerging technology that has the potential to attract and amaze people. The purpose of AR is to improve the physical and visual environment of a person. This is achieved by overlapping a (3-D) three-dimensional virtual image on an object or environment in the real world. Therefore, Augmented Reality is described as an emerging technology that demands a strong consideration as a learning tool in educational programs. Recently, there has been an increasing effort to incorporate this technology in different educational environments. It is noticeable that there are initiatives for the incorporation of ICT, specifically AR technologies. Since the State is developing a framework for innovation in this topic, thanks to educ.ar [5]. In order to encourage creativity in an artistic field, various projects that helped to achieve this goal were developed. For example, colAR Mix [6], an application that allows coloring on different drawings to bring them to life in a 3D animated world. This tool is mainly aimed at increasing and/or encouraging the creative development of children. Other project is Re + Public [7], Re + Public's mobile application digitally resurfaces walls and buildings in urban centers by overlaying digital content onto the physical environment. In doing so, Re + Public challenges our notions about private property boundaries and user access. Additionally, how the user chooses to interact with the mural alters the mural's digital content, which provides anonymous data in terms of how individuals are engaging with the art, and ultimately the space that situates that art. The fusion of creativity and technology can uncover new modes of relaying ideas and create innovative interfaces between digital design and physical worlds in ways that provoke the imagination and problematize existing styles of art, design, and interaction. Picture Puzzle Augmented Reality System for Infants Creativity [8] Visualizes an 3D model with spacial and sounds effects on the block puzzle work with the purpose to make infants or children feel a sense of achievement and interest. It allows to build creativity, fine motor skills, perception of objects, and language education at the same time. EduAR [9] application applies image detection and augmentation techniques to present virtual content on markers in real environments. It offers different activities like AR puzzles, continent geography information on markers and mathematics operations. wARna [10] is a mobile-based interactive Augmented Reality coloring book that identifies and maps the texture color from the image of their coloring book, to the corresponding 3D content augmented on them. AIR-EDUTECH: Augmented Immersive Reality (AIR) Technology for High School Chemistry Education [11]. The application presents Chemistry related topics, using physical cards to represent different chemical elements. It can play audio files to pronounce the names of them when they are detected by the user application. In addition, it augments 3D scenes of chemical reaction between elements when a user collides two or more cards. The framework presented here differs from other proposals [8, 10, 11] in their customizations of contents to be adapted dynamically to different subject areas. For example, Students can create different sets of virtual contents, to integrate their knowledge of different subjects in the same match or make different matches with one subject each one to go deeper on that dominion. In addition, Students can work all together to make contents which will be later shared and to improve their knowledge basis attractively. In the next section, we will describe the creator workflow, the goose game mechanics of the proposed framework and the results of proof of concept.

3   Framework Description

The framework consists of three modules. A web application working as editor, which allows the content creator user to create learning categories and upload video questions; an android AR application which performs the augmentation and implements the game logic; and a backend which manages persistence and communication between the other two.

For the creation of the augmented contents, the minimum requirements are a computer with a web browser and the virtual contents to add (pre-recorded videos). For the consumption of the augmented content, a modern Android smartphone with internet access is required. The web editor that is in charge of the content creation has a workflow consisting of three steps. This procedure guides the content creator through the augmentation process of reality over the game board. The first step consists in selecting or capturing a picture of the physical element to serve as a marker. Each marker will be the target or anchor to the augmented content for a given learning category. The second step consists in incorporating and linking the augmented contents to a corresponding marker. Each content consists of one video, which represents a question and different options to select as answers. The last step requires the content creator to set the relative spatial location of each content in relation to its corresponding marker for a correct visualization by the client mobile application. This step can be greatly simplified by the use of a template, allowing to set the relative locations of the contents once and apply it to all the different markers.

3.1   Goose Game Mechanics

To play the game, students need the Android mobile application and the goose board with the pictures loaded as AR markers as slots. Each marker represents a learning category previously created by the content creator user in the web editor. To start the game, users must focus the physical board with their device to view the virtual dice and the two player pieces (Fig. 1) through the device's screen. At the start of a turn, the participating student must touch the virtual dice to determine how many slots to advance. The piece associated with the student player on turn will automatically move over the related physical slot.

Fig. 1. Virtual dice and player pieces

Upon focusing the device camera on the slot, the student will be able to answer one multiple choice question randomly selected from the category's pool. The application plays the videos over the surface of the category slot on the board, providing the feeling that the video is actually positioned and executed in the physical world as shown in Fig. 2. Each video offers three options of which the player will choose one by tapping

Fig. 2. Player selects an option to answer a question to continue playing.

on the screen of the device. If the student selects the correct one, he will continue playing. If he selects the wrong one, the other Player will start to play. The game finishes when one player reaches the finish line.

4   Framework Implementation

This framework is based on our previous work, the Augmented Catalogs System [12] and Template Framework for the Augmented Catalogs System [13].

4.1   The Visualization Module

The visualization module application was developed for the Android operating system with the support of Unity3D as graphic engine and Vuforia's AR engine. By using the integrated camera, built-in sensors and processing capabilities of any Android mobile device it augments the students' reality with the virtual content of the game. This module is divided into four layers and a central controller which maintains and provides access to the different workflow elements. After markers, and optionally their contents, are downloaded from the web editor module though the internet and initialized by the AR layer, the visual recognition and positioning system works together with the different content visualization components in a local or online fashion for its proper exploitation. Figure 3 shows a relational diagram of the framework components described above. The main controller has the responsibility of coordinating the framework tasks. Figure 4 shows the sequence of component activation at runtime. The main controller performs the invocation of AR system to start recognition of the AR markers. This AR system in turn triggers marker detection and performs tracking to align virtual contents over the physical elements. When a marker is detected by the AR system, it notifies the Content Viewer so the current content is directly displayed or streamed from the internet.

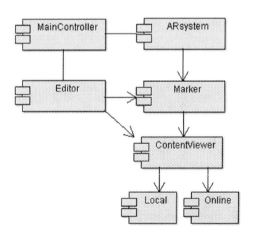

Fig. 3. Relational diagram among framework's components

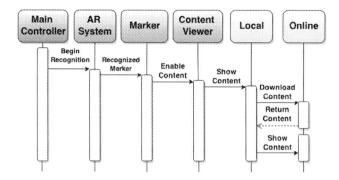

Fig. 4. Sequence diagram for the detection of a marker and display of its contents.

In addition, the visualization module has a component to manage the game divided into different classes. The game controller manages the general logic of the game and delegates specific functions to another objects. For example, the board manager class handles virtual elements on physical board, question controller chooses a content randomly from the category associated to the marker where a player piece is at. The Fig. 5 shows the framework's classes and their relationships.

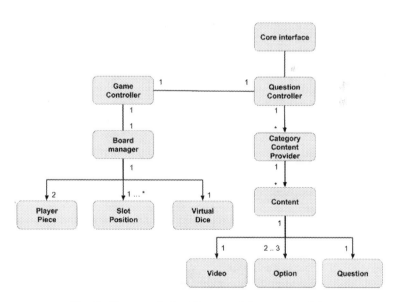

Fig. 5. Conceptual class diagram of the game module.

4.2   The Web Editor Module

The purpose of this application is to be an online editor to allow anyone with internet access and a modern web browser to create, edit and then share AR content into the visualization module. After logging in to the web application users may proceed to create new game instances and empty markers representing a category. Figure 6 shows the menu to select and work with markers. Each marker has to be loaded with a certain amount of augmented contents as seen in Fig. 7. Additionally, each content has a position and rotation relative to the Marker that owns them. The web editor is supported by a Java back-end running in an Apache Tomcat server and Spring IO Platform. This configuration of frameworks and technologies provide us a great flexibility and possibility of reutilization which dramatically decreased implementation times. For example, during a technology transference project to the Arts Department of our institution, the editor was easily adapted for other purposes such as content augmentation of gallery Artworks. Likewise, this module allowed augmentation of didactic materials like maps and posters presented on an initial prototype [14].

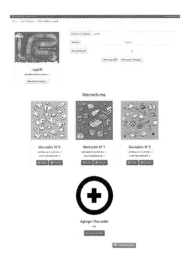

Fig. 6. UI of user marker selection

Fig. 7. Contents for a marker: questions and video upload

4.3   The Backend Module

The main application of the framework plays the role of the backend of the web application providing services to create, edit and storage markers and contents through a Web Service. This Web Service exposes a RESTful (Representational State Transfer) API using the HTTP protocol and URL mapping, increasing the system's reusability and providing access to any application that is compatible with the RESTful services [15].

The API provides the four basic functions of CRUD (Create, Read, Update and Delete) to any content contained in Markers. Served by a Java environment using the Spring Framework and Apache Tomcat it uses Protocol Buffer serialization and the LZMA library for data compression. The data storage can be handled by any DBMS (Database Management System) with JDBC support. Therefore, H2 database was used in the development environment and MySQL in the testing environment for the first prototype of the framework. Figure 8 shows components that were used in the backend module of the framework. The spring framework provides the MVC architect model to organize the backend service on Model, View and Controller components. The model component contains the business data of the service, in our case markers and virtual contents like videos, questions and their answers. Controllers which can handle user requests, make state changes on the business model and choose views to show on web browser of the user. Finally, the view components present the web editor to users to interact with the framework using html web pages where they create virtual contents to send them to the backend service.

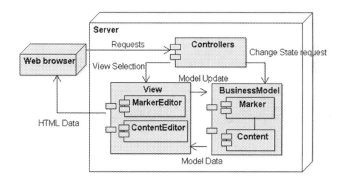

Fig. 8. Conceptual component diagram of the framework main application

5 Specific Proofs of Concept

In the educational context, it was detected that there is a growing need to transmit contents dynamically between teachers and students. We made a proof of concept with high school students who attended the exhibition expo Project. For this scenario, we created learning categories with their markers. The news category (Fig. 9a) is about different current issues in Argentina., Music Category (Fig. 9b) is about different music group of this country, The History category (Fig. 9c) is about origins Argentine Independence, Movies category (Fig. 9d) is about curiosities in international movies. Finally, the sports category (Fig. 9e) about football, volleyball and tennis players of Argentine teams.

In this case, we designed a physical board which is shown in Fig. 10, where the player's virtual pieces are moved over the path on the side of the learning category slots showing virtual questions with video associated. Each one shows questions of their own type.

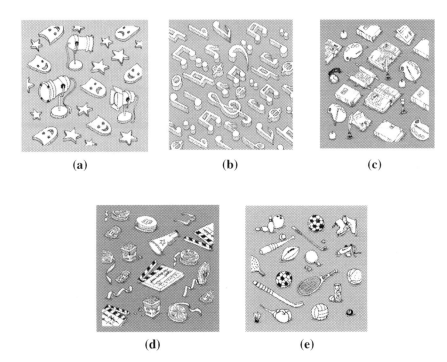

Fig. 9. a. News category **b.** Music category **c.** History category **d.** Movie category **e.** Sports category

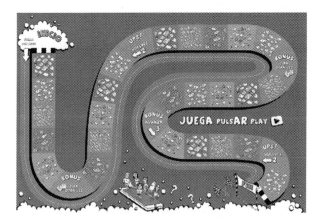

Fig. 10. Goose physical board

6   Exhibition Test and Results

Our research group carried out tests of this framework in which high school and university students from different fields were invited to participate in test games. During the 3-day exhibition, satisfactory results were observed, where the students showed great interest in the mechanics of the game that rewards knowledge and learning. We performed the test with 50 different students. They played the game with five categories with multiple choice questions about topics:

- Argentine News (AN): Emergent Community issues.
- Argentine History (AH): Argentine Commanders and leaders, Argentine independence war campaigns.
- Argentine Music (AM), Cultural identity origins: Tango and main interpreters, Cultural identity origins: Folkore and main interpreters.
- Argentine Sports (AS): Historical Football players and main achievements, Tennis, basketball and volleyball players and main achievements.
- International Movies(IM): Actors and their main interpretations.

After that, a multiple choice quiz which contained a mix of 20 questions of five categories was carried out to test their knowledge about the contents of the game. They need a min of 3 of 5 categories approved to pass the test. 40 out of 50 students passed through the exam. There was also a high level incorporation of the contents exposed in the exam instance by students who participated in the test more than once. Table 1 shows the knowledge improvement on each area:

Table 1. Student knowledge retention results

Category of users/topics	AN	AH	AM	AS	IM
Users who disapproved the category	10	5	6	10	10
Users who approved the category (Play the game once)	15	15	18	14	12
Users who approved the category (Play the game twice or more times)	25	30	26	26	28

7   Conclusions and Future Lines of Work

This paper involves the use of Augmented technology generating new alternatives which improve teaching methods by creating program contents. The physical board and markers should be designed according to the proposed themes since the categories are used as representative markers of themselves. It was also possible to generate the image of the board and markers projected on the board or wall in order to save costs and time on the physical manufacture of them. Due to the results obtained in the experiences previously mentioned and tests of the tool presented, it is concluded that the paper contributes with the teaching of games strategy. Future lines of work are focused on improving the User interface and allowing the contents generation through this AR framework. Finally, we have intended to adapt this framework to the Augmented Reality lenses like Epson Moverio BT-200.

References

1. Moralejo, L., Sanz, C., Pesado, P., Baldassarri, S.: Avances en el diseño de una herramienta de autor para la creación de actividades educativas basadas en realidad aumentada (advances in the design of an author's tool for the creation of ducational activities based on augmented reality). In: XIX congreso argentino de ciencias de la computación, 1st edn., pp. 516–525, October 2013
2. Pictogram room. http://www.pictogramas.org/proom/init.do?method=inittab. Accessed Mar 2018
3. Yuen, S.C.-Y., Yaoyuneyong, G., Johnson, E.: Augmented reality: an overview and five directions for ar in education. J. Educ. Technol. Dev. Exchange **4**(1), 119–140 (2011)
4. Thornton, T., Ernst, J.V., Clark, A.C.: Augmented reality as a visual and spatial learning tool in technology education. Technol. Eng. Teach. **71**(8), 18–21 (2012)
5. Educ.ar. http://recursos.educ.ar/aprendizajeabierto/realidad-aumentada. Accessed Mar 2018
6. Colar mix. http://colarapp.com. Accessed Nov 2014
7. Re + public. http://www.republiclab.com. Accessed Mar 2018
8. Oh, Y., Suh, Y., Kim E.: Picture puzzle augmented reality system for infants creativity. In: Eighth International Conference Ubiquitous and Future Networks (ICUF 2016), pp. 343–346, July 2016
9. Imrattanatrai, W., Hanittinan, C., Tanachaihirunsiri N., Kamnoonwatana, N.: Real-time recognition and augmented reality for education. In: 2014 Third ICT International Student Project Conference (ICT-ISPC 2014), pp. 17–20, May 2014
10. Norraji, M. F., Shahrizalsunar, M.: wARna - mobile-based augmented reality coloring book. In: 2015 4th International Conference on Interactive Digital Media (ICIDM), Bandung, Indonesia, 1–5 December 2015, pp. 17–20, September 2015
11. Al Qassem, L.M.M.S., Al Hawai, H., Al Shehhi, S., Zemerly, M.J., Ng, J.W.: Air-EDUTECH: augmented immersive reality (AIR) technology for high school chemistry education. In: 2016 IEEE Global Engineering Education Conference (EDUCON), Abu Dhabi, UAE, 10–13 April 2016, pp. 842–847 (2016)
12. Ierache, J., Mangiarua, N., Bevacqua, S., Verdicchio, N., Becerra, M., Sanz, D., Sena, M., Ortiz, F., Duarte, N., Igarza, S.: Development of a catalogs system for augmented reality applications. Int. J. Comput. Electr. Autom. Control Inf. Eng. **9**(1), 1–7 (2015). E-ISSN: 1307-6892. World Academy of Science, Engineering and Technology, International Science Index 97. http://waset.org/publications/development-of-a-catalogs-system-for-augmented-reality-applications/10000077x. Accessed Mar 2018
13. Mangiarua, N., Montalvo, C., Petrolo, F., Sanz, D., Verdicchio, N., Becerra, M., Igarza, S., Ierache, J.: Framework para la generación de templates en sistemas de catálogos de realidad aumentada (framework for the generation of templates in catalog systems of augmented reality). In: XIX workshop de investigadores en ciencias de la computación (WICC 2017), itba, buenos aires, pp. 393–397 (2017). ISBN: 978-987-42-5143-5
14. Ierache, J., Igarza, S., Mangiarua, N., Becerra, M., Bevacqua, S., Verdicchio, N., Ortiz, F., Sanz, D., Duarte, N., Sena, M.: Herramienta de realidad aumentada para facilitar la enseñanza en contextos educativos mediante el uso de las tics (increased reality tool to facilitate teaching in educational contexts through the use of ICT). Revista latinoamericana de ingeniería de software **2**(6), 365–368 (2014). ISSN 2314-2642
15. Fielding, R.T.: Architectural styles and the design of network-based software architectures. Doctoral dissertation, University of California, Irvine (2000)

Augmented Reality as a New Marketing Strategy

Cristian Gallardo[✉], Sandy P. Rodríguez[✉], Irma E. Chango[✉],
Washington X. Quevedo[✉], Jaime Santana[✉], Aldrin G. Acosta[✉],
Julio C. Tapia[✉], and Víctor H. Andaluz[✉]

Universidad de las Fuerzas Armadas ESPE, Sangolquí, Ecuador
cmgallardop@gmail.com, {sprodriguez5,iechango,
wjquevedo,agacosta,jctapia3,vhandaluz1}@espe.edu.ec,
jaimesantana1@hotmail.com

Abstract. This article proposes the development of an augmented reality application that allows the user to preview in real time the product you want to buy, in the same way you can modify the characteristics you want to adjust it to your tastes and needs before making the purchase. The proposal includes the design of the application that incorporates a catalog of living room, dining room and bedroom furniture; the user will be able to modify characteristics of size, color and texture in a way that emphasizes the interaction with the consumer, to this is added the possibility of showing relevant information about the furniture as they are visualized and modified, it allows to reduce the uncertainty of the user and at the same time allow a participatory action where the user is the protagonist. The augmented reality application My Style AR can be used in handheld devices that have support for augmented reality level 2.0.

Keywords: Augmented reality · Marketing · Technology · Unity
Arkit · Swift4

1 Introduction

The main objective of marketing is the satisfaction of consumer needs [1, 2]. In order to maximize sales, marketing has made use of the internet as a means of promotion, since the access of visitors to websites facilitates knowledge of the brand and allows its positioning in the market [3]. All this has shown that marketing adapts to the constant changes that have arisen as technology continues to evolve.

The accelerated growth of companies along with new technologies converges in a reality where marketing must constantly adapt to changes in it. Although marketing strategies have been studied extensively and are directly oriented to traditional methods, the inclusion of various methods based on technological advances facilitates the promotion of new products in a more interactive way. By appreciating that new technologies help to better campaign deployment, we reach the conclusion that marketing must innovate its way of diffusion, strongly considering technological advances, in this way, commerce begins to tend to use ubiquitous technology (smartphones) [4–7].

© Springer International Publishing AG, part of Springer Nature 2018
L. T. De Paolis and P. Bourdot (Eds.): AVR 2018, LNCS 10850, pp. 351–362, 2018.
https://doi.org/10.1007/978-3-319-95270-3_29

Since technology is involved in different areas of marketing, it adapts and evolves according to the new requirements that arise, where tools such as virtual reality, augmented reality, and so on, are added to marketing strategies [8]. At the level of technological proposals, new advances and concepts based on virtual reality -VR- have been developed that generate virtual environments in real time with the help of computer systems, which allows some degree of immersion to the user [9, 10]. In a parallel area of development, the augmented reality -AR- incorporates digital objects in 2D and 3D over spaces and between real physical objects, so that the user has a vision of how their environment could be when making desired modifications [11]. To be able to perceive scenarios in augmented reality it is essential to use a visualization medium, where Handheld devices capture the real environment by means of an integrated digital camera and locate the virtual objects on it, offering a mixed visualization.

The use of these technologies can be applied in different areas of knowledge, such as: *(i) Health* which facilitates the professionals in this area to carry out their activities by giving them a much broader perspective of the reactions that the patient has to a stimulus and the subsequent treatment that should be followed [12–14]. The *(ii) Industrial Field* (focused in assembly tasks) allows the user's work to be more interactive, in addition to providing accurate information of assembly instructions [15]. The *(iii) Construction field* analyzes and aims to mitigate the risk to which people working in this sector are exposed through virtual environments [16]. In the case of *(iv) Tourism,* there is a synergy between tourism and new technologies, facilitating the birth of e-tourism, which among its multiple proposals is the possibility of the interaction of several tourists within a virtual scenario that allows sharing experiences, observations, recommendations or simply interact with each other [8]. In the same way, *(v) Marketing* has opted for the use of these technologies in order to improve the line of dissemination of products and services, which improves their competitive advantages [17–21]. As described above, it shows how virtual and augmented reality are adaptable to any area of knowledge, specifically in marketing, since with the help of augmented reality sales can be exponentially enhanced.

In this context, the following article focuses on promoting a new marketing strategy through augmented reality; using as a test object the elements of a furniture store for the generation of an application (My Style.AR). The application allows adapting the set of furniture to the liking of the user, prior to the acquisition of this. The design of the application is made up of a furniture catalog of different segments such as living room, dining room, and bedroom, where the user can also modify features such as color and texture, according to their requirements. As a final result, the application facilitates reducing the uncertainty of the client when making a purchase.

The work is organized into 5 sections, including the Introduction. Section 2 presents the formulation of the problem before the uncertainty which the client has when making the purchase of a piece of furniture; while in Sect. 3 the structure of the application with augmented reality developed is presented; Sect. 4 illustrates the experimental results of the application's performance; and finally the conclusions of the work are described in Sect. 5.

2 Problem Formulation

Currently companies faced with a constant competitiveness that exists in the market, looking for ways to implement tactics that contribute to their development, for their position in the market and for their profitability. Although traditional marketing is effective, its presence implies a high cost and the difficulty of interacting and offering a personalized service to the client since you can not adjust a service that recognizes your requirements or opinions, so that the ways of learning are modified, nowadays, people use more technological devices such as cell phones and computers because of the continuous technological change in the world [22, 23].

The uncertainty in the consumer during a purchase increases the chances that a negotiation is not defined by the lack of knowledge, little information or inability to know how to choose a specific product, then increases the risk of tearing down the confidence of the consumers, these problems within of a company create a gap waiting for new tactics to reach the customer, the interest and satisfaction for a specific product. Another negative factor with respect to the consumer is the lack of time incurred daily in a negotiation; for the disorganization and inefficient planning when buying, which directly affects the consumer's expectations and directly with the company's objective ad the fulfilling; its commitments avoiding wasting time in inefficient marketing strategies that do not positively infer the attention of the client [23]. The problems described to are often due to the implementation of marketing strategies without prior study, which can generate considerable losses or even the closure of activities within the companies.

By described earlier in this paper, it is proposed to promote marketing in synergy with augmented reality through an application, which will offer ease and comfort to the client at the time of making a specific purchase, with personalized and interactive attention, experimenting with innovative products located in a desired real space; in the same way it allows to adapt and modify desired characteristics using a Handheld device [23, 24]. Therefore, in this way the furniture commercialization companies are taken as a case study, where the use of said application for the purpose of marketing development becomes relevant.

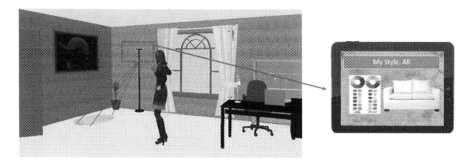

Fig. 1. Use of application in a real space.

As shown in Fig. 1, it is proposed to design a new way to disseminate a product and customize it before being purchased; quickly, easily and interactively with the use of an application based on augmented reality (AR), which allows the consumer to simulate the prototype of the required product over a real space with the ability to customize relevant features such as: size, color, texture; characteristics that allow to satisfy the clients liking. Thus, it is intended to capture the customer's attention through a personalized and interactive service, so that for furniture trading companies generate higher sales, causing an important strategy to be taken into account by companies with the probability of increasing sales and at the same time have a satisfied customer to meet their expectations and requirements.

3   System Structure

To offer a customizable and scalable application which allows the integration of future features for the user, a modular programming is carried out in which the functionalities offered by a simplified data exchange between modules are obtained.

The scheme proposed in Fig. 2 can be presented in three well-defined blocks such as: Unity3D AR Screen output, functions scripts and input/output.

The block of Unity3D AR screen output consists of the scenes that consume the 3D objects, audio user interface components, the game object, the user interaction and the functionalities programmed in the scripts, all this is located on the captured image through The camera of the mobile device achieves a location tracking in 3 dimensions of objects and animations on each video frame. In the scene presented to the user, 3D objects are integrated, which have been modeled and textured in external applications. After this the 3D models are imported into Unity3D to be able to program their behavior, this applies to animate or inanimate objects.

In the block of scripts, a main point in this marketing proposal uses augmented reality is the management of arkit plugin, which uses visual-inertial odometry manages to track the environment and its three-dimensional characteristics in order to recognize the surfaces of the environment that allow locating the desired objects in such a way that they mix with the real environment. For the location of objects the FocusSquare scripts are used, which offer a preview of the furniture on the space that will be tracked in real time, once the desired object is located in the desired place the object editor allows to modify characteristics such as color, texture and rotation; rotation is achieved with the use of Lean Touch plugin specifically with the use of the Lean Rotate script, so that the location and rotation of the 3D model works perfectly it is necessary to add to the 3D object characteristics of Box Collider and Rigid Body.

The input/output block shows the flow of information both received and emitted by the mobile device's hardware, as input means is the camera, accelerometer, gyroscope and gps, as output means is the screen of the mobile device and the speakers (Fig. 3).

For offering an application that works both online and offline, it is necessary to synchronize the database on the internet with the local database.

The entities for which the database is formed are shown in the diagram entity relationship of Fig. 4 in the same proposed a simple but functional structure for the storage of furniture and business information. The relationships proposed between the

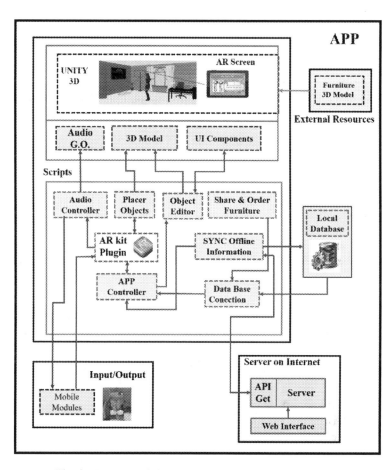

Fig. 2. Structure of the augmented reality (AR) application.

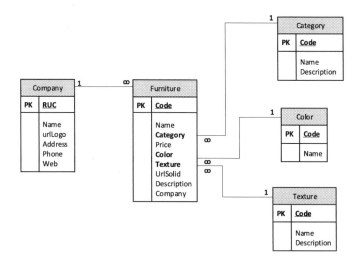

Fig. 3. Diagram entity relationship, database.

entities give rise to having pre-loaded categories, colors and textures that are eligible within a piece of furniture, in the same way to allow carrying the inventory of several companies at the same time a one-to-many relationship is created between entity and entity piece of furniture.

With the structure of the application and the database defined, in Fig. 4 the web administration interface is shown, which is based on frameworks, libraries and snippets that with the use of programming languages HTML, CSS and Javascript offers the interfaces and interactions necessary for the system administrator to create, read, update and delete information from the database.

To optimize the communication between the server and the web client, the communication is made through requests HTTP requests to an API hosted on the server, each request to the API goes through a validator before performing any action on the

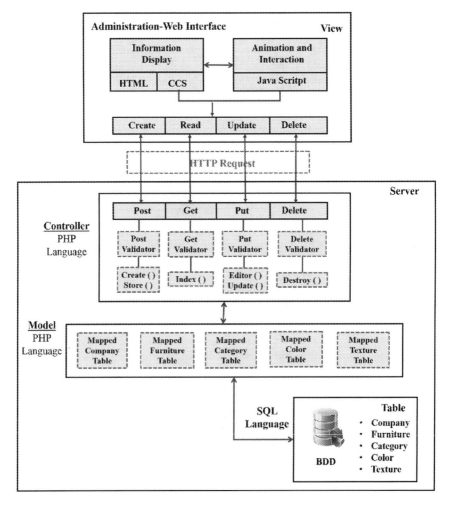

Fig. 4. Scheme of the server and web administrator.

database. For manipulate the data of the database hosted on the server, entity mapping layer is implemented, in this way a modularity is achieved between the DBMS used and the manipulation methods. This allows that in the future it is desired to change the DBMS. and there would be no problem with the rest of the application.

4   Results and Discussion

This section shows how the augmented reality application My Style.AR facilitates the process of selection, adaptation, approval, and purchase of a piece of furniture. In this case, the user can make use of the application to preview the furniture he/she wants to acquire in the desired environment. To use this application, it is required to have a Handheld device which has support for augmented reality level 2.0. For experimentation, it is used an iPhone 6s with 4.7-in. widescreen multi-touch LCD screen (diagonal) with IPS technology, resolution of 1334 by 750 pixels at 326 ppi, A9 64-bit chip and integrated M9 motion coprocessor. The sensors of the Iphone 6s are: fingerprint sensor, touch ID, barometer, three-axis gyroscope, accelerometer, proximity sensor, ambient light sensor, and the operating system installed is IOS 11.2.

In order to have information available on the offered products, it is necessary to preload information in the centralized database on the internet, for which an administrative web interface is used which allows to load the information of all the attributes contained in the BDD (Fig. 5).

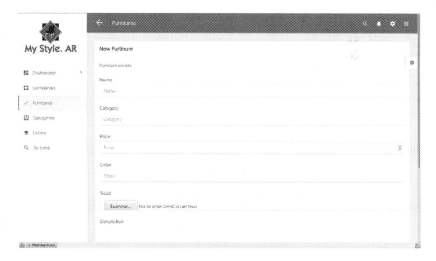

Fig. 5. Web page administration

When starting the prototype application, the user displays icons which allow access to the catalog of products available for the home such as: living room, dining room, and bedroom offered by the furniture store. (Figure 6).

Fig. 6. Presentation of the application

With the My Style.AR application, the user selects the furniture of the segment that he/she requires, visualizing the commercial name of the product and the sale price (Fig. 7). In order for the user to preview the desired element, the place where the furniture will be placed must be indicated, thus improving its perspective and reducing the uncertainty of purchase. Through sensors integrated in the device, features such as three-dimensional visualization are allowed, in addition to keeping the object in the configured place even though the device stops visualizing the configured display point. As a result, it is anticipated that the use of the My Style.AR application will reduce costs, time, and increase furniture sales given the proposed level of immersion (Fig. 8).

Fig. 7. Product catalog

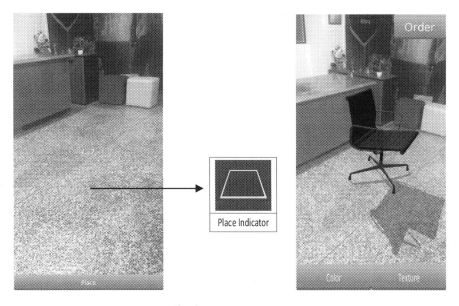

Fig. 8. Furniture display

Fig. 9. Assignment of characteristics.

When selecting the product, the user will be able to assign characteristics of his/her preference such as colour and textures, in order to adapt the piece of furniture to the environment and in the according to his/her liking and needs (Fig. 9).

Once the user has finished the selection stage, the product can be purchased, where its price is displayed and a description of the furniture's characteristics (Fig. 10).

Fig. 10. Selected product.

5   Conclusions

Augmented reality contributes to the development of marketing, providing benefits which contribute to the image of the company, strengthen the interaction with the customer and increase sales. The new technologies currently developed positively enhance marketing and take great relevance in it. Under this paradigm, the present work shows the development of the My Style.AR application which offers characteristics adjusted to the needs of the consumer and adaptable to the sales environment. In turn, the application generates new shopping experiences with a personalized service given that it offers a catalog of objects to choose quickly, easily, and interactively within a real physical space. Finally, the application presents various selection options which allow meeting consumer expectations and needs.

Acknowledgement. The authors would like to thanks to the Corporación Ecuatoriana para el Desarrollo de la Investigación y Academia –CEDIA for the financing given to research, development, and innovation, through the CEPRA projects, especially the project CEPRA-XI-2017-06; *Control Coordinado Multi-operador aplicado a un robot Manipulador Aéreo*; also to Universidad de las Fuerzas Armadas ESPE, Universidad Técnica de Ambato, Escuela Superior

Politécnica de Chimborazo, and Universidad Nacional de Chimborazo, and Grupo de Investigación en Automatización, Robótica y Sistemas Inteligentes, GI-ARSI, for the support to develop this work.

References

1. Kotler, P., Keller, K.L.: Marketing Direction. Pearson education, New Delhi (2009)
2. Ferrell, O.C., Hartline, M.D.: Marketing Strategy. Cengage Learning Editors (2012)
3. Sundjaja, A.M., Naviri, E.: The adoption of Facebook as internet marketing strategies in journal promotion. In: 2016 International Conference on Information Management and Technology (ICIMTech), Bandung, pp. 205–209 (2016)
4. Tardan, P.P., Shihab, M.R., Yudhoatmojo, S.B.: Digital marketing strategy for mobile commerce collaborative consumption startups. In: 2017 International Conference on Information Technology Systems and Innovation (ICITSI), Bandung, Indonesia, pp. 309–314 (2017)
5. Editorial Vértice. Marketing digital. Editorial Vértice (2010)
6. Leung, P.P.L., Wu, C.H., Ip, W.H., Ho, G.T.S., Cho, V.W.S., Kwong, K.K.Y.: Customer loyalty enhancement of online-to-offline marketing in beauty industry. In: 2016 4th International Conference on Enterprise Systems (ES), Melbourne, VIC, pp. 51–59 (2016)
7. Yu, Z., Zhang, D., Yu, Z., Yang, D.: Participant selection for offline event marketing leveraging location-based social networks. IEEE Trans. Syst. Man Cybern. Syst. **45**(6), 853–864 (2015)
8. Castro, J.C., Quisimalin, M., Córdova, V.H., Quevedo, W.X., Gallardo, C., Santana, J., Andaluz, V.H.: Virtual reality on e-Tourism. In: Kim, K.J., Kim, H., Baek, N. (eds.) ICITS 2017. LNEE, vol. 450, pp. 86–97. Springer, Singapore (2018). https://doi.org/10.1007/978-981-10-6454-8_13
9. Klempous, R., Kluwak, K., Idzikowski, R., Nowobilski, T., Zamojski, T.: Possibility analysis of danger factors visualization in the construction environment based on Virtual Reality model. In: 2017 8th IEEE International Conference on Cognitive Infocommunications (CogInfoCom), Debrecen, Hungary, pp. 000363–000368 2017
10. Jerald, J.: The VR Book: Human-Centered Design for Virtual Reality. Morgan & Claypool, New York (2015)
11. Butkiewicz, T.: Designing augmented reality marine navigation aids using virtual reality. In: OCEANS 2017– Anchorage, Anchorage, AK, pp. 1–9 (2017)
12. Skulimowski, S., Badurowicz, M.: Wearable sensors as feedback method in virtual reality anti-stress therapy. In: 2017 International Conference on Electromagnetic Devices and Processes in Environment Protection with Seminar Applications of Superconductors (ELMECO & AoS), Nałęczów (Naleczow), Poland, pp. 1–4 (2017)
13. Quevedo, W.X., Sánchez, J.S., Arteaga, O., Álvarez V., M., Zambrano, V.D., Sánchez, C.R., Andaluz, V.H.: Virtual reality system for training in automotive mechanics. In: De Paolis, L. T., Bourdot, P., Mongelli, A. (eds.) AVR 2017. LNCS, vol. 10324, pp. 185–198. Springer, Cham (2017). https://doi.org/10.1007/978-3-319-60922-5_14
14. Andaluz, V.H., Castillo-Carrión, D., Miranda, R.J., Alulema, J.C.: Virtual reality applied to industrial processes. In: De Paolis, L.T., Bourdot, P., Mongelli, A. (eds.) AVR 2017. LNCS, vol. 10324, pp. 59–74. Springer, Cham (2017). https://doi.org/10.1007/978-3-319-60922-5_5

15. Nugraha, I.E., Sen, T.W., Wahyu, R.B., Sulistyo, B., Rosalina.: Assembly instruction with augmented reality on Android application "assembly with AR". In: 2017 4th International Conference on New Media Studies (CONMEDIA), Yogyakarta, Indonesia, pp. 32–37 (2017)
16. Klempous, R., Kluwak, K., Idzikowski, R., Nowobilski, T., Zamojski, T.: Possibility analysis of danger factors visualization in the construction environment based on Virtual Reality model. In: 2017 8th IEEE International Conference on Cognitive Infocommunications (CogInfoCom), Debrecen, Hungary, pp. 000363–000368 (2017)
17. Kollatsch, C., Schumann, M., Klimant, P., Lorenz, M.: [POSTER] industrial augmented reality: transferring a numerical control connected augmented realty system from marketing to maintenance. In: 2017 IEEE International Symposium on Mixed and Augmented Reality (ISMAR-Adjunct), Nantes, pp. 39–41 (2017)
18. Adrianto, D., Hidajat, M., Yesmaya, V.: Augmented reality using Vuforia for marketing residence. In: 2016 1st International Conference on Game, Game Art, and Gamification (ICGGAG), Jakarta, pp. 1–5 (2016)
19. Irshad, S., Awang, D.R.B.: User perception on mobile augmented reality as a marketing tool. In: 2016 3rd International Conference on Computer and Information Sciences (ICCOINS), Kuala Lumpur, pp. 109–113 (2016)
20. Jimenez, R.J.P., Becerril, E.M.D., Nor, R.M., Smagas, K., Valari, E., Stylianidis, E.: Market potential for a location based and augmented reality system for utilities management. In: 2016 22nd International Conference on Virtual System & Multimedia (VSMM), Kuala Lumpur, pp. 1–4 (2016)
21. Rajappa, S., Raj, G.: Application and scope analysis of Augmented Reality in marketing using image processing technique. In: 2016 6th International Conference - Cloud System and Big Data (2016)
22. Liao, T.: Augmented or admented reality? The influence of marketing on augmented reality technologies. Inf. Commun. Soc. **18**(3), 310–326 (2015)
23. Yaoyuneyong, G., Foster, J., Johnson, E., Johnson, D.: Augmented reality marketing: consumer preferences and attitudes toward hypermedia print ads. J. Interact. Advertising **16**(1), 16–30 (2016)
24. Zhang, X., Navab, N., Liou, S.P.: E-commerce direct marketing using augmented reality. In: 2000 IEEE International Conference on Multimedia and Expo. ICME 2000. Proceedings. Latest Advances in the Fast Changing World of Multimedia (Cat. No. 00TH8532), New York, NY, vol. 1, pp. 88–91 (2000)
25. Scholz, J., Smith, A.N.: Augmented reality: designing immersive experiences that maximize consumer engagement. Bus. Horiz. **59**(2), 149–161 (2016)

Live Mixed Reality Video Production for Educational Presentation

Yanxiang Zhang[(✉)] and Ziqiang Zhu

Department of Communication of Science and Technology,
University of Science and Technology of China, Hefei, Anhui, China
petrel@ustc.edu.cn, monders@mail.ustc.edu.cn

Abstract. By using Microsoft Kinect, virtual objects could be fused with presenter in a real-time video for educational purpose. Unfortunately Kinect's video quality is not good also it could not overcome the issues of occlusion. In this paper, real-time high quality RGB video from a professional video camera was calibrated with the depth image from Kinect to achieve real-virtual fusion, and a hand shape blue-color mask was attach to the presenter's hand to realize high quality occlusion between virtual objects and real presenter.

Keywords: AR · TV · High-resolution camera · Kinect

1 Introduction

Presentational video is paying a more and more important role in online learning. But in the teaching of structure of some materials or objects in the field of chemistry or engineering for example, it is not convenient to present the contents the form of traditional video. In such scenario, allowing the presenter to fuse and interact with 3D geometry of these objects will provide the learners a more immersive, more vivid and more realistic experience, thus enhance the cognition effects for their learning.

Traditionally such effects could be realized by video post-production special effects, but such approach is slow and requires a very high cost. Some researchers tried to use Kinect's depth image to realize such composition [4, 5, 9, 10], but existing works did not deal with the issues of occlusion between real and virtual, with the edge of occlusion being very coarse and low quality, which is not acceptable for the audience.

2 System Design

One approach for achieving mixed reality with Kinect is by firstly retrieving skeleton data with the Kinect 2 sensor and then using those data information to generate and manipulate virtual objects, resulting in the interaction between the real presenter and the virtual objects.

However, the color image of such MR systems is the one acquired with the color camera of the Kinect2 sensor with visual quality that does not meet or match the requirements of online and broadcast TV program videos.

© Springer International Publishing AG, part of Springer Nature 2018
L. T. De Paolis and P. Bourdot (Eds.): AVR 2018, LNCS 10850, pp. 363–372, 2018.
https://doi.org/10.1007/978-3-319-95270-3_30

Hence, in order to build Kinect-based MR systems with high quality video data, it is important to couple and match video data recorded by an additional high definition video camera with the depth data recorded by the sensor. The Kinect2 sensor is equipped with two cameras: a depth camera and a color camera which are perfectly parallel one two each other with a small distance separating them and are relatively fixed, with the depth image and the color image of the sensor matching each other. The fixed spatial relationship and small distance between the two cameras make matching easily.

The content recorded by two parallel cameras, under the same focal length, naturally cannot completely overlap, however, with Kinect2, because of the small distance separating both cameras, the overlapping portion is also small and deleting that portion does not affect the final image result.

Besides, the camcorders used for HD broadcast are of big size, whereas the size of the kinect2 itself is not negligible. Under the same focal length, applying the original image from Kinect2 to match an additional HD camcorder will also result in a small overlapping region, and if the non-overlapping part is deleted, this will result in a loss of information contained in the pixel of the camera. Moreover, by adjusting or changing the focal length, the information contained in the images captured by both cameras cannot be fully use.

In addition, the sizes of these two devices vary considerably, which makes it difficult to achieve a perfect parallel placement.

Therefore, this article considers two cameras positioned at a slight angle (Fig. 1), in order to closely match their field of view and so that fewer image information is lost.

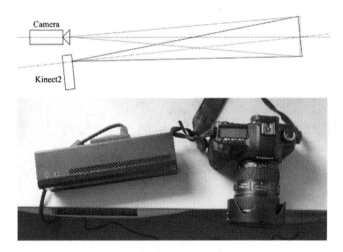

Fig. 1. Angle between camera and Kinect2

Since the skeletal information provided by Kinect2 is obtained through calculations performed by the depth camera, it is possible to obtained skeletal information that match video recorded by a HD camcorder after matching the camcorder with the depth camera of the Kinect2.

During an interaction between real and virtual elements, occlusion is necessary to build the spatial relationship between real presenter and virtual objects to make the MR video more realistic. Depth image from Kinect could be utilized to roughly build up the spatial structure of the presenter and the present space, then virtual objects could be integrated into the MR video according to the spatial structure that Kinect captured.

There are three possible fusion scenarios between the virtual objects and the real presenter:

(1) The virtual objects is in front of the presenter.
(2) The virtual objects is behind the presenter.
(3) The virtual objects is in front of some body parts of the presenter while some other body parts of the presenter, usually a hand, are in front of the virtual objects.

Gesture recognition will be utilized to decide in which scenario virtual objects will be fused with real presenter. In the first scenario, virtual objects could be directly composited over the video according to the presenter's gesture. In the second scenario, the presenter's image should be extracted from the background first, then virtual objects could be directly composited between the background and the extracted video image of the presenter according to the presenter's gesture. A blank background without presenter should be recorded first so that the presenter's image could be extracted by difference algorithm. In the third scenario, it usually happens that the presenter is manipulating a virtual object. A blue mask was tightly attached to the presenter's hand so that the hand part could be extracted separately and that the virtual objects could be placed between the performer's hand and body. The workflow of the system is shown as Fig. 2.

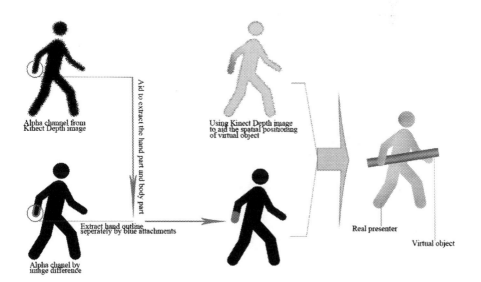

Fig. 2. Workflow of the system (Color figure online)

3   Method and Implementation

There are two steps to realize the mixed reality video with interaction and occlusion. Firstly, the video camera should be calibrated with Kinect sensor's depth camera. Next, a rough alpha channel of body part will be extracted from image difference between RGB video stream and RGB background. Then, an alpha channel of the outline of hand will be extracted with the aid of hand's blue attachments from RGB video stream, and finally the alpha channel of hand part and body part will be finished with the aid of Kinect sensor's depth image.

3.1   Calibration of Video Camera and Kinect Sensor's Depth Camera

A difference in angle between Kinect2 and the camcorder will also lead to a difference in angle between the depth information obtained by Kinect2 and skeletal information. Because the depth information and the skeletal information provided by kinect2 include depth data, in essence, we obtain three-dimensional coordinates of real points; during calibration we can then perform rotation and translation of skeletal information base on the three-dimensional coordinate, align and match them with the camera color image to effectively solve the problem of difference in angle.

1. Depending on the usage scenario, put the Kinect2 and the high definition camera in a holder and keep them fixed. A fixed spatial relationship being the precondition for the calibration in order to keep the perspective of both camera the same.
2. Use the chessboard to calibrate the HD camera and depth camera of Kinect2, and get their intrinsic parameters (H_{dep}, H_{rgb}) [1].
   Because the infrared ray sent by Kinect2 is not consistent, which may influence the calibration, its emitter is covered during the calibration process and is replaced with an external LED infrared light source.
3. Shoot the same chessboard under the same conditions with both cameras and then calculate their rotation matrix and translation vector (R_{dep}, T_{dep}, R_{rgb}, T_{rgb}).
4. Use the matrix transformation to perform the calibration (Fig. 3).

Fig. 3. Calibration

Let P_{dep} be the spatial coordinate of a point in depth camera's coordinate system. Let p_{dep} be the projection of this point in image plane (a 3D coordinate, Z representing the depth value). Intrinsic value (H_{dep}) of depth camera is obtained in step 2. Therefore,

$$p_{dep} = H_{dep}P_{dep} \qquad (1)$$

Let P_{rgb} be the spatial coordinate of a point in HD camera's coordinate system. Let p_{rgb} be the projection of this point in image plane (a 2D coordinate). The intrinsic value (H_{rgb}) of the HD camera is obtained in step 2. Therefore,

$$p_{rgb} = H_{rgb}P_{rgb} \qquad (2)$$

The coordinates of a point in different coordinate system can be unified by a rotation matrix R and a translation vector T. Therefore

$$P_{rgb} = RP_{dep} + T \qquad (3)$$

Let P be a point in the global coordinate system.

$$P_{dep} = R_{dep}P + T_{dep} \qquad (4)$$

$$P_{rgb} = R_{rgb}P + T_{rgb} \qquad (5)$$

Derived from (4),

$$P = R_{dep}^{-1}P_{dep} - R_{dep}^{-1} + T_{dep} \qquad (6)$$

Substitute (6) into (5),

$$P_{rgb} = R_{rgb}R_{dep}^{-1}P_{dep} - R_{rgb}R_{dep}^{-1}T_{dep} + T_{rgb} \qquad (7)$$

Contrast (3) and (7),

$$R = R_{rgb}R_{dep}^{-1}$$

$$T = -R_{rgb}R_{dep}^{-1}T_{dep} + T_{rgb}$$

Substitute (3) into (2),

$$p_{rgb} = H_{rgb}RP_{dep} + H_{rgb}T \qquad (8)$$

Substitute (1) into (8),

$$p_{rgb} = H_{rgb}H_{dep}^{-1}Rp_{dep} + H_{rgb}T \qquad (9)$$

To sum up, by (9), p_{dep} can be used to calculate p_{rgb}, meaning the pixel in depth information can be transformed to match the coordinate system of RGB information. Because the skeletal information is stored in the depth camera's coordinate system, therefore it can be transformed to match the RGB information in this way.

Keep the Kinect2 and the camera in a fixed relative position at a small angle to ensure that their vision is almost same. Then, get the broadcast RGB image and skeleton information, Fig. 4(A).

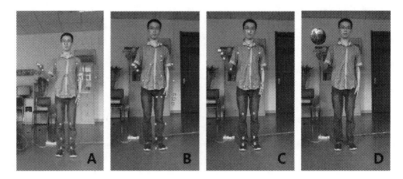

Fig. 4. Calibration result.

Directly adding the skeleton information to the RGB image before calibration leads to the result shown in Fig. 4(B) whereas Fig. 4(C) shows the result after calibration. Figure 4(D) are the mixed reality effects examples implemented after calibration.

3.2   Channel Operation of Depth and Alpha to Achieve Real-Virtual Fusion

After depth image of Kinect2 and the video stream of RGB camera were calibrated, two alpha channel will be necessary to realize the real-virtual interaction and fusion, one is the alpha channel for the whole body of the presenter, and the other is the alpha channel for the hand part of the presenter.

Video stream of the blank environment background was recorded firstly (Fig. 5), then a rough alpha channel for the whole body of the presenter (Fig. 6) could be obtained by difference and threshold operation (Fig. 7); its outline and inner could be post-modified by the depth channel from Kinect (Fig. 8) to obtain a rather clean alpha channel (Fig. 9). By using this alpha channel, virtual objects could be composited between real presenter and the environment (Fig. 10).

But in many cases, it is necessary to place a virtual object between the presenter's body part and hand part to achieve a more realistic and more immersive experience for the audience; a rough composition could be obtained by using Kinect's depth image, but it has a very coarse edge due to Kinect's low resolution in the depth image.

Small slips of blue paper were cut and attached to the presenter's hand part as mask (Fig. 11), and the outline of the hand could be extracted easily as an alpha channel. With the aid of Kinect's depth image, a clean alpha channel of the hand part could be

Fig. 5. Recorded blank environment background

Fig. 6. Whole body of the presenter

Fig. 7. A roughly alpha channel for the whole body of the presenter could be obtained by difference and threshold operation

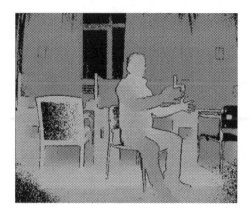

Fig. 8. Depth channel from Kinect

Fig. 9. Clean alpha channel from post modification

Fig. 10. Virtual object was composited between real presenter and the environment

obtained. Then the hand part could be extracted cleanly and virtual object could be placed between the hand and the body of the presenter to realize a realistic composition (Fig. 12).

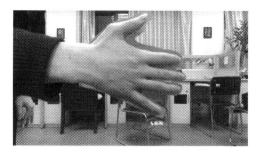

Fig. 11. Blue mask for hand part

Fig. 12. Composition

In order to allow natural interaction, gesture recognition was utilized to define the triggering and interaction patterns. Virtual objects was placed behind the performer when initialization, then by using specific gesture the performer could bring forward the virtual object and place it between two hands. A serial of gestures were recorded as patterns to realize movement, rotation, and resizing operation; dynamic time wrapping algorithm (Fig. 13) was used to match the real-time gestures with the recorded gestures patterns, then corresponding action will be triggered when they match.

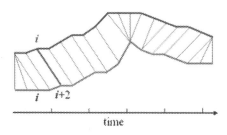

Fig. 13. Dynamic time wrapping algorithm

4   Conclusion

The research conducted in this paper introduced a method to calibrate Kinect2 together with a professional high definition camera in order to match the skeletal information of Kinect2 with the RGB image of the high definition camera. By positioning both cameras one to another at a small angle, the scene image captured by both of them are almost the same hence allowing us to fully use their pixel information. Thanks to this calibration, the research achieved an AR effect that mixes virtual and real elements in online video and TV program production, thus, making it possible to enhance their contents and effects.

In order to improve the channel operation result, presenters could make the presentation in front of a pure color background with uniform light which have large contrast with their costumes, resulting in a rather clear result from the channel operation performed in Fig. 7.

References

1. Bouguet, J.-Y.: Camera Calibration Toolbox for Matlab. http://www.vision.caltech.edu/bouguetj/calib_doc/
2. Kim, C., Yun, S., Jung, S.-W., Won, C.S.: Color and depth image correspondence for kinect v2. In: Park, J., Chao, H.-C., Arabnia, H., Yen, N.Y. (eds.) Advanced Multimedia and Ubiquitous Engineering. LNEE, vol. 352, pp. 111–116. Springer, Heidelberg (2015). https://doi.org/10.1007/978-3-662-47487-7_17
3. Zeller, N., Quint, F., Guan, L.: Kinect based 3D scene reconstruction. In: 22nd International Conference in Central Europe on Computer Graphics, Visualization and Computer Vision, WSCG 2014-in co-operation with EUROGRAPHICS Association, 2 June 2014–5 June 2014, pp. 73–81 (2015)
4. Yang, R.S., Chan, Y.H., Gong, R., Nguyen, M., Strozzi, A.G., Delmas, P., Gimel'farb, G., Ababou, R.: Multi-Kinect scene reconstruction: calibration and depth inconsistencies. In: 2013 28th International Conference on Image and Vision Computing New Zealand, IVCNZ 2013, 27 November 2013–29 November 2013, pp. 47–52 (2013)
5. Shibo, L., Qing, Z.: A new approach to calibrate range image and color image from kinect. In: 2012 4th International Conference on Intelligent Human-Machine Systems and Cybernetics, IHMSC 2012, 26 August 2012–27 August 2012, pp. 252–255 (2012)
6. Landau, M.J., Choo, B.Y., Beling, P.A.: Simulating Kinect Infrared and Depth Images (2015)
7. Zhang, Z.Y.: Microsoft kinect sensor and its effect. IEEE Multimedia **19**, 4–10 (2012)
8. Khoshelham, K., Elberink, S.O.: Accuracy and resolution of kinect depth data for indoor mapping applications. Sensors **12**, 1437–1454 (2012)
9. Han, J., Shao, L., Xu, D., Shotton, J.: Enhanced computer vision with microsoft kinect sensor: a review. IEEE Trans. Cybern. **43**, 1318–1334 (2013)
10. Herrera, D.C., Kannala, J., Heikkila, J.: Joint depth and color camera calibration with distortion correction. IEEE Trans. Pattern Anal. Mach. Intell. **34**, 2058–2064 (2012)

A Study on Narrative Design of Augmented Reality Publications

Yanxiang Zhang$^{(\boxtimes)}$ and Weiwei Zhang

Department of Communication of Science and Technology,
University of Science and Technology of China, Hefei, Anhui, China
petrel@ustc.edu.cn, anna5ll@mail.ustc.edu.cn

Abstract. This paper combs the pattern of the combination of contents in physical book and augmented reality content in AR publication. Through case studies on narrative patterns which have emerged in different types of augmented reality publications, the authors summarize the respective advantages in the integration between traditional text-narration and AR-narration, and come to some noteworthy points emerged in the narration design. These considerations and discussions can be useful for guiding the design and implementation of augmented reality publication, thus promote the communication effect and social function of AR publication.

Keywords: Augmented reality · Publication · Narrative design

1 Introduction

Augmented Reality is a promising technology with which the virtual information can be viewed as co-existing with the real environment through real-time calculation of the position and angle parameters of computer camera. Users are given the ability the sense of the real world while interacting with the virtual and physical object. User's reading & learning experience also can be improved vastly through this process of interaction. Three characteristics of augmented reality technology which includes: (1) 3D Registration. Adding and locating the virtual objects in 3D-space and achieving tracing registration on both virtual object and real object. According to the change of the user action and angle of view, computer-generated information on virtual object will be adjusted for the correlation between virtual environment and users. (2) Real-virtual Fusion. Integrate real objects and virtual objects in the real world. (3) Real-time Interaction. It means that completing a real-time three-dimensional human-machine interaction in real-virtual syncretic scene. Nowadays, Augmented Reality is prevailing as a new technology in many fields of the society such as: military; medicine; engineering design; robotic; telerobotic; learning; entertainment; education; edutainment; stage design, etc. Although the application of augmented reality in the publishing industry is a rather new trend, it does have opened a new road of digital publishing and new narration method of physical book.

In the way of reading, the AR markers contained augmented content on the paperback of the AR publication can be identified by the scan of the camera of the handheld terminal. As a result, it is possible for the reader to see the integration

L. T. De Paolis and P. Bourdot (Eds.): AVR 2018, LNCS 10850, pp. 373–381, 2018.
https://doi.org/10.1007/978-3-319-95270-3_31

environment of virtual object and the paper page. In addition, the reader can also interact with the virtual object such as 3D model by selection, move, translation, rotation. Figure 1 explains briefly the usage of augmented reality publication at present.

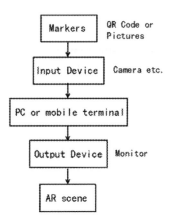

Fig. 1. Usage of augmented reality publication at present

Several works have already been presented for augmented reality publication. However, some researches focus on the design of AR book with the development and application of AR technology in education [1, 2]. Some are devoted to carding and clarifying the problems existed during the application and collaboration, thereby to make their suggestions accordingly from a technical perspective [3]. Others keep eyes on expanding application of AR as a storytelling medium in journalism, art and so on [4]. There are few studies which pay attention on the narrative strategies in different types of AR publication and advantages between the traditional text-narration and AR-narration. Porter Abbott emphasizes that the only difference between the electronic narrative and traditional narrative is reading off a screen rather than a page [5]. One of the character of electronic narrative is to use hypertext linking, which makes non-linearity become common to narrative discourse. Today, using augmented reality in publishing has changed the narrative discourse. It is no doubt that the communication effect of the publications is closely related to the narrative methods of both the content and form of the publication. This paper discusses in the following aspects. First, present the pattern of text content on combination of augmented reality content in AR publication with some representative examples. Then paying close attention to the various narrative strategies in different types of augmented reality publication. Next, illuminate the advantages of traditional text-narration and AR-narration. In the end, raise some noteworthy points emerged in the period of integration of traditional text-narration and AR-narration in order to enhance the promotion of the communication effect of the AR publication and play the social function better.

2 The Combination Pattern of Physical Book and Augmented Reality Content in the Narration of AR Publication

2.1 AR-Narration as the Complement to Text-Narration

Base on the content of traditional physical book, this kind of augmented reality publication adds the content of augmented reality narration to physical book, such as the link to audio and video materials, animation or three-dimensional model. The reader just needs to scan the quick response code or picture on the physical book and point at every button on the monitor so that the 3D model or animation of respective markers will show. In spite of the simple form of this kind of combination between the two narration methods, it can surely expand the information on paper content effectively and enrich the reading layers compared with physical book.

For example, Augmented Reality has been used in *We Love Science*, a children popular science magazine of China Children's Press and Publication Group since 2015. Readers can view 3D animation content by scanning the images on the page, which enhances the interactivity greatly. Phoenix Fine Arts Publishing. LTD has published a pop-up lift-the-flap book named AR language map, on which the map of each continent are shown double spread with different language means hello of different countries and regions. The content of text-narration of this book shows abundant text introduction on geography, local customs and the atmosphere of culture while the content of audio information in AR-narration contains more than 50-kind of greetings and expand 20,000 words content and some of the 3D animation cartoon characters.

2.2 AR-Narration and Text-Narration Complement Each Other

This kind of augmented reality publication is suitable for themes which are often demonstrated through 3D model or interactive animation, such as Physics, Chemistry, biologic, Mechanics and Engineering. These themes are often difficult to be sensed in the real world lacking of more directly understanding. By means of showing 3D model and animation using augmented reality, this kind of AR publication clarifies the material of content intuitively, which make a better comprehension for learners. The complementary relationship between the AR-narration as well as traditional text-narration makes the reader get command with the abstract concept on physical book more easily. Thus, it has become a mainly current form of the augmented reality publication.

For example, an augmented reality application designed for a traditional medicine textbook named Human Anatomy and Histology and Embryology has gone well with the learner. It was published by the cooperation of Suzhou Dreamer technology Co. Ltd and Science and Technology Press. Three-dimensional modeling of organ will be shown while the reader scanning the pictures of the body part through this application using camera of mobile terminal. It can also adjust the angle automatically according to the change of the position of the camera. The learner can have a close-up view of 3D biomedical model from different angle of view. Thus, the learner can have a good command of knowledge in this new textbook with the combination of traditional strict content of the text-narration and vivid augmented reality narration.

2.3   AR-Narration as the Subject of the Content of the AR Publication

The content of the AR-narration carries main information in this kind of augmented reality publication. Through scanning AR marker on the paper, a fund of AR information will be provided for the reader. This narrative method of integration with the application on publishing has broken down the form of the traditional text-narration, which supplements the simplex linear narrative method in physical book with interactive multi-dimensional AR narration. The multi-sensory and stereo narrative method of the augmented reality publication can deepen the comprehension and memory of the content of publication. It brings a new experience of reading and learning for the reader.

3   The Media Fusion Pattern of Narration in Augmented Reality Publications

The element of the narrative design using in the AR publication is decided by the different ways of the combination of the narrative medium. In the Augmented reality publication, there are two aspects: the text, picture in the content of physical book and the sound, model, animation in the content of augmented reality scene. Different patterns of augmented reality publication are formed by integrating the content of AR-narration and interactive effect with the content of the text-narration. Integrating AR-narrative into a physical book will convert a traditional static text reading experience into a dynamic, vivid and interesting reading experience for the reader.

3.1   The Fusion of the Sound Narration and Text Narration in AR Publication

The text of the physical book may be adjusted structurally according to the sound of the augmented reality scene when necessary. As a result, the reader can trigger the audio player separately and independently. Here are the mainly sound elements in the content of augmented reality narration: voice-over as the sound narration, background music, sound effect along with the model and animation, and the interactive sound between the virtual character and the reader.

As the subject of the sound narration, voice-over added in the augmented reality scene plays an important role in supplement the text on the physical book while reading. In the existing AR publication, reader may usually find that the voice-over is still played when he has finished reading on account of the discrepancy between the speed of voice-over and the reader's rate of reading. It brings about a non-equivalent of the rhythm of the narration to some extent. Therefore, it is necessary to refine the text of voice-over and adapt more colloquial expression on the basis of the text on the physical book and realize the complementation of design of the two kind of narration methods. The important component of the context narration is composed of the background music and sound effect. The sound effect matched with model and animation makes the 3D virtual character more vivid. The accurate and automatic speech recognition brings about a more natural and fluent experience kind of interactive narration. AR publication can give the reader a stronger sense of immersion through its excellent context narration.

3.2   The Fusion of the Title or Subtitle Narration and Text Narration in AR Publication

The title or embedded subtitle in the augmented scene also belongs to text information. However, when it comes to the integration between the traditional text-narration and AR-narration, this kind of narration method can make supplementary effect. Hint and guidance of the content of narration are given to the reader through the title or subtitle, but also realize the communication with man and machine, which can further reinforce the interactivity of the narration of the augmented reality publication. As one of the indispensable role in the scene of augmented reality narration, readers can take truly participate in the process of narration with this way of narration while reading. It is mainly used in the field of interactive gaming. Caption or enquiry in the virtual text box is set in the game level to adjust the rhythm of game.

Few attempts have been taken in the augmented reality publication due to the effect of title or subtitle in virtual scene are usually unsatisfactory and the pre-existing traditional text-narration has already quite logical. In addition, the narration through title or subtitle has less visual impact than the visual effect of the virtual 3D model and animation. However, it is irrational to ignore the role of the narration of title and subtitle. For example, titles can be put in the virtual scene of narration to illustrate the plot development or put forward questions according to the antecedent in an augmented reality story book. It can provoke the thinking or conjecture towards the following episode of the story and even can let the reader decide the destiny of the protagonist and change the way of the plot development. The experience of reading compare with the way of traditional reading can be promoted.

3.3   The Fusion of Visual Narration of 2D Animation or Video and Text Narration in AR Publication

The information processing mode of human brain makes the processing speed of text message slower than the speed of image processing. That is due to the additional processing to visualize the abstract text message transferred into brain. 2D animation and video of the AR-narration form the basis for visual narration of augmented reality publication. The reader can play the video or watch the animation through the application of AR in the reading process. These 2D animation and video content can also be used in other time whenever necessary for the reader as independent learning resources. It can expand the amount of information on the physical book and enrich the layer of the narration in the augmented reality publication.

This kind of narration method is widely used in the field of Education publication which may be called more suitably with the word "edutainment". With the combination of the content of text-narration and the video and 2D animation of the AR-narration, the learner can understand deeply towards the content of publication. Not long ago, PEP Digital Publishing Corporation Limited together with Tencent QQ software present the Primary English textbook which is the first AR textbook in China [6]. After logging

Tencent QQ software and clicking on the button "scan", student users can get the multimedia teaching resources by scanning main picture of every unit. There is a consensus that augmented reality technology is an appropriate narrative method as the AR publication itself. The majority of participants indicated that the augmented reality publication was a stimulating educational resource that can enrich the learning method and increase the student's desire to learn [7].

3.4 The Fusion of Spatial Narration of 3D Model Structure and Text Narration in AR Publication

The display of the 3D model is one of the important superiority of AR-narration. Existing augmented reality publications apply 3D model into the integration between the text-narration and AR-narration expertly. 3D models combined with the text of physical book give full play to multi-dimensional characteristic and the benefit of dynamics of the stereoscopic space narration of augmented reality. On the basis of the detailed explanation in the text-narration of the physical book, 3D models in the virtual scene give a clearer and more vivid illustration on physical structures complementing each other's advantages. Representative examples can be found in the popular scientific publications [8] such as the introduction to C60, Carbon nanotube, the double helix structure of DNA, and 3D geometric designed for learning mathematics and geometry.

Digital Culture Center of University of Science and Technology of China has developed an AR system. It contains various field of knowledge such as physics; chemistry; biology; mechanics and new energy. When the user put the recognizable card in front of the camera of the computer, a 3D virtual object is shown or an animation starts on the monitor. For another example, a science picture book series "Banana & Rocket" published by Jieli Publishing House, integrating augmented reality technology with the traditional picture book. Finding the AR markers on the back cover of the book, scanning the Quick Response code, and the reader can observe the 3D model of animal and plant from different views. Reading experience is enlarged by the real-virtual environment within a computer-generated 3D-world.

3.5 The Fusion of Interactive 3D Animation and Text Narration in AR Publication

3D interactive animation is the brightest spotlight of the augmented reality publication. It is suitable for the trend of human towards visual information. The demonstrations of the three-dimensional interactive animation in AR publication transfer the simplex content of the text-narration into the dynamic interactive narration of scene of augmented reality. Compared with the traditional static explanatory charts, these three-dimensional dynamic progresses are better understood for the reader. A new search space is provided for readers through the integration between the advantages of the linear logical text-narration and the strength of the interactive narration of 3D interactive animation [9].

An augmented reality book named Monsters, Inc published by Carlton Books Ltd. also uses the technology of QR recognition to obtain the augmented reality animation content. Book series "Digital Magic" are popular for its interesting content of interactive animation, which can be get after download the assorted application free of charge. For example, in this book named Transformers Robots in Disguise: Where Crown City Comes to Life [10], young reader can complete the interaction with the virtual transformer robot in the scene of AR and select favorite components for his exclusive transformer robot. After that, the transformer robot made personally will be showed in the way of 3D animation in AR environment. For other example, the AR cards "Pocket Zoo" series belong to Neobear. Scanning the animal card with the application of Pocket Zoo, 3D animation of each animal will be shown on the screen. Using different prop card can generate corresponding virtual prop to play with the virtual animal characters such as killing bugs with the pesticide, let sea lion play with a ball. When the reader turn on the function of off-card, it is able to interact with 3D virtual animal even take away the AR card.

4 The Harmonious Unification of Traditional Text-Narration with AR-Narration

Traditional narrative in physical books allows many interactions and sensory feedback between readers and the publication such as speech through the narration, vision through pictures and touching through the turning and pointing at the pages. However, reading experience can be a monotonous activity as actions are usually descriptive based and illustrated through static graphics. Traditional narrative takes the paper page as medium unit. Therefore, readers have to read and analyze the content of physical book in order which is too simplex to limit the thinking of reader. As an assistant multimedia, augmented reality technology can enlarge the range of information contained by the physical book changing the format of carrying information of the publication. In a word, the text-narration based on the text content is linear, static, and unidirectional while the AR-narration based on the visual content is multi-dimensional, dynamic, and interactive.

Regarded as a new means of narrative method rather than a new means of media, augmented reality surely enriches the narrative layers of the AR publication. The narration method of the AR publication can be classified into three types according to the way of the combination of the text-narration and AR-narration. First: Linear narrative. The sequence of narration carries on by the single clue and adds the content of AR when it is necessary. This kind of narration method is closer to the traditional physical book. Second: Juxtaposition narrative. The text and AR content of the publication interact with each other. That is to say, the reader can enjoy the AR content such as video and audio materials for commentary while reading. Third, Cross narration. It means to put some part of text content into the scene of augmented reality. The reader will get the reminders through the interactive operation in AR scene and go back to the reading on the physical book.

The organic unification of traditional text-narration with AR-narration requires the coincidence of two main elements which are "speed" and "depth" [11]. The response speed along with the stability of the augmented reality application itself decides the quality of the interaction of AR publication. The "depth" which means the level of the publication content builds the foundation of the narrative design as well as the foundation of the augmented reality publication. On the one hand, to realize the integration of text-narration and AR-narration, the narrative logic of the publication should be noted and put the quality of the content as the first consideration no matter when. On the other hand, augmented reality technology should be adopted in proper position to show readers the richness of the content using the interactive multi-dimensional narrative method. Above all, the design of AR publication on narrative is expected to increase to grab the reader's attention as well as increase reader's participation or interaction.

5   Noteworthy Points Emerged in the Period of Integration of Traditional Text-Narration and AR-Narration

Here are the design considerations in planning and implementing AR publications on narrative.

First of all, handle properly the relationship between the static text message and dynamic AR images. Especially avoid throwing the reader into confusion which is due to a mass of content both in the text and AR scene. The 3D model or interactive animation is surely more attractive. It is likely that the reader is attracted with them and absorbed in the fun of interaction without thinking about the knowledge in the publication. It is also probably that the reader pays no attention to the content of AR because of the fussy accession. Thus, the organic unification of traditional text-narration with AR-narration is required to make the content of AR-narration become an important and irreplaceable part of the publication. Augmented reality can not only become a selling point or gimmick of AR publication.

Next, it is important to deal with the relationship between the reader and the AR publication. Compared to traditional book, AR book needs some initial setup before usage which is often associated with markers. Thus, to reduce the learning curve for reader as well as to increase the interactivity between reader and publication, the narrative design of AR publication should be more convenient and humanized. The graphical reader interface can be divided into 3 main areas which are the display space, main button and the narration spaces. It is obviously that the reader wants a more succinct and easy-to-control interface and operation methods. Excessive pursuit of the visual effect or the application of the new technology can only lead to the flashy development of publishing.

Furthermore, humanistic concern also should be taken into consideration for an augmented reality publication. Readers can switch into the immersive virtual world to view the 3D model, animation, and other interactive element more clearly while reading the AR book. However, this new technology used in publication also can brings some negative effects, such as the harm to eyesight especially for young readers still in the period of growing. The designer of the augmented reality publication should think about how we want this AR book to be perceived according to the different reading habits of different readership such as the reading habits, information demands and reading expectations. The relationship between narrative design and the acceptance degree of the readers towards contents of the AR publications should be considered while doing the design of narration.

6   Conclusion

Based on a number of typical cases of AR publications, this paper presented some desirable characteristics for augmented reality narrative methods. No doubt, AR has broken down the linear narrative represented for traditional physical text narrative and enriched the narrative format of publication. The convergence of augmented reality narration and traditional text-narration defines the outer borders of the book system, around which society is shaped. Through cases studies, we can feel deeply with the new reading method bringing along with augmented reality technology. Nevertheless, every application of new technology in the field of publishing is nothing but change or update the format of the publications. The core value of the publication is the premium content for all time. Therefore, the discussion on the narrative design is extremely necessary. For future work, there will be more reflection and thinking on how to integrate the text-narration and the AR-narration in order to improve the communication effect of the AR publication and bring up both social benefit and economic benefit.

References

1. Akcayir, M., Akcayir, G.: Advantages and challenges associated with augmented reality CrossMark for education: a systematic review of the literature. Educ. Res. Rev. **20**, 1–11 (2017)
2. Mohd. Zainuddin, N.M., Zaman, H.B., Ahmad, A.: A participatory design in developing prototype an augmented reality book for deaf student. In: IEEE 2nd International Conference on Computer Research and Development (2010)
3. Kim, K., Lepetit, V., Woo, W.: Scalable real-time planer targets tracking for digilog books. Vis. Comput. **26**, 1145–1154 (2010)
4. Perey, C.: Print and publishing and the future of augmented reality (2012). http://www.perey.com/White_Paper_for_ARCHP&P_January_12.pdf. Accessed 23 Oct 2013
5. Porter Abbott, H.: The Cambridge Introduction to Narrative. Cambridge University Press, Cambridge (2002)
6. http://www.sohu.com/a/210055320_177795
7. Ibáñez, M.B., Di Serio, A., Villarána, D., et al.: Experimenting with electromagnetism using augmented reality: impact on flow student experience and educational effectiveness. Comput. Educ. **71**, 1–13 (2014)
8. Wolle, P., Müller, M.P., Rauh, D.: Augmented reality in scientific publications—taking the visualization of 3D structures to the next level. ACS Chem. Biol. **13**(3), 496–499 (2018)
9. Ryan, M.-L.: Narrative as Virtual Reality: Immersion and Interactivity in Literature and Electronic Media. Johns Hopkins University Press, Baltimore (2001)
10. Rowlands, C.: Transformers Robots in Disguise: Where Crown City Comes to Life. Carlton Books Ltd., London (2016)
11. Crawford, C.: Chris Crawford on Interactive Storytelling. New Riders Press, San Francisco (2004)

Realistic Shadow Augmented Reality of Rare Animals from Indonesia

Mohammad Fadly Syahputra[(⊠)], Muhammad Iqbal Rizki Siregar, and Romi Fadillah Rahmat

Department of Information Technology, Faculty of Computer Science and Information Technology, Universitas Sumatera Utara, Medan, Indonesia
{nca.fadly,romi.fadillah}@usu.ac.id,
m.iqbalrizki@students.usu.ac.id

Abstract. Indonesia is a country known for its natural resource. Various flora and fauna lives on this fertile land in the country, such as one-horned rhinoceros (Javanese rhinoceros), Sumateran elephant, Bawean deer or even komodo can be found here. But as the technology evolves, author will apply Augmented Reality (AR) technology to present these Indonesia's animals in real scale without disturbing their population. This technology is equipped with features to apply realistic shadow so the object of virtual animals will have shadow similar to real animals. Phase to create this realistic shadow is receive light, which is a process receiving light from sun object in virtual environment, then setting plane is a setting in virtual plane to receive shadow's projection and projection shadow is method to projecting shadow on a plane in virtual environment. The result of applying realistic shadow augmented reality is a projection reference on virtual objects. Applied realistic shadow will give a realistic impression on virtual animals of Indonesia that is showed.

Keywords: Realistic shadow · Augmented reality
Rare animal from Indonesia

1 Introduction

Population of rare animals in Indonesia is getting smaller as illegal hunting and narrowed habitat which happened because of narrowed forest land in Indonesia (Iqbal et al. 2014) [3]. That is the reason why presenting those animals directly to introduce them to public society is hard. This introduction aims for society learn about various Indonesia's rare animals without disturbing their population.

Currently, as the times evolves, Augmented Reality (AR) technology is developed to create possibility to mixes reality and virtual (Satrioadi 2014) [9], which can benefit in many aspect in life. Such as education, entertainment, tourism and trades. Basically, AR has advantages to give experience and deep understanding to its subject of learning (Nugraha 2014) [8]. This does not rule out the possibility that this technology could be presented as a media to introduce Indonesian rare animals in its real size.

The use of shadows is very important in the application of augmented reality applications. What needs to be noticed and understood for the application of

© Springer International Publishing AG, part of Springer Nature 2018
L. T. De Paolis and P. Bourdot (Eds.): AVR 2018, LNCS 10850, pp. 382–393, 2018.
https://doi.org/10.1007/978-3-319-95270-3_32

appropriate shadows to objects is the relationship between spatial objects within a scene such as location, shape and object volume (Jacobs 2006) [4]. Realistic shadow is a blend of soft shadow and hard shadow then it is displayed and adjusted to the state of the virtual object view environment so that virtual objects look real (Tassio 2012) [10].

2 Identification of Problems

Augmented reality is a technique that can bring Indonesia's rare animals into 3 dimensional form. However, unsuitable lighting and shadows make the virtual object look stiff and does not blend with the real world. In order to present a virtual object more visible to the real world, it requires lighting and shadow mapping that can be adapted to the conditions and situation of the marker area. Therefore we need a method to be able to map the shadow that can be used as a support for augmented reality of rare animals of Indonesia

3 Previous Research

In 2014, applications that implement augmented reality for museum zoology have been created by Gonidjaja and Mayongga [1]. They make markers in the form of brochures that can display the floor plan, description of the room and animals that exist in a particular room. Grosch [2] in his research used the algorithm Goniometric Light Construction to produce objects that look natural. The way the algorithm works is to create a pixel block to find the source of light coming in and overwrite the real object. So the app can reconstruct the existing light on the object according to the light in the virtual object environment is displayed. However, this study only works optimally if there is one light source in the virtual object display environment. Kolivand [5] in 2014 conducted research to map the shadows using the Z-Gaf Shadow Maps algorithm on virtual objects to display more visible objects. The research done by Kolivand is devoted to the performance of virtual object outdoors. In 2011 Lim et al. [6] conducted Implementation of A Study on Web Augmented Reality based Smart Exhibition System Design for User Participating. It provides designs on Augmented Reality (AR) based on intelligent exhibition systems to encourage user participation. If the conventional way to observe the exhibit is only on the visual of the product at hand, a smart exhibit that uses augmented reality will allow users to get in-depth information not only through text, images, and video but also through virtual 3D objects in real-time. In 2010, Tian [11] Implemented "Real-time Occlusion Handling in Augmented Reality Based on an Object Tracking Approach". Applications to produce realistic enlargement in augmented reality, the relative position of true objects and virtual objects is essential. In their writing, they proposed a real-time method of handling novel occlusion-based on a tracking object approach. Our method is consist of three steps: selection of occluding objects, object tracking and handling occlusion. The user selects the occluding object using interactive segmentation method. The contour of the selected object is tracked in the next frame real-time. In handling occlusion step, all pixels on the traced object are redrawn in the augmented image and processed to generate a new synthesized image where the relative positions between real and virtual objects are correct. The proposed method has several advantages. First, it is powerful and stable, as it remains effective when the camera moves through large changes of viewing angle and volume or when objects and backgrounds have the same color. Second, it is fast because real objects can be tracked in real-time. Finally, the smoothing technique provides a seamless merger between augmented and virtual objects. Several experiments were provided to validate the performance of the proposed method. 2014 Mauro et al. [7] carried out the Augmented Reality implementation tools for teaching and learning. In this paper, they present some educational activities created using augmented reality without tools and require no programming knowledge to be used by any teacher. The research includes markers and less markers based on augmented reality technology to show how teachers can create learning activities to visualize additional information such as animations and 3D objects that help students understand educational content [13, 14]. Currently there are many augmented reality applications as our previous research, they are augmented reality for historical building [12] with skin detection [14]. They see the most popular augmented reality ecosystem. Our goal is to find an AR system that can be used in everyday learning activities. Augmented reality systems is user friendly, as they can be used by teachers who generally have no programming knowledge.

4 Methods

The method to display the shadow of virtual objects look realistic or realistic shadow consist of several stages of receiving light and projecting shadow. The general architecture that describes the method in this study is shown in Fig. 1.

4.1 Marker Scanning

The process of marker scanning is a process of marker reading which can be an image of 2 dimension, cylinder or 3 dimensional object. This process works by capturing images of objects that have been stored as markers and then displaying virtual objects that have been programmed to be displayed as augmented reality.

4.2 Matching Data

After performing the marker reading process, image data that captured by the camera is adjusted to the existing database and from this process selected virtual object to be displayed.

4.3 Setting Shadow

This stage consist of several process such as receive light, set plane and draw shadow. Once the 3D object is selected by the light database derived from the directional light object which is received by the outer texture of the object and plane, this process is

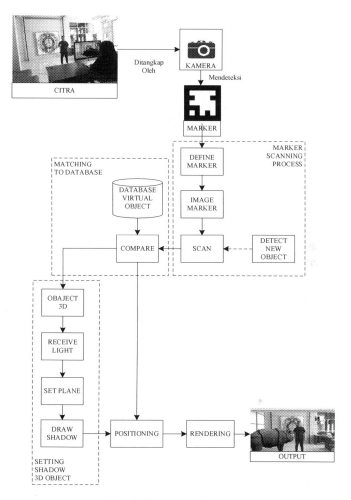

Fig. 1. General architecture

called the receive light. On the plane, shadow material is mounted which has been provided specifically by Unity. The function of this shader is to capture and project the shadow of virtual objects on the plane that has been installed.

4.4 Receive Light

This stage is the stage of lighting arrangements in the virtual environment in an augmented reality environment. Light source in the form of directional light is adjusted its position with the sun in the real world so as to display the appropriate lighting. Appropriate lighting is influential in projecting shadows. The more similar the lighting to the real world the more similar the shadow of a virtual object with a shadow on the objects in the real world. Light settings in this application by default can be seen in Fig. 2.

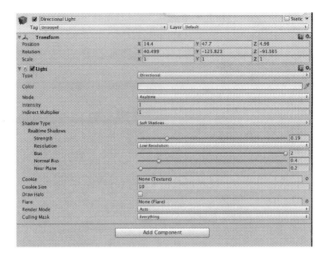

Fig. 2. Directional light setting.

4.5 Setting Plane

At this stage of plane setting, plane or plain is created under virtual animals, serves as a virtual shadow object of projected virtual animals. For that, there are several steps that must be done so the shadow of virtual animals can be projected like a real shadow. The first stage is the stage of making the plane which its size is adapted to the real space environment of augmented reality appearance and positioned just below the feet of virtual animals. The first stage of plane setting can be seen in Fig. 3.

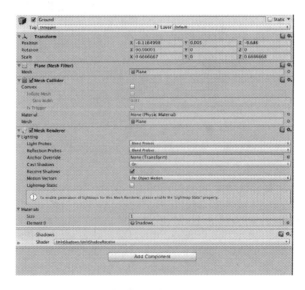

Fig. 3. Plain setting

In this second stage, to make the plane or artificial plane visible transparent, a shader is inserted into the plane that has been set the position and size. The function of this shader, besides making the plane becomes transparent, is arranging shader as shown in Fig. 4, which can also activate the material on part or all of the plane when light is not on the plane part.

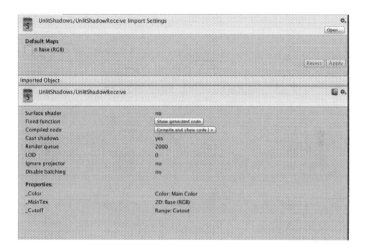

Fig. 4. Shader setting.

4.6 Draw Shadow

Draw shadow is the stage of shadow depiction on the plane area. This process of shadow depiction begins by placing the gray colored material on the plane which will become the base material for the shadow to be projected, the example of shadow material can be seen in Fig. 5.

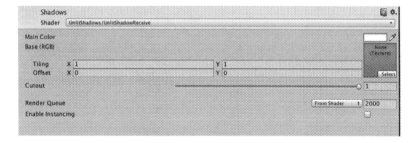

Fig. 5. Texture shadow setting.

This process occurs after the unknown part of the plane is not exposed to light or plane areas that do not get the light due to closed or blocked virtual objects in the area of the virtual environment.

4.7   Object Positioning

In this positioning object stage, the virtual object moves according to the path that already installed. This path is installed above the plane to determine the route of the virtual object path.

4.8   Rendering

Rendering is the final process of the whole process of computer modeling or animation. In rendering, all the data has been included into the modeling, animation, texturing, lighting with certain parameters will be translated in an output form (final display of the model and animation).

5   Result and Discussion

In testing this realistic shadow application, a testing is done to know how the condition of the shadow at the position of the sun moves. In this testing, the researchers made four scenarios in which each scenario has different conditions such as bright or dark lighting and also the distance of the sun.

Scenario 1: Simulation is done when the sun is in the 12 PM direction. Distance of camera position with marker is 5 m and camera height from floor is 1.5 m.

Fig. 6. Scenario 1

The result of light and shadow testing at direction of 12 PM direction is shown in Table 1 which its overall has 100% accuracy. Compared to Fig. 6 the shadow on the real object is the same as the shadow of the virtual animal.

Table 1. Testing result of Scenario 1

Game object	Sum of testing (n)	Conformity of shadow thickness	Conformity of shadow depth	Accuracy (%)
Javanese rhinoceros	5	5	5	100
Sumateran elephant	5	5	5	100
Sumateran tiger	5	5	5	100
Komodo	5	5	5	100
Bawean deer	5	5	5	100

Scenario 2: The test is done when the sun is in 3 PM direction. Distance of camera position with marker is 5 m and camera height from floor is 1.5 m.

Fig. 7. Scenario 2.

The result of light and shadow testing at 3 PM direction position is shown in Table 2 with its overall is 100% accuracy. Compared to Fig. 7 the shadow on the real object is the same as the shadow of the virtual animal.

Table 2. Testing result of Scenario 2

Game object	Sum of testing (n)	Conformity of shadow thickness	Conformity of shadow depth	Accuracy (%)
Javanese rhinoceros	5	5	5	100
Sumateran elephant	5	5	5	100
Sumateran tiger	5	5	5	100
Komodo	5	5	5	100
Bawean deer	5	5	5	100

Scenario 3: The test is done when the sun is in the 6 PM direction. Distance of camera position with marker is 5 m and camera height from floor is 1.5 m.

Fig. 8. Scenario 3.

Table 3. Testing result of Scenario 3

Game object	Sum of testing (n)	Conformity of shadow thickness	Conformity of shadow depth	Accuracy (%)
Javanese rhinoceros	5	5	5	100
Sumateran elephant	5	5	5	100
Sumateran tiger	5	5	5	100
Komodo	5	5	5	100
Bawean deer	5	5	5	100

In Table 3 above, we can see the results of light and shadow testing at 6 PM direction. The projected shadow of virtual animals has 100% accuracy. Compared to Fig. 8 the shadow on the real object is the same as the shadow of the virtual animal.

Scenario 4: The test is done when the sun is at 9 AM. Distance of camera position with marker is 5 m and camera height from floor is 1.5 m.

Fig. 9. Scenario 4.

The result of light and shadow test at 9 AM direction position is shown in Table 4 with its overall is 100% accuracy. Compared to Fig. 9 the shadow on the real object is the same as the shadow of the virtual animal.

Table 4. Testing result of Scenario 4

Game object	Sum of testing (n)	Conformity of shadow thickness	Conformity of shadow depth	Accuracy (%)
Javanese rhinoceros	5	5	5	100
Sumateran elephant	5	5	5	100
Sumateran tiger	5	5	5	100
Komodo	5	5	5	100
Bawean deer	5	5	5	100

6 Conclusion

After doing the implementation process and testing the system, we can draw some conclusions such as; The application can run properly while detecting and showing the 3D object, the accuracy of the shadow projection in dimensions and depth between virtual world with real world reaches 100% during sunny weather and radiation conditions in good experimental space, and the optimum space to detect the marker is up to 5 m. Suggestions that can be given for further research includes it is expected to detect the source of light with real time, it is expected to show the Augmented Reality without using marker, and it is also expected to detect the shadow in areas that have more than one source of light.

References

1. Gonydjaja, R., Mayongga, Y.: Aplikasi Museum Zoologi Berbasis Augmented Reality. Universitas Gunadarna, Depok (2014)
2. Grosch, T., Müller, S., Kresse, W.: Goniometric Light Reconstruction for Augmented Reality Image Synthesis. Institut für Computervisualistik, Universität Koblenz-Landau (2002)
3. Iqbal, M., Kurnia, M.P., Susanti, E.: Tinjauan Yuridis Terhadap Kepemilikan dan Penjualan Satwa Langka Izin di Indonesia. Universitas Mulawarman (2014)
4. Jacobs, K., Loscos, C.: Classification of illumination methods for mixed reality. Comput. Graph. Forum **25**(1), 29–51 (2006)
5. Kolivand, H., Sunar, M.S.: Realistic Real-Time Outdoor Rendering in Augmented Reality. Universiti Teknologi Malaysia, Skudai (2014)
6. Lim, J.: A Study on Web Augmented Reality Based Smart Exhibition System Design for User Participating. Hannam University (2014)
7. Mauro, F.: Augmented reality tools for teaching and learning. Int. J. Adv. Educ. Res. **1**, 22–34 (2014)
8. Nugraha, I.S.: Pemanfaatan Augmented Reality Untuk Pembelajaran Pengenalan Alat Musik Piano. Universitas Diponegoro (2014)
9. Satrioadi, R.B.: Pengenalan Budaya Papua dengan Augmented Reality Berbasis Android. Universitas Muhammadiyah Surakarta (2014)
10. Tassio, K.C., Luiz, H.F., Luiz, V.: Realistic shadows for mobile augmented reality. In: 14th Symposium on Virtual and Augmented Reality. Visgraf Lab, IMPA, Rio de Janeiro, Brazil (2012)
11. Tian, Y.: Real-time Occlusion Handling in Augmented Reality Based on an Object Tracking Approach. Huazhong University of Science and Technology (2010)
12. Syahputra, M.F., Siregar, R.K., Rahmat, R.F.: Finger recognition as interaction media in augmented reality for historical buildings in Matsum and Kesawan Regions of Medan City. In: De Paolis, L.T., Bourdot, P., Mongelli, A. (eds.) AVR 2017. LNCS, vol. 10325, pp. 243–250. Springer, Cham (2017). https://doi.org/10.1007/978-3-319-60928-7_21
13. Rahmat, R.F., Anthonius, M.M.A., Hizriadi, A., Syahputra, M.F.: Virtual reality interactive media for Universitas Sumatera Utara – a campus introduction and simulation. J. Phys: Conf. Ser. **978**(1), 012101 (2018)

14. Syahputra, M.F., Rizki, M.I., Fatimah, S., Rahmat, R.F.: Implementation of player position monitoring for Tanjung Pura palace virtual environment. In: De Paolis, L.T., Bourdot, P., Mongelli, A. (eds.) AVR 2017. LNCS, vol. 10325, pp. 328–334. Springer, Cham (2017). https://doi.org/10.1007/978-3-319-60928-7_29
15. Rahmat, R.F., Chairunnisa, T., Gunawan, D., Sitompul, O.S.: Skin color segmentation using multi-color space threshold. In: 2016 3rd International Conference on Computer and Information Sciences (ICCOINS), Kuala Lumpur, pp. 391–396 (2016)

Simulation System Based on Augmented Reality for Optimization of Training Tactics on Military Operations

Fabricio Amaguaña[1], Brayan Collaguazo[1], Jonathan Tituaña[1], and Wilbert G. Aguilar[1,2(✉)]

[1] CICTE Research Center, Universidad de las Fuerzas Armadas ESPE, Sangolquí, Ecuador
wgaguilar@espe.edu.ec
[2] GREC Research Group, Universitat Politècnica de Catalunya, Barcelona, Spain

Abstract. In this article, we proposed an augmented reality system that was developed in Unity-Vuforia. The system simulates a war environment using three-dimensional objects and audiovisual resources to create a real war conflict. Vuforia software makes use of the database for the creation of the target image and, in conjunction with the Unity video game engine resources, animation algorithms are developed and implemented in 3D objects. That is used at the hardware level are physical images and a camera of a mobile device that combined with the programming allows to visualize the interaction of the objects through the recognition and tracking of images, said algorithms are belonging to Vuforia. The system allows the user to interact with the physical field and the digital objects through the virtual button. To specify, the system was tested and designed for mobile devices that have the Android operating system as they show acceptable performance and easy integration of applications.

Keywords: Military strategy · Augmented reality · Warlike simulator

1 Introduction

At present, the augmented reality technology is used in various fields such as education, campaigns tours, museums, marketing, military [1–4]. In the state art referred to multiple military applications used in operations in urban areas through monitoring and guidance of the head of the user and superimposes graphics together with annotations that are aligned with the real objects in the visual field of the user [5].

Our purpose is to implement a system of augmented reality that will serve as a tool for military tactics, using specialized software in vuforia image processing and 3D environments developer Unity. Initial-mind is used a database of vuforia, where they are hosted images goals, the recognition algorithm runs on the application of unity. A bed-ra captures a physical image and compares it with the database by using the Algoritmos monitoring and detection vuforia, established the relationship is des-fold the animated 3D objects on the physical area.

© Springer International Publishing AG, part of Springer Nature 2018
L. T. De Paolis and P. Bourdot (Eds.): AVR 2018, LNCS 10850, pp. 394–403, 2018.
https://doi.org/10.1007/978-3-319-95270-3_33

The algorithms of animation is developed in C# (C Sharp) IDE pro-provided by Microsoft's Visual Studio. The motion of objects was achieved with the implementation of an algorithm that modifies the position and speed using a set time of displacement according to the coordinate axis that is agreed-niebnte. To start the animation on the Stage that the virtual button is activated by the user making it possible for the interaction between the real world and the physical world.

As a contribution to the military level the focus is on giving a perspective of the field where the military personnel will be deployed, through the simulation we can analyze possible actions to be followed, anticipating events that may or may not occur within the battlefield, this is achieved more visually and interactively the introduction of augmented reality technology, since it can combine 3D objects and physical objects being these parts of the scenario where simulation is required; so the motivation to develop the application is related to allowing the making of better decisions in military tactics.

This paper is organized as follows: Sect. 2 describes the state of art. Next, our proposal for augmented realty system, the creation of the algorithms are described in Sect. 3. In Sect. 4 we present the results. Finally conclusions and future works are presented in Sect. 5.

2 Related Works

In the literature, many projects based on the augmented reality technology have been developed for the military camp. NRL [5] created a prototype, bars that tracks the position and orientation with an overlay of objects and indications mounted on real structures. Eyekon developed by Hicks, Jeffrey, is a system running on a laptop where the soldier has access to information about your equipment. The information is superimposed on the screen of the weapon using augmented reality techniques [6].

DARPA [7] in the year 2009 iARM implements digital system oriented to the decision-making of military personnel. This project uses artificial intelligence main features of obtaining improvements in the performance to meet the tactical objectives. HEaDS-UP is a military device developed for the US Army to inform soldiers who are on the battlefield. It consists of a helmet that integrates a ballistic vision on which health information and maps of the site are projected [8].

The University of the Andes in Colombia presented in 2010 a work of visualization of urban information through augmented reality on georeferenced targets, information that can be manipulated through an iPhone mobile phone. Interactive Environment for tourist sites, is an application developed by researchers from the Pedagogical University of Colombia in 2010, to visualize tourist sites in specific geographical places for Android and iOS mobile devices. It collects geographic data such as altitude and longitude to determine the tourist sites of interest [9].

[10] exposes the main applications that Virtual Reality has in the design of environments for the evaluation and intervention of people with intellectual disabilities, focusing on the utilities that Virtual Reality has for neuropsychology in general, and for this particular population. [11] that talks about games with augmented reality for evaluation and rehabilitation of people with disabilities, where it is described the use of

Augmented Reality technology in a simulation system oriented towards evaluation and rehabilitation of cognitive patients. In particular, it is detailed the operation of a platform for patients with Attention Deficit Hyperactivity Disorder (ADHD) and patients with frontal lobe damage. He designed tests of increasing complexity, in of labyrinths with dynamic objects since the use of a labyrinth editing tool allows therapists, without knowledge of 3D modeling [12–14] and programming, design specific tests for each patient. Once the tests proposed by the therapists, the system returns performance parameters that measure quantitatively the different abilities of the patients and their evolution.

[15] describes that the RA is capable of providing experiences of learning outside the classroom, more contextualized, uniting links between reality and the situation of learning in which students participate, stating that any physical space can become a stage Academic stimulant. [16, 17] presents the progress made in the design of an author tool, called AuthorAR, oriented towards the creation of educational activities by the teacher, based on augmented reality (RA). This application allows generating exploration and structuring activities of phrases, which can favor the acquisition processes of the language and communication training. Also It is suggested that most of the projects studied augmented reality present a particular interest, given its application to the 'educational environment and to people with some type of disability in particular, but none of these applications is especially oriented to the creation of activities educational.

3   Our Approach

For what is the development of the application makes use of the Vuforia program for the creation of data base where they are staying the different objectives that will be included in the Image Target and to generate the activation key of the application that subsequently use in Unity. In Unity is exported the objectives of the database and adds in the prefabs Image Target in which the 3D elements, with this we have a way to fund the selected image where it is displayed objects.

To carry out stage of animation, there are models that we can find them already with your animations which you must specify where and when to run the animation for this we rely of the programming language that uses Unity, the language C# (pronounced C-sharp), an industry-standard language similar to Java or C, one can say that is a programming oriented to objects which by means of algorithms we insert the animation of each one.

The audio was introduced to supplement, by means of an algorithm which detects the image and plays the sound corresponding to it.

Finally all tested from the computer is the next step to the creation of the application on the Android operating system, it is done directly from Unity by configuring the application name, logo or a characteristic image of the same and the minimum system in which you can run and chose Android 4.4 and later for reasons of stability which was considered doing their respective field trials. In Fig. 1 shows the process of conditioning. The prefabs used in Unity are shown in Fig. 2. And the attributes of the images objectives are presented in Fig. 3.

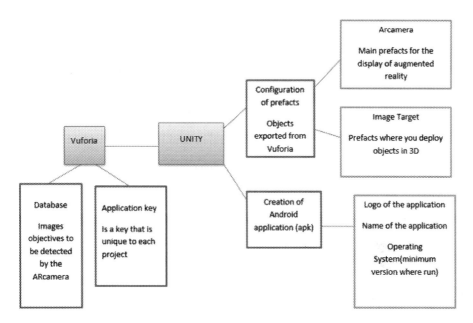

Fig. 1. Conditioning of software.

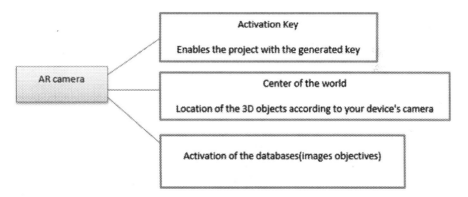

Fig. 2. Prefabs AR camera.

For the detection of images the database created in vuforia is used, previously the image is loaded using natural patterns of the target image as shown in Fig. 4.

The Algorithm 1 defines the trajectory that the object "Bullet" will follow; If bullet crash with the object "enemy" the object position changes and generates a call to object "explosion". So that we have the follow algorithm.

Algorithm 1 : Shooting behavior
1: speed=10, explosion, bullet;
2: bullet=V(0,0,1)*speed*Time;
3: destroy objetc
4: **If** collide with "enemy" **then** ;
5:     enemy = random(V2(1,0,1));
6:     Instantiate explosion ;

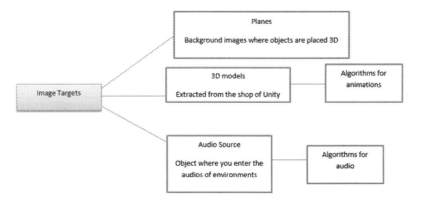

Fig. 3. Image Targets.

Fig. 4. Patterns of image.

"Bullet" variable represents the 3D object of a tank bullet; "Enemy" is a tag assigned to an object that is represented by the enemy tank; "explosion" is an object that is displayed when a coalition occurs.

An inconvenience was generated in the use of the virtual button, it was sought to generate a shot at a time when it is pressed, however, the result was a burst of projectiles being fired either when this was pressed or kept in action; so a solution was arrived at by taking, the concept of bistable circuit RS was used to achieve that when pressing the button, only one bullet leaves the tank.

The next-state equation of a SR flip-flop is given by the following function.

$$Q^{t+1} = S + \bar{R}Q^t \tag{1}$$

Algorithm 2: Virtual Button

1: control =0,variable=1;
2: **If** button == on **then**
3:     control=0,variable=1;
4: **Else**
5:     control=1;
6: **Return** control;
7: **Return** variable;

We use two local flags "control" and "variable" that send their states according of virtual button activation; the variables values will be used in the shooting algorithm.

Algorithm 3: Shooting

1: c1,c2,a;
2: c2=control;
3: **If** a=0 **then**
4:     c1=variable;
5:     **If** c1=1 and c2 =0 **then**
6:         instantiate shooting ;
7:         c2=2;
8:         a=1;
9:     **If** c2 =1 **then**
10:        a=0;

In the Algorithm 3 we use "c1", "c2" and "a" flags and the variable "c1" takes "variable" flag value; "c2" takes "control" variable value; To execute the shooting action the condition c1 = 1 and c2 = 0 should occurs that guarantees the shoot of only one projectile every time when the virtual button is pushed.

Algorithm 4: Audio

1:Audio;
2: **If** image target = detected or tracked or extended tracked **then**
3:     Audio = play;
4:**Else**
5:     Audio = stop;

We introduce an audio track in mp3 format that contains a war conflict environment; when the scene image is detected this track is played.

Algorithm 5: Shooting behavior

1: speed, enemy, initial ,final;
2: enemy=V(0,0,1)*speed*Time;
3: reset objetc ;
4:**If** enemy(1,0,0)<=final;
5:     enemy = V2(initial,0,random());

The Algorithm 5 shows the behavior of the enemies that move randomly in the field. The coordinate's values and the velocity are modified; also, the region where the enemies are created is delimited.

Enemy object is created and a movement vector in the Z axis is assigned. Using velocity and time the object is positioned randomly along of Z axis if the condition of the final variable is true.

4   Results and Discussion

This section shows images of the application developed running on Android operating system. Algorithms results will be visualize interacting together through three dimensional objects.

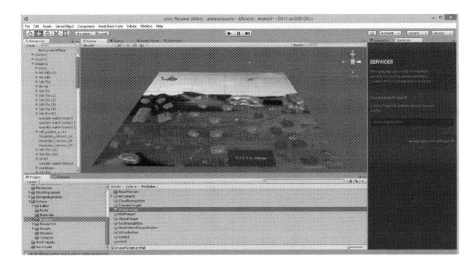

Fig. 5. Unity development environment

The Fig. 5 shows Unity development environment which is used to realize war conflict animation; The environment has like components 3D objects and the target will be recognize by the mobile device camera for later create the corresponding animation.

Fig. 6. Display of the war field

He Fig. 6 shows user and physic image interaction which is executed at the moment when the camera is focused on the image.

Fig. 7. Detection and tracking of objects

Figure 7 shows from different vision angles the objects with more details when the device approximates to the scene image.

In Fig. 8 the user interacts with the virtual button that initiates the simulation.

Video results are provided on https://www.youtube.com/watch?v=o3iNL7agedQ.

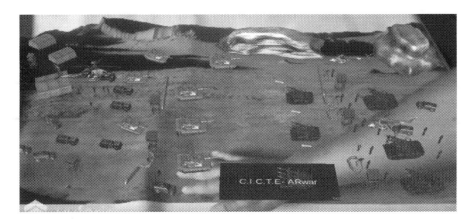

Fig. 8. Physical and virtual world interaction

5   Conclusions and Future Work

The detection and tracking algorithms of Vuforia make possible the digital object scaling according the physic image size where the scene is visualized. With this way we can appreciate objects details according the distance and focusing angle.

The application was tested on android platform and we guarantee a optimum performance for upper versions to Android 4.2. Also we recommend use on devices with RAM memory upper to 1 G. For the installation 87 Mb of space memory is necessary.

In the future we propose implement artificial intelligence algorithms that allow simulate tactical operations. Also different modeled scenes in 3D can be implemented to have more realism.

The implementation of a graphic interface of user will give us the control of different tactics operations scenes in real time, and improves the human computer interaction like [18–20].

References

1. Aguilar, W.G., Abad, V., Ruiz, H., Aguilar, J., Aguilar-Castillo, F.: RRT-based path planning for virtual bronchoscopy simulator. In: De Paolis, L.T., Bourdot, P., Mongelli, A. (eds.) AVR 2017. LNCS, vol. 10325, pp. 155–165. Springer, Cham (2017). https://doi.org/10.1007/978-3-319-60928-7_13
2. Aguilar, W.G., Morales, S., Ruiz, H., Abad, V.: RRT* GL based path planning for virtual aerial navigation. In: De Paolis, L.T., Bourdot, P., Mongelli, A. (eds.) AVR 2017. LNCS, vol. 10324, pp. 176–184. Springer, Cham (2017). https://doi.org/10.1007/978-3-319-60922-5_13
3. Aguilar, W.G., Morales, S.: 3D environment mapping using the kinect V2 and path planning based on RRT algorithms. Electronics 5(4), 70 (2016)

4. Aguilar, W.G., Morales, S., Ruiz, H., Abad, V.: RRT* GL based optimal path planning for real-time navigation of UAVs. In: Rojas, I., Joya, G., Catala, A. (eds.) IWANN 2017. LNCS, vol. 10306, pp. 585–595. Springer, Cham (2017). https://doi.org/10.1007/978-3-319-59147-6_50

5. Livingston, M.A., Rosenblum, L.J., Julier, S.J., Brown, D., Baillot, Y., Swan II, J.E., Gabbard, J.L., Hix, D.: An augmented reality system for military operations in urban terrain. In: Proceedings of Interservice/Industry Training, Simulation & Education Conference (I/ITSEC), Orlando, Florida, 2–5 December, p. 89 (abstract only) (2002)

6. Hicks, J., Flanagan, R., Petrov, P., Stoyen, A.: Eyekon: Distributed Augmented Reality for Soldier Teams. © Copyright 21st Century Systems, Inc. (2003)

7. Juhnke, J., Kallish, A., Delaney, D., Dziedzic, K., Chou, R., Chapel, T.: Tanagram Partners. Final Project Report. Aiding Complex Decision Making through Augmented Reality: iARM, an Intelligent Augmented Reality Model (2010)

8. Quintero, A.: Augmented reality on the battlefield, October 2013. http://gglassday.com/3103/la-realidad-aumentada-en-el-campo-de-batalla/

9. Callejas, M., Quiroga, J., Alarcón, A.: Interactive environment for tourist sites, implementing augmented reality layar. Technological University of Bogotá

10. Perez, C.P.: Virtual reality: a real contribution for the evaluation and treatment of people with intellectual disability, Santiago (2008)

11. García, R.: Serious games with augmented reality for evaluation and rehabilitation of persons with disabilities (2012)

12. Aguilar, W.G., Rodríguez, G.A., Álvarez, L., Sandoval, S., Quisaguano, F., Limaico, A.: Real-time 3D modeling with a RGB-D camera and on-board processing. In: De Paolis, L.T., Bourdot, P., Mongelli, A. (eds.) AVR 2017. LNCS, vol. 10325, pp. 410–419. Springer, Cham (2017). https://doi.org/10.1007/978-3-319-60928-7_35

13. Aguilar, W.G., Rodríguez, G.A., Álvarez, L., Sandoval, S., Quisaguano, F., Limaico, A.: Visual SLAM with a RGB-D camera on a quadrotor UAV using on-board processing. In: Rojas, I., Joya, G., Catala, A. (eds.) IWANN 2017. LNCS, vol. 10306, pp. 596–606. Springer, Cham (2017). https://doi.org/10.1007/978-3-319-59147-6_51

14. Aguilar, W.G., Rodríguez, G.A., Álvarez, L., Sandoval, S., Quisaguano, F., Limaico, A.: On-board visual SLAM on a UGV using a RGB-D camera. In: Huang, Y., Wu, H., Liu, H., Yin, Z. (eds.) ICIRA 2017. LNCS (LNAI), vol. 10464, pp. 298–308. Springer, Cham (2017). https://doi.org/10.1007/978-3-319-65298-6_28

15. Carracedo, J., Martínez, C.L.: Augmented Reality: An Alternative, Nicaragua (2012)

16. Moralejo, L., Sanz, C.V., Pesado, P., Baldassarri, S.: Advances in the design of an author tool for the creation of educational activities based on augmented reality. Sedici, La Plata (2014)

17. Kato, H., Blanding, R., Azuma, R.: Image processing and the Artoolkit. Osgart project, Artoolworks

18. Orbea, D., Moposita, J., Aguilar, W.G., Paredes, M., León, G., Jara-Olmedo, A.: Math model of UAV multi rotor prototype with fixed wing aerodynamic structure for a flight simulator. In: De Paolis, L.T., Bourdot, P., Mongelli, A. (eds.) AVR 2017. LNCS, vol. 10324, pp. 199–211. Springer, Cham (2017). https://doi.org/10.1007/978-3-319-60922-5_15

19. Aguilar, W.G., Angulo, C.: Real-time model-based video stabilization for microaerial vehicles. Neural Process. Lett. **43**(2), 459–477 (2016)

20. Aguilar, W.G., Angulo, C.: Real-time video stabilization without phantom movements for micro aerial vehicles. EURASIP J. Image Video Process. **1**, 1–13 (2014)

Development of Practical Tasks in Physics with Elements of Augmented Reality for Secondary Educational Institutions

Yevgeniya Daineko, Madina Ipalakova, Dana Tsoy[(✉)],
Akmedi Shaipiten, Zhiger Bolatov, and Tolganay Chinibayeva

Department of Computer Engineering and Telecommunication,
International IT University, 050040 Almaty, Kazakhstan
{yevgeniyadaineko, m.ipalakova, danatsoy, ahiko.dk,
zhiger.ali, ttemirbolatova}@gmail.com

Abstract. The current work demonstrates the use of augmented reality technology for the development of an application that can be employed as an additional teaching tool within physics in secondary educational institutions in Kazakhstan. The application contains a set of problem tasks in "Mechanics". The physical processes within tasks are visualized with help of augmented reality and this helps pupils to imagine and understand deeper the studied phenomena. One of the advantages and distinctive features of the developed application is that it provides the user interface in Kazakh, Russian and English languages. This corresponds to the multilingual policy adopted by the government of the country. In the article the existing analogs worldwide are presented, development software is described and the main results of the project are discussed.

Keywords: Physics · Augmented reality · Secondary education

1 Introduction

Nowadays, it is hard to think about modern education without employing information and communication technologies (ICT) that evolves at a rapid pace. Not only higher, but secondary and even primary educational institutions apply ICT within the educational process.

Today any teacher has many opportunities to use various ICT tools during classes, such as the Internet, electronic books, dictionaries and directories, presentations, software, communication means like chats, forums, blogs, electronic mail, teleconferences, webinars and much more. Besides, application of ICT helps teachers to:

- continuously motivate pupils;
- activate cognitive abilities;
- attract passive pupils;
- accelerate educational process;
- provide up-to-date materials;
- teach pupils to work with different sources of information;

© Springer International Publishing AG, part of Springer Nature 2018
L. T. De Paolis and P. Bourdot (Eds.): AVR 2018, LNCS 10850, pp. 404–412, 2018.
https://doi.org/10.1007/978-3-319-95270-3_34

- promote research activities;
- provide flexibility of education process.

Among the software for schools different types of virtual laboratories are worth to be mentioned. They allow not only observing, but conducting virtual experiments of various subjects [1]. Simple animations are also useful tools that can be used by pupils for deeper understanding of studied processes and phenomena. And the augmented reality (AR) is one of the technologies for developing such interactive applications. They can be used by teachers within lessons as an additional tool for visualization of the material explained.

The area of application of software with augmented reality involved is very wide. For example, with help of such programs it is possible to conduct complex physical or chemical experiments in real time absolutely safe. On the geography lesson the maps in textbooks become "alive" and are able to move showing how countries' boundaries or population are changing in time. Also there is a chance to travel across the wonders of the world sitting in class. It is possible to study historical battles or play a role of a soldier. Descriptive video onto complex biological schemas can help understand and remember studied material easily. In such countries like USA and Japan the lessons with the use of augmented reality technology have been being conducted already for a long time. The surveys show that as a result of such classes pupils are more involved into the educational process and master new material easier.

In the article the authors present a computer application that allows solving a set of practical tasks in physics, section "Mechanics". The application is implemented using the technology of augmented reality and is designed for secondary educational institutions. The application is developed at the Department of Computer Engineering and Telecommunication of the International Information Technology University, Almaty, Kazakhstan.

2   Related Works in the Field of Development and Introduction of Computer Learning Systems Based on the Augmented Reality

Modern technologies evolve very fast and nowadays the term "Augmented reality" is not fiction. AR technology is able to change the notion of the modern world and make it more convenient and interactive. The fields of application of this technology are quite wide: medicine, warfare, education, public services, etc.

In the present article the use of augmented reality in education is shown. It is generally known that human brain perceives visual images better, rather than just text. A lot of research exists [2, 3], which shows that AR technology in education enriches visual and contextual learning, improving the content of information. During lectures only 25% of information is retained, but if visual support is used 80% of information can be perceived. As a result of these studies, it turned out that application of augmented reality in education is beneficial for all people and for children especially.

Below several examples of foreign experience in using AR in education are presented.

In [4] the application of mobile augmented reality in teaching physics is shown. The obtained results showed that the using of this technology by physics teachers is rather effective. Besides, it allows developing skills to teach natural sciences in the modern world of digital technologies.

In [5] the authors studied the problem of merging of their own devices and the technology of augmented reality in education. It is shown that the use of this integration allows increasing the quality of teaching of pupils and students in any institutions at any level of education.

In [6] the application of AR technology in teaching natural sciences for pupils of 7th grade of a private college was studied. According to the teachers and pupils opinion studying the subjects with this technology was pleasant, easy and useful.

In [7] the use of AR technology in math studying and exactly in studying of solids rotation was considered. The authors are convinced in advantages that AR technology provides for math studying and intend to use it for explaining the calculations of volume of rotation solids and other problems. In future the application of the technology will be widen in developing skills of spatial visualization.

The main idea in [8] is the investigation of the impact of AR on improving students' performance and their physiological state. The second year students took part in the research. They studied the course "Presentation of information on computers" using the AR technology and the Internet. The results showed that both technologies contributed to improving of students' performance.

The article [9] is about using AR technology to support "Software" course and to test various studied effects with help of interactive on-line and AR teaching strategies. The obtained results showed the potential of using AR methods for increasing students' motivation and for interaction between peers. It was concluded that when introducing of AR applications into the course, technology developers must carefully study the teaching target audience, information volume depicted on the screen of mobile phone and accessibility of training equipment and audience environment in order to archive appropriate teaching scenarios.

In [10] the efficiency of using AR technology on lectures is shown. It is demonstrated that AR has a positive effect on students learning process, increases their self-esteem and motivation.

In such a way, training software with the use of AR technology is a promising tool with completely new visualization possibilities.

3   Software Support of the Project

The main criteria for choosing the development tool for creating the application for teaching physics with help of AR technology were speed of project development, the quality of visualization and cheap cost.

3D graphics is used to display models, processes and phenomena. And as a development tool Unity 3D was chosen.

Unity 3D is a cross-platform engine for the development of interactive application with real-time graphics. This engine is most common among developers of 3D large-scale games. It has its own editor; the programming language C# is used for the development. This allows creating applications that display complex physical processes. The development process of 3D environments is object-oriented, which means environment creation is divided into objects with behavior. The engine is implemented using C++ language, and this fact makes it fast and productive.

The Unity 3D engine meets the following requirements:

- the end product is a multimedia 3D object, embedded into an HTML page;
- the end product is an object of high level of abstraction of object prototypes;
- high quality of graphical presentation of information;
- the library of 3D objects can work with many formats of modern 3D graphics, such as *.3ds, *.dae, *.fbx, *.flt;
- the support of high level languages (C++, C#, Java);
- the license for free use for non-commercial purposes;
- the editor for software and graphical objects development;
- the possibility to connect third-party object libraries.

The Vuforia library was chosen for the realization of augmented reality functions. The library is cross-platform and free, it allows performing visual search. Vuforia simplifies scanning target object using the built-in scanner Vuforia Object Scanner. Also it is possible to include virtual buttons and map additional elements with help of OpenGL. The library is cross-platform, which means the application can be used on any device. And the time for the development of the versions is minimal.

Free license decreases the cost of project realization, which is important factor during the project implementation.

Also Vuforia allows creating various visual effects, like night vision or X-rays simulation. Another useful feature of this library is that it is possible to play video on any given surface. Occlusion control in Vuforia allows tracking objects even if they are visible only partially.

Thus, Vuforia library provides all the necessary functionality and fully justifies its use in the project.

4 Main Scientific Results

As a result of the project implementation in the International Information Technology University at the Department of Computer Engineering and Telecommunication an application with a set of practical tasks in physics for secondary educational institutions is developed. The tasks are realized with elements of augmented reality. The application meets all the requirements for such type of systems, provides realization of large number of complex effects; has simple but functional design and user-friendly interface.

One of the distinctive features of the current application is its three-language interface. A user is able to choose Kazakh, Russian or English language to interact with the system. In Fig. 1 the main window of the application with English language interface is shown.

The main idea of the current work is the development of animated tasks in physics of school curriculum, which would be closest to the real world. The problem tasks for

Fig. 1. Main window of the application with English language interface

the application were chosen in cooperation with the physics teacher of the Republican Physics and Mathematics School (Almaty, Kazakhstan). The tasks are taken from the pool of tasks for Olympiad in physics and require additional visual support for better understanding. The problem visualization along with its given solution allows pupils to understand thoroughly the physical nature of the studied processes and will facilitate solving similar problems independently in future. Also the application allows pupils to take part in the simulation, not only to passively observe it. He or she can change the tasks parameters, and in such a way examine the process in different conditions. Thus, visual demonstration of how the task elements depend on the physical parameters makes the material easier to understand (Fig. 3).

Besides, the tasks are implemented with 3D scenes, so that experiments are shown in space. A user can control an experiment by him/herself by modeling various situations of its conducting. For example, he/she is able to move in space of a task and watch its simulation from any position or angle of view. It helps to perceive and assimilate the material. A keyboard and a camera are used to control the simulation and rotate the 3D scenes in different directions. Also it is possible to zoom out the objects for more detailed observation. The dialog window is refreshed when a view point and position are changed. The visual representation is the main advantage of the application, which provides visibility and quick assimilation of the material. Moreover, in the application it is possible to make mathematical calculations of experiments within problem tasks.

Let us consider the problem task, which is presented in Fig. 2.

After a user has chosen the problem task above, its camera is turned on and needs to be pointed on a special marker. A scene with problem task simulation will appear on the screen (Fig. 3). At the beginning a stone and two textboxes appear. Using them it is possible to set the velocity and the angle of the stone throw. The simulation changes depending on these parameters.

After the parameters of the task are set, using the key U on the keyboard it is possible to throw the stone. The directions of the velocity and stone gravitational force

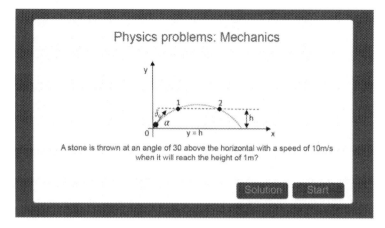

Fig. 2. The application screenshot with a problem task

Fig. 3. The application screenshot with the problem task simulation at the starting point

are displayed using arrows on the next scene. Also the angle of the stone throw appears. Since the solution of the problem is the time after which the stone reaches a certain height, in the scene after the throw the points where this height is reached are marked and the time is shown (Fig. 4). After the simulation using the keyboard it is possible to proceed to the problem task solution.

The main feature of the developed application is visualization using augmented reality. This approach makes pupils involved in experiments and the game form of the application allows delivering material in a simple and easy way (Fig. 5). Besides, such experiments will be much better mastered thanks to the interaction of the application virtual elements and real physical objects.

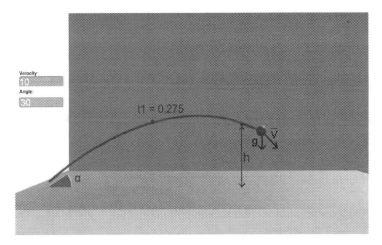

Fig. 4. The application screenshot with the problem task simulation at the end point

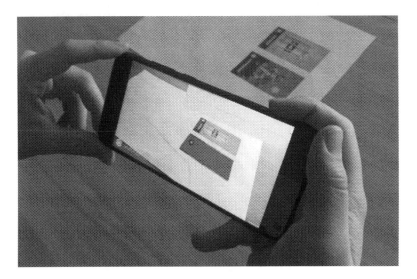

Fig. 5. Demonstration of the developed application

In the application there is an access to the set of problem tasks from "Mechanics" section so far. Currently 12 problem tasks are implemented. The problem tasks from "Electricity" and "Optics" sections are under the development right now and will be added to the application in the near future. New problem tasks can be easily integrated into the application. All the tasks are taken from the physics course of a secondary school curriculum. Each task contains an animated scene and a solution.

For each problem task a separate 3D model was created and a physical engine was implemented. The engine calculates the interaction of the model's objects. The models were realized in Blender, and the main functionality is implemented in C#.

In Fig. 6 the component diagram of the application developed is displayed. All the components can be divided into 3 groups: (1) starting point; (2) problem tasks – main components; (3) additional components, which are problem tasks solutions. The main project part is a set of 12 problem tasks. Each problem has an access to the shared collection of 3D objects. Besides, all the problem tasks follow the common structure of classes.

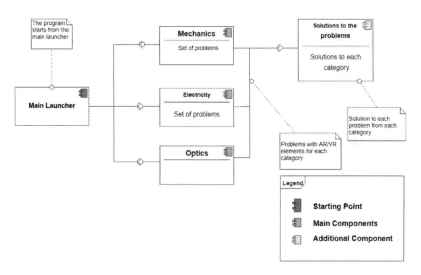

Fig. 6. The component diagram of the application

5   Conclusion

The efficiency of the developed application was estimated in the following way. 20 pupils of the 9th grade of the RFMW were interviewed. The question was "Is the application with augmented reality effective supplementary learning tool to study physics?". The results of the interview are presented in the Table 1.

Table 1. The results of the interview

Possible answer	Percentage of pupils
Not effective at all	1,2
Rather not effective	3,7
Do not know	6,1
Rather effective	27,4
Very effective	61,6

The interview shows that 89% of the respondents believe that the developed application is effective and convenient in use. The pupils noted that such application increase the interest in physics in general.

In such a way, new information technologies open wide perspectives for improving the quality of education. Such technologies like Augmented Reality allow transforming the process of solving traditional physical problem tasks into an interactive game. Thus, pupils become more involved into the studied process. Such visualization helps in understanding the problem and solving it. And as a long-term result pupils become more motivated and interested in the subject in general.

The authors continue to work on the current project and develop new animated problem tasks from other physics sections to be integrated into the application.

Acknowledgments. The work was done under the funding of the Ministry of Education and Science of the Republic of Kazakhstan (No. AP05135692).

References

1. Daineko, Y., Dmitriyev, V., Ipalakova, M.: Using virtual laboratories in teaching natual sciences: an example of physics courses in University. Comput. Appl. Eng. Educ. **25**(1), 39–47 (2017). https://doi.org/10.1002/cae.2177
2. Nesloney, T.: Augmented Reality Brings New Dimensions to Learning [Electronic resource]. http://www.edutopia.org/blog/augmented-reality-new-dimensions-learning-drew-minock. Accessed 30 Mar 2018
3. Mitra, A.: U Dopolnennoi Realnosti problem s Otobrazheniyem (in Russian) [Electronic resource]. http://holographica.space/articles/blippar-1774. Accessed 30 Mar 2018
4. Craciun, D., Bunoiu, M.: Boosting physics education through mobile augmented reality. In: TIM1 Physics Conference, AIP Conference Proceedings, vol. 1916, p. 050003 (2017). https://doi.org/10.1063/1.5017456
5. Sanchez-Garcia, J.M., Toledo-Morales, P.: Converging technologies for teaching: Augmented Reality, BYOD, Flipped Classroom. Red-Revista de Educacion a Distancia **55**, 5–15 (2017)
6. Karagozlu, D., Ozdamli, F.: Student opinions on mobile augmented reality application and developed content in science class. TEM J. **6**(4), 660–670 (2017)
7. Salinas, P., González-Mendívil, E.: Augmented reality and solids of revolution. Int. J. Interact. Des. Manuf. **11**(4), 829–837 (2017)
8. Giasiranis, S., Sofos, L.: Flow experience and educational effectiveness of teaching informatics using AR. Educ. Technol. Soc. **20**(4), 78–88 (2017)
9. Wang, Y.H.: Using augmented reality to support a software editing course for college students. J. Comput. Assist. Learn. **55**(5), 532–546 (2017)
10. Mumtaz, K., et al.: An e-assessment framework for blended learning with augmented reality to enhance the student learning. EURASIA J. Math. Sci. Technol. Educ. **13**(8), 4419–4436 (2017)

ARtour: Augmented Reality-Based Game to Promote Agritourism

Juan Garzón[1(✉)], Juan Acevedo[1], Juan Pavón[2], and Silvia Baldiris[3]

[1] Catholic University of the East, Rionegro, Colombia
{fgarzon,jacevedo}@uco.edu.co
[2] Complutense University of Madrid, Madrid, Spain
jpavon@gfdi.ucm.es
[3] International University of La Rioja, La Rioja, Spain
Silvia.baldiris@unir.net

Abstract. Agritourism is an extension of ecotourism, which encourages visitors to experience agricultural life at firsthand. The growing interest in this industry worldwide poses new challenges to the environment. Traditional tourism models have somehow endangered local biodiversity and, consequently, it is necessary to promote new models that include education. Eco-education is commonly conducted through passive learning approaches within educational institutions, which often result in poor student performance in real life. Therefore, it is necessary to generate active methodologies to enrich learning experiences. Augmented Reality holds the power to add multiple benefits to the learning processes. Accordingly, this study introduces "ARtour". ARtour combines an Augmented Reality experience with on-site experiences to learn about agritourism while encourages tourists to maintain responsible environmental behavior. The project considers two outdoor learning scenarios: aquaponics and subsistence crops. We posit that ARtour will enhance outdoor learning experiences and will be a useful guide to promote agritourism.

Keywords: Agritourism · Augmented reality · Eco-education
Ecotourism

1 Introduction

Agritourism is form of ecological tourism of growing interest around the world. It includes a wide variety of activities such as farm stays, bed-and-breakfast, pick-your-own produce, agricultural festivals, farm tours, and others [1]. Weaver and Fennell [2] provided a widely accepted definition of agritourism as rural enterprises which incorporates both a working farm environment and a commercial tourism component. This industry has experienced a rapid growth in the last two decades [3], posing new opportunities and challenges for natural and social environments. If properly planned and implemented, agritourism can generate positive impacts on nature and communities. Among other benefits of agritourism, we can find income generation, employment opportunities, a stronger economy, and environmental education. Some studies have

L. T. De Paolis and P. Bourdot (Eds.): AVR 2018, LNCS 10850, pp. 413–422, 2018.
https://doi.org/10.1007/978-3-319-95270-3_35

found that farmers who participate in agritourism activities are likely to obtain higher income levels than farmers who do not undertake such activities [4–6].

However, like other forms of tourism, environmental degradation is a potential problem of agritourism, which highlights the need to promote sustainable tourism models [7–9]. These models aim to ensure the balance between economic development and nature conservation and must include eco-education as an important component [10].

Eco-education is present in educational programs around the world. However, it is often conducted through passive teaching methodologies within the classrooms and occasional field trips are reduced to a sightseeing. These strategies do not encourage students to develop interest for ecological education, which usually results on poor student performance in real life [11, 12]. Many studies have found that learning processes become more significant when students develop feelings on the subjects they are taught [13–15]. That is, for knowledge to be meaningful for students, they need to feel motivated and develop emotional attachment. Therefore, it is important to consider active teaching methodologies that enhance real environment experiences to support the learning processes.

Augmented Reality (AR) is an important technology that has been successfully implemented in many fields [16, 17]. This technology helps enrich education by transforming passive learning materials into interactive multimedia learning materials [18–21]. Since the integration of AR technologies into mobile devices [22], the development of AR applications to support learning has rapidly increased and has effectively taken root in educational settings [21, 23, 24]. Caudell and Mizell [25] introduced the term "Augmented Reality" to describe the group of technologies that allow users to augment the visual field through the use of heads-up display technologies. However, current AR systems involve not only the sense of sight but also all the other senses. In this way, Akçayir and Akçayir [23] proposed a wider definition of AR as a technology that overlays virtual objects into the real world.

The integration of AR systems into educational environments, provides multiple benefits that have been identified by different studies. These studies have concluded that learning gains and motivation are the two most reported advantages of AR systems for education [19, 21, 23]. Another important advantage reported by the studies, has to do with the fact that the integration of AR systems into mobile devices favors "mobile learning" [24]. Mobile learning allows learning processes to be carried out in outdoor learning environments, providing learners with different strategies to acquire the knowledge.

This paper presents an Augmented Reality-based game to promote agritourism named "ARtour". The project is in an early stage of development and includes the design, implementation and validation of the system through outdoor learning experiences at the final stage. ARtour is a wise farmer, who introduces basic concepts of agritourism and at the same time encourages tourists to maintain responsible environmental behavior. In addition, this research proposes to identify the impact of the ARtour system on the users learning effectiveness, addressing the following research questions (RQ):

RQ1: What is the effect of an augmented reality-based educational game on users learning gains in real-world observations?

RQ2: Are there statistically significant differences in the users' motivation according to the learning scenario they use?

RQ3: What is the degree of user satisfaction after using the ARtour application in outdoor learning scenarios?

The project considers two outdoor learning scenarios: (1) Aquaponics and, (2) Subsistence crops. To evaluate the effectiveness of the system, we propose two case studies (one per learning scenario). To identify the effect of an augmented reality-based educational game on users learning gains (RQ1), we propose to evaluate the Effect Size (ES) of ARtour on the learning effectiveness of the users. In this context, learning effectiveness is defined as the improvement in a user's learning between the beginning and the end of the intervention through the AR application. Likewise, "user" refers to the "tourist" who participates in the field trip. To evaluate users' motivation (RQ2) we propose the motivational measurement instrument Instructional Materials Motivation Survey (IMMS) [27]. Finally, to measure the degree of user satisfaction, we propose a satisfaction survey that uses a 7-point Likert scale.

2   Related Work

Many studies have found that the integration of AR systems into educational environments adds multiple benefits to teaching-learning processes. A literature review study conducted by Garzón et al. [21], analyzed 50 studies published between 2011 and 2017 (40 case studies and 10 literature review studies. This review analyzed the reported advantages and challenges of AR systems for education. Likewise, the study identified the most common target groups as well as the most common fields of education in the studies. The review found that the most reported advantages are learning gains and motivation and the most reported challenges is that AR systems are difficult for students to use. Regarding target group, the study found that most studies are focused on students from primary education, secondary education, or bachelor education. In contrast, there are some target groups such as vocational education students that have not been considered in the studies. As for fields of education, the study found that AR is most applied to teach subjects related to Natural Sciences or Mathematics. On the other hand, some fields of education such as Agriculture and Forestry have not been considered in the studies. Another important finding of the review is that only one study included aids for users with particular needs, which represents a stepback in terms of social inclusion. However, although Natural Sciences is the most common field of education in AR systems, most of these applications are related to physics, chemistry, anatomy, and biology. In contrast, applications related to eco-education are limited in number [12, 28–30], and none is related to agriculture or forestry.

3   ARtour

3.1   Concept of the Project

ARtour is a game based on AR technologies that promotes agritourism while encourages tourists to maintain responsible environmental behavior. By using ARtour, tourists will be the protagonists of an adventure that will immerse them in a journey of exploration. They will have the opportunity to learn and discover about the treasures that are hidden in Colombian landscapes. ARtour (Fig. 1), a wise farmer who represents the spirit of Colombian farmers, will guide this trip. He will provide users with the information and instructions to interact with the platform on which the experience is developed.

Fig. 1. ARtour, the wise spirit of Colombian farmers

The objective is to involve users in a story with the mission of learning about agritourism activities. They will be the protagonists of the mission and will assume an active role throughout the learning adventure. It is an immersive experience that seeks to impact users, so that they are motivated to take this experience to another level.

3.2   Description

When executing the application for the first time, the user is received by ARtour who presents himself as the guide of the experience and names the user "Explorer". ARtour is a wise farmer with the ability to communicate in multiple ways such as speech, images, texts and sounds. ARtour's guidance will allow the explorer to know beforehand the principles of agritourism and the rules that must be followed to be environmentally responsible.

The video game will involve the Explorer into a wonderful interactive audiovisual journey that stimulates his/her senses and mind. Unimaginable sounds, fantastic animals, and colorful flora are part of biodiversity that are presented in this amazing expedition. At the end of each stage of the trip, in addition to the experience and knowledge that has been collected, the Explorer becomes the creditor of a representative virtual piece. The Explorer accumulates virtual pieces as a reward which are added to a piggy bank. Each piece has a magical power and can be used to access other digital content to learn additional information about the treasures of Colombian agriculture.

4 Learning Scenarios

The ARtour project comprises two initial learning scenarios: (1) Aquaponics and (2) subsistence crops. Further projects will expand the experience, including other forms of agriculture.

4.1 Aquaponics

Aquaponics combines aquaculture (raising fish) and hydroponics (the cultivation of plants without soil) to produce fish and plants together in a single integrated system [31]. The implementation of these systems in Colombia increased over the last decade and became an important component of Colombian government's intention to increase food self-sufficiency of farmers.

It is estimated that the volume of production varies between 25–35 kg/month of fish and between 45–50 kg/1.5 month of vegetables for an aquaponic system of 16 m^2. This supposes a large extent of the monthly food requirement of a family of 4–6 people. Furthermore, surplus production volumes can be marketed to generate additional revenue.

ARtour gives the Explorers basic information about the main functions of an aquaponic system. The trip consists of four stages. The first stage explains basic information about aquaculture. The second stage explains basic information about hydroponic systems. The third stage explains how these two systems are integrated into a single system and, finally, the fourth stage gives important information about the rules of responsible behavior to apply when interacting with this type of system. When the Explorer finishes the experience, he/she can exchange the accumulated credit into new information. This information is related to the process of construction of aquaponic systems.

4.2 Subsistence Crops

Subsistence agriculture is a self-sufficiency farming system that farmers grow to use or eat themselves and their families, rather than to sell [32]. According to the Food and Agriculture Organization (FAO) of the United Nations, Colombia is one of the countries with the greatest potential for expanding land for agricultural use in the world. Accordingly, the Colombian government and the former guerrilla group of the Farc, presented a plan that seeks to replace 50000 hectares of illicit crops with subsistence crops. This initiative has to objectives: (1) to reduce the number of illicit crops in Colombia and (2) to secure food self-sufficiency of Colombian farmers.

ARtour gives the Explorers basic information about the main functions of a Subsistence crop. The trip consists of four stages. The first stage explains basic information about subsistence agriculture. The second stage explains what type of food can be grown in a subsistence crop according to the climatic conditions and the size of the crop. The third stage gives important information about the rules of responsible behavior to apply when interacting with this type of system. When the Explorer finishes the experience, he/she can exchange the accumulated credit into new information. This information is related to the process implementing urban subsistence crops.

5   Case Studies

We propose to conduct two case studies, one per learning scenario, each of which will be carried out in a locality of the province of Antioquia, Colombia. To assess the effectiveness of the system, we propose a quasi-experimental research structure that includes quantitative and qualitative methods.

5.1   Participants

Each case study will adopt vocational education students as a target group. Vocational education students refers to students who have finished secondary school but are not willing to enroll in a university [33]. These students have been labeled as promising research partners for validation and for demonstrating the possibilities of AR learning scenarios [34]. However, as many literature review studies have reported [20, 21, 23], these students have barely been taken into account as a target group in AR applications. The study by Garzón et al. [21], emphasizes the importance of the inclusion of these unexplored target groups to benefit such students from the affordances that AR systems adds to the learning processes.

Each case study will have an approximate number of 50 students and will be made up of experimental and control groups. Both groups will be trained by the same instructor to eliminate the confounding factors on the experimental results of different personalities, teaching styles, and teaching methods [35].

5.2   Experimental Instruments

The search includes as experimental instruments the pre-test, the post-test, the motivational measurement instrument IMMS, and the satisfaction survey. The pre-test aims to identify previous knowledge of users about agritourism. This test is taken by students from experimental and control groups. Users of both groups take the post-test at the end of the experience. This test aims to identify the knowledge acquired by users after having been trained by either of the two methodologies. The credibility of both the pre-test and the posttest, will be assessed using the Kuder-Richardson reliability formula.

To assess the impact of the learning approaches on the students' learning motivation, we propose the motivational measurement instrument IMMS. It includes 36 questions in 4 subscales, scored using a 5-point Likert scale. Each level ranges from "strongly disagree" (1) to "strongly agree" (5). The main components in the IMMS are attention, relevance, confidence, and satisfaction. Finally, the satisfaction survey aims to measure the degree of user satisfaction when using the ARtour application.

It consists of 10 statements that used a 7-point Likert scale. Each level ranges from "strongly disagree" (1) to "strongly agree" (7).

6 Results

As explained above, the project is at an early stage. Therefore, this section does not present obtained results but results that are expected after the validation of the project.

6.1 RQ1: What Is the Effect of an Augmented Reality-Based Educational Game on Users Learning Gains in Real-World Observations?

To guarantee equivalent prior knowledge of the students in the experimental and control groups, a t-test is proposed in terms of their pre-test grades. Next, to identify the outcomes of the students when using different learning methodologies, a t-test is proposed to compare the post-test grades between the two groups. Finally, to measure the effect of the ARtour System on the learning effectiveness of the users, we propose to calculate the ES based on Cohen's d ES using the following formula:

$$ES = \frac{\left(\bar{X}_{1\_post} - \bar{X}_{1_{pre}}\right) - \left(\bar{X}_{2\_post} - \bar{X}_{2\_pre}\right)}{SD_{post}} \tag{1}$$

Where, $\bar{X}_{1\_post}$ and $\bar{X}_{1\_pre}$ are the mean scores of the post-test and pre-test of the experimental group, respectively. $\bar{X}_{2\_post}$ and $\bar{X}_{2\_pre}$ are the mean scores of the post-test and pre-test of the control group, respectively. Finally, SD_{post} is the pooled standard deviation for the post-test:

$$SD_{post} = \sqrt{\frac{\left(n_{2\_post} - 1\right)S^2_{2\_post} + \left(n_{1\_post} - 1\right)S^2_{1\_post}}{\left(n_{2\_post} + n_{1\_post} - 2\right)}} \tag{2}$$

Where n_{2_post} and n_{1_post} are the sample sizes of the experimental and control groups, respectively. S_{2_post} and S_{1_post} are the standard deviations for the experimental and control groups respectively for the post-test.

6.2 RQ2: Are There Statistically Significant Differences in the Users' Motivation According to the Learning Scenario They Use?

To evaluate users' motivation (RQ2) we use the motivational measurement instrument Instructional Materials Motivation Survey (IMMS) [27]. This instrument measures learner motivation following the ARCS model and is particularly relevant to evaluate the impact of technology as a motivational factor in learning [36].

6.3 RQ3: What Is the Degree of User Satisfaction After Using the ARtour Application in Outdoor Learning Scenarios?

An additional test is proposed to be applied to users, once the educational experience is completed. It is a satisfaction survey (Table 1) validated and used in other investigations [37] and modified to be applied in this research.

Table 1. Satisfaction survey.

Question/affirmation
1. I am comfortable using the application
3. It is easy to navigate within the application
4. The information displayed in the application is accurate
5. The application has given me a positive impression about agritourism
6. The application has given me important information for my learning
7. The graphic design of the application is visually appealing
9. I was given enough information for the use of the application
10. I like the information that shows the application

The users are requested to rate the degree of agreement with each of the 10 statements based on a Likert type scale with 7 levels. Each level ranges from "strongly disagree" (1) to "strongly agree" (7). This instrument will allow us to know the perception of the users, their feelings and the degree of satisfaction with the use of the proposed system. In addition, to gain more qualitative feedback, we propose to conduct a short an informal interview to some of the users of the application.

7 Conclusion and Future Work

We posit that the use of ARtour will improve outdoor learning experiences and allow tourists to learn basic principles of agritourism. ARtour will motivate and facilitate the learning experience of tourists while having fun playing an AR game. ARtour intends to extend the concept of agritourism to a broader concept of Eco-agritourism, by showing tourists the importance of protecting and conserving of nature. In addition, ARtour encourages the tourists to build their own agricultural systems, if possible at their own spaces. Further research is pretended to be developed along with the ministry of tourism in Colombia. This research will focus on developing a wider set of options for tourist to visit and learn about agritourism activities.

Acknowledgement. The authors are deeply grateful to Catholic University of the East - Colombia, for having fully supported this project.

References

1. McGehee, N.G., Kim, K., Jennings, G.R.: Motivation for agri-tourism entrepreneurship. Tour. Manag. **28**(1), 280–289 (2007)
2. Weaver, D.B., Fennell, D.: The vacation farm sector in Saskatchewan: a profile of operations. Tour. Manag. **18**, 357–365 (1997)
3. Melstrom, R.T., Murphy, C.: Do agritourism visitors care about landscapes? An examination with producer-level data. J. Travel Res. **57**(3), 360–369 (2018)
4. Govindasamy, R., Vellangany, I., Arumugam, S.: Bed and breakfast: an analysis of consumer preferences for eco-agritourism. J. Food Distrib. Res. **45**(1), 69–70 (2014)
5. Abelló, F.J., Palma, M.A., Waller, M.L., Anderson, D.P.: Evaluating the factors influencing the number of visits to farmers' markets. J. Food Prod. Mark. **20**(1), 17–35 (2014)
6. Trends, C., Zurbriggen, M., Nitzsche, P., Vanvranken, R.: Farmers Markets (1998)
7. Holden, A.: Environment and Tourism. Routledge (2016)
8. Mowforth, M., Munt, I.: Tourism and Sustainability: Development, Globalisation and New Tourism in the Third World. Routledge
9. Paramati, S.R., Shahbaz, M., Alam, M.S.: Does tourism degrade environmental quality? A comparative study of Eastern and Western European Union. Transp. Res. Part D Transp. Environ. **50**, 1–13 (2017)
10. Wearing, S., Tarrant, M.A., Schweinsberg, S., Lyons, K.: Cultural and environmental awareness through sustainable tourism education: exploring the role of onsite community tourism-based work-integrated learning projects. In: Handbook of Teaching and Learning in Tourism, Chap. 27, p. 402 (2017)
11. Reis, G., Roth, W.M.: A feeling for the environment: Emotion talk in/for the pedagogy of public environmental education. J. Environ. Educ. **41**(2), 71–87 (2009)
12. Huang, T.C., Chen, C.C., Chou, Y.W.: Animating eco-education: to see, feel, and discover in an augmented reality-based experiential learning environment. Comput. Educ. **96**, 72–82 (2016)
13. Pekrun, R.: Emotions and learning. Int. Acad. Educ. Bur. Educ. IEA (http://www.iaoed.org), IBE (http://www.ibe.unesco.org/publications.htm) (2014)
14. Villarroel, J.D., Antón, Á., Zuazagoitia, D., Nuño, T.: Young children's environmental judgement and its relationship with their understanding of the concept of living things. Environ. Socio Econ. Stud. **5**(1), 1–10 (2017)
15. Torkar, G.: Learning experiences that produce environmentally active and informed minds. NJAS - Wageningen J. Life Sci. **69**, 49–55 (2014)
16. Martin, S., Diaz, G., Sancristobal, E., Gil, R., Castro, M., Peire, J.: New technology trends in education: Seven years of forecasts and convergence. Comput. Educ. **57**(3), 1893–1906 (2011)
17. Billinghurst, M., Clark, A., Lee, G.: A survey of augmented reality. Found. Trends Hum. Comput. Interact. **8**(2–3), 73–272 (2015)
18. Yuen, S.C., Yaoyuneyong, G., Johnson, E.: Augmented reality: an overview and five directions for AR in education. J. Educ. Technol. Dev. Exch. **4**(1), 119–140 (2011)
19. Diegmann, P., Schmidt-kraepelin, M., Van Den Eynden, S., Basten, D.: Benefits of augmented reality in educational environments – a systematic literature review. Wirtschaftsinformatik **3**(6), 1542–1556 (2015)
20. Bacca, J., Fabregat, R., Baldiris, S., Graf, S., Kinshuk: Augmented reality trends in education: a systematic review of research and applications. Educ. Technol. Soc. **17**, 133–149 (2014)

21. Garzón, J., Pavón, J., Baldiris, S.: Augmented reality applications for education: five directions for future research. In: De Paolis, L.T., Bourdot, P., Mongelli, A. (eds.) AVR 2017, Part I. LNCS, vol. 10324, pp. 402–414. Springer, Cham (2017). https://doi.org/10. 1007/978-3-319-60922-5_31

22. Mekni, M., Lemieux, A.: Augmented reality : applications, challenges and future trends. In: Applied Computational Science Anywhere, pp. 205–214 (2014)

23. Akçayir, M., Akçayir, G.: Advantages and challenges associated with augmented reality for education: a systematic review of the literature. Educ. Res. Rev. **20**, 1–11 (2016)

24. Chen, P., Liu, X., Cheng, W., Huang, R.: A review of using augmented reality in education from 2011 to 2016. In: Popescu, E., et al. (eds.) Innovations in Smart Learning. LNET, pp. 13–18. Springer, Singapore (2017). https://doi.org/10.1007/978-981-10-2419-1_2

25. Caudell, T.P., Mizell, D.W.: Augmented reality: an application of heads-up display technology to manual manufacturing processes. In: Proceedings of the Twenty-Fifth Hawaii International Conference on System Sciences, vol. 2, pp. 659–669 (1992)

26. Tekedere, H., Göker, H.: Examining the effectiveness of augmented reality applications in education: a meta-analysis. Int. J. Environ. Sci. Educ. **11**(16), 9469–9481 (2016)

27. Keller, J.M.: Motivational Design for Learning and Performance: The ARCS Model Approach. Springer, New York (2009). https://doi.org/10.1007/978-1-4419-1250-3

28. Tarng, W., Ou, K.-L., Yu, C.-S., Liou, F.-L., Liou, H.-H.: Development of a virtual butterfly ecological system based on augmented reality and mobile learning technologies. Virtual Real. **19**(3–4), 253–266 (2015)

29. Kamarainen, A.M., et al.: EcoMOBILE: integrating augmented reality and probeware with environmental education field trips. Comput. Educ. **68**, 545–556 (2013)

30. Huang, T.C.: Seeing creativity in an augmented experiential learning environment. Univ. Access Inf. Soc. **129**, 1–13 (2017)

31. Wharton, C.R.: Towards commercial aquaponics: a review of systems, designs, scales and nomenclature (1969)

32. Wharton, J.: Subsistence Agriculture and Economic Development. Routledge (2017)

33. UNESCO, The International Standard Classification of Education (2011)

34. Bacca, J., Baldiris, S., Fabregat, R., Kinshuk, Graf, S.: Mobile augmented reality in vocational education and training. Procedia Comput. Sci. **75** (Vare), 49–58 (2015)

35. Chen, C.-H., Chou, Y.-Y., Huang, C.-Y.: An augmented-reality-based concept map to support mobile learning for science. Asia-Pacific Educ. Res. **25**(4), 567–578 (2016)

36. Di Serio, Á., Ibáñez, M.B., Kloos, C.D.: Impact of an augmented reality system on students' motivation for a visual art course. Comput. Educ. **68**, 585–596 (2013)

37. Joo-Nagata, J., Martinez Abad, F., García-Bermejo Giner, J., García-Peñalvo, F.J.: Augmented reality and pedestrian navigation through its implementation in m-learning and e-learning: evaluation of an educational program in Chile. Comput. Educ. **111**, 1–17 (2017)

Robust Outdoors Marker-Based Augmented Reality Applications: Mitigating the Effect of Lighting Sensitivity

Vlasios Kasapakis[1(✉)], Damianos Gavalas[2], and Dzardanova Elena[2]

[1] Department of Cultural Technology and Communication,
University of the Aegean, Mytilene, Greece
v.kasapakis@aegean.gr
[2] Department of Product and Systems Design Engineering,
University of the Aegean, Hermoupolis, Greece
{dgavalas,lena}@aegean.gr

Abstract. Marker-based AR is widely used in outdoors applications enabling the augmentation of physical objects with virtual elements. However, the diversification of lighting conditions may severely affect the accuracy of marker tracking in outdoors environments. In this paper we investigate the effectiveness of geolocative raycasting, a technique which enables the real-time estimation of the user's field of view in outdoors mobile applications, as a complementary method for enhancing the robustness of marker-based AR applications, thus mitigating the effect of lighting sensitivity.

Keywords: Augmented Reality · Marker-based · Marker identification
Vuforia · Occlusion · Field of view · Raycasting · Lighting sensitivity

1 Introduction

Recent advancements in mobile computing have enabled the diffusion of mobile Augmented Reality (AR) applications. Two popular paradigms for implementing outdoors AR are marker-based AR and sensor-based AR. Marker-based AR is based on vision tracking and relies on the placement of fiducial markers in the real world, which are then tracked by the built-in camera of mobile devices. While experiencing marker-based AR, users perceive the real world through the camera feed, superimposed with virtual elements, based on the location of the tracked fiducial markers [1]. On the other hand, outdoors sensor-based AR applications utilize multiple commodity sensors, commonly integrated in smartphones, to estimate the device's rotation and direction. This information allows the appropriate positioning of virtual elements on top of the real world, which are typically projected through the user's camera feed. Outdoors sensor-based AR also utilizes GPS, to acquire user location and provide accurate placement of the virtual elements which are often associated with real locations [2].

Outdoors sensor-based AR applications require only a limited amount of the user's field of view (FoV) to be superimposed with computer-generated graphics, while the rest of the user's view perceives the physical world [3]. The augmentation of the

L. T. De Paolis and P. Bourdot (Eds.): AVR 2018, LNCS 10850, pp. 423–431, 2018.
https://doi.org/10.1007/978-3-319-95270-3_36

physical world by virtual elements provides the user with a better sense of her location and surroundings, thus improving her overall perception. In typical urban settings, though, the to-be-augmented physical spot is often hidden from the user's FoV due to surrounding buildings. This effect is known as *occlusion*. In such cases, the projection of virtual elements meant to augment the occluded physical spot has been found to compromise the depth judgment of users, thereby resulting in misconceptions and wrong pursuance of tasks assigned to them [13]. Moreover, GPS and sensors used in outdoors sensor-based AR applications have limited accuracy, hence, they fall short in accurately positioning virtual elements, occasionally resembling a directional hint rather than an overlay matched to an exact location [8].

Outdoors marker-based AR applications are far more accurate than their sensor-based counterparts. In marker-based AR the virtual elements are visually attached to specific identified parts of the fiducial markers; the latter are commonly created using photographs of physical items which are to be augmented (e.g. the photograph of the side part of a building could serve as a fiducial marker). When the user aims her camera towards a physical item (whose photograph is registered as a fiducial marker), the item is detected and subsequently augmented, as the AR 'engine' matches common feature points of the fiducial marker image and the real image (as captured by the user device's camera) [2]. However, the accuracy of the matching process depends heavily on the actual lighting conditions on the real environment; even slight differences in the environmental lighting conditions (among the time that the fiducial marker's photograph was taken, and the time the user's camera captures the physical item) may severely affect the ability of the AR application to detect the fiducial marker and project virtual elements upon it. In fact, experimental tests have revealed that the sensitivity to environmental lighting conditions increases during nighttime, presumably due to the high variance of artificial lighting in urban environments [5].

The work presented herein attempts to enhance the robustness of outdoors AR applications through mitigating the effect of lighting sensitivity on marker-based AR. Our approach enables -by default- a 'standard' marker-based AR framework to detect registered physical items and accurately superimpose AR content upon them. In the event that marker tracking fails due to improper lighting conditions, we propose the complementary use of a FoV estimation technique (normally used in sensor-based AR apps); the FoV estimation algorithm detects whether the physical item is indeed within the user's FoV and then attempts to project AR content as accurately as possible. Our approach borrows research results from two relevant works recently undertaken by the authors. The first work involved the development of an efficient geometric technique, aiming at assisting developers of outdoors sensor-based AR applications in generating a realistic FoV for the users. The second work involved the evaluation of an outdoors marker-based AR application to annotate and promote architectural heritage in urban environments.

The remainder of this article is structured as follows: Sect. 2 presents previous research related to our work. Section 3 details the design principles and technical aspects of a research prototype which implements the above discussed hybrid approach to enhance the robustness of outdoors marker-based AR applications under non-uniform lighting conditions. Finally, Sect. 4 concludes our work and draws directions for future work.

2   Related Work

To the best of our knowledge, the problem of inaccurate tracking of fiducial markers has received little interest in the (marker-based) AR literature so far. Existing research [9, 10] has investigated the tracking of custom, barcode-like, grayscale fiducial markers (i.e. not created from photographs) in indoors environments. In particular, Naimark and Foxlin proposed a modified form of homomorphic image processing to eliminate the effect of non-uniform lighting on images [8]. Pintaric introduced an algorithm for selecting adaptive thresholds for fiducial segmentation to cope with generic lighting phenomena, such as shadows or reflections off a marker's surface [7]. Both the proposed solutions have been demonstrated on desktop (rather than mobile) applications. The remainder of this section presents previous works of the authors, the combination of which enables the development of lighting-insensitive outdoors marker-based AR applications.

2.1   FoV Estimation in Sensor-Based AR Applications

Outdoors sensor-based AR applications commonly fail to effectively handle the occlusion effect, thus superimposing virtual elements even when the associated to-be-augmented physical items do not lie within the users' FoV [6]. An example of this issue is illustrated in Fig. 1a, wherein the AR content attached to a venue is projected on the user's camera, although the venue is occluded by another building, thus resulting in misjudgments.

To address occlusion, in classic video games, the visibility of virtual objects is estimated utilizing the raycasting technique. Raycasting refers to the act of casting imaginary light beams (rays) from a source location (typically the point of view of the character or object controlled by the player) and recording the objects hit by the rays [11] (see Fig. 1b). The combination of several rays aiming towards different angles (centered around the characters' current direction) may be used to estimate the user's FoV (see Fig. 1c).

In a previous work [6], we extended this idea to mobile gaming wherein, unlike video games, the game space is not pre-registered and occlusion typically occurs due to surrounding buildings. Our focus has been on determining the user's FoV, whilst satisfying critical requirements of mobile games such as (a) real-time performance; (b) suitability for execution on average mobile equipment; and (c) support of popular map platforms. Along this line, we introduced a geolocative raycasting method which allows mobile game developers to detect buildings (or custom-generated obstacles) in location-based AR game environments, thereby reliably handling the object occlusion issue. Essentially, our method receives inspiration from the raycasting technique utilized in classic video games. It employs an efficient geometric technique generating several ray segments which are derived based on the users' location (as measured by the GPS receiver of the user's device), while their direction is set based on the smartphone's direction (as estimated by its magnetic sensor). Finally, the rays' intersection points with nearby building polygons (deconstructed in sides) are calculated to estimate the users' FoV.

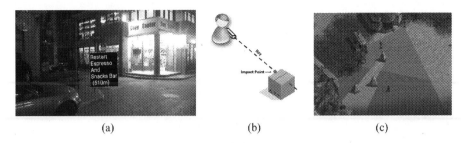

(a)   (b)   (c)

Fig. 1. (a) Demonstration of occlusion in GPS-enabled sensor-based AR; (b) raycasting in classic video games; (b) FoV determination in classic video games (http://store.steampowered.com/app/6800/Commandos_Behind_Enemy_Lines/).

To test geolocative raycasting we created an outdoors sensor-based AR game for Android smartphone devices, the Order Elimination[1]. In Order Elimination the user has to hunt down a zombie, which moves along a pre-defined route in the real world. To eliminate the zombie, the user has to approach in a distance up to 50 m, and shoot it down while it lies within her FoV, as generated by the geolocative raycasting algorithm (see Fig. 2a and b).

The performance and effectiveness of our method has been thoroughly evaluated under realistic game play conditions by twelve (12) players. The evaluation results have been encouraging as they highlighted the responsiveness and accuracy of the geolocative raycasting technique [6].

2.2   Marker-Based AR Architectural Heritage Guide Application

A typical application of AR technology in cultural heritage involves the use of the marker-based AR to effectively promote heritage assets through projecting virtual content over physical objects, thereby serving as an attractive interpretation and guidance tool [4, 7, 14]. Our previous work with marker-based AR challenged this narrow view suggesting its utilization as an effective annotation tool; in particular, as a means for (a) spatially correlating archival photos with the current form of a building; (b) annotating particular architectural or decorative elements of a building; (c) facilitating the development of AR content by end users (i.e., citizens and tourists) participating in crowdsourcing campaigns.

To demonstrate this idea, we have developed Flaneur [5], an outdoors marker-based AR application which offers dual operation: the 'projection' mode of Flaneur serves as a 'typical' mobile architectural heritage guide which projects pre-edited content over selected heritage buildings; the 'annotation' mode of the application invites a crowd interested in architecture to wander around a city and actively contribute in highlighting its architectural assets. In particular, the user may use the Flaneur application to capture a photo of a building, register it as a fiducial marker (as long as the building view has

---

[1] A video demonstration of *Order Elimination* can be found at: https://www.youtube.com/watch?v=iiY5aTasKPg .

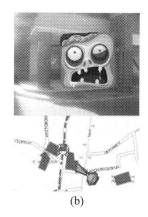

(a)   (b)

Fig. 2. (a) Zombie lying within the player's FoV; (b) Zombie lying out of the player's FoV (occluded by surrounding buildings).

enough identification points) and then accurately position augmented information, such as text, upon the captured image [5]. Thereupon, the annotated building along with the augmentation content are available for end users to retrieve and consume through operating the 'projection' mode of Flaneur (see Fig. 3).

The evaluation of Flaneur by eighteen (18) participants, revealed that the most critical issue which severely affected and caused frustration to end-users has been the failure of the application to track buildings (i.e. fiducial markers) under diverse lighting conditions. For example, the photograph of a real location captured by a user during the morning, and registered as a fiducial marker, could not be detected by other users of Flaneur during the evening. This was mainly due to varying illumination levels as well as lighting phenomena like shadows or reflections off a marker's surface.

3 Supporting Marker-Based AR Applications Under Non-uniform Lighting Conditions

Inspired by the works presented in the preceding section, we have developed a prototype application wherein the geolocative raycasting technique is used to enhance the robustness (i.e. the accuracy level) of outdoors marker-based AR apps under diverse environmental lighting conditions. To validate our solution, we firstly implemented an application for Android smartphone devices based on the Vuforia[2] AR framework (also utilized in Flaneur). As a case study, we have taken photographs (under clear sky, daylight conditions) of two sides of an important cultural heritage building located in Lesvos (Mytilene, Greece); those photographs have been later registered as fiducial markers in the Vuforia cloud service. Figure 4a presents the two building sides along with the locations where the user can stand and aim her camera to display AR content.

---

[2] https://www.vuforia.com/.

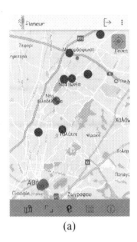
(a)

(b)

Fig. 3. The *Flaneur* application: (a) map view illustrating the location of AR-enhanced buildings; (b) identification of a marker (building's side) and projection of AR content.

Figure 4b demonstrates the augmentation of the building side with virtual content upon the successful tracking of the respective fiducial marker by the Vuforia engine. Figure 4c illustrates a 'bad' scenario, wherein the application fails to detect the fiducial marker during a cloudy day, thus preventing the projection of the AR content.

To address this issue, we 'hybridized' the application through incorporating sensor-based AR capability; the latter has been enhanced by our geolocative raycasting implementation so as to accurately detect events wherein the user is indeed in line-of-sight with the registered building's polygon sides. Firstly, we created a custom polygon resembling the cultural heritage building. Figure 4d presents the building polygon, two sides of which have been annotated with the same AR content as in the respective marker-based AR mode of the application. We have confined the overall user's FoV to 4 rays, representing a 4° FoV. This narrow FoV ensures that in order to enable the AR content (through geolocative raycasting), the user should target exactly the same part of the building as in the marker-based version of the application. Finally, Fig. 4e presents the result perceived by the user, when she aims at a building side annotated with AR content. Evidently, the user views the same AR content, as in the marker-based version of the application, even if the lighting conditions are inappropriate for tracking the fiducial marker[3].

Even though our preliminary field tests revealed that the geolocative raycasting technique can effectively complement marker-based AR application, a number of limitations have been identified. First, the GPS accuracy may affect the accuracy of geolocative raycasting. However, our tests revealed that the 5 m–10 m GPS accuracy, which is common among smartphone devices [12], is acceptable. Users who evaluated the Order Elimination game shared the same view, further supporting this claim [6].

---

[3] A video demonstrating geolocative raycasting, used to support outdoors Marker-Based AR applications, can be found at https://youtu.be/pYIIEQEtgTc.

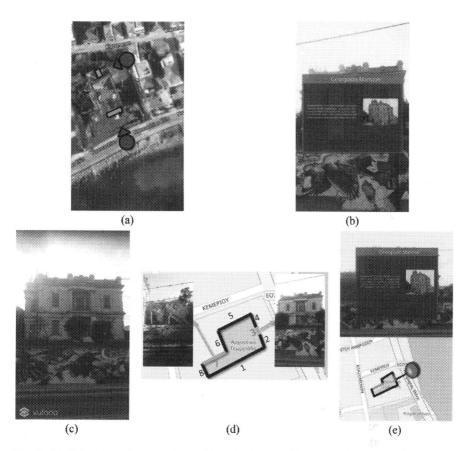

Fig. 4. (a) Fiducial markers locations; (b) projection of AR content by means of 'standard' outdoors marker-based AR; (c) marker-based AR under non-ideal lighting conditions: failure to track the marker; (d) the polygon sides of the cultural heritage building; (e) projection of AR content in sensor-based AR, enhanced by geolocative raycasting.

Moreover, considerable attention should be paid when annotating polygon sides with AR content. As shown in Fig. 5b, the user should register the whole building's side photograph as a fiducial marker, and associate it with AR content.

However, when using geolocative raycasting, the polygon side to be tracked (i.e. to be targeted by the rays) should be significantly shorter than the actual building side, and be center-aligned on the building side. This requirement is meant to address the lower accuracy of sensor-based AR applications, which is mainly due to the inaccurate estimation of the device's GPS location. Moreover, it enforces the sensor-based AR mode of the application to resemble its marker-based counterpart with respect to the location wherefrom the user may trigger the projection of the AR content. As shown in Fig. 5a, for example, the total length of the building side registered as a fiducial marker is 15 m, while the respective polygon side length fed into the geolocative raycasting algorithm is only 5 m. Thus, the application correctly enables or disables the projection

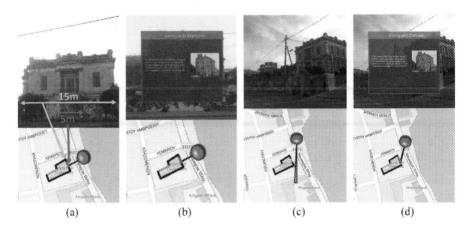

Fig. 5. (a) Adjusted polygon side; (b) AR content correctly enabled based on the user's FoV; (c) AR content correctly disabled based on the user's FoV; (d) AR content erroneously enabled (due to registering a polygon side which matches the actual length of the building's side).

of AR content depending on whether the rays intersect with the narrow (5 m long) building's polygon side (see Fig. 5b and c). On the other hand, if the polygon side matches the full length of the building side (i.e. the 15 m used to create the fiducial marker), the user will be able to view AR content from locations which would be unsuitable for the marker-based version of the application (see Fig. 5d).

4   Conclusion

Outdoors marker-based AR applications commonly fail to track fiducial markers (often created using photographs of real physical locations) under non-uniform lighting conditions. In this work, we propose a hybrid method for enhancing the robustness of AR applications: we use a standard marker-based AR framework to track registered markers; in parallel, we execute an efficient geometric method to detect events where the user actually targets a marker which, however, remains untracked due to inappropriate environmental lighting conditions. This method is based on an existing geolocative raycasting technique which enables real-time determination of the user's FoV in outdoors sensor-based AR applications.

Our preliminary field tests revealed that geolocative raycasting may effectively complement standard marker-based frameworks to counteract their sensitivity to diverse lighting conditions. In the future, we aim at incorporating device inclination in our raycasting algorithm, to enable virtual elements annotation at specific building parts (e.g. interesting architectural details such as decorative elements), apart from building sides.

References

1. Azuma, R., Baillot, Y., Behringer, R., Feiner, S., Julier, S., MacIntyre, B.: Recent advances in augmented reality. IEEE Comput. Graph. Appl. **21**, 34–47 (2001)
2. Azuma, R.T.: A survey of augmented reality. Presence: Teleoper. Virtual Environ. **6**(4), 355–385 (1997)
3. Billinghurst, M., Clark, A., Lee, G.: A survey of augmented reality. Found. Trends Hum. Comput. Interact. **8**, 73–272 (2014)
4. Feiner, S., MacIntyre, B., Höllerer, T., Webster, A.: A touring machine: prototyping 3D mobile augmented reality systems for exploring the urban environment. Pers. Technol. **1**, 208–217 (1997)
5. Ioannidi, A., Gavalas, D., Kasapakis, V.: Flaneur: augmented exploration of the architectural urbanscape, In: Proceedings of the Symposium on Computers and Communications (ISCC), pp. 529–533 (2017)
6. Kasapakis, V., Gavalas, D.: Occlusion handling in outdoors augmented reality games. Multimedia Tools Appl. **76**, 9829–9854 (2017)
7. Kasapakis, V., Gavalas, D., Galatis, P.: Augmented reality in cultural heritage: field of view awareness in an archaeological site mobile guide. J. Ambient Intell. Smart Environ. **8**, 501–514 (2016)
8. Langlotz, T., Wagner, D., Mulloni, A., Schmalstieg, D.: Online creation of panoramic augmented reality annotations on mobile phones. Pervasive Comput. **11**, 56–63 (2012)
9. Naimark, L., Foxlin, E.: Circular data matrix fiducial system and robust image processing for a wearable vision-inertial self-tracker. In: Proceedings of the 1st International Symposium on Mixed and Augmented Reality, p. 27 (2002)
10. Pintaric, T.: An adaptive thresholding algorithm for the augmented reality toolkit. In: Proceeding of the International Augmented Reality Toolkit Workshop, p. 71 (2003)
11. Schroeder, J.: Andengine for Android Game Development Cookbook. Packt Publishing Ltd., Birmingham (2013)
12. Singhal, M., Shukla, A.: Implementation of location based services in Android using GPS and web services. Int. J. Comput. Sci. Issues **9**, 237–242 (2012)
13. Tian, Y., Long, Y., Xia, D., Yao, H., Zhang, J.: Handling occlusions in augmented reality based on 3D reconstruction method. Neurocomputing **156**, 96–104 (2015)
14. Vlahakis, V., Ioannidis, M., Karigiannis, J., Tsotros, M., Gounaris, M., Stricker, D., Gleue, T., Daehne, P., Almeida, L.: Archeoguide: an augmented reality guide for archaeological sites. Computer Graph. Appl. **22**, 52–60 (2002)

Computer Graphics

Write-Once, Transpile-Everywhere: Re-using Motion Controllers of Virtual Humans Across Multiple Game Engines

Fabrizio Nunnari[1(✉)] and Alexis Heloir[1,2]

[1] DFKI-MMCI, SLSI group, Saarbrücken, Germany
fabrizio.nunnari@dfki.de
[2] LAMIH UMR CNRS/UVHC 8201, Valenciennes, France

Abstract. Transpilation allows to write code once and re-use it across multiple runtime environments. In this paper, we propose a software development practice to implement once the motion controllers of virtual humans and re-use the implementation in multiple game engines. In a case study, three common human behaviors – blinking, text-to-speech, and eye-gaze – were developed in the Haxe programming language and deployed in the free, open-source Blender Game Engine and the commercial Unity engine. Performance tests show that transpiled code executes within 67% faster to 127% slower with respect to an implementation manually written in the game engine target languages.

Keywords: Virtual humans · Motion controller
Software architecture · Transpilation · Haxe

1 Introduction

Animated Virtual Agents are used in many industrial and academic contexts, such as videogames, avatars for immersive social experiences, visual front-ends for chat-bot systems, precisely controlled and reproducible psychological experiments, and virtual interpreters for sign language.

Regardless of the application domain, creating and deploying a virtual character implies a considerable development effort. A research team, or a software company, starting the development of a new virtual character today, must support already established hardware (Desktop and Mobile) and software (Window, MacOSX, Linux, Android, iOS, WebGL) platforms as well as look ahead to future available human-computer interaction devices, such as Immersive or Holographic Head-Mounted Displays.

Implementing such a system from scratch implies mastering high-performance languages and APIs, managing a plethora of required libraries, accounting for the undocumented subtleties of every possible target platform, and maintaining a sprawling build system. No reasonably-sized team can tackle all these tasks while conducting research and development related projects.

© Springer International Publishing AG, part of Springer Nature 2018
L. T. De Paolis and P. Bourdot (Eds.): AVR 2018, LNCS 10850, pp. 435–446, 2018.
https://doi.org/10.1007/978-3-319-95270-3_37

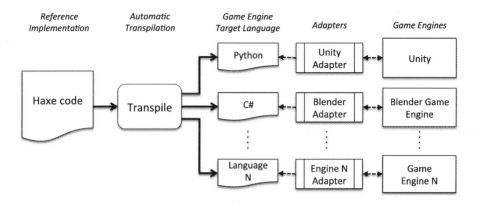

Fig. 1. How a single game-agnostic implementation can be re-used across multiple game-engines.

A number of existing game engines offer a *write once, deploy everywhere* support: developers do program the application using the engines' own API and elected programming language regardless of the target platform. The game engine not only offers a significant amount of pre-existing libraries for 3D programming, but it also hides the complexity of a building system able to deploy of multiple platforms. Among others, game engines such as Unity[1] or Unreal[2] have gained a significant market share and, thanks to a permissive licensing system, have been widely adopted by academics in the fields of Virtual Reality, Augmented Reality, Conversational Agents, and more.

However, for-profit closed-source game-engine companies might unpredictably change their pricing and licensing system. Not to mention that unforeseen marketing conditions might lead to their closure. Those, or any other reasons, such as the need to deploy on an unsupported platforms, might force a team to switch to a new game engine; leading to a significant re-implementation effort. Often, this re-implementation effort is frustrating and consists of both rewriting existing code into a new language as well as mapping the API of the previous game engine on the API of the new game engine.

Transpilation, together with a suitable software engineering, fosters the portability of code across multiple platforms. Given a game-engine-specific implementation of a functionality that must run in several game engines, it is possible to identify the set of features offered by any game engine and factorize them out of the existing implementation. The resulting game-engine-agnostic implementation would offer an API in the form of an elegant Domain Specific Language (DSL), abstracting away the technical subtleties of every engine.

Figure 1 illustrates the global idea. A developer implements and maintains a single game-engine-agnostic version of some functionality. A transpiler converts the reference implementation into the target language of each game engine.

---

[1] https://unity3d.com/ – 30 Apr 2018.

[2] https://www.unrealengine.com/ – 30 Apr 2018.

At this point, the developer must only write an adapter which interfaces the functionality code with the specific game engine API.

This paper presents the results of a study using the open-source Haxe[3] toolkit and programming language to steer the surfacing behavior of an animated character. The same code was used in two game engines: the Blender Game Engine[4] and Unity. In order to compare the performances of an Haxe transpilation with respect to hand coding, each behaviour was implemented in both Haxe and in the native language of the game engine (Python for the Blender Game Engine and C# for Unity) and their execution time were measured.

Section 2 presents some related work on transpilation. Section 3 presents the implementation guidelines and the software architecture which we used to *write-once, transpile everywhere* motion controllers. Section 4 describes the characteristics of the three motion controllers. Section 5 reports the result of the performance test comparing transpilation vs. hand-made implementation. Section 6 concludes the paper.

2   Related Work

Transpiling (or transcompiling, or source-to-source compilation) refers to the process of translating source code written in one language into another language with similar level of abstraction[5].

Transpilation is already successfully used in many industrial applications. Emscripten[6] allows for the translation of C/C++ code in to JavaScript for execution of native applications in modern web browsers: it is employed by Unity and Unreal to run games inside web browsers with WebGL support. The Google Web Toolkit[7] is a widget toolkit to develop web client graphical frontends. The front ends are programmed in Java and then translated into JavaScript. Xamarin[8] is dedicated to the development of mobile apps. Thanks to transpilation, applications can be written once in C# and deployed on Android, iOS, and Windows Mobile platforms as native applications.

Despite its wide usage in the industry, the practice of transpilation has been scarcely addressed in scientific contexts. Among the few works that we found, Maheshwari and Reddy [8] present a solution to transpile legacy ActionScript3 code into JavaScript in order to convert Flash web sites into HTML5. Still on the domain of web development, Bouraqadi and Mason [1] use transpilation to convert SmallTalk code into Javascript. Hirzel and Klaeren [6] investigated how to perform tests of code coverage in transpiled code. Finally, Bysiek et al. [2] use transpilation to convert legacy Fortran code into modern, type-hinted, Python code.

---

[3] https://haxe.org/ – 30 Apr 2018.

[4] https://www.blender.org/ – 30 Apr 2018.

[5] https://en.wikipedia.org/wiki/Source-to-source_compiler – 30 Apr 2018.

[6] https://github.com/kripken/emscripten – 30 Apr 2018.

[7] http://www.gwtproject.org/ – 30 Apr 2018.

[8] https://www.xamarin.com/ – 30 Apr 2018.

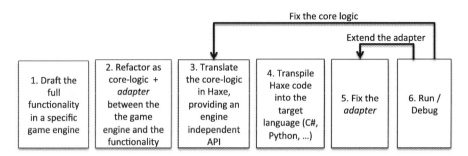

Fig. 2. From left to right, the steps needed to develop and maintain a new functionality across multiple game engines.

None of the above mentioned work deals with the specific case of transpilation in the context of game or real-time 3D application development. As such, they do not address the implications on the performance of high-frequency frame refresh cycles nor the use of geometric libraries. We make up for this absence by using transpilation to develop real-time simulation of human behavior and deploy it on multiple game engines.

The work presented in this paper uses Haxe as a cross-platform programming language. Haxe was initially developed as a platform independent language for the Neko virtual machine [9] and later used as an alternative language to develop Flash applications [3]. In the recent years, Haxe extended its list of target languages to include JavaScript, Lua, PHP, C++, Java, Python, and C#. As such, it has been adopted by many software companies as primary language for cross-platform game development.

3   Development Pipeline and Software Architecture

This section presents the software architecture and the development guidelines needed to implement a motion controller that can be re-used across multiple game engines.

Fig. 2 shows the steps needed to implement and maintain a functionality across different game engines.

1. The development process starts by coding a draft implementation of the desired functionality in a chosen game-engine. This step is needed because, according to our experience, it is realistically impossible to "blindly" develop a new functionality without any visual feedback to help debugging.

2. Once the draft works, the developer will split the code into a *core-logic* and an *adapter*; the latter being the name of a popular *Design Pattern* which is presented more in detail later in this section. The purpose of this step is to abstract and insulate into a self-contained class the logic driving the motion of the virtual human, independently from the technicalities of the surrounding game-engine. At the same time, the adapter will perform only technical operation, like datatype conversions, unaware of the data processing logic contained in the core. Such refactoring will result in defining an API for the core-logic which is independent from the game engine, in the form of *domain specific language*, and thus likely to be re-usable in other environments.

3. The next step consists of manually translating the core-logic into a meta-programming language like Haxe.

4. The new Haxe-based core-logic can be transpiled into the language of the game engine. This step is performed by the Haxe interpreter.

5. After the first transpilation, the developer might need to adjust the API of the core-logic in order to adapt it to the data-types provided by the Haxe language and libraries. Consequently, the wrapping adapter must be updated accordingly.

6. The new motion controller, made of a combination of hand-written adapter and transpiled core-logic, is ready to be used and enter an enhancement and debug cycle. At each debug iteration, the developer might have to fix either the Haxe core-logic or the native-language adapter (or both).

Once the first implementation is accomplished, supporting a new game engine will only require the implementation of a new adapter, essentially skipping steps 1 and 3 of the initial development pipeline.

As mentioned above, step 2 implies the use of the *adapter design pattern*. Design patterns, introduced by Gamma et al. [5], are "recipes" describing how to organise classes and methods in Object Oriented languages in order to solve recurring software architecture problems.

The *adapter* design pattern[9] is used when a Client class offers an interface to implement a functionality and another class already implements such functionality, but using a different interface. As a solution, the developer writes an *adapter* class which wraps the existing class (*adaptee*) and forwards the calls of the client's interface to the methods of the adaptee, conveniently converting method names and signatures. Figure 3 (left) depicts the situation with an UML diagram.

In game engines, developing a new functionality means implementing a new class containing two mandatory methods: an *initialization* method, invoked only one time when the game starts, and an *update* method, invoked at high frequency (e.g., 60 times per second), every time the engine generates a new frame. Each game engine relies on a specific programming language and defines its own API concerning the signatures of the mandatory methods.

In Unity (the Client), developers add functionalities to game objects by implementing a concrete class that extends the abstract class `MonoBehaviour` (the interface). Figure 3 (right) shows how the *adapter* design pattern is used in the eye-gaze functionality, which is presented in the next section. The logic of the eye gaze motion is encapsulated in the Haxe-generated `EyeGazeLogic` class (the adaptee). The class `EyeGazeController` (the adapter) maps the calls to `Start()` and `Update()` to `init()` and `updateEyesRot()`, respectively.

In addition, the `EyeGazeController` provides a clean public interface, as domain specific language primitives, to the eye gaze behaviour with the

---

[9] https://en.wikipedia.org/wiki/Adapter_pattern – 30 Apr 2018.

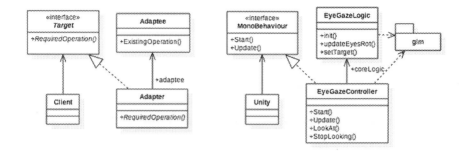

Fig. 3. Left: description of the *adapter* design pattern. Right: class diagram of the eye-gaze functionality, where the EyeGazeController acts both as *Adapter* and as *Façade*.

public methods `LookAt()` and `StopLooking()`, which comply to the Unity code standards (method names start with capital letters). Finally, the controller hides the complexity of converting the 3D data types (vector and quaternions) from Unity to/from the `glm` math library embedded with Haxe. As such, the `EyeGazeController` effectively implements the *Façade* design pattern[10], also described by Gamma et al. [5].

4   Motion Controllers

This section describes the three motion controllers implemented using the development pipeline proposed in Sect. 3. The controllers have been implemented in Haxe 3.4.2 and transpiled in Python and in C# in order to run in the Blender Game Engine v2.79 and in Unity 2017.3, respectively. All the source code is available as supplemental material[11].

Figure 4 shows, side-by-side, the same virtual character as viewed in the two rendering engines in realtime. The three functionalities are simultaneously executed. The supplemental material contains a demonstration video.

The virtual character has been created in Blender using the free add-on ManueBastioniLAB[12]. The character has been augmented with extra bones in order to gather the absolute location of the eyes. For both engines, the materials have been manually edited for better (not necessarily equal) aesthetics.

Eye blinking This is the simplest of the three motion controllers and provides the virtual character of irregular eye-blink animations. The implementation logic is based on a simple state machine cycling between CLOSING, OPENING, and WAITING states. The closing and the opening times are fixed at 1/8th and 1/10th of a second, respectively. The waiting time is randomized between 4 and 8 seconds, as reported in [7].

---

[10] https://en.wikipedia.org/wiki/Facade_pattern – 30 Apr 2018.

[11] http://www.dfki.de/~fanu01/SalentoAVR2018/ – 30 Apr 2018.

[12] http://www.manuelbastioni.com/ – 30 Apr 2018.

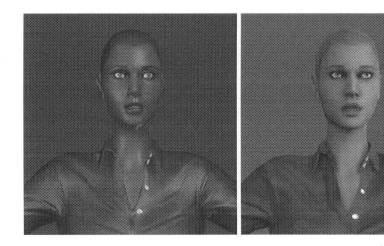

Fig. 4. The same virtual human performing the three behaviours in the Blender Games engine (left) and in Unity (right).

The high-frequency update method of the core-logic takes as input the current time stamp (float, in seconds) and fills a 4-elements vector with the weights of the blend shapes driving the eyes. The two adapters only forward the time stamps from the relative game engine and copy back the calculated blend shape weight into the character's mesh data structure.

As an example, Listing 1.1 shows the code of the eye-blink adapter for Unity.

Text-to-Speech. This controller gives the ability to the virtual human to speak out arbitrary sentences, given as string, and simultaneously move the lips in synch. The implementation uses the MaryTTS[13] [10] speech synthesiser to get (i) an audio file of the spoken sentence and (ii) a time-table associating a timestamp to a phoneme to be pronounced. The core logic of this controller contains, first of all, the code to parse the time-table. Then, during the high-frequency updates, the controller acts as sequencer, locating at each call the phoneme that has to be currently spoken. Each phoneme is mapped to a morph target of the mouth that matches with the emitted sound. The update method performs the smooth animation of the blend shapes values.

The MaryTTS engine works as a remote server and can be inquired through HTTP requests. The role of the adapter is to use the platform-depended network APIs to connect to the server and retrieve both the audio as wav file and the time-table as text file. Also, the adapter invokes the engine-specific audio devices in order to playback the sound. Similarly to the blinking functionality, the interaction with the core logic consists of copying the weight of the blend-shapes calculated by the logic into the character's mesh.

---

[13] http://mary.dfki.de/ – 30 Apr 2018.

```
 1  public class EyeBlinkController : MonoBehaviour {
 2
 3      // The core-logic
 4      private EyeBlinker blinker = new EyeBlinker() ;
 5      // Buffer for blendshape weights
 6      private double[] viseme_weights = new double[EyeBlinker.
            get_viseme_count()] ;
 7
 8      private SkinnedMeshRenderer skinnedMeshRenderer;
 9      private Mesh skinnedMesh;
10
11      void Start () {
12          skinnedMeshRenderer = GetComponent<SkinnedMeshRenderer>();
13          skinnedMesh = GetComponent<SkinnedMeshRenderer>().sharedMesh;
14      }
15
16      void Update () {
17          // updates the weights vector
18          blinker.update (Time.time, this.viseme_weights);
19
20          // Update the BlendShapes' weight
21          for(int i=0 ; i < EyeBlinker.get_viseme_count() ; i++) {
22              string viseme = (string)(EyeBlinker.VISEMES [i]);
23              int blendShapeIdx = this.skinnedMesh.GetBlendShapeIndex (
                    viseme);
24              skinnedMeshRenderer.SetBlendShapeWeight(blendShapeIdx, (float)
                    (this.viseme_weights[i] * 100.0f));
25          }
26      }
27  }
```

Listing 1.1. The C# adapter for eye-blink in Unity.

Coordinated Eye-Head Gaze. This functionality gives the ability to the virtual human to move the eyes and the neck to watch at a given 3D point in space. The eyes move first, involving the rotation of the neck when the angle between the straight-forward direction and the target point exceed an amplitude of 30° horizontally or 12° vertically [4]. The eye/head gaze logic is the most complex of the three as it not only modulates the blend shapes to rotate the eyes, but also rotates the neck bone in order to move the whole head towards the requested point. As such, the initialization of the core-logic requires the information about the 3D reference frame in terms of *forward, up,* and *side* vectors. The *update* method of the core-logic takes as input the current timestamp, the current absolute location and rotation of both eyes-bones, and the current rotation of the neck. It returns the new rotation of the neck together with the weight of the 4 blend shapes driving the rotation of the eyes. The core-logic public API allows to set a target 3D point to watch. The update method smoothly animates neck and eyes rotation in order to converge to the desired target with a natural-looking animation. The core-logic needs to expose data types for vectors and quaternions in order to define its API and to perform its 3D calculations. Hence, the 3D math library for Haxe glm[14] (v2.1) was downloaded and included in the source code.

---

[14] https://lib.haxe.org/p/glm/ – 30 Apr 2018.

Like for the other controllers, the adapter must update the character mesh with the weight of the blend shapes driving the eyes. In addition, for this functionality it also has to read and write the bones locations and rotation from and to the skeleton of the character. Here, some extra code is needed to translate the 3D data types (vectors and quaternions) between the native types and the types exposed by the Haxe-based *glm* library.

All the functionalities were written to operate on a specific virtual human, hence expecting the presence of a given set of blend shapes and bones. As such, the functionalities are currently not portable across different characters. Of course, it would be possible to create a further layer of abstraction and implement the core-logic independently from a specific skeletal structure or set of morph targets. Such choice will result in a more complex architecture of classes, needing an intermediate translation between abstract body activators and the actual data structure of the virtual characters, thus increasing the complexity of the adapters.

5   Performance Tests

In order to assess the performance of the Haxe-generated code, we manually implemented Hand-made versions of the core-logic of all the three functionalities, each using the native language of the two game engines. Hence, in each of the two game engines, for each of the three functionalities we have one adapter and two implementations of the core logic. Each adapter can use either of the two implementations by simply setting a flag or by defining a macro. We compared the execution speed between Transpiled and Hand-made versions.

The summary of our comparison is reported in Table 1. Each column reports information about the source code, divided in three sections: Haxe code, Python code for the Blender Game Engine, and C# code for Unity, either manually written (Hand-made) or generated by the Haxe compiler (Transpiled). The Python code was executed by the CPython interpreter v3.5.3 embedded in Blender 2.79, while the C# code is executed by a Mono Develop 5.9.6 environment embedded in Unity 2017.3.

We measured the size of the source code in terms of both number of lines and size of the source file. It was not possible to report the size of the single controllers for the transpiled Python code because Haxe generates one single module with all classes.

As it can be seen from the lines Source Size (lines/bytes), the size of the source codes is comparable among hand-written versions, while it grows of a factor between 2x and 4x when comparing between manually written and transpiled versions. The growth raises to +460% (Python) to +1405% (C#) when comparing the total amount of generated code, which includes the extra library `glm`.

The performance tests measured the execution time of the `update()` method of the core-logics. The table reports the results of 10 seconds measurements: the number of iterations, the average time per iteration in micro seconds (usec), and

Table 1. Results of the translation and performance test of the execution of the three controllers for 10 s.

		Haxe	Python (Blender)		C# (Unity)	
		Hand-made	Hand-made	Transpiled	Hand-made	Transpiled
Blink	Source Size (lines)	133	99	see tot	134	395
	Source Size (bytes)	3759	3299	see tot	3266	9524
	Exec Iterations	-	601	601	602	602
	Exec Time Mean (usecs)	-	13.041	6.006	0.520	0.171
	Exec Time SD	-	2.318	1.511	0.979	0.375
	Relative Exec Time (pct)	-	-	**−53.95%**	-	**−67.15%**
TTS	Source Size (lines)	384	410	see tot	379	720
	Source Size (bytes)	13742	15242	see tot	12727	21649
	Exec Iterations	-	439	439	440	438
	Exec Time Mean (usecs)	-	41.442	47.915	2.445	2.665
	Exec Time SD	-	7.505	6.683	1.984	0.931
	Relative Exec Time (pct)	-	-	**+15.62%**	-	**+9.01%**
Gaze	Source Size (lines)	375	300	see tot	320	967
	Source Size (bytes)	13852	13061	see tot	11701	37782
	Exec Iterations	-	601	601	602	601
	Exec Time Mean (usecs)	-	46.859	106.334	5.974	9.062
	Exec Time SD	-	6.783	11.861	2.259	12.410
	Relative Exec Time (pct)	-	-	**+126.92%**	-	**+51.70%**
Total	Extra Libs	glm	-	glm	-	glm
	Source w/Libs (bytes)	132167	31602	176831	27694	416670
	Relative Source size (pct)	-	-	**+459.56%**	-	**+1404.55%**

its standard deviation. As expected, it can be noticed how any C# implementation runs faster than the Python version, mainly thanks to the compiled vs. interpreted nature of the language.

The last line (Relative Exec Time, bold text) reports the percentage of time execution needed by the transpiled code compared with the one hand-made. A Welch's t-test[15] on the execution time between the two conditions (Hand-made vs. Transpiled) shows a statistically significant difference with $p < 0.05$ for the TTS functionality in Unity ($+9.01\%$) and $p < 0.001$ for all the remaining cases.

Concerning which of the two code versions (hand-made or transplied) is the fastest, and to what extent, depends on the controller.

The code of *blinking* is mostly characterized by comparison of values and basic algebraic operations, few if/then branches, and for loops limited to two iterations. It contains a single call to a native library for the computation of a random float. In this case, the transpiled code clearly outperforms the one hand-made. The code for *Text-to-speech* features more complex conditionals and a more intense use of both loops and dictionaries, but no calls to native libraries. In this case the performances are comparable, with the transpiled code requiring no more than 16% additional time for computation. Finally, the *eye-gaze* code

---

[15] https://en.wikipedia.org/wiki/Welch's_t-test – 30 Apr 2018.

features no loops, very limited use of dictionaries, a moderate use of native mathematical functions (abs, sign), and a heavy use of operations between vectors and quaternions. The transpiled code is in this case 127% slower in Python and 51% slower in C#. However, it is worth noticing the fundamental difference of the vector/quaternion operations between Haxe and C#. The C# implementation uses the Unity's native `Vector` and `Quaternion` types, which are implemented as `struct` definitions and hence operate efficiently on the stack memory when executing operators. Differently, the Haxe implementation of the `glm` library uses heap memory allocation, generating a new instance as result of every operator. Said this, we are pretty confident than a more careful use of the `glm` library, where the developer pre-allocates instances in order to reduce instantiations, might limit the gap between the hand-made and the transpiled code.

6   Conclusions and Future Work

We presented an implementation methodology that takes advantage of two well-established design patterns (adapter and façade) and transpilation to *write-once* the code of motion controllers for virtual humans and re-use them across multiple game engines. Our tests show that, for both the Blender Game Engine and Unity, the performance of Haxe transpiled code is comparable to code manually translated by humans. As such, we would suggest Haxe as a reasonable choice to encode of the core logic of motion controllers when the support of multiple game engines is a requirement.

At the moment, the main limitation of this approach is the difficulty in debugging the Haxe code during its development. The code transpiled by Haxe is in most cases non human readable, and this is the code seen by the engine's own debugger. Hence, in order to effectively improve the quality of the development pipeline, it is worth investigating a technical solution to step-by-step debug the original Haxe code rather than its transpiled version. That would effectively drop the need of step 1 (implementation of an initial draft) from the development pipeline. In future development of our character animation suite, we would like to include Unreal in the set of game engines and test C++ as target language.

Virtual humans, also known as virtual characters, virtual agents, or avatars, are used in many research fields. However, the research community misses standards for the interoperability of different virtual human software, mainly also due to the significant differences in the underlying technologies. New teams starting a research in those fields rely on the latest gaming technologies to (re-)implement fresh new virtual humans. However, off-the-shelf game engines mainly offer production pipelines and tools for the playback of motion captured human motion, while there are no integrated libraries for procedural animation control. Small research teams or companies do not have budget to re-implement and integrate in a single platform the multitude of motion controllers that have been conceived and implemented in the last years by many unconnected investigators.

This work suggests that it is possible to write reusable and portable motion controllers with limited implementation overhead and an acceptable impact on performances. The authors hope for the creation of a shared web repository of motion controllers, each presented as a combination of one core-logic and several adapters, where researches in the field can jointly store their contributions. This would allow the research community to more easily share, compare and improve their results, reduce the effort of migrating between game engines, and have access to a catalog of controllers in order to more easily setup multi-functional virtual humans.

Acknowledgments. The authors wish to thank our student Timo Gühring for his precious help in the development and translation of the TTS and the eye-gaze modules. We also thank Kiarash Tamaddon for the Unity project setup.

References

1. Bouraqadi, N., Mason, D.: Mocks, Proxies, and Transpilation as development strategies for web development. In: Proceedings of the 11th Edition of the International Workshop on Smalltalk Technologies, IWST 2016, pp. 10:1–10:6. ACM, New York (2016)
2. Bysiek, M., Drozd, A., Matsuoka, S.: Migrating legacy Fortran to Python while retaining Fortran-level performance through transpilation and type hints. In: 2016 6th Workshop on Python for High-Performance and Scientific Computing (PyHPC), pp. 9–18. IEEE, November 2016
3. Cannasse, N.: Using HaXe. In: The Essential Guide to Open Source Flash Development, pp. 227–244. Apress, Berkeley (2008)
4. Fang, Y., Nakashima, R., Matsumiya, K., Kuriki, I., Shioiri, S.: Eye-head coordination for visual cognitive processing. PloS One **10**(3) (2015)
5. Gamma, E., Helm, R., Johnson, R., Vlissides, J.: Design Patterns: Elements of Reusable Object-Oriented Software. Addison-Wesley, Reading (1994)
6. Hirzel, M., Klaeren, H.: Code coverage for any kind of test in any kind of transcompiled cross-platform applications. In: Proceedings of the 2nd International Workshop on User Interface Test Automation, INTUITEST 2016, pp. 1–10. ACM, New York (2016)
7. Johnston, P.R., Rodriguez, J., Lane, K.J., Ousler, G., Abelson, M.B.: The interblink interval in normal and dry eye subjects. Clin. Ophthalmol. **7**, 253–259 (2013)
8. Maheshwari, Y., Reddy, Y.R.: Transformation of flash files to HTML5 and JavaScript. In: Proceedings of the ASWEC 2015 24th Australasian Software Engineering Conference, pp. 23–27. ACM, New York (2015)
9. Ponticelli, F., McColl-Sylveste, L.: Professional HaXe and Neko. Wiley, Hoboken (2008)
10. Schrder, M., Trouvain, J.: The German text-to-speech synthesis system MARY: a tool for research, development and teaching. Int. J. Speech Technol. **6**(4), 365–377 (2003)

Non-photorealistic Rendering and Sketching Supported by GPU

Bruno Ježek[✉], David Horáček, Jan Vaněk, and Antonín Slabý

University of Hradec Králové, Hradec Králové, Czech Republic
{bruno.jezek,david.horacek,antonin.slaby}@uhk.cz,
vanek.conf@gmail.com

Abstract. One of the methods of non-realistic rendering - sketching and its use and outcomes with utilization of modern graphic cards is presented in the paper. First we outline individual aspects of the drawing and their basic inscriptions. The goal of the proposed sketching method and the subject of its visualization outputs are artist-made-like images. We describe the process of this kind of creation. Our goal is also real-time processing. Therefore, the proposed method combines CPU and GPU processing. Multi-passes through the graphical pipeline of programmable GPUs are used. Finally appropriate evaluation criteria are set and evaluation is performed using this criteria.

Keywords: NPR · GPU · Sketching · Real-time rendering

1 Introduction

Computer visualization includes also methods of non-photorealistic rendering (NPR). Unlike realistic rendering methods, NPR methods do not try exact rendering, but highlight certain scene properties, such as shape or mutual spatial relationships. Therefore, line drawings can be widely found in specialized publications [1, 2]. NPR methods use findings and knowledge of artistic creation, which cover for example ways to find significant edges in the image or spatial representation, along with the application of selected drawing techniques. The aim of computer visualization outputs is creation of hand-made-like images. They use different techniques such as hatching and sketching [3–5].

In this paper NPR sketching is described in more details. First are defined individual aspects and some basic facts and features of this kind of drawing. Then its implementation details using the possibilities and advantages of modern programmable graphics cards are presented. They are then applied to the program solution. Proposed method and design and implementation of the accompanying algorithm and results of their application are shown and evaluated.

© Springer International Publishing AG, part of Springer Nature 2018
L. T. De Paolis and P. Bourdot (Eds.): AVR 2018, LNCS 10850, pp. 447–463, 2018.
https://doi.org/10.1007/978-3-319-95270-3_38

2   Sketching

Sketching is a drawing style that includes several different techniques. The design and results may vary in stroke lengths and repetition, the type of pencil used, or the stroke force applied. The difference in stroke length greatly affects the resulting sketch appearance. Short strokes allow more precise design that is particularly suitable for beginners, while long strokes make the sketch result cleaner and smoother. Longer strokes are more demanding as to following the exact line. The sketch possessing long strokes seems to be more relaxed and at the same time is faster and consequently it is commonly used in sketches (animation designs, drawings, constructions, etc.). Important factors defining the visual outline of the results is imitation of the differences in strokes that are characterized by the hardness or sharpness of the used pencil, the ways of holding it and the way the stroke is lead. It is also worth considering the pressure force that can be distinguished by different types of strokes. The hardness of the pencil and the applied pressure result in the differences in saturation of the resulting color, and the shade of the resulting trace. Likewise, the shape of the pencil makes it possible to simulate minor nuances in the created footprints. The shape of the pencil tip can be represented by a polygon. Pencil stroke representation - the path of the pencil can be defined as the set of several connected segments and then smoothed by e.g. approximation using appropriate parametric curves. A polygon tip changing to color of the individual pixels according to the relevant parameters of the paper (canvas) is applied along the path. For more details see Sousa and Buchanan's Architecture [6].

2.1   Edge Identification Methods for Sketching

Sketching methods require identification of edges that are subsequently rendered by some of the NPR methods. Here rises some problems. If we use raster representation, it is first necessary to detect the individual edges in the image. Common methods find significant color or shade changes using edge filters detectors. It is not possible to determine with certainty that each edge found is suitable to be used in the sketch. Some edges may for example form the boundary of areas created by shadows casting etc.

In case, the object representation is used, the individual edges forming the input model of the object are known, but it is necessary to classify them and divide into two groups: significant edge contours and less significant edges not used in the sketch. The models are mostly composed of many relatively short edges placed near the boundary of the facets. These edges enable to shape the sketch finely. It is but necessary to remove some less important edges to prevent the resulting sketch to be overburdened by edges.

2.2   Detection Edges in Raster Image

Edge detectors are typically used to find quick and substantial changes in the colors (shades) of neighboring pixels. One of them is Sobel's operator, which calculates the gradient based on surrounding pixel values [7]. Another possible approach is detection proposed by John F. Canny. Its procedure is based first on eliminating possible noise that could influence the results and then on finding a gradients and their local maxima, eliminating excess edges and subsequent final thresholding to pick only significant edges. Canny Edge Detection modification and improvement of the algorithm is discussed for example in [8]. A comparison of these two and other possible methods can be found for example in Image Edge Detection [9].

2.3   Determining the Spatial Scene Silhouette

The silhouette indicates the contour, shade, or preview of the image. A common form of silhouette is the black drawing on the white background. The term silhouette in this contribution refers to a set of edges forming an outline of an object, otherwise known as a contour. The prerequisite for drawing a silhouette is rendering a scene consisting of oriented polygons that include information about their front (i.e. site facing to the observer). The first step in the process aims to find the edges whose adjacent polygons are visible from the opposite sides, one of them has its front and the other the back facing the viewer. The second step solves the problem of possible overlapping of two or more polygons and enables the plotting only actually visible ones. The disadvantage of raster approaches is absence of vector representation necessary for further processing.

Vector approach does not look up the silhouette in the picture, but uses directly the wireframe model of the spatial scene. Consequently the required boundaries are obtained, but it is still necessary to remove and/or cut the hidden edges or their parts. The commonly used method is based on the Appel algorithm that divides each edge at all points where it intersects (from the viewpoint of the observer). All created separate segments are then tested against all polygons to find whether they are in the front and are therefore visible. The disadvantage of this approach is the high computational complexity disturbing in solution of complex scenes with a large number of objects [10].

3   Stroke Generation

The proposed processing chain described in the following text includes own insights and observations by the authors confirmed by testing. The individual steps are based on just described general approach. It is used vector input and output model. The proposed method solves the sketching technique by plotting a sequence of short curves that resembles pencil strokes. The steps of the input model processing chain and its implementation using the hardware support of the graphics card are described further.

The process of making a sketch can be understood as a sequence of steps of gradual processing of the input model, usually given in the form of surface triangles, to obtain the resulting raster image. The whole process is composed of the following steps:

- Finding edges forming adjacent surfaces,
- Deleting duplicate and insignificant edges to find silhouette,
- Division edges into edge segments at intersections,
- Removing invisible segments,
- The final artist-made-like visualization of strokes based on making strokes and their subsequent rounding.

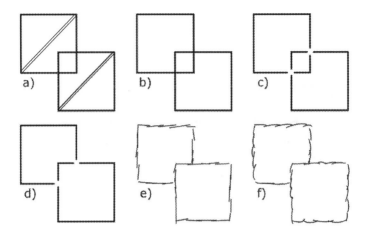

Fig. 1. Visualization of steps of the processing a) Initial model; b) Deleting duplicate and insignificant edges; c) Division edges into edge segments; d) Removing invisible segments; e) Making strokes from edges; f) Rounding strokes

The following figure (Fig. 1) demonstrates, on a simple sample of the model consisting of two planar squares, composed of triangles, this procedure and illustrates achieved gradual results of individual steps.

3.1   Finding Adjacent Surfaces Forming Edges

Input surface model for the whole chain has boundary representation and is composed of individual triangles determined by three vertices without knowledge of the mutual relations of triangles. The adjacent primitives, important for further processing, need to be traced further. The loaded model is stored in the form of a common vertex and index buffer. Vertex buffer is a list of vertices that stores spatial coordinates of individual points. The index buffer contains information about linking of points to triangles. Each triple of items (vertices) in the index buffer forms one triangle and any pair of points of the triangle forms the triangle edge. It is important, that the common vertices are placed in the list of vertices as a single point, so that the neighbors could be identified correctly. In addition to it, the order of vertices in the triangle is important, because the sequence of vertexes determines the orientation of the sides and determines front and back sides.

The triangle search algorithm goes through the edges of all triangles and searches for common vertices in all other triangles. Vertex comparison is performed in the index buffer based on the consistency of vertex indexes. When finding the same edge in two triangles, their third point in the triples the sought-after point of adjacency of the opposite triangle. Although this is the most demanding operation as each edge is compared to the edges of all the following triangles in the list, then fact does not matter as it is required only when the model is first processed and does not affect the rendering speed later on.

3.2   Removing Duplicate Edges

The processing of this step uses the fact, that the edges are all represented in a closed model twice as edge of two adjacent triangles. Therefore, all duplicates must first be removed from the list of edges. This is done by scanning all triangles and their edges. Each edge is included into the silhouette only if it is first found in search.

3.3   Removing Invisible Edges

The aim of this step is to exclude invisible edges that do not belong to the silhouette. The method used to remove hidden edges, or their parts, which form the triangles of the surface model of the object, is used to check. It is based on Appel's algorithm. The edges are first divided into parts determined by intersections from the viewer's perspective. Subsequently, each of the resulting segments is tested for visibility against all model polygons. For more details see [11]. The result of this step is illustrated on the following figure (Fig. 2).

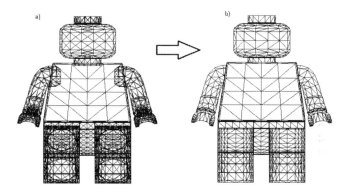

Fig. 2. Removing invisible edges, a) original model; b) visible segment of the model

The simplest approach is to test each edge against all others. Operation has asymptotic computational complexity n^2. There are alternatives that simplify the problem by editing edges. One possibility is explained in the Bentley-Ottmann algorithm described in [12]. It uses the so called sweep line to sweep the space [13] and reduces the computational complexity to $n\log(n)$. But two other conditions are required. The endpoints do not lie on different edges and more than two edges does not meet at one point. In general, these conditions cannot be guaranteed, since it is not possible to determine in advance what the intersections will be. A simplified naive approach having complexity n^2 establishes testing the edge with only all edges following it in the list, and writing the potential intersection to both edges.

The visibility test follows. Since comparison of each segment with all polygons is time consuming operation, a segment comparison is based on testing chosen single point of the segment against the depth of the model in the same location. It is necessary to render the model (using common approach) and save to a depth buffer in the texture first for this purpose. This texture subsequently serves as a mask against which individual segments are tested.

3.4   Removing Minor Edges

This step enables to choose which edges will remain as a part of the silhouette. The results of removing less significant edges for more complex models are shown in the figure (Fig. 3). The testing is based on comparing the mutual angle of the normal vectors of the two adjacent triangles. The dot products of normal vectors determines the limit of boundary.

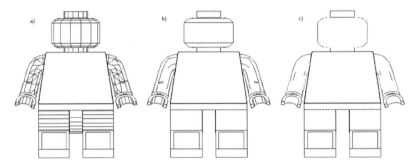

Fig. 3. Removal of insignificant edges with a minimum angle set to the limit of boundary – a) 0.99; b) 0.9; c) 0.7

3.5   The Final Artist-Made-like Visualization of Strokes Based on Strokes and Their Subsequent Rounding

After finding all the visible segments of the model, the next step is its final art redraw. This step consists of two phases: dividing the edges into sections that represent single strokes and their subsequent visualization. Each stroke is defined by its length and its repetition parameters. The first phase divides individual edge segments into separate strokes, according to the selected parameters. It is necessary to apply the partially random casting, which brings the resulting visualization closer to artist-made drawings. The repeating parameter defines the percentage of length of overlapping of the two consecutive strokes. The second phase of strokes visualization is their shaping. Since man is unable to draw perfectly straight lines and the strokes mostly resemble arcs of some kind, each generated stroke is replaced by an arc. The next figure (Fig. 4) demonstrates this approach at the sample square visualization.

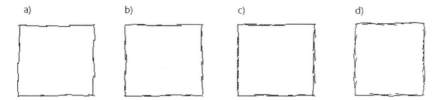

Fig. 4. Results of applying setting repeating parameter that defines the percentage of length of overlapping of the two consecutive strokes to the value – a) 0.05; b) 0.2; c) 0.4; d) final rounded strokes

4   Hardware Support of Methods

The visualization pipeline is a sequence of steps in which data is processed into the resulting image (typically using graphics card). In recent years significant changes in the internal GPU structure that allows some of the steps to program for GPU and modify the data flow have been introduced. Each of the steps then has to be adapted to the use of GPU when implementing the individual steps of the proposed methodology. The technology of separate programmable shaders included in the visualization chain is selected from the variety of possibilities provided by programmable graphics cards and the OpenGL API is selected for programming.

The shader unit is a self-running kernel programmable by its own code-shader program. Vertex shader (VS) processes all vertices of the input model and performs transformation operations and calculations of parameters sent with vertices. After linking the vertices to the appropriate structures (triangles, lines, points), the geometry shader (GS) allows to expand or completely change their structure – generate new vertices, or convert from triangles into lines. After data processing, rasterization takes place. Fragment shader (FS) processes specific pixel primitives and serves primarily for color editing. In addition to color, there is a very important z-coordinate of the fragment that determines its visibility. Z-buffer is the same size as the image buffer (the resulting image displayed on the monitor) and stores the depth of the nearest fragment in the given location. Each fragment before saving the color to the image buffer is first tested to the depth, if it is visible, and if so, the data in both buffers is overwritten.

Transforms feedback (TF) is an alternative to outgoing GS data that does not serve for rasterization but is stored in a buffer that is available for further processing. The data can be repeatedly processed by multiple passes, including the exchange of programmed shaders.

4.1   Generation a Depth Mask

The entire model passes through standard visualization pipeline in the first step of algorithm with the only difference that the resulting depth of the fragments is written into the special texture (depth buffer equivalent). The reason is in the use of the depth mask in the visibility test against all polygons in Appel's algorithm. In VS, the vertex coordinates are multiplied by the transformation matrices into the resulting projection.

In FS, the outgoing color is replaced by the depth, that is, the calculated and inter-polated z-coordinate of each fragment.

4.2   Finding the Silhouette

The next steps are performed at the level of individual vertices or geometric entities, so option Rasterization is set from this step on until the last one. All calculations are stopped on GS and consequently execution time is saved by stopping rasterization and other operations. The result of processing in VS and GS is buffered using TF. Com-pleted models are sent again to the pipeline, and the first sorting of the edges that may be part of the silhouette is established. Each incoming triangle is sent with adjacent vertices and the normals of all four neighboring (adjacent) triangles are calculated.

4.3   Segmentation

It is necessary to exclude all hidden or partially hidden segments of otherwise visible edges after selecting the possible edges of the silhouette. Intersections are found for each edge with the other edges and separate parts are created according to which the segments are divided into separate segments. Removing of invisible separated seg-ments is based on method described above (see 3.3).

4.4   Pre-processing of Strokes

The sketching itself comes after rendering the silhouette. The first step leads to dividing edges into separate strokes and includes some variability. A noise texture is generated once during initialization to represent the randomness. Pixel colors of the texture are set by the random method from Math class in Java. The noise texture is sent subsequently to the shader. The random number is selected according to the current position of the end point of the stroke. Different color components for the start and end points of the strokes are used to minimize the likelihood of the phenomenon that two vertices of the same position will be equally shifted.

4.5   Drawing of Strokes

Final rendering and rounding of strokes is performed during the last pass through the chain. The reason for this pass is in the fact, that in the previous step, dozens of vertexes can occur in case of long edges and short strokes. Each of the strokes is then composed of several vertices that are connected to represent the arc. In the application is used six vertices. GS has a limited number of outgoing vertices (170 in the tests performed) and consequently it is possible to produce up to 28 strokes coming from a single edge. The rounding direction has already been defined as a positive or negative half-space at the segment (denoted by +1 or −1). The definition and calculation of the arc uses Ferguson's cubic segment expression. The segment is defined by the end points and the directional vectors belonging to them.

4.6   Optimization of Calculations

The segmentation algorithm with the computational complexity n^2 proved to be computationally most demanding part of the processing during the initial test. Since detailed surface models are made up of a plenty of facets, the amount of calculations for edge segmentation is rapidly growing with the dependence of this number. Deleting hidden parts of edges by a depth test, which reduces the amount of edges processed, takes place after segmentation. Edge segmentation must always occur when the transformation is changed, so it is appropriate to design a suitable optimization method.

Optimization is usually based on splitting of the space into smaller parts and then testing edges with those located in the same sub-space only. The first possibility is a breakdown edges when creating silhouettes. SSBO buffers used to send a list of edges to the segmentation shader allow GS to write, and the individual buffers can represent the appropriate sub-spaces for sorting in the process of searching for silhouettes.

Therefore, the QuadTree Quadrate method is selected in the application. Its substance is in a gradual splitting of the space into four regular sections, and all the objects contained in the parental space are divided into newly created descendant parts. Subsequently, each edge is tested for the intersection with only the group of edges in the respective descendant of the space.

4.7   GPU Programming Interface

The proposed solution uses functionality of GPU programmable in Shading Language (GLSL), part of OpenGL standard. GLSL language is a higher-level language, derived from C language and is designed to program graphics cards and define entities to process. It supports the most common language structures (cycles, conditions, etc.) and basic data types. In addition to it, special types (e.g. vectors and matrices) are available, including operators and functions needed for various calculations including matrix multiplication and vector normalization, etc.

The OpenGL version 4.3 and higher is required for the functionality of our application implementation. Support of the format of the GL_TRIANGLE_ADJA-CENCY graphic entities is necessary for implementation of our proposed algorithm, as it serves in the shader geometry to store three adjacent triangle vertices, which are necessary for finding the silhouette. Another requirement for the graphics card is its support of Transforms Feedback technology, which allows the shader geometry results to be stored in the GPU memory, instead of being sent to rasterization and to resubmit the data from it for further processing. The use of this technology allows to keep the vector structure of the model up to stage of final rendering.

Shader Storage Buffer Object is the last important technology used is. This is a buffer format similar to the older Uniform Buffer Object format, but having new options and possibilities. This buffer is used to send silhouettes edges to the GPU, where they are tested at intersections and divided into separate segments.

The figure (Fig. 5) gives a summary of previous information and shows architecture of our framework. Part of the calculation takes place on the CPU and most of the demanding operations are performed by the GPU. The complexity of the proposed

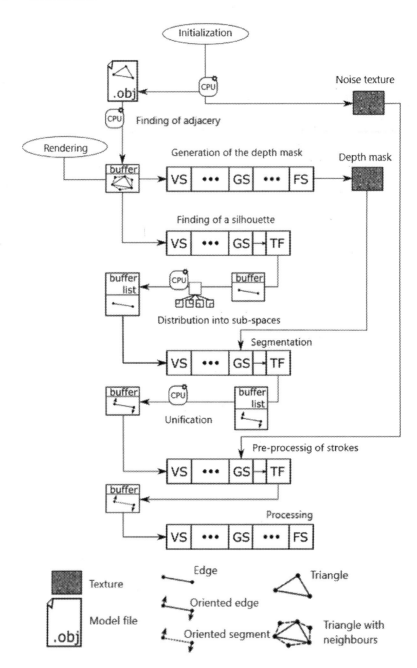

Fig. 5. Architecture of the framework combine both, CPU and GPU processing VS – vertex shader, GS – geometry shader, TF – transfer feedback, FS – fragment shader

process requires multi passes through graphic pipeline and some of them are terminated before rasterization by transfer feedback operation.

Loading the OBJ model, finding adjacent surfaces and creating an index buffer in the GL_TRIANGLE_ADJACENCY format takes place on the CPU and that is processed only once at initialization. Creating the image itself, which depends on the position of the model, starts with the generation of a depth map performed by a single pass of GPU pipeline. The silhouette of the distinguished edges is determined by the truncated GPU pass finished before rasterization. Subsequently, the Quadtree subspaces optimization is performed on the CPU. The silhouette edges are segmented in another GPU pass together with hidden segments removing based on deep map texture sampling. At the same time, the edge orientation is added at this step. Gained visible segments are joined by unification to the edges on the CPU. The resulting edges form a complete silhouette ready for sketching. The edges are divided into strokes in the preprocessing according to the specified threshold parameters. This is done through one restricted GPU pass. The last step is the rounding of the strokes and the final rendering.

5   Results

The implemented algorithm was tested on freely available OBJ models; Hulk [17] (Fig. 6a), HammerShark [18] (Fig. 7), Lizard [19] (Fig. 9), Gun [20] (Fig. 8) and LEGO Man [21] (Fig. 10). The complexity of the model expressed by the number of vertices is given in the table (Table 1). The visual evaluation of the rendered results, and comparison of time and computational complexity was made.

5.1   Visual Evaluation and Control

The primary and suitable evaluation of the results of the proposed sketching methods is visual control of their result images. First they are compared with samples of related hand-made works (Fig. 6). Models are chosen with varied complexity and displayed in several variants with different settings of two selected parameters L, R. The parameter R represents a repetition of strokes and is defined as the percentage of the edge length. The parameter L determines the stroke length in units of the model space dimension. The total height and width was set to be 2 units. Samples of visual outputs show the original model with all the edges, the silhouette found, and the result of the sketching obtained with different parameter L, R settings. Hand-made artefact of a similar object is also available for visual comparison of the achieved results. Further drawings illustrate the results obtained by the same sketching method with different stroke repeat parameters and other successive selected results, e.g., R = 0.6; 0.3 and their lengths, e.g. L = 0.01; 0.2 (Figs. 9 and 10).

5.2   Computational Complexity

Another measure of usability of the proposed algorithm is its computational complexity and efficiency for solving the problem. The essential steps parts of the algorithm are evaluated in terms of their complexity and the amount of time required to process test

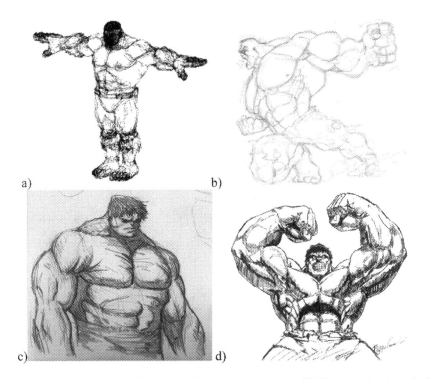

Fig. 6. Visual comparison of sketching with artist-made works of Hulk a) rendered result; b) [14]; c) [15]; d) [16]

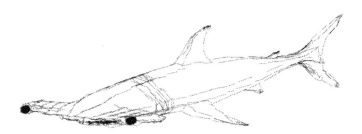

Fig. 7. Result of HammerShark model sketching

Fig. 8. Result of Gun model sketching

Table 1. Complexity of the model

	Number of vertexes	Number of indices	Number of quads
HammerShark	2646	15840	5280
Gun	7 166	40 761	13 587
Lizard	718	4 296	1 432
LEGO Man	285	31 488	10 496

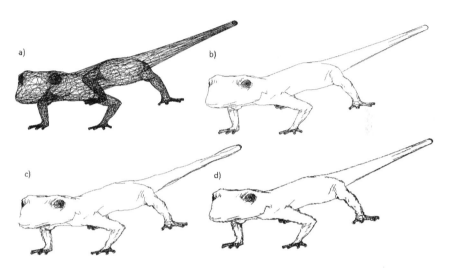

Fig. 9. Lizard rendering results a) input model; b) visible segments; c) sketching visualization with parameters R = 0.3, L = 0.2; d) and R = 0.6, L = 0.01

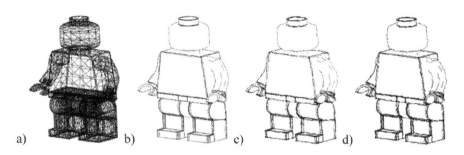

Fig. 10. LEGO man rendering results; a) input model; b) visible segments; c) sketching visualization with parameters R = 0.3, L = 0.2; d) and R = 0.3, L = 0.01

models. The lizard model is rather a plain test object, while the remaining three models have higher quality.

Initialization of the model

The purpose of the first step of the algorithm is to load a model file and preprocess it. This step is followed finding the necessary adjacency for proper visualization functionality.

The following table (Table 1) lists the complexity of tested models in terms of the number of geometric entities for surface definition.

The next Table 2 lists the time amount necessary to process individual files on the CPU. The program runs in a single thread, and the time interval needed to loading and preprocessing is in the order of seconds. However, as this is only an initialization step and mentioned operations are performed only once, a relatively longer time is acceptable.

Table 2. File processing times

	File read time	Time to find neighbours	Overall time
HammerShark	0.033 s	0.862 s	0.895 s
Gun	0.057 s	5.346 s	5.403 s
Lizard	0.022 s	0.080 s	0.102 s
LEGO Man	0.050 s	2.543 s	2.593 s

Complexity of Processing and Visualization

This section discusses the rendering itself. The object is processed in five steps.

1. Generation the depth mask. The complexity of rendering depends linearly on the number of triangles of the model.
2. Finding the silhouette. The complexity here again depends linearly on the number of triangles, and the processing is limited to the GS performance, where the normals of the adjacent triangles are calculated and compared (i.e. four times per triangle).
3. Edge segmentation. The computation complexity depends quadratically (n^2) on the number of edges in the given sub-space due to necessity of testing each edge relative to all other ones. In positive case the intersection coordinates are calculated.
4. Preprocessing of strokes. The incoming segments are divided according to the required length of the strokes into smaller sections. The complexity of preprocessing depends linearly on the number of segments.
5. Drawing of strokes. The last stroke refinement is performed here. The complexity of each incoming segment is determined by the number of operations per vertex.

The only time-critical step is just the segmentation, which includes the edge sorting using the QuadTree method. The next table (Table 3) lists the number of edges or

Table 3. Number of primitives in individual processing steps

	Origin	Silhouette	Segments	Pre-processing
HammerShark	15 840	10 411	672	3 749
Gun	40 761	28 328	11 266	12 324
Lizard	4 296	735	370	450
LEGO Man	31 488	12 010	4 516	4 571

segments processed in each of the silhouette processing steps where the original value is the number of triangles multiplied by 3.

Segmentation of Edges

Segmentation consists of two separate steps. First step includes finding intersections, division of strokes into segments and instant execution of the depth-test for finding the segment's visibility using GPU. The second step is CPU sorting using QuadTree structure. The times required for tested artefacts are summarized in table (Table 4). The following parameters were used for sorting. Maximum number splitting levels into sub-spaces: 15 and Maximum number of segments achieved as a result of repeated splitting: 400.

Table 4. Segment processing times on CPU a GPU

	CPU sorting time [s]	GPU segmentation time [s]
HammerShark	0.025	0.195
Gun	0.015	0.280
Lizard	0	0.015
LEGO Man	0.010	0.105

In spite of the fact, that the splitting resulted in creation of many sub-spaces, the increase in their number did not reduce the resulting time. This was caused by the higher CPU load, increased number of segmentation passages (each sub-space is being processed separately) and small splitting areas at greater depths, as in the final demanding details of the models, the high number of edges is clustered in very tight distances.

6   Conclusion and Future Work

We have presented a framework for non-photorealistic rendering method – sketching. Our implementation combines both CPU and GPU multi pass processing that enable real time rendering of quite complicated models. Visual comparison of rendered sketches and art-made drawings prove applicability of designed solution. Sketching parameters of rendering methods enable set up different styles of pencil drawings.

In further research we will focus on the application of other specific visualization styles replacing the individual strokes themselves and optimizing the algorithm. In particular, we will try to use edge classifications for the purpose of their emphasis and use in the resulting image. The degree of emphasis can be determined based on the prominence of the edge in terms of curvature of the surface of the model and apply the appropriate thickness, repeatability, or edge length. Another direction for expansion would be to focus on shading some parts of a drawing based on the shape and rotation of the surface of the model.

There are still a several possibilities to refine and optimize the algorithm and reduce the number of necessary calculations. This improvements may include for example saving the tested center point, or running individual QuadTree branches on separate process threads and take advantage of parallelization options in subdividing into subspace. However, since CPU time comprises up to 10% of total processing time, greater emphasis should be placed on speeding up or simplifying segmentation itself.

Acknowledgements. This work and the contribution were supported by a project of Students Grant Agency (SPEV) - FIM, University of Hradec Kralove, Czech Republic. The authors of this paper would like to thank Milan Košťák, a student of Applied Informatics at the University of Hradec Kralove, for help with GPU implementation.

References

1. Hertzmann, A.: Introduction to 3D non-photorealistic rendering: silhouettes and outlines. In: SIGGRAPH 1999 (1999). Non-Photorealistic Render
2. Gooch, A., Gooch, B., Shirley, P., Cohen, E.: A non-photorealistic lighting model for automatic technical illustration. In: Proceedings of the 25th Annual Conference on Computer Graphics and Interactive Techniques, pp. 447–452. ACM, New York (1998)
3. Suarez, J., Belhadj, F., Boyer, V.: Real-time 3D rendering with hatching. Vis. Comput. **33**, 1319–1334 (2017)
4. Hertzmann, A., Zorin, D.: Illustrating smooth surfaces. In: Proceedings of the 27th Annual Conference on Computer Graphics and Interactive Techniques, pp. 517–526. ACM Press/Addison-Wesley Publishing Co., New York (2000)
5. Grabli, S., Turquin, E., Durand, F., Sillion, F.X.: Programmable style for NPR line drawing. In: Rendering Techniques 2004 (Eurographics Symposium on Rendering). ACM Press, Norrköping (2004)
6. Sousa, M.C., Buchanan, J.W.: Computer-generated graphite pencil rendering of 3D polygonal models. Comput. Graph. Forum. **18**, 195–208 (1999)
7. Gao, W., Zhang, X., Yang, L., Liu, H.: An improved Sobel edge detection. In: 2010 3rd International Conference on Computer Science and Information Technology, pp. 67–71 (2010)
8. Bao, P., Zhang, L., Wu, X.: Canny edge detection enhancement by scale multiplication. IEEE Trans. Pattern Anal. Mach. Intell. **27**, 1485–1490 (2005)
9. Maini, R., Aggarwal, H.: Study and comparison of various image edge detection techniques. Int. J. Image Process. IJIP. **3**, 1 (2009)
10. Raskar, R., Cohen, M.: Image precision silhouette edges. In: Proceedings of the 1999 Symposium on Interactive 3D Graphics, pp. 135–140. ACM, New York (1999)
11. Markosian, L., Kowalski, M.A., Goldstein, D., Trychin, S.J., Hughes, J.F., Bourdev, L.D.: Real-time nonphotorealistic rendering. In: Proceedings of the 24th Annual Conference on Computer Graphics and Interactive Techniques, pp. 415–420. ACM Press/Addison-Wesley Publishing Co., New York (1997)
12. Bentley, J.L., Ottmann, T.A.: Algorithms for reporting and counting geometric intersections. IEEE Trans. Comput. **C-28**, 643–647 (1979)
13. Shamos, M.I., Hoey, D.: Geometric intersection problems. In: 17th Annual Symposium on Foundations of Computer Science (SFCS 1976), pp. 208–215 (1976)
14. Gavin, M.: Hulk Smash. https://gavinmichelli.deviantart.com/art/Hulk-Smash-329337385
15. Heron: Hulk. http://prettygoodcomics.blogspot.com/2012/02/warm-up-sketch-hulk.html
16. Cremonini, F.: Hulk (sketch), http://filippocremonini.com/?portfolio=hulk-sketch
17. Hulk Free 3D Model. http://tf3dm.com/3d-model/hulk-77446.html

18. Hammerhead SHark. https://www.blender-models.com/model-downloads/animals/fish/id/
hammerhead-shark/
19. Lizard. https://www.blender-models.com/model-downloads/animals/amphibians/id/lizard/
20. Colt M4A1 Free 3D Model. https://free3d.com/3d-model/colt-m4a1-8099.html
21. LEGO Man Free 3D Model. https://free3d.com/3d-model/lego-man-25498.html

The Effect of Gait Parameters on the Perception of Animated Agents' Personality

Santi P. Badathala, Nicoletta Adamo[✉], Nicholas J. Villani, and Hazar N. Dib

Purdue University, West Lafayette, USA
{sbadatha, nadamovi, nvillani, hdib}@purdue.edu

Abstract. The esthetics and personality of animated agents play an important role in enhancing the experience of human-computer interactions. In the context of online learning and instruction, research shows that the personality of pedagogical agents can have a significant impact on students' learning. The study reported in the paper focused on the expression of agents' personality through non-verbal cues. In particular, it investigated whether certain gait parameters affect how the audience perceives the personality of a stylized animated pedagogical agent walking in a virtual classroom. While evidence exists that the way a character walks can affect the viewer's perception of his/her personality, it is not clear yet which specific gait attributes contribute the most to identifying the personality of the character. In this study, six different parameters of gait were examined to see how slight changes in their values could help the audience perceive the agent as an extrovert. The study included 18 video stimuli and data was collected from 79 participants. Findings confirmed the effect gait can have on the perception of personality. They further suggest that stride length, beat of the walk (e.g. walking speed) beltline tilt, and upper body twist contribute the most towards this end.

Keywords: Animated pedagogical agents · Character animation
Gait · Personality · Five-factor model

1 Introduction

Johnston and Thomas made a quote in their book about Grumpy from Snow White and the Seven Dwarfs, that he (Grumpy) could not put his head on someone's shoulder like Dopey. True to his personality, he must turn away and cry alone [1]. These words explain the emphasis traditional animators placed on conveying the personality of animated characters in films.

The personality of animated agents is equally important, as it can help enhance the human-computer interactions that persist increasingly in our lives. In particular, the personality of animated pedagogical agents (APA) could have a significant effect on learners' engagement, motivation, and therefore learning. With the advance of technology it is now possible to design computer-based learning environments that support simulated social interactions between learner and computer [2]. Pedagogical agents

© Springer International Publishing AG, part of Springer Nature 2018
L. T. De Paolis and P. Bourdot (Eds.): AVR 2018, LNCS 10850, pp. 464–479, 2018.
https://doi.org/10.1007/978-3-319-95270-3_39

with emotional capabilities can provide such interactions with the learner. According to Kim, Baylor and Shen, it is "the provision of such simulated emotional interactions that may distinguish pedagogical embodied agents from traditional computer-based tutoring, seemingly offering a unique instructional impact" [2].

The goal of our research is to investigate how a pedagogical agent's non-verbal cues, such as facial expressions, gestures, and body movement affect the perception of his/her personality. More specifically, the objective of the study reported in the paper was to determine whether 6 parameters of the character's gait (e.g. stride length, walk beat, beltline tilt, upper body twist, backward/forward body lean, and angle of the foot) contribute to the perception of the agent as an extrovert.

2 Animated Agents with Personality

The presence of animated agents in day-to-day lives has increased significantly in the past few years. Many companies make a place for themselves in the virtual world in order to interact directly with consumers and streamline their products to consumer needs [3]. A study that investigated how animated agents can influence the consumer shopping behavior found that the attractiveness of the agent played a greater role towards persuading customers than how informative the agent was [4]. In their article, Can computer personalities be human personalities? Nass et al. [5] emphasize the importance of the agent's personality in human-computer interactions. They state that people respond much better to agents similar to them in personality, and argue that the personality of the agent can be presented with a few minimal cues and superficial manipulations rather than richly defined agents, sophisticated pictorial representations, natural language processing, or artificial intelligence (p. 223) [5]. Based on this proposition, the study reported in the paper predicted that simple body language of an animated agent could be used to give the audience a cue to the agent's personality.

Animated Pedagogical Agents (APA) are characters embedded within a computer based learning environment to facilitate student learning. Many studies confirm the positive learning effects of systems using these agents [6–9]. Cassell [10] one of the first researchers who studied the use of animated agents in learning and communication, developed the Embodied Conversational Agent, an interactive virtual agent that can speak and exhibit nonverbal behaviors. Cassell argued that well-designed embodied pedagogical agents could enrich one's learning experience and foster motivation. A fairly recent meta-analytic review of 43 papers shows that APAs enhance learning in comparison with learning environments that do not feature agents [11].

Research indicates that the manipulation of the APAs' affective behavior (e.g. their personality and emotions) can significantly influence learner beliefs and learning efficacy [12–14]. Erdle et al. [15] suggest that the personality and charisma of the teacher plays an important role in ensuring effective communication with the student and enhancing the classroom experience. The instructor's personality is as important when the teacher is an animated agent in a virtual classroom. It has been noted that people interact much more freely with animated agents when the agents act realistically or exhibit behavioral similarities to the users [16]. Konstantinidis et al. [17] have explored the effectiveness of virtual learning environments featuring pedagogical agents specifically in the case of autistic children. In their paper they state that expressing the emotional state and personality of the agent through the agent's body language and facial expressions can greatly enhance the students' experience.

3 The Five-Factor Model of Personality

Personality has been, and still is, a subject of active debate. However, for several years, the five-factor model, or the big five model, has been accepted by many as the most fundamental and comprehensive model of personality. McCrae and John describe the five-factor model of personality as a hierarchical organization of personality traits in terms of five basic dimensions: Extraversion, Agreeableness, Conscientiousness, Neuroticism, and Openness to Experience (p. 1) [18]. In their article, McCrae & John summarize various studies on the categorization of personality types and their appropriate taxonomies, and classify the five-factor model as a break-through in psychology, and a fundamental stepping-stone on which future studies of personality may be based. They describe each personality type with the following adjectives: Extraversion-active, assertive, energetic, enthusiastic, outgoing; Agreeableness-appreciative, forgiving, generous, kind, sympathetic, trusting; Conscientiousness-efficient, organized, reliable, responsible, thorough; Neuroticism-anxious, self-pitying, tense, touchy, unstable, worrying; Openness to Experience-artistic, curious, imaginative, insightful, original, wide interests. Of the five types of personalities mentioned in the big five model, extraversion has been correlated most to positive emotions and leadership.

The terms 'extraversion' and 'introversion' were coined by Carl Jung. As the founder of analytical psychology, Jung made many breakthroughs about personality and its significance. Jung believed that every person has an extroverted and an introverted side. But one side is more dominant than the other, thus classifying a person as an extrovert or an introvert [19]. Eysencks model describes the extrovert personality as sociable, lively, active, assertive, sensation seeking, carefree, dominant, venturesome (p. 22) [20]. Neff et al. following the big five model suggest that extroverts talk more, at a faster pace, more loudly and more repetitively than introverts [21].

In this paper the focus is on the extrovert personality type, as research suggests that teachers who are Extroverted-Intuitive-Feeling-Perceiving are assets to the field of education [22].

4 The Role of Non-verbal Cues in the Expression of Personality

The expression of emotion and personality relies greatly on non-verbal cues such as facial expressions, gestures and body movement. Neff et al. suggest that spatial attributes such as body position, gesture amplitude, motion smoothness, motion direction and fluency could be key indicators of personality [21]. They hypothesize that as the measure of extraversion increases, the spatial stroke of the persons gesture also increases. That is, extroverts converse with more outward gesture, characterized by greater distance of the limbs from the body. They also suggest that extroverts have greater gesture speed and smaller response time, a forward lean in the posture, upward direction of palms and a general smoothness of gestures. Riggio and Friedman carried out research that indicated that, though gender differences exist, extraversion is generally characterized by outward, fluent gestures, and fluent speech. Their study also shows that these factors directly contribute to the perception of the personality type [23].

Gait is an important factor that contributes to the perception of personality. Sakaguchi and Hasegawa observed that viewers were able to arrive at a conclusion regarding the subjects' personality by watching point light walk cycles of the person [24]. It is a popular opinion that people suffering depression or general dysphoria would walk with heavy treads or a slouching posture. Studies also suggest that psychological factors can have a significant effect on gait. Satchell et al. conducted a study to see the correlation between the big five personality types and various gait parameters. Their results showed that gait speed for extroverts is relatively high and that strong positive correlation exists between the pelvis movement and gait [25].

While a few studies have investigated how emotion may affect the gait of a person, the effect of personality on the parameters of gait still remains, at best, loosely correlated. This research explores how stride length, speed, tilt of the beltline, upper body twist, forward and backward lean, and angle of the foot of a walking animated agent affect the perception of the agent as an extrovert. Although the study reported in the paper focused on animated pedagogical agents, the results of this research can help establish guidelines that may be extended to applications outside virtual learning.

5   Methodology

Based on the data available on the differences between non-verbal cues of extroverts versus introverts, the following hypotheses were drawn and tested in this research. Each hypothesis refers to an animated walking agent.

Hypothesis 1(0): Spatial scale of stride does not have an effect on subjects' perception of the agent's degree of extroversion.

Hypothesis 1(a): Spatial scale of stride has an effect on subjects' perception of the agent's degree of extroversion. Walking characters with a large spatial scale of stride are perceived as more extroverted.

Hypothesis 2(0): Beat of the walk does not have an effect on subjects' perception of the agent's degree of extroversion.

Hypothesis 2(a): Beat of the walk has an effect on subjects' perception of the agent's degree of extroversion Walking characters with a low beat (e.g. low number of frames per step, hence faster walk) are perceived as more extroverted.

Hypothesis 3(0): Beltline tilt does not have an effect on subjects' perception of the agent's degree of extroversion.

Hypothesis 3(a): Beltline tilt has an effect on subjects' perception of the agent's degree of extroversion. Walking characters with a pronounced beltline tilt are perceived as more extroverted.

Hypothesis 4(0): Upper body twist does not have an effect on subjects' perception of the agent's degree of extroversion.

Hypothesis 4(a): Upper body twist has an effect on subjects' perception of the agent's degree of extroversion Walking characters with a pronounced upper body twist are perceived as more extroverted.

Hypothesis 5 (0): Forward/backward upper body lean does not have an effect on subjects' perception of the agent's degree of extroversion.

Hypothesis 5(a): Forward/backward upper body lean has an effect on subjects' perception of the agent's degree of extroversion. Walking characters with a pronounced forward/backward upper body lean are perceived as more extroverted.

Hypothesis 6(0): Foot inward/outward rotation around the heel joint does not have an effect on subjects' perception the agent's degree of extroversion.

Hypothesis 6(a): Foot inward/outward rotation around the heel joint has an effect on subjects' perception the agent's degree of extroversion Walking characters that place their feet facing far away from the center of the body are perceived as more extroverted.

The animated agent used in the study is shown in Fig. 1. His legs and arms are rigged using Inverse Kinematics; his spine is rigged using Forward Kinematics.

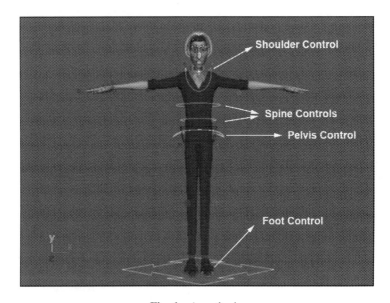

Fig. 1. Agent's rig

5.1 Video Stimuli

The stimuli of the experiment included 18 animated clips featuring the agent walking in a classroom in front of a white board. The agent was animated using keyframe animation technique. The movements of the character were restricted to walking in front of the whiteboard and the value of the six gait parameters were varied to three different levels, e.g., low, neutral and high. For each of the parameters, the levels of variation were achieved differently. Stride length is measured as the distance covered from the initial contact of one foot to the following contact of the same foot. The normal stride length of the character depends on its height and build. In the stimuli produced for this research, the length of the character's legs and the normal stride of the character follow a ratio of 1:1. For the chosen character, the length of the leg was approximately 10 units. Therefore, the neutral stride length of the character also covers 10 units of distance per step. For the shorter stride length (low level) the character covers 6 units per step and for the larger stride length (high level) the character covers 12 units per step.

Beat is the speed of the gait (e.g., the number of frames needed to take one step). In a fast walk, the character takes a smaller number of frames to complete one step. In a slow walk, the character takes a larger number of frames to complete one step. Therefore, the low level of this parameter pertains to the smaller number of frames, i.e., faster speed. In this study the character takes 24 frames to complete one step when walking at a neutral pace. At a fast pace the character takes one step every 16 frames, and at a slow pace the character takes one step in 32 frames, at a playback speed of 30 frames per second.

Belt line tilts occur when the weight of the body shifts from one leg to the other while walking. The shoulder line also tends to tilt with this shift of weight. Unlike the lean and upper body twist, which are most noticeable during the contact positions, the beltline tilt is observed in the passing positions of the walk. For a neutral walk, the pelvis control of the character (which controls the rotation of the pelvis joint – see Fig. 1) was rotated 7° along the z-axis in the direction of the leg/foot on the ground. The lower level of this parameter was 3.5 and the higher level was 10.5° respectively. The shoulder control (which controls the rotation of the collar joint – see Fig. 1) was rotated the same number of degrees as the pelvis control in the same direction in all cases.

The upper body also rotates as the person puts one foot in front of the other. The upper body twist in the animations was produced by rotating the pelvis control along the y-axis on the contact positions, and simultaneously rotating the shoulder and spine controls (which control the spine joints – see Fig. 1) in the opposite direction. The pelvis control was rotated by 20° for a normal walk. This number was halved and doubled to get the low and high levels of variation. The amplitude of rotation of the shoulder control was the same as the pelvis control but in the opposite direction. Rotation of the shoulder control was half the amplitude of the pelvis control rotation, also in the opposite direction.

People tend to lean their upper bodies forward or backward while walking. The three levels of variation for this parameter are forward lean, straight or subtle lean, and backward lean. The lean of the character is more pronounced on the contact positions and less pronounced on the passing positions. In this study, the pelvis control of the character was rotated 10° along the x-axis to produce the forward lean (high level). Similarly, the pelvis control was rotated −7 along the x-axis to produce the back-ward lean (low level). For a walk with subtle lean (neutral level), the pelvis control was rotated by 3.5° along the x-axis.

The outward angle of the foot was the sixth gait parameter considered in the study. The feet of the avatar point straight ahead for the low level of this parameter. This means the y-rotation of the foot control (which pivots the foot around the heel joint) was kept at zero. The foot was rotated 10 and 20° away from the center of the body for the neutral and high levels respectively.

The values of all the gait parameters used in the study are based on best practices in character animation [26] and were selected in such a way that the walk of the agent did not appear too exaggerated or out of the ordinary at any point. After creating a baseline animation where all six parameters are kept at a neutral level, the values of the parameters were modified in Maya 3D software graph editor to obtain the variations of the walk. A pilot study with 5 graduate students in animation was conducted on the baseline animation to see if the walk was perceived as acceptable and neutral. 3 experts in the field further validated the completed animations. A total of 18 walk animations were produced. In each animation, all the parameters were varied together to different levels. 18 different combinations of the parameters and their respective levels were selected based on the Fractional Factorial Design [27], which is explained in Sect. 6. Table 1 shows the 18 different combinations of the 6 parameters' values. The numbers 0, 1 and 2 in Table 1 indicate the low, neutral and high levels of the parameters respectively. The order of the 6 parameters is the following: (1) stride length, (2) number of frames per step, (3) beltline tilt, (4) upper body twist, (5) forward and backward lean, and (6) angle of the foot. The ordering of the parameters was chosen randomly. The combination 111111 represents the baseline animation where all six parameters are kept at the neutral level. Similarly, 000000 represents a combination where all parameters are kept at the low level, and 222222 represents a combination where all parameters are kept at the high level. A combination such as 000210 represents a walk in which stride length, number of frames per step and beltline tilt are kept at the low level, upper body twist is kept at the high level, forward and backward lean are kept at the neutral level, and angle of the foot is kept at the low level. From here on in the paper, the videos will be referred to by the combination of the parameters' values (ex. Video 210120). Figure 2 shows the beginning, middle and end frames of videos 000000, 111111 and 222222.

The animations were captured in a medium/long shot in both side and front views (see Fig. 3, top), such that the limbs and other channels were easily observable. The duration of each animation ranged from 10 to 20 s. The actions performed in all the animations were the same. The completed animations were then presented to subjects who rated the personality of the character on a scale of 1 to 10, with 1 being extremely introvert, and 10 being extremely extrovert.

Work of Albright et al. suggests that observing a person of zero acquaintance for about 10 s can help the observers form a judgment about his/her personality [28]. Hence, this study adopted a methodology where stimulus videos of the same animation of approximately 10 to 20 s in length were created and presented to the audience, who then rated the degree of extraversion of the character.

5.2   Subjects

This study used simple random sampling and anyone over the age of 18 was eligible to participate in the experiment. A total of 134 responses were collected from students and faculty in the departments of Computer Graphics Technology, Engineering Technology, English, and Computer Science at Purdue University. 50.39% of the respondents

Table 1. The 18 combinations of the parameters' values used in the study

Parameter 1 (stride length)	Parameter 2 (number of frames per step)	Parameter 3 (beltline tilt)	Parameter 4 (upper body twist)	Parameter 5 (forward & backward lean)	Parameter 6 (angle of the foot)
0	0	0	0	0	0
1	1	1	1	1	1
2	2	2	2	2	2
0	0	1	1	2	2
1	1	2	2	0	0
2	2	0	0	1	1
0	1	0	2	1	2
1	2	1	0	2	0
2	0	2	1	0	1
0	2	2	1	1	0
1	0	0	2	2	1
2	1	1	0	0	2
0	1	2	0	2	1
1	2	0	1	0	2
2	0	1	2	1	0
0	2	1	2	0	1
1	0	2	0	1	2
2	1	0	1	2	0

were from the department of Computer Graphics Technology and had some experience in computer animation. 47.29% of the participants were females. Age of the participants ranged from 18 to 66 years. 53 of the collected responses were incomplete and were, therefore discarded. Two more responses were discarded because the participants had marked the same degree of extraversion of the character across all 18 videos. Hence, these responses were classified as faulty.

5.3   Experimental Setup

The participants were sent an email with a brief summary of the research study and a link to an online survey. The web survey consisted of 3 demographics questions and 18 screens, one screen per video. The demographics questions related to subjects' age, background, and gender. Each screen included one of the 18 video stimuli. The videos were presented one after the other and the order of presentation was randomized. All participants viewed all the 18 animations and after each video clip they were presented with 2 questions. First, they were asked to rate the personality of the character in the clip they had just watched on a scale of 1 to 10, 1 being extremely introvert and 10 being extremely extrovert. The second question asked the participants to specify whether the character may fall under one of the 4 personality types other than extraversion. This was a multiple-choice question with the other 4 personality types

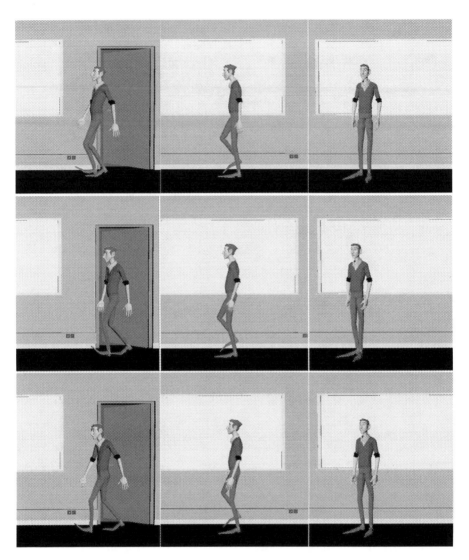

Fig. 2. Frames from videos 000000 (top), 111111(middle) and 222222 (bottom)

from the big five model as the options, along with a fifth option "none" and a sixth option "other". In the options, each personality type was described with a few adjectives to make sure that the subjects understood what each personality type represented.

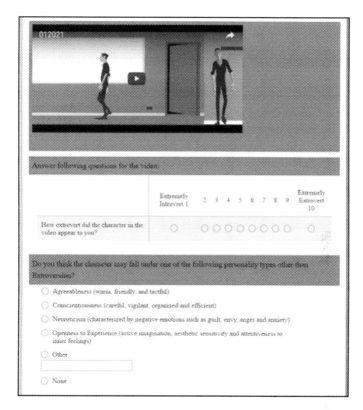

Fig. 3. Screenshot from the online survey

6   Findings

This study adopted a fractional factorial design as opposed to a full factorial design [27]. Since the study used 6 different factors, each varied at 3 discrete levels, a full factorial design would have required 729 experimental runs. Due to various constraints, it was not possible to produce 729 animations and include them in the online survey. Hence, 18 representative combinations of the factors were created according to the fractional factorial model. The study collected both qualitative and quantitative data. Quantitative data was recorded in the form of subjects' ratings of the agent's extraversion on a 10-point scale. The answer to the other question in the survey was recorded as qualitative data.

For the purpose of statistical analysis, this study assumed that the data collected had a constant variance, followed a normal distribution and that all responses were independent of each other. The data set was parsed to separate out the qualitative data from the quantitative data. The ratings of the degree of extroversion were analyzed as the quantitative data. By simply comparing the means of the scale values for each of the 18 combinations, it was observed that the combination 120102 had the lowest rating of extroversion and the combination 202101 had the highest. Table 2 shows the means of ratings of degree of extroversion for each of the videos. Table 3 gives the results of the ANOVA test, which was conducted to assess if the six parameters being tested had a significant effect on subjects' perception of the agent's degree of extroversion.

Table 2. Means of the ratings of extroversion for each video

Stimulus video	Mean
000000	5.8228
001122	5.6203
010212	5.3924
012021	5.2025
021201	4.62
022110	4.443
100221	6.165
102012	6.114
111111	5.6582
112200	6.481
120102	4.0127
121020	4.873
201210	6.519
202101	6.785
210120	5.684
211002	6.354
220011	5.2405
222222	5.0253

With a chosen significance level of 0.05, the p-values for Hyp1, Hyp2, Hyp4, and Hyp5 (reported in Table 3) indicate that stride length, walk beat, beltline tilt, and upper body twist, respectively, had a significant effect on subjects' perception of the agent as an extrovert. Hence we rejected null hypotheses H1(0), H2(0), H3(0) and H4(0). For hypotheses 5 and 6 the p-values are >0.05 (see Table 3) therefore we could not reject null hypotheses H5(0) and H6(0) and no further analysis was conducted.

The interactions between the hypotheses were also tested. Interaction between Hyp1 and Hyp2 (p = 0.0336), and interactions between Hyp1 and Hyp4 (p = 0.0456) were significant. Table 4 shows linear regressions performed on Hyp1, Hyp2, Hyp3 and Hyp4. As mentioned earlier, each parameter was varied to 3°. For the purpose of this analysis, the 3° are labeled 0, 1 and 2, '0' being low, '1' being neutral and '2' being high. The estimate of the 'intercept' indicates the value where all parameters were held at level '0'. The first column indicates Hyp(n)(m) where n is the number of the hypothesis from 1 to 6 and m is the level at which the parameter was held. For example, Hyp1(2) denotes parameter 1 at level 2.

The positive values of Hyp1(1) & Hyp1(2), which correspond to the stride length of the character at neutral and high levels respectively, indicate that the ratings of extroversion increased as the stride length increased. Estimate of Hyp1(2) is greater

Table 3. ANOVA model for the 6 parameters

	Degrees of freedom	Sum of squares	Mean of squares	f-value	p-value
Hyp1	2	132	66.02	19.980	2.71e−09
Hyp2	2	545	272.37	82.430	<2e−16
Hyp3	2	21	10.70	3.238	0.0393
Hyp4	2	27	13.71	4.150	0.0158
Hyp5	2	15	7.38	2.235	0.1069
Hyp6	2	13	6.61	2.000	0.1352

Table 4. Linear mixed model

Hyp(n)(m)	Estimates
(Intercept)	5.6069959
Hyp1(1)	0.21519
Hyp1(2)	1.26582
Hyp2(1)	−0.6962
Hyp2(2)	−1.41772
Hyp3(1)	0.06329
Hyp3(2)	0.18987
Hyp4(1)	−0.1519
Hyp4(2)	0.26582

than the estimate of Hyp1(1). Negative values of Hyp2(1) and Hyp2(2), which correspond to the neutral and slow pace of the character respectively, indicate that the ratings of extroversion decreased considerably as the speed with which the character walked decreased. The positive values of Hyp3(1) and Hyp3(2), which correspond to the beltline tilt of the character at the neutral and high levels respectively, indicate that the ratings of extroversion increased slightly as beltline tilt increased. The value of Hyp4(1), which corresponds to the upper body twist at the neutral level, indicates that the ratings of extraversion decreased significantly when the upper body twist was neutral. Lastly, the value of Hyp4(2), which corresponds to the upper body twist at the high level, indicates that the ratings of extroversion increased very slightly when the upper body twist was high.

Based on the analysis of interactions, the following conclusions could be drawn for each of the parameters: *the animated agent with larger stride length had significantly higher ratings of extroversion; the ratings of extroversion decreased as speed of the character decreased; ratings of extroversion increased slightly with an increase in the beltline tilt; the ratings of extroversion decreased slightly when the upper body twist of the agent went from low to neutral, but increased again when the twist was high.*

Since hypotheses 1&2 and hypotheses 1&4 interacted significantly, further testing the interactions of these hypotheses resulted in the following conclusions: when speed and stride length of the character were both held at the neutral level, ratings of extroversion of the avatar went up significantly (estimate = 0.93671), when speed and upper body twist were both high the ratings of extroversion decreased (estimate = −0.78481).

In summary, results of the statistical analyses show that *characters that walk with a larger stride length and with a more pronounced beltline tilt are perceived as more extroverted. Characters that walk with a lower beat (e.g. higher speed) are perceived as more extroverted when the value of upper body twist is not high.* In regard to upper body twist, although the results showed a significant effect, there was not enough evidence to draw meaningful conclusions and additional testing is needed.

Gender, age and background (e.g. home department) were the only demographic data collected from the participants. All three types of data were found to have a significant effect on the participants' ratings. It was found that participants from the department of Computer Graphics Technology (e.g., participants with a background in animation) rated the characters slightly higher than the average (estimate = 0.51396) on the extroversion scale than participants from other departments. Male participants rated slightly lower than the average on the rating scale (estimate = −0.33403). It was found that participants rated slightly lower than average as age increased (estimate = −0.015797).

In addition to rating the degree of extroversion of the character, participants were asked whether they thought the character might fall under any of the personality types of the big five model other than extraversion. Figure 4 visualizes the data collected for this question for each of the 18 videos. The options given to the participants were neuroticism, agreeableness, openness to experience, conscientiousness, other and none. Participants could leave their own comments under the other option. Although this research focused on the extrovert personality type, the graph in Fig. 4 gives some insights on how to animate a character so that he/she appears as one of the other four personality types. For example, the bars of 022110, 120102 and 222222 in the graph (speed of the character is slow in all three videos), show that agents with slow pace were perceived as neurotic by many of the participants. Similarly, the agent with neutral or large stride length was more likely to be perceived as agreeable, when accompanied by a fast or neutral speed. The agent with slow pace, large strides and less pronounced upper body movements was often perceived as conscientious.

7 Conclusion and Future Work

The results of the study are consistent with existing literature in this area and help conclude that the gait of the character can inform the audience significantly about the character's personality. Of the six parameters tested, it is observed that only four have a significant effect on the perception of personality namely, stride length, speed, beltline tilt and upper body twist. Therefore, it may be stated that these parameters should be given the most priority while designing an animated agent with extrovert personality.

As mentioned previously, the study adopted a fractional factorial design to produce the videos. Each video was a combination of each of the 6 parameters at 3 different levels and the differences between the 18 videos were subtle. While the changes in stride length and speed of the avatar are the most easily discernible, followed by beltline tilt and upper body twist, it may have been difficult to identify the changes in the other parameters. This could be the reason behind the lack of significant effect in the case of body lean and angle of the foot of the agent. The short duration of the videos may also have contributed to this end. The results also show that not all the

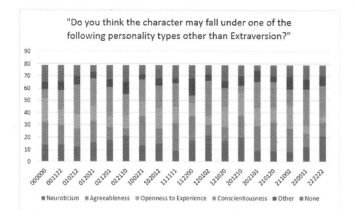

Fig. 4. Graph showing the frequency of each personality type for the 18 videos

parameters interact with each other. The interactions between the parameters as well as the interactions of the parameters with factors such as age, gender and department should be studied more thoroughly in the future with a larger data set.

The dressing style of the agent and the agent's build and facial features may have influenced the decisions of some of the participants. Even though the avatar was chosen to look unintimidating and plainly clothed with a neutral facial expression, making the agent even more plain and maybe without a face, could eliminate the role of these factors completely and yield more meaningful results. The study assumed that the participants were familiar with the concepts of extraversion and introversion. However, if some of the participants were unfamiliar with these concepts, this might have influenced the outcome of the study.

This study tested the effect of a limited set of gait parameters on the perception of personality. Other gait parameters may prove to have a significant impact if tested. Similarly, other animation parameters may also contribute largely to the perception of personality. For instance, the effect of specific facial articulations, eye movements and body/hand gestures could be investigated in future research.

This study used a white male stylized agent in his late twenties-early thirties. Agents of different ethnicities, gender and ages, and with different degrees of stylization (e.g. from iconic to realistic) could be used in future experiments to see if the conclusions drawn from this study would still hold true.

Despite its limitations, this study provides a set of initial guidelines for animators and instructional designers for designing effective extroverted animated agents.

Acknowledgements. This work is supported in part by NSF award #1217215, and by Purdue Provost Instructional Innovation Grant 2017–2018. The authors would like to thank Purdue Statistical Consulting for their help with the statistical analysis of the data.

References

1. Thomas, F., Johnston, O., Rawls, W.: Disney Animation: The Illusion of Life, vol. 4. Abbeville Press, New York (1981)
2. Kim, Y., Baylor, A.L., Shen, E.: Pedagogical agents as learning companions: the impact of agent emotion and gender. J. Comput. Assist. Learn. **23**, 220–234 (2007)
3. Blisle, J.F., Bodur, H.O.: Avatars as information: perception of consumers based on their avatars in virtual worlds. Psychol. Mark. **27**(8), 741–765 (2010)
4. Holzwarth, M., Janiszewski, C., Neumann, M.M.: The influence of avatars on online consumer shopping behavior. J. Mark. **70**(4), 19–36 (2006)
5. Nass, C., Moon, Y., Fogg, B.J., Reeves, B., Dryer, C.: Can computer personalities be human personalities? In: Conference companion on Human Factors in Computing Systems, pp. 228–229. ACM (1995)
6. Lester, J., Converse, S., Kahler, S., Barlow, T., Stone, B., Bhogal, R.: The persona effect: affective impact of animated pedagogical agents. In: Proceedings of CHI 1997, pp. 359–366 (1997)
7. Holmes, J.: Designing agents to support learning by explaining. Comput. Educ. **48**, 523–547 (2007)
8. Moreno, R., Mayer, R.: Interactive multimodal learning environments. Educ. Psychol. Rev. **19**, 309–326 (2007)
9. Lusk, M.M., Atkinson, R.K.: Animated pedagogical agents: does their degree of embodiment impact learning from static or animated worked examples? Appl. Cogn. Psychol. **21**, 747–764 (2007)
10. Cassell, J.: Embodied Conversational Agents. The MIT Press, Cambridge (2000)
11. Schroeder, N., Adesope, O.O., Barouch Gilbert, R.: How effective are pedagogical agents for learning? A meta-analytic review. J. Educ. Comput. Res. **49**(1), 1–39 (2013)
12. Zhou, L., Mohammed, A.S., Zhang, D.: Mobile personal information management agent: supporting natural language interface and application integration. Inf. Process. Manag. **48**(1), 23–31 (2012)
13. Kim, Y., Baylor, A.L.: Pedagogical agents as social models to influence learner attitudes. Educ. Technol. **47**(01), 23–28 (2007)
14. Guo, Y.R., Goh, D.H.L.: Affect in embodied pedagogical agents: meta-analytic review. J. Educ. Comput. Res. **53**(1), 124–149 (2015)
15. Erdle, S., Murray, H.G., Rushton, J.P.: Personality, classroom behavior, and student ratings of college teaching effectiveness: a path analysis. J. Educ. Psychol. **77**(4), 394 (1985)
16. Bailenson, J.N., Yee, N., Merget, D., Schroeder, R.: The effect of behavioral realism and form realism of real-time avatar faces on verbal disclosure, nonverbal disclosure, emotion recognition, and co-presence in dyadic interaction. Presence Teleop. Virtual Environ. **15**(4), 359–372 (2006)
17. Konstantinidis, E.I., Hitoglou-Antoniadou, M., Luneski, A., Bamidis, P.D., Nikolaidou, M. M.: Using affective avatars and rich multimedia content for education of children with autism. In: Proceedings of the 2nd International Conference on Pervasive Technologies Related to Assistive Environments. ACM (1995). Article No. 58
18. McCrae, R.R., John, O.P.: An introduction to the five factor model and its applications. J. Pers. **60**(2), 175–215 (1992)
19. Jung, C.G.: Memories, Dreams. Reflections. Vintage, New York (1989)
20. Eysenck, H.J.: The Biological Basis of Personality. Transaction Publishers, New Brunswick (1967)

21. Neff, M., Wang, Y., Abbott, R., Walker, M.: Evaluating the effect of gesture and language on personality perception in conversational agents. In: Allbeck, J., Badler, N., Bickmore, T., Pelachaud, C., Safonova, A. (eds.) IVA 2010. LNCS (LNAI), vol. 6356, pp. 222–235. Springer, Heidelberg (2010). https://doi.org/10.1007/978-3-642-15892-6_24
22. Rushton, S., Morgan, J., Richard, M.: Teacher's Myers-Briggs personality profiles: identifying effective teacher personality traits. Teach. Teach. Educ. **23**, 432–441 (2007)
23. Riggio, R.E., Friedman, H.S.: Impression formation: the role of expressive behavior. J. Pers. Soc. Psychol. **50**(2), 421 (1986)
24. Sakaguchi, K., Hasegawa, T.: Person perception through gait information and target choice for sexual advances: comparison of likely targets in experiments and real life. J. Nonverbal Behav. **30**(2), 63–85 (2006)
25. Satchell, L., Morris, P., Mills, C., O'Reilly, L., Marshman, P., Akehurst, L.: Evidence of big five and aggressive personalities in gait biomechanics. J. Nonverbal Behav. **41**, 35–44 (2016)
26. Williams, R.: The Animator's Survival Kit: A Manual of Methods, Principles and Formulas for Classical, Computer, Games, Stop Motion and Internet Animators, 4th edn. Farrar, Straus and Giroux, New York (2012)
27. Wu, C.J., Hamada, M.S.: Experiments: Planning, Analysis, and Optimization. Wiley, New York (2011)
28. Albright, L., Kenny, D.A., Malloy, T.E.: Consensus in personality judgments at zero acquaintance. J. Pers. Soc. Psychol. **55**(3), 387 (1988)

Vulkan Abstraction Layer for Large Data Remote Rendering System

Primož Lavrič, Ciril Bohak$^{(\boxtimes)}$, and Matija Marolt

Faculty of Computer and Information Science, University of Ljubljana,
Večna pot 113, 1000 Ljubljana, Slovenia
pl9506@student.uni-lj.si,
{ciril.bohak,matija.marolt}@fri.uni-lj.si

Abstract. New graphics APIs require users to implement a lot of needed functionality, such as memory management, by themselves. In this paper we present an abstraction layer build on top of such API, in our case the Vulkan API, for purpose of off-screen rendering of large data. We also present a use case for such abstraction layer implementation – a remote rendering system for simple Path Tracing accessible through web-based client-side application. The preliminary evaluation results show that implementation of simple Path Tracer is significantly faster then comparable implementation in OpenCL. In conclusion we also present possible extension and improvements of the developed abstraction layer.

Keywords: Vulkan API · Graphics library abstraction layer
Real-time rendering

1 Introduction

Graphical pipeline for real-time rendering has gone through substantial changes throughout its development since early 1990s. Over the years, the developers have gained substantially more control over what is happening in individual stage of the pipeline with added support for programmable stages. Most recent graphical APIs (Vulkan [1], DirectX 12, Mantle and Metal) are providing the developers with even more control, but on the other hand also require of them to implement a lot of additional functionality (e.g. memory management), previously handled by the APIs (OpenGL and DirectX 1–11).

The remote rendering concept of large datasets is not a new concept. It was implemented for different domains such as large volumetric data [2] and was implemented on different platforms (e.g. a web-based approach [3]). The researchers have also proposed different approaches for transferring the information between client- and server-side. Authors of [4] propose to transfer the information in form of 3D video. An interesting approach on high-resolution remote rendering system with collaborative features for grid environments is presented in [5]. Our approach distinguishes from the above presented implementation in several ways: (1) developers can implement their own rendering

© Springer International Publishing AG, part of Springer Nature 2018
L. T. De Paolis and P. Bourdot (Eds.): AVR 2018, LNCS 10850, pp. 480–488, 2018.
https://doi.org/10.1007/978-3-319-95270-3_40

solution (in our case we present shader-based path-tracing implementation), (2) the approach is very general and allows the extension for use with different kind of data and (3) our approach supports broad specter of hardware (e.g. not limited to specific manufacturer like CUDA) and does not necessarily need a GPU.

The rest of the paper is structured as follows: in Sect. 2 we present the developed abstraction layer, in Sect. 4 we present preliminary evaluation and results and in Sect. 5 we give the pointers for future work and present the conclusions.

2   Vulkan API Abstraction Layer

Unlike OpenGL, Vulkan provides only basic functionality on top of the driver and requires the developer to implement the rest. The implemented abstraction layer is on a similar level as OpenGL, but unlike OpenGL, it is not implemented as a state machine, because that would hinder the multi-thread performance. Rather than implementing a state machine, we implemented high-level wrappers that employ RAII programming idiom, each wrapping one or more Vulkan objects. Figure 1 presents the diagram of the abstraction layer. Unlike Vulkan objects which are independent of each other, the presented objects form a hierarchy in which each child object is dependent of its parent. This way we enforce that the objects are created in the correct order and that the child objects and their resources are automatically disposed of upon its parent's disposal. Each object is retrievable from its parent in a form of a raw pointer and all operations that operate on some object take a raw pointer as input parameter (for example a Descriptor Set requires a pointer to Descriptor Set Layout). Raw pointers are used to emphasize that the objects are owned by the parent of the object and not by the developer, and also to prevent the developer from accidentally disposing of the object.

The abstraction layer provides a base-class for the renderer implementation. This class provides interface for managing Vulkan instance and more importantly Vulkan devices. Vulkan device objects are the core of the abstraction layer. Vulkan device allows developer to manage enabled features, extensions and to query the device properties, but more importantly, it provides the structures for compute and graphical operations. In the following sections we present four key components provided by Vulkan device: Program Manager, Allocation Manager, Descriptor Pool and Queue Families and their integration within the abstraction layer.

2.1   Program Manager

The task of the Program Manager is to load shaders and to construct pipeline layouts and render passes. The Program Manager requires that the developer specifies the directory that contains shaders and a shader configuration file. Shader configuration file contains relative paths to all shaders' source files and a

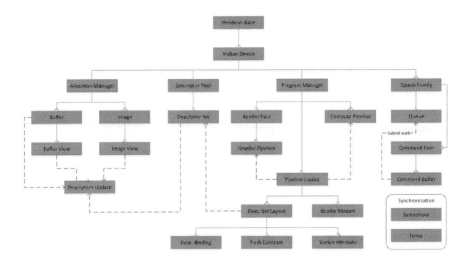

Fig. 1. Diagram showing the structure of our Vulkan API abstraction layer. Blue lines represent the composition association with either one-to-one or one-to-many relation. Orange arrows indicate that the object is used by the object the arrow is pointing to. (Color figure online)

list of pipeline configurations, each equipped with IDs of shaders that form the pipeline.

After the shaders are loaded, we need to perform shader reflection in order to build the pipeline layouts. Shader reflection is a process in which we extract the types, sets, bindings, layouts and array counts of shader uniforms, attributes and sub-pass attachments from the shader source code. Unlike OpenGL, which has integrated shader reflection, Vulkan requires the developer to either implement shader reflection on his own or provide pipeline layout configuration using other means. In our implementation, we used library SPIRV-Cross [6,7] to decompile SPIRV shaders and perform shader reflection. Because shader loading is intended to occur during the configuration time, the speed is not of crucial importance and we can afford to perform shader decompilation. We use the acquired data to populate pipeline layout descriptor sets, attributes and push constants and finally build the pipeline layout. Using the generated Pipeline Layout objects Program manager initializes the Compute Pipelines.

In the current implementation we only support Compute Pipelines, but intend to provide support for Graphical Pipelines in the future. Graphical Pipelines differ from Compute Pipelines as they are required to specify additional graphic related configuration, such as: vertex shader input, assembly configuration and depth and stencil state. In addition to that, Vulkan allows us to specify complex Render Passes, that consist of many Shader Programs given in a directed acyclic graph. This means that we need to specify the dependencies between the programs and connect the inputs and the outputs between the connected programs. In our implementation, we decided to let user provide additional graphic related configuration via a Pipeline State object and Render

Pass configuration as additional data in shader configuration file. Pipeline State object encodes the configuration in a bit field using only 423 bits while maintaining a 32/64 bit hash of the bit field to speed up pipeline querying. As for the Render Pass configuration, it is better that we provide it in th configuration file, because a typical application usually uses a small number of different Render Passes and they do not change in runtime.

2.2   Allocation Manager

In terms of memory management, there is a huge difference between Vulkan and OpenGL. In OpenGL, the memory management was handled implicitly by the API. In Vulkan though, developer needs to allocate and manage the memory used by buffers and images.

For memory management, we decided to use Vulkan Memory Allocator library provided by AMD GPUOpen [8]. We decided to use this library, because it provides very efficient memory management, by allocating very large chunks of memory and implementing paging on top of it, thus minimizing the number of operating system allocation calls. It also provides all of the needed functionalities and allows developer to provide custom allocator implementation.

Vulkan Memory Allocator allocations are managed by the Allocation Manager and are completely hidden from the developer. The developer can request either Buffer or Image object from the Allocation manager simply by specifying its size and format. The user can then manipulate the Buffers and the Image by either writing/reading the data via the provided interface (CPU visible memory only) or by submitting Command Buffer object containing write/copy commands to the Queue.

Developer can also create View objects for both Images and Buffers (limited to texel buffers). A view is quite literally a view into an image/buffer. It describes how to access the image/buffer and which part of the image/buffer to access, for example, if it should be treated as a 3D texture, which mip-map levels should be used and so on. Created Views are used to bind the image/buffer to either frame buffer or descriptor set.

2.3   Descriptor Pool

We already presented the Descriptor Sets in Subsect. 2.2, more specifically Descriptor Set Layouts. But before Descriptor Sets can be used, they have to be allocated from the Descriptor Pool. In Vulkan, the Descriptor Pool requires that the maximum number of allocated Descriptor Sets and bindings of each type is specified in advance. One could set these to maximum possible value, but this would be very inefficient. Because of that, the abstraction layer allow the developer to query the number of Descriptor Sets and bindings from the Program Manager and provide it to the Descriptor Pool object. This way, the Descriptor Pool knows the exact number of Descriptor Bindings, and the developers are also still able to modify the count manually. For example, multiply it by two for implementation of double buffering.

After the Descriptor Pool is initialized one can start allocating Descriptor Sets. The Descriptor Sets can be filled with the data using Descriptor Update object that records write/copy operations and executes them once submitted to Vulkan Device object. After the data has been written to the Descriptor Set, one can bind it via a bind command submitted to the command buffer.

2.4   Queue Families

Each device can have up to three Queue Families: graphic, compute and transfer queues. Graphic Family supports all operations (including compute and transfer operations), Compute Family supports both compute and transfer operations and the Transfer Family supports only transfer operations. This means one could use graphic family to perform all operations, but it is usually better to perform transfer operations on the Transfer Family queue and compute operations on the Compute Family queue because of the driver optimization.

Because of that, we allow the developer to specify how many Queues of each family he wants to create during the Vulkan device initialization. This allows the distribution of the operations on different Queues to achieve better performance. Note that using too many Queues may hinder the performance due to the excessive synchronization.

Each Queue Family object also has a Command Pool object associated with it. Command Pool allows the allocation of the Command buffer objects for its Queue Family. One can use the Command buffer objects to record and submit the commands to the queue. In order to synchronize the command execution among multiple Command buffers and the host, we can use fences and semaphores wrapped in Fence and Semaphore objects.

3   Use Case: Remote Rendering

The developed Vulkan abstraction layer was used for implementation of remote rendering system. Using the Vulkan abstraction layer, we implemented a show-case example with a simple GPU Path Tracing renderer that renders and transmits the image to the user in real time, and listens for the user input.

3.1   System Architecture

The remote rendering system roughly consists of three parts: (1) NodeJS server, (2) web client and (3) remote renderer. NodeJS servers only task is to provide HTTP server that serves the web page to the client (Fig. 2).

Web client is used as an interface to the remote renderer. Its job is to display the images that are broadcasted from the server and to capture the user input and forward it to the server. To display images, we implemented a basic WebGL renderer that renders a given texture to the quad and displays it on HTML canvas. In the future we also intend to perform some lightweight rendering (2D, 3D annotations) on the client side and merge it with the remote renderer

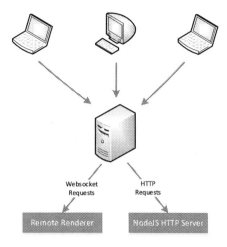

Fig. 2. Diagram showing the communication paths between clients and the server.

output. All the communication between the client and the remote renderer occurs via HTML Websockets, because of their very low overhead latency. The client is always listening for the remote renderer updates, which contain rendered images in the binary format. Because the remote renderer provides the image encoded in the format supported by WebGL, the client can simply forward the received image to its WebGL renderer and display it. In the showcase implementation, we also use mouse input information to move around the scene. We capture the mouse input on the client and transmit the data in JSON format to the remote renderer.

The remote renderer's primary task is to broadcast the rendered images and handle user input requests. First it opens up a socket and waits for the client to connect. When the first client connects it starts rendering the scene using renderer implemented on top of our Vulkan abstraction layer. Each rendering iteration computes one sample per pixel and send the updated image to all connected clients. When the remote renderer receives input update request (containing mouse position), it computes a new camera position, writes it to uniform buffer and triggers a redraw.

3.2   Rendering Example

Renderer computes the image by solving the rendering equation [9] using numerical integration. We implemented Monte Carlo path tracing with Russian roulette early path termination in GLSL compute shaders (compiled to SPIR-V). The implementation is loosely based on [10, 11]. Shader program inputs are scene data (spheres and planes), camera transformation and timestamp (updated each iteration), used for pseudo-random number generation. Upon execution, the shader program adds the radiance to the storage buffer that is used to accumulate radiance. When the shader program finishes, the data is read from the GPU and forwarded to the client (Fig. 3).

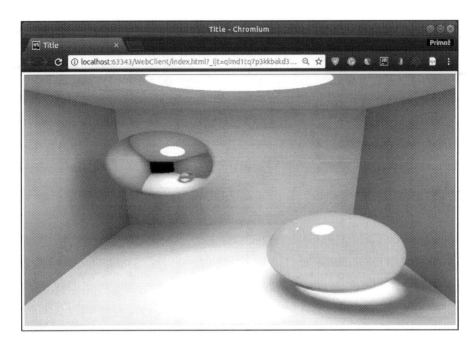

Fig. 3. Shows the image of the Cornell Box that was rendered by the remote renderer implemented on our Vulkan abstraction layer and the streamed to the web client.

4   Evaluation and Results

We conducted a preliminary performance evaluation by comparing three different implementations of the same path tracer algorithm: C# (CPU), OpenCL (GPU) and Vulkan (GPU) implementation. On both GPU implementations only one SPP was computed each kernel/shader program execution. On CPU implementation we parallelized the work and used 8 threads for the benchmark. We rendered a 1920 × 1080 image and measured the time required to reach 1000 SPP (GPU) and 100 SPP (CPU). The performance was evaluated on the following

Table 1. Performance evaluation results of CPU, OpenCL and Vulkan path tracer implementations.

	CPU (100 SPP)	OpenCL (1000 SPP)	Vulkan (1000 SPP)
Average	4850 s (∼80 min)	4.27 s	3.91 s
STD	157 s	0.04 s	0.06 s

machine: CPU - Intel i7 6700k, RAM - 16 GB and GPU - NVIDIA GeForce GTX 1080Ti. We performed 10 time measurements for each implementation. Results of our testing are presented as average time required to reach 1000 SPP (100 SPP for CPU) and standard deviation in Table 1.

The results show that the OpenCL implementation and the Vulkan implementation on top of the Vulkan abstraction layer both perform very similarly, but the Vulkan implementation is on average 9% faster.

5   Conclusions and Future Work

In this work we present an abstraction layer built on top of the Vulkan API, which allows faster and easier development of graphics application. The abstraction layer was developed for purpose of implementing headless remote rendering application connected to web-based client-side end-user application. The preliminary evaluation, based on example use case application, shows that the developed system outperforms OpenCL implementation. Such rendering system could be used for visualizing large data on lightweight client devices (e.g. smart phones or tablets) by exploiting the processing power of dedicated server-side system.

There are still many possible extensions of the presented system, for example: implementation of swapchain abstraction that could be optionally used to display the content window of local application, implementation of streaming compression (GPU/CPU) for faster transfer of render results and adaptive streaming based on connection quality, structures that would enable seamless multi GPU support and buffer streamers that would enable rendering of large data that does not fit the memory of the GPU.

We are also planning to fully implement the remote rendering presented as use case and integrate it with an existing web-based medical data visualization framework.

References

1. Sellers, G., Kessenich, J.: Vulkan Programming Guide: The Official Guide to Learning Vulkan. Addison-Wesley Professional, Boston (2016)
2. Guthe, S., Wand, M., Gonser, J., Strasser, W.: Interactive rendering of large volume data sets, November 2002
3. Yoon, I., Neumann, U.: Web-based remote renderingwith IBRAC (image-based rendering acceleration and compression). Comput. Graph. Forum 19(3), 321–330 (2000)
4. Shi, S., Jeon, W.J., Nahrstedt, K., Campbell, R.H.: Real-time remote rendering of 3D video for mobile devices. In: Proceedings of the 17th ACM International Conference on Multimedia, MM 2009, pp. 391–400. ACM, New York (2009)
5. Karonis, N.T., Papka, M.E., Binns, J., Bresnahan, J., Insley, J.A., Jones, D., Link, J.M.: High-resolution remote rendering of large datasets in a collaborative environment. Future Gener. Comput. Syst. 19(6), 909–917 (2003). 3rd Biennial International Grid Applications-Driven Testbed Event, Amsterdam, The Netherlands, 23–26 September 2002

6. Arntzen, H.K., et al.: KhronosGroup/SPIRV-Cross. https://github.com/KhronosGroup/SPIRV-Cross. Accessed 15 Feb 2018
7. Arntzen, H.K.: Using SPIR-V in practice with SPIRVcross (2016). https://www.khronos.org/assets/uploads/developers/library/2016-vulkan-devday-uk/4-Using-spir-v-with-spirv-cross.pdf
8. Sawicki, A., et al.: Vulkan Memory Allocator 1.0 - GPUOpen. https://gpuopen.com/vulkan-memory-allocator-1-0/. Accessed 15 Feb 2018
9. Kajiya, J.T.: The rendering equation. In: ACM SIGGRAPH Computer Graphics, vol. 20, pp. 143–150. ACM (1986)
10. Beason, K.: smallpt: Global Illumination in 99 lines of C++. http://www.kevinbeason.com/smallpt/ (2014). Accessed 15 Feb 2018
11. Shirley, P., Morley, R.K.: Realistic Ray Tracing, 2nd edn. A. K. Peters, Ltd., Natick (2003)

Using Applications and Tools to Visualize *ab initio* Calculations Performed in VASP

Viktors Gopejenko[1,2(✉)] and Aleksejs Gopejenko[3]

[1] ISMA University, Riga, Latvia
[2] Ventspils University College, Ventspils, Latvia
viktors.gopejenko@venta.lv
[3] Institute of Solid State Physics, University of Latvia, Riga, Latvia

Abstract. Visualization of the results of the *ab initio* calculations is important for the analysis of these results. It improves the quality of the analysis by supplementing the plain numbers received as the output of the calculations with various graphical images and facilitates the analysis of the results. In addition to that visualization helps avoiding some mistakes or inconsistencies. Various tools have been used in this work to construct the unit cell models of the calculated lattices, to check and analyze the calculated lattice structure before and after the relaxation, to plot total and difference electron charge density maps.

Keywords: Visualization of the *ab initio* calculations · Model
Crystalline lattice · Total and difference electron charge density map

1 Introduction

There are numerous freeware applications available for the visualization of the results of *ab initio* calculations. Some of these applications are developed to be used with a specific computer code used to perform the *ab initio* modelling. Within this work the visualization of the *ab initio* results is performed based on the first principle calculations of the interactions between Y, Ti, and O defects in *fcc*-Fe lattice performed using VASP computer code [1].

These calculations are performed in order to understand the formation principles of the oxide particles in the oxide dispersed strengthened (ODS) steels. ODS steels are promising structural materials for future fusion and advanced fission reactors [2]. Implementation of the ODS steels compared to conventional reduced activation ferritic-martensitic steels allows increasing the operating temperature of the reactors by 100 °C [3, 4], thus improving the reactor efficiency. Both size and spatial distribution of the oxide particles affect the mechanical properties of the material as well as the radiation resistance.

ODS steels are produced by mechanical alloying, followed by a powder consolidation at the temperatures of around 1000–1200 °C and pressure 100 MPa. Oxide particles found after the powder consolidation are the remnants of the initial oxide powder crushed by mechanical alloying incorporated in the steel matrix. This view is supported by the fact that the powder consolidation temperatures are much lower than

© Springer International Publishing AG, part of Springer Nature 2018
L. T. De Paolis and P. Bourdot (Eds.): AVR 2018, LNCS 10850, pp. 489–496, 2018.
https://doi.org/10.1007/978-3-319-95270-3_41

the melting temperature of yttria and therefore the thermal processes of oxide particle transformation should be excluded.

Experimental evidence has been found that after milling a significant part of Y and O atoms can be decomposed from yttria clusters in steel matrix with concentrations above their equilibrium solubility [5, 6]. This might mean that the precipitation of Y and O particles occurs already during the hipping stage as a result of yttrium-oxygen co-precipitation [7].

0.3wt% concentration of Ti leads to the formation of different Y-Ti-O oxides effectively reducing the size of the oxide particles, which increases the homogeneity of the oxide cluster distribution in the steel matrix and might have a significant role in pinning the dislocations and improving the mechanical and radiation resistance properties of ODS steels. The average size of the oxide particles is reduced from 10 ± 3 nm for ODS steels without Ti to 5 ± 2 nm for ODS steels with 0.3wt% Ti [8].

Some of the crucial modelling details might be hidden behind the plain numbers received in the results of the *ab initio* modelling, which might lead to some mistakes during the analysis. This is the reason why the visualization of the *ab initio* results is crucial as it allows avoiding such mistakes and improves the quality of the analysis.

The analysis of the available freeware visualization tools compatible with VASP computer code has been performed. Basing on this analysis the most convenient visualization tools have been chosen to visualize the models used in the calculations, to analyze the relaxation of the calculated configurations as well as to plot the total and difference electron charge density maps.

The paper consists of 5 sections including introduction. The second section of the paper describes the methods used to perform *ab initio* calculations as well as some important computational parameters required to receive plausible results. In addition to that a brief description of the visualization tools is also provided in this section. Visualization examples of the results of the *ab initio* calculations and their detailed description are provided in the Sect. 3. The conclusion is provided in the Sect. 4 and acknowledgements are provided in Sect. 5.

2   Computational Details

VASP 5.4 computer code has been used to perform *ab initio* calculations [1]. It is based on the Density Functional Theory (DFT) approach with a plane-wave (PW) basis set [1, 9] and Perdew-Wang-91 GGA non-local exchange-correlation functional [10], which operates with Fe core electrons of ($4s^1 3d^7$ outer shell), O ($2s^2 2p^4$), Y ($4s^2 4p^6 5s^1 4d^2$), and Ti ($3p^6 4s^2 3d^4$) atoms with 8, 6, 11, and 12 external electrons, respectively. The core electrons are described within the Projector-Augmented Wave (PAW) method [11] and have been treated with PAW-PW91 pseudopotentials. The calculations have been performed on *fcc* Fe lattice, which is stable at the temperatures of the powder consolidation. It is assumed that at high temperatures the magnetic moments of iron atoms are disordered, and iron can be considered as paramagnetic.

To define the calculation parameters necessary to achieve the plausible results various test calculations have been performed in order to reproduce the basic experimental data for fcc-Fe lattice, such as lattice constant a0, bulk modulus, cohesive energy per atom Ecoh, etc. The analysis of the convergence of the results depending on the supercell size, the cut-off energy as well as the k-point set in the corresponding Brillouin zone has also been performed. The cubic supercell size with the extension of $4a0 \times 4a0 \times 4a0$ containing 64 atoms has been used in the calculations. The Brillouin zone should be sampled with at least $7 \times 7 \times 7$ k-mesh for the supercell [12]. The estimated cut-off energy value required to achieve plausible results has been found to be 800 eV [13–16].

Transition State Tools for VASP (VTST tools) contain various scripts that perform common tasks to help with VASP calculations [17]. E.g. pos2rdf.pl script calculates the radial distribution around a specific atom, this allows analyzing the atoms displacement during the relaxation as well as it helps to position the defect atoms at the desired distances relating to each other to perform the calculations. chgsum.pl is used to calculate the sum or the difference between two CHGCAR files, which contain the electron charge data for the calculated lattice and is required to plot difference electron charge density maps.

Jmol has been primarily used to visualize the models that were in the calculations for inclusion in the scientific papers [18].

Visualization for Electronic and STructural Analysis (VESTA) [19], which is compatible with VASP input and output files has been used to visualize the calculated lattice and to check whether the defects has been placed correctly. Visualization of the lattice after the relaxation allows assessing the displacement of the atoms during the relaxation and comparing the positions of the atoms with the configuration before the relaxation. In addition to that Vesta allows visualization of the electron charges in the calculated structure, which is important in assessing the interactions between the atoms in the calculated lattice.

LEV00 is another freeware tool [19], which is compatible with various *ab initio* calculation packages including VASP. It allows processing the output data in a way that allows constructing such important plots as the Density of States, total, and partial electron charge densities etc. Within this work this tool has been used to construct the total and difference electron charge densities.

3 Visualization

As it was mentioned above Jmol is used simply to construct the models of the calculated lattices. It is important to note that this is only a small cut (a unit cell) from the larger supercell that is actually calculated. Such unit cell allows showing the model with the distance between the defects up to the fourth nearest neighbors (NN). The model of the ideal *fcc*-Fe lattice is shown in Fig. 1a, *fcc*-Fe lattice with O atom in the octahedral (Fig. 1b), tetrahedral (Fig. 1c) interstitial, and substitutional position (Fig. 1d).

It is easy to construct the models of the more complex defects under investigation. E.g. Figure 2a–c demonstrates the model of *fcc*-Fe lattice containing Y-Ti-O triple defect. O and both Y and Ti atoms are positioned as the first nearest neighbors in all these models, while Y and Ti are positioned as the 1NN (Fig. 2a), 2NN (Fig. 2b), and 3NN (Fig. 2c).

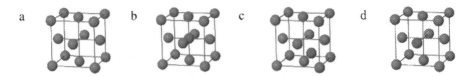

Fig. 1. a–d. Ideal *fcc*-Fe lattice (a), the model of O in the octahedral interstitial position in *fcc*-Fe lattice (b), the model of O in the tetrahedral interstitial position in *fcc*-Fe lattice (c), the model of O substitutional atom in *fcc* Fe lattice.

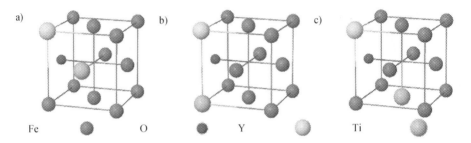

Fig. 2. a–c. Model of Y_{Fe} and Ti_{Fe} atoms as 1NN (a), 2NN(b) and 3NN (c) and O_{Fe} as the 1NN to both Y_{Fe} and Ti_{Fe} atoms.

It is quite obvious from both Figs. 1 and 2 that the demonstrated models are very compact allowing a compact placement of the several models side by side, while the image of the whole calculated lattice consisting of 64 atoms would occupy at least one-half of the page making it inconvenient to compare the models as shown in Fig. 3 as created in VESTA.

It is worth noting that the lattice constructed by VESTA contains more atoms than were actually calculated as VESTA automatically makes a periodic projection of some of the atoms. As VESTA applies these settings automatically it might make the model cumbersome and inconvenient to embed in the scientific presentations and papers. However, the advantage of VESTA is that it allows inspecting the lattice structure as it has been calculated and visualizes atom displacements during the relaxation. It is also easy to rotate and zoom in and out the calculated lattice.

The example of the visualization possibilities is provided basing on the results of the actual calculations provided in Table 1.

The first column of the table provides the list of the configurations that have been calculated. Obviously, it might be quite hard and confusing to understand the placement of the defect atoms in the lattice from the table. However, using Jmol it is possible to create compact visualization models of these configurations, which allows everyone to easily understand the difference between the calculated configurations (Fig. 4).

VTST tools allow extracting the electron charge data and relative atom displacements from the output files. These data are summarized in Table 1.

Some of the data presented in Table 1 such as the values of the binding energy and atom displacements relating to their initial positions are self-explanatory, however, the

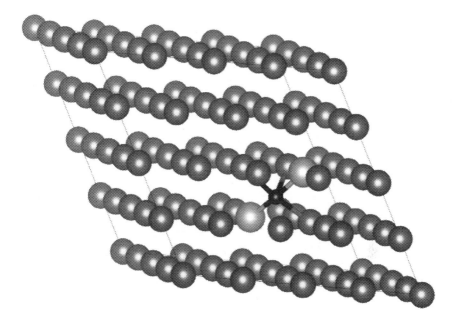

Fig. 3. The calculated lattice containing Ti-O-Ti defect created by Vesta from the VASP file.

Table 1. Calculated parameters for two Ti_{Fe} and one O_{Fe} atoms

Configuration	E_{bind}, eV	$\Delta q, e*$ (Ti_{Fe})	$\Delta q, e*$ (Ti_{Fe})	$\Delta q, e*$ (O_{Fe})	$\delta r_{Ti(1)}$, Å	$\delta r_{Ti(2)}$, Å	δr_O, Å
1NN**	0.88	1.15	1.15	−1.22	0.22	0.22	0.86
2NN**	1.58	1.22	1.22	−1.27	0.20	0.20	1.58
3NN**	1.35	1.24	1.24	−1.18	0.22	0.22	0.81

*estimated within the Bader topological analysis [21]
**distance between two Ti_{Fe} atoms, O_{Fe} is the 1NN to both Ti_{Fe} atoms

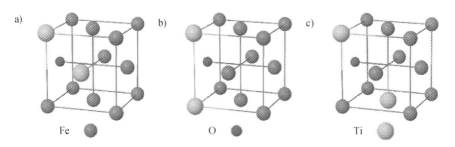

Fig. 4. a–c. Model of two Ti_{Fe} atoms as 1NN (a), 2NN(b) and 3NN (c) and O_{Fe} as the 1NN to both Ti_{Fe} atoms.

electron charge redistribution requires some additional explanation and the easiest way to demonstrate how the electron charge transfer occurs is by constructing electron charge redistribution map across the plane projected through the defect atoms.

Using LEV00 it is possible to process VASP output file and to create a data file with the projection of the electron charge density across the plane, while Origin [22] is used to construct the plots. The total charge density map (Fig. 5b) is used as a reference showing the atom positions in the plane, while electron charge density map shown in Fig. 5a nicely supplements the data provided in the columns 3–5 of the Table 1 for the 2NN configuration showing the electron charge transfer from both Ti atoms towards O atom and the closest Fe atoms, while O atom attracts the electrons from both Ti atoms and from the closest Fe atoms.

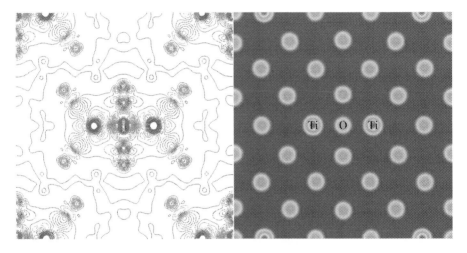

Fig. 5. Difference and total electron charge density maps for and Ti_{Fe}-O_{Fe}-Ti_{Fe} 2NN, where oxygen substitute atom is the first nearest neighbour (1NN) for both Ti atoms, during the relaxation O_{Fe} has moved from the regular lattice site exactly to the octahedral interstitial position. Solid (red), dash (blue) and dash-dot (black) isolines (with the increment of 0.002 $e/Å^3$) represent positive, negative and neutral electronic charge, respectively (Color figure online).

In addition to that Fig. 5 shows that after the relaxation O atom is positioned exactly in the octahedral interstitial position where it has moved from the regular lattice site.

4   Conclusions

Various visualization applications have been used to supplement the *ab initio* calculations with model and result visualization. Jmol implementation allows construction of the compact models used in the calculations. Compact models can be placed side by side making it easy to demonstrate the defect configurations under investigation. VESTA, which requires VASP input or output files allows rotating and zooming in and out the configuration under investigation. Unfortunately, some of the settings are applied automatically, which might make it impossible to use the resulting image for the presentation purposes, however, it is very useful in understanding the atom displacements during the relaxation. The last but not the least is LEV00, which allows processing the output files to construct such plots as total and difference electron charge density maps, which show the electron charge transfer between the defect atoms as well as between the defect and lattice atoms.

Acknowledgment. This research has been supported by Ventspils International Radio Astronomy Centre Ventspils University College.

Ab initio calculations have been carried out using the Marconi supercomputer system at the Cineca computational HPC Simulation Centre (Italy).

References

1. Kresse, G., Hafner, J.: VASP the Guide. University of Vienna (2007)
2. Lindau, R., Möslang, A., Rieth, M., Klimiankou, M., Materna-Morris, E., Alamo, A., Tavassoli, A.-A.F., Cayron, C., Lancha, A.-M., Fernández, P., Baluc, N., Schäublin, R., Diegele, E., Filacchioni, G., Rensman, J.W., Van der Schaaf, B., Lucon, E., Dietz, W.: Fusion Eng. Des. **75–79**, 989–996 (2005)
3. Klimiankou, M., Lindau, R., Möslang, A.: J. Nucl. Mater. **367–370**, 173–178 (2007)
4. Lindau, R., Möslang, A., Schirra, M., Schlossmacher, P., Klimiankou, M.: J. Nucl. Mater. **307–311**, 769–772 (2002)
5. Okuda, T., Fujiwara, M.: J. Mater. Sci. Lett. **14**, 1600–1603 (1995)
6. Odette, G.R., Alinger, M.J., Wirth, B.D.: Ann. Rev. Mater. Res. **38**, 471–503 (2008)
7. Miller, M.K., Kenik, E.A., Russell, K.F., Heatherly, L., Hoelzer, D.T., Maziasz, P.J.: Mater. Sci. Eng., A **353**, 140–145 (2003)
8. Rogozhkin, S., Bogacheva, A., Korchuganova, O., Nikitin, A., Orlov, N., Aleev, A., Zaluzhnyi, A., Kozodaev, M., Kulevoy, T., Chalykh, B., Lindau, R., Hoffmann, J., Möslang, A., Vladimirov, P., Klimenkov, M., Heilmaier, M., Wagner, J., Seils, S.: Nucl. Mater. Energy **9**, 66–74 (2016)
9. Kresse, G., Furthmueller, J.: Phys. Rev. B **45**, 11169–11186 (1996)
10. Perdew, J.P., Wang, Y.: Phys. Rev. B **45**, 13244–31249 (1992)
11. Kresse, G., Joubert, D.: Phys. Rev. B **59**, 1758–1775 (1999)
12. Monkhorst, H.J., Pack, J.D.: Phys. Rev. B **13**, 5188–5192 (1976)
13. Gopejenko, A., Zhukovskii, Y., Vladimirov, P.V., Kotomin, E.A., Möslang, A.: J. Nucl. Mater. **406**, 345–350 (2010)
14. Gopejenko, A., Zhukovskii, Y., Vladimirov, P.V., Kotomin, E.A., Möslang, A.: J. Nucl. Mater. **416**, 40–44 (2011)
15. Gopejenko, A., Zhukovskii, Y.F., Vladimirov, P.V., Kotomin, E.A., Möslang, A.: Interaction between Oxygen and Yttrium impurity atoms as well as vacancies in fcc iron lattice: Ab Initio modeling. In: Shunin, Y., Kiv, A. (eds.) Nanodevices and Nanomaterials for Ecological Security. NATO Science for Peace and Security Series B: Physics and Biophysics. Springer, Dordrecht (2012). https://doi.org/10.1007/978-94-007-4119-5_14
16. Gopejenko, A., Zhukovskii, Y., Kotomin, E.A., Mastrikov, Y., Vladimirov, P.V., Borodin, V.A., Möslang, A.: Phys. Status Solidi B **253**, 2136–2143 (2016)

17. http://theory.cm.utexas.edu/vtsttools/
18. http://jmol.sourceforge.net/
19. http://jp-minerals.org/vesta/en/
20. https://nms.kcl.ac.uk/lev.kantorovitch/codes/lev00/index.html
21. Henkelman, G., Arnaldsson, A., Jónsson, H.: Comput. Mater. Sci. **36**, 354–360 (2006)
22. https://www.originlab.com/

Secure Lossy Image Compression via Adaptive Vector Quantization

Bruno Carpentieri, Francesco Palmieri, and Raffaele Pizzolante[(✉)]

Dipartimento di Informatica, Università degli Studi di Salerno,
Via Giovanni Paolo II, 132, 84084 Fisciano, SA, Italy
bc@dia.unisa.it, {fpalmier,rpizzolante}@unisa.it

Abstract. In this paper we propose a secure lossy image compression method based on Adaptive Vector Quantization. The proposed approach is founded on the principles of the Entropy-restricted Semantic Security and the logical functioning of the Squeeze Cipher algorithm. It could be useful in several application domains, including Virtual Reality (VR) or Augmented Reality (AR), for its security aspects and for its asymmetrical compression/decompression behavior. Indeed, decompression is more efficient and significantly faster with respect to compression. This aspect could be relevant in many scenarios where images are compressed once and decompressed several times, sometimes on devices with limited hardware capabilities. In the proposed approach a single key is used for the compression and the simultaneous encryption of the input image. Such a key must also be used for decryption (and the associated simultaneous decompression). We report preliminary experimental results achieved by a proof-of-concept implementation of our approach. Such results seem to be quite promising and meaningful for future investigations of the proposed approach.

Keywords: Image compression · Lossy compression
Entropy-restricted security · Adaptive Vector Quantization

1 Introduction

Compression makes possible the efficient encoding of data by minimizing the digital length of the associated representation [1]. The compression of images and of other digital multimedia data (such as video, audio, etc.) is motivated by the need to minimize the usage of storage space, as well as by the need to save bandwidth in communications (e.g., client/server and/or client/cloud services transactions, etc.).

These needs become more significant in real-time scenarios, for example when Virtual Reality (VR) and Augmented Reality (AR) applications are involved.

In general, the preferred techniques for the compression of images are lossy, because the end user is often human and cannot sense a few pixel differences between an original and a decompressed image.

In this paper, we introduce a secure, lossy image compression algorithm that is based on Adaptive Vector Quantization (AVQ) (see for example [4]). The proposed scheme relies on the concepts and the definitions related to Entropy-restricted Semantic Security [6] and on the basic ideas used to design the Squeeze Cipher algorithm [7].

L. T. De Paolis and P. Bourdot (Eds.): AVR 2018, LNCS 10850, pp. 497–505, 2018.
https://doi.org/10.1007/978-3-319-95270-3_42

Our approach becomes particularly meaningful in presence of some AR/VR and real-time applications, mainly because of its "asymmetrical" nature concerning the compression and the decompression processes. More precisely, the decompression is significantly faster with respect to the compression and this aspect may be relevant for all the applications in which compression is performed just once, or at most a few times, but decompression is performed several times and on heterogenous devices (e.g., ranging from devices with plenty of hardware resources to ones with constrained hardware capabilities).

In addition, the proposed approach is also able to encrypt an image according to the definition of entropy-restricted semantic security. A user-defined key is used for the compression and the simultaneous encryption of the input image. The decryption and the simultaneous decompression must use the same key that was chosen for the compression/encryption process.

This paper is organized as follows: Sect. 2 shortly reviews the underlying ideas and the compression process of the AVQ algorithm. In Sect. 3 we highlight the characteristics of our scheme and in Sect. 4 we report the preliminary results we achieved by a proof-of-concept implementation of the proposed approach. Finally, in Sect. 5, we draw our conclusions and highlight future research directions.

2   Adaptive Vector Quantization

The AVQ algorithm [3] combines dictionary-based schemes (such as the LZ2, etc.), and vector quantization.

It uses a dictionary (denoted as D) and operates on two-dimensional data, i.e. full color or grayscale images or generic binary images. However, AVQ extensions are also capable to work with image sequences (see, for instance, [2]).

The basic idea, on which AVQ relies on, is that an input image I can subdivided into several two-dimensional blocks b_k, which can have different sizes.

During the compression process, each block b_k will be gradually substituted, with an index i in the dictionary D. The entry $D[i]$ (i.e., the i-th entry of the dictionary D) shall contain a block that is similar (according to a given distortion measure) to the block b_k. In this way, the block b_k will be *approximated* with the block stored in the entry $D[i]$) and hence it will be substituted by an integer: i.e., the index i of the dictionary. Notice that these are precisely the basic principles on which the *Vector Quantization* (VQ) encoders are based.

Indeed, a VQ-based encoder divides the input data into *vectors* (such as data blocks, etc.), and each vector is replaced by a similar vector that is maintained into a static dictionary of codebook vectors (denoted as *codewords*) [3].

The new blocks that the AVQ algorithm dynamically adds to the dictionary D play an essential role in the compression process. By using these new blocks, the algorithm can continue the encoding by processing the parts of the input image that have not yet be encoded.

The main components of the AVQ algorithm are essentially three: the *growing points* (GPs), the *growing point pool* (GPP) and the dictionary D.

A *growing point* can be any point in the not yet encoded portion of the image: from a growing point the AVQ algorithm can continue the compression process. Considering the two-dimensional nature of the processed data, we can have several different GPs at the same time.

In Algorithm 1, we report the pseudo-code of the AVQ algorithm used for the compression process.

First, the growing point pool (GPP) is initialized with at least one growing point (that is generally the one at the upper-left corner of the image: it has coordinates $(0, 0)$). Subsequently, the dictionary D is initialized with the *alphabet* that is composed, for grayscale images, by all the 256 values that a pixel can assume, according to an *initialization dictionary heuristic* (IDH).

At each step of the compression process, the AVQ algorithm selects, by means of a *growing heuristic* (GH), a GP (the GPs are maintained into the GPP). After that, the block b_k, anchored to the selected GP, is obtained. The algorithm finds the best match (according to a given distortion measure) between the block b_k and each block of the same sizes of b_k in the dictionary D.

The match is performed through a *match heuristic* (MH). Some MHs permits to manipulate the behavior of the matching logic, by considering several user-defined parameters (e.g., quality, distortion, etc.).

The logical functioning of a MH is graphically shown in Fig. 1, in which the not yet coded part of the input image is reported in white, and the already coded part of the image, is reported in uniform light grey.

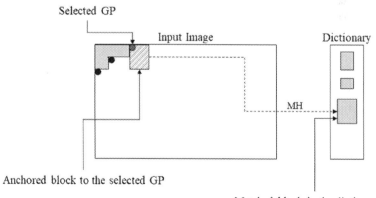

Fig. 1. Logical functioning of the match heuristic (MH).

Algorithm 1. Pseudo-code of the *compression process* of the AVQ algorithm.

- Initialize the *growing point pool* (GPP) with at least one *growing point* (e.g., the one at coordinates (0, 0));
- Initialize the dictionary *D*, by using an *initialization dictionary heuristic* (IDH);
- **while** GPP has more elements **do begin**
  - ○ Individuate the next *growing point* (GP) to process, by using a *growing heuristic* (GH);
  - ○ Individuate the match between the block b_k, anchored to the current GP, and a block in the dictionary *D*, by using a *match heuristic* (MH);
  - ○ Transmit or store the index *i* of the dictionary *D* related to the matched block;
  - ○ Update the dictionary *D* with the new generated blocks, by using a *dictionary update heuristic* (DUH);
  - ○ **if** the dictionary *D* is full
    - ■ According to a *deletion heuristic* (DH), delete some entries in the dictionary *D*
  - ○ **end**
  - ○ Update the *growing point pool* (GPP) with the new growing points, derived from the selected matched block, by using a *growing heuristic* (GH);
  - ○ Remove the current growing point (GP) from the growing point pool (GPP);
- **end**

Once the match is found, if the block b_k has matched (according to the MH heuristic) with the block stored in the entry $D[i]$, then the AVQ algorithm transmits the index *i* to the receiver.

After this, the dictionary *D* is updated with one or more blocks, through a *dictionary update heuristic* (DUH). When the dictionary is full, a *deletion heuristic* (DH) is invoked to eventually make space in *D*.

The GPP is then updated, by using a *growing pool update heuristic* (GPUH), and the processed GP is removed from the GPP (therefore this GP will be not further processed).

Once the GPP is empty then the algorithm terminates the compression process.

In [4, 5], further details concerning the logical functioning of the compression and decompression processes and concerning the heuristics of the AVQ algorithm are reported.

3 Secure, Lossy, Image Compression via the AVQ Algorithm

In this paper we design a modified version of the AVQ algorithm that we denote as AVQ_S. It relies on ideas and assumptions that are similar to the ones that were used to design the Squeeze Cipher algorithm, which is fully described in [6], and is a modified version of the Lempel-Ziv-Welch (LZW) algorithm that is discussed in [7].

It is proved to be secure, according to the *Entropy-restricted Semantic Security* definition in [6]. It substantially modifies the behavior of the dictionary *D* of LZW, by "randomizing" it. Essentially, the Squeeze Cipher algorithm provides a uniform distribution of the entries in D.

At each step of the compression process, once an entry is used then this entry is swapped with another one, which is pseudo-randomly selected in D (when possible, an empty entry is preferred). In this way, most of the entries of D, are unmodified and this improve the efficiency.

Furthermore, when a new entry is added to the dictionary D, the position of this entry is pseudo-randomly selected. If the position does not refer to a non-empty entry, another position is selected until a position that refers to an empty entry is encountered. In this manner, the Squeeze Cipher algorithm compresses and encrypts an input stream of character.

Starting from these ideas, we designed the AVQ_S algorithm with the objective of compressing and encrypting an input image by means of a user-defined key K.

The AVQ_S algorithm is also able to decompress and decrypt the compressed stream, but only if the correct key is provided.

Algorithm 2 reports the pseudo-code of the AVQ_S compression algorithm.

Algorithm 2. Pseudo-code of the *compression process* of the AVQ_S algorithm.

- Initialize the *growing point pool* (GPP) with at least one *growing point* (e.g., the one at coordinates $(0, 0)$).
- Initialize a Pseudo-Number Random Generator (PRNG) G, by using a seed, obtained by a user-defined key K
- Initialize the dictionary D_S, by using a *secure initialization dictionary heuristic* (SIDH) in conjunction with the PRNG G;
- **while** GPP has more elements **do**
  - ○ Individuate the next *growing point* (GP) to process, by using a *growing heuristic* (GH);
  - ○ Individuate the match between the block b_k, anchored to the current GP, and a block in the dictionary D_S, by using a *match heuristic* (MH);
  - ○ Transmit or store the index i of the dictionary D_S related to the matched block;
    - ▪ Swap the entry at index i with an empty entry in D_S, which is selected by means of the PRNG G;
  - ○ Update the dictionary D_S with the new generated blocks, by using a *secure dictionary update heuristic* (SDUH) in conjunction with the PRNG G;
  - ○ **if** the dictionary D_S is full
    - ▪ According to a *deletion heuristic* (DH), delete some entries in the dictionary D_S
  - ○ **end**
  - ○ Update the *growing point pool* (GPP) with the new growing points, derived from the selected matched block, by using a *growing heuristic* (GH);
  - ○ Remove the current growing point (GP) from the growing point pool (GPP);
- **end**

The main differences between the AVQ_S algorithm and the AVQ algorithm are therefore related to the dictionary management.

The initialization of the dictionary D_S is driven by a modified initialization dictionary heuristic, denoted as *secure initialization dictionary heuristic* (SIDH).

The SIDH heuristic locates the initial entries (i.e., the 256 pixels) to pseudo-random positions. Such positions are selected by means of the PRNG G (based on the user-defined K).

Analogously to the AVQ algorithm, also the AVQ_S algorithm transmits or stores the index i, which represents the index of the matched block b, obtained at the previous step. However, the AVQ_S algorithm performs an additional step: the entry at index i is swapped with an empty one in the dictionary D_S. This latter entry is selected by using the PRNG G.

Finally, a modified dictionary update heuristic, which we denoted as *secure dictionary update heuristic* (SDUH), adds new blocks to D_S. In detail, each new block is added to a pseudo-randomly selected position of D_S.

The position is selected by using the PRNG G. It should be observed that the position is selected by considering the whole dictionary, therefore it could occur that the position refers to a non-empty entry. In this case, a new position is cyclically selected until a position that refers to an empty entry is identified.

4   Preliminary Results

In this section, we report the preliminary results achieved by a *proof-of-concept* implementation of the proposed approach. The dataset we used is composed by six grayscale images (from the USC-SIPI dataset [8]) and is synthetized in Table 1.

Table 1. Description of the used dataset.

Images	5.1.09	5.1.10	5.1.11	5.1.12	5.1.13	5.1.14
Width	256	256	256	256	256	256
Height	256	256	256	256	256	256

The main objective of our testing phase is to evaluate the behavior of the dictionary D_S, during the AVQ_S compression process, by analyzing the number of accesses of each entry. We expect to obtain a uniform-like distribution of the accesses, since each entry, once accessed, is pseudo-randomly swapped with another one. Consequently, also the accesses to the dictionary should be distributed in a uniform manner.

All the experiments are performed with the following parameters:

- Dictionary Size: 4096 entries;
- Match Heuristic (MH): MSE MH (described in [2, 4])
  - MSE MH Parameter set to 6;
- Deletion Dictionary: Freeze [2];
- User-defined Key (only for the AVQ_S algorithm): '12345'.

In Table 2, we report the achieved results in terms of compression performances. For each image of the used dataset (columns from the second to the seventh), we report the Compression Ratio (C.R.), in the second row, and the Peak-Signal-to-Noise-Ratio (PSNR), in the third row.

Table 2. Results in terms of compression performances.

Images	5.1.09	5.1.10	5.1.11	5.1.12	5.1.13	5.1.14
C.R.	1.91	1.59	1.54	3.66	11.16	1.77
PSNR	38.64	40.04	30.23	27.13	43.75	39.50

Figures 2, 3, 4, 5, 6 and 7 graphically show, for each image, the number of accesses (on the Y-axis) for each entry (on the X-axis), at the end of the compression processes of the AVQ algorithm (sub-images on the left) and of the AVQ_S algorithm (sub-images on the right).

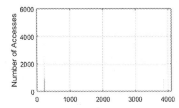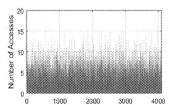

Fig. 2. Number of the accesses during the compression process of the AVQ algorithm (*left*) and of the AVQ_S algorithm (*right*), related to the '5.1.09' image.

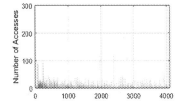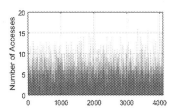

Fig. 3. Number of the accesses during the compression process of the AVQ algorithm (*left*) and of the AVQ_S algorithm (*right*), related to the '5.1.10' image.

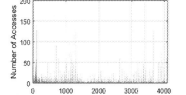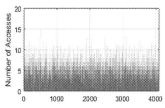

Fig. 4. Number of the accesses during the compression process of the AVQ algorithm (*left*) and of the AVQ_S algorithm (*right*), related to the '5.1.11' image.

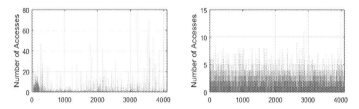

Fig. 5. Number of the accesses during the compression process of the AVQ algorithm (*left*) and of the AVQ$_S$ algorithm (*right*), related to the '5.1.12' image.

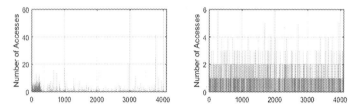

Fig. 6. Number of the accesses during the compression process of the AVQ algorithm (*left*) and of the AVQ$_S$ algorithm (*right*), related to the '5.1.13' image.

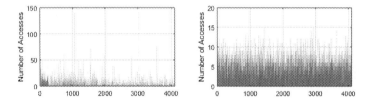

Fig. 7. Number of the accesses during the compression process of the AVQ algorithm (*left*) and of the AVQ$_S$ algorithm (*right*), related to the '5.1.14' image.

As it is observable from the above figures, in all the cases, the accesses, related to the dictionary D_S (right sub-image for each image) follow a uniform-like distribution, as expected.

For each image, we have also measured the execution time of the AVQ and of the AVQ$_S$ algorithms, regarding the compression process. In detail, AVQ$_S$ results to be slower at most of about 14% (due to the swapping of each entry, after its usage).

In addition, we also observed that the decompression (and the contemporary decryption) is faster than the compression (and the contemporary encryption) of about 15 times, in average, for what concern the AVQ$_S$ algorithm.

5   Conclusion and Future Works

In this paper, we introduce a novel approach for the secure lossy compression of images based on the AVQ algorithm. The proposed approach, which we denote as AVQ_S, relies on the ideas, addressed in [6], and could be considered for Virtual Reality (VR) and/or Augmented Reality (AR) applications.

The AVQ and the AVQ_S algorithms are asymmetrical for what concerns the compression and the decompression operations. Indeed, the decompression is much more efficient and significantly faster with respect to the compression. In AR/VR applications, this aspect could become meaningful, since the images and other multimedia are generally compressed once and can be decompressed several times, in an efficient manner, even on devices with limited capabilities.

Future works will include further experiments on different and larger datasets, and more detailed analysis of the results, considering several statistical parameters. In addition, further optimizations should be designed to improve the swapping of the entries and the general management of the dictionary.

Acknowledgements. Bruno Carpentieri would like to thank its students Giovanni Festa and Michele Roviello, for the implementation of a preliminary version of the AVQ_S approach.

References

1. Carpentieri, B., Weinberger, M.J., Seroussi, G.: Lossless compression of continuous-tone images. Proc. IEEE **88**(11), 1797–1809 (2000)
2. Pizzolante, R., Carpentieri, B., De Agostino, S.: Adaptive vector quantization for lossy compression of image sequences. Algorithms **10**(2), 51 (2017)
3. Gersho, A., Gray, R.M.: Vector Quantization and Signal Compression, vol. 159. Springer, New York (2012)
4. Pizzolante, R., Carpentieri, B., Castiglione, A., De Maio, G.: The AVQ algorithm: watermarking and compression performances. In: 2011 Third International Conference on Intelligent Networking and Collaborative Systems (INCoS), pp. 698–702. IEEE, November 2011
5. Constantinescu, C., Storer, J.A.: Online adaptive vector quantization with variable size codebook entries. Inf. Process. Manage. **30**(6), 745–758 (1994)
6. Kelley, J., Tamassia, R.: Secure Compression: Theory & Practice. IACR Cryptology ePrint Archive, 2014, 113 (2014)
7. Zhou, J., Au, O.C., Fan, X., Wong, P.H.W.: Secure Lempel-Ziv-Welch (LZW) algorithm with random dictionary insertion and permutation. In: IEEE Multimedia and Expo 2008, pp. 245–248. IEEE, June 2008
8. The USC-SIPI Image Database. http://sipi.usc.edu/database/

Trivial Algorithm for Interactive Water Simulation

Jan Vaněk[(✉)], Jan Tobola, Karel Petránek, Bruno Ježek,
and Miloslava Černá

University of Hradec Králové, Hradec Králové, Czech Republic
vanek.conf@gmail.com, tobola.jan@gmail.com,
{karel.petranek, bruno.jezek, miloslava.cerna}@uhk.cz

Abstract. The paper introduces a simple and computationally efficient algorithm for dynamic and interactive water simulation in applications where physical accuracy is not required, but a credible look and little impact on rendering speed are of crucial importance.

Keywords: Water rendering · Real-time simulation · GPU

1 Introduction

Water and other liquids are complex phenomena; during their simulation it is necessary to compromise between physical accuracy and computational speed. Scientific and industrial simulations are based on an accurate theoretical model described by the Navier-Stokes equations, these simulations are computationally very demanding. But in case of simulations used in virtual reality systems with real-time response the low computational complexity is crucial and the emphasis is placed on visual credibility instead of physical accuracy. A simplicity of the simulation implementation is also important together with an easy integration with other algorithms and subsystems of virtual reality. The paper deals with real-time water rendering.

2 Current Methods

Approaches which are used for water rendering in virtual reality systems can be basically divided into two groups according to the sort of the water mass which they simulate.

For dynamic simulations of flowing water interacting with the environment, particle systems are currently being used with the best results. They are defined in computer graphics as sets of points in space with clearly specified characteristics and rules defining their behavior and appearance [1]. Each particle has its own parameters such as position, direction, speed and color. Values of these parameters depend on the environment and surrounding particles. During the simulation individual particles disappear and new come into existence. New particles are assigned with initial values of the parameters, according to these parameters they are transformed and subsequently rendered [2].

© Springer International Publishing AG, part of Springer Nature 2018
L. T. De Paolis and P. Bourdot (Eds.): AVR 2018, LNCS 10850, pp. 506–513, 2018.
https://doi.org/10.1007/978-3-319-95270-3_43

If a sufficiently precise mathematical model describing water behavior is selected (Navier-Stokes equations), the simulation which is carried out using particle systems can look very realistic, see e.g., the Smoothed Particle Hydrodynamics method. This method was originally designed for astrophysics, later it began to be applied in other fields, as well. The method and its implementation on the GPU are described in [3]. The amount of particles has a major influence on the visual quality of the result, but it also has a strong negative impact on the computational complexity of the system. Therefore, the applicability of particle systems for simulating water effects in real time is only confined to small-scale water masses. Commercial systems of virtual reality, especially in the field of interactive entertainment, apply primarily algorithmically and computationally inexpensive, non-dynamic and non-interactive water rendering solutions whose visual credibility is the work of artists.

The other group of approaches is used to render large areas of water like the sea or lake, whose main visual element is not the flow of water masses but the motion of waves over the surface. Water is represented by height field in this kind of approaches, a function of two variables which returns the height to the desired point in two-dimensional space [4]. A flat two-dimensional triangular grid is most frequently used for rendering; it gets transformed into three-dimensional space by translating the individual points to the heights obtained from the height field. Both simple procedural models based on multi-octave Perlin noise [4] and statistical models based on Fourier analysis of oceanographic data, see [5] or [6], are used to perturb the height fields.

There are also solutions which extend the water height field representation with dynamic and interactive simulation models. They have thus the potential to unify the rendering of watercourses and vast undulating water surface. Such solutions are found in the work of e.g. [7–9], they are based on the iterative solution of greatly simplified Navier-Stokes equations. These solutions are still very computationally demanding and do not bring visually convincing results.

3   Proposed Solution

The proposed water rendering solution utilizes height field and a regular triangular grid, so that all the data required for the simulation can be stored compactly as an array, for example in the form of GPU textures. The algorithm is iterative and calculations of the water height field in the individual grid cells are independent of each other. All calculations can therefore run in parallel on the GPU. Simulation data are stored in the total of five textures: two textures for storing of terrain heights and water levels, one texture for storing calculations of water flow and two textures as a repository of previous values of water levels and water flow.

Calculation of the water level takes place in two stages resulting in a single simulation frame. In the first step, the change of the current water column depending on the four adjacent columns is calculated. At this stage, the algorithm only computes how much water may drain away in each direction. The situation in one dimension is illustrated in Fig. 1. The arrows show the direction and outflow amount from the water column, the columns without arrows have nowhere to flow.

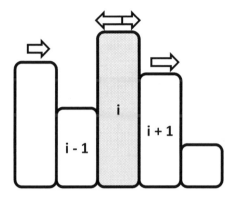

Fig. 1. Water column outflows

The value of flow inertia is calculated from each outflow value by adding it to the previous value of inertia. It is important that the inertia is computed and stored for each direction separately. Due to the fact that the inertia calculation is evaluated only in four directions, a single RGBA texture is sufficient where each color channel is used to store the inertia value of one direction.

The second stage of the algorithm deals with the calculation of a new water level depending on the height of the previous and current values of inertia.

A simplified outline of the algorithm is listed below; the two stages are described in detail in the two sections following. The algorithm for calculating the water levels iteratively updates four textures. Let us denote them 0–3. The texture labelled 0 is used to store four calculated inertia components, texture 1 contains final water level and textures 2 and 3 are copies of previous textures which are created at the end of each iteration and serve as the input for the next. The general outline of the algorithm is as follows:

1. Bind textures 2 and 3 for reading.
2. Calculate the four-component inertia from texture 2 and 3 values. Store the calculated values into the texture 0.
3. Bind textures 0 and 3 for reading.
4. Calculate a new water level from textures 0 and 3. Store the calculated value into the texture 1.
5. Bind texture 0 for reading and copy all its values into the texture 2.
6. Bind texture 1 for reading and copy all its values into the texture 3.
7. Update the triangular grid according to the height values in the texture 1.

3.1   Calculation of the Four-Component Inertia

The outflow value of the water column is obtained as the difference between the previous water level and the previous levels of the adjacent columns. To create a flow, it is necessary to take the elevation into consideration. In the Fig. 2 different heights can be seen.

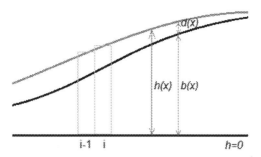

Fig. 2. The depth and height levels

In the Fig. 2, $d(x)$ is the water depth, $b(x)$ is the terrain elevation and h(x) is the water level. The water level is given by $h(x) = b(x) + d(x)$.

The calculation of the outflow in the two-dimensional space is described by the Eq. 1, where x is the position of the water column and x_a the position of the adjacent column. Negative values, i.e. tributaries, are not considered, the resulting value in such a case is zero.

$$f_{outflow}(x, x_a) = \max((b(x) + d(x)) - (b(x_a) + d(x_a)), 0) \tag{1}$$

The calculation of the inertia s of the outflow from x to x_a is given by the Eq. 2, where s' is the value of the inertia from the previous frame and k is a constant in the interval <0; 1>, which specifies the attenuation of waves which can be perceived as a parameter influencing the apparent viscosity of water. The parameter p_1' is a constant defining the speed at which water can flow depending on the water level difference.

$$s(x, x_a) = k \cdot s'(x, x_a) + p_1 \cdot f_{outflow}(x, x_a) \tag{2}$$

The entire algorithm for the calculation of all four components of inertia is as follows:

1. Load all inertia components from the previous frame.
2. Load the previous water depth and height of the terrain.
3. Calculate the inertia for all four directions.
   (a) Load the previous water depth of the adjacent column in the given direction.
   (b) Load the height of the terrain at the adjacent point in the direction.
   (c) Calculate the outflow according to the Eq. 1.
   (d) If the adjacent point in the given direction is off the grid (i.e. the current point is the boundary of the area), then the value of the outflow is 0.
   (e) Calculate the inertia according to the Eq. 2.
4. Calculate the sum of all current inertia components, see Eq. 3.

$$\sum_{i=1}^{4} s(x, x_{a_i}) \tag{3}$$

5. If the previous value of depth is less than the inertia sum, recalculate all the inertia components according to the Eq. 4, where $d'(x)$ is the previous water depth.

$$s(x, x_a) = \frac{d'(x) \cdot s(x, x_a)}{\sum_{i=1}^{4} s(x, x_{a_i})} \tag{4}$$

6. If the inertia sum is higher than a parameter p_2, store individual inertia components into the texture, otherwise store only zeros into the texture.

Step 5 prevents the situation in which more water could be withdrawn from the water column than the column actually contains. Constant p_2 in step 6 defines the minimum level difference that causes overflow.

Constants p_1 and p_2 are adjustable algorithm parameters that enable customization of water behavior as needed so that the water can reach the desired impression.

3.2 Final Water Level Calculation

Calculation of the final water depth is the step that follows the inertia calculation. The depth is stored into the texture together with the terrain elevation; their sum gives the height to which the individual vertices of the water surface triangular grid will be translated.

The algorithm is as follows:

1. Load the previous water depth.
2. Load all the current inertia components of this column.
3. Calculate the sum of all current local inertia (first sum in Eq. 5, see Fig. 3 – blue components)
4. Load all the current inertia components of all the adjacent columns.
5. Calculate the inertia sum from the inertia components of adjacent columns leading to the current column (second sum in Eq. 5, see Fig. 3 – red components).

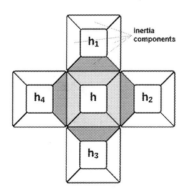

Fig. 3. Local and adjacent inertia components (Color figure online)

6. Calculate the new depth according to Eq. 5, where d' is the water depth from the previous frame, s represents the inertia components of the current column and s_a denotes the relevant inertia components of the adjacent columns.

$$d = d' - \sum_{i=1}^{4} s_i + \sum_{i=1}^{4} s_{a_i} \qquad (5)$$

7. Store the elevation and the new depth into the texture.

3.3   Results

The simulation was tested on a computer equipped with common hardware (Intel Core i5 processor and NVIDIA GeForce GTX 560 Ti GPU). The average number of FPS in dependence on changes in the water grid resolution was logged during the simulation. The performance was measured with water grid resolutions of 256 × 256, 512 × 512, 1024 × 1024 and 2048 × 2048 vertices. The terrain grid was fixed during all the measurements at 512 × 512 vertices.

Measurements were performed with different combinations of image quality improvement settings. MSAA was used for anti-aliasing and anisotropic filtering (AF) to improve texture sampling at oblique viewing angles. The simulation was tested at the screen resolution of 1440 × 900 pixels. The simulation showed a steady rendering rate, it scaled with the change of water grid resolution as expected, see Fig. 4.

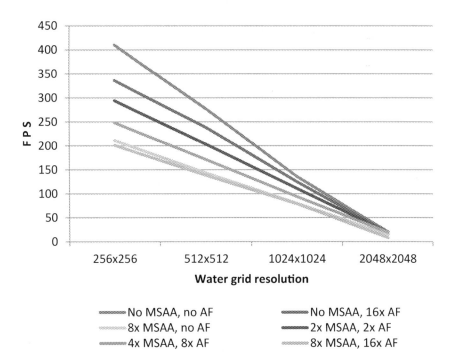

Fig. 4. Performance graph

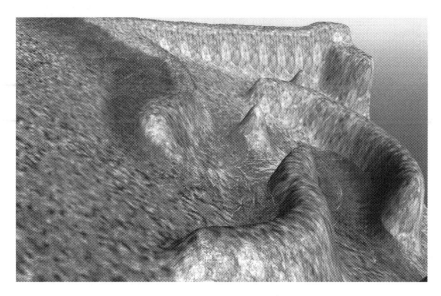

Fig. 5. Sample of prototype implementation

In spite of its simplicity the simulation brings very convincing results. As a consequence of the interaction with the terrain, a complicated flow emerges with fully dynamic waves that exhibit properties of chaotic systems even though the simulation is completely deterministic. Figure 5 shows a picture of the prototype implementation of simulation.

The simulation can be seen in action in the following YouTube videos:

https://youtu.be/rP1uy05i6NA
https://youtu.be/gZi54fVD-iE
https://youtu.be/yZstIXDlBT4
https://youtu.be/YCtVQuCYzjU

The videos are also accessible via the following playlist:

https://www.youtube.com/playlist?list=
PLNabMQGG1XM84ZDn7JPOnFZQjYhS17N1Y

4 Conclusion

This paper proposes an interactive simulation of flowing water based on height field and a regular grid. The simulation is computationally inexpensive yet achieves visually impressive results. Its implementation is uncomplicated, it uses simple and coherent data structures. It is assumed that the area with which the simulated water should interact is described by a height field, which is currently the most common representation of large terrain models. The simulation is therefore suitable for integration with existing solutions for rendering scenes in real time. A side-result of the simulation is also the flow vector field that can act as an input to other algorithms, which could for instance control objects moving across the water surface. The simulation can also be easily integrated with level-of-detail algorithms and the procedural and statistical models generating waves over large areas of stagnant water mentioned in the introduction such as [4–6].

Acknowledgements. This work and the contribution were supported by a project of Students Grant Agency (SPEV) - FIM, University of Hradec Kralove, Czech Republic. Jan Tobola is a student member of the research team. The authors of this paper would like to thank Jan Budina, a PhD student of Applied Informatics at the University of Hradec Kralove, for testing the simulation prototype.

References

1. Hastings, E.J., Guha, R.K., Stanley, K.O.: Interactive evolution of particle systems for computer graphics and animation. IEEE Trans. Evol. Comput. **13**, 418–432 (2009)
2. Reeves, W.T.: Particle systems—a technique for modeling a class of fuzzy objects. ACM Trans. Graph. **2**, 91–108 (1983)
3. Harada, T., Koshizuka, S., Kawaguchi, Y.: Smoothed particle hydrodynamics on GPUs. In: Computer Graphics International, pp. 63–70. SBC Petropolis (2007)
4. Johanson, C.: Real-time water rendering: introducing the projected grid concept (2004). http://fileadmin.cs.lth.se/graphics/theses/projects/projgrid/
5. Tessendorf, J.: Simulating ocean water. Simul. Nat. Realistic Interact. Tech. SIGGRAPH. **1**, 5 (2001)
6. Jensen, L.S., Golias, R.: Deep-water animation and rendering. In: Game Developer's Conference (Gamasutra) (2001)
7. Kass, M., Miller, G.: Rapid, stable fluid dynamics for computer graphics. In: Proceedings of the 17th Annual Conference on Computer Graphics and Interactive Techniques, pp. 49–57. ACM, New York (1990)
8. Miklós, B., Müller, M.: Real time fluid simulation using height fields (2004). http://www.balintmiklos.com/layered_water.pdf
9. Noe, K., Trier, P.: Implementing rapid, stable fluid dynamics on the GPU (2004). https://users-cs.au.dk/noe/projects/GPU_water_simulation/gpu-water.pdf

Author Index

Printed in the United States
By Bookmasters